Essays on Medieval Music
in Honor of
David G. Hughes

Isham Library Papers 4

David G. Hughes

Photograph by Nathan Logus. Courtesy of Harvard Division of Continuing Education.

Essays on Medieval Music

in Honor of David G. Hughes

edited by

GRAEME M. BOONE

Isham Library Papers 4
Harvard University Department of Music
1995

Distributed by Harvard University Press
Cambridge, Massachusetts ❖ London, England

Printed and bound in the United States of America

Design and production by Elaine Benfatto, E&P Ware

Library of Congress Cataloging-in-Publication Data
Essays on Medieval music : in honor of David G. Hughes / edited by Graeme M. Boone.
p. cm. -- (Isham Library papers : 4)
Includes bibliographical references.
ISBN 0-674-26706-0
1. Music--500–1400--History and criticism. I. Hughes, David G.
II. Boone, Graeme M. (Graeme MacDonald), 1954– .
ML 172.E87 1994
780'.9'02--dc20 94-48626
CIP
MN

Contents

Editor's Preface vii
GRAEME M. BOONE

Conference Program ix

Welcome xi
CHRISTOPH WOLFF

David Hughes: An Informal Portrait xiii
ALEJANDRO E. PLANCHART

De Accentibus Toni Oritur Nota Quae Dicitur Neuma: *Prosodic Accents, the Accent Theory, and the Paleofrankish Script* 17
CHARLES M. ATKINSON

Chant Notation in Eleventh-Century Roman Manuscripts 43
JOHN BOE

The Antiphon Cantantibus Organis *and Dante's* Organi Del Mondo 59
THOMAS H. CONNOLLY

Thoughts on Responsories 77
RICHARD L. CROCKER

Prolegomena to a History of Music and Liturgy at Rome in the Middle Ages 87
JOSEPH DYER

The Tabula Monochordi *of Magister Nicolaus de Luduno* 117
LAWRENCE GUSHEE

The Repertory of Sequences at Winchester 153
DAVID HILEY

The Origin of the Monodic Chants in the Codex Calixtinus 195
MICHEL HUGLO

Rome and Jerusalem: From Oral Tradition to Written Repertory in Two Ancient Liturgical Centers 207
PETER JEFFERY

Structure and Ornament in Chant: The Case of the Beneventan Exultet 249
THOMAS FORREST KELLY

Gregorian Chant and Oral Transmission 277
KENNETH LEVY

Antiphonal Psalmody in Christian Antiquity and Early Middle Ages 287
EDWARD NOWACKI

A Sommacampagna Codex of the Italian Ars Nova? 317
NINO PIRROTTA

Notes On The Tropes in Manuscripts of the Rite of Aquileia 333
ALEJANDRO ENRIQUE PLANCHART

Ways of Telling Stories 371
SUSAN RANKIN

Guido's Theory of Organum after Guido: Transmission—Adaptation—Transformation 395
FRITZ RECKOW

Rithmus 415
ERNEST H. SANDERS

Once More, Music and Language in Medieval Song 441
LEO TREITLER

Ut Hic: *Announcing a Study of Musical Examples in the Thirteenth-Century Music Treatises* 471
JEREMY YUDKIN AND TODD SCOTT

GRAEME M. BOONE

Editor's Preface

The present volume incorporates a series of essays originally presented at a conference in honor of the sixtieth birthday of David G. Hughes, Fanny Peabody Mason Professor of Music at Harvard University. The conference took place on October 6-9, 1990 in Harvard's Paine Hall; twenty papers were given, to an audience of over 100 participants from all over the country and abroad. In this volume the papers are presented in alphabetical order by author. The discussions have been recorded and are available on tape in the Isham Memorial Library. Our gratitude is due to Alejandro Planchart, former student of David G. Hughes and Harvard Ph.D. of 1971, who organized the conference and served as its *spiritus rector.*

Many have assisted in the preparation of the manuscript, and I shall list them here in alphabetical order: Alexandra Amati, Elaine Benfatto, Liane Curtis, Carol DeFeciani, Sean Gallagher, John Johnson, Mark Kagan, Tom Kozachek, Ann Morrison, Sharon Prado, Nancy Shafman, Jenny Shallenberger, and Stephanie Wollny.

It has been my pleasure to work as editor on this book, thanks not only to the breadth and quality of its contents, but particularly to the warmth and esteem I, as so many of my colleagues, feel for its dedicatee. May it stand as a small repayment for a debt we have incurred from David Hughes, wise professor, scholar, mentor, and friend.

CONFERENCE PROGRAM

From Rome to the Passing of the Gothic: Western Chant Repertories and their Influence on Early Polyphony A Conference in Honor of David G. Hughes

PROGRAM COMMITTEE
Reinhold Brinkmann, Rodney Dennis, Lewis Lockwood, Michael Ochs, Christoph Wolff, Alejandro E. Planchart (*Chair*)

Friday, October 5, 1990

GREETINGS

Christoph Wolff (*Harvard University*)

Alejandro E. Planchart (*University of California, Santa Barbara*)

AESTHETICS AND TRANSMISSION OF CHANT

David Hiley (*University of Regensburg*), *Chair*

Richard Crocker (*University of California, Berkeley*)
"Thoughts on Roman Responsories"

David Hiley (*University of Regensburg*)
"The Repertory of Sequences at Winchester"

Leo Treitler (*CUNY*)
"Once More, Music and Language in Medieval Song"

CHANT IN ITALY

Lewis Lockwood (*Harvard University*), *Chair*

John Boe (*University of Arizona*)
"Chant Notation in Roman Manuscripts Written before 1071"

Lawrence Gushee (*University of Illinois*)
"The *Tabula Monochordi* of Magister Nicolaus de Luduno"

Thomas Kelly (*Oberlin Conservatory*)
"Context of the Italian Exultet"

Kenneth Levy (*Princeton University*)
"What Is Oral Transmission?"

Saturday, October 6, 1990

CHANT AND ITS CULTURAL CONTEXTS

Ruth Steiner (*Catholic University of America*), *Chair*

Charles Atkinson (*Ohio State University*)
"*De accentibus toni oritur nota quae dicitur neuma:* Prosodic Accents, the Accent Theory, and the Paleofrankish Script"

Thomas Connolly (*University of Pennsylvania*)
"The Antiphon *Cantantibus organis* and Dante's *organi del mondo*"

Michel Huglo (*CNRS*)
"The Origin of the Songs in the Codex Calixtinus"

Craig Wright (*Yale University*)
"A 16th-Century Plainsong Manuscript at Yale"

EARLY POLYPHONY

Reinhold Brinkmann (*Harvard University*), *Chair*

Nino Pirrotta (*Harvard University*)
"A Sommacampagna Codex of the Italian Ars Nova?"

Fritz Reckow (*University of Erlangen-Nürnberg*)
"Guido's Organum after Guido: Transmission and Context"

Ernest Sanders (*Columbia University*)
"The Earliest Phases of Measured Polyphony"

Sunday, October 7, 1990

SYMPOSIUM: NEW DIRECTIONS IN MEDIEVAL SCHOLARSHIP

Janet Knapp (*Pittsboro, NC*), *Chair*

Joseph Dyer (*University of Massachusetts, Boston*)

Peter Jeffery (*University of Delaware*)

Edward Nowacki (*University of Cincinnati*)

Susan Rankin (*Emmanuel College, Cambridge University*)

Jeremy Yudkin (*Boston University*)

CHRISTOPH WOLFF

Welcome

On behalf of the Department of Music and the Isham Memorial Library I welcome you all most cordially here at Harvard. We are very pleased indeed that you followed our invitation to a three-day scholarly conference on medieval music. Whether you participate as lecturer, discussant, moderator, performer, or listener, whether you have come from far away or from just around the corner, it means a lot to us that you are contributing to this conference.

We have held a number of one-day symposia in the past—on the music of Alban Berg, on topics in ethnomusicology, or on Americanism in European music of the 1920s, to mention only the most recent ones—but up until now we have not been able to mount elaborate three-day conferences more than once in a decade. Perhaps we will manage to increase the frequency slightly in the future, but we wouldn't want to do it at the expense of overall quality. Technically speaking, we shall count this as the fourth Isham Library Conference, whose basic idea continues to be intensive and extensive discussions of subject areas and source-related problems in the history of music. The first conference in 1957 (chaired by Curt Sachs) was devoted to early instrumental music, the second in 1961 (chaired by Gustave Reese) to the chanson and madrigal, the third in 1979 (chaired by Lewis Lockwood, then of Princeton) to the string quartets of Haydn, Mozart, and Beethoven. This time (and again following the principle of having an outside chairman, Alejandro Planchart of the University of California at Santa Barbara) we turn to a central medieval topic, that is, western chant repertoires and their influences on early polyphony. As with the previous conferences, we should like to keep a record of the proceedings in the form of a published volume, which we hope will appear soon after the event.

There is, however, one noticeable difference between this conference and its predecessors. We did not simply choose a subject area of general importance or of particular current interest, but we decided to develop a theme that is closely identified with the scholarly concerns and career of our esteemed and distinguished colleague, David Hughes. Therefore, we members of the Harvard Music Department are particularly pleased that you are joining us in the realization of a long-standing plan to honor David. As the current Chairman of this Department—and believe it or not, the one next in line, however distant after David, in terms of length of service at this institution—let me very briefly speak to this point and leave the more specific *laudatio* to Alejandro. To be sure, we are not celebrating David's sixtieth or sixty-fifth birthday (we "missed" the first and consider it premature to think of the second date), nor are we throwing a retirement party (anyway, age is hardly an applicable category as far as David Hughes is concerned). We are taking this opportunity to acknowledge publicly what the presence of this most private, modest, dedicated, and congenial colleague means to us. This is the thirty-fifth year of David's teaching at Harvard, a very appropriate moment for us to think about the impact he has had not only on our Department but on the profession as a whole, and to express our appreciation and gratitude.

I am especially pleased that our remarkably active emeritus faculty is well represented today, that we have among us a respectable number of David's former and present students (among them Tom Connolly, Tom Kelly, Alejandro Planchart, and Craig Wright are on the program), and that we have been joined by an impressive and varied crowd of distinguished medievalists. The heterogeneity of this body promises to create the appropriate atmosphere for productive scholarly exchange and debate.

At this point, it is my great pleasure to thank the Conference Organizing Committee consisting of Reinhold Brinkmann, Rodney Dennis, Lewis Lockwood, and Michael Ochs for their manifold efforts, without which this conference would not have been possible. I should like to single out Alejandro Planchart, whose imaginative guidance has made a big difference from the outset. We are also obliged to the members of the Local Arrangements Committee, Phyllis Benjamin, Mark Kagan, and David Kilroy, as well as the staff of the Department Office who provided competent, reliable, and most valuable assistance regarding the logistics and many organizational details.

It remains for me now to wish this conference every success. Let us all look forward to a series of stimulating papers and refreshing meetings, to the establishment or renewal of personal contacts, and to an altogether memorable affair.

ALEJANDRO E. PLANCHART

David Hughes: An Informal Portrait

To write about David Hughes seems almost a subversive act because in all his public utterances in print, in conferences, in classes and seminars, and even in private conversation, he has always presented his ideas in a profoundly self-effacing manner that belies both his extraordinarily broad command of the general tradition of Western art music and his incisive grasp of his specialized fields: Gregorian and medieval chant, music theory in the central Middle Ages, thirteenth-century liturgical polyphony, and the transition from the *ars subtilior* to the "new style" of the fifteenth century.

The major part of David's research and work has consistently been geared towards maximum utility by other scholars. Nearly thirty-five years after it was born into a genre usually doomed to obscurity, his groundbreaking dissertation remains a gold mine of insight and information for students of musical style in the late fourteenth and early fifteenth century. Pursuing the implications of any of his research essays, works where the lucidly presented surface opens up on careful reading to present an extraordinary number of ideas tightly compressed and carefully interwoven, could easily occupy the better part of a scholarly career. His long standing labor, which is seeing the light of print slowly and relatively "late" in his career, is the kind of work that has kept the entire atelier of Solesmes occupied for the better part of a century, namely the disentangling and explication of the different traditions of Gregorian chant between the ninth and the fourteenth century. It is the kind of Herculean but quiet and unassuming work without which most of what else we do in this field is but built upon shifting sand. As a distinguished colleague some years ago pointed out to me, "David is actually creating the ground upon which we walk."

With his concern for others, a great deal of David's published work has been in the form of reviews, usually long and detailed reviews that are research articles in their own right and where he brings his own sharp perceptions to bear upon a musicological or a historiographic issue. But these reviews, unlike the newer review articles that are increasingly fashionable now, seldom call attention to themselves as articles. Instead, David's keen yet unfailingly civilized commentary seems geared to increase the value and accuracy of the work discussed, to point out, and sometimes to work out, important implications that the author left unsaid or barely sketched, so that indeed the reader finds in the review an expanded intellectual world that enhances the reading of the work reviewed.

This same breadth of vision and quickness of mind have made David an extraordinary teacher. In him many of us found a seemingly impossible combination of extremely high standards and a sympathetic understanding for our own failings, so that he was able to guide students through countless seminars in a gentle and seemingly effortless style, always appearing to be just another member of the seminar rather than the professor. With the same light and humane touch, he has directed a large number of young scholars through their doctoral work and the beginning of distinguished careers. In his unassuming way, David Hughes has been a major force behind the remarkable flowering of the study of chant and its traditions in America over the last two decades. He has, moreover, provided students and colleagues with a model of scholarly integrity, devotion to the field, and human kindness that remains a treasure for all who have come into contact with him.

Essays on Medieval Music in Honor of David G. Hughes

CHARLES M. ATKINSON

De Accentibus Toni Oritur Nota Quae Dicitur Neuma: *Prosodic Accents, the Accent Theory, and the Paleofrankish Script*

An anonymous Frankish author probably writing in the tenth century begins his treatment of chant as follows:

> What is chant? It is skill in the musical art, the inflection and modulation of the voice. Why is it called 'chant'? From 'chanting,' that is, from skill in the musical art or in the modulation of the voice. Its origins and its structure are revealed in the accents of tone or from the feet of syllables. Indeed, it is founded in acute, grave, and circumflex accents of tone.

The author then makes the statement quoted in the title of this paper:

> De accentibus toni oritur nota quae dicitur neuma (From the accents of tone arises the notational sign which is called neume).[1]

This passage is drawn from the treatise *Quid est cantus*, sometimes referred to as the Vatican Anonymous, first edited by Peter Wagner in the

[1] "Quid est cantus? peritia musicae artis, inflexio vocis et modulatio. Quare dicitur cantus? a canendo, idest, a peritia musicae artis vel vocis modulatione. Ortus quoque suus atque compositio ex accentibus toni vel ex pedibus syllabarum ostenditur. Ex accentibus vero toni demonstratur in acuto et gravi et circumflexo. Ex pedibus denique syllabarum ostenditur in brevi et longa. De accentibus toni oritur nota [a later hand has added above this 'figura'] quae dicitur neuma." Biblioteca Vaticana, Cod. lat. Palat. 235, fol. 38ᵛ, ed. Peter Wagner, "Un piccolo trattato sul canto ecclesiastico in un manoscritto del secolo X–XI," *Rassegna gregoriana* 3 (1904): 481–84. A fascimile of the passage in question may be found in Enrico Marriott

third volume of *Rassegna gregoriana* in 1904. I quote it here because it is one of the only medieval statements I know of concerning the origins of neumes. Given its temporal proximity to the events it is reporting and given the clarity of its statement about the basis of the neumes, one is surprised to find that if mentioned at all, it has been treated only in passing in several recent articles on the beginnings of music-writing in the West.[2] Moreover, given the Vatican Anonymous's unequivocal statement that the neumes were derived from prosodic accents, it is a bit surprising to find a large portion of one of those articles devoted to a demonstration that "Carolingian notation could not possibly have been derived from the accents."[3]

The apparent conflict between what medieval and modern scholars have had to say about accent and its relation to the origins of neumes is the subject of the present paper. It will not be my purpose here to attempt a new "Universale Neumenkunde," or to outline a new theory of the origins of neumes, or even to resurrect an old one. Instead, I should like to examine the concept of accent at its source, in the grammatical treatises of antiquity and within the educational milieu of the Carolingian court, so that we may better understand what we mean when we talk about prosodic accents and the theory of such accents as they relate to the advent of practical musical notation in the West.[4]

Our first task in this endeavor must be to ascertain whether and how Carolingian musicians might have acquired a knowledge of prosodic accents. To approach this question we must examine at least briefly the educational system of the Frankish court.

Upon his ascent to the Frankish throne in 771, Charlemagne became the ruler of an empire that was increasing in size and importance, and would become even larger and more influential during his reign. New techniques of administration were required, and indeed were forthcoming. One of the

Bannister, *Monumenti Vaticani di Paleografia musicale latina* (Leipzig: Harrassowitz, 1913), no. 1. It is given in parallel Latin and German in Peter Wagner, *Einführung in die gregorianischen Melodien: Ein Handbuch der Choralwissenschaft* 2: *Neumenkunde* (Leipzig: Breitkopf & Härtel, 1911–12), 355–56.

[2] See, for example, Leo Treitler, "The Early History of Music Writing in the West," *Journal of the American Musicological Society* 35 (1982): 237–79, and "Reading and Singing: On the Genesis of Occidental Music-Writing," *Early Music History* 4 (1984): 135–208; Helmut Hucke, "Die Anfänge der abendländischen Notenschrift," in *Festschrift Rudolf Elvers zum 60. Geburtstag*, ed. Ernst Hettrich and Hans Schneider (Tutzing: Hans Schneider, 1985), 271–88, and "Gregorianische Fragen," *Die Musikforschung* 41 (1988): 304–30; and Kenneth Levy, "On the Origin of Neumes," *Early Music History* 7 (1987): 59–90.

[3] Treitler, "Reading and Singing," 184.

[4] Although he does not treat this topic *expressis verbis*, Mathias Bielitz offers much information useful for its pursuit in his *Musik und Grammatik: Studien zur mittelalterlichen Musiktheorie*, Beiträge zur Musikforschung 4 (Munich-Salzburg: Katzbichler, 1977). See in particular 114–20.

administrative techniques that Charlemagne adopted is of special interest here. Under his rule the administration of both secular and ecclesiastical affairs became increasingly dependent upon written documents, especially in the period after 800.[5] As Ganshof has pointed out, "Whatever the field, Charlemagne attached great importance to setting things down in writing."[6] His administrators obviously needed to know how to read and write—and they needed to know how to do those things well. One Carolingian author reports that Charles "devoted just as much ardor to abolishing imperfections of language as he devoted to vanquishing his enemies on the field of battle."[7]

As Ganshof and others have shown, the ability to read and write was a skill that was not in great supply in the Frankish kingdom in the mid- to late eighth century.[8] Thus, Charlemagne had to create an educational system that could provide trained administrators in both sacred and secular realms. In order to do that he brought to his court some of the most gifted men of the day—Paulinus of Aquileia, Peter of Pisa, and Theodulf of Orléans among them—and convinced Alcuin of York to take over the direction of the palace school and to assist him in implementing a program of educational reform.[9]

Unfortunately, we have little direct information about Alcuin's organization of the palace school, but we can reconstruct its outlines from various

[5] François Louis Ganshof, "The Use of the Written Word in Charlemagne's Administration," in *The Carolingians and the Frankish Monarchy*, trans. Janet Sondheimer (Ithaca, N.Y.: Cornell University Press, 1971), 125–42. Ganshof remarks that from about the middle of the seventh century until the time of Pippin III "the only use for written records seems to have been to furnish proof of individual rights, or to assist in such proof." He continues: "So far as we can judge from the sources, the use of the written word for administrative purposes started to revive under Pippin III, though only to a very modest extent. . . . When we come to the reign of Charlemagne we find a change in the situation. The number of sources to enlighten us about administrative records becomes more plentiful; and although more numerous for the period after the imperial coronation, they are spread over the entire reign. This abundance of documentation is novel and revealing" (125–26).

[6] Ganshof, "The Use of the Written Word," 126.

[7] *MGH*, Poetae latini aevi carolini I, 89–90. Cited after Pierre Riché, *Écoles et enseignement dans le Haut Moyen Age: Fin du ve siècle—milieu du xie siècle* (Paris: Picard, 1989), 112.

[8] Ganshof, "The Use of the Written Word," 135. See also Max Ludwig Wolfram Laistner, *Thought and Letters in Western Europe, A.D. 500 to 900* (Ithaca, N.Y.: Cornell University Press, 1931/1966), 191–92, and Joseph Dyer, "The Monastic Origins of Western Music Theory," in Laszlo Dobszay et al., eds., *International Musicological Society Study Group "Cantus Planus": Papers Read at the Third Meeting, Tihany, Hungary, 19–24 September 1988* (Budapest: Hungarian Academy of Sciences, Institute for Musicology, 1990), 199–225, particularly 210–11.

[9] On this see Franz Brunhölzl, "Der Bildungsauftrag der Hofschule," in *Karl der Große: Lebenswerk und Nachleben* 2: *Das geistige Leben*, ed. Bernhard Bischoff (Düsseldorf: Schwann, 1965), 28–41, and Laistner, *Thought and Letters*, 192–99.

sources, such as the program he later established at St. Martin of Tours. The school at Tours had one division for Bible study, a second one for the liberal arts (among which the discipline of astronomy received special treatment), and a third devoted specifically to grammar.[10] From this outline and from Alcuin's *Disputatio de vera philosophia*, the preface to his treatise on grammar, one can deduce that the ultimate and highest goal of instruction was the study of the Bible, but one would progress to that through study of the liberal arts.[11] The first of these—in both a literal and a figurative sense—was grammar. Beyond the most fundamental types of elementary instruction, such as the learning of reading and writing and the memorization of certain liturgical texts,[12] the discipline of grammar was the one liberal art whose study we can reasonably assume to have been expected of everyone.[13] As the testimony of Alcuin's own treatise on grammar, along with ninth-century library catalogues as well as editions and commentaries by Paul the Deacon, Peter of Pisa, Smaragdous, Walafrid Strabo, Murethach, Sedulius Scotus, and Remigius of Auxerre tell us, the chief authority for grammar was

[10] Brunhölzl, "Der Bildungsauftrag," 30. On this, see Alc. epist. 121 in *MGH*, Epist. IV 176, 32ff. In another instance an unknown bishop tells Alcuin that he should oversee instruction, and names grammar, reading, and study of the Bible as subjects (Alc. epist. 161; *MGH*, Epist. IV 260, 13ff.). In Brunhölzl's view, such witnesses tell us that Alcuin's poem 26 also depicts the court school itself.

[11] Brunhölzl, "Der Bildungsauftrag," 33–34. For the text of the *Disputatio*, see Migne *PL* 101, 849–54. In the *Disputatio*, Alcuin is asked by his students to explain the stages leading up to philosophy. Alcuin responds by quoting the Bible: "Wisdom hath builded her house, she hath hewn out her seven pillars" (Prov. 9:1). The seven pillars are to be understood not just as the seven Gifts of the Holy Spirit, but also as the seven liberal arts. Cf. *PL* 101, 853–54. On Alcuin as a teacher, see Eleanor Shipley Duckett, *Alcuin, Friend of Charlemagne: His World and His Work* (Hamden, Conn.: Archon Books, 1965), 109–17.

[12] The texts in question are the Pater noster, the Credo, and the Psalms. Cf. Bernhard Bischoff, "Elementarunterricht und Probationes Pennae in der ersten Hälfte des Mittelalters," in *Classical and Medieval Studies in Honor of Edward Kennard Rand*, ed. Leslie Webber Jones (New York: the editor, 1938), 9–20, the expanded form of this article in Bischoff, *Mittelalterliche Studien: Ausgewählte Aufsätze zur Schriftkunde und Literaturgeschichte* 1 (Stuttgart: Hiersemann, 1966), 74–87, and Brunhölzl, "Der Bildungsauftrag," 39.

[13] Cf. Riché, *Écoles et enseignement*, 111–12, and Brunhölzl, *Geschichte der lateinischen Literatur des Mittelalters* 1: *Von Cassiodor bis zum Ausklang der karolingischen Erneuerung* (Munich: Fink, 1975), 246–47. Brunhölzl characterizes grammar as the "Grundlage aller Wissenschaften," and goes on to say (247): "Es ist dabei von sekundärer Bedeutung, daß man in der Praxis von den artes liberales zunächst fast nur die Fächer des Triviums—Grammatik, Dialektik, Rhetorik—pflegte, unter denen wiederum die Grammatik den weitaus größten Raum einnahm, während die Einbeziehung der rechnenden Disziplinen des Quadriviums—Arithmetik, Geometrie, Musik und Astronomie—in nennenswertem Umfang erst etwa seit der Mitte des 9. Jahrhunderts und auch da allmählich und an den verschiedenen Schulen in sehr verschiedenem Maße erfolgte."

Donatus.[14] The saying that "every schoolboy had his Donatus" was no less true in the Carolingian period than it was in late antiquity.

In our quest to learn what the Carolingians would have learned about prosodic accents, we must therefore turn our attention to Donatus, along with the sections on grammar in two of the three manuals of the liberal arts that were the "standardized textbooks" for the Carolingians—namely, Isidore of Seville and Martianus Capella.[15] (The third of those textbooks is, of course, Cassiodorus, but the chapter on grammar in his *Institutiones* is simply a two-page précis of Donatus's *Ars maior.*)[16]

Excerpt 1 presents the opening sentences of each of the six chapters of Donatus's *Ars maior*, Book I, drawn from the new critical edition by Louis Holtz.[17]

Excerpt 1
from Donatus, Ars maior, *Book I*

1. De Voce

Vox est aer ictus, sensibilis auditu, quantum in ipso est. Omnis vox aut articulata est aut confusa. Articulata est, quae litteris conprehendi potest; confusa, quae scribi non potest.

2. De Littera

Littera est pars minima uocis articulatae. Litterarum aliae sunt uocales, aliae consonantes. Consonantium aliae sunt semiuocales, aliae mutae. Vocales sunt, quae per se proferuntur et per se syllabam faciunt. Sunt autem numero quinque a e i o u.

[14] Cf. Alcuin, *Grammatica, PL* 101, cols. 854–902. Donatus is cited early in the treatise (855C: "Ut reor, in Donato legimus . . .") and several times subsequently. Cf. Brunhölzl, "Der Bildungsauftrag," 39. For listings of Donatus in ninth-century library catalogues, see Paul Lehmann, *Mittelalterliche Bibliothekskataloge Deutschlands und der Schweiz* 1 (Munich: Beck, 1918), in particular the catalogues from St. Gall and Reichenau. For a listing of the most important extant manuscripts, as well as a discussion of medieval editions of and commentaries upon Donatus, see Louis Holtz, *Donat et la tradition de l'enseignement grammatical: Étude sur l'Ars Donati et sa diffusion (IVe–IXe siècle) et édition critique*, Documents, études et répertoires publiés par l'Institut de recherche et d'histoire des textes (Paris: Centre national de la recherche scientifique, 1981), 354–421 (manuscripts) and 438–41 (Carolingian editions and commentaries).

[15] On this point as it pertains to instruction in music, see Michel Huglo, "Le développement du vocabulaire de l'*Ars musica* à l'époque carolingienne," *Latomus* 34 (1975): 131–51.

[16] See *Cassiodori Senatoris Institutiones*, ed. R. A. B. Mynors (Oxford: Clarendon, 1937), 94–96.

[17] Holtz, *Donat et la tradition*, 603–12.

3. De Syllaba
Syllaba est conprehensio litterarum uel unius uocalis enuntiatio temporum capax. Syllabarum aliae sunt breues, aliae longae, aliae communes.

4. De Pedibus
Pes est syllabarum et temporum certa dinumeratio. Accidunt uni cuique pedi arsis et thesis, numerus syllabarum, tempus, resolutio, figura, metrum. Pedes disyllabi sunt quattuor, trisyllabi octo, duplices sedecim.

5. De Tonis
Tonos alii accentus, alii tenores nominant. Toni igitur tres sunt, acutus, grauis, circumflexus.

6. De Posituris
Tres sunt [omnino] positurae uel distinctiones quas θέσεις Graeci uocant, distinctio, subdistinctio, media distinctio.

Following the opening chapter on articulate versus inarticulate speech—with inarticulate being defined as that which cannot be written down using letters—the five remaining chapters provide a syntactic description of Latin, proceeding from the smallest element, the letter, up to the sentence or period.[18] (Larger divisions, such as paragraphs or sections of a speech, would be covered in rhetoric and logic.) Two chapters, *De pedibus* and *De tonis*, are devoted to the treatment of whole words, while the final chapter treats the sentence and its subdivisions of colon and comma.

But the chapters in which we are most interested are the final two, *De tonis* and *De posituris*. Excerpt 2 presents sections of these two chapters.[19]

Excerpt 2
from Donatus, Ars maior, *Book I, chapters 5 and 6*

5. De Tonis
[A] Tonos alii accentus, alii tenores nominant. Toni igitur tres sunt, acutus, grauis, circumflexus. Acutus cum in Graecis dictionibus tria loca teneat, ultimum, paenultimum et antepaenultimum, apud Latinos paenultimum et antepaenultimum tenet, ultimum numquam. Circumflexus autem, quotlibet syllabarum sit dictio, non tenebit nisi paenultimum locum. Grauis poni in eadem dictione uel cum acuto uel cum circumflexo potest, et hoc illi non est commune cum ceteris.

[18] Holtz, *Donat et la tradition*, 58–62, points out that the organization of this book of the *Ars maior* is based on principles set forth in Melampous, a commentator on the grammar of Dionysios of Thrace (see edition cited in n. 20 below), and is quite close to the τὲχνη περὶ φωνῆς of Diogenes of Babylonia.

[19] Holtz, *Donat et la tradition.*

[B] Acutus accentus est nota per obliquum ascendens in dexteram partem /, grauis nota a summo in dexteram partem descendens \, circumflexus nota de acuto et graui facta ^, longus linea a sinistra in dexteram partem aequaliter ducta —, breuis uirgula similiter iacens, sed panda atque contractior ˘, hyfen uirgula subiecta uersui: hac nota subter posita duo uerba, cum ita res exigit, copulamus, ut *ante‿tulit gressum* et *Turnus ut ante‿uolans.* Huic contraria est diastole, dextera pars [quaedam] circuli ad imam litteram adposita: hac nota male cohaerentia discernuntur, ut est *ereptae, uirginis ira* et *uiridique in litore conspicitur, sus.* Apostrophos circuli item pars dextera, sed ad summam litteram adposita: hac nota deesse ostendimus parti orationis ultimam uocalem, cuius consonans remanet, ut est *tanton' me crimine dignum Duxisti?* Ceterum dasian ⊢ et psilen ⊣ apud Latinos H littera uocali addita uel detracta significat.

6. De Positvris

[C] Tres sunt [omnino] positurae uel distinctiones quas θέσεις Graeci uocant, distinctio, subdistinctio, media distinctio. Distinctio est, ubi finitur plena sententia: huius punctum ad summam litteram ponimus. Subdistinctio est, ubi non multum superest de sententia, quod tamen necessario separatum mox inferendum sit; huius punctum ad imam litteram ponimus. Media distinctio est, ubi fere tantum de sententia superest, quantum iam diximus, cum tamen respirandum sit: huius punctum ad mediam litteram ponimus. In lectione tota sententia periodos dicitur, cuius partes sunt cola et commata.

A close connection with music is established by the very first sentence of chapter 5: "Tonos alii accentus, alii tenores nominant" ("Some call tones accents, others tenors"). Although it echoes a passage in Quintilian, this definition ultimately goes back to the Greek grammarians, for whom *tonos* (from the verb τείνω) is the standard term for vocal inflection and the most important element of προσῳδία.[20] Its direct lineage from the Greek may be seen in the fact that two of its terms, *tonus* and *tenor*, have Greek cognates, and that the term *accentus* is a translation of the Greek προσῳδία.[21]

After listing the three types of accents—acute, grave, and circumflex—Donatus contrasts Greek usage with Latin, stating, for example, that the

[20] See Marcus Fabius Quintilianus, *Institutio oratoria*, ed. L. Radermacher (Leipzig: Teubner, 1907), I.v.22. For examples of the Greek usage, see *Dionysii Thracis Ars grammatica et Scholia in Dionysii Thracis Artem grammaticam*, ed. Gustav Uhlig, Grammatici Graeci, 1/1 and 3 (Leipzig: Teubner, 1883/1901).

[21] On this see the excerpts from Isidore and Martianus below, as well as the article "Tenor" by Dagmar Hoffmann-Axthelm in *Handwörterbuch der musikalischen Terminologie.*

acute can appear in any of three positions within a word in Greek,[22] but in only two positions in Latin. He also mentions that the grave accent can be placed in the same word with either an acute or circumflex, but that this trait does not pertain to the other two—that is, an acute and a circumflex may not appear together in the same word.

Following a set of examples demonstrating the placement of accents in words of varying numbers of syllables and quantities of vowel sounds, Donatus finally tells us what the accents actually are (see section B of excerpt 2): "An acute accent is a *nota* [a graphic sign] ascending toward the right in oblique motion; a grave accent is a *nota* descending toward the right from above; a circumflex accent is a *nota* made from acute and grave." He goes on to describe the *notae* used for long and short syllables, the hyphen, diastole, and apostrophe, and closes the chapter with examples of the *dasia* and the *psile*, signifying the addition or absence of the letter H in Latin. (Musicologists will recognize the *dasia* as the stem for most of the notational signs in the *Musica enchiriadis.*)[23]

The final chapter of *Ars maior*, Book I (section C in excerpt 2) discusses the *positurae* or punctuation signs: a high point placed at the end of a sentence or distinction; a low-level point placed at the end of a subdistinction or comma, where not much of the sentence is left; and a mid-level point for a medial distinction or colon, where enough of the sentence is left so as to require a new breath. To provide examples of these distinctions, Murethach of Auxerre, an early ninth-century commentator on Donatus, used the text for the Introit *Iubilate Deo omnis terra:* " 'Iubilate Deo omnis terra,' here is a medial distinction; 'psalmum dicite nomini eius,' here is a subdistinction; 'date gloriam laudi eius,' here a distinction."[24]

[22] Holtz, *Donat et la tradition*, 62, states that Donatus's word *dictio* is his equivalent of λέξις in Diogenes, and is used to signify a word as a sounding and written entity, apart from its meaning.

[23] Cf. *Musica et Scolica enchiriadis, una cum aliquibus tractatulis adiunctis*, ed. Hans Schmid, Bayerische Akademie der Wissenschaften: Veröffentlichungen der Musikhistorischen Kommission 3 (Munich: Verlag der Bayerischen Akademie der Wissenschaften, 1981). The treatise is also available in Martin Gerbert, *Scriptores ecclesiastici de musica sacra potissimum* 1 (St. Blasien: Typis San-Blasianis, 1784; repr. Milan: Bollettino bibliografico musicale, 1931), 152–73.

[24] The passage with its lemma is as follows: "HUIUS PUNCTUM AD MEDIAM LITTERAM PONIMUS (372, 21). Et recte ad mediam litteram, quia medius sensus est ibi. Cuius rei exemplum est 'Iubilate Deo omnis terra,' ecce media distinctio; 'psalmum dicite nomini eius,' ecce subdistinctio; 'date gloriam laudi eius,' ecce distinctio." Murethach (Muridac), *In Donati Artem maiorem*, ed. Louis Holtz, Corpus Christianorum: Continuatio mediaevalis 40 (Turnhout: Brepols, 1977), 45. According to Holtz, *Donat et la tradition*, 439, Murethach taught at Auxerre before 840. "Iubilate Deo omnis terra" is the text of the Introit for the third Sunday after Easter.

In keeping with the progressive, systematic character of the six chapters of Book I of the *Ars maior*, Donatus's treatment of the accents and *positurae* in the last two of these chapters provides a complete set of graphic signs to convey the inflection and articulation of a text, from individual syllables to phrases, to the totality of a complete sentence. With regard to the accent signs themselves, I believe it is significant that Donatus does not define them in terms of their pitch inflections, but rather in terms of their appearance as graphic figures. His use of the term *nota* for these signs is completely in keeping with the use of that word in late antiquity as a notational sign for various linguistic purposes and even for music: Boethius uses the same term when he presents the Alypian notation in his *De musica.*[25]

Even though Donatus himself does not describe the accents in terms of their pitch inflections, ninth-century commentators such as Murethach and Sedulius Scotus do. But they derive their own descriptions from two intervening sources—Isidore of Seville and Martianus Capella.

As Louis Holtz has pointed out, the sections on grammar in Isidore's *Etymologiarum* incorporate and expand upon Donatus's work.[26] This is readily apparent from Isidore's treatment of *accentus* and *positura*, which appears in slightly abbreviated form in excerpt 3.[27]

Excerpt 3
from Isidore of Seville, Etymologiarum, *I*

[A] *De Accentibus.* Accentus, qui Graece prosodia dicitur [ex Graeco nomen accepit]. Nam Graece πρός Latine "ad," ᾠδή Graece, Latine "cantus" est. Hoc enim nomen de verbo ad verbum expressum est. Latini autem habent et alia nomina. Nam accentus et tonos et tenores dicunt, quia ibi sonus crescit et desinit. Accentus autem dictus, quod iuxta cantum sit, sicut adverbium quia iuxta verbum est. Acutus accentus dictus, quod acuat et erigat syllabam, gravis, quod deprimat et deponat. Est enim contrarius acuto. Circumflexus, quia de acuto et gravi constat. Incipiens enim ab acuto in gravem desinit, atque ita dum ascendit et descendit, circumflexus efficitur.

[B] *De Figvris Accentvvm.* Figurae accentuum decem sunt, quae a grammaticis pro verborum distinctionibus adponuntur. 'Οξεῖα, id est acutus accentus, linea a sinistra parte in dexteram partem sursum ducta, fit

[25] Boethius, *De institutione musica,* IV, 3.

[26] Holtz, *Donat et la tradition,* 250 and 432.

[27] Isidore of Seville, *Etymologiarum,* I, xviii–xx, excerpts, from *Isidori Hispalensis Episcopi Etymologiarum sive Originum Libri XX,* ed. W. M. Lindsay, Scriptorum Classicorum Bibliotheca Oxoniensis (Oxford: Clarendon, 1911).

ita: /. Βαρεῖα, id est gravis, linea a summo sinistrae in dexteram deposita, fit ita: \. Περισπωμένη, id est circumflexus, linea de acuto et gravi facta, exprimitur ita: ^. Μακρός, id est longa, virgula iacens est ita: —. Βραχύς, id est brevis, pars est circuli inferior, iacens ita: ◡. Ὑφέν, id est coniunctio, quia duo verba conectit, subiecta virgula versui circumflexa, fit ita: ‿. Diastole, id est distinctio, quae e contrario separat, dextra pars circuli supposita versui, fit ita:). Apostrophus pars item circuli dextra et ad summam litteram adposita, fit ita:), qua nota deesse ostenditur in sermone ultima vocalis, ut "tribunal' " pro "tribunale." Δασεῖα, quod interpretatur aspiratio, id est ubi H littera poni debet, tali figura notatur: ⊢. Ψιλή, quod interpretatur siccitas, sive purum, id est, ubi H littera esse non debet, tali nota ostenditur: ⊣. Quorum duorum accentuum figuram Latini ex ipsa littera aspirationis fecerunt. Vnde si coniungas has, fecisti eandem aspirationis notam. Rursus si medium eius apicem scindis, δασεῖαν et ψιλήν facis.

[C] *De Positvris.* Positura est figura ad distinguendos sensus per cola et commata et periodos, quae dum ordine suo adponitur, sensum nobis lectionis ostendit. Dictae autem positurae vel quia punctis positis adnotantur, vel quia ibi vox pro intervallo distinctionis deponitur. Has Graeci θέσεις vocant, Latini posituras. Prima positura subdistinctio dicitur; eadem et comma. Media distinctio sequens est; ipsa et cola. Vltima distinctio, quae totam sententiam cludit, ipsa est periodus; cuius, ut diximus, partes sunt cola et comma; quarum diversitas punctis diverso loco positis demonstratur.

He begins by providing an etymology for the term "accent": "Accent, which is called 'prosodia' in Greek [takes its name from the Greek]. For 'pros' in Greek is 'ad' in Latin, 'odé' in Greek is the Latin 'cantus'"—hence the Latin "ad-cantus" or "accentus." He then echoes Donatus in saying that the Latins have other names for accent, "For they call accents both tones and tenors, because here the sound rises and falls."[28] The way the sound "rises and falls" is then described:

The acute accent is so called because it elevates and lifts up a syllable; the grave is so called because it depresses and pushes it down. It is thus the opposite of the acute. The circumflex is so called because it consists of the acute and grave. Beginning from the acute, it ends in the grave, and thus a circumflex is made because it both ascends and descends [*ascendit et descendit*].

[28] Isidore's terms are "crescit et desinit," which could mean "increases and ends." I have chosen to translate somewhat freely, "rises and falls," in consideration of the context.

The next section follows Donatus in demonstrating the placement of accents in words of varying numbers of syllables and quantities. This discussion is in turn followed by treatments of the graphic signs for the accents (*De figuris accentuum*) and of the punctuation marks (*De posituris*). In comparing these sections with Donatus, one finds that Isidore does little but add the Greek names for the accents and provide an expanded treatment of the *positurae.*

The close parallels between Donatus and Isidore become all the more obvious when those two authors are compared with the third we wish to examine, Martianus Capella. In Book III of his *De nuptiis Philologiae et Mercurii*, Martianus provides an extensive treatment of prosodic accents. In the main it follows the precepts we have already seen in both Donatus and Isidore, but it differs from both of those authors in some rather important details, as seen in excerpt 4.[29]

Excerpt 4
from Martianus Capella,
De nuptiis Philologiae et Mercurii, *Book III*

[A] Hactenus de iuncturis; nunc de fastigio uideamus, qui locus apud Graecos περὶ προσῳδιῶν appellatur. Hic in tria discernitur: unaquaeque enim syllaba aut grauis est, aut acuta, aut circumflexa, et ut nulla uox sine uocali est, ita sine accentu nulla. Et est accentus, ut quidam putauerunt, anima uocis et *seminarium musices*, quod omnis modulatio ex fastigiis uocum grauitateque componitur, ideoque accentus quasi adcantus dictus est.

[B] Omnis igitur uox latine simplex siue composita habet unum sonum aut acutum aut *circumflexum;* duos autem acutos aut *inflexos* habere numquam potest, graues uero saepe. Acutum habet in prima syllaba, si dicas Caelius, in secunda Sallustius, in tertia Curiatius, inflexum item in prima, si dicas caelum, syllaba autem paenultima numquam acuitur natura ipsa breuis, sed praecedens eius, id est ab ultima tertia, siue breuis siue longa sit, ut Cicero Caelius. *Flexus* autem sonus in ea tantummodo syllaba consistit, quae praecedit ultimam, nec aliter quam ut ipsa natura longa sit et ultima tamen breuis, ut Galenus. At si longa, aut si paenultima positione longa, licet ultima breuis, acutus tamen sonus fiet, Galeni Camilli. Inflexi proprium hoc est, ut

[29] Martianus Capella, *De nuptiis Philologiae et Mercurii*, Book III, excerpts, ed. Adolph Dick, with Addenda by Jean Préaux, Bibliotheca Scriptorum Graecorum et Romanorum Teubneriana (Stuttgart: Teubner, 1969), 98–103.

> nisi longis natura syllabis non adhaereat, acutus autem et in longis et in breuibus inuenitur. Omnis autem uox aut acutum aut circumflexum sonum habeat necesse est, etiam si monosyllaba sit; monosyllabae enim graui carent. Omnis uox monosyllaba, cum aliquid significat, siue breuis est siue positione longa, acuetur, ut dicimus far ars, si autem natura longa, flectetur, ut lux mos.
>
> [C] Acutus accentus notatur uirgula a sinistra parte in dexteram ascendente /, grauis autem a sinistra ad dexteram descendens \. Inflexi signum est sigma super ipsas litteras deuexum ⌒. Accentus partim fastigia uocamus, quod litterarum capitibus apponantur, partim cacumina, tonos uel sonos, Graeci prosodias. Sciendum etiam uni uocabulo accidere omnes tres accentus posse, ut est Árgìlêtum.

Some of the differences just mentioned occur in the first section of excerpt 4 (labeled A), in which Martianus begins his discussion of the accents:

> Every single syllable is either grave, acute, or circumflex; and just as there is no utterance without a vowel, so too there is none without an accent. As some assert, accent is the soul of utterance and the seed-plot of music [*seminarium musices*], because every melody is composed of elevation or depression of the voice. Thus accentus is called "ad-cantus"—"toward song"—so to speak.

The section following this (labeled B), which discusses the placement of the accents within words, is primarily interesting in that Martianus uses two different Latin terms as synonymous with circumflex. One of these terms is *inflexus*, the other simply *flexus*. Like any good author, Martianus was conscious of the need for *variatio sermonum*, but it is striking that he applied this technique only to the circumflex.

The final section of excerpt 4 (labeled C) offers a view that contrasts rather markedly with Donatus and Isidore. Both of the other authors had stated that the grave accent could be placed in a single word together with one of the other accents, but that it could not appear with both of the others. But after describing the *notae* for the acute, grave, and *inflexus* accents—the last of which he describes as a sigma facing downwards—Martianus states: "It should be known that all three accents can occur together in one word, as is the case in *Árgìlêtum*." Thus, according to Martianus at least, the inflections on all syllables of a word could be represented via the accent signs, irrespective of whether those signs were acute, grave, or circumflex.

Following the discussions of prosodic accents in Donatus, Isidore, and Martianus Capella, we find that: (1) acute, grave, and circumflex were the principal accents, the circumflex also being called "flexus" or "inflexus" by

Martianus; (2) these accents were names for inflections of the voice applied to syllables of a text; (3) at the same time, the accents were graphic signs, *notae*, used to represent these vocal inflections; (4) the inflections themselves are described as "ascending," "descending," or a combination of both (not merely "high" or "low"); (5) the accents were applied over individual syllables of words, and according to Martianus every syllable could carry an accent; (6) in conjunction with the system of *positurae*, the accents provided a cohesive system for the graphic representation of the melodic inflections and articulations of a complete text, from syllable to sentence.

Assuming that the elements of accent just discussed were being taught in Carolingian schools, we must now ask ourselves whether any of this material could have played a role in the advent of our earliest preserved examples of practical musical notation, those copied in Frankish manuscripts in the ninth century. In order to do this, I should like to start in the same place Professor Treitler did. He began his discussion of the role of accent in the rise of occidental music-writing by providing a concise version of what I am calling the "accent theory" as articulated by Peter Bohn in 1887. It reads as follows in Treitler's translation:

> In neumatic script, the *accentus acutus* was usually written in a vertical position and received a special name; it was called *virga* and signified a note that is higher than the preceding or following note. The *accentus gravis* was at first written in a declining oblique position, shortened itself gradually into a point . . . after which it received the name *punctum*. It signifies a note that is lower than the preceding or following one. In compound neumes it retains its original form [the grave accent]. The *accentus circumflexus* is called *clivis, clinis*, or *flexa;* it designates two notes of which the first is higher than the second.[30]

The attentive reader will have noticed that there is no accentual model for the ascending two-note neume, the *pes* or *podatus*, in this description. In order to provide one, Bohn invented an accent, the "accentus anticircumflexus." (I have found no evidence for an accent by that name.) He says (again in Treitler's version): "The *accentus anticircumflexus* was given the name *podatus* or *pes;* it signifies two notes of which the second is higher than the first."[31]

[30] Peter Bohn, "Das liturgische Rezitativ und dessen Bezeichnung in den liturgischen Büchern des Mittelalters," *Monatshefte für Musikgeschichte* 19 (1887): 31–36; taken from Treitler, "Reading and Singing," 181.

[31] Ibid.

Obviously there are problems with Bohn's description, problems that are both logical and philological. To get at some of them, let us look at one of the earliest and most famous examples of musical notation in the Middle Ages—the partially notated setting of the *Doxa in ipsistis theo* in the manuscript Paris 2291, dating from 875 or 876.[32] It appears in plate 1.

This piece was discussed by Jacques Handschin in his article "Eine alte Neumenschrift" of 1950.[33] The neumatic script in question is one of the oldest types of practical musical notation, the so-called Paleofrankish script.

By comparing this setting of the *Doxa* with that in thirteen other manuscripts, Handschin was able to establish a close connection between the Paleofrankish neumes in Paris 2291 and what he seems to have felt were the neumes described by Aurelian of Réôme with designations such as *acutus accentus* and *circumflexio* or *circumvolutio*.[34] Handschin found that the oblique upward stroke answering the grammarians' descriptions of an acute accent—which one sees here, for example, in line 2 over *-e-* in *theo*, in line 3 over *y-* in *yrini* and over *-o-* in *anthropis*, and in lines 5–9 over the syllable *-men* in the phrase "enumense, eulogumen se, proskynumen se, doxologumen se eukaristumen sy"—actually stands for an ascending two-note melodic gesture, not the single high note or *virga* postulated by the accent theory. The oblique downward stroke corresponding to the grammarians' description of the grave accent—here at the beginning of the second line and over *-men* in lines 5–9—represents a descending two-note gesture, not the single low *punctum* predicted by the accent theory. Finally, the note in lines 10 and 11 that looks like a letter *C* facing downward—a downward

[32] Jean Deshusses, "Encore les sacramentaires de Saint-Amand," *Revue bénédictine* 89 (1979): 310–12. This is a postscript to his article "Chronologie des grands sacramentaires de Saint-Amand," *Revue bénédictine* 87 (1977): 230–37. Here he is concerned with the three youngest of the St. Amand sacramentaries: Reims 213, Paris 2291, and Stockholm A 136. Deshusses had proposed a date of "vers 871" for Paris 2291. Now, he proposes between Christmas of 875 and October of 877 (most likely between 875 and 876) for Paris 2291, and between 876 and 877 for Stockholm A 136. The reason is that the word "rex" has been crossed out and the word "imperator" substituted for it in both manuscripts. Charles the Bald was crowned emperor on Christmas, 875, and died in October, 877. For further discussion of the St. Amand sacramentaries and the Greek pieces they contain see Charles M. Atkinson, "Zur Entstehung und Überlieferung der 'Missa graeca,'" *Archiv für Musikwissenschaft* 39 (1982): 113–45; "*O amnos tu theu:* The Greek Agnus Dei in the Roman Liturgy from the Eighth to the Eleventh Century," *Kirchenmusikalisches Jahrbuch* 65 (1981): 7–30; and "The *Doxa*, the *Pisteuo*, and the *ellinici fratres:* Some Anomalies in the Transmission of the Chants of the 'Missa graeca,'" *The Journal of Musicology* 7 (1989): 81–106.

[33] Jacques Handschin, "Eine alte Neumenschrift," *Acta Musicologica* 22 (1950): 69–97, with further observations in "Zu 'Eine alte Neumenschrift' (Acta 22, 71ff.)," *Acta Musicologica* 25 (1953): 87–88.

[34] Handschin, "Eine alte Neumenschrift," 69–73 and 78–79.

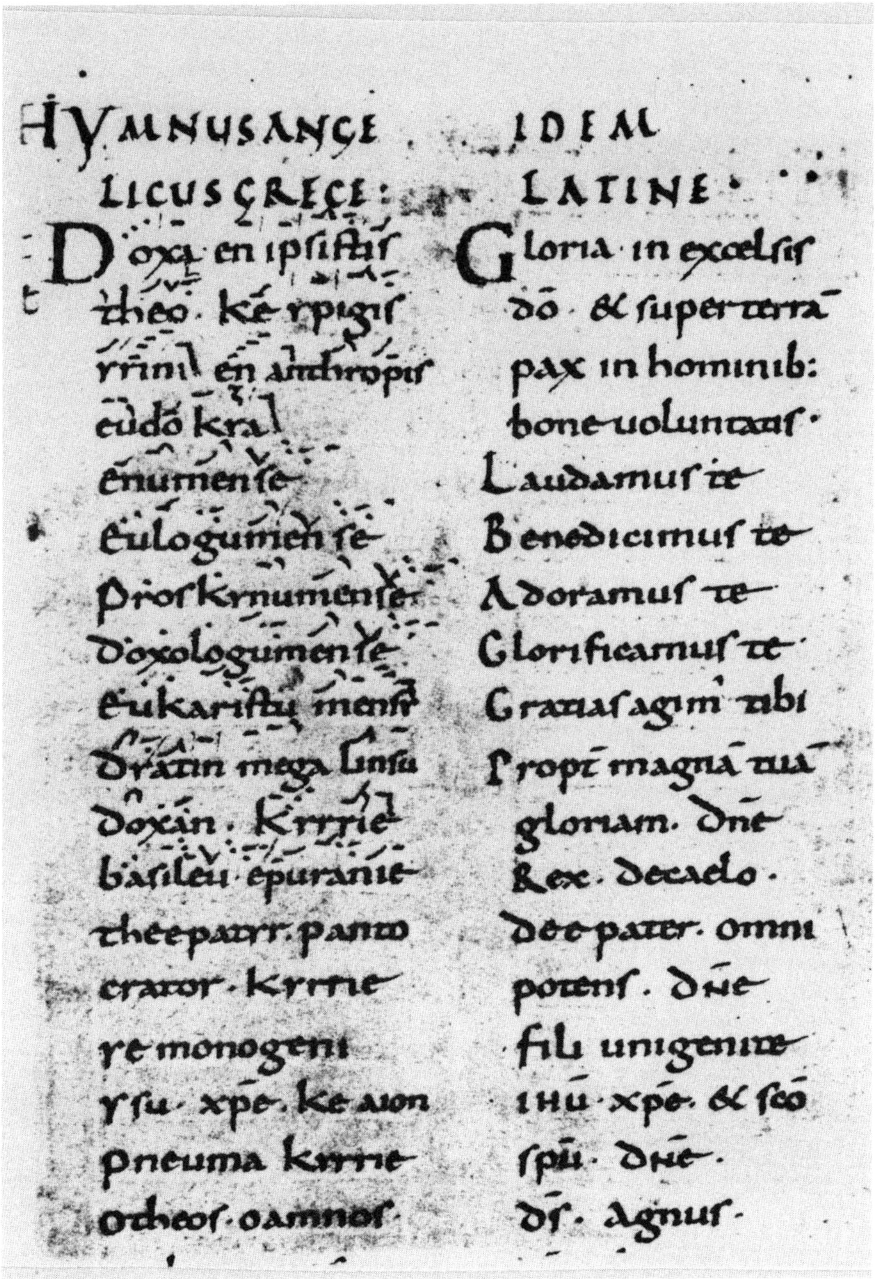

Plate 1: *Doxa in ipsistis theo* in Paris, Bibliothèque Nationale, lat. 2291, fol. 16. Reproduced by permission.

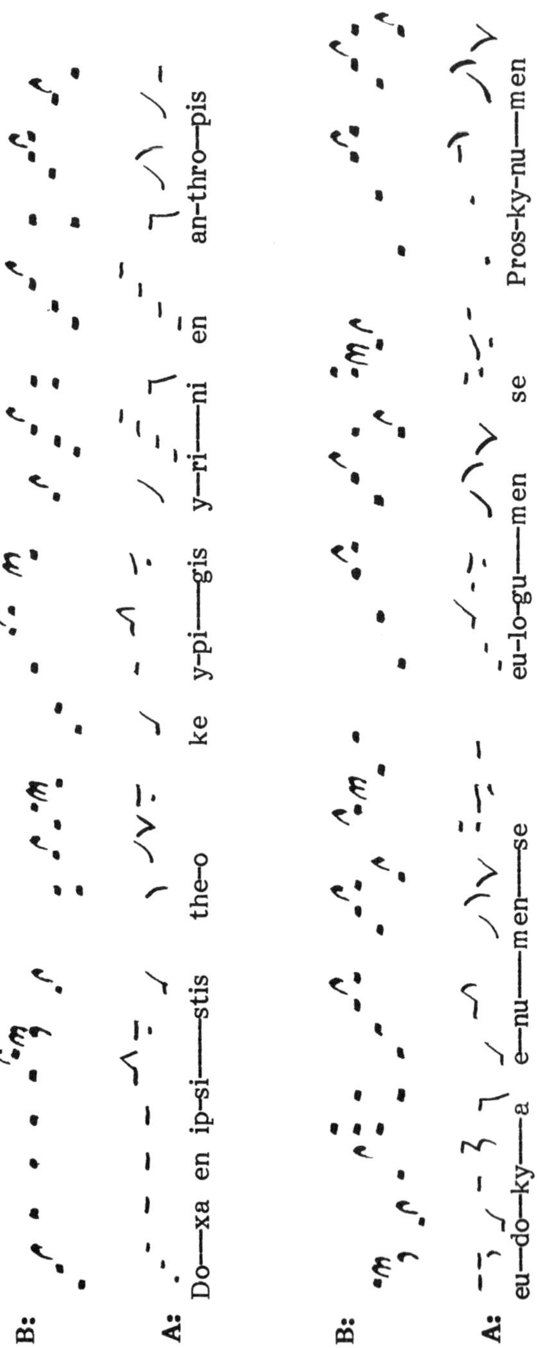
B:
A: Do—xa en ip-si—stis the-o ke y-pi—gis y—ri—ni en an-thro—pis
B:
A: eu—do—ky—a e—nu—men—se eu-lo-gu—men se Pros-ky-nu—men

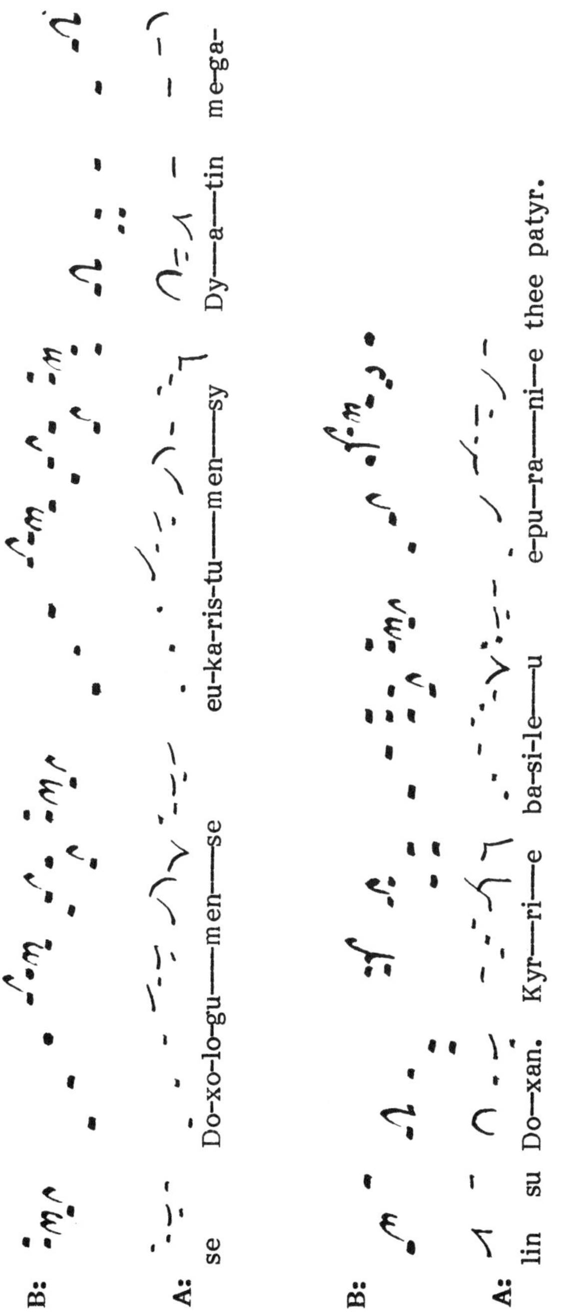

Example 1: *Doxa in ipsistis theo* in Paris, Bibliothèque Nationale, lat. 2291, fol. 16 (A), and in Paris, Bibliothèque Nationale, lat. 1118, fols. 67v–68v (B).

sigma as Martianus would describe it—does not correspond to the *clivis* as the "accent theory" states, but rather to a *torculus*, consisting of a three-note ascent and descent.[35]

Handschin had discovered that the Paleofrankish script incorporated the signs for prosodic accents, but he then proceeded to deny that these signs had anything to do with the accents! There were two reasons for this. First, his understanding of the relationship between accents and neumes was based upon the "accent theory," as summarized a few moments ago, not upon a reading of the ancient grammatical treatises themselves or their Carolingian commentaries. The fact that the acute, grave, and circumflex signs in the notation in Paris 2291 did not correspond to *virga*, *punctum*, and *clivis* as postulated by the accent theory led Handschin to conclude that those signs could not have been derived from prosodic accents. (At one point he does ask whether the grammarians might not have understood the acute accent as an ascent, rather than a high tone, but he carries this no further.)[36] The second kind of evidence against any putative role for accents in the Paleofrankish script came from a different characteristic of this script itself—namely, its heighting.

As can be seen in example 1, which compares the neumatic settings of the *Doxa* in Paris 2291 and Paris 1118, the neumes in Paris 2291 are rather carefully heighted so as to convey the fundamental shape of the melody.

Handschin went so far as to say that the Paleofrankish script had "diastematic character."[37] It is not diastematic—it does not indicate all intervals, including half and whole steps, unequivocally—but the script is certainly a good example of what Leo Treitler has called "iconic" notation.[38] At all events, the relatively good heighting of the neumes in Paris 2291 led Handschin to the following conclusion: "The principle of this neumatic script is clear: the higher or lower position on the parchment corresponds to pitch-level; insofar as a rising or falling line is used, it serves to link such positions, but it is not itself a notational character. Therefore no *virga* = *accentus acutus* in the sense of the grammarians. . . ."[39]

[35] Handschin, "Eine alte Neumenschrift," 72–78.

[36] Handschin, "Eine alte Neumenschrift," 79. In his words: "Man könnte übrigens fragen, ob nicht schon die Grammatiker beim 'Acutus' manchmal an Aufstieg statt an Hochton gedacht haben." A bit later, on p. 80, he suggests further doubts about the "accent theory" when he states: "Man mag immerhin den letzteren Typus weiterhin als 'Akzent-Neumen' bezeichnen (dies unter der *nicht ganz zutreffenden Voraussetzung, daß der Acutus immer nur den Hochton und nicht die steigende Folge bezeichnet hat*) . . ." (my italics).

[37] Handschin, "Eine alte Neumenschrift," 74.

[38] Cf. Leo Treitler, "Reading and Singing," and his earlier article, "The Early History of Music Writing," where this concept was presented for the first time.

[39] Handschin, "Eine alte Neumenschrift," 78–79.

Unfortunately, Handschin had apparently not studied many other examples of the Paleofrankish script.[40] Had he been able to do so, he would have realized that most of them are not as carefully heighted as is the *Doxa* in Paris 2291.[41] One such example appears in plate 2.

This is the setting of the Introit *Ad te levavi* as it appears in the sacramentary Düsseldorf D 1. The sacramentary itself dates from the ninth century; the Paleofrankish neumes were probably entered in the tenth century.[42] I have provided a synoptic, diplomatic transcription of *Ad te levavi* from several early manuscripts in example 2.

As comparison of plate 2 and example 2 will quickly reveal, the script in Düsseldorf D 1 cannot be described as being "carefully heighted." If it were, the ascent on *le-* of *levavi* would be larger than that on *an-* of *animam,* to name just one example. Heightedness, not to mention diastematy, is clearly not the persistent, commanding feature of this notation. If one compares the various scripts in example 2 from the point of view of accent, however, a different picture emerges. Wherever the Paleofrankish setting has an oblique upward stroke, the sign for an acute accent, the other manuscripts have a *pes* (e.g., over the syllables *le-* of *levavi, an-* and *-mam* of *animam*). Whenever it has a descending oblique stroke, the sign for a grave accent, the other sources have a *clivis* (e.g., over the syllables *me-* in *meus, e-* in *erubescam, -de-* of *irrideant,* and *me-* in *mei*). Wherever it has a downward *C* or sigma, the circumflex, the other manuscripts have a *torculus* (e.g., over the syllables *-que* of *neque, -ri-* of *irrideant,* and *ex-* and *-tant* of *expectant*). The significance of the "accent" signs in Düsseldorf D 1 is thus precisely the same as it was in Paris 2291—they represent two-note ascending and descending gestures and the three-note ascent/descent respectively. They do

[40] Handschin also discusses in detail the examples of the Paleofrankish script in Valenciennes, Bibliothèque municipale, MS. 148, containing the *Musica disciplina* of Aurelian of Réôme, as well as the isolated examples in Valenciennes 294, 337, 399, and 107. For a listing of the sources for the Paleofrankish script, see p. 216 of Jacques Hourlier and Michel Huglo, "Notation paléofranque," *Études grégoriennes* 2 (1957): 212–19. Of these, Handschin had apparently not consulted Douai, Bibliothèque municipale, MSS. 6 and 246; Düsseldorf, Universitätsbibliothek, MSS. D.1, D.2, and D.3; Leiden, Bibliotheek der Rijksuniversiteit, MS. B. P. L. 28; Paris, Bibliothèque Nationale, MSS. lat. 2717, lat. 7972, lat. 15614, lat. 17305, lat. 17306, and n. a. lat. 1618; or Boulogne-sur-Mer (St. Omer), Bibliothèque municipale, MS. 666.

[41] On this see Solange Corbin, *Die Neumen,* Palaeographie der Musik I:3 (Köln: Arno Volk, 1977), 3.77.

[42] On this setting see Bruno Stäblein, *Schriftbild der einstimmigen Musik,* Musikgeschichte in Bildern III/4 (Leipzig: VEB Deutscher Verlag für Musik, 1975), 106–07; Ewald Jammers, *Die Essener Neumenhandschriften der Landes- und Stadtbibliothek Düsseldorf* (Ratingen: Aloys Henn, 1952), 25ff. and Tafeln 5–7; and Jacques Hourlier and Michel Huglo, "Notation paléofranque," 216.

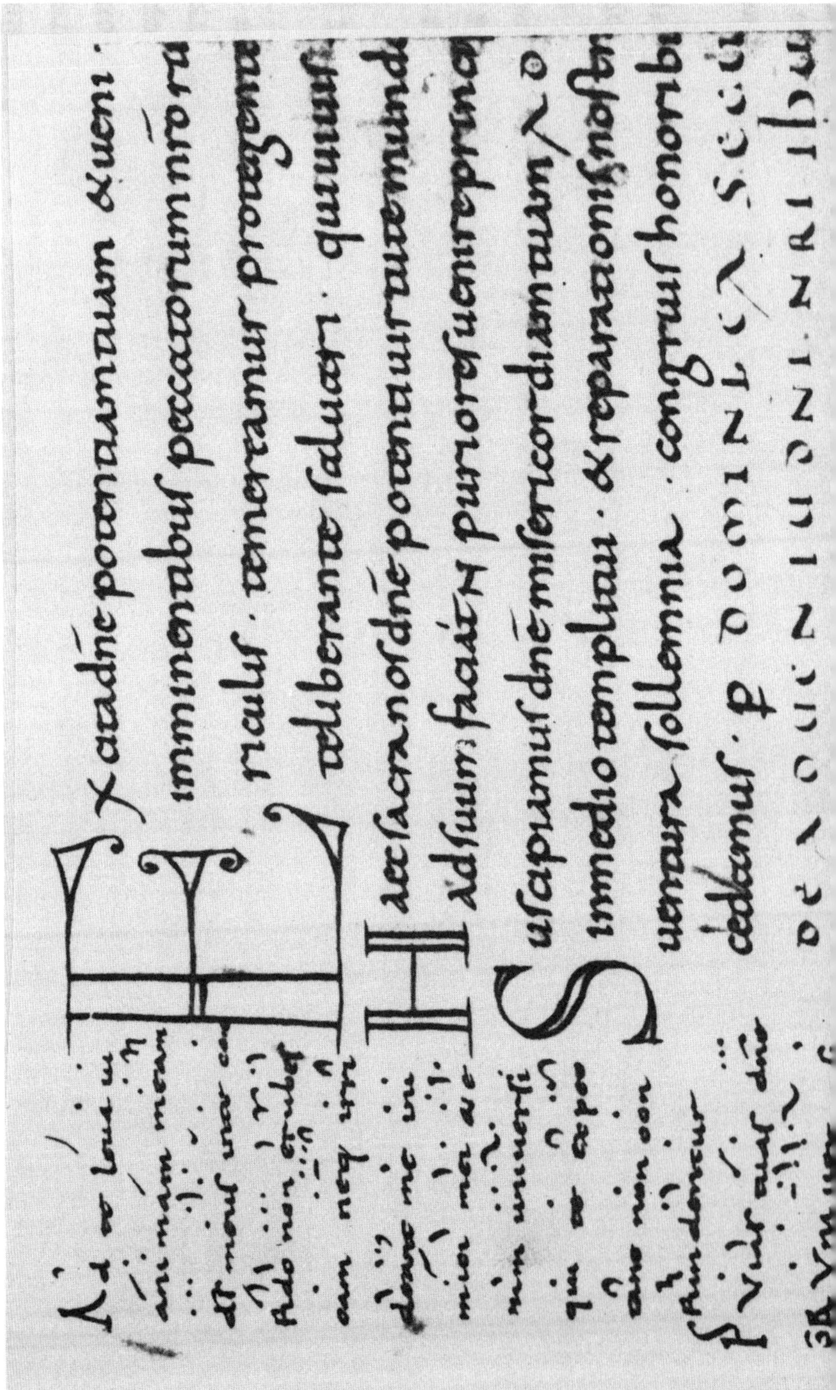

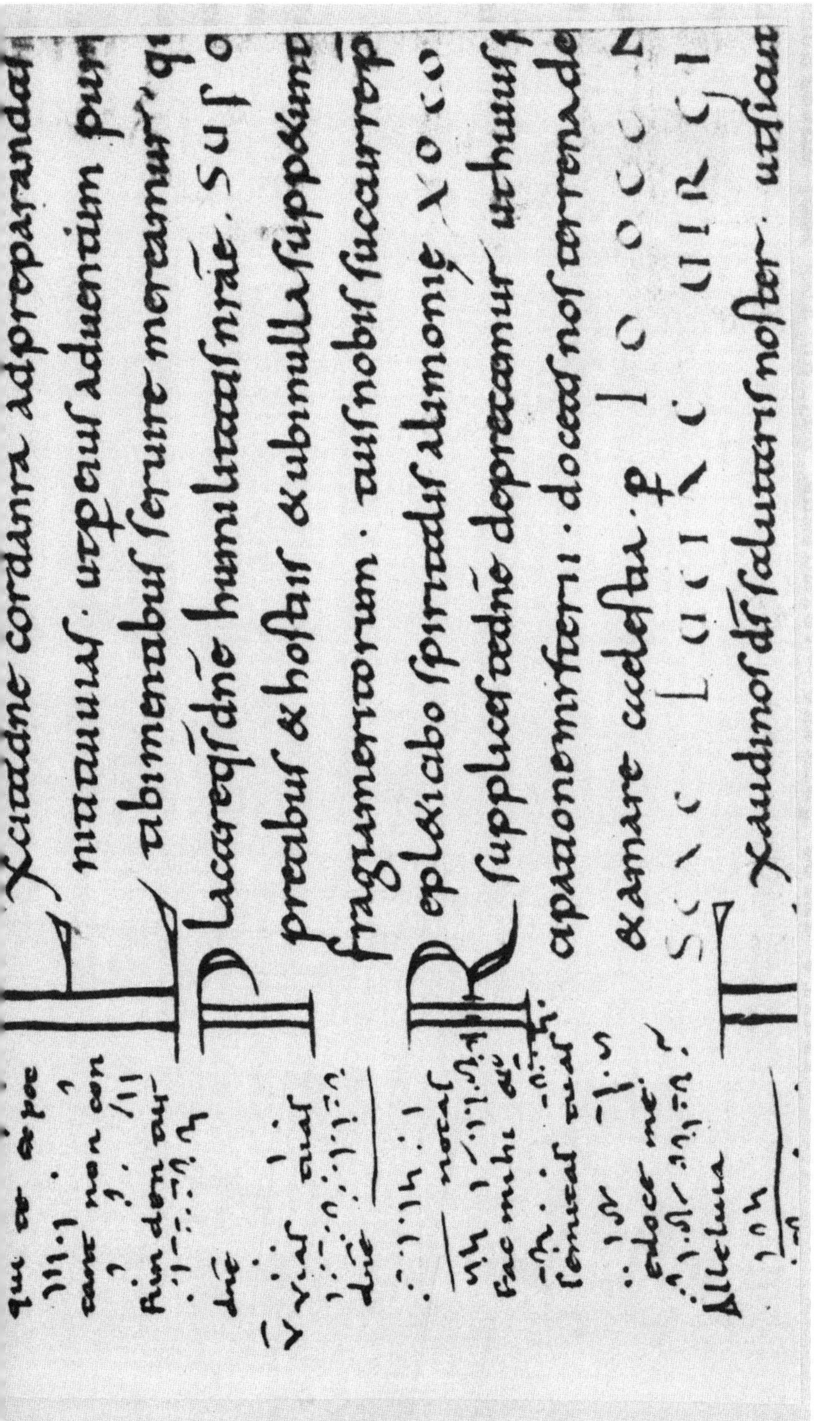

Plate 2: *Ad te levavi* in Paleofrankish script (Düsseldorf, Universitäts- und Landesbibliothek, MS. D 1, fol. 126v; on loan from the city of Düsseldorf). Reproduced by permission.

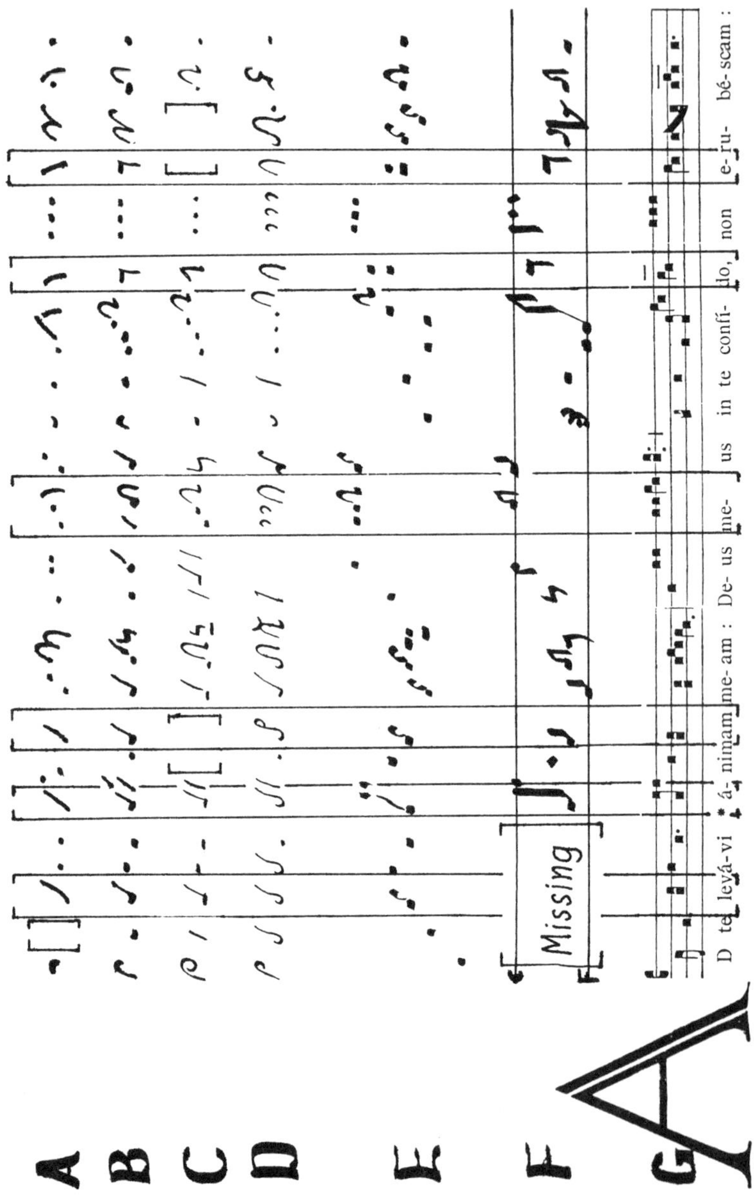
A
B
C
D
E
F
G
Missing
A D te levá-vi * á- nimam me-am : De- us me- us in te confí- do, non e-ru- bé-scam :

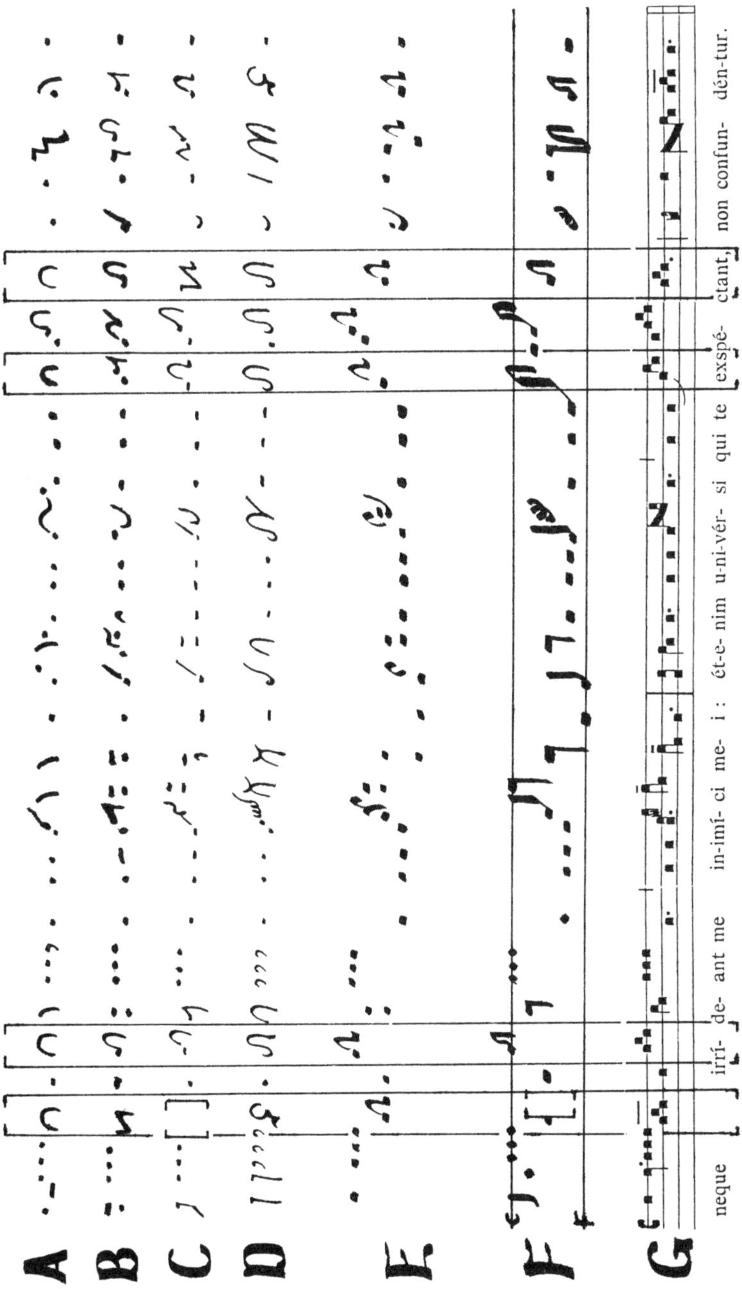

Example 2: *Ad te levavi* in Paleofrankish (A: Düsseldorf D 1), Bretonic (B: Angers 91), French (C: Chartres 47), St. Gall (D: St. Gall 339), Aquitanian (E: Paris 903), and Beneventan (F: Ben VI.34) scripts, and in *Graduale Romanum* (G).

not represent the *virga*, *punctum*, and *clivis* postulated by the accent theory—and they do not serve as links between positions on a diastematic matrix as Handschin supposed. Instead, they are employed in both manuscripts in a fashion completely consistent with the descriptions of the prosodic accents in ancient grammatical treatises and in their Carolingian commentaries.

Thus far I have been trying to avoid applying the name "accent" to the notational signs we have been discussing in Paris 2291 and Düsseldorf D 1. There is, however, some ninth-century evidence that the specific melodic gestures these signs represent were called by the names of the accents. I am speaking of course about the treatise of Aurelian of Réôme. As is well known, Aurelian's work shares with the *enchiriadis* treatises and the *Commemoratio brevis* a strong preference for the use of grammatical terminology as a means of discussing plainchant.[43] For example, in the nineteenth chapter of his *Musica disciplina* Aurelian describes the Introit psalm-tone of the first mode (see excerpt 5 and example 3) by saying that it has an acute accent on the second syllable, if that syllable is a dactyl or short, and on the fourth syllable if that syllable is long. He goes on to say that the eighth syllable "will be circumflexed," and that the ninth "will be made acute." The twelfth syllable "will be wound around" (*circumvolvetur*),[44] and the fifteenth will receive a three-fold percussion of the voice.[45]

Excerpt 5
from Aurelianus Reomensis, Musica disciplina, *chapter 19*

Igitur in reciprocatione introituum, si versus eiusdem XVI in se continuerit syllabas, ut est "Gloria patri et filio et spiritui sancto," mediocriter prima initiabitur syllaba, id est "Glo-," et *secunda acuto enunciabitur accentu,* videlicet "-ri-." Ea tamen ratione, si dactilus fuerit, vel quelibet correpta syllaba; sin autem producta fuerit, fuerit tunc circumflexione gaudebit.

[43] On this see Calvin M. Bower, "The Grammatical Model of Musical Understanding in the Middle Ages," in *Hermeneutics and Medieval Culture*, ed. Patrick J. Gallacher and Helen Damico (Albany: State University of New York Press, 1989), 133–45.

[44] Here and elsewhere in the treatise, Aurelian uses the verbs "circumvolvo" and "circumflecto" and the nouns "circumvolutio" and "circumflexio" interchangeably, with all four terms referring to a three-note ascending/descending melodic gesture, insofar as one can determine. See the articles on these terms in *Mittellateinisches Wörterbuch.* Cf. Martianus's use of *variatio sermonum* with respect to the circumflex accent, as discussed above.

[45] *Aureliani Reomensis Mvsica disciplina*, ed. Lawrence Gushee, Corpus Scriptorum de Musica 21 ([Rome]: American Institute of Musicology, 1975), 119. My paraphrase is based on the translation by Joseph Ponte, "Aureliani Reomensis Musica Disciplina: A Revised Text, Translation, and Commentary" (Ph.D. diss., Brandeis University, 1961), 2:156–58. Cf. Bielitz, *Musik und Grammatik*, 116.

> Tertia vero, scilicet "-a," suspensa tenebitur voce. *Quarta* post haec, hoc est: "Pa-," si producta fuerit veluti haec eadem syllaba quae positione producitur, in ea *acutus accendetur vocis accentus.*
>
> Quinta autem, sexta ac septima, vicelicet he "-tri et Fi-," gravi tenebuntur tenore. *Octava vero, hoc est "-li," circumflectetur. Nona acuetur, id est "-o."*
>
> Decima et undecima, scilicet he "et Spi-" graviter pronunciabuntur, [ac] *duodecima, hoc est "-ri-," circumvolvetur.* Tercia autem decima atque quartadecima, id est "-tu-" et "-i," in imis deponentur.
>
> Quartadecima vero, videlicet "Sanc-," terna gratulabitur vocis percussione. Sane sextadecima syllaba, scilicet "-to," sive prima fuerit, secundave seu tertia divisio iuxta normam superius insitam eorum erit distributio divisionum; sin alias uberior fuerit versus, interpolatio ilico fiet modulationis iuxta congeriem litterarum ut hic:

The Valenciennes manuscript of Aurelian's treatise does not carry any neumes over this description. Therefore, for illustrative purposes in example 3, I have supplied prosodic accents in the places he specified.

Example 3: Gloria Patri for *Protus autentus* in *Graduale Romanum* (from Bruno Stäblein, "Psalm," in *Die Musik in Geschichte und Gegenwart*, vol. 10, cols. 1668–90).

Although Aurelian's version and the modern one differ in details, it is nonetheless clear that the melodic gesture to which he refers when he specifies an acute accent is an upward ascent of two notes; the gesture referred to as *circumflexio* or *circumvolutio* is an ascent and descent of three notes. Thus, there is the same congruence of accent name and melodic gesture in Aurelian as there was between accent shape and melodic gesture in the Paleofrankish script. As a result, the question of whether Aurelian was referring to actual written signs or not is moot:[46] the melodic gestures represented by graphic signs in the Paleofrankish script and by the terms *accentus acutus* and *circumflexus* in Aurelian are the same in either case.

I hope that it has become clear from what I have had to say above that both the prosodic accents themselves, as well as the terms used to describe them, are a part of the conceptual matrix of ninth-century musical notation. In saying that, I must insist again upon adherence to the concept of prosodic accents as presented in the grammatical treatises themselves, and not that given in the "accent theory" of musical notation. Professor Treitler has said that "it is time the accent theory was abandoned."[47] I agree with him completely; it was a flawed theory to begin with. At the same time, however, it should be clear that a fully adequate theory of the origins of the neumes in the medieval West must take account of both prosodic accents and punctuation signs as a means for representing musical discourse. Finally, as regards the Paleofrankish script, I believe that when he said "De accentibus toni oritur nota quae dicitur neuma," the Vatican Anonymous was right after all.

[46] Cf. Corbin, *Die Neumen*, 3.18, and Treitler, "Reading and Singing," 152.
[47] Treitler, "Reading and Singing," 186.

JOHN BOE

Chant Notation in Eleventh-Century Roman Manuscripts

Was music notated at Rome before the St. Cecilia gradual, finished in 1071, was begun? Obviously yes, although according to common wisdom, no examples of Roman notation before 1071 have survived.[1] Nevertheless, might one find bits of notation written in urban or suburban Rome before 1071, if one looked hard in the right places? Probably: the search through Roman sacramentaries, epistle and gospel books, office lectionaries, bibles, homiliaries, etc.—books that did *not* perish under Nicholas III (1277–80)—would be worth undertaking. (Of course, notation added to an earlier manuscript text is hard to date.) If the search should turn up bits of notation, what might they show? They might show an earlier stage of Roman notation: that

[1] The St. Cecilia gradual, now Cologny-Geneva, Bibliotheca Bodmeriana, Codex 74 (henceforth "Bodmer 74"), was written at and for the basilica of Santa Cecilia in Trastevere. Max Lütolf, editor of the handsome facsimile edition, *Das Graduale von Santa Cecilia in Trastevere, Cod. Bodmer 74* (Cologny-Geneva: Fondation Martin Bodmer, 1987), aptly remarks, ". . . nach der heutigen Quellenlage setzt mit dieser Handschrift die musikalische Überlieferung des sogenannten 'altrömischen' Chorals ein," but continues "Von der Frage der altrömischen Tradition . . . abgesehen, stellt C 74, *die als die älteste heute bekannte Musikhandschrift römischer Provenienz überhaupt gelten darf*, auch für die Rezeption der sogenannten gregorianischen Überlieferung sowie für die Aufnahme einer beträchtlichen Zahl an Stücken aus dem Tropen- und Sequenzenschatz des 9.–11. Jahrhunderts in Rom eine bemerkenswerte Quelle dar" (vol. 1, p. 14). It is to the phrase I have italicized that this paper is addressed.

is, the same type of neumes as those found in the St. Cecilia gradual but *in campo aperto*. Such neumes would presumably have developed within an indigenous tradition for writing music reaching back before the eleventh century, especially if found with pieces from the local Roman repertory. One could then reasonably hypothesize a mixed oral and written tradition for that repertory during most of the tenth and early eleventh centuries. On the other hand, pre-1071 notation appearing in undoubtedly Roman manuscripts might instead have been borrowed or imported, either so generally as to have been adopted by Roman scribes in Roman scriptoria for Roman manuscripts, or else casually, penned now and then in Roman ink but by non-Roman hands. Also, such notation might only have served to record pieces foreign to the local repertory, leaving local Roman chant to oral tradition. And finally, if bits of notation should appear to have been imported, where were they imported from?

Toward the end of the eleventh century, chant notation at Rome was broadly similar to central-Italian notation as found in manuscripts from Lucca, say, or Norcia. This Roman notation survives in three manuscripts from the eleventh century, which by luck remain of the "fifty antiphoners, graduals, missals, and other old service books" destroyed by order of Pope Nicholas III between 1277 and 1280.[2] Of these three manuscripts, two graduals, Bibliotheca Bodmeriana 74 and Vaticanus latinus 5319, have been

[2] The Brabantian observer and comparative liturgist Radulph de Rivo (ca. 1345–1403), who spent 1381 and 1396–97 in Rome, is the authority for this event. In his *De canonum observantia liber* (1397), he writes:

> Sciendum tamen, quod Nicolaus papa tertius, natione Romanus de genere Ursinorum, qui coepit anno Domini millesimo ducentesimo septuagesimo septimo et palatium apud sanctum Petrum construxit, fecit in ecclesiis Urbis amoveri antiphonarios, gradualia, missalia, et alios libros officii antiquos quinquaginta et mandavit, ut de cetero ecclesiae Urbis uterentur libris et breviariis Fratrum Minorum, quorum regulam etiam confirmavit. Unde hodie in Roma omnes libri sunt novi et Franciscani, et forma notularum in cantu antiqua, qua tum Ambrosiani quam Alemaniae nationes utuntur, cum pluribus aliis observationibus ecclesiasticis ab Urbe relegata.

I take this passage from the convenient quotation in *Monumenta Monodica Medii Aevi* 2, ed. Bruno Stäblein and Margareta Landwehr-Melnicki (Kassel: Bärenreiter, 1970), 141, where further references are given. I have not found a specific decree of Nicholas III (Giovanni Gaetano Orsini, a native noble Roman) touching this matter in *Regesta Pontificum Romanorum* 2, ed. August Potthast (Berlin: Decker, 1875), 1719–56, except perhaps decree no. 21, 531, dated 3 February 1279, dealing with the ordering of various matters at St. Peter's, presumably after he had established papal residence at the Vatican. Nicholas III had been named protector of the Franciscans by Urban IV before Nicholas became pope, and did much for the friars throughout his pontificate. There seems to be no reason to doubt Radulph de Rivo's careful testimony, though he wrote more than a hundred years after the event he describes. He was curious about the Roman Liturgy and made careful inquiries on the spot.

published. A third, less well-known manuscript, Archivio San Pietro F 11, containing the office and several masses for the dead, the wedding mass, and other items, is notated in the same style. These manuscripts come from the Caecilian, Lateran (?), and Vatican basilicas, respectively. There must have been others like them that perished. Later collections of Roman chant repertory also survive.[3]

When did the late eleventh-century Roman version of central-Italian notation originate? I wish I knew for sure. Guido's famous visit to the court of the Tusculan pope John XIX must have taken place in 1032 or just before. The use of Guido's yellow line for c and red line for F at Rome can hardly antedate the decade 1025–35. It may be that similar uncleffed but diastematic notes *in campo aperto* were used at Rome before Guido's lines graphically established the place of the semitone in the scale. In any case, during the scant fifty years 1020–70, scribes working at Rome borrowed, adapted, or developed the Roman dialect of central-Italian notation and fixed the rules of its script. These rules—as for instance when to use a *virga* and when a *punctum* and what kind of slant, if any, to give the *punctum*—are different from those of south-Italian Beneventan notation. Furthermore, liquescents are employed much less often in Roman manuscripts than in Beneventan. The unfortunate misconception that Roman notation is a mere variety of Beneventan notation is, alas, still being propagated. Bruno Stäblein was right to assign Roman notation to central Italy; and it is to central Italy that we must look for notation parallel to the Roman variety.

The hypothesis preferred in this paper is that Roman notation developed between 1020 and 1070 by imitating central-Italian notation. But, for the moment, I revert to the alternative: that Roman notation developed indigenously over a period of a hundred years or longer before 1070. South of Rome, there is evidence both direct and indirect that Beneventan notation developed over a long span of time: tenth-century ur-Beneventan notation[4] exists. It is not fanciful to argue for the presence of notation of

[3] Namely the well-known MSS Archivio San Pietro F 22, a thirteenth-century gradual; London, B.L. Add. 29988, a twelfth-century office antiphoner; and Archivio San Pietro B 79, another office antiphoner from the late twelfth or early thirteenth centuries.

[4] As in a tenth-century bishop's roll for the blessing of the font on Easter Even, and an originally separate roll for pontifical ceremonies (both now cut up and bound together with a somewhat later Exultet roll, in Rome, Biblioteca Casanatense 724). The pontifical roll—and probably the *Benedictio fontis*—belonged to Landulf, bishop of Benevento 957–69, and archbishop 969–82. The preface for the blessing of the font has partial notation for certain cadences and a few complete passages. The notation is probably a later addition, but not much later than the text. In Montecassino, Compactiones VII, a piece is stuck to the verso of the missal fragment Alban Dold called "Missal II," the notation of which piece has to be read in a mirror. The hand is small, early Beneventan; the notation, fine and spidery early Beneventan, perhaps from a tonary, and must date from the early tenth century or possibly still earlier.

some sort in southern Italy by the late ninth century.[5] I have not yet seen any such evidence for Rome. On the contrary, such sparse evidence as I have gathered, some of it perhaps from the late tenth century, argues instead for the opposite notion that the kind of music writing found in late eleventh-century Roman books was created earlier in that same century, though not *ex nihilo*. Other kinds of notation were known and used in Rome before 1020 and perhaps earlier. I have found a few such examples. But the later eleventh-century Roman style could hardly have developed directly from the style of notation found in these few and isolated passages.

Another objection to the alternative hypothesis of a long and gradual development of notation at Rome must be taken into account. Throughout most of the tenth century, from at least 930 to 985, Rome seems to have been unable to support scriptoria on any continuing basis. No entries were made at Rome in the *Liber pontificalis* after 891. The state of affairs in the tenth century has been regarded by some as irrelevant to chant transmission at Rome: it is *not* irrelevant and it influences what can reasonably be hypothesized about the development of notation. The French liturgical scholar Pierre Jounel writes:

> The tenth century has not transmitted any Roman liturgical manuscripts to us, with the possible exception of a *Capitulare evangeliorum*, Barb. lat. 637. [This statement is a slight exaggeration. Examples that may date from the *end* of the century are cited by Jounel himself.] One should not be surprised, for the Roman clergy had fallen into a state of extreme decadence, on the intellectual plane as well as the moral plane.[6]

Under such conditions, a continuing local evolution of a native Roman style of notation during most of the tenth century is hard to imagine. *If* there was written notation in use at Rome towards the end of the ninth century—which proposition is doubtful but hard to disprove—books containing such notation may have continued in use: they were certainly not much copied.

Before delivering this paper, I was able to examine slightly more than half of the Roman liturgical books (mainly sacramentaries and lectionaries of various sorts, including bibles) that survived Nicholas III's bonfire. The earliest, a ninth-century evangeliary-capitulary, Vaticanus latinus 5465, has

[5] See Kenneth Levy, "Charlemagne's Archetype of Gregorian Chant," *Journal of the American Musicological Society* 40 (1987): 1–30.

[6] Pierre Jounel, *Le culte des saints dans les basiliques du Latran et du Vatican au douzième siècle*, Collection de l'École Française de Rome 26 (Rome: École Française de Rome, 1977), 129.

no notation, not even at *Eli Eli* in the Palm Sunday passion, where it might be expected. Of the others, I wish here to mention four, of which the first was listed in Bannister's survey of Vatican manuscripts with notation. (Bannister did not include manuscripts held outside the Vatican Library in his systematic list. In his day, codices in the Archivio San Pietro were not accessible through the Vatican Library.) The first instance, the St. Cecilia Bible, BAV Barberianus 587, was prepared ten to twenty years later than the Caecilian gradual of 1071 but at the same scriptorium. Notation occurs where one might expect in a Roman bible—that is, to notate passages of chant arising in the context of unnotated readings that were recited to lesson tones. These more lyrical chant passages were notated in bibles—or in liturgical extracts from bibles—because such books were used for reading the lessons, particularly at the night office; and because, in most cases, the reader who chanted the lesson also sang the canticle, prayer, or exclamation given special musical treatment but imbedded in or attached to the lesson. So much is implied by the recurrent rubric *hic mutatur uox* or *hic mutat tonum*. In this example from the St. Cecilia bible, the Lamentations for the last three days of Holy Week are notated in the margins, with lines and clefs. The notation, added not long after the completion of the manuscript, is typical of late eleventh-century Roman style, except for two Beneventan liquescents; other liquescents use the normal Roman forms.[7]

The only instance I can here present of the kind of notation that ought to have *preceded* the familiar Caecilian variety—that is, diastematic notation *in campo aperto*, with *custodes* but without lines and clefs—is hardly earlier than Caecilian examples and moreover is infected with Beneventan symptoms: an *acuasta* at the start; the restriction of the *virga* to the top of the phrase and the use of upward slanting *puncta* for rising notes neither highest nor lowest. The notation is found in a Roman office lectionary containing the scriptural books of the prophets, BAV Archivio San Pietro C 92,

[7] The most reliable attribution and dating of the St. Cecilia bible is that by Knut Berg in "Notes on the Dates of Some Early Giant Bibles," *Institutum Romanum Norvegiae, Acta ad Archaeologiam et Artium Historiam Pertinentia* 2 (Rome: Bretschneider, 1965), 167–76. Berg makes his case that the body of the text of the bible dates from "shortly before 1097"; comes not from Santa Cecilia in Trastevere but from another scriptorium; and in 1097 or just before was edited at and for Santa Cecilia by the insertion of several folios and marginal additions, including the lists of altar dedications, clergy, and donors. In this essay and in his later *Studies in Tuscan Twelfth-Century Illumination* (Oslo: Universitetsforlaget, 1968), Berg refers to and corrects the various opinions on the bible expressed by the art historian E. B. Garrison in the four volumes entitled *Studies in the History of Mediaeval Italian Painting* (Florence: L'Impronta, 1953–62). (Also see revised extracts from Garrison's essays, published after his death in 1981 as *Early Italian Painting: Selected Studies* [London: Pindar, 1984], vol. 2: Manuscripts.)

certainly used at St. Peter's towards the end of the eleventh century. In his admirable study of the manuscript, Jean Gribomont has shown that the last part of it, from Ezekiel to the end, was largely written by Belizo, *sacer indignus*, to be identified with a priest of the basilica whose unusual name is found in a legal document of 28 April 1083.[8] Isaiah (the beginning of which is lost), Jeremiah, and Lamentations—at the end of which the notated passage is found—are by other and earlier hands. The acrostic Prayer of Jeremiah, *Oratio Hieremię prophetę* is notated *in extenso* on fol. 138[v], only the announcement *Incipit oratio hieremię prophetę* being notated in the margin. Liquescents are notably absent: there are only three, though properly Beneventan in shape, over the syllables *gau-* of *gaudium*, *au-* of *autem*, and *prin-* of *principio*. Otherwise this notation could be described as "anachronistic ur-Beneventan" penned above the Roman minuscule text.

See H. M. Bannister, *Monumenti Vaticani di Paleografia musicale latina*, Codices e Vaticanis selecti phototypice expressi 12 (Leipzig: Harrassowitz, 1913), no. 415 (without plate and with inaccurate description of clefs); Thomas Connolly, "The *Graduale* of S. Cecilia in Trastevere and the Old Roman Tradition," *Journal of the American Musicological Society* 28 (1975): 418–20; and Lütolf, *Das Graduale von Santa Cecilia in Trastevere*, 1:36–37.

Notation in the St. Cecilia Bible is entered in the top margin of fol. 155[v] above the tiny script for *Incipit lamentatio hieremię prophetę. Aleph. Q[uonia]m̊ sedet sola ciuitas . . . facta ē[st] sub tributo*, as a model for the rest of the lesson. Similar notation appears for *Heth Cogitauit dominus . . . Teth* in the bottom margin of fol. 156[r] (rubric in the left margin of main text: *Fr̄ vi in PARASCEVEN*); for *Heth Misericordie dn̄i qui n̄ sumus cs̄up̄ti* in the bottom margin of fol. 156v (rubric: *IN SAB̄B̄ SC̄Ō.*); and for *Incipit oratio hieremie prophętę Recōdare dn̄ē quid accideret nōb* in the bottom margin of fol. 157[r].

[8] Jean Gribomont, "Les Prophètes de Belizo (San Pietro C 92)," in *Miscellanea Codicologica F. Masai Dicata*, ed. Pierre Cockshaw et al. (Ghent: Story-Scientia, 1979), 1:189–201. Cosmas Stornajolo, "Inventarium Codicum Manuscriptorum Latinorum Archivii Basilicae S. Petri in Vaticano . . ." (Città del Vaticano, typescript in the Sala Barberini, BAV, 1968) dates it "saec. xi." Also see Paola Supino Martini, *Roma e l'area grafica romanesca, secoli x–xii* (Alessandria: dell'Orso, 1987), 66–68 and nn. 60–64: "Per quanto riguarda le Sacre Scritture, sembra che un solo manoscritto in minuscola romanesca, contenente la tradizione Vulgata dei *Profeti*, Vat. Arch. S. Pietro C 92, possa essere attribuito con certezza allo *scriptorium* vaticano . . . . Se le prime 138 carte sono da riferirsi a due o tre mani diverse, tutte romanesche, Belizo di certo attese alla maggior parte del lavoro di copia (cc. 139–305)." Also see Garrison, *Studies*, 4:241–50. Garrison thought the manuscript came from the monastery of San Saba on the basis of records of financial transactions on the last folio (see Gribomont, "Les prophètes," 197–98); but Supino Martini corrects the interpretation of these: "È dunque probabile che il monastero di S. Saba possedesse alcune case nei pressi della basilica—adibite a dormitorio per i pellegrini o ad altro uso—i cui proventi furono percepiti talora dagli *actionarii* [general administrators of the patrimony of St. Peter's?] di S. Pietro e da essi successivamente versati ai monaci di S. Saba, talora direttamente da questi ultimi."

The melody of the Prayer of Jeremiah in San Pietro C 92 is similar to that found in a Farfa lectionary for the office, Rome, Biblioteca Nazionale, Farfense 32, fol. 138[v].

I turn to an extensive example of surviving notation written during the eleventh century in Rome: an epistle book or mass lectionary, now Rome, Biblioteca Angelica, MS. 1383 (henceforth RoA 1383), that must antedate the St. Cecilia gradual and in Jounel's view and mine must come from the monastery of San Saba. The monastery of San Saba on the "false" or "little" Aventine was founded some time between 650 and 710 by Greek monks and was still occupied by them in 870. The *Liber pontificalis* records gifts to the monastery by Leo III (792–816) and Gregory IV (827–44). After 870 and until 1145, when the house was formally placed under Cluny by Pope Lucius II, its history is obscure; but Benedictines must have been in place by the eleventh century, when the Latin rite was clearly in use.[9]

In agreement with Pierre Jounel and against Paola Supino Martini's opinion, I hold that the epistolary or *Lectionarium vetus*, now RoA 1383, was undoubtedly written for the eleventh-century Abbey of San Saba in Rome. In this manuscript, the feast of St. Saba has a vigil—a vigil otherwise unknown in the West in the period and explicable only as preceding the patronal festival. Moreover, the vigil is calligraphically embellished with the same degree of elaboration as is Easter. The folios at the end of the manuscript have been torn out: as Jounel remarks, they must have contained a specially grand illumination, probably of the Judean anchorite St. Saba himself.[10] The elegant but otherwise not sumptuous manuscript resembles

[9] But there is no evidence for the Benedictines at San Saba being Cassinese, as was surmised by Paul Fridolin Kehr, *Italia Pontificia sive Repertorium privilegiorum et litterarum a Romanis pontificibus . . .* (Berlin: Weidmann, 1906–1935), 1:118 (quoted in Supino Martini, *Roma e l'area grafica romanesca*, 142, n. 109). See n. 8 above for evidence that the monastery of San Saba owned a house or houses near St. Peter's, probably for the use of pilgrims, by the late eleventh century. One of Gregory VII's documents against the anti-pope Wibert (Clement [III]), dated *noui anni*—that is, 1081–82—was subscribed by *Maurus abbas s̄c̄e sabe* and *Ioh̄s archipb̄r de s̄c̄a cecilia*. A copy of the document is appended to Gregory I's *Liber pastoralis* in MS. Vaticanus latinus 586. So far as I know, the subscription has not been cited in connection with either institution.

[10] See Jounel, *Le culte des saints*, 33, 66, and 67, and Supino Martini, *Roma e l'area grafica romanesca*, 140–42 and pl. 28. Supino Martini thinks Jounel's attribution of the manuscript to San Saba is not justified because the manuscript has vigils for other feasts as well, namely for the feasts of St. John Baptist, SS. Peter and Paul, St. Mary on 15 August; All Saints' Day on 1 November; and St. Andrew: ". . . è possibile, a mio avviso, avanzare soltanto una più generica ipotesi di origine in ambiente monastico urbano." She seems unaware of the fact that all of these vigils (except All Saints') are found in *all* Roman kalendars and liturgical books of the mid-eleventh century. Most of them are ancient (the ancient vigil for St. Lawrence is unaccountably missing here), although the vigil for the Assumption of the B.V.M. is not quite so ancient as the others. The vigil for All Saints was being added to Roman observance in the latter part of the eleventh century. No other Roman manuscript or kalendar has a vigil for St. Saba: in fact, the feast itself is found in only three of the twelve Roman kalendars from the ninth to the early twelfth century edited by Jounel, namely RoV E 15 from St. Lawrence in Damaso, SP F 14 from St. Tryphon, and Archivio di Stato Italiano, MS. 997 (now lost), from the Lateran, where the feast of course had no vigil.

the Roman manuscripts Vaticanus latinus 5319 and Bodmer 74 in a general way. The rubrics disclose a kalendar conservative by later eleventh-century standards.[11] To the solidly Roman core have been added the feasts of St. Saba and St. Benedict, the feasts of the evangelists Matthew and Luke, the Nativity of the Blessed Virgin in September, the feast of All Saints on 1 November, and the feast of the Transfiguration of Christ. (According to Jounel, the manuscript is one of the earliest to attest the celebration of the Transfiguration at Rome.) However, the Sundays after Pentecost are numbered consecutively and entered all in a group after Pentecost. Moreover, the twenty-fifth Sunday is followed by *Dōm de scā Trinitate*, a distinctly non-Roman addition, redolent of Cluny.

The first instance of notation in the epistolary is found in the Easter vigil on Holy Saturday. The lesson from Jonah, *Lēc Ione Prop̄he* (beginning on fol. 75ᵛ) has extensive notation for the Prayer of Jonah, *Oratione Prophete*, beginning with *Clamaui* (fols. 76ʳ–77ᵛ), in the same ink as the main text. The *Lēc Daniēl. Prophetae cum cantico* (fol. 79ᵛ onwards) is also neumed intermittently and rubricked for singing.[12] The *Trac.* (more properly, canticle) following the Isaiah lesson *Vinea facta est* (fol. 74ʳ) was notated but the notation has faded badly, although the beginning is still legible. The *Tractum* [sic] *Cantemus Domino* (on fol. 69ᵛ) and the canticle *Attende celum* are also notated. *Sicut ceruus* (fol. 87ᵛ), which is not an appendage or continuation of a lesson sung by the reader but an independent processional chant, is not neumed in this lector's book. In all the notated passages, sufficient space was left for notation and the text was written smaller than elsewhere, after the manner of notated propers in missals. Thus there is reason to think that the notation with its consistent style is contemporary with the rest of the manuscript or nearly so.

It is at once clear that the three canticles *Vinea*, *Cantemus domino*, and *Attende celum* all have the Gregorian melody, which is also found in the old Roman mass antiphoners. That this should be so on the Easter vigil, the "mother of vigils," has always seemed strange. The conventional explanation that Gregorian versions have replaced lost old Roman versions—of which no single trace remains in three Roman graduals!—is hard to accept. Putative old Roman versions for the vigil canticles would presumably have resembled other eighth-mode tracts in the Roman repertory. At least it seems unlikely that they resembled the responsorial alternative *Vinea* found

[11] Printed in Jounel, *Le culte des saints*, 65–66.

[12] The lesson continues without notation on fols. 80–81ʳ. Notation again appears on fols. 82ᵛ–83ʳ for the Prayer of Azarias, the Song of the Three Children *Benedictus es domine* and *Benedicite omnia opera domini* continuing on fols. 84ʳ–86ʳ.

in Pistoia 121 and Rome, Biblioteca Vallicelliana C52.[13] Since Peter Jeffery's recognition that a leaf in an Hungarian library comes from an eighth-century Italian and possibly Roman gradual without notation but with old Roman text,[14] an explanation of sorts has appeared, one however that raises further questions. Jeffery's leaf fortunately contains masses from the offertory of Thursday before Palm Sunday through the introit of the Saturday after Easter. According to Jeffery's transcription, the Easter vigil mass was missing altogether from the manuscript in its original state and was only added in the margin with the following items: *pro introitu letania; deinde gloria in excelsis. alleluia. redemptionem. cum laudate dominum*—that is, the mass without the preceding vigil (I follow Jeffery's expansion of the abbreviations). Here is not the place to consider why the Easter vigil and mass might have originally been omitted from the manuscript; but the omission would account for the adoption of the Gregorian tracts for the canticles of the vigil, now seen in the old Roman books.

Setting aside the question of the Roman Easter vigil canticles, I turn to the notation employed in the San Saba manuscript, as shown in plate 1, the canticle *Cantemus domino* (fol. 69[v]); in plate 2, the introduction and start of *Benedictus es domine, deus patrum nostrorum* (fol. 84[r]); in plate 3, the ending of *Benedictus es domine* and the start of *Benedicite omnia opera domini dominum* (fol. 84[v]); and in plate 4, the conclusion of *Benedicite omnia opera domini* and the continuation of the lesson from the book of Daniel.

This notation is entirely adiastematic. It is not East Frankish: added significative letters nowhere occur. The descending three-note group  , as at *salutem* in the canticle *Cantemus domino* (end of third line), is indeed used in the Winchester Tropers; but the *ductus* of the San Saba manuscript lacks the perpendicular axis of the Winchester notation. The similarity of this notation to the neumes of Montpellier H 159 and to other manuscripts influenced by the monastic discipline of William of Dijon (otherwise known as William of Volpiano or Fécamp) is obvious. It is true, however, that San Saba does not use the "descending *quilisma*" of Montpellier H 159, and the *virga* is employed even more consistently as the normal note for recitation in the San Saba manuscript than in Montpellier H 159. Although

[13] The argument that the alternative *Vinea* in Pistoia 121 and RoV C 52 is old Roman seems to rest solely on the observed presence of certain *texts* in RoV C 52 that are drawn from the Roman psalter or Itala versions of the bible and occur in old Roman sources. See Michel Huglo, "Le chant 'vieux-romain': Liste des manuscrits et témoins indirects," *Sacris Erudiri* 6 (1954): 96; Dom Georges Frénaud, "Les témoins indirects du chant liturgique en usage à Rome aux IXe et Xe siècles," *Études grégoriennes* 3 (1959): 41–74; but especially Joseph Dyer, "Latin Psalters, Old-Roman and Gregorian Chants," *Kirchenmusikalisches Jahrbuch* 68 (1984): 11–30.

[14] As reported at the Fifty-Seventh Annual Meeting of the American Musicological Society, Chicago, November 1991.

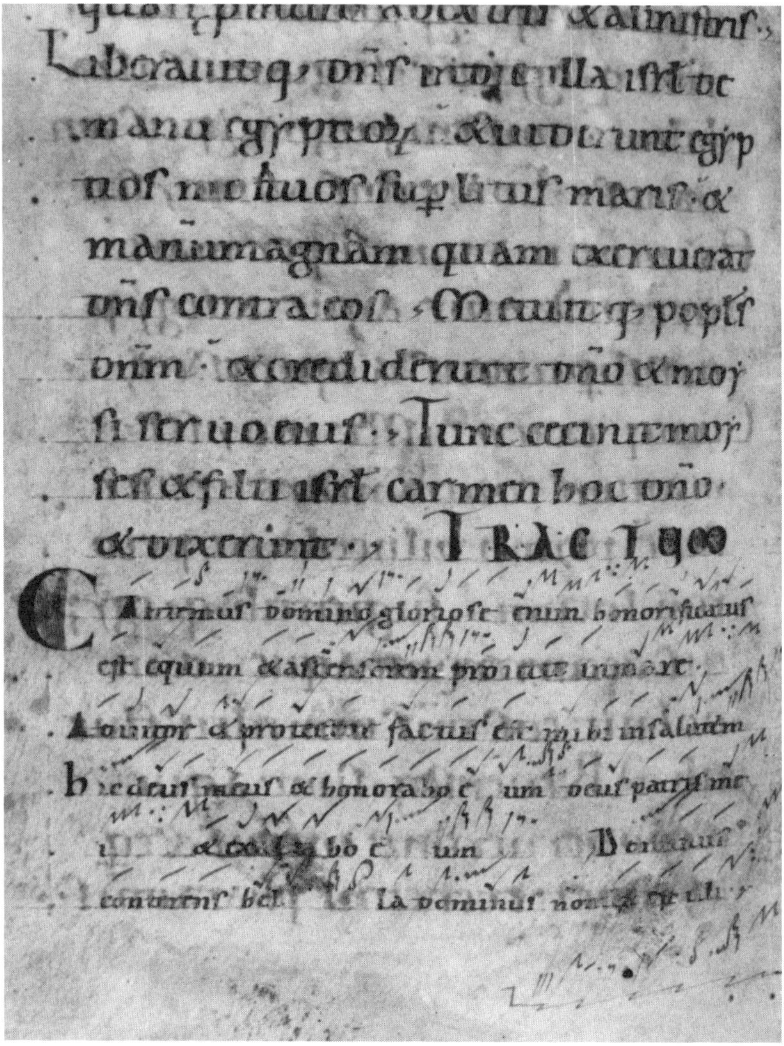

Plate 1: Rome, Biblioteca Angelica 1383, fol 69^{v}. Epistolary from San Saba monastery, Rome, last half, 11th c. Holy Saturday canticle, *Tractum Cantemus domino gloriose.* Reproduced by permission of the Italian Government, Ministerio per i Beni Culturali ed Ambientali. Further reproduction of any kind forbidden without express authorization.

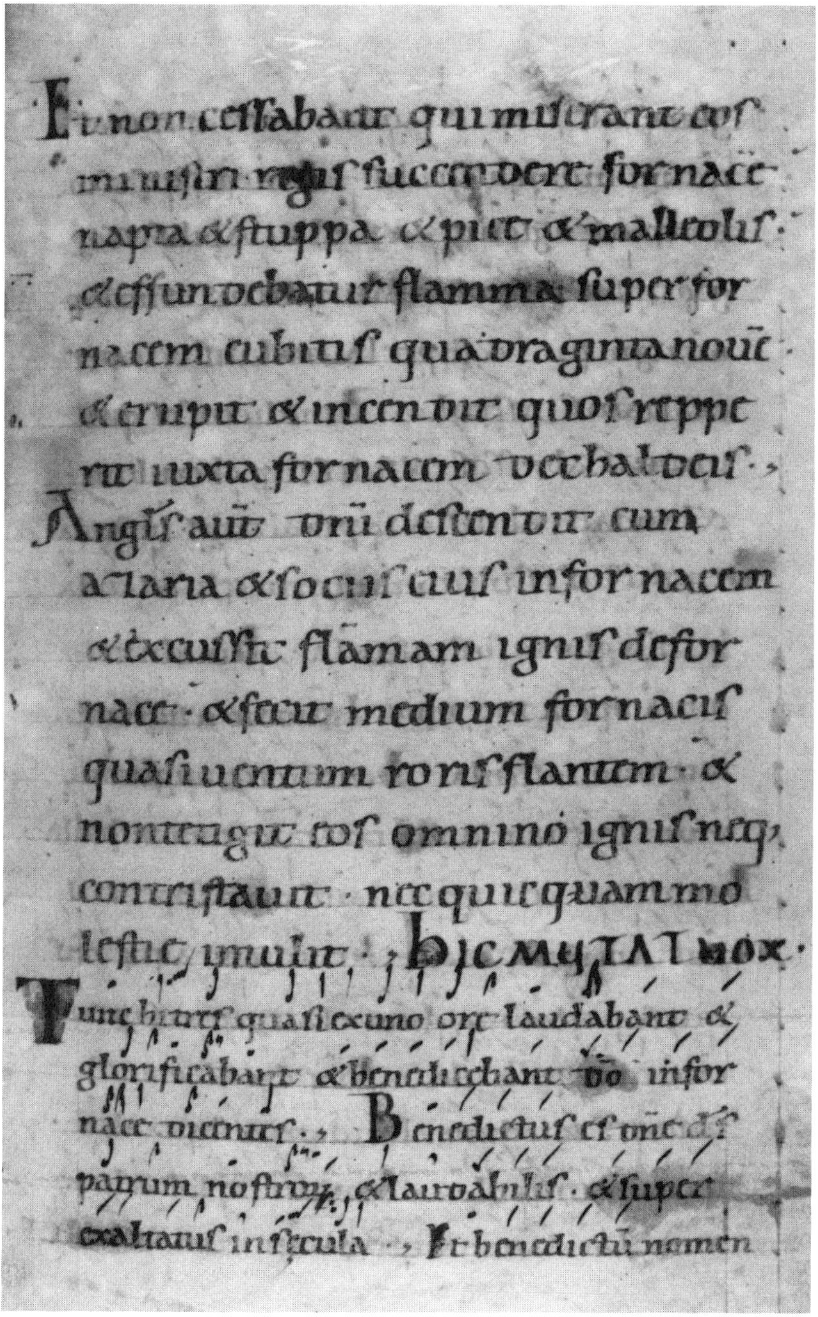

Plate 2: Rome, Biblioteca Angelica 1383, fol. 84[r]. Introduction and beginning of *Benedictus es domine deus patrum nostrorum.* Reproduced by permission of the Italian Government, Ministerio per i Beni Culturali ed Ambientali. Further reproduction of any kind forbidden without express authorization.

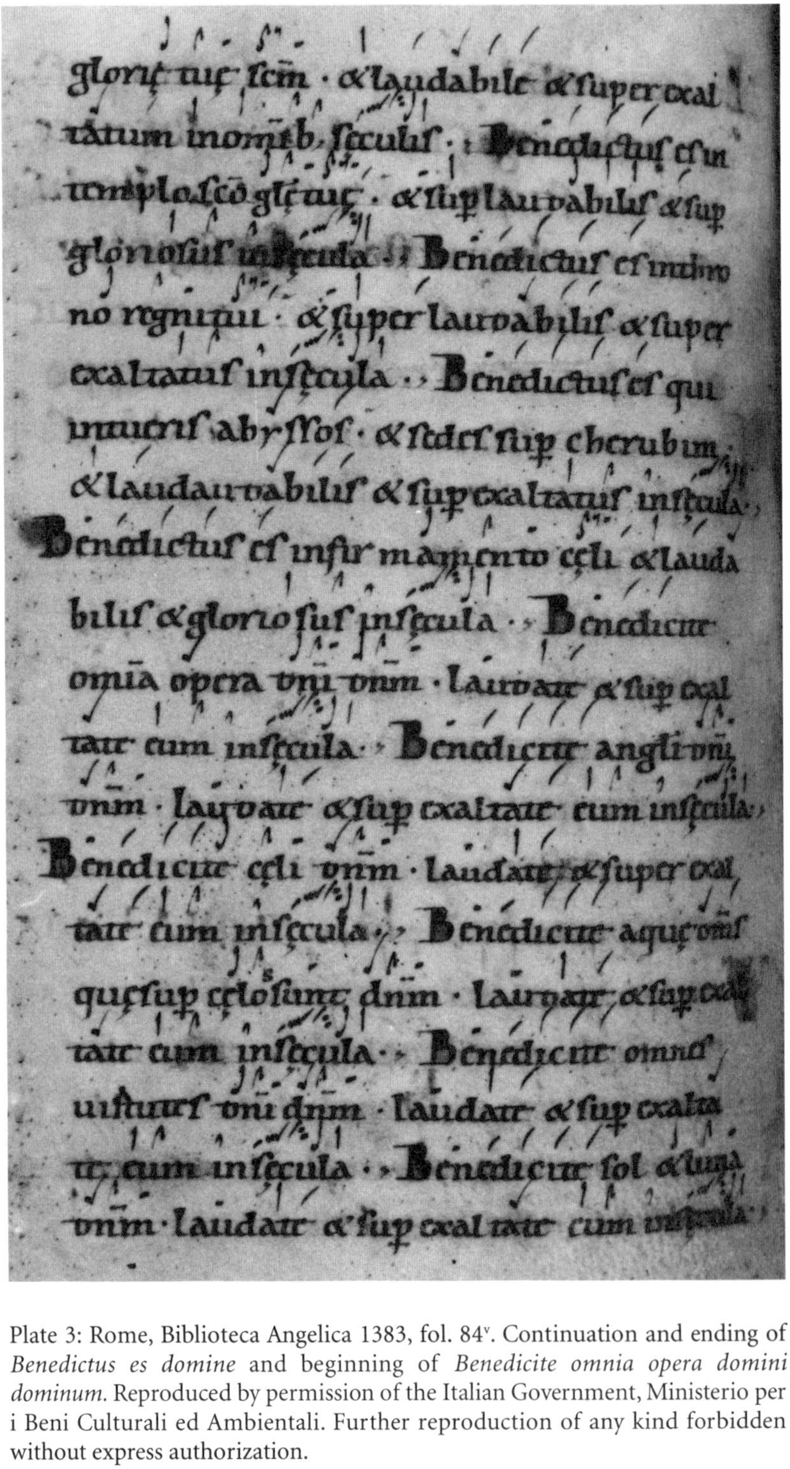

Plate 3: Rome, Biblioteca Angelica 1383, fol. 84v. Continuation and ending of *Benedictus es domine* and beginning of *Benedicite omnia opera domini dominum*. Reproduced by permission of the Italian Government, Ministerio per i Beni Culturali ed Ambientali. Further reproduction of any kind forbidden without express authorization.

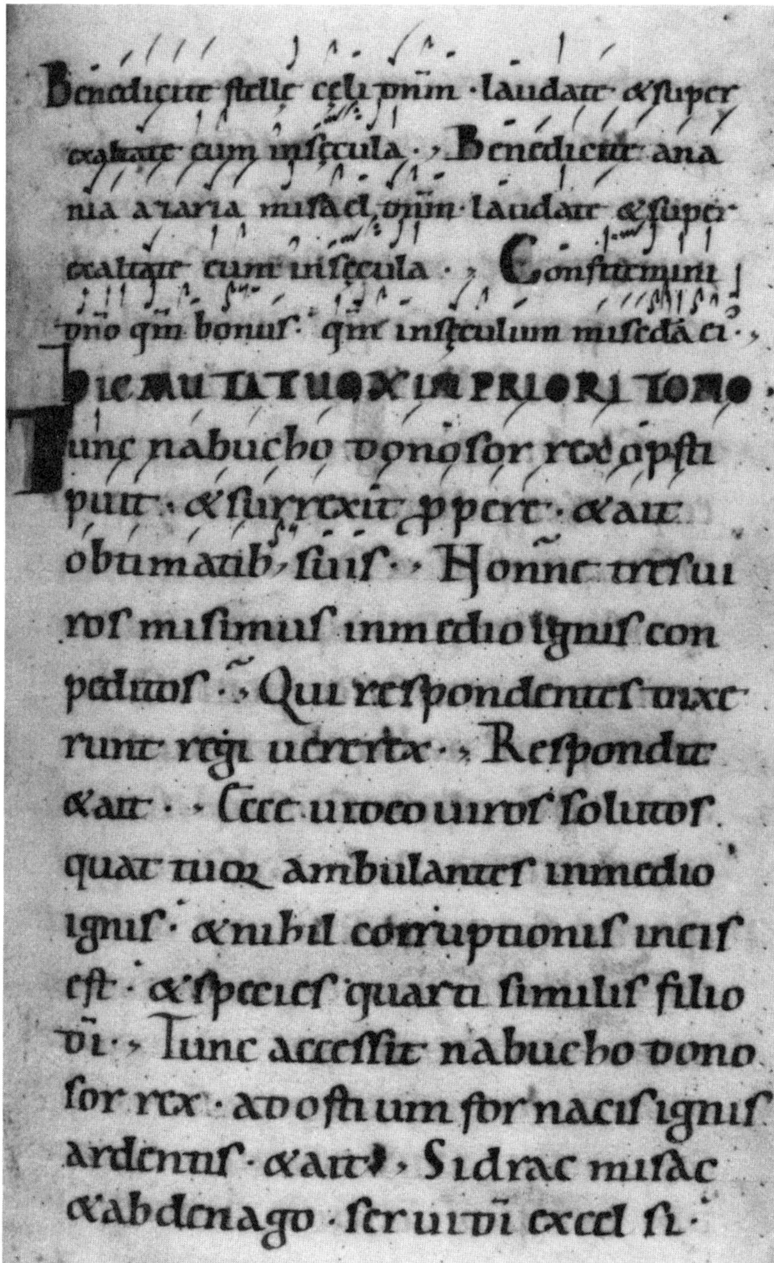

Plate 4: Rome, Biblioteca Angelica 1383, fol. 85r. Conclusion of *Benedicite omnia opera domini* and continuation of the lesson from the Book of Daniel. Reproduced by permission of the Italian Government, Ministerio per i Beni Culturali ed Ambientali. Further reproduction of any kind forbidden without express authorization.

the San Saba manuscript has Roman minuscule script with typically Roman interlaced zoomorphic decorative initials and a Roman kalendar, its chant was neumed with Dijonesque central-French neumes of the type used in reformed French monastic houses of the tenth and early eleventh centuries, especially those reformed or founded by William of Volpiano.[15]

Finally, I turn to the codex Archivio San Pietro H 58, a manuscript sometimes described as "a copy of the martyrology of Bede"; but the martyrology begins only at fol. 59^{r}. Down to fol. 49^{v}, the contents make up a sort of votive missal plus manual, with many masses for the dead and the Palm Sunday mass, with two orders for the visitation of the sick. The manuscript has been variously dated from the end of the tenth century to the middle or end of the eleventh century. Jounel adduces reasons for its having been written for and used at St. Peter's; but Supino Martini assigns it "una localizzazione genericamente romana."[16] In the *Mīs in dominicis ad palmas*, beginning on fol. 4^{r}, *HELI. HELI. Lama sabacthani. Hoc est d̄s ms Ds ms. ut quid dereliquisti me.* of the passion is notated. This notation, probably added to the verbal text a little later and at the same time as the letters *c* and *l* and the sign + in the passion, and at the same time as the verbal text was corrected, is of the same kind as in the San Saba epistolary. The peculiar descending group  occurs over *ds.*

In summary: my examination of Roman manuscripts before 1071 has thus far disclosed no evidence for notation of the old Roman repertory nor even firm Roman evidence for notation that could be seen as a direct forerunner of that used for the old Roman repertory in Bodmer 74 and Vaticanus latinus 5319. On the basis of these slight negative findings, I suggest for now that Roman notation as found in the St. Cecilia gradual was perfected during the fifty years between 1020 and 1070, using central-Italian notation as a model but with Guidonian clefs and colored lines. (Of

[15] See my sequel to this paper (likewise dedicated to David G. Hughes), "Music Notation in Archivio San Pietro C 105 and in the Farfa Breviary, Chigi C. VI. 177," in *Chant in Rome*, ed. Thomas Forrest Kelly (Colloques de Royaumont, 1993), forthcoming.

William, born at Isola San Giulio, Novara, entered the abbey of San Michele, San Gennario (or San Genuario), Lucedio (or Locedio), in the diocese of Vercelli at the age of seven. In 987, at the age of twenty-seven, William irregularly left his monastery to join Cluny, where he stayed until 990. He was then sent out as a brilliant disciple of Cluniac reform to St. Bénigne at Dijon, where he became and remained abbot. In 1001 he reformed the abbey of Fécamp in Normandy, also becoming abbot. In the course of his several trips to Italy, William and his family founded and endowed the abbey of Fruttuaria (or Fructuaria) northeast of Turin. The charter for Fruttuaria, drawn up between 1003 and 1005, provided for full exemption from the control of the diocesan bishop of Ivrea or of any lay patron. At the many monasteries reformed by him, "on cultivait en particulier le chant et la musique."

[16] Jounel, *Le culte des saints*, 24, and Supino Martini, *Roma e l'area grafica romanesca*, 72–75.

course much central-Italian notation in its turn derived from central-French notation.) The slight evidence can be set forth as follows. (1) The last liturgical book surviving from the ninth century, the evangeliary Vaticanus latinus 5465 first mentioned earlier, has no notation for *Eli Eli*, where it might be expected. (2) Other Roman liturgical books, not described in this paper, from the very late tenth and early eleventh centuries, which might also be expected to show neumed passages, do not do so—suggesting that native Roman notation—if it was at hand—was not much used. (3) The importation of central-French notation to the monastery of San Saba during the first half of the eleventh century, as shown in a book intended for use at this house and written in native Roman minuscule, would seem to imply that native Roman notation was either not available or that use of it was not firmly enough rooted to keep out the intruding style of notation from the north.

Thus my tentative conclusion must be that there was no native Roman notation in general use before about 1020 (I mean a notation in which the old Roman repertory might have been handed on by native Roman scribes) and that the notation we see in Bodmer 74, Vaticanus latinus 5319, and Archivio San Pietro F 11 was developed after 1020 in imitation of post-Guidonian central-Italian notation. This conclusion is preliminary: it could easily be overturned by the discovery of even one passage in a manuscript written at and intended for use at Rome employing a notation foreshadowing that of Bodmer 74, preferably a passage from an old Roman version of the repertory. But on the basis of those manuscripts I have so far been able to examine—including about twenty-five Roman homiliaries, office lectionaries, bibles or extracts from bibles, lives of saints, etc., that contain absolutely no notation—I rather expect that what may turn up will be more of the same: examples from monasteries under the influence of the Cluny-Dijon reform of 930–1050 that use a variety of central-French notation.

If this conclusion holds, then we may guess that the fifty books destroyed under Nicholas III were notated between 1020 and 1280—by no means an impossible number to have been written over a span of 250 years for several important basilicas of Rome during a period of intense artistic and cultural revival. If so tentative a conclusion can be trusted, it would follow that the old Roman repertory was handed down for the most part orally until sometime around or after A.D. 1000.*

*More vestiges of Roman notation recovered in 1991 have in part altered these conclusions. Dedicated to David G. Hughes, a sequel to the present article, entitled "Music Notation in Archivio San Pietro C 105 and in the Farfa Breviary, Chigi C. VI. 177," will appear in a collection of essays edited by Thomas Forrest Kelly, *Chant in Rome* (Colloques de Royaumont, 1993).

THOMAS H. CONNOLLY

The Antiphon Cantantibus Organis *and Dante's* Organi Del Mondo

I am going to compare two texts, both well known in the Middle Ages, both no doubt well known to many of you. Far removed from each other in time—they were composed eight hundred years apart—they seem on the surface to be quite unrelated, and you will no doubt ask at once why I bring them together. Their single point of contact is their use of the word "organs," yet each seems to use it in a sense quite different from the other. One, from the second canto of Dante's *Paradiso*, is part of a learned discourse by Beatrice about instrumentality—instrumental causality—in the transfer of influence from the divine realms, the Empyrean, into the mutable universe, through the moving spheres and even into the sublunar world. These organs of the universe, *organi del mondo*, are implements of divine power, of divine love; they are not musical instruments.

> Questi organi del mondo così vanno,
> come tu vedi omai, di grado in grado,
> che di su prendono e di sotto fanno.[1]

[1] *Paradiso* 2:121–23. "These organs of the universe proceed thus, as thou now seest, step by step, receiving from above and operating below." Throughout this paper I have used the text and translation, and have benefited from the lucid comments, of John D. Sinclair, *The Divine Comedy of Dante Alighieri*, 3 vols. (Oxford: Oxford University Press, 1977).

The other text is an antiphon from the feast of St. Cecilia. It was taken from the saint's *Passio*, a document written about 500 A.D., and seems to be a strictly narrative passage which describes Cecilia's wedding: the musical instruments that played during the festivities, the saint's spiritual predicament as she is being forced to wed, her state of soul, and her prayer for God's help. These organs seem to be musical instruments pure and simple, implements for making musical sounds and nothing more.

> Cantantibus organis Cecilia domino decantabat dicens: Fiat cor meum immaculatum ut non confundar.[2]

The comparison will become more palatable when I point out that my concern will be not so much with the original sense of the antiphon, which was presumably a purely narrative sense, but with the meaning or meanings given it in the later Middle Ages, much closer to Dante's time.[3] My attention will, however, be given to the word "organ," and I will show that its significance in each text goes rather deeper than its literal and surface meaning. This is easier to see in Dante, for the music of the turning spheres was, to earlier minds, inseparable from their other instrumental functions. In discussing various medieval references to the antiphon, I aim to show that the opposite is true of it: that whereas its primary sense is narrative, and tells us of musical instruments making music, the medieval mind had no hesitation in understanding these *organa* as instrumentalities of the human soul, transmitting, by grace, divine influence or "impetus." My aim, then (and the point must be insisted upon), is to demonstrate the opposition, yet at the same time the complementarity, of the two texts: Dante's *organa* are primarily causal instruments, yet music-making is inseparable from them in medieval understanding; the *organa* of the *Passio Caeciliae* are primarily music-making instruments, yet those who discuss them at about the time of Dante readily apply them to the work of grace within the soul. These references to *organis cantantibus* have given us a rare insight into the ways in which the medieval mind understood the interdependence of *musica mundana, musica humana, musica instrumentalis,* into its conception of the all-pervasiveness of music, expressed in Cassiodorus's famous dictum: "Whatever

[2] "While instruments played Cecilia kept on singing to the Lord: 'May my heart be kept spotless so that I may not be put to shame.'"

[3] One cannot altogether rule out that the author of the *Passio Caeciliae* had some mystical and allegorical intent in much that he wrote. This is especially true of passages like *cantantibus organis,* which always played a prominent role in discussion of St. Cecilia and which was generally put to symbolic purpose.

heavenly or earthly occurrence takes place in a manner consistent with the ordering of its Author is said not to be exempt from this science."[4]

Let us proceed by examining the texts in a little more detail, beginning with Dante. With Beatrice for guide, the poet has just begun his journey through the spheres towards the divine realm, the Empyrean. He has arrived in the first of the nine spheres, that of the moon, and immediately questions his guide about a problem that much occupied medieval thinkers, the reason for the dark marks on the face of the moon. It was a question about a natural phenomenon, but Beatrice, in line with Dante's larger aims, turns it to a spiritual end. The canto becomes the vehicle for the poet to explain the essential function of nature, the manner in which divine impulse is transmitted to the visible universe.

> Within the heaven of the divine peace spins a body [the *primum mobile*] in whose virtue lies the being of all that it contains; the next heaven [the starry sphere], which has so many different sights, distributes that being among different existences, distinct from it and contained in it; the other spheres, by various differences, direct the distinctive qualities which they have in themselves to their ends and fruitful working. These organs of the universe [the spheres] proceed thus, as thou seest now, grade by grade, each receiving from above and operating below. . . .

Dante's argument in this passage, understood in the light of the general cosmological thought of his age, places all primal impulse in God, dwelling in the Empyrean. This impulse, this vital principle—it is important to notice, as Dante himself does in the last lines of his poem, that it is nothing else than the divine love—is transmitted first to the ninth and outermost sphere, the *primum mobile*. This sphere, however, being utterly homogeneous and containing no stars, does not analyze the divine impulse, nor distribute it in any discriminated fashion, but merely passes it on to the eighth sphere as a simple force, though now a material one. The stars in the eighth sphere, which is the region of the fixed stars, have a power to distribute the received impulse in a discriminating way as required by the needs of the lower spheres. This differentiated impulse is then channelled to the earth through the other spheres, each of which transmits to it new energies and powers which belong to the particular sphere's own essence. Thus modified, and perhaps marred, by intervening forces and entities, the initial divine

[4] Cassiodorus, *Institutiones*, II.9; trans. Leslie Webber Jones, *An Introduction to Divine and Human Readings*, 2nd ed. (New York: Octagon, 1969), 196. We still apply musical metaphors to things that operate effectively: an engine that runs well, for instance, is said to "hum."

impulse is disseminated throughout the sublunar world and the abode of humankind.[5]

Let me note two things here, the first of which has already been stated, but will bear repeating. First, even though *organi* here refers to the spheres and clearly means cosmic mechanisms, causative implements, with no primary reference to the making of music, it was a given that these *organi* did in fact make music as they revolved, so that the sense of musical instrument is not far from the surface. Second, I want to spend a little time sketching what I call Dante's spiritual map of the universe. By this I mean the plan of the cosmos that Dante describes, with its attendant spiritual states. Dante's references to music at particular points in his journey correlate with this plan in revealing ways, and this correlation is the aim of my excursus on his cosmography.

The extremes of his travels are on the one hand the center of the earth, the frozen river Cocytus which is the domain of Beelzebub, the Emperor of the Woeful Kingdom (*Inferno* 34:28), and on the other the Empyrean, the unchallenged home of God. In Cocytus all is hatred and sadness—even the name means "wailing." Beelzebub—or Lucifer, or Satan—stands like a huge windmill, immersed in the ice. He is three-faced, a terrible parody of the triune God he had once tried to overthrow; and from the flapping of his three pairs of wings there issues the three winds that keep all of Cocytus frozen. He is the complete contrary of what he had once been, and of the divinity he had rebelled against. "If he was as fair as he is now foul, and lifted up his brows agains his Maker, well may all sorrow proceed from him."[6]

The Empyrean, the goal of Dante's journey after he leaves Cocytus, is of course the contrary of the Woeful Kingdom. In place of fixed, endless hatred and sadness, there are now infinite, substantive love, and infinite joy. Trite though this contrast may sound, it has both important roots and important consequences in medieval thought, which we have not the time to explore in this paper. I do want to note that at the extremes Dante's progress is from utter sadness and hatred to utter joy and love; and that this progress is marked throughout the *Commedia* by specific allegorical devices. Two of these concern us deeply, the use of the smile, especially the smile of Beatrice, and of ever more joyful music, to indicate the poet's progress.

[5] See for example the summary by Charles H. Grandgent, ed., *La Divina Commedia di Dante Alighieri* (Boston: Heath, 1933), 663–64.

[6] *Inferno* 34:34–36. "S'el fu si bello com'elli è or brutto, / e contra 'l suo fattore alzò le ciglia, / ben dee da lui procedere ogni lutto."

I want to suggest that these three things—the spiritual progress from sin to grace that is allegorized in Dante's journey, the passage from sadness/hatred to joy/love that this journey encompasses, and the ever more joyous music and smile—are closely related in the poet's intent. His progress is in fact a reversal of the change that transpires as the power of love sifts down from the Empyrean through the spheres. The effects of love are stultified as the divinely authored impulse enters the sublunar world, the abode of sin, and approaches its centre, which is Cocytus. That love which moves the sun and the other stars is subverted in its passage to the center of the human habitat; there, instead of love, from which springs joy, reigns hatred, from which springs sadness.

Dante's use of smile and song to indicate the degree of sadness or of joy that characterize the human soul as it goes on its journey between sin and grace is a traditional device, but one that seems to have gone unstudied. The clearest, and probably most fecund, use of the figure seems to have been in the pulpit. Medieval preachers made great use of scripture texts that expressed the flux of sin and grace as a flux of sadness and joy. Matthew 5:5 is an obvious example: "Blessed are those who mourn, for they shall be comforted." So too is John 16:20: "I tell you the truth, you will weep and mourn while the world rejoices. You will grieve, but your grief will be turned into joy." Among the many texts of this kind, there exists a small group which use the image of music to express the flux of sadness and joy. Job 30:31 is such a text: "My harp is turned into mourning, my organ into the voice of those who weep." Another example, and one that was very popular, is Lamentations 5:15–16: "The joy of our heart is fled, our singing is turned to mourning, the crown has fallen from our head. Woe unto us, for we have sinned!" One of the foremost modern authorities on preaching in the middle ages, Siegfried Wenzel, has noted how prevalent this text was, calling it one of the "common tags" of the medieval pulpit.[7]

Interestingly, and importantly, these scripture texts expressing the flux of sadness and joy in musical terms were given striking visual expression in the Middle Ages and the Renaissance. Most notably, the common miniature of David Repentant that is found especially at the head of the Seven Penitential Psalms in Books of Hours often shows a musical instrument or a crown on the ground beside the kneeling king, an illustration of these two texts from Job and Lamentations.

[7] Siegfried Wenzel, *Verses in Sermons: "Fasciculus morum" and Its Middle English Poems*, Mediaeval Academy of America Publications 87 (Cambridge, Mass.: The Mediaeval Academy of America, 1978), 89–90.

A similar text is the concluding words of the mass-lesson for the Wednesday after the Second Sunday of Lent, Esther 13:17, "Turn our mourning into rejoicing . . . and do not close the mouths of those who sing your praises, O Lord." They were chosen often as *thema* for sermons on that day, and in their lenten context had a peculiar aptness for the musical expression of conversion, of turning from sin and sadness to joy and grace. One notes that they reverse the thought of the texts from Job and Lamentations—where these speak of joy turned to mourning, Esther 13:17 asks God to turn mourning into joy. They also constitute a critical point in our argument, for on this Wednesday the Roman station was observed at the basilica of S. Cecilia in Trastevere, the saint to whose legend and office the text *Cantantibus organis* belongs.[8] Like the texts just cited from Job and Lamentations, this text from Esther receives a remarkable visual translation: at the very time when the repentant David begins to be shown with instruments discarded, images of Cecilia appear holding the organ which was to become her most common symbol. It was as if Cecilia took up the instrument David had laid down, in mimicry of the way the text of the lesson from her station-day reversed the thought of the texts from Lamentations and Job.[9]

Before we consider the antiphon *Cantantibus organis*, we must point to some of the places in which Dante associates song and smile with progress from sadness to joy and from sin to grace. Two of these are of special significance, for they mark the major points of arrival in the soul's progress, the boundaries between the three stages of Bonaventure's three ways—the transition respectively from the purgative way to the illuminative, and from the illuminative to the unitive.

[8] The words will also be found to play a critical role in the development of St. Cecilia's association with music. This lies outside the scope of this paper, but is explained at length in my recently completed book, "Mourning Into Joy: Music, Raphael, and Saint Cecilia" (New Haven: Yale University Press, 1995).

[9] Given the popularity of the text of Esther 13:17 as a *thema* of medieval sermons, one can confidently surmise that the influence of the pulpit was strong in the rendering of these images of David and Cecilia. The first images of David Penitent with the musical instrument discarded appear towards the end of the thirteenth century. Scholars have been loath to put the date of the earliest representations of Cecilia with the organ as emblem as early as this, yet the evidence is now sure. The statue of Cecilia holding an organetto in the Castelvecchio Museum in Verona is securely dated around 1325. Illustrations of this statue and descriptions of possible musical Cecilias of even earlier date will be found in two studies of mine. See Thomas H. Connolly, "L'iconografia di S. Cecilia prima di Raffaello," in *L'Estasi di Santa Cecilia di Raffaello da Urbino nella Pinacoteca Nazionale di Bologna*, Documenti del tempo 1 (Bologna: ALFA, 1983), 228–34 [catalogue of an exhibition held in Bologna on the occasion of the five-hundredth anniversary of Raphael's birth]; and "The Cult and Iconography of St. Cecilia before Raphael," in *Indagini per un dipinto: La santa Cecilia di Raffaello*, ed. Andrea Emiliani (Bologna: ALFA, 1983), 119–40.

The first transition is symbolized by Dante's arrival at the borders of the Earthly Paradise, after climbing the mountain of Purgatory (*Purgatorio* 28). Here, having passed through the way of purgation, he encounters a fair lady, who sings and smiles as she gathers flowers by the stream. She will later be identified by name as Matilda, and is often thought to be the mystic Matilda of Hackeborn. In response to the poet's question, she identifies this river-bank as a place where her smile is appropriate: it is the place originally intended by God for mankind, but in which man stayed but a short time because "through his own fault he changed honest laughter and sweet sport into weeping and toil." As with almost all medieval references to "mourning and joy," or "tears and laughter," these words of the smiling, singing lady echo the familiar "common tags" of the preacher, with their implication of the passage between sin and grace. In the context of Dante's spiritual journey, at any rate, such an interpretation is eminently supportable. The turning of joy to sadness was part of the process by which the impulse of divine, joyful love was subverted into the hatred and misery of Cocytus, and was thus allied with the functioning and misfunctioning of the *organi del mondo*. How appropriate that the reversal of the already subversive process—the passage from sin to grace, the motion from sadness to joy—should be marked by joyous song and smiling countenance!

If the encounter with Matilda marks the end of the purgative stage, the encounter which immediately follows, and with which the first is inseparably connected, marks the beginning of the illuminative way. This second encounter is the meeting with Beatrice, who becomes Dante's guide for the remainder of his journey. Her ever-brightening smile, and the increasingly joyful music they meet as they make their way through the spheres—the menacing concupiscence of the sublunar world now left behind—symbolize the heightened spiritual powers and the swelling joy of the middle stage of the soul's progress, the illuminative way. Dante breaks this pattern, however, with a literary device of uncommon power, when he wishes to depict the second major transition, from the illuminative to the unitive way. This occurs when they enter the sphere of Saturn, which the poet represents as the sphere of the contemplative spirit.

There are many reasons for so depicting this sphere, some of them obvious. The god Saturn had reigned over the golden age of the ancients. The farthest and the coldest of the planets, Saturn was considered to be the sphere of temperance, which both influenced and represented abstraction from the sensible world in favor of the spiritual. As the furthest and last of the planetary spheres, it was closest to the Empyrean and thus best able to represent the soul's movement from illumination to divine union.

In the sphere of Saturn Dante suggests the second of the soul's two great transitions, from illumination to union, not by describing an even more joyous music and an even brighter smile of Beatrice, but by silence and gravity. Here, he hears no more music and Beatrice smiles no more. The reason is pointed out by a great contemplative whom they encounter, St. Peter Damian. The song is still, the smile vanished, he says, not because this is a joyless place—rather, the opposite is true. This sphere of contemplation is so joy-filled that Dante's still-mortal powers would be unable to withstand the music and the smile that would here be appropriate. "Your hearing is mortal, like your sight," says Peter Damian, "and it is for this reason that there is no singing here, for the same reason that Beatrice does not smile."[10] As Dante and Beatrice mount the ladder that will lead them through the starry sphere to the Empyrean, she reinforces the point. He should realize, from the intense emotion he felt when he heard the cry of indignation uttered by the contemplatives at the parlous condition of the church, just how unready he was for the surge of joy that her smile and the song of the spirits in this place would have enkindled. He would have been wholly changed, "transmutated."[11]

Music, progress through the spheres, fluctuations of joy and sadness, radical change—all of these are inseparably intertwined in this remarkable passage. As the divine impulse of joyous love was transmitted to the created universe through the agency of the choiring spheres, until frustrated and subverted in the sublunar world, where joyous music was replaced at the center of the earth by the wailing and lament of the Inferno, so the soul's progress from that horrid and lugubrious center through the spheres to the divine realms was accompanied by signs of burgeoning joy, not least among them the sign of swelling music and song. It remains to me to show that the second of the two texts I am considering, that which speaks of the instruments that played at Cecilia's wedding, carried for the contemplative medieval mind these same associations, of spiritual progress, the flux of joy and sadness, and radical, interior change. This will be apparent in the several examples of its use that I shall cite. First, however, we must consider the text itself, and its position in the document from which it was drawn, the *Passio Caeciliae.*

This *Passio* is a curious document, known to have been composed about 500 A.D. Hippolyte Delehaye's penetrating study of 1936 remains the

[10] *Paradiso* 21:61–63. "'Tu hai l'udir mortal sì come il viso;' / rispuose a me 'onde qui non si canta / per quel che Beatrice non ha riso.'"

[11] *Paradiso* 22:10–12. "Come t'avrebbe trasmutato il canto, / e io ridendo, mo pensar lo puoi, / poscia che'l grido t'ha mosso cotanto. . . ."

clearest statement of its history and its problems. While scanning with a cold eye its complications and contradictions, and while casting an unhesitating vote for denying even existence to the saint (he held that she developed from the mistaken attribution of martyr-status to a pious lady of the *gens Caecilia* who had been granted burial next to the Crypt of the Popes in the Catacomb of St. Callistus), the great Bollandist noted, perhaps intuitively, that the fictitious tale was "illuminated with mystical glimmerings."[12] Intuitively, I say, because some of the most important medieval statements about Cecilia, certainly those which help define the special characteristics of her cult, were made later in the writings of the medieval mystics, or in spiritual counsel given to those who had ventured on the mystic's path. We shall consider some of these after we have discussed the text of the antiphon *Cantantibus organis*, and its context in the *Passio*.

The *Passio* tells of Cecilia, a Christian maiden vowed secretly to virginity, who was constrained by her parents to accept as husband a young pagan named Valerian. A practicing contemplative (this is what the *Passio* means by saying that "she kept the gospel always in her heart") who wore a hairshirt beneath her patrician robes, she redoubled her prayers and fasting in this predicament. On the wedding night, *cantantibus organis*, "while instruments played, she went on singing in her heart, to God alone," a prayer for deliverance from her plight: "May my heart and my body be kept spotless, *ne confundar*, lest I be cast into confusion." She is able to convert her husband, Valerian, and his brother, Tiburtius. The rest of the legend describes their good works: their preaching and converting, their work for the poor, and eventually their arrest, their trials, their long disputes with the judge, and their martyrdom.

Several features of the story serve to explain its appeal to the mystics of the later Middle Ages. One is the constant appeal to light and light-giving—everything is explained as a function of divine light and vision bestowed on those who are spiritually blind. Another is its dwelling on nuptial imagery, the principal imagery of mystical union. Yet another, more germane to this study, is the activity of the heart. Two of the most potent passages of the legend tell us that Cecilia "kept the gospel in her heart," and that she "sang to God in her heart." Both images are dear to contemplatives, even fundamental to their thinking and expression. The gospel, the word of God, in the heart, is not meant as a description of one endowed with a good memory

[12] ". . . un thème intéressant, éclairé de lueurs mystiques." Hippolyte Delehaye, *Étude sur le légendier romain: Les saints de novembre et de décembre*, Subsidia hagiographica 23 (Brussels: Société des Bollandistes, 1936), 78. Delehaye's edition of the *Passio Caeciliae* appears in the same volume, 194–220. It will be used hereafter, abbreviated as *Passio*.

and familiar with the text of the Scriptures; rather it is a clear statement of the divine indwelling, of the presence of the Word, in the grace-filled soul, and is thus a statement of one of the doctrines on which Christian mysticism is founded. "Singing in the heart" is not meant as a description of one who imagines melody (though that too). It derives from St. Paul's counsel to the Ephesians: "Speak to one another with psalms, hymns, and spiritual songs. Sing and make music in your hearts to the Lord."[13] This injunction is the culmination of Paul's mature thought on the doctrine of the Mystical Body: his readers' life-in-Christ demands that charity, centered in their hearts, overflow in their daily living. Their inner music is the perfect harmony that flows out from the primal divine impulse of love, and overflows through their working "in Christ."

The Cecilia of the *Passio* is the embodiment of Paul's counsel to the Ephesians: she might be called Ephesians in action. At the core of her being is the Word she has accepted and nourishes; the harmony of charity is never silent within her, and flows out in her actions to those she encounters. She instructs, she preaches, she argues, all in the cause of true charity. So busy is she about the working-out of the impulse of love that Pope Urban (who baptizes Valerian and Tiburtius in the story) declares that she is ever busy in the Lord's service, like a "disputatious bee." His words became an antiphon at lauds and vespers for St. Cecilia's feastday, and their rumination by the contemplative mind formed the related image of Cecilia that Chaucer knew and described when he retold the legend in *The Second Nun's Tale.*[14] Chaucer offers a unique and valuable perspective on the saint, one that must be examined before we pass on to contemporary applications of the *cantantibus organis* passage.

The singular and most valuable elements in Chaucer's view of Cecilia are found in the prologue to his tale, and are drawn in part from Jacques de Voragine's Golden Legend, in part from sermons, and in part from contemporary interpretation of the significance of the saint. Much of what Chaucer says is strikingly consonant with the view of Cecilia I have advanced, which

[13] Ephesians 5:19.

[14] The context of the passage in the *Passio* suggests, in agreement with at least some of the manuscripts, that the original image was of a "disputatious sheep" rather than of a bee. In the edition of Delehaye, Urban gives thanks for Cecilia's unceasing service with the words: "Domine Iesu Christe, pastor bone, Caecilia famula tua quasi ovis argumentosa deservit. Nam sponsum, quem quasi leonem ferocem accepit, ad te quasi agnum mansuetissimum destinavit." ("Lord Jesus Christ, good shepherd, your servant Cecilia goes on serving you like a disputatious sheep. For her spouse, a raging lion when she received him, she now brings to you as the meekest of lambs.") Both the manuscripts Delehaye used have *ovis.* In one of them, *ovis* has been erased and *apis* inserted in its place. As an antiphon, the passage seems more often to have read *apis.*

would understand the *Cantantibus organis* antiphon as signifying a kind of cosmic force of charity working within the heart in accordance with musical law, just as the divine charity descended through the spheres with their ethereal strains. Praising her "busyness"—he has Pope Urban call her "a busy bee"—Chaucer compares her ceaseless charity, her active divine love, to the motion of the heavenly spheres. She is the model of Christian works and working. As people look to the heavens and see there sun, moon, and sundry stars, so in Cecilia they see the magnanimity of faith (the sun), the clarity of wisdom (the moon), and "sundry works, bright of excellence" (the stars). She was in this like the heavens themselves: as they are—so the philosophers tell us—swiftly moving, round, and ever burning, so too was Cecilia. For she was "swift" and "busy" in "good working"; "round and whole in persevering"; and, finally and most importantly, "burning ever in charity full bright." Her "working" led, as it was bound to do, to perfect love of God. She was, for Chaucer (following, I believe, the conventional wisdom of his age), a saint intimately bound up with the radical change wrought by charity, with change "in the heart."

That Chaucer viewed her thus is confirmed by his deliberately juxtaposing *The Second Nun's Tale* with a tale of alchemy, *The Canon's Yeoman's Tale.* The Chaucerians have for some years been deeply interested in this juxtaposition, though not totally convincing in their explanations.[15] Chaucer's strategy becomes much more understandable when we view Cecilia as one who is concerned with the most profound kind of change, change in the human spirit. She is, in fact (and this I believe was Chaucer's intent) a spiritual alchemist, one who brings about the transmutation of the innermost being. Interestingly, there are passages in the *Passio* itself that suggest this. To the arresting officers, grieved that one so young and beautiful should be about to die, she answers that she will not lose her life but will change it—it will be like giving clay for gold, a common stone for a precious gem, a mean house for a court adorned with pearls.[16] Chaucer intended an acute opposition between Cecilia, the alchemist of the spirit, and the conniving,

[15] The fundamental studies for this are those of Joseph E. Grennen and Bruce Rosenberg. See for instance Grennen, "Jargon Transmuted: Alchemy in Chaucer's Canon's Yeoman's Tale" (Ph.D. diss., Fordham University, 1960); "The Canon's Yeoman's Alchemical Mass," *Studies in Philology* 62 (1965): 546–60; and "Saint Cecilia's 'chemical wedding': The Unity of the Canterbury Tales, Fragment VIII," *Journal of English and Germanic Philology* 65 (1966): 466–81. See also Rosenberg, "The Contrary Tales of the Second Nun and the Canon's Yeoman," *The Chaucer Review* 2 (1967): 278–91. A splendidly nuanced consideration of the matter, with deep consideration of the iconographic evidence, is the study by V. A. Kolve, "Chaucer's *Second Nun's Tale* and the Iconography of St. Cecilia," in *New Perspectives in Chaucer Criticism*, ed. Donald M. Rose (Norman, Oklahoma: Pilgrim Books, 1981), 137–74.

[16] *Passio*, 215.

fraudulent practitioners of "the great work" (one notes the contrast between their "working" and Cecilia's). Interestingly, he even alludes to their trade as one that "turns a man's joy to sorrow," echoing as Dante did, in his story of Matilda at the entrance to the earthly paradise, the medieval pulpit's common image of the changes of grace and sin.[17]

The overview we have just essayed, first of Dante's cosmography, his use of the figure of mourning turning to joy as a symbol of the flux of sin and grace, and second of the reflection of these same ideas in Chaucer's treatment of Cecilia, has yielded a perhaps unconventional image of this saint. She was a figure in whom the impulse of the divine love was *not* subverted, a figure in whom charity was ever active and productive, "working" as alchemy was reputed to work in effecting radical change, spiritual transmutation. The popularity in the medieval pulpit of the scriptural texts of mourning and joy, and especially of those which equated this flux with a musical phenomenon, may be a cause, but is certainly a concomitant, of the developed view of St. Cecilia as one who was intimately involved in the transformation of the deepest recesses of the human heart and spirit, a transformation that the Middle Ages of necessity perceived as musical in the ancient and medieval sense. It remains for us to discuss some examples of such a view of Cecilia in medieval spiritual writing and discourse. In these we will find confirmation of the idea that *cantantibus organis* was perceived as a description not simply of audible music, but of radical, inner change, effected "in the heart" by the impulse of divine love. More than anywhere else, such confirmation is found in the lives and writings of the late medieval mystics.

Julian of Norwich is the most famous of these. Her whole spirituality was founded on her memory of a preacher or a spiritual adviser who spoke of the three wounds suffered by Cecilia at her martyrdom. Julian based her spiritual life on a wish for "three wounds," and from her petition for these sprang the revelations she received. There is a further suggestion of the importance of St. Cecilia to the mystics, to those who sought their destiny in the contemplative way, in the fact that the little bands of contemplative women who first established the great female orders of the Dominicans and of the Poor Clares included, in each case, a young woman who took the name of Cecilia. Legend associates both Dominic and Francis with the saint, as a model of contemplation. There is a story of Dominic's being granted a vision of the Virgin Mary accompanied by St. Cecilia and St. Catherine of Alexandria; both were contemplatives as well as great

[17] *The Canon's Yeoman's Tale*, lines 1402–03. "Lo! swich a lucre is in this lusty game, / A mannes mirthe it wol torne unto grame. . . ."

preachers, and thus embodied the Dominican ideal *contemplata aliis tradere*.[18] It is, however, among the Franciscans, and especially among their female branch, the Poor Clares, that we find the most interesting and convincing treatment of Cecilia as a model for contemplatives. And it reflects exactly the kind of reference to the *cantantibus organis* text that we have described: a reference that combines musicality with instrumentality, spiritual progress, and radical, interior change.

Camilla Battista da Varano was a Poor Clare of the convent at Camerino in the *Marche*. In her *Vita spiritale*, a vivid account she left of her spiritual formation (as a daughter of the ruling family of Camerino, a cultivated humanist court, she had received an excellent education), Battista wrote about Cecilia and about Cecilian themes and texts in ways that strongly suggest a special influence of the saint's legend on the schooling of contemplatives. She began her spiritual journey, she says, under a divine command to "keep her body and her heart immaculate as Cecilia had done."[19] She describes her time of bitter trial and testing—an experience she shared with almost all the mystics—by citing, in the fifteenth chapter, the words of Job 30:31, " . . . and therefore the harp of my trusting was turned into mourning." She goes on, in the succeeding chapter, to describe her liberation from her torment. For three months, she says, she experienced a feeling of interior flame, a burning desire to be freed and to be with Christ. It was not a feeling of dying, but rather "a going to nuptials while 'organs pulsed'" ("uno andare a noze 'pulsantibus organis'").[20]

The phrase *pulsantibus organis* is, of course, a reference to *cantantibus organis*, which in its original context described Cecilia's wedding and her reaction to it. In employing the phrase to describe her passage to the state of divine union, Battista adopts the image of this union that is most profoundly rooted in both Scripture and the mystical tradition, the image of marriage-union. This suggests some subversion of the original context. The instruments that played in the *Passio Caeciliae* were musical instruments played at Cecilia's perfectly human wedding to the pagan, Valerian. Yet any contemplative reading the *Passio* as an exercise of spiritual reading, of *lectio divina*, would have been well aware of Cecilia's insistence to her earthly husband that she had another and deeper lover—Valerian must not infringe on

[18] It is told, in fact, by the Sister Cecilia who was one of the first Dominican nuns. See Suor Cecilia, *Miracula Beati Dominici*, ed. with introduction by A. Walz in "Die 'Miracula Beati Dominici' der Schwester Cäcilia," in *Miscellanea Pio Paschini: Studi di storia ecclesiastica* 1 (Rome: Facultas Theologica Pontificii Athenaei Lateranensis, 1948), 293–326.

[19] Camilla Battista da Varano, *Le opere spirituali*, ed. Giacomo Boccanera (Iesi: Scuola tipografica francescana, 1958), 18 (in chapter 6 of the *Vita spirituale*).

[20] *Le opere*, 55 (*Vita spirituale*, chapter 16).

the claims of that lover, who is clearly a spiritual husband with a more profound claim upon her. The *noze* to which Battista is led are the spiritual nuptials of mystical experience, like those of St. Catherine of Alexandria, for instance.

But what of the phrase *pulsantibus organis?* Is it simply a casual allusion meant to color and heighten the nuptial imagery? I suggest not, but that it is rather a studied reference to the kind of spiritual instrumentality of which St. Cecilia was a model, the working of divine love, through the agency of the spiritual faculties. This is the instrumentality of Dante's *organi del mondo*, though operating in the spiritual plane; it is the instrumentality that Chaucer associates with Cecilia, in his description of her "busyness" and "working." Battista's substitution of *pulsantibus* for *cantantibus* intensifies this interpretation. For while *pulsantibus* can indeed be said of playing musical instruments, especially keyboards, or percussion instruments, or even bells, its primary meaning better supports the sense of *organa* as agencies or instrumentalities of the human person—instrumentalities of the physical organism, but here, even more felicitously, of the human spirit. Without denying to the phrase its sense of audible music being performed, Battista has at the same time indicated those inner, spiritual agencies or organs (the spiritual senses, for example) through which charity, divine love, operated within the heart and soul. Such operation, let it be repeated, was a musical operation in the ancient and medieval sense, an operation of the *musica humana.*

The view of Cecilia I have advanced finds confirmation in a variety of diverse medieval texts and images. Many of these at the same time support the linking of music and spiritual instrumentality, of which in this view Cecilia is a model. Preaching yields many examples. Why else, for instance, would an unnamed Benedictine preacher of the late thirteenth century take the text of *Cantantibus organis* as the starting-point for a discussion of the varieties of impulse to which the soul is subject?

> *Cantantibus organis* Cecilia the virgin sang to the Lord in her heart, saying: "Lord, let my heart and my body be spotless lest I be cast into confusion." As Blessed Gregory says, in the elect and the reprobates there are different impetuses. For the elect follow the impetus of the spirit, the reprobates are ruled by the impetus of the flesh. But the impetus of the spirit is to spiritual things, that of the flesh to fleshly. The former is to interior gifts, the latter to exterior. . . .[21]

[21] Paris, Bibliothèque Nationale, MS. lat. 12412, fol. 157^r. "Cantantibus organis cecilia virgo in corde suo domino decantabat dicens: Fiat domine cor meum et corpus meum immaculatum ut non confundar. Sicut ait beatus Gregorius in electis et reprobis divisi sunt

This preacher seems to have linked the phrase *cantantibus organis*, and Cecilia's singing in her heart, to the motions of the human spirit, rather in the way that Camilla Battista da Varano did. As Dante and his readers knew that the *musica mundana* accompanied the moving organs of the universe, so the preacher and his hearers knew that Cecilia's musicalizing betokened the motion and change that the divine impulse effected within the heart.

The kind of musical-spiritual allusiveness we have observed in Dante and Chaucer, in sermons and the writings of contemplatives, is perhaps more explicit in the visual arts of the late Middle Ages and the Renaissance. Many paintings and statues of St. Cecilia, of course, and particularly those which display the organ or some other musical motif as her emblem, take on new meaning when viewed from the stance I have proposed: the scenes in the central vaults of the Cathedral at Albi, for instance; or Riccardo Quartararo's painting of her in Palermo Cathedral, listening reflectively to an angel-lutenist; or Anton Woensam's *Mystical Nuptials of St. Cecilia and St. Valerian* in the Wallraf-Richartz Museum in Cologne. But other images, too, share in related symbolisms: the instruments cast down in miniatures of David in Prayer; the hat on the ground in paintings of St. Jerome; unplayed instruments in a number of paintings and contexts.

The image which best reveals the symbolism I have been describing is Raphael's famous altarpiece in Bologna, *L'Estasi di Santa Cecilia*. Its perfection of form and color, but also its mysterious display of musical instruments, painted with obvious symbolic intent, have drawn the attention of a remarkable array of critics: Richardson, Addison, Winckelman, Reynolds, De Brosses, Burney, Goethe, Wackenroder, Shelley, Stendhal, Liszt, Balzac, Schopenhauer, Mommsen, Ruskin, the Goncourts, Nietzsche, these are but some of the names of those who made the famous painting a small stop on the grand tour, and left their impressions and reflections about it in a variety of essays, books, memoirs and letters.[22] Though it was for centuries the most admired of Raphael's paintings (it headed a list of Italian masterworks that the French removed to Paris during the Napoleonic conquests), its strange musical iconography has continued to resist satisfactory critical explanation. This resistance yields, I believe, to the insights offered in this study.

The painting shows Cecilia standing in an open landscape amid four saints—Paul, John the Evangelist, Augustine, and Mary Magdalene. Broken

impetus. Nam electi impetum spiritus subsecuntur; reprobi autem carnis impetu dominantur. Impetus autem spiritus ad spiritualia, impetus carnalis ad carnalia. Hic ad interiora dona, ille ad exteriora. . . ."

[22] The pertinent passages have been anthologized in *L'estasi di Santa Cecilia*, 253ff.

and discarded instruments lie about Cecilia's feet.[23] She is in seeming ecstasy, distracted from everything around her, gazing heavenwards towards a point somewhere above and in front of her. Behind her, through a rent in the clouds, can be seen six angels in the guise of boy choristers, singing from two choir-books. In her hands, held carelessly upside down as if she had just ceased to play it at the moment when the celestial strains enthralled her, and were now about to discard it without further thought, is a portative organ from which the pipes are beginning to slide to the ground. This organ, like many other representations of the instrument in medieval and Renaissance times, is reversed; that is to say its longer, lower-pitched pipes are to the right, its shorter, higher-pitched pipes to the left, an arrangement opposite to that of an actual organ.

All the explanations I have read of this musical design, with one notable exception, see here an opposition of two musics. Cecilia is said to reject earthly music for heavenly, to favor vocal music over instrumental, or church music over secular. The exception is the more remarkable in that it correctly and persuasively insists on three rather than two zones of music in the painting—this without any benefit of the historical evidence I have advanced but on purely visual grounds from which the author draws eloquent and accurate conclusions. This is Oskar Fischel, who in addition recognizes the dynamic aspect, the symbolism of spiritual change, that lies in the little organ Cecilia holds in her hands: "But for Raphael also the tones of the organ formed the transition between this world and the next. . . . We pass from the obtrusively earthbound, through the zone of agitation and effort, to the soaring transfiguration of light. . . ."[24]

Raphael's musical imagery is of a passage through three stages, not a contrast of two. The broken and abandoned instruments at Cecilia's feet are in the same tradition as the instruments David has discarded in the miniatures of the David-in-Prayer. The most common situation of this miniature, before the Seven Penitential Psalms, indicates the character of these instruments. They are the music that must be abandoned if one is to enter on the path of perfection, a symbol then of St. Bonaventure's first way, the way of purgation.[25] Like the harp discarded by the penitent David, they set before

[23] They are a viola da gamba with broken strings and its bow lying across its broken belly, three recorders, two tambourines, two small kettledrums (one with its skin pierced) with their drumsticks, a triangle, and a pair of cymbals.

[24] Oskar Fischel, *Raphael*, trans. Bernard Rackham (1948; repr. London: Spring Books, 1964), 245.

[25] The interpretation is confirmed by the fact that the texts the David-in-Prayer miniature accompanies in medieval sources are used in the liturgy of Cecilia. The incipit of the First Penitential Psalm, "Domine ne in furore tuo arguas me" (Psalm 6), is the same as the incipit of the

us the words of Job and Lamentations, "my harp is turned into mourning . . . ," "the joy of our heart is fled, our singing is turned into mourning . . ." Spurning them, Cecilia has taken up the organ, reversing the motion from grace to sin, from joy to mourning, in the words from Esther, "turn our mourning into rejoicing, and do not close the mouths of those who sing your praises." This is the second stage of the spiritual journey, the way of illumination. And the organetto in her hands is the spiritual dynamic by which she has come thus far, been transformed and changed. Yet Cecilia has here so clearly passed beyond the illuminative way to the goal of the spiritual journey, the third of Bonaventure's ways, the state of union and even of ecstasy. This instrument, which has transformed her and brought her to this state, and which she seems to have been playing until this moment, she now lets fall from her grasp as a still higher melody makes its claim upon her.

There are other grounds than those advanced here for the interpretation I have offered of the three zones of music in Raphael's scheme. They are found in the circumstances of the painting's commissioning. The principal commissioner, Elena Duglioli Dall'Olio, was known as a mystic and ecstatic with a great devotion to St. Cecilia and an undoubted understanding of the character of her cult.[26] It can be shown that through her spiritual director, Pietro da Lucca, she was in touch with the precise manner of symbolic thought about music and spirituality that this paper has proposed, but to do so here would take us beyond our purpose and must await the appearance of my longer study of St. Cecilia's relation to music. My purpose here has been simply to show that in the late Middle Ages there was abroad a way of thinking about music that allied it with the working of the *musica humana*, with the changes that divine love could effect within the human spirit. Such power of transformation lies at the heart of Raphael's symbolism, just as it does of Dante's, and of the medieval understanding of St. Cecilia's music as it was encapsulated in the antiphon *Cantantibus organis.*

Third Penitential Psalm (Psalm 37), which is the entrance psalm for the mass of the station day at S. Cecilia in Trastevere. The second most common situation of the miniature is before the entrance psalm of the First Sunday of Advent, Psalm 24, "Ad te domine levavi animam meam"; but this is the offertory antiphon of the same stational mass at S. Cecilia.

[26] The best published account of this person and of her part in the commissioning of the painting is by Gabriella Zarri, "L'altra Cecilia: Elena Duglioli dall'Olio (1472–1520)," in *Indagini per un dipinto*, 81–118.

RICHARD L. CROCKER

Thoughts on Responsories

This paper presents prolegomena to a study of the chant responsories of the Night Office. It seems to me, as I work through the whole repertory of responsories, that careful thought has to be given certain basic issues; this paper summarizes my positions on some of these issues.[1]

[1] Principal studies on the responsories: Walter Howard Frere, "Introduction," *Antiphonale Sarisburiense*, ed. Walter Howard Frere (London: Plainsong & Mediaeval Music Society, 1901–25); Peter Wagner, *Einführung in die gregorianischen Melodien* 1: *Ursprung und Entwicklung der liturgischen Gesangsformen bis zum Ausgange des Mittelalters*, 3rd ed. (Leipzig: Breitkopf & Härtel, 1911); 3: *Gregorianische Formenlehre* (Leipzig: Breitkopf & Härtel, 1921); Paolo Ferretti, *Esthétique grégorienne, ou traité des formes musicales du chant grégorien*, trans. A. Agaësse (Paris: Société de Saint Jean l'Évangéliste, 1938); Willi Apel, *Gregorian Chant* (Bloomington: Indiana University Press, 1958); Hans-Jörgen Holman, "The Responsoria Prolixa in the Codex Worcester F 160" (Ph.D. diss., Indiana University, 1961); Helmut Hucke, "Das Responsorium," *Gattungen der Musik in Einzeldarstellungen: Gedenkschrift Leo Schrade in Verbindung mit Freunden, Schülern und weiteren Fachgelehrten*, ed. Wulf Arlt et al. (Bern: Francke, 1973).

Responsories can be studied in one of the medieval antiphonales available in facsimile edition: *Antiphonaire de l'office monastique transcrit par le B. Hartker: MSS Saint-Gall 390–391 (980–1011)*, 2nd ed., Paléographie musicale, 2nd. ser., 1 (repr. Bern: Lang, 1970), cited here as "Hartker's Antiphonale"; *Antiphonaire monastique (XIIe siècle): Codex 601 de la Bibliothèque capitulaire de Lucques*, Paléographie musicale 9 (Tournai: Desclée, Lefebvre, 1906); *Antiphonaire monastique (XIIIe siècle): Codex F.160 de la Bibliothèque de la Cathédrale de*

Symon Petre[2]

Symon Petre, antequam de navi vocarem te, novi te:
super plebem meam principem te constitui:
et claves regnarum caelorum tradidi tibi.

(Simon Peter, before I called thee from the ship, I knew thee:
I placed thee as leader of my people:
and I gave thee the keys to the kingdom of heaven.)

The words of responsories are extremely important; some day a book will be written on them alone. But the relationship of words and music has many dimensions, and not all of them are employed in any one musical style. John Stevens has argued—persuasively, I think—that sacred and also secular medieval chant is mostly concerned with the formal and phonetic aspects of words.[3] But with David Burrows's evocative article on "Singing and Saying" in mind,[4] we can go much further towards a positive appreciation of the role of music in responsories. Singing is different from saying. The difference is due specifically to the resonance that accumulates from the use of discrete as opposed to continuous pitch (to use the standard Greek distinction).[5] Responsories seem to pay relatively little attention to the words simply because they are paying so much attention to the purely musical qualities of the flow of sound. Words and music proceed on parallel but separate tracks, coordinated in a few respects, merely coexisting in others.

The one respect in which words and music are consistently coordinated is in the large syntactic articulations of the words: these are always accommodated by the phrasing of the melody. This consistent relationship was pointed out by medieval writers, in terms of *cola* and *commata*,[6] which has suggested to modern scholars that many other relationships between words

Worcester, Paléographie musicale 12 (Tournai: Desclée, Lefebvre, 1922). *Antiphonale Sarisburiense*, ed. Walter Howard Frere.

I have been using the St. Denis Antiphonale, Paris B. N. lat. 17296; inventory in Réné-Jean Hesbert, *Corpus Antiphonalium Officii* 2: *Cursus monasticus*, Rerum Ecclesiasticarum Documenta, Series maior, Fontes 8 (Rome: Herder, 1965).

[2] Responsories were sung from time to time in the course of this paper to illustrate the genre. The versions used followed Hartker's Antiphonale. "Symon Petre" is for St. Peter (29 June), Hartker's Antiphonale, 280.

[3] John E. Stevens, *Words and Music in the Middle Ages: Song, Narrative, Dance, and Drama, 1050–1350* (Cambridge: Cambridge University Press, 1986).

[4] David Burrows, "Singing and Saying," *The Journal of Musicology* 7 (1989): 390–402.

[5] Aristoxenus, "Elementa harmonica" I, 8, in *Greek Musical Writings* 2: *Harmonic and Acoustic Theory*, ed. Andrew Barker (Cambridge: Cambridge University Press, 1989), 132.

[6] For instance, in the *Scolica enchiriadis:* see *Musica et Scolica Enchiriadis*, ed. Hans Schmid (Munich: Verlag der Bayerischen Akademie der Wissenschaften, 1981), 82–83.

and music should be sought out. But I think this is the wrong conclusion to draw from what the medieval authors say, or how the chants themselves are constituted. I find no relationship suggesting that the melody *consistently* conformed to, or responded to, or imitated the words in aspects such as word accent, image, mood, meaning, idea. There is a clear division of labor here: the words can speak for themselves. The word accent, for instance, can be there in the rendition, perfectly audible, with no accommodation provided by the melody. The words project all aspects of their meaning perfectly well by themselves; they do it nicely without music, they can do it with music. Music has other things to do. Indeed, music is another thing to do with words, another mode in which words can be presented, as an alternative to conversation, or recital, or exposition, or argumentation, or narrative. And in this musical mode the words can be given other inflections, other accentuations, other rhythms.

I can illustrate quickly the familiar discrepancy between the rhythm of words and the rhythm of melody in responsories, by reciting the words of the next responsory, *Hodie nobis de caelo*, using the durations but not the pitches of the melody, that is, in continuous not discrete pitch. This shows how the durations are grouped relative to the words in ways that are undeniably rhythmic, yet have little perceptible relationship to the rhythms the words would have by themselves in a recital mode.

> *Hodie nobis de caelo* [spoken]

Of course, these rhythms are much more persuasive when projected through the discrete pitches of the melody.

> *Hodie nobis de caelo*[7] [sung]

> Hodie nobis de caelo pax vera descendit:
> hodie per totum mundum melliflui facti sunt caeli.

> *(Today true peace descends to us from heaven:*
> *today throughout all the world the skies are made sweet.)*

I do not mean to deny any accommodation of melody to words; in fact, when the melody is understood in terms I hope to suggest, there is much more accommodation than is usually allowed. I do mean that the words as a system do not generate the melody, and the melody does not merely reflect the words.

[7] Christmas Matins; Hartker's Antiphonale, 45.

It seems to me that our problems in understanding pitch relationships in Gregorian chant stem not from the repertory itself (which has continued to be immediately comprehensible to succeeding generations, including our own) but rather from the aesthetic apparatus and analytic tools we bring to it. I find it extremely fruitful—indeed, essential—to approach the tonal structure of chant with a sense of what I call the "pitch environment," or "the overall pitch set." I use the term "pitch environment" to refer to several closely related aspects. The first is the long-range historical continuum in which eighth-century Roman chant occurs. The continuum supplies a seven-toned diatonic system, in which the intervals that include four or five adjacent pitches are (with one exception) tuned in perfect fourths or fifths. In the millenium leading up to the eighth century A.D. the system was known by the Greek terminology "Greater Perfect System" and "Lesser Perfect System,"[8] but as a system it had been in place in the Near East at least since the second millenium B.C.[9] Also in place since whenever was the corollary set of "octave species"; inflected variants, "chromatic" or "enharmonic" genera, were in use from time to time, but not by Christians.

I mean "pitch environment" in another sense as well, concerning the way music sounded in Rome just before and during the emergence of Christian musical practice. I want to refer to Gunther Wille's massive book, *Musica romana;*[10] Wille's four thousand textual references make Roman musical practice inescapable, if still in some respects inscrutable. It is clear that there was much music sounding in Rome along a broad spectrum from high art to low art, from public to private performance, involving various combinations of voices and instruments, from voice and cithara or lyre through large, and probably noisy, ensembles; and choral ensembles, sometimes also large.[11] This was not music one pitch at a time, which would be especially apparent in the practice of cithara or lyre accompaniment to

[8] See Isobel Henderson, "Ancient Greek Music," in *Ancient and Oriental Music,* ed. Egon Wellesz, New Oxford History of Music 1 (London: Oxford University Press, 1957), 346.

[9] As shown in the interpretation of the "tuning tablet" from second millenium Mesopotamia; see Hans M. Kummel, "Zur Stimmung der babylonischen Harfe," *Orientalia* 39 (1970): 252–63.

[10] Gunther Wille, *Musica romana: Die Bedeutung der Musik im Leben der Römer* (Amsterdam: Schippers, 1967).

[11] To pass over the gross instances mentioned in texts quoted by Wille (356, n. 543: one hundred trumpeters, also one hundred of each of three kinds of aulos players; another time, six hundred singers and three hundred kithara players), Claudian (quoted ibid.) includes an impressive wedding ensemble in two hexameters:

> tympana chorda simul symphonia tibia, buxus
> cymbala, bombylium cornus, aes, fistula, sistrum.

The "Carmen saeculare" of Horace was sung in Rome in 17 B.C. by twenty-seven boys and twenty-seven girls (238–39).

song—which, tangentially, is the origin and basic meaning of the term "lyric."[12] All of that would lead us far afield, and is not relevant here simply because by patristic injunction instruments and instrumental accompaniment were excluded from Christian practice.[13] Roman Christian music became one pitch at a time; but I think the prior Roman practice makes it inescapable that a pitch environment, the "overall pitch set," was sounding implicitly as the precondition of any melodic rendition, either as the diatonic system (the Greater Perfect System) or the segment needed for the song to be sung.

Hodie nobis caelorum[14]

Hodie nobis caelorum rex de virgine nasci dignatus est,
ut hominem perditum ad regna caelestia revocaret:
gaudet exercitus angelorum, quia salus aeterna humano generi apparuit.

(Today for us the king of heaven deigned to be born of a virgin,
that he might recall man, once doomed, to the kingdom of heaven:
let the host of angels rejoice, for eternal salvation has appeared to human kind.)

From an analytic point of view the most important factor is that the pitch set was *pre-tuned,* exactly as the lyre had been tuned explicitly.[15] Being tuned, the system was resonant with itself, and it is this pre-tuned, resonant pitch set that can bear the burden of structure in Gregorian chant. The overall pitch set is the best generality for understanding the structure of a responsory—better than the usual assumption of an armature consisting of, say, a fifth, or a fourth, or a couple of thirds. The melody seems to explore freely the whole pitch set, moving to any part of it at any time. In its way of moving, the line seems to accept little responsibility for the structure of the chant. It is restless, fluttery, unpredictable; it may dwell for a while on a subset, reiterating the pitches of the subset, but then it can cadence on any of those pitches, or can escape from the subset to cadence somewhere else [an

[12] The standard Latin term is "cantus ad lyram." The Greek tradition for this genre began with Alcaeus and Sappho, who developed the meters later called "lyric," and sang them to asiatic lyre-type instruments called variously *lyra, barbitos,* or *kithara;* perhaps harp-type instruments were also used, but the instrument the Greeks specifically called "lyra" gave its name to the genre. See Barker, *Greek Musical Writings,* 1:47–53.

[13] See *Music in Early Christian Literature,* ed. James McKinnon (Cambridge: Cambridge University Press, 1987), 1–4.

[14] Christmas Matins; Hartker's Antiphonale, 45.

[15] I have in mind here the most common, "default," kind of tuning to a scale of about an octave extent in diatonic genus. This tuning can be presumed "pythagorean," that is, by perfect fourths and fifths, any time from the second millenium B.C. on; see n. 9.

example was sung, showing the formula that starts G a b a G a a G, ending variously on G, F, a, c, E, D].

In his dissertation on responsories, Hans-Jürgen Holman catalogued the formulae by ending pitches, on the tacit assumption that a cadence, by definition, is on the pitch that best represents the phrase to be ended. This gives him, for example, 103 different formulae ending on D; but in some of them the D is much less expected than in others.[16] The point is, the last pitch of a subset is no better index for the pitch set than is any other. It was Dom Jean Claire who emphasized that discussion of tonal structure in chant must deal primarily with where a chant spends most of its time, not where it ends.[17] If we ask, "Where is the principal residence of a responsory?" the answer must be, "In the pitch set as a whole."

This is not to say that the line lacks musical meaning, or purpose, or expressiveness, only that it avoids clear location, direction, goal. Its purpose seems to be variability. Its avoidance of regularity is so systematic as to be not just intentional, but a principle, I think a basic one. This avoidance of repetition is especially noticeable at the level of detail, in the rhythmic arrangement of the number of notes per syllable, as well as in the movement up and down by tone and semitone. This free play with tone—in the absence of all those other good things the church fathers prohibited—comes close to being the essence of music.

To understand this kind of melody we need tools far more sophisticated than the simple outline of a psalm tone, so often used as a model for the tonal plans of Gregorian chants. As analytic tools, psalm tones are suspect on several counts; here I am concerned only that the assumption of a reciting tone as a structural referent for florid chant is neither useful nor believable. Instead of the calculus of sameness provided by this and other traditional methods of analysis, we need a calculus of successive difference in order to track this restless, exploratory, seemingly random melody.

Quem vidistis pastores[18]

How to reconcile this kind of melody with the extensive use of formula or idiom that has always been observed in responsories? Holman catalogued all these formulae, demonstrating the full extent of their usage, but also their great number and variety. Holman also defined melody type carefully, and, I think, correctly: he allowed a melody type only when two chants selected the same number of the same standard phrases and presented them

[16] Holman, "The Responsoria Prolixa," 431–36.

[17] Jean Claire, "Les répertoires liturgiques latins avant l'octoéchos: L'office férial Romano-Franc," *Études grégoriennes* 15 (1975): 79 and passim.

[18] Christmas Matins; Hartker's Antiphonale, 46.

in the same order.[19] He identified relatively few melody types—one in mode 2, one in mode 7, three in mode 8, accounting all together for a hundred or so responsories out of the repertory of seven or eight hundred. It is important to understand that a melody type is not a thing in itself, rather it is a statistical generality. It is useful to think of the whole repertory spread out on a field, with responsories that share idioms placed next to each other. Given the tendency toward differentiation of detail, the responsories will be distributed widely and more or less evenly throughout the field. There will, however, be dense clusters where a number of responsories share idioms almost exactly, and those we call melody types. Still, the reality is a collection of seven or eight hundred melodies, each with its own set of words.

Formulae are used for many different purposes in the history of music. The most important use in the eighth and ninth centuries, while well known, has not been given its due importance. Use of idioms is obviously the way the liturgist extends the repertory throughout the "circle of the year." It is essential, I feel, to distinguish between a musician generating or developing new melodies, with whatever materials and just for the sake of making music, from a liturgist or liturgical musician adapting them for new requirements in the calendar. We know that such requirements were presenting themselves during the sixth, seventh, eighth centuries, and beyond. We should not automatically attribute the formulaic methods of musical composition used for those liturgical purposes to musical activity in general, or to the development of other kinds of new melodies.

Formulae are often mentioned in connection with improvisation, and rightly so; but some careful distinctions are called for. The word "improvise" means "not to foresee." Now, anyone who has improvised music knows that you do not stand up to do it in public without *some* kind of provision. It is customary to come armed with a store of formulae, as well as extensive experience in generic music-making. What is not foreseen is exactly which materials will be used, in what order, and for how long.

Since formulae are used for many other purposes (such as the liturgical one I just mentioned), the presence of formulae by itself does not necessarily indicate the use of improvisation. And we have no documentation indicating such use by eighth-century Roman cantors. Nonetheless, we can assume they used it, simply because standing up to make music without knowing exactly what is going to happen is such a basic and universal practice. The interesting question is, what did they use it for, and did they use it in public or private?

[19] Holman, "The Responsoria Prolixa," 85.

Another distinction. Musicians sometimes work very hard to improvise music so that it will sound as if it had been composed. And they sometimes work very hard at composing music so that it will sound as if it had been improvised. Indeed, if a skillful musician stands up to perform music that is unfamiliar to you, you have no way of knowing how many times he has been through it before by himself. There may be very little correlation in this respect between how a piece of music was made and how it sounds. The words and concepts "composition" and "improvisation" still need much reflection, which I leave to others; for the moment I will use the words "improvise" and "improvising" to refer to making music without knowing in advance how it will be, and the word "improvisatory" for music that *sounds as if* it had been improvised.

We need this distinction to deal with a paradox.[20] Why and how did this eighth-century Roman chant style, with its seemingly random contours, become so fixed by the time of its earliest written records prepared some time later? I believe the answer lies in the nature of the chant and its production in the eighth century. I believe that while it may *seem* improvisatory, as if produced by spontaneous, impulsive singing, it was in fact very precisely controlled and stabilized. I can identify three essential moments in the production of a new piece of chant, that is, a way of singing a new set of words not previously provided with a melody. First, the materials to be used were indeed generated by improvising—in private. Second, and most important, the results of improvising were scrutinized, selected, and refined; for it is surprisingly difficult to produce results that sound truly random, given the closure of the pitch set on one hand, and the needs of stylistic consistency on the other. Only some of the results of improvising are acceptable. This process leads inescapably, I feel, to the third essential moment, fixation, on the spot, of the results so achieved, so that they will not have to be re-invented next time.

One of the most important things Leo Treitler has done is to remind us that music most truly resides in ourselves, not in graphics on a page. I go on

[20] The following paragraphs address issues raised in connection with "oral tradition," discussed intensively in a series of articles that appeared 1987–90: Kenneth Levy, "Charlemagne's Archetype of Gregorian Chant," *Journal of the American Musicological Society* 40 (1987): 1–30; David G. Hughes, "Evidence for the Traditional View of the Transmission of Gregorian Chant," *Journal of the American Musicological Society* 40 (1987): 377–404; Leo Treitler, Kenneth Levy, David Hughes, in "Communications," *Journal of the American Musicological Society* 41 (1988): 566; Helmut Hucke, "Gregorianische Fragen," *Die Musikforschung* 41 (1988): 304–30; Hendrik Van der Werf, David Hughes, in "Communications," *Journal of the American Musicological Society* 42 (1989): 432; Kenneth Levy, "On Gregorian Orality," *Journal of the American Musicological Society* 43 (1990): 185–227; see also Levy, "Gregorian Chant and Oral Transmission," in the present volume.

to say, the eighth-century Roman cantor pre-arranged and stabilized responsory melodies inside himself, so that he could faithfully reproduce them, then teach them to the chorus. These pre-arranged and stabilized melodies, one for each set of words, are, I believe, faithfully preserved in the written records prepared some time later. Treitler also reminded us that a given piece of music could proceed differently in certain respects without materially affecting either its identity or its quality. I go on to say, this kind of alternative (which I find extremely important in music) is at a given point in a given chant very limited in number, and to be very precisely specified. This kind of alternative is also preserved in the variants of the earliest sources.[21]

There is a much more interesting paradox that involves the question, why did the Romans want such an improvisatory style in their responsories? For the other term of this paradox is that the Romans showed a passion for ceremonial precision in all aspects of their liturgical practice except musical style.[22] There are at least two possible answers. I think it would be possible to track through Roman culture, pagan as well as Christian, a desire that cult musicians should show an inspired spontaneity indicative of the indwelling of the deity—a divine raptus. Then, more specifically Christian is the nature and purpose of monastic meditation. Here there is the problem of responsories for some of the Roman martyrs, responsories that relentlessly recount the agony of the martyrs in the unspeakable tortures they suffered; these were recorded in the *vitae*, and thence abstracted for the responsories.—Unspeakable, apparently not unsingable. But if singable, then not to be musically expressed in any of the meanings of "expression" familiar to us from later Western practice. How is music to express the feelings of the martyrs, or of the devout contemplating the martyrs—of Laurence roasting in the grill, of Hypolitus watching his whole household decapitated in front of him, of Agatha—never mind about Agatha. What music *can* do, with a suitably effusive style such as we find in the responsories, is induce in the devout a meditative ecstasy that is at least an intimation of that ecstasy that caught up the martyrs in their agony, transfiguring it and transporting them through it—which is why the monastics were concerned with the martyrs in the first place. And why, I believe, they were concerned with all those responsories.

[21] See especially the discussion of variants by Hughes, "Evidence for the Traditional View," and "Communications" (1989).

[22] Most clearly apparent in, say, "Ordo Romanus I," ed. Michel Andrieu, *Les Ordines Romani du haut moyen age* 2 (n.p.: Louvain, 1948), 81.

JOSEPH DYER

Prolegomena to a History of Music and Liturgy at Rome in the Middle Ages

The "new direction" in medieval scholarship which I offer for consideration will be devoted to a review of the topics relevant to the study of music and liturgy at Rome during the Middle Ages. Due to the city's status as the spiritual capital of Western Christendom and to the prestige of its bishop, Rome presents the researcher with distinctive challenges which require an unusually broad contextual approach. The musical and liturgical sources must be read in conjunction with urban topography, archeology, art history, monasticism, and the organization of the urban and papal clergy. Because of the complexity inherent in the coordination of such diverse sources, the following remarks can pretend to be no more than a sketch of the sources with suggestive illustrations of how they can enrich studies of the Roman liturgy and its music.

The history of medieval Rome and the grand sweep of events which shaped that history establish an obvious framework for research on the city's liturgy and music.[1] Naturally, events elsewhere on the Italian peninsula cannot be ignored, for they often had repercussions within the walls of

[1] For its detailed treatment one still looks to the classic study of Ferdinand Gregorovius, *Geschichte der Stadt Rom im Mittelalter.* Originally published between 1859 and 1870, there are several subsequent German editions. It is available in English as *History of the City of Rome in*

Rome.[2] The papacy, an institution with a history of its own, was deeply involved not only in local pastoral care and political struggles but also in events with wider European and Eastern resonances. The popes were invariably drawn into the turbulent doctrinal and jurisdictional controversies with Byzantium and the churches of the East.[3] Our understanding of the medieval city itself has advanced markedly thanks to the admirable synthesis of Richard Krautheimer, *Rome: Profile of a City, 312–1308*, the superb fruition of a lifetime of study devoted to the complex evolution of Rome from Constantinian times until the removal of the papal court to France in the early fourteenth century.[4] This richly illustrated and documented volume is filled with extensive references to primary and secondary source material. John Boe has recently demonstrated how awareness of the broad historical context can engender fascinating insights about the interaction of music and liturgy in medieval Rome.[5]

the Middle Ages, trans. Mrs. G. W. (Annie) Hamilton (London: Bell, 1906; repr. New York: AMS Press, 1967). See also the studies of Peter Llewellyn, *Rome in the Dark Ages* (New York: Praeger, 1971); Robert Brentano, *Rome before Avignon* (New York: Longman, 1974); Thomas F. X. Noble, *The Republic of St. Peter: The Birth of the Papal State, 680–825* (Philadelphia: University of Pennsylvania Press, 1984).

[2] See Ludwig Moritz Hartmann, *Geschichte Italiens im Mittelalter*, 3 vols. in 5 (Gotha: Perthes, 1897–1911); Thomas Hodgkin, *Italy and Her Invaders*, vols. 5–7 (Oxford: Clarendon, 1892–99); and Charles Wickham, *Early Medieval Italy: Central Power and Local Society, 400–1000* (London: Basingstoke, 1981).

[3] Of the several histories of the papacy the most authoritative are those of Franz Xaver Seppelt, *Geschichte der Päpste*, 5 vols. (Munich: Kösel, 1954–59); Horace K. Mann, *The Lives of the Popes in the Early Middle Ages*, 18 vols. (London: Paul, Trench, Trübner, 1925–32); Erich Caspar, *Geschichte des Papsttums von den Anfängen bis zur Höhe der Weltherrschaft*, 2 vols. (Tübingen: Mohr, 1930–33); Jeffrey Richards, *The Popes and the Papacy in the Early Middle Ages, 476–752* (London: Routledge and Kegan Paul, 1979); and Bernhard Schimmelpfennig, *Das Papsttum: Grundzüge seiner Geschichte von der Antike bis zur Renaissance*, 2nd ed. (Darmstadt: Wissenschaftliche Buchgesellschaft, 1987). For quick reference J. N. D. Kelly, *The Oxford Dictionary of Popes* (Oxford: Oxford University Press, 1986) is quite useful. The primary source of information for the earlier Middle Ages is the *Liber pontificalis*. See Louis Duchesne, ed., *Le Liber pontificalis*, 2 vols. (Paris: Thorin, 1886–92); a second edition of this work, ed. Cyrille Vogel, reproduces Duchesne's additions and corrections in a third volume, and provides an excellent bibliography on pp. 23–42 (Paris: Boccard, 1955–57). An English translation of the papal biographies up to the year 817 has been published by Raymond Davis, *The Book of the Pontiffs (Liber Pontificalis): The Ancient Biographies of the First Ninety Roman Bishops to AD 715* ([Liverpool]: Liverpool University Press, 1989), and *The Lives of the Eighth-Century Popes*, Translated Texts for Historians 5 and 13 (Liverpool: Liverpool University Press, 1992).

[4] Richard Krautheimer, *Rome: Profile of a City, 312–1308* (Princeton: Princeton University Press, 1980).

[5] John Boe, "Italian and Roman Verses for Kyrie leyson," *La tradizione dei tropi liturgici: Atti dei convegni sui tropi liturgici, Parigi (15–19 ottobre 1985)—Perugia (2–5 settembre 1987)*, ed. Claudio Leonardi and Enrico Menesto (Spoleto: Centro di studi sull'alto medioevo, 1991), 337–84. Contextual themes are treated, not always with satisfying results, by S. J. P. van Dijk,

A grasp of urban topography provides another essential foundation for the study of the liturgy of Christian Rome in late Antiquity and the Middle Ages.[6] As Krautheimer and others have emphasized, Constantine's decision to establish the Basilica Salvatoris and the ecclesiastical administrative center on the outskirts of the city, far from the monumental area and, as it happened, far from what were to be the areas of maximum population density in the Middle Ages, proved to be unfortunate.[7] Situated just within the walls, but at the southeast corner of the city, the Lateran was not close to the medieval population centers located at the bend of the Tiber—in the Campus Martius and across the river in Trastevere. Furthermore, many of the old community centers (*tituli*) and basilicas established between the third and the fifth centuries no longer had sizable resident congregations. All of this population movement forced the popes to build new churches to accommodate the altered topographical distribution of urban settlements.

The remoteness of the pope's cathedral church and the impossibility of accommodating the entire Roman congregation at the Lateran fostered—even necessitated—the development of what is known as "stational" liturgy. The pope or his representative travelled with a retinue from church to church across the city to celebrate the liturgy on important days of the year.

"The Urban and Papal Rites in Seventh- and Eighth-Century Rome," *Sacris Erudiri* 12 (1961): 411–87; "The Medieval Easter Vespers of the Roman Clergy," *Sacris Erudiri* 19 (1969–70): 261–363; and "Gregory the Great: Founder of the Urban *Schola Cantorum*," *Ephemerides Liturgicae* 77 (1963): 335–56. I have interpreted the evidence on the latter topic rather differently in "The Schola Cantorum and Its Roman Milieu in the Early Middle Ages," in *De Musica et Cantu: Studien zur Geschichte der Kirchenmusik und der Oper: Helmut Hucke zum 60. Geburtstag,* Musikwissenschaftliche Publikationen, Hochschule für Musik und Darstellende Kunst 2, ed. Peter Cahn and Ann-Katrin Heimer (Hildesheim: Olms, 1993), 19–40.

[6] I can cite here only a few of the many works on Roman topography: the many volumes of the *Guide rionali di Roma* from the Roman publisher Palombi; Carlo Ceccarelli, "Roma medioevale" in *Topografia e urbanistica di Roma*, ed. Ferdinando Castagnoli et al., Istituto di studi Romani (Bologna: Capelli, 1958), 189–341; Louis Duchesne, "Notes sur la topographie de Rome au moyen-âge," I–XIII, repr. in his *Scripta Minora* (Rome: École française de Rome, 1973); Amato Frutaz, *Le piante di Roma*, 3 vols. (Rome: Istituto di studi Romani, 1962); Umberto Gnoli, *Topografia e onomastica di Roma medioevale e moderna* (Rome: Staderini, 1939; repr. Foligno: Edizioni dell'Arquata, 1984); Sylvia Pressouyre, *Rome au fil du temps* (Boulogne: Cuenot, 1973). Primary documents are printed in Roberto Valentini and Giuseppe Zuchetti, *Codice topographico della città di Roma*, 4 vols., Fonti per la storia d'Italia 81, 88, 90, 91 (Rome: Istituto storico italiano per il medio evo, 1940–53); *Itineraria et Alia Geographica* (Notitia ecclesiarum urbis Romae, De locis sanctis martyrum, Itinerarium Malmesburiense, Itinerarium Einsidlense), Corpus Christianorum Series Latina 175–176 (Turnhout: Brepols, 1965); and Karl L. Urlichs, *Codex urbis Romae topographicus* (Würzburg, 1871).

[7] Richard Krautheimer, *Three Christian Capitals: Topography and Politics* (Berkeley: University of California Press, 1983), 7–40 and 93–121; idem, *Rome: Profile of a City*, 3–31. For a list of Constantine's lavish donations to the church of Rome see the *Liber pontificalis*, ed. Duchesne, 1:172–87.

The stational churches were extensions of the bishop's own church, not autonomous parishes with pastors who exercised independent jurisdiction in coordination with the bishop. The prominent role eventually assumed by the great cemeterial basilicas must also be brought into proper perspective.[8] These included St. Peter's, St. Paul's, St. Lawrence outside the walls, and St. Agnes (the latter now extant only as a ruin near Sant'Agnese on the Via Nomentana). They were not originally intended as places for regular worship, but the desire of pilgrims to focus their devotions on the sites hallowed by the graves of the martyrs soon elevated their liturgical importance.[9] Both the Constantinian church of St. Peter and the papal foundation of St. Mary Major were very important stational churches. Subsequently, certain food-distribution centers known as *diaconiae* also became sites where the stational liturgy was celebrated.

Though at first unsystematic, this liturgical circuit gradually crystallized into the fully developed stational system. In its definitive form it encompassed twelve Sundays and fifty-four ferias (mostly in Lent and the week following Easter), not counting optional stations which the pope might celebrate at the tombs of martyrs outside the walls.[10] The *Ordines Romani* are a rich source of information about the celebration of this papal liturgy, though they vary widely in the amount of detail they offer. As the fifty *ordines* are grouped in the critical edition of Michel Andrieu, they include directions for the papal (or episcopal) Mass (1–10), baptism (11), lists of chants and readings for the Office (12–14), prescriptions concerning monastic discipline and liturgy (15–19), miscellaneous ceremonies of the liturgical year (20–33, 37–38,), ordinations (34–36, 39–40), the dedication of a church (41–44), the coronation of the emperor (45–48), funeral rites (49),

[8] Richard Krautheimer, "Mensa-Coemeterium-Martyrium," *Studies in Early Christian, Medieval, and Renaissance Art* (New York: New York University Press, 1969), 35–58.

[9] Pilgrims made up an important part of the non-resident Roman "congregation." *Ordo Romanus* 15 mentions a "copiosa multitudo peregrinorum de quacumque provintia congregati," gathered at the church of S. Adriano on the Forum, ready to participate in the Candlemas procession to St. Mary Major (*Ordo* 15.79; ed. Michel Andrieu, *Les Ordines Romani du haut moyen-âge*, Spicilegium Sacrum Lovaniense, Études et documents 11 [Louvain: n.p., 1931–61], 3:113).

[10] See John F. Baldovin, *The Urban Character of Christian Worship: The Origins, Development, and Meaning of Stational Liturgy*, Orientalia Christiana Periodica 228 (Rome: Pont. Institutum Studiorum Orientalium, 1987). The older surveys of Johann Kirsch are still valuable: *Die römischen Titelkirchen im Altertum* (Paderborn: Schöningh, 1918) and *Die Stationskirchen des Missale Romanum* (Freiburg-im-Breisgau: Herder, 1926). The study of G. G. Willis, "Roman Stational Liturgy," in his *Further Essays in Early Roman Liturgy*, Alcuin Club Collections 50 (London: Alcuin Club, 1968) is useful, but not always accurate in matters concerning the history of the stational churches themselves.

and the *Ordo Romanus antiquus* (50).[11] Topographical information is included only incidentally in these documents when for example a procession from the papal residence or from one church to another forms part of the ritual. In the descriptions of papal ceremonies found in the *Liber politicus* (ca. 1142) of Canon Benedict of St. Peter's, the author traces the course of some papal processions with reference to the ancient monuments found along the route.[12]

Even when the pope was not personally present at a liturgical celebration, the union with his clergy and people across the city was cemented by dispatching to the priests in the *tituli* a portion of the consecrated bread (*fermentum*) from the Mass he was celebrating concurrently with them. The ritual of the *tituli* must have been a modified and reduced version of the papal liturgy. Indeed, instructions found in a few of the *Ordines Romani* confirm this. *Ordo* 22 grants permission for independent presbyteral celebration during Lent, if attendance at the papal stational Masses is impossible.[13] The second half of *Ordo* 15 describes how Mass was to be celebrated "in cenubiis, sive in civitatibus vel in vicis, aut ubicumque sacerdus missas celebraverit . . . sive cum clero puplice, vel etiam cum duabus aut unum ministrum."[14] Viewed as an ensemble, however, the *ordines* offer little precise information about the liturgy as it was carried out daily in the Roman *tituli*. In addition to the liturgical activity of the pope and his court, the great basilicas and the *tituli*, there were in Rome many monastic establishments, which had the special charge of chanting the Divine Office.

Since the *Ordines Romani* describe the conduct of ceremonies within a church building, a full understanding of the *ordines* often requires a knowledge of the interior configuration of the buildings in question. Repeated renovations have obscured the medieval interiors of virtually all Roman churches. Unfortunately, modern historical archeology has paid little heed

[11] Andrieu, *Les Ordines Romani*. See the grouping of the *ordines* in Cyrille Vogel, *Medieval Liturgy: An Introduction to the Sources*, rev. and trans. William Storey and Niels Rasmussen (Washington, D.C.: Pastoral Press, 1986), 191–93.

[12] *Liber politicus*, ed. Paul Fabre and Louis Duchesne in *Le Liber Censuum de l'Eglise romaine*, Bibliothèque des Écoles françaises d'Athènes et de Rome, 2nd ser., vi/2 (Paris: Thorin, 1910), nos. 16, 29, 48, 50. A guide book to Roman antiquities has been attributed to Benedict. For the Latin text of the original version ("Descriptio plenaria totius urbis") see Urlichs, *Codex urbis Romae topographicus*, 91–112. The translation by F. M. Nichols incorporates later additions: *The Marvels of Rome (Mirabilia urbis Romae)*, trans. and ed. Francis Morgan Nichols, 2nd ed. prepared by Eileen Gardiner (New York: Italica Press, 1986).

[13] *Ordo* 22.16; Andrieu, *Les Ordines Romani*, 3:261. *Ordo* 17 (*Breviarium ecclesiastici ordinis*) is destined for a monastic environment (Andrieu 3:157–93).

[14] *Ordo* 15.121; Andrieu, *Les Ordines Romani*, 3:120.

to evidence about the permanent (marble or masonry) "furniture" which accommodated the needs of the liturgy within medieval Roman church buildings.[15] The evidence is scanty, to be sure, but drawings of hypothetical interior reconstructions, once published, tend to be reproduced again and again in subsequent studies without any critical reexamination of the evidence. In fairness it must be granted that information on early church "furnishings" can be recovered only with exceeding difficulty from excavation reports. Some efforts have been made to link floor decoration with liturgical movements, but this approach is unavoidably speculative.[16] Yet the importance of such evidence, interpreted by scholars steeped not only in the history of art but also in the liturgy, can hardly be overemphasized. Both are essential for a complete reconstruction of successive stages in the history of the medieval Roman liturgy.

I first turned my attention to the question of such interior arrangements while conducting research on the *schola cantorum*, the special papal choir whose existence can be traced back to approximately the end of the seventh century. Art historians are accustomed to calling a structure in the nave of certain Roman churches (San Clemente, Santa Maria in Cosmedin, Santa Sabina) a "schola cantorum." The one at San Clemente, extant since the beginning of the twelfth century, is the only such enclosure with a continuous history since the Middle Ages. Both of the others are modern reconstructions based on archeological evidence or earlier reports about the buildings' interiors.

[15] Richard Krautheimer expressed the need for joint liturgical-architectural investigations in a postscript to "The Transept in the Early Christian Basilica," *Studies in Early Christian, Medieval, and Renaissance Art*, 67. Only Thomas Mathews, "An Early Roman Chancel Arrangement and its Liturgical Functions," *Rivista di archeologia cristiana* 38 (1962): 73–95, has attempted to coordinate the internal arrangements of a (in some respects hypothetical) Roman church with its function. Theodor Klauser's suggestion that the seven silver *altaria* donated to the Lateran by Constantine were for the reception of liturgical offerings assumes an excessively early date for the introduction of this part of the liturgy: "Die konstantinischen Altäre der Lateransbasilika," *Römische Quartalschrift für christliche Altertumskunde und Kirchengeschichte* 43 (1935): 179–86, repr. in his *Gesammelte Arbeiten zur Liturgiegeschichte, Kirchengeschichte und christlichen Archäologie*, ed. Ernst Dassmann, Jahrbuch für Antike und Christentum, Ergänzungsband 3 (Münster in Westfalen: Aschendorff, 1974), 155–60.

[16] The most complete presentation of data on the architectural history of Roman churches is Richard Krautheimer, *Corpus basilicarum Christianarum Romae,* 5 vols. (Rome: n.p., 1937–77) with additional bibliography in *Rome: Profile of a City*. On floor markings in Byzantine churches see George P. Majeska, "Notes on the Archeology of St. Sophia at Constantinople: Notes on the Green Marble Bands on the Floor," *Dumbarton Oaks Papers 32* (1978): 299–308; Neil K. Moran, "The Musical 'Gestaltung' of the Great Entrance Ceremony in the Twelfth Century in Accordance with the Rite of Hagia Sophia," *Jahrbuch der österreichischen Byzantinistik* 28 (1979): 167–93. An important related study is Thomas Mathews, *The Early Churches of Constantinople: Architecture and Liturgy* (University Park, Penn.: Pennsylvania State University Press, 1971).

Upon closer examination the connection between the architectural term and the *schola cantorum* seems to reach back no further than the sixteenth century, when a Roman historian, Pompeo Ugonio, commenting on the structure in San Clemente, remarked that "*dicono* che serviva per la scola de Cantori, che oggi chiamiamo Cappella" (emphasis added).[17] A slightly earlier contemporary, Onofrio Panvinio, mentioned a "coro di marmo" at San Lorenzo fuori le mura.[18] Panvinio's term proves to be a far more accurate description of its true function, as art historians might have surmised, had they realized that the papal *schola* visited some of these churches only once or twice a year. The so called "schola cantorum" is actually a large architectural choir for the singing of the Office.[19] None of these structures, however, nor any of the others that once adorned Roman churches has any link whatsoever with the eminent college of papal singers.

A recent publication by Sible de Blaauw, *Cultus et decor: Liturgie en architectuur in laatantiek en middeleeuws Rome, Basilica Salvatoris, Sanctae Mariae, Sancti Petri*, has placed the study of the interaction between liturgy and architecture on a new footing.[20] This monograph traces the history of each building through successive remodelings and relates the available liturgical evidence to the author's (newly conceived) reconstruction drawings. De Blaauw's documentation is exemplary, and this book will surely represent a model for all future investigations of the churches of Rome and the liturgy which took place within their walls. The fact that nearly seven hundred pages are needed to do justice to the three most important churches hints at the potential for further research along these lines.

[17] Ugonio noted similar features at San Eusebio and Santi Giovanni e Paolo in his *Historia delle stationi di Roma, che si celebrano la Quadragesima* (Rome: n.p., 1588).

[18] Onofrio Panvinio, *De praecipuis urbis Romae sanctioribusque basilicis quas septem ecclesias vulgo vocant liber* (Rome: n.p., 1570). A splendid ambo, presumably once part of this enclosure, still exists in the church.

[19] This was the conclusion of Theodor Bogler, "Mönchschor und Presbyterium," *Liturgie und Mönchstum* 29 (1961): 56–63; for a review of the evidence see Elaine De Benedictis, "The '*Schola Cantorum*' in Rome During the High Middle Ages" (Ph.D. diss., Bryn Mawr College, 1983). To the churches she discusses I can add an eighteenth-century reference to S. Silvestro in Capite: "Di Silvestro crediamo perciò quell'*Ambone,* o come altri dicono, coro con pulpito, e legili di marmo, i quali rimasero nella nostra Chiesa fino al tempo del celebre Cardinal Baronio" [who removed the structure to SS. Nereo e Achilleo on the Via Appia]. Some people called the pulpit an ambo: "altri poi pensano che tutto il coro, detto talvolta *Schola Cantorum* insieme co[n] pulpiti si denominasse *Ambone.*" Giuseppe Carlotti, *Memorie istorico-critiche della chiesa e monastero di San Silvestro in Capite di Roma* (Rome: n.p., 1795), 28–29.

[20] Sible de Blaauw, *Cultus et decor* (Delft: Eburon, 1987), with an Italian summary, 647–57. A useful general orientation was provided by the earlier survey of C. J. A. C. Peeters, *De liturgische dispositie van het vroegchristelijk kerkgebouw* (Assen: Van Gorcum, 1969). On papal donations see Herman Geertman, *More Veterum: Il Liber Pontificalis e gli edifici ecclesiastici di Roma nella tarda antichità e nell'alto medioevo*, Archeologia Traiectina 10 (Groningen: Tjeenk

The relationship between the liturgy (or liturgical texts), the Roman churches, and their decoration remains to be explored in depth. A few years ago, an article by Marchita Mauck drew attention to a possible link between a Gregorian antiphon and the mosaic of the triumphal arch in the Roman church of Santa Prassede.[21] The decorative program of the church was carried out during the pontificate of Paschal I (817–24), presumably in coordination with his transfer of relics from cemeteries (mainly S. Alessandro on the Via Nomentana) to safety within the city. For the mosaic of the apse and its arch the mosaicist sought inspiration from the nearby church of SS. Cosma e Damiano, but the mosaic of the triumphal arch (plates 1a and 1b) seems to be an original design.[22] In an important and novel attempt at developing a contextuality between a Roman church building and the liturgy which transpired within it, Mauck linked scenes depicted on the arch with the antiphon *In paradisum* from the funeral liturgy.

While it seems conceivable that the scenes on the triumphal arch do in fact allude to Paschal's massive translation of relics, one might ask whether or not they constitute a satisfactory visual representation of *In paradisum.*

> In paradisum deducant te angeli,
> in tuo adventu suscipiant te martyres,
> et perducant te in civitatem sanctam hierusalem.[23]

Willink, 1975) and the same author's "L'Illuminazione della basilica paleocristiana secondo il Liber Pontificalis," *Rivista di Archeologia Cristiana* 64 (1988): 135–60.

[21] "The Mosaic of the Triumphal Arch of S. Prassede: A Liturgical Interpretation," *Speculum* 62 (1987): 813–28.

[22] P. Jonas Nordhagen, "Un problema di carattere iconografico e technico a S. Prassede," *Roma e l'età carolingia: Atti delle giornate di studio, 3–8 maggio 1976* (Rome: Multigrafica, 1976), 159–66. Nordhagen concerns himself only with the "legame fra l'iconografia dell'abside e dell'arco absidale de S. Prassede e l'iconografia del mosaico nella chiesa dei SS. Cosma e Damiano al Foro Romano" (159).

[23] Some early sources read "in paradiso." For the text variants see Damien Sicard, *La liturgie de la mort dans l'église latine des origines à la réforme carolingienne*, Liturgiegeschichtliche Forschungen und Quellen 64 (Münster in Westfalen: Aschendorff, 1978), 135. *In paradisum* does not occur in the manuscripts containing urban (Old Roman) chant. The most important studies of the antiphon are Bernard Capelle, "L'antienne In Paradisum," *Questions liturgiques et paroissiales* 8 (1923): 161–76, repr. in his *Travaux liturgiques* (Louvain: Centre liturgique, Abbaye de Mont César, 1955), 3:252–67; Hieronymous Frank, "Römische Herkunft der karolingischen Beerdigungsantiphonen," *Mélanges en l'honneur de monseigneur Michel Andrieu*, Revue des sciences religieuses, vol. hors série (Strasbourg: Palais universitaire, 1956), 161–71; and idem, "Der älteste erhaltene *Ordo Defunctorum* der römischen Liturgie und sein Fortleben in Totenagenden des frühen Mittelalters," *Archiv für Liturgiewissenschaft* 7/2 (1962): esp. 360–79. A Gallican or Milanese origin for the antiphon is rejected by Sicard, *La liturgie de la mort*, 215–20.

Some of the images in the mosaic (angels, martyrs, Jerusalem) can indeed be seen as relevant to *In paradisum*, but there is a serious textual problem in linking the mosaic with this particular antiphon. The exclusive use of the optative subjunctive (*deducant, suscipiant, perducant*) in a petitional sense cannot easily be explained in the context of the early Christian belief that those who confessed Christ with their blood gained immediate access to the beatific vision and the company of the blessed. The Roman martyrology normally commemorates the *natalis* of a saint: simultaneously the day of his or her death and triumphal entrance into eternal life. The antiphon, furthermore, asks the martyrs to receive the soul of the departed ("deducant te, suscipiant te, perducant te") while the mosaic shows the martyrs themselves bearing their crowns as they are welcomed by angels.

I would propose an alternative solution: that the Roman antiphons for the procession of relics at the dedication of a church, listed in table 1, offer a better analogue of the scene depicted at Santa Prassede.[24] The text of the sixth antiphon, "Ambulate sancti dei, ingredimini in civitatem domini; hedificatum est enim vobis ecclesiam novam; tibi populus adorare debeat maiestatem dei," is particularly apposite to the translation of relics. The entry of the martyrs into the heavenly Jerusalem—and possibly the relocation of their earthly remains to Santa Prassede—is also the subject of the previous antiphon (no. 5): "Ambulate sancti dei ad locum destinatum quod vobis preparatum est ab origine mundi." The texts of several of the others seem to me equally consistent with the mosaic, though none of them explicitly mentions the angels seen welcoming the martyrs. Given the presumed protective power of the saints' bodies, there may likewise be a connection between a phrase in the third relic antiphon ("De hierusalem exeunt reliquie et salvatio de monte syon, propterea protectio erit huic civitati . . .") and Paschal's deposition of their bodies within a city often needing their protection. The right side of the arch depicts Peter and Paul, possibly representing the city of Rome, welcoming the blessed into the heavenly Jerusalem.

Relating the mosaic program with these Roman antiphons also avoids the problem of the contested provenance (Gallican or Roman?) of *In paradisum*.[25] The antiphon probably predates the mosaic, since its incipit (as "In paradiso deducant te") is found in the Gelasian Sacramentary of

[24] Rome, Biblioteca Apostolica Vaticana, Vat. lat. 5319, fols. 135–36, transcribed in *Monumenta Monodica Medii Aevi*, ed. Bruno Stäblein (Kassel: Bärenreiter, 1970), 2:552–56.

[25] Sicard defends a Roman origin of *In paradisum* and states that Frank now agrees with him on this point (*La liturgie de la mort*, 219).

Plate 1a: Rome, Santa Prassede. Detail of the triumphal arch (left side). Alinari / Art Resource.

Plate 1b: Rome, Santa Prassede. Detail of the triumphal arch (right side). Alinari / Art Resource.

Table 1

Old Roman Antiphons In Dedicatione Ecclesie

1. Ecce populus custodiens iudicium et faciens veritatem; in te speraverunt, domine; usque in eternum viam iustorum recta facta est et iter sanctorum preparatum est. *Ps.*Venite exultemus. *V.*Preoccupemus.

2. Cum iocunditate exibitis et cum gaudio deducimini, nam et montes et colles exilient expectantes vos cum gaudio.

3. De hierusalem exeunt reliquie et salvatio de monte syon; propterea protectio erit huic civitati et salvabitur propter david famulum meum.

4. Ad honorem sanctorum concurrite populi videntes gloriam dei; ecce qui meruerunt, qui dominum hiesum xrictum non negaverunt.

5. Ambulate sancti dei ad locum destinatum, quod vobis preparatum est ab origine mundi.

6. Ambulate sancti dei, ingredimini in civitatem domini; hedificatum est enim vobis ecclesiam novam; tibi populus adorare debeat maiestatem dei.

7. Platee hierusalem gaudebunt et per omnes vicos eius canticum letitie dicunt.

8. Sub altare domini sedem* accepistis, intercedite pro nobis per quem meruistis.

Rome, Vat. lat. 5319, fols. 135–36

*corrected from *sedes.*

Rheinau which dates from the late eighth or early ninth century.[26] There it is prescribed to be sung as the body is taken *out* of the church. The earliest Roman liturgical source with the antiphon places its singing *in* the church.[27] Yet another Roman *ordo* calls for the antiphon as the body is brought *into* the church.[28] The employment of *In paradisum* for the Santa Prassede dedication would entail the transfer of a piece rooted in the funeral liturgy to a ceremony honoring the martyrs. I believe that the evidence speaks against this transfer. Whether any of the relic antiphons were actually composed for the renovation of Santa Prassede, whether the mosaics take up the theme of already extant antiphons, or whether the mosaic program draws from other sources are not the essential questions. The presumed relation between the dedication antiphons and the mosaic suggests that a closer examination of visual records might offer insights into the development of liturgy and music in Rome. The Santa Prassede mosaics add perhaps yet another instructive dimension to Antoine Chavasse's observation that "la vieille liturgie romaine a toujours été très 'circonstanciée.' "[29]

The origins and development of the Roman liturgy have occupied the interests of scholars for centuries, and to mention even the most important relevant scholarship would be impractical. Instead, I would like to focus on one type of liturgical book, the Sacramentary, recently the object of intense research which has succeeded in focussing attention both on the layers of euchological development and on the disparity of practice within the city of Rome.[30] This research has clarified the existence of separate books for papal

[26] Zürich, Zentralbibliothek, cod. Rh30, fols. 151–55 (pp. 305–12). See Capelle, "L'antienne," 170; the text of the *ordo* is given in Frank, "Der älteste erhaltene *Ordo*," 362–63.

[27] *Ordo* 49.5; Andrieu, *Les Ordines Romani*, 4:529. There the text of the antiphon reads: "In paradiso D[e]i ducant te angeli [in tuo] adventu suscipiant te martyres, perducant te in civitatem sanctam Hierusalem." Though the manuscript containing this *ordo* (Rome, Vat. Ottob. 312) dates from the eleventh century, Andrieu believes that it derives from a Roman model of the first half of the eighth century.

[28] This tenth-century (monastic) *ordo*, once in the Archivio di S. Pietro (no. 1), is now lost. An extract is printed in *Venerabilis viri Josephi Mariae Thomasii opera omnia*, ed. Antonius Franciscus Vezzosi (Rome, 1749), 4:330–41.

[29] Antoine Chavasse, *Le sacramentaire gélasien (Vaticanus Reginensis 316): Sacramentaire presbytéral en usage dans les titres romains au VIIe siècle* (Tournai: Desclée, 1958), 514. On other connections between the visual arts and the liturgy see G. A. Wellen, "Sponsa Christi: Het Absismozaiek van de Santa Maria in Trastevere te Rome en het Hooglied," *Feestbundel F. van der Meer* (Amsterdam: Elsevier, 1966), 148–59; and Ernst Kitzinger, "A Virgin's Face: Antiquarianism in Twelfth-Century Art," *Art Bulletin* 62 (1980): 6–19.

[30] For a summary of current research see Vogel, *Medieval Liturgy*, 61–106, and Jean Deshusses, "Les Sacramentaires," *Archiv für Liturgiewissenschaft* 24/1 (1982): 19–46 (English translation in *Liturgy* 18 [1984]: 13–60). Difficult, yet important, is Antoine Chavasse's recent "Évangéliaire, épistolier, antiphonaire et sacramentaire: Les livres romains de la messe au VIIe et au VIIIe siècle," *Ecclesia Orans* 6 (1989): 177–255.

and presbyteral uses and established the probable dates of their compilation. The summary which follows is based largely on the conclusions of the two most important researchers, Antoine Chavasse and Dom Jean Deshusses.

The Gregorian Sacramentary was created as a book for papal services.[31] During the late seventh century, probably during the pontificate of Vitalian (657–72), a liturgical reorganization produced a revised Gregorian Massbook. This book, known as the "type-II" Gregorian Sacramentary, was an adaptation of the papal Sacramentary for use by priests at an important basilica, generally presumed to be St. Peter's. This revision provided the full round of daily services expected by the pilgrims who frequented the basilica: Masses for Sundays, the weekdays of Lent, feasts of the Lord, and saints' days. This is exactly what is found in the earliest preserved representative of this type-II Gregorian Sacramentary, the Sacramentary of Padua. Although the manuscript of the *Paduense* was copied somewhere in North Italy or in the northern part of the empire (Neustria or Austrasia) while Lothair was sole emperor (840–55), an analysis of its contents reveals a state of liturgical development reached almost two centuries before.[32] Simultaneously with this revision, high-ranking papal clergy were assigned to celebrate the liturgy at the basilica. At about the same time (ca. 685), a revision of the papal liturgy for use at the Lateran basilica resulted in the creation of yet another Sacramentary (type-I Gregorian), represented by a manuscript now preserved at Trent.[33]

It might not be entirely coincidental that the foundation of the papal *schola cantorum* seems to be roughly contemporary with this liturgical activity. What better complement to a liturgical renewal than a choir of professional singers entrusted with a share in its implementation? (Perhaps at the same time the resident singers of the principal basilicas were also reorganized.) A well known, but generally discredited remark by the thirteenth-century chronicler Ekkehard V of St. Gall to the effect that a special choir of

[31] Deshusses's introduction to his edition of the Gregorian Sacramentary traces a history of that book, see *Le sacramentaire grégorien: Ses principales formes d'après les plus anciens manuscrits*, Spicilegium Friburgense 16 (Freiburg, Switzerland: Éditions universitaires, 1971), 50–75.

[32] Padua, Bibl. Cap. D47, ed. Cunibert Mohlberg, *Die älteste erreichbare Gestalt des Liber Sacramentorum anni circuli der römischen Kirche*, Liturgiewissenschaftliche Quellen und Forschungen 11–12 (Münster in Westfalen: Aschendorff, 1927; repr. 1967).

[33] Edited by F. Dell'Oro and Bonifacio Baroffio, *Monumenta liturgica ecclesiae Tridentinae saeculo XIII antiquiora* 2 (Trent: Società studi trentini di scienze storiche, 1985); see also Jean Deshusses, "Le sacramentaire grégorien de Trente," *Revue bénédictine* 78 (1968): 261–82; idem, "Le sacramentaire grégorien pré-hadrianique," *Revue bénédictine* 80 (1970): 213–37; and Vogel, *Medieval Liturgy*, 97–102.

"Vitaliani," named after Pope Vitalian (657–72), sang in the papal presence could be a dim recollection of these seventh-century Roman developments.[34] The outlines of the urban presbyteral liturgy are much more difficult to reconstruct. The texts of its Mass prayers are preserved in the Gelasian Sacramentary, but urban documents comparable to the papal *Ordines Romani* seem not to have been preserved.[35] The impressive ceremonial and music of the papal stational services had to be adapted for the modest daily and Sunday needs of the *tituli.*

The loss of medieval Roman liturgical manuscripts has been large, especially considering the fact that many were transported north of the Alps and as far away as Britain. There still remains, however, a significant number of liturgical sources earlier than the fourteenth century that can be identified as either (1) written or used in Rome, or (2) very closely modeled on urban practices. Table 2 (pp. 108–15) offers a provisional list of these sources, arranged according to liturgical category. Within each broad category (Mass, Office, Varia) the manuscripts deposited in the Vatican Library and other Roman libraries are cited first, followed by those deposited outside of Rome. A separate section lists the most important manuscripts of non-Roman provenance which very closely reflect Roman use at a stage earlier than that represented by the surviving Roman manuscripts. All of the churches and monasteries listed are located in Rome unless otherwise indicated. The fact that a manuscript can be identified with a specific Roman institution does not, of course, mean that it was either written there or originally destined for that institution. The script employed in many of the manuscripts was common to central Italy in the eleventh and twelfth centuries.[36] For attributions and dating I have relied on published catalogues, principally the inventory of Dom Salmon, and scholarly discussions.[37] Most of the manuscripts

[34] "Hic est Vitalianus praesul, cuius adhuc cantum quando Apostolicus celebrat, quidam qui dicuntur Vitaliani, solent edere in praesentia eius," as quoted in Bruno Stäblein, *Monumenta Monodica Medii Aevi,* 2:142*. On the foundation of the *schola* see the article cited in n. 5 above.

[35] Antoine Chavasse, *Le sacramentaire gélasien;* for a discussion of the Gelasian Sacramentary see Vogel, *Medieval Liturgy,* 64–70. Only portions of a few *ordines* (*Ordo* 2.16, *Ordo* 15.133–51, *Ordo* 17, *Ordo* 22.15) could be applied to liturgies celebrated by an ordinary priest (Andrieu, *Les Ordines Romani,* 3:281). *Ordo* 37B.5–6 (Andrieu 4:250) notes that the observance of the Ember Days by the "parrochianos cleros" will differ from that of the "domnus apostolicus" and his clergy, "qui dicuntur cardinales."

[36] See Paola Supino Martini, *Roma e l'area grafica romanesca (secoli X–XII),* Biblioteca di scrittura e civiltà 1 (Alessandria: Edizione dell'Orso, 1987).

[37] Pierre Salmon, *Les manuscrits liturgiques latins de la Bibliothèque Vaticane,* 5 vols., Studi e testi 251, 253, 260, 267, 270 (Vatican City: Biblioteca Apostolica Vaticana, 1968–72); H. Ehrensberger, *Libri liturgici Bibliothecae Apostolicae Vaticani manuscripti* (Freiburg im Breisgau: n.p., 1897); Robert Amiet, "Inventaire des manuscrits liturgiques conservés dans les bibliothèques et les archives de Rome," *Scriptorium* 39 (1985): 109–18; idem, "Catalogue des

from the Vatican Library have been examined either directly or on microfilm.[38] In the case of liturgical books preserved in the Archives of St. Peter's, the assumption is that they were destined for use at the basilica. Manuscripts from the Lateran are fewer in number. Perhaps the fortunes of that church, depending as they did on the presence or the absence of the papal court, created a less stable environment for the preservation of liturgical texts. A break in the Lateran tradition occurred in the early twelfth century when Paschal I (1099–1118) installed the canons of St. Fridian of Lucca at the basilica.

Some of the documents preserve the papal liturgy, while others represent service books produced for use by members of the court. The pattern of manuscript distribution among Roman churches and monasteries undoubtedly reflects the vicissitudes of accident rather than the liturgical importance of the establishments whose liturgical books have survived. A thorough examination and close comparison of these apparently random survivals would certainly add to our appreciation of the diversity of the urban liturgy. Of all the prolegomena to a history of liturgy and music in Rome the task of assessing these sources is surely one of the most urgent.

The extraordinarily strong representation of Legendaries and Homiliaries indicates not only their usefulness under changing liturgical conditions, but also the continuing value of saints' lives and patristic writings for spiritual edification. The undoubted loss of many Sacramentaries must be regretted. Since a Sacramentary or Missal was a prerequisite for the celebration of the Eucharist, we must assume that every church in Rome possessed at least one copy. The Office is not particularly well represented among the surviving manuscripts, particularly when one recalls the number of monasteries which existed in Rome, some of them with papal commissions to celebrate the Divine Office solemnly in public.[39] While the few remaining

livres liturgiques conservés dans les archives et les bibliothèques de la Ville de Rome," *Studi medievali*, 3rd ser., 27/2 (1986): 925–97; Cosimo Stornajolo, *Inventarium codicum manuscriptorum latinorum Archivii basilicae S. Petri in Vaticano maxima ex parte e recensione Cosimi Stornajolo depromptum* (available for consultation at the Vatican Library, Sala Barberini, no. 411). See also Klaus Gamber, *Codices Liturgici Latini Antiquiores*, 2nd ed., 2 vols., Spicilegii Friburgensis Subsidia 1 (Freiburg, Switzerland: Universitätsverlag, 1968) and the Ergänzungs- und Registerband, ed. Bonifacio Baroffio et al. (Freiburg, 1988). I am grateful to Dom Baroffio for providing many citations to liturgical codices presently located in libraries in and outside of Rome. Without his generous help the listing in table 2 would have been far less complete. Although the rather extensive bibliography on the manuscripts cannot be cited here, the most important studies are mentioned in Cyrille Vogel, *Medieval Liturgy*.

[38] I would like to express my thanks to Dr. Charles J. Ermatinger, director of the Vatican Film Library at St. Louis University, and to the Andrew W. Mellon Fellowship Program, for enabling me to pursue research at the Vatican Film Library.

[39] An important, but as yet unexploited source for musical aspects of the Office of the Roman Curia in the late thirteenth century is the *Practica artis musice* (chapters 10–11) by the

books of Old Roman chant, three for the Mass and two for the Office, may seem a meager remnant, they furnish a quite complete record of the repertoire. They represent, furthermore, a comparatively high rate of survival for a written tradition which did not commence until the end of the eleventh century with the *graduale* (1071) of S. Cecilia in Trastevere.[40] We do not know, of course, how avidly the idea of committing the oral Old Roman tradition to notation was taken up by Roman singers. Undoubtedly, many churches preserved the local oral tradition until their entire repertoire was replaced by Gregorian chant.

Certain types of liturgical books are well served by modern scholarly editions; some of these are listed at the end of table 2. Almost all of the pure Roman sources which came north of the Alps were altered by Frankish additions. It is the merit of Michel Andrieu and other scholars that they have attempted to distinguish the latter from the fundamental Roman elements. The best known of the *Ordines Romani* prescribe the manner in which the Eucharist is to be celebrated, but others provide directions for the readings at the Office, the ceremonies of Lent and Eastertide, ordinations, the dedication of churches, and the coronation of the emperor. Related to the *ordines* are the ceremonial notes gathered by Canon Benedict of St. Peter's (*Liber politicus*, ca. 1142), Prior Bernhard of the Lateran (*Ordo Lateranensis*, 1140–45), and by the papal chamberlain Censius Savelli in his *Liber censuum* (ca. 1188–97).

The Roman Pontifical of the twelfth century was not a single official book promulgated by papal decree. Rather, there were various private compilations which shared certain common features. The later Pontifical of the Roman Curia emanated from the liturgists of the Lateran palace for use in the city and surrounding region. It gained wider currency when the papal court left Rome for France in the fourteenth century. The Ordinal of Innocent III embodies, according to van Dijk, a reform of the court Office carried out during the years 1213–16. Although the manuscripts collated by Dom Hesbert for his *Antiphonale Missarum Sextuplex* originated in France, and the chants in them were in all likelihood sung to Gregorian melodies, the text form (Roman Psalter) and liturgical ordering derive ultimately

priest Amerus, ed. Cesarino Ruini, Corpus Scriptorum de Musica 24 (Rome: American Institute of Musicology, 1977).

[40] Edited in facsimile with commentary by Max Lütolf, *Das Graduale von Santa Cecilia in Trastevere (Cod. Bodmer 74)*, 2 vols. (Cologny-Geneva: Fondation Martin Bodmer, 1987). A companion antiphoner might have been produced at the same time, as Lütolf points out (*Das Graduale*, 1:49). On earlier and contemporary fragments see John Boe, "Chant Notation in Eleventh-Century Roman Manuscripts," in the present volume.

from Roman models. Pierre Jounel's splendid study of the sanctoral cycle observed at the Lateran in the twelfth century contains twelve previously unedited Roman calendars.

The liturgical divisions within the city (papal-presbyteral or stational-titular) reflected a division within the Roman clergy between (1) those attached primarily to the papal service and (2) those who served the urban churches.[41] In the first half of the eighth century a reorganization of the clergy sharpened this distinction between the two Roman "churches." The highest echelons of the Roman clergy, namely the chief presbyter of each *titulus*, the original seven deacons, the twelve new regional deacons, and the bishops of the seven suburbican sees (also known as the hebdomadary bishops of the Lateran), became more closely tied to the papal administration. The twenty-eight cardinal priests (the title borne by the the leading Roman presbyters) had duties not only at their *tituli* but also weekly liturgical obligations at four of the patriarchal basilicas (St. Peter's, St. Paul's, St. Mary Major, and St. Lawrence). Service at the Lateran was reserved to the cardinal bishops.

Neither the details nor the implications of Roman ecclesiastical structures and their history can be addressed here, but the gap between urban and papal clergy was a real one. A strong indication of this distinction in function and status between the two groups occurs in the description of a Mass of ordination in *Ordo* 35. The non-papal priests and deacons (*forenses*) are not accorded the same honors as their papal counterparts. The new urban deacons are not clothed with the dalmatic, and evidently the new urban priest does not take his place with the cardinal priests (". . . et exit quo iturus est"). The priests and deacons destined for urban service cannot even approach the papal throne or altar. As the *Ordo*

[41] For further information see Noble, *The Republic of St. Peter*, 212–55; Vincenzo Monachino, *La cura pastorale a Milano, Cartagine e Roma nel secolo IV*, Analecta Gregoriana 41 (Rome: Università gregoriana, 1947), 279–407; Louis Halphen, *Études sur l'administration de Rome au moyen âge: 751–1252* (Paris: Champion, 1907); Michel Andrieu, "L'origine du titre de cardinal dans l'Église romaine," *Miscellanea Giovanni Mercati* 5, Studi e testi 125 (Vatican City: Biblioteca Apostolica Vaticana, 1946), 113–44; Walter Croce, "Die niederen Weihen und ihre hierarchische Wertung," *Zeitschrift für katholische Theologie* 70 (1948): 257–314; Carl Gerold Fürst, *Cardinalis: Prolegomena zu einer Rechtsgeschichte des römischen Kardinalscollegiums* (Munich: Fink, 1967), 14–71; Rudolf Hüls, *Kardinäle, Klerus und Kirchen Roms (1049–1130)*, Bibliothek des Deutschen historischen Instituts in Rom 48 (Tübingen: Niemeyer, 1977), 3–44 ("Die Entwicklung der kardinalizischen Ordines bis zum 12. Jahrhundert"); and Hans-Walter Klewitz, *Reformpapsttum und Kardinalkolleg* (Darmstadt: Gentner, 1957), 11–134 ("Die Entstehung des Kardinalkollegiums").

explains: "quomodo potest fieri ut super illud altare communicent, ubi licentiam non habent ministrare nec corpus domini consecrare."[42] Similarly, when in 1018 Pope Benedict VIII gave the bishop of Porto, one of the cardinal bishops, jurisdiction over Trastevere and the Tiber island, he included the right of ordination. The bishop of Porto could not, however, ordain "cardinales presbyteri, cardinales diaconi vel subdiaconi vel acolythi sacri palatii Lateranensis."[43] I suggest that this division raises interesting questions about the Old Roman and Gregorian chant traditions and their relationship to the urban liturgy. The cardinal priests were required (1) to celebrate Mass in their *tituli,* (2) to officiate at the patriarchal basilica assigned to their region, and (3) to participate in the papal stational Masses in their own region and on the most solemn feasts. Can we imagine that they encountered a different musical repertoire in all or some of these locations? I think that the circumstances argue strongly for a substantially unified musical practice in Rome. How long it might have lasted is a question which cannot be answered at the present moment, but I think the answer depends somewhat on the degree to which the elite levels of the Roman clergy eventually began to see themselves more as functionaries of an "international" church—whose music was Gregorian chant—rather than as humble priests, deacons, and singers serving local Roman congregations.

Another factor in the Roman ecclesiastical structure was the presence of scores of monasteries within the city walls. The early history of monasticism in Italy is not easy to trace, and this obscurity shrouds Rome as well.[44] Monks may have been integrated into the liturgical life of the city as early as the pontificate of Sixtus III (432–40), who established a monastery "in Catacumbas," conceivably to chant the hours of the Divine Office.[45] Successive foundations of other popes were situated in proximity to the major basilicas to assure that the Office would be celebrated day and night. Because St. Benedict depended on the basilical monasteries for the formulation of

[42] *Ordo* 35.36; Andrieu, *Les Ordines Romani,* 4:40. See also n. 35 above.

[43] P. Jaffe and S. Lowenfeld, *Regesta Pontificum Romanorum,* 2nd ed. (Leipzig: n.p., 1885–88), no. 4024, as quoted in Fürst, *Cardinalis,* 19 and 28.

[44] See Gregorio Penco, *Storia del monachesimo in Italia,* 2nd ed. (Milan: Jaca Book, 1983); G. D. Gordini, "Origine e sviluppo del monachesimo a Roma," *Gregorianum* 37 (1956): 220–60; Jean-Marie Sansterre, *Les moines grecs et orientaux à Rome aux époques byzantine et carolingienne (milieu du VIe-fin du IXe siècle),* 2 vols., Mémoires de la classe des Lettres, 2nd ser., vol. 66/1 (Brussels: Académie royale de Belgique, 1983); *Dizionario degli Istituti di Perfezione,* s.v. "Roma," by Peter Llewellyn et al., 7:1895–1912.

[45] *Liber pontificalis,* 1.234 and n. 13 (p. 236); it was located near the basilica of S. Sebastiano on the Via Appia. See Guy Ferrari, *Early Roman Monasteries,* Studi di antichità cristiana 23 (Vatican City: Biblioteca Apostolica Vaticana, 1957), 163–65.

the liturgical code of his Rule, the practice of these Roman monasteries took on a fundamental role in the history of the Divine Office.[46] The custom of St. Peter's, where Leo I (440–61) established one of the earliest basilical monasteries (dedicated to Sts. John and Paul), was later regarded as the paradigm to be followed by other Roman monasteries. When Gregory III (731–41) renewed a foundation at St. Crysogonus, he obliged it to celebrate the Office "secundum instar officiorum ecclesiae beati Petri apostoli." When he restored the monastery of S. Pancrazio near the Lateran basilica, he imposed the same requirement.[47] There is no reason to believe, however, that Roman monks at this time followed the Rule of Benedict with respect to the Office. Robert Taft cautions that even the distinction between the cathedral (Lauds and Vespers) and monastic (Matins and the other hours) Office, accepted by most modern scholars as normative elsewhere in the Christian world, might not be applicable to Rome.[48] Our knowledge of the monasteries' participation in the liturgical life of the city is not very complete, however.[49] There seems to have been hostility on the part of the Roman clergy toward followers of the monastic life as early as Jerome, who had to leave the city in 385 following the death of his patron, Pope Damasus. Even as late as the seventh century, elements of the Roman clergy sought to bar monks from the reception of sacred orders. Though more and more monks were ordained to the priesthood, it would be too simple to assume that the division of labor decreed by Gregory III when he established a chapel at St. Peter's in honor of Mary and all the saints (". . . a monachis vigiliae celebrentur, et a presbyteris ebdomadariis missarum solemnia") held through out the Middle Ages or was even applicable to other situations.[50] We do not yet understand to what extent the monks collaborated liturgically with the urban clergy over the centuries, though this is clearly an important question. The controversy became moot as the priest-monks were gradually transformed into canons regular in the eleventh and twelfth centuries.

[46] This has been recognized since the pathbreaking studies of Camillus Callewaert, conveniently gathered together and reprinted in his *Sacris Erudiri* (Steenbrugghe: Abbatia S. Petri de Aldenburgo, 1940), 53–168.

[47] *Liber pontificalis*, 1.419. The monastery was also under the patronage of St. John the Baptist and St. John the Evangelist, see Ferrari, *Early Roman Monasteries*, 252–53.

[48] Robert Taft, *The Liturgy of the Hours in East and West* (Collegeville, Minn.: Liturgical Press, 1986), 130–34, 143.

[49] Ildefonso Schuster, *Liber Sacramentorum: Note storiche e liturgiche sul Messale Romano* (Turin: Marietti, 1930), 5:12–74 ("L'opera del Monachesimo nella vita liturgica a Roma").

[50] *Liber pontificalis*, 1.421.

The importance of Rome for the development of music and liturgy throughout the West in the Middle Ages has long been acknowledged, yet much remains to be known about the city that provided much of the framework and content of the wider European practice. Exactly how the history of liturgy and music at Rome in the Middle Ages will be realized still needs to be defined. In the foregoing remarks I have sought to emphasize that such a history entails a panorama broader than that of the special urban repertoire and its relationship to Gregorian chant. I have also tried to stress that in many aspects the Roman church was unique, and that one cannot approach the study of medieval Rome with concepts derived from other Western cities. Charlemagne's admonition to his querulous cantors that they "return to the source" would be a suitable motto for our endeavor. But I might just as reasonably borrow a remark made by Kenneth Levy during one of the stimulating discussions which pervaded this conference in honor of David G. Hughes: "the Roman question—that's the one we really need an answer to!"

Table 2

Sources of the Roman Liturgy before the Fourteenth Century

Part One: Manuscripts of Roman Provenance

MASS

Sacramentaries—Missals

Arch. di S. Pietro F 11A (fols. 101v–166)	Sacramentary (11–12 c.)	St. Peter's
Arch. di S. Pietro F 12 (fols. 87–209)	Sacramentary (late 11 c.)	St. Peter's
Arch. di S. Pietro F 14	Sacramentary (early 12 c.)	S. Salvatoris in Primicerio (S. Trifone)
Arch. di S. Pietro F 15	Sacramentary (mid-12 c.)	Rome (Spoleto/Fermo?)
Arch. di S. Pietro F 16	Sacramentary (early 14 c.)	St. Peter's
Arch. di S. Pietro F 18	Sacramentary (12–13 c.)	St. Peter's
Arch. di S. Pietro H 58 (fols. 1–59; 81–151v)	Ritual-Sacramentary (11–12 c.)	Rome (S. Vito in Macello?)
Barb. lat. 536	Sacramentary (late 12 c.)	Rome
S. Maria Maggiore 40	Sacramentary (ca. 1230)	Monastery of Sts. Andrew and Bartholomew?
S. Maria Maggiore 52	Sacramentary (13 c.)	S. Maria Maggiore?
Ottob. lat. 356	Sacramentary (ca. 1288–90)	Papal; used at S. Maria in Aquiro
Vat. lat. 12989	Sacramentary (after 1230)	Papal
Rome, Bibl. Vallic. B 43	Sacramentary (late 12 c.)	Used at S. Maria di Ninfa (Rome or Velletri)
Rome, Bibl. Vallic. E 15	Sacramentary (early 11 c.)	S. Lorenzo in Damaso
Rome, Bibl. Vallicell. F 4	Sacramentary (12 c.)	S. Maria in Trastevere
Rome, Arch. di Stato 997 (lost)	Missal (ca. 1180)	Ospedale del Ssmo. Salvatore (near Lateran)
Rome, Arch. di Stato 1001		Ospedale del Ssmo. Salvatore (near Lateran)
(fols. 1–310)	Sacramentary (ca. 1300)	
(fols. 311–416) (lost)	Missal (ca. 1300)	
Rome, Bibl. Angelica 1606 (18-c. copy of lost orig.)	Sacramentary (13 c.)	S. Maria ad Martyres

Avignon, Bibl. mun. 100	Sacramentary (late 13 c.)	Use of papal chapel
Florence, Bibl. Riccardiana 299	Antiphoner-Sacramentary (late 11 c.)	Papal chapel
Florence, Bibl. Riccardiana 300	Votive Masses (late 11 c.)	Rome
Madrid, BN MS. lat. 730	Sacramentary (early 13 c.)	Papal; used at S. Lorenzo fuori le mura
Malibu, Getty Museum, Ludwig I.5	Sacramentary (13 c.)	Rome
Montpellier, Bibl. mun. 25	Sacramentary (13–14 c.)	Papal chapel
New York, Pierpont Morgan Library, MS. 713	Votive Masses, Sacramentary (early 14 c.)	Use of the Curia

Mass Lectionaries—Graduals

Arch. di S. Pietro F 1	Epistolary (late 13 c.)	St. Peter's
Arch. di S. Pietro F 5	Evangelary (14 c.)	Rome? (Use of the Curia)
Arch. di S. Pietro F 7	Evangelary (12 c.)	St. Peter's
Arch. di S. Pietro F 12 (fols. 4–86^{v})	Evangelary (late 11 c.)	Monastery of St. Martin near St. Peter's
Chigi A VI 164	Cap. Evang. (10–11 c.)	Rome (monastic)
S. Maria in Via Lata I 45 (almost illegible)	Cap. Evang. (10 c.)	Used at monastery of Sts. Cyriacus and Nicholas
Vat. lat. 44	Cap. Evang. (early 12 c.)	Rome?
Vat. lat. 5465 (fols. 171–176^{v})	Cap. Evang. (8–9 c.)	Rome (S. Matteo?)
Vat. lat. 12985	Evangelary (12 c.)	S. Maria ad Martyres
Rome, Bibl. Ang. lat. 1383	Epistolary (mid-11 c.)	S. Saba?
Rome, Bibl. Casanat. 4906 (17-c. copy of lost orig.)	Epistolary (12 c.)	Lateran
London, S. B. Cron Coll. (olim Cod. Cockerell)	Lectionary-Epistolary (11 c.)	S. Cecilia in Trastevere
Cambridge, Corpus Christi College 286	Evangelary (late 6 c.)	Rome?
Florence, Bibl. Laur. F 17.27	Evangelary (11 c.)	S. Cecilia in Trastevere
London, Brit. Lib. add. 6156	Evangelary (late 11 c.)	S. Maria in Trastevere
Arch. di S. Pietro F 22	Old Roman Grad. (late 12 c.)	St. Peter's
Vat. lat. 5319	Old Roman Grad. (11–12 c.)	Lateran
Cologny, Bibl. Bod. C 74	Old Roman Grad. (1071)	S. Cecilia in Trastevere

OFFICE

Psalters—Antiphoners—Breviaries

Arch. di S. Pietro B 79	Old Roman Ant. (ca. 1181–87)	St. Peter's
Arch. di S. Pietro B 87	Antiphoner (14 c.)	St. Peter's
Arch. di S. Pietro D 150	Psalterium Romanum (late 11 c.)	Rome (originally monastic)
Arch. di S. Pietro D 156	Psalt.-Hymn. monast. (mid-12 c.)	S. Clemente (Rome)? S. Maria Maggiore (Tivoli)?
Arch. di S. Pietro E 14	Calendar-Psalt.-Hymn. (mid-13 c.)	S. Martino ai Monti
Vat. lat. 4406	Calendar-Psalterium Romanum (early 13 c.)	S. Pancrazio near Lateran
Rome, Bibl. Vallicell. B 79	Breviary (late? 12 c.)	SS. Anastasio e Vincenzo ad Aquas Salvias (Tre Fontane)
Rome, Bibl. Vallicell. C 5	Antiphoner (early 12 c.)	Monastic (S. Sisto Vecchio?)
Rome, Bibl. Vallicell. C 62	Capitular-Orational (late 11 c.)	SS. Anastasio e Vincenzo ad Aquas Salvias (Tre Fontane)
Faenza, Bibl. communale	Antiphoner	SS. Anastasio e Vincenzo
London, BL add. 29988	Old Roman Antiphoner. (12 c.)	Rome
Naples, Bibl. Naz. I.B.22	Breviary (13 c.)	Rome

Homiliaries—Legendaries

Arch. di S. Pietro A 2	Legendary (late 11 c.)	St. Peter's (+ A 4 and A 5)
Arch. di S. Pietro A 3	Legendary (late 12 c.)	St. Peter's
Arch. di S. Pietro A 4	Legendary (late 11 c.)	St. Peter's
Arch. di S. Pietro A 5	Legendary (late 11 c.)	Monastic (S. Saba?)
Arch. di S. Pietro A 6	Legendary (14 c.)	Monastic (S. Saba?)
Arch. di S. Pietro A 7	Lectionary (13 c.)	St. Peter's
Arch. di S. Pietro A 13	Homiliary (mid-12 c.)	St. Peter's?
Arch. di S. Pietro B 42	Homilies of Gregory the Great in liturgical order (13 c.)	Rome?
Arch. di S. Pietro B 50	Lectionary (frags. 11 c.)	Rome? (monastic)
Arch. di S. Pietro C 92	Lectionary (late 11 c.)	St. Peter's
Arch. di S. Pietro C 105	Homiliary pars hiemalis (10 c., on 7-c. model)	St. Peter's

Arch. di S. Pietro C 106	Homiliary (14 c.) (adaptation of C 105)	St. Peter's
Arch. di S. Pietro C 107	Homiliary (12–13 c.) (adaptation of C 105)	St. Peter's
Arch. di S. Pietro D 144	Bruno: Expositio in psalmos with liturgical notes (late 12 c.)	St. Peter's?
Arch. di S. Pietro D 212	Homiliary (12 c.)	St. Peter's
Arch. di S. Pietro F 40	Lectionarium stationum (14 c.)	St. Peter's
Barb. lat. 587	Bible (ca. 1080)	S. Cecilia in Trastevere
S. Maria Maggiore 3	Lectionary (13 c.)	S. Maria Maggiore
S. Maria Maggiore 122	Homiliary (late 11 c.)	Rome
S. Maria Maggiore EE IV 1	Bible	S. Maria Maggiore
Vat. lat. 1189	Legendary-Homiliary (10–11 c.)	Monastery of SS. Andrea e Gregorio in Clivo Scauri
Vat. lat. 1191	Legendary (late 12 c.)	S. Maria in Trastevere (+ VL 1193, 1194, 10999)
Vat. lat. 1192	Legendary (mid 12 c.)	Lateran
Vat. lat. 1193	Legendary (late 12 c.)	S. Maria in Trastevere
Vat. lat. 1194	Legendary (late 12 c.)	S. Maria in Trastevere
Vat. lat. 1195	Legendary-Homiliary (late 11 c.)	SS. Giovanni e Paolo
Vat. lat. 1196	Legendary (11–12 c.)	Rome?
Vat. lat. 1274	Homiliary (late 11 c.)	Monastery of SS. Andrea e Gregorio in Clivo Scauri
Vat. lat. 3835/3836	Homiliary (8 c.)	Sts. Philip and James
Vat. lat. 5696	Legendary (late 12 c.)	S. Maria ad Martyres
Vat. lat. 5736 (fols. 1–2; 57–58)	Frag. (12–13 c.) of Haimo of Auxerre, *Expositio in Pauli epistolas*	S. Cecilia in Trastevere
Vat. lat. 10999	Legendary (12 c.)	S. Maria in Trastevere?
Vat. lat. 12958	Bible (12 c.)	Probably Rome
Rome, Arch. S. Giovanni in Laterano 65	Legendary (late 12 c.)	Lateran
Rome, Arch. S. Giovanni in Laterano 67	Legendary (13–14 c.)	Lateran
Rome, Arch. S. Giovanni in Laterano 77	Homiliary (10 c.)	Lateran
Rome, Arch. S. Giovanni in Laterano 78	Homiliary (late 12 c.)	Lateran

Rome, Arch. S. Giovanni in Laterano 79 and 81	Legendary (12 c.)	Lateran
Rome, Arch. S. Giovanni in Laterano 80	Legendary (early 12 c.)	S. Clemente
Rome, Arch. S. Giovanni in Laterano 82	Legendary (late 12 c.)	Lateran
Rome, Archivio di Stato 12950	Homiliary	Rome?
Rome, Bibl. Angelica 1273–1274	Bible (ca. 1125)	Probably Rome
Rome, Bibl. Vallicell. A 14 (17-c. copy in Rome, Vat. lat. 6075/6)	Augustine: *Tract. in Johannem* with liturgical notes (9 c.)	Rome?
Rome, Bibl. Vallicell. tomo V	Legendary (11 c.)	S. Lorenzo in Damaso; used at S. Sebastiano ad Catacumbas in 13 c.
Cape Town, So. African Lib., Grey 6 b 4	Office elements (late 13 c.)	Used at S. Cecilia in Trastevere
Cape Town, So. African Lib., Grey 48 b 4–5 (17-c. copy in Rome,Vat. lat. 6075/6)	Legendary (late 11 c.)	Used at S. Cecilia in Trastevere
Novara, Bibl. Cap. S. Maria LXXXVIII (58)	Homiliary (ca. 1100)	Rome
Paris, BN lat. 755 + BN lat. 3278	Legendary (ca. 1253)	Rome
Perugia, Bibl. Com. Augusta L.59	Bible (early 12 c.)	Probably Rome

Martyrologies

Arch. di S. Pietro H 56	Usuard Martyrology (13 c.)	St. Peter's
Arch. di S. Pietro H 58 (fols. 59–80)	Bedan Martyrology (after 1000)	St. Peter's
Barb. lat. 646 (fols. 1–8^{v}) + VL 4885	Martyrology derived from Bede (mid-late 11 c.)	Monastery of SS. Andrea e Gregorio in Clivo Scauri
Barb. lat. 646 (fols. 9–44)	Bedan Martyrology with adds. from Jerome (ca. 1000)	Monastic; used at Rome
Ottob. lat. 38 (fols. 1–25)	Bedan Martyrology (ca. 1050)	Rome
Vat. lat. 378 (fols. 1–70)	Usuard Martyrology (late 11 c.)	Monastery of S. Maria in Pallara
Vat. lat. 1351	Martyrology (1059/63–1067/68)	S. Lorenzo in Damaso
Vat. lat. 4885	Martyrology (late 11 c.)	S. Paolo fuori le mura

Rome, Archivio di Stato 72 (olim Lancisana 262) (fols. 1–46)	Usuard Martyrology (late 13 c.)	Ospedale di S. Spirito in Sassia
Rome, Bibl. Vallicell. F 85	Bedan Martyrology (1024–43) with additions from Jerome	Monastery of SS. Cyriaco e Nicolò in Via Lata
London, BL add. 14801 (fols. 4–45)	Bedan Martyrology (ca. 1061–91) with additions from Jerone	S. Maria in Trastevere
Monte Cassino, Cod. 179	Bedan Martyrology (ca. 1050)	Rome
Oxford, Bibl. Bod., lat. liturg. d.43 (fols. 49–71v)	Martyrology (late 12 c.)	S. Saba

VARIA

Arch. di S. Pietro B 78	Holy Saturday (13–14 c.)	St. Peter's?
Arch. di S. Pietro F 11A (fols. 1–101)	Ritual-Orationale (mid-12 c.)	St. Peter's
Chigi C VI 173	Liber precum-Calendar (11–12 c.)	Monastic (Rome?)
Barb. lat. 549	Pontifical of the Curia (13–14 c.)	Rome
Ottob. lat. 270	Pontificale Romanum (12 c.)	Rome
Vat. Lat. 9135 (fols. 358–62)	Copy of wall calendar (11 c.)	S. Maria dell'Aventino
———	Wall calendar (before 1246)	SS. Quattro Coronati
———	Wall calendar	S. Saba
Rome, Bibl. Alessandrina 173	Romano-Germanic Pontifical (1000–25)	Rome? (on model from Salzburg)
Rome, Bibl. Naz. Vitt. Emm. 2096 (Sess. 52)	Ordines (11–12 c.)	Used at monastery of S. Croce in Gerusalemme
Messina, Bibl. Seminario 5	Chapter book (13 c.)	SS. Vincenzo e Anastasio
Novara, Arch. Stor. Dioces.	Corpus Domini (13 c.)	Rome
Paris, Bibl. Nat., lat. 1143	Corpus Domini	Rome
Stockholm, Riksarchivet Fr. Br. 2323	Corpus Domini (13 c.)	Rome

Part Two: Manuscripts of Non-Roman Provenance Reflecting Roman Use

Bibl. Apost. Vat., Regin. 316 + Paris, BN lat. 7139	Gelasian Sacr. (ca. 750)	Chelles (Roman presbyteral book)
Padua, Bibl. cap. D.47	Gregorian Sacr. (type II)	Reflects pre-680 St. Peter's use
Trent, C. del Buon Consiglio	Gregorian Sacr. (type I)	Reflects St. Peter's use (685–90)
Cambrai 164 (Hadrianum)	Gregorian Sacr. (type I) (ca. 790)	Papal use (735)
Cambrai, Bibl mun. cod. 553	Comes of Alcuin (ca. 800)	Roman model (ca. 626)
Monte Cassino MS. 175	Cap. Evang. (10 c.)	Roman model (Chavasse IIIA)
Monte Cassino MS. 271	Sacramentary-Lect. (ca. 700)	Roman model (660–80)
Ottob. lat. 79 (fols. 129–135)	Cap. Evang. (10 c.)	Frankish-Roman use of 755 (Klauser Σ)
Vat. lat. 46	Cap. Evang.	Roman model (7 c.)
Vat. lat. 3828 (fols. 122–236^v)	Homiliary (10 c.)	Rome?
Vat. lat. 8523	Cap. Evang. (9–10 c.)	No. France; Roman use of 650 (Klauser Δ)
Malibu, Getty Museum	Evangelary (ca. 800)	Carolingian, on 7-c. Roman model
Würzburg, UB, M.p.Th.f.62 (fols. 2^v–10^v)	Cap. lectionum (ca. 750)	Roman use of 7 c.
Würzburg, UB, M.p.Th.f.62 (fols. 10^v–16^v)	Cap. Evang. (ca. 750)	Roman use of 645 (Klauser Π)
Rome, Bibl. Casanat. 116	Psalter-Collectar-Hymnary (13 c.)	Capua (Calendar of St. Peter's, Rome)
Oxford, Bibl. Bodl., Canon. lit. 379	Breviary (late 13 c.)	Use of papal court
Paris, BN lat. 3798	Homiliary (12 c.)	Roman model (6 c.)
Berlin, D. Staatsbibl., Phillipps 1676	Homiliary of Eugenio of Verona (ca. 796–99)	St. Peter's use of 7 c.
London, BL add. 57528	Pontifical (late 12 c.)	Apamea (Antioch) on Roman model
Lyons, Cod. 570, fols. 289–344^v (17 c. copy of above)	Pontifical (late 12 c.)	Apamea (Antioch) on Roman model
Paris, Bibl. de l'Arsenal, lat. 526 (fols. 89–119)	Pontifical (ca. 1300)	Model ca. 1243/74 (Gregory X)
Paris, BN lat. 4124A	Ordinal of Innocent III (1365)	Model of early 14 c.

Part Three: Published Sources of the Liturgy of Rome

Andrieu, Michel. *Le Pontifical romain au moyen age* 1: *Le Pontifical romain du xii*[e] *siècle;* 2: *Le Pontifical de la Curie romaine au xiii*[e] *siècle;* 3: *Le Pontifical de Guillaume Durand;* 4: *Tables alphabétiques.* Studi e testi 86–88, 99. Vatican City: Biblioteca Apostolica Vaticana, 1938–41.

———. *Les Ordines Romani du haut moyen-age.* 5 vols. Spicilegium Sacrum Lovaniense 11, 23, 24, 28, 29. Louvain: Spicilegium Sacrum Lovaniense, 1931–61.

Dykmans, Marc. *Le Cérémonial papal de la fin du moyen âge à la Renaissance* 1: *Le cérémonial papal du xiii*[e] *siècle;* 2: *De Rome en Avignon ou le cérémonial de Jacques Stefaneschi.* Bibliothèque de l'Institut Historique Belge de Rome 24–25. Brussels-Rome: Institut Historique Belge de Rome, 1977–81.

Fabre, Paul and Duchesne, Louis. *Le Liber Censuum de l'Église romaine.* Bibliothèque des Écoles françaises d'Athènes et de Rome, 2nd ser., vi/1. Paris: n.p., 1910. (Vol. 2 includes the *Liber politicus* of Canon Benedict of St. Peter's.)

Fischer, Ludwig. *Bernhardi cardinalis et Lateranensis ecclesiae prioris Ordo officiorum ecclesiae Lateranensis.* Historische Forschungen und Quellen 2–3. Munich-Freising: Datterer, 1916.

Frere, Walter Howard. *The Roman Epistle-Lectionary.* Alcuin Club Collections 32. Oxford: Alcuin Club, 1935.

Grégoire, Réginald. *Homéliaires liturgiques médiévaux: Analyse de manuscrits.* Biblioteca degli "Studi medievali" 12. Spoleto: Centro italiano di studi sull'alto medioevo, 1980.

Hesbert, Jean. *Antiphonale Missarum Sextuplex.* Brussels: Vromant, 1935.

Jounel, Pierre. *Le culte des saints dans les basiliques du Latran et du Vatican au douzième siècle.* Collection de l'École Française de Rome 26. Rome: École Française de Rome, 1977.

Klauser, Theodor. *Das römische Capitulare evangeliorum.* Liturgiegeschichtliche Quellen und Forschungen 28. Münster in Westfalen: Aschendorff, 1935.

Van Dijk, S. J. P. *The Ordinal of the Papal Court from Innocent III to Boniface VIII and Related Documents.* Spicilegium Friburgense 22. Freiburg, Switzerland: Universitätsverlag, 1975.

Vogel, Cyrille and Elze, Reinhard. *Le pontifical romano-germanique du dixième siècle.* 3 vols. Studi e testi 226–27, 269. Vatican City: Biblioteca Apostolica Vaticana, 1963–72.

LAWRENCE GUSHEE

The Tabula Monochordi *of Magister Nicolaus de Luduno*

. . . *for David Hughes,* magistro egregio.

Although David has become known to the world of musical scholarship for his devoted attention to matters concerning plainchant and monophonic song, we also know that he arrived there *a rovescio*, beginning with a dissertation in which he laid "Gothic" polyphonic music to rest . . . or at least so he may have thought. The seeds for the present Gothic paper were planted by David in—could it possibly have been in 1958?—during a year's visitation to New Haven. The mixture of admiration, fascination, pity, and mock bewilderment—but without a trace of condescension—with which he approached such worthies as Aribo of Freising or Petrus dictus Palma ociosa is hard to describe, but was certainly unforgettable, and in the cases of Marion and myself, the beginning of a lifelong interest.

The more general objective of this paper is to stimulate scholarly discussion of an important manuscript source of fourteenth-century music theory rather than to solve all its mysteries. It's not that various parts of the manuscript have lacked for serious attention—*au contraire*—but due to an eighteenth-century dismemberment, it has been difficult to gain equal access to the two sections of the book. Another factor has delayed a synthetic view of the manuscript, namely the relative lack of attention given to cisalpine writing about music until the last twenty-five years or so. This paper is not that synthesis, but prolegomena of a predominantly descriptive character.

The chief topic, however, is but one work of the many found in the reconstituted manuscript: a *Tabula monochordi* ascribed in the source to Nicholas of Luduno. Knowledge of the existence of such a work has been available to scholars at least since the publication of the third volume of Martin Gerbert's *Scriptores*, which included as the lower half of the frontispiece an engraving of part of the *tabula*, with a caption stating that it was taken from a fourteenth-century manuscript of the Sankt Blasien library (plate 1).

Gerbert's preface tells us nothing about the manuscript but does give the reason for including this illustration: as the *minima* as discussed by Johannes de Muris represented a stage in the development of music notation beyond that of Franco of Cologne, so the flagged minims of the *tabula* are a stage beyond Johannes. Why nothing more was done with the work of Nicholas, as well as with the other works from this source, is not difficult to understand. Some of them would have presented a considerable challenge to the engravers or printers, and at least one of the others, a work by Imbertus of France, was rejected as completely derivative from Johannes de Muris.[1]

Although some of the manuscripts used by Gerbert for his *Scriptores* were destroyed in a catastrophic fire at the monastery in 1768, this was not one of them. It is now in the collection of the Stiftsbibliothek of Sankt Paul im Lavantthal, having come to rest there with other books once in the possession of Sankt Blasien. It is immediately evident from the fact that its folios are numbered 17 to 24 at the top of each recto that they were once part of a larger manuscript. Somewhere between volume 1 of the *RISM* catalogue of manuscripts of medieval music theory, published in 1961, in which the Sankt Paul fascicle was not even listed, and volume 2 of 1968, it was recognized that the larger manuscript to which it belonged was a manuscript of the Vatican Library, viz., Barberini 307. It probably was Gilbert Reaney who first publicly testified to the relationship in 1964, although not in time to inform the edition of Philippe de Vitry's (or pseudo-Philippe's) *Ars nova* published in that year.[2] I was able to see and photograph the Sankt Paul

[1] Martin Gerbert, *Scriptores ecclesiastici de musica sacra* (St. Blasien, 1784; repr. 1963), 3, praefatio: "Hunc [i.e., ultimam augmentationem] ad amussim sequitur IMBERTUS de Francia in regulis de mensurabili musica non ultra progrediens, quam iam citato loco de IOANNE de Muris notavi, cuius exscriptor & compendiator fuit IMBERTUS, hic a nobis ideo omissus."

[2] Gilbert Reaney, "The Question of Authorship in the Medieval Treatises on Music," *Musica disciplina* 18 (1964): 16.

Plate 1: Martin Gerbert, *Scriptores ecclesiastici de musica sacra,* vol. 3, frontispiece: facsimile of part of the *Tabula monochordi* of Nocholas of Luduno.

fascicle in the spring of 1965, although I can't recall whether I was aware at the time of the connection between it and the Barberini codex.

The Barberini manuscript has been described a number of times with varying degrees of detail. One important description and inventory is not cited in musicological sources, viz., that of Theodore Silverstein in his provisional catalogue of medieval Latin scientific writings in the Barberini collection, which, however, does not cite the present location and contents of the missing fascicle. In point of fact, all five published descriptions are faulty in varying degrees. While this state of affairs would clearly justify a totally new inventory made from the ground up, it will not be attempted here inasmuch as a research trip to the Vatican library would be absolutely essential in order to avoid yet another incomplete or inaccurate report.[3]

The Sankt Paul manuscript has been catalogued only twice to my knowledge, once in 1890 by Koller, and by Ulrich Michels in Corpus Scriptorum de Musica 17, published in 1972.[4] The first of these was quite preliminary, the

[3] In chronological order, the descriptions are as follows:

1) Raffaele Casimiri, "Teodono de Caprio, non Teodorico de Campo, teorico musicale italiano del sec. XV," *Note d'archivio per la storia musicale* 1911–12 (January–April, 1942): 38–42; continued in 1914–15 (July–October, 1942): 93–100. While eschewing the succinct tabular form of the other inventories, Casimiri includes most of the important information along with some useful interpretation.

2) Theodore Silverstein, *Medieval Latin Scientific Writings in the Barberini Collection: A Provisional Catalogue* (Chicago: University of Chicago Press, 1957), 87ff. Painstaking measurements and effort to distinguish the several scribal hands, not subsequently attempted by later scholars.

3) *Philippi de Vitriaco Ars nova*, ed. Gilbert Reaney et al., Corpus Scriptorum de Musica 8 ([Rome]: American Institute of Musicology, 1964), 10f., with the siglum V.

4) Pieter Fischer, ed., *The Theory of Music from the Carolingian Era up to 1400*, 2: *Italy* (Munich: Henle, 1968) [*RISM* B III^2], with incomplete analysis of the original structure and wrong shelf-mark for the missing fascicle.

5) *Johannis Vetuli de Anagnia Liber de musica*, ed. Frederick Hammond, Corpus Scriptorum de Musica 27 ([Rome]: American Institute of Musicology, 1977), 10ff., with accurate collation and citation of the missing fascicle.

6) Christian Meyer, "Le *De synemmenis* et sa tradition: Contribution à l'étude des mesures du monocorde vers la fin du xiiie siècle," *Revue de musicologie* 76 (1990): 83–91, his siglum V_2, with incorrect dimensions due to a typographical error and no citation of Corpus Scriptorum de Musica 27. This brief reference repeats the dating and provenance of *RISM.*

An important discussion of certain aspects of the manuscript appears in *Anonymus de musica mensurabili*, ed. Cecily Sweeney, Corpus Scriptorum de Musica 13 ([Rome]: American Institute of Musicology, 1971).

[4] Oswald Koller, "Aus dem Archive des Benedictinerstiftes St. Paul im Lavantthal in Kärnten," *Monatshefte für Musikgeschichte* 22/3 (1890): 39–41; Johannes de Muris, *Notitia artis musicae et Compendium musicae practicae*, ed. Ulrich Michels, Corpus Scriptorum de Musica 17 ([Rome]: American Institute of Musicology, 1972), 111–14.

second exceptionally thorough. With some hesitation I've proceeded to stitch together a Frankenstein's monster using Silverstein's and Hammond's catalogues, with the necessary supplement for the Sankt Paul fascicle taken from Ulrich Michels (table 1).

A few remarks on the unique authors of our two manuscripts would not be out of place here, inasmuch as musicological aim has been wobblier than usual for works of this comparatively recent date. First of all, the author of the first work, now known as Johannes Vetulus de Anagnia, i.e., Giovanni Vecchi, used to be Johannes Verulus due to a misreading of the *explicit* in which the family name was clumsily overwritten. This seemingly insignificant change may in fact permit an approximate dating and identification of our music theorist with the notary of the same name cited in a 1372 document from Frosinone, barely fifteen miles to the southeast of Anagnia.[5]

The second unique author of the Barberini manuscript is one Theodonus de Caprio, according to Coussemaker and other early sources "Theodoricus de Campo" but most punctiliously self-described in the manuscript as "Frater Theodonus de Caprio [or perhaps Capro, depending on how an abbreviation is resolved] de Civitate Sancte Agathe, prior Capuanus ordinis sacri monasterii Montis Virginis." Casimiri gets the credit for having cleared up the confusion nearly half a century ago, along with the identification of Sant' Agata de Goti in the province of Benevento, and the Benedictine monastery in Capua which, depending on the abbey of Montevergine, had a prior as chief administrator. Not only that, Casimiri published the notice of his death dated July 4, 1434, from an entry in the necrology of the abbey, along with two other documents from 1432 and 1433. These dates correspond very closely with the two dates found in Theodonus's Barberini *incipits*, namely, July 7, 1431 and March 31, 1432.[6]

[5] Gallo, citing G. Caetani, *Regesta chartarum: Regesto delle pergamene dell'archivio Caetani* (San Casciano Val di Pesa, 1928), 21, cautiously suggests that while such an identification is rather uncertain, "sembra peraltro abbastanza probabile che a tale famiglia, a tale epoca, a tale ambiente egli sia appartenuto." F. Alberto Gallo, *La teoria della notazione in Italia dalla fine del XIII all'inizio del XV secolo*, Antiquae musicae Italicae, subsidia theorica 2 (Bologna: Tamari, 1966). I have not been able to consult Caetani's publication.

[6] Casimiri, "Teodono de Caprio, non Teodorico de Campo." Casimiri suggested as the Italian form of the Latin name a Totone or Todone, similar to a modern Neapolitan pet name of Totonno (which, however, is short for Antonio). The codicological joke here is that the treatise published by Coussemaker under the distorted name (not his fault, but that of the scribe of the eighteenth-century manuscript he employed) of Theodoricus de Campo is in fact anonymous. Theodoricus/Theodonus is responsible only for a relatively brief set of *contrapunctus* rules, and a version of the *Libellus cantus mensurabilis* attributed to Johannes de Muris, both written in an informal hand in some of the unoccupied space at the end of the sixth fascicle.

Table 1

Inventory of the Barberini/Sankt Paul Manuscript compiled from the inventories of Silverstein, Hammond, and Michels

[Theodore Silverstein, *Medieval Latin Scientific Writings in the Barberini Collection: A Provisional Catalogue* (Chicago: University of Chicago Press, 1957), 87]

Rome, Biblioteca Apostolica Vaticana. Barberini lat. 307 (X.125: Pieralisi I, 402–4; n.a. 841 and VII.D.18); 15th c., parchment, 32 fols., written in various hands.

(1)	fols. 1–16^{v}	19.2 x 6.3	cms.	43 ll.
(2)	17–29^{v}	18.9 x 16.3		40
(3)	29^{v}–30	18 x 6.4		34
(4)	30–30^{v}	19–24 x 7.7		30–47
(5)	31–31^{v}	18.3 x 7		41
(6)	31^{v}	21.4 x 8		43

N.B. This is the modern foliation.

[Johannis Vetuli de Anagnia, *Liber de musica*, ed. Frederick Hammond, Corpus Scriptorum de Musica 27 ([Rome]: American Institute of Musicology, 1977), 10.]

V Rome, Biblioteca Apostolica Vaticana, Barberini lat. 307 (*olim* 841), ca. 1400–32; cod. membr., 205 x 270 mm., 33 fols. (originally 62: the original fols. 17–24 are in the Abbey Library of St. Paul in Carinthia (cf. infra); the original fols. 41–61 are lost) (cf. H. M. Bannister, *Monumenti Vaticani di paleografia latina*, Rome, 1913, 196–98). Collation: 1^{8}, 2^{8}, [a^{8}], 3^{6}, 4^{6}, 5^{6} (2 missing), 6^{2} (2 missing)

fols. 1^{r}–16^{v} Iohannis Vetuli de Anagnia liber de musica. "Magistri jo. de Anagnia." *a m rec.* Inc. "Cum igitur de arte musice tractare debeamus . . ." Expl. ". . . aut minima prolatio cum minore. Finito libro sit laus gloria Christo. Dexteram scriptoris salvet eam deus cunctis horis Amen. Explicit liber de musica magistris Johannis Vetuli de Anagnia."
"Amen" and "Magistris . . . Anagnia" *a m rec* (cf. Plate II). (*CS* III, 129–77)

[Johannis de Muris, *Notitia artis musicae* et *Compendium musicae practicae* etc., ed. Ulrich Michels, Corpus Scriptorum de Musica 17 ([Rome]: American Institute of Musicology, 1972), 111–14.]

S_R St. Paul, Archiv des Benediktinerstiftes 135/1, = fragmentum (fols. 17–24) codicis: Rom, Bibl. Vat., Barberini lat. 307, XV° s. (ca. 1400–32), cod. membr., 4°, 27 x 21 cm., olim 62 folia, sed desunt fols. 17–24 (= S_R) et fols. 41–61; codex igitur nunc consistit 33 foliis novis numeris ordinatis. Descriptionem vide: G. Reaney, A. Gilles, J. Maillard, *Philippi de Vitriaco Ars nova*,

CSM 8, Rome 1964, p. 10s. In primo folio huius codicis invenitur index scriptus a manu posteriori (XVIII° s.?): "In hoc volumine continentur Tractatus diversi de musica, quorum Auctores sunt in francia, videlicet:

Johannis Veruli de Anania	fols. 1–16
Imbertus de Francia	fol. 17
Johannis de Muris	fols. 22v–24v
Philippus de Vitry	fols. 25–28v
Isidorus Hispalensis	fols. 35–37
Theodoricus de Campo	fol. 38–38v"

Tempore cuius indicis scriptoris codex continuit etiam fols. 17–24v, quae tempore Abbatis M. Gerberti in Bibliothecam St. Blasii venisse videntur. M. Gerbert utebatur hoc fragmento, quod *codicem alterum San. Blasianum* (*GS* III 190 et 301) nuncupavit, in editione sua (*GS* III 301–08). Folia fragmenti recto in margine superiori novis numeris (fols. 1–8) signata sunt, sed in descriptione sequenti dantur numeri originales Codicis Romanensis, quae medio in margine superiori inveniuntur. Cf.: O. Koller, Aus dem Archiv des Benediktinerstiftes St. Paul im Lavanthal in Kärnten, *MfM* 22, 1890, Nr. 3, pp. 39ss.; G. Reaney, The Question of Authorship in the Medieval Treatises on Music, *MD* 18, 1964, pp. 16s.

fol. 17 Imbertus de Francia, *Regulae de mensurabili musica.* Quae regulae partim conveniunt cum Secundo libro *Notitiae artis musicae* Johannis de Muris (cf. N 2 IX 15, XI 4, IX 16, VI 4, VII 4). Imbertus veresimile Hubertus de Salinis sit, qui in codice Chantilly, Musée Condé 1047, fol. 46 *Ymbert* nominatur (cf. G. Reaney, *MD* 18, 1964, p. 16). Inc. "Notula duo in se includit, scilicet formam et significationem . . ." Expl. ". . . ad perfectionem reducuntur ut hic «exemplum». Expliciunt regule domini Imberti de Francia de mensurabili musica."

fol. 17v Rota compositionis monochordi.

fol. 18 "Turris quem totum comprehendit rerum originem creaturarum."

fols. 18v–19 Compositio notis nigris et rubris (cf. *GS* III folium primum; O. Koller, l.c., p. 40).

fols. 18v–22 Nicolaus de Luduno, Tabula et explicationes monochordi; mediis in foliis 18v–19 legitur: "Explicit tabula monochordi Magistri Nicolai de Luduno. Deo Gratias. Amen."

fol. 21v Marchettus de Padua, *Lucidarium*, tract. IV, cap. I: Inc. "Proportio est quedam habitudo . . ."
Expl. ". . . numeralis in musica" (*GS* III 78a/b).
Quod capitulum alia manu in margine inferiori insertum est.

fol. 22 Item in margine inferiori manu posteriori:
"Ait philosophus: lege et relege, sivis scientiam invenire/

Assiduitas legendi animus aperit a discendi."
"Multi dicunt, illi sciunt, qui componunt musicam. Nam qui facit, quod non sapit, diffinitur bestia.
Igitur qui cantandi desiderat et artem non intelligat plus errorem quam magisterium.
Bestia non cantor, qui non canit arte sed usu.
Non vox cantorem facit, sed artis documentum."
(cf. Guido, *GS* II 25; Lambertus, *CS* I 252; Jacobus Leod., CSM 3, I, 64; etiam in G, fol. 49^{v} b; cf. D. Bartha, Studien zum musikalischen Schrifttum des 15. Jahrhunderts, *AfM* 1, 1936, p. 187, n. 20).

fols. 22^{v} a–24 a Johannes de Muris, *Compendium musicae practicae* (*GS* III 301a–306b, cf. annotationes in calce pertinentes ad hunc codicem). In margine superiori alia manu: "Joannes de Muris."
Inc. "Et est sciendum quod partes prolationis . . ."
Expl. ". . . ut in thoma tibi obsequia."

fol. 24 a Sequitur sine spatio: "longa imperficitur per brevem . . . quod ternarius numerus ipsum habeatur" (*GS* III 306a; initium secundum Johannem de Muris, *Notitia artis musicae*, Secundus liber, cap. VIII, 2: conclusiones 1, 2, 3, 6, 9).

fols. 23^{v} a/b–24 a Philippotus Andreas, Tractatus versificatus de contrapuncto (*CS* III 116–18; etiam in Einsiedeln, Stiftsbibl. 689, fol. 45^{v}; Florenz, Bibl. Laurentiana, Ashburnham 1119, fols. 75^{v}–77^{v}; Mailand, Bibl. Ambros., I 20 Inf., fol. 36–36^{v}; Rom, Bibl. Corsiniana e dell'Accademia dei Lincei 36 D 31, fol. 13; etiam in codice Ch, cf. p. 12), hic sine nomine autoris manu posteriori in margine inferiori insertus est. Exempla desunt. Inc. "Post quintam tertiam semper tenere memento . . ."
Expl. ". . . post quintam sextam habetur."

fols. 24 a–24^{v} a Tractatus anonymi de discantu (*GS* III 306a–07b).
Initium aequat capitulo ultimo *De speciebus compositis* compilationis *Regule contrapunctis ordinate per . . . Theodonum de Caprio* in codice originali Rom, Bibl. Vat., Barb. lat. 307, fols. 38–39 (cf. K.-J. Sachs, Der Contrapunctus im 14. und 15. Jahrhundert, Diss. Freiburg i.Br. 1966, mschr., 194f.).
Inc. "De discantu. Sex sunt species discantus, per quas . . ."
Expl. ". . . per falsam illicitum est discantare. Explicit tractatus de musica Magistri Johannis de Muris de Francia. Amen." Hoc Explicit soli compendii Johannis de Muris est.

fol. 24 b Quaedam annotatio addita alia manu in margine superiori (*GS* III 306 n.a.).
"Supradicte vero sex species . . . simplices consonantias componendo."

fol. 24^{v} b Tractatus de musica mensurabili (fragmentum? *GS* III 307b–08b).
Inc. "Que differentia est inter notem alteratam et imperfectam . . ."
Expl. ". . . et talis opinio michi occurrit salvo dicto magistro."

[Johannis Vetuli de Anagnia, *Liber de musica*, ed. Frederick Hammond, Corpus Scriptorum de Musica 27 ([Rome]: American Institute of Musicology, 1977), 11–12. © by American Institute of Musicology/Hänssler-Verlag. Reproduced by permission.]

fols. 25–28^{v} *Ars nova* Philippi de Vitriaco. Inc. "Musice tria sunt genera mundanum humanum et instrumentalem . . ." Expl. "explicit ars nova magistri philippi de vetri. deo gratias amen. amen. amen:" (ed. G. Reaney, A. Gilles, and J. Maillard, *MD* 10 (1965), 13–33, and CSM 8, 1964)

fols. 29–35 a Tractatus anonimi. Inc. "Omni ars sive doctrina . . ." Expl. ". . . quelibet in numero suo, salvo semper dicto meliori" (*CS* III, 177–93, attributed to "Theodoricus de Campo"; new ed. by C. Sweeney, CSM 13, 1971)

fol. 35 b Fragmentum: "quomodo musica derivatur a moys . . ." Expl. ". . . qui verberat tamen."

fols. 35–37 Isidori *Musica.* Inc. "Incipit capitulum de musica. 1. Musica est peritia modulationis sono . . ." Expl. ". . . id est elevatione et positione" (*GS* I, 20–24)

fol. 37 De Aureliani *Musica Disciplina.* Inc. "De octo tonis. Gregorius presul . . ." Expl. ". . . aut duo aut iij aut v. faciunt neomam. Explicit tractatus de musica beati Ysodori Yspalensis episcopi."

fol. 37–37^{v} De musis. Inc. "Ut superius dictum est per multos . . ." Expl. "Nablum hebraice, grece psalterium, latine organum dicitur."

fols. 37^{v}–38 "Ars et modus pulsandi organa . . ." Expl. "semitonium quod est inter .G. et .a." (ed. R. Casimiri, *Note d'Archivio* 19, 1942, 100–1)

fols. 38–39^{v} *Regulae contrapuncti* fratris Theodoni de Capua. Inc. "Incipiunt regule contrapuncti ordinate per venerabilem virum fratrem Theodonum de caprio de civitate sancte Agathe priorem Capuanum ordinis sacri monasterii montis virginis. In anno domini 1431 . . ." Expl. ". . . sol mars. Jovis Saturnus. Terra spera celestis." (ed. Casimiri, *Note d'Archivio* 19, 38–42, 93–98)

fol. 39^{v} *Libellus cantus mensurabilis* Johannis de Muris. Inc. "Sancti spiritus assit nobis gratia. Incipit ars magistri Johannis de muris de francia scripta per venerabilem virum et religiosum fratrem Theodonum de sancta Agatha priorem Capuanum ordinis sancti monasterii montis virginis. sub anno domini 1432. ultimo mensis marcii . . ." Expl. "Imperfecta sive mi [nor quando semibrevis valet duas minimas]" (*a m rec*) (*CS* III, 46–47)

fol. 40–40^{v} *vacat*

fol. 62^{r} Rota paschalis et dominicalis: "Habito preterito paschate, inde enumerare incipe versus."

While the actual contribution of Theodonus is of little interest compared to the work formerly attributed to him (reedited in Corpus Scriptorum de Musica 13), it does provide us with a reasonably secure date before which the rest of the manuscript was copied. It's also of importance that these two authors who bracket the other contents are both apparently from the same region of the Italian peninsula.

This brings us to dating and provenance on grounds other than biography. The manuscript is handsomely illuminated, including artfully colored and finely rendered musical diagrams. The first opinion known to me comes from the authors of a standard work on illuminated manuscripts in Austrian libraries, who suggested that the style was Italian, probably Bolognese.[7] Other opinions reported by Frederick Hammond—for example, from Millard Meiss—suggest an "Umbrian or Neapolitan" origin, which, combined with the earlier notion, begins to embrace most of the Italian peninsula. This is a rather more crucial matter than the date of copying, it seems to me, although the date at which the components of the contents of the missing fascicle were copied is certainly not without interest. So far as the former is concerned, I see no objection to settling for 1400 plus or minus thirty years. This span is rather wider than one would like, but it's not immediately obvious how it can be improved upon.

These topics will, however, be approached again, once the contents of the detached Sankt Paul fascicle, and in particular the work of Nicholas of Luduno, have been examined. As a preamble to that more extended investigation, however, it is of no little interest to look into the circumstances which resulted in the removal of the Sankt Paul fascicle. By a stroke of good fortune, it is in fact possible to say rather more about this than usual.

To believe *RISM* and Hammond's edition—which evidently rely on Gilbert Reaney in his much-cited and ground-breaking 1964 article on questions of attribution—the entire manuscript was once in the possession of Sankt Blasien.[8] This misinterprets Reaney's words, however, and almost certainly is the reverse of what happened.

Among the thousands of letters addressed to Padre Martini, there are some half dozen written in 1759 by his faithful Roman correspondent Girolamo Chiti, choir master of San Giovanni Laterano, that deal with the

[7] The opinion is that of Robert Eisler, *Beschreibendes Verzeichnis der illuminierten Handschriften in Oesterreich* 3:123, as reported by Trende in *Carinthia* 1 (1952): 662.

[8] Hammond, Corpus Scriptorum de Musica 27, 14: "In the earlier part of the eighteenth century the manuscript had belonged to Gerbert's monastery of St. Blasien, and the original folios 17–24 . . . were removed . . . ." *RISM* B III², 102: "Originally this codex, which belonged to the monastery of Sankt Blasien in the eighteenth century . . ." (describing Barberini 307).

problems of copying codex 841 of the Biblioteca Barberini. The first letter of the series, dated March 8, 1756, makes it virtually certain that this codex is identical with today's Barberini 307. Chiti refers to the uncertainty of Abbate Ballerini, the custodian of the library, regarding how much has already been copied, and whether Martini took a partial copy back to Bologna or left it in Rome for further copying:

> Il Signore Ballerini stà in dubbio se Lei il già copiato se lo portasse a Bologna, o per proseguire la serie come desiderava lo lasciasse nelle mani del Padre Maestro S. Giorgi, o vero essendo selo portato seco, ci dica, fino a qual segno fù copiato, ove si sono osservate tutte le figure gerogifliche d'Alberi, Torri, Circoli, Rote, etc. per le quali vogliono miniature, e colori diversi et intelligenza di caratteri . . .[9]

The present Barberini manuscript does, of course, contain trees illustrating the treatise of Johannes Vetulus, but no circles, towers, or wheels. Since both a circle and a tower are prominent features of the Sankt Paul fascicle, it seems clear that the two manuscripts were still united in 1756.

The copying of the graphic elements of the manuscript presented extraordinary difficulties. The copyist who had been working on it—presumably Father San Giorgi—had lost heart seeing how much time and effort would be involved and didn't want to continue, given the limited hours during which the Barberini library was open, and the fact that he understood little regarding either music or miniatures. Besides, he had died.

> . . . per la qual cosa dificile, e longa quell' Ecellentissimo Riverenze, vedendo che portava gran tempo, e lavoro, si perdette di animo, e non volle proseguirne l'opera, non solo perche la Libreria sta aperta due sole volte la settimana, ma perche ancora poco intelligente di musica, e miniature, non gli bastò l'animo, e ben che fosse pratico, e forse capace, in oggi l'è passato a miglior vita.[10]

Without conducting a more thorough investigation of Martini's manuscripts and correspondence, one can't be certain of exactly what happened, but the following scenario is at least plausible. Martini, fascinated by the Barberini codex during his visit to that library probably in 1747,[11] put it

[9] The letters are nos. 1631, 1632, 1633, and 1636 of Schnoebelen's index (Anne Schnoebelen, *Padre Martini's Collection of Letters in the Civico Museo Bibliografico in Bologna: An Annotated Index* [New York: Pendragon, 1979]), written between March 8 and August 7, 1756. Signora Bonavera of the Civico Museo Bibliografico Musicale of Bologna most graciously provided photocopies of the relevant documents, and assistance in translating Chiti's rambling prose was kindly extended by John Hill and Laura Callegari Hill.

[10] From the same letter as the previous extract.

[11] Schnoebelen lists a letter of introduction for Martini from Girolamo Chiti to Abbate Ballerini, the librarian of the Barberini Collection. Although it is apparently undated, it almost certainly is contemporaneous with Martini's visit to Rome in 1747.

high on his list of desiderata and commissioned a partial copy of the musical sections. Nearly a decade later Chiti, wearying of the problem of finding an artist capable of rendering the drawings, prevailed on the Barberini librarian to take the manuscript apart and send the really difficult fascicle to Martini in Bologna—the trees illustrating Vetulus's theories were not so difficult to copy. Martin Gerbert, who visited Martini in Bologna in 1762, saw the fascicle and Martini honored his German colleague's interest by loaning it to him, either then or later.

Since Gerbert's letters to Martini contain no mention of the fascicle, its contents, or its authors—relying once again on the published summaries of Martini's correspondence—it seems more likely that Gerbert took it back with him to Sankt Blasien, where, fortunately, it survived the 1768 fire. There a rather carefully rendered[12] engraving was made of a peculiar 24-line staff with all sorts of mensural notation strewn about it. This then served as part of the frontispiece to the third volume of the *Scriptores* (plate1).

This imagined account helps to explain another codicological twist that I've so far concealed from you, and which is absent from the majority of published descriptions, namely, that the Barberini manuscript had originally 62 folios, to judge by the original foliation, so that fols. 41–61 have also gone astray. This could easily have occurred when the book was taken apart to remove the fascicle now in Austria, at which time a decision may have been made to put fols. 41–61—perhaps because they did not deal with music—with others of a similar character. There are at least two Barberini volumes comprised of miscellaneous fascicles with scientific content that may preserve these other wandering folios.

It also helps explain why the eighteenth-century listing of authors now prefacing the Barberini manuscript does not include Nicholas of Luduno, but Martini's inventory affixed to his copy still preserved in Bologna does. The importance of all this, quite apart from the inherent interest of any puzzle, is that a southern Italian provenance is considerably more probable for the entire manuscript if it was first in the Barberini collection than if it had been in the Sankt Blasien library. The possibly surviving fols. 41–61 might offer additional clues regarding authorship, provenance, and date.

The eight folios of the Sankt Paul fascicle comprise five principal components, not counting various marginal additions more than adequately listed

[12] Careful up to a point, that is. Substantial parts of the notation were omitted, as also the distinction between red and black notation. Koller included with his article "Aus dem Archive" a quite accurate plate, without, however, distinguishing the colors.

by Michels. Unless bracketed, the titles are as given in the manuscript; the foliation is that of the complete manuscript.

1)	fol. 17	*Regule Domini Imberti de Francia de mensurabili musica*
2)	fol. 17v	*Rota compositionis monocordi*
3)	fol. 18	*Turris quem totum comprehendit rerum originem creaturarum*
4)	fol. 18v	*Tabula monochordi Magistri Nicolai de Luduno*
5a)	fol. 22v	[*Compendium musicae practicae Johannis de Muris*]
5b)	fol. 24	[*Tractatus anonymi de discantu*]
5c)	fol. 24v	[*Fragmentum de notis alteratis et imperfectis*]

The elaborate initial of the next fascicle—of the Barberini manuscript, originally fol. 25—signals the beginning of the principal manuscript source of de Vitry's so-called *Ars nova* along with the important post-Vitriacan Anonymous once called Theodoricus but now Theodonus, and a number of supplementary comments.[13] In none of these do we find any mention of Jehan des Murs, something which would have been perfectly appropriate in a number of instances. The first of the supplements—by a writer one might be inclined to dub the Master of the Semiminimissima—makes important mention of differences between Italian and French practice as well as of Marchetto da Padova; the second, of Johannes Vetulus. The overall impression is of a relative conservatism which strikes one as a significant point of difference from the contents of the Sankt Paul fascicle to which we now return.

The first author, Imbert of France, presumably would not have been called that in his native country. Be that as it may, his rules are unadventurous adaptations of the early doctrine of Jehan des Murs and need not detain us in this context except as an indication of a *terminus a quo*. Michels's (and Reaney's)[14] notion that the author is identical with Hubertus de Salinis, because the latter is designated "Ymbert" in the Chantilly manuscript, seems uncoercive.[15]

[13] For my part, I am convinced by the arguments of Sarah Fuller, "A Phantom Treatise of the Fourteenth Century? The *Ars Nova*," *Journal of Musicology* 4 (1985–86): 23–50, to the effect that there was no such treatise and that, in particular, the text found in Barberini 307 should not be ascribed to the famous musician.

[14] Reaney, "The Question of Authorship," 16.

[15] There is a possibility that there exists or existed in the last century another manuscript with a work or works by Imbert. At least, so reports Fétis in his *Biographie universelle*, according to which J. L. F. Danjou had, on the occasion of his library tour of Italy in 1847, found a thirteenth-century treatise on music by Imbert de France at the Biblioteca Malatestiana in Cesena. No mention is made of this author in the article contributed by Danjou to his *Revue de musique réligieuse, populaire et classique*, which does mention two manuscripts from the Malatestiana; perhaps Danjou communicated the information to Fétis in personal correspondence. Be that as it may, no manuscript in this library with a work on music by this author is mentioned in more recent scholarship, so it must remain for the moment a tantalizing ghost.

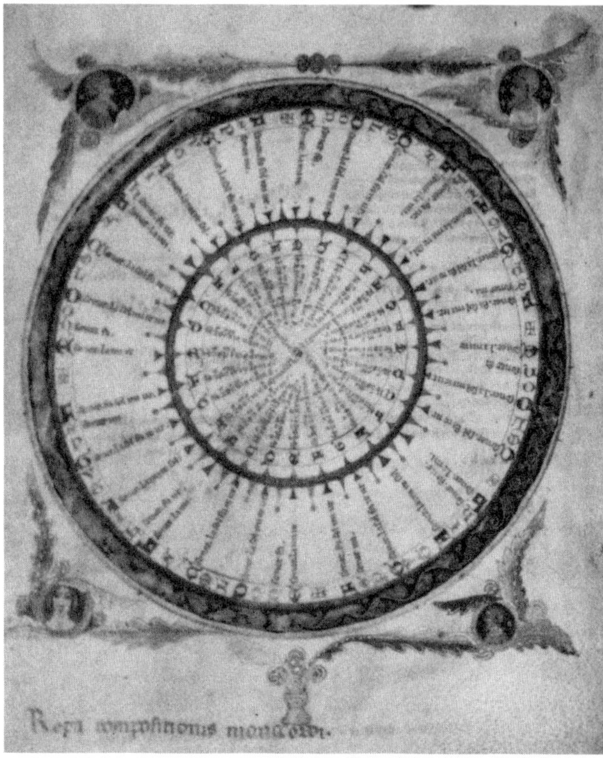

Plate 2: St. Paul, Archiv des Benediktinerstiftes 135/1, fol. 17^{v}: *Rota compositionis monocordi.* Reproduced by permission.

Table 2

Text of the Rota compositionis monocordi

Outer rim	Spokes	Inner circle	Spokes	Hub
A	sonet la mi re sol	A	h̄t iͦs uͫ cͦ m u aͩ aspiratū ī	h
I				
♭	sonet fa ut			
♮	sonet la mi	H	h̄t iͦs uͫ cͦ m ı aͩ r m	c
S				
C	sonet sol fa re ut	C	h̄t iͦs uͫ cͦ m l aͩ r m	b
M				
L				
D	sonet la sol mi re ut	D	h̄t iͦs cͦ uͫ m m aͩ m	n
O				
N	sonet fa			
E	sonet la mi re	E	h̄t iͦs uͫ cͦ m o aͩ r m	f
⊞				
F	sonet fa sol mi ut	F	h̄t iͦs uͫ cͦ m p aͩ r m	e
S	sonet mi			
P				
G	sonet la sol fa re ut	G	h̄t iͦs cͦ uͫ m t aͩ m	s
U				
T				
A	sonet la mi re sol	[and so on for three more cycles]		

The next item is the "Rota compositionis monocordi" (plate 2).

The photograph is barely legible, but in any event a transcription of the text in tabular form is required as a basis for discussion (table 2).

Around the outer rim we find the standard diatonic A–G series with both the round and square forms of B. Each whole step brackets two intermediate letters, with a cross separating the pitches of the minor semitone E–F.[16] These additional letters appear to be assigned pairwise in a more or less regular way, beginning with the A to B natural whole step. The quasi-letters J and K are omitted, as also R and Q. S has to do double duty between B natural and C, as well as between F and G. Going inwards

[16] This symbol simply indicates that there is no intermediate pitch between the minor semitone E to F. By the same token, there should be a *crux* or some similar sign between B and C as there is no intermediate pitch, C flat being lower than B and B sharp higher than C. The

towards the hub, the first set of "spokes" gives the hexachordal names of the steps of the gamut, with two hexachords based on B flat and D added to the standard ones on C, F, and G. Thus, the pitches G and D are each members of all five hexachords, whereas the chromatic pitches E flat and F sharp—to use modern terminology—necessary for B flat and D hexachords are members only of their own hexachords.

The arrangement is not without additional anomalies. If the extraordinary letters are intended to represent the two possible semitones between two pitches a whole step apart, they appear in the wrong order, if the spatial arrangement of the wheel is meant to correspond to that of the monochord. That is, the "fa" between D and E should be positioned closer to D than it is to E, and the "mi" between F and G closer to G. Furthermore, F is designated "fa sol mi ut," but the only way for it to be "mi" is to assume an improbable hexachord beginning on D flat.

We must wonder about the purpose of going to the trouble to construct such a diagram in the form of a wheel. What does it clarify, what relationships does it illustrate? Medieval manuscripts are full of circles, to be sure, given the ease of manipulating a compass, but I don't want to assume that the four-fold cycle has only a decorative function.

The innermost circle of spokes contains a highly abbreviated text which, assuming that my resolution of the abbreviations is correct, has a separate terminological interest. I assume here that the *c* with an *o* over it is to be read as "comes," "comitem," or "comites" according to need, i.e., companion; and that *r* is to be expanded as "rectum."[17] The *compendia* for "duos," "unum," "aliud," and "habet" seem relatively unproblematic and have not been indicated below by italics. Words in brackets have been supplied by me. Accordingly, the text reads as follows:

A habet duos [comites], unum co*mitem* in *u*, aliud aspiratum in *h*.
H habet duos [comites], unum co*mitem* in *i*, aliud r*ectum* in *c*.
C habet duos [comites], unum co*mitem* in *l*, aliud r*ectum* in ♮.
D habet duos comites, unum in *m*, aliud in *n*.[18]
E habet duos [comites], unum co*mitem* in *o*, aliud r*ectum* in *f*.

letter S which intervenes between B and C has no business being there, and is in fact found in its logical place between F and G.

[17] It's true that there is an apparent disagreement of gender between the masculine *comes* and the neuter *aliud*. Such disagreement would exist no matter how we expanded the abbreviation, since *duos* should also be masculine. Neuter alternatives to *comes* are (at least): *conjunctum, confinium, complementum*. One can always invoke—albeit reluctantly, as a last resort—shaky or inconsistent grammar to explain the situation.

[18] In two of the cycles, the order of *m* and *n* is reversed.

F habet duos [comites], unum co*mitem* in *p*, aliud r*ectum* in *e*.
G habet duos comites, unum in *s*, aliud in *t*.[19]

Consequently, with each of the letters of the A to G scale are associated two "conjoined notes" or "companions," one of them higher, the other lower; the letters correspond to those of the outermost rim of the wheel. Thus, the lower companion of E is given as O, which is correctly positioned with respect to D, rather than as N, despite the fact that N is labelled *fa*.

The procedure generally is that the companion pitches are a major semitone lower or higher, except where there is a scale step of the traditional diatonic gamut in the vicinity—i.e., only a comma away. In that case the normal ("rectum") diatonic pitch is substituted. Thus, the higher companion for E is F, the lower companion for C is B, rather than the difficult E sharp (which would be a double *mi*, as it were), or C flat (a double *fa*).

All well and good, but the lower companion to B should, by the same reasoning, be B flat or B *fa*, already represented in the natural series, but instead is stated to be I. Final sticking point: the nomenclature for raising A is anomalous, i.e., "aspiratum in ♮" where one might expect it to be "rectum in ♮" as was the case for C, B flat, F, and E.

The decorative and conceptual *tour de force* of the fascicle—and indeed the entire manuscript reassembled—is the "Tower which comprises the entire origin of things and created beings"[20] (plate 3). Although the caption might strike the modern reader as something of an overstatement, this architectural fantasy nevertheless manages to festoon a relatively ordinary graphic display of the note forms of the four levels of developed mensural notation with a number of quite fundamental dichotomies—no less powerful for being predictable.

perfectum — imperfectum
mulier — masculus
forma — materia
agens — patiens
rectum — obliquum
[ignis — terra][21]

[19] The order of the letters is reversed in two of the A–G series, but not the same two as the letters *m* and *n* mentioned in the preceding footnote. These variations in order are not reflected in the order of the letters around the "rim," which is the same in all four repetitions of the series.

[20] Arriving at this translation requires reading "quae" for "quam" and the addition of a missing "et" or "atque."

[21] The intermediate elements of water and air are placed—as they should be—between earth and fire.

Plate 3: St. Paul, Archiv des Benediktinerstiftes 135/1, fol. 18: *Turris quem totum comprehendit rerum originem creaturarum.* Reproduced by permission.

Table 3

Turris quem totum comprehendit rerum originem creaturarum

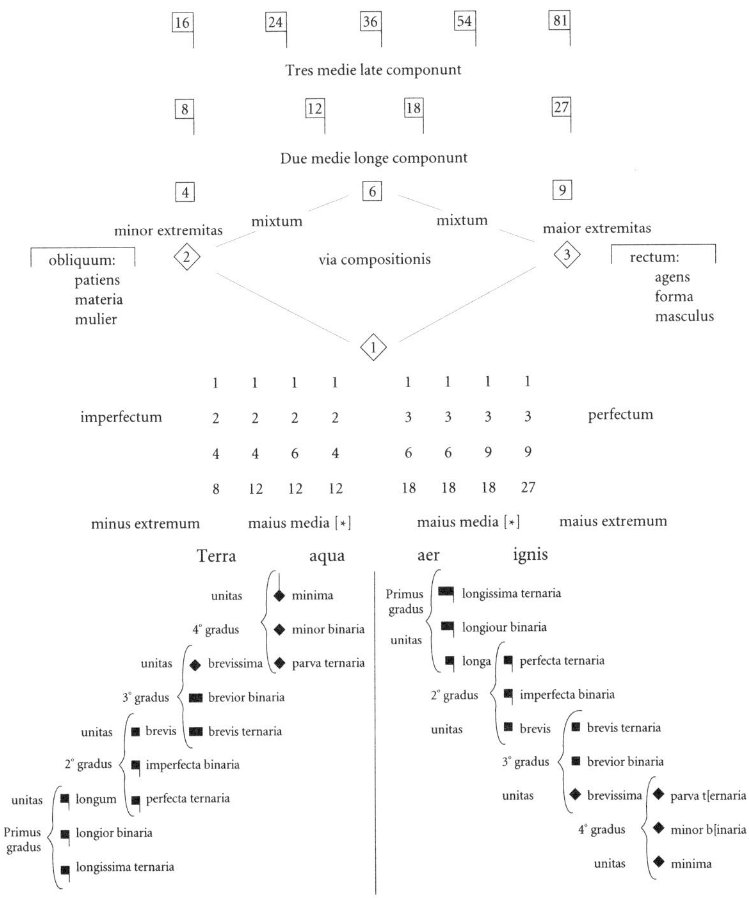

[*] This barely legible abbreviated word may be "proportionale"

Once again, a transcription of the text apart from the graphic design is probably desirable to facilitate legibility and understanding (table 3).

From the point of view of mensural notational theory, the avoidance of the term "semibrevis perfecta" or "semibrevis imperfecta" in favor of "parva" or "minor" is not uninteresting, as well as the graphic link between levels (e.g., the ternary *brevis* of the third degree equated with the unitary *brevis* of the second). Hope for some congruence of terminology between the tower and the theories of the highly original Johannes Vetulus is not realized, however, although Vetulus's association of the right hand with perfection and length, the left with imperfection and brevity is cut from the same philosophical cloth as the dichotomies listed above.[22]

The nomenclature of the *semibrevis* does correspond with that of Jacques de Liège/Mons/Audenaarde,[23] who comments in the seventh book of the *Speculum* on the mensural theory of an unnamed "doctor modernus." In so doing, Jacques refers to the *semibrevis* in the following terms: "Semibrevis tam parva quam minor seu perfecta et imperfecta," and later "Quartus [gradus] sic: semibrevis major, minor et minima, vel parva, minor, minima." The "doctor modernus" is, to be sure, Jehan des Murs, who uses this nomenclature in his so-called *Musica practica* (or, *pace* Michels, the second book of the *Notitia artis musicae*).[24]

The mensural terminology would be particularly appropriate for the second quarter of the fourteenth century, before semiminims, not to speak of other subdivisions of the *minima*, became an issue. To be sure, the long after-life of the doctrine of Jehan des Murs, particularly in Italy (to judge by the extant manuscripts), warns us not to take 1350 as any kind of limit. So far as the *conjunctae*—the extra chromatic pitches implying or requiring hexachords beyond the Guidonian three—are concerned, an E flat *fa* and an F sharp *mi* are hardly "modern," given their frequency in actual composition in the thirteenth century. On the other hand, matters had so far advanced by 1375 that the author of the so-called Berkeley theory manuscript, edited by Oliver Ellsworth,[25] proposes transposed hexachords on F, A, B flat, D, and E flat, sufficient to account for a semitone between each whole step,

[22] Corpus Scriptorum de Musica 27:64. One of the lengthier disquisitions on the association of the right-handedness with perfection and left-handedness with imperfection is, to be sure, in Marchetto's *Pomerium*. See Gerbert, *Scriptores*, 3:129f., and Corpus Scriptorum de Musica 7. One suspects that there may be a quite specific source for this particular association of traits.

[23] May the reader forgive this graceless mode of citing Jacobus's name, necessitated by recent well-founded doubts regarding his identity and place of origin (or family name).

[24] Corpus Scriptorum de Musica 17:78f. This is *not* the nomenclature of pseudo-Philippe de Vitry.

[25] Oliver Ellsworth, *The Berkeley Manuscript: University of California Music Library, MS. 744 (olim Phillipps 4450)* (Lincoln: University of Nebraska Press, 1984), 53–67.

although not a fully chromatic Pythagorean gamut. And we might well remember that the notorious "Fumeux fume" of Solage—from around the time of the Berkeley theory manuscript, so it is said—uses an even larger repertory of non-diatonic pitches.[26]

I'm not sure how much we should expect to erect a chronology of the adoption either in theory or in practice of *conjunctae* or added hexachords. The crucial step was not a matter of comfortable evolution, it seems to me, but a decision to go against or to adapt long established practice and powerful authority. Once that decision was taken, then a great variety of new gamuts and hexachords could be constructed. But making that decision would not result in the dismantling of tradition, not least because plain chant remained as a body of music not requiring these new-fangled constructions. Rather frequently, then, authors both accept and reject non-diatonic pitches; symptomatic of the situation is the varying nomenclature: *musica falsa, musica ficta, conjunctae,* and so forth.

Finally we turn to the *raison d'être* of this paper: the *Tabula monochordi* of Master Nicholas of Luduno.[27] (plate 4) His identification, alas, is no easier than that of Imbertus. The first difficulty is presented by the toponym, which some transcribers have assumed must be either "Lauduno" or "Lugduno."[28] If the latter, we might opt for Lyon; if the former, "Loudun" between Poitiers and Angers, or "Laudun" in the present-day department of Gard, not far from Orange.[29] Diligent search in sources of Italian place

[26] *Polyphonic Music of the Fourteenth Century* 19, ed. Gordon K. Greene (Monaco: Editions de l'Oiseau-Lyre, 1982), 185ff.

[27] Certainly an obscure figure of medieval music theory, Nicholas has nonetheless attracted attention from Joseph Levitan in his article "Adrian Willaert's Famous Duo *Quidnam ebrietas,*" *Tijdschrift van de Vereniging voor Nederlandse Muziekgeschiedenis* 15 (1939): 227–28, and in Karol Berger, "The Expanding Universe of *musica ficta* in Theory from 1300 to 1500," *Journal of Musicology* 4 (1985–86): 417–18 (taken over word for word in Berger's *Musica ficta* [Cambridge: Cambridge University Press, 1987], 33). Neither Berger nor Levitan comment on the notation or the enigmatic text purportedly explaining it, or the *tabula* of numbers. It seems likely that they were using Gerbert's frontispiece, rather than photographs of the manuscript.

[28] For Lugdunum see Hammond, Corpus Scriptorum de Musica 27:11; Koller, "Aus dem Archive," 40, and drawing upon him, Robert Eitner, *Bibliographie der Musik-Sammelwerke des XVI. und XVII. Jahrhunderts* (Berlin: Liepmanssohn, 1877). For Laudunum see the listing of authors in Codex Barberinus MS. 841 offered by Giovanni Battista Martini, *Storia della musica* (Bologna: Leliodalla Volpe, 1757–81), 1:447ff., where we read "contin. Tract. de Musica Joan. Veruli de Anania . . . M. Nicolai de Lauduno."

[29] Cottineau, *Dictionnaire,* lists at Laudun a priory of the Celestins of Avignon and for Loudon a Benedictine priory. Of course, de Ludunum may simply be intended as a commune, not a monastic or other ecclesiastical establishment. The quite well-known northern French city of Laon seems to be ruled out, as its name as a rule takes the form (Civitas) Laudunensis (see also next n.).

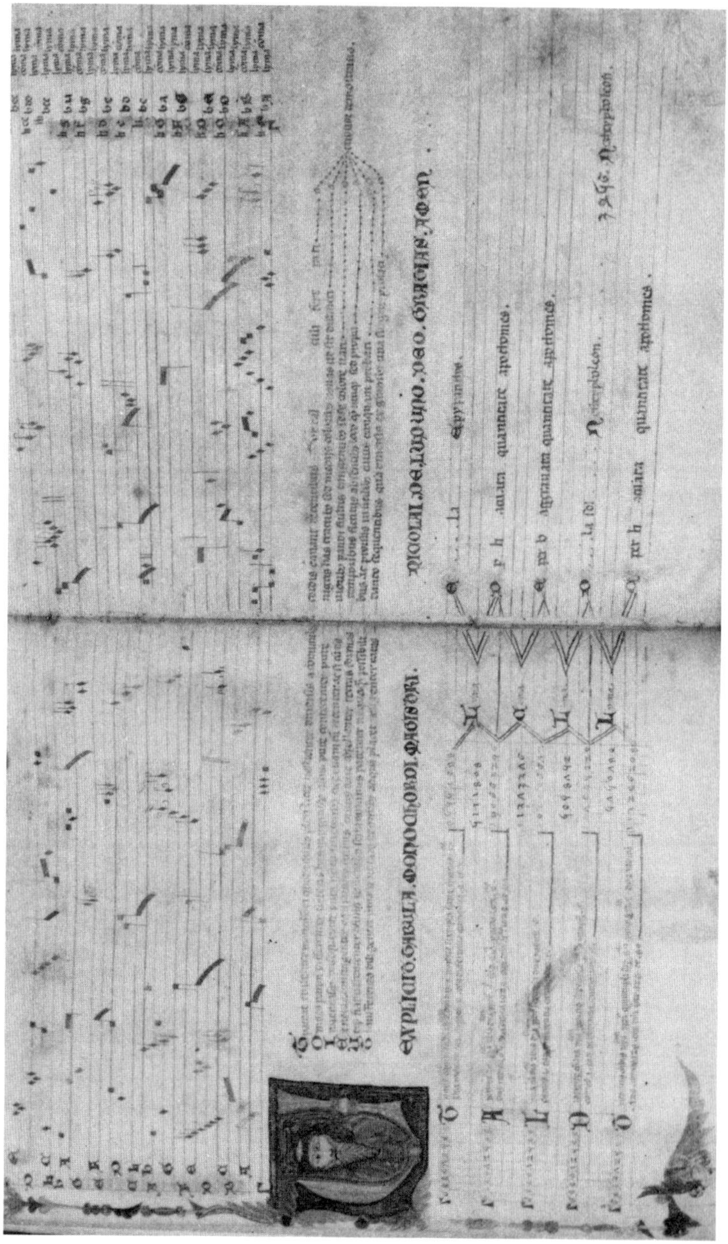

Plate 4: St. Paul, Archiv der Benediktinerstiftes 135.1, fols. 18v–19, containing the *Tabula monochordi* of Nicholas of Luduno. Reproduced by permission.

names has not turned up any likely candidates. I'm assuming for the time being a French origin for our author.[30]

The second difficulty is that there are no known—known to me, that is—literary or scientific works by a Master Nicholas of Ludunum, Laudunum or Lugdunum. Neither does he appear in the indices of fourteenth-century papal registers, normally a fertile prosopographical source. For the moment then, his identity, other than as the author of a "Tabula monochordi," is unknown.

But indeed, what is the *tabula?* The *explicit*—"Explicit tabula monochordi Magistri Nicolai de Luduno, Deo gratias. Amen"—appears between the fanciful 24-line staff and the table of numbers, leaving the latter without any indication of authorship, although the two clearly belong together. This has led at least one transcriber (Koller) to read "Explicatio" rather than "Explicit" even though the word is not abbreviated, and even though this would play hob with the grammar, requiring a further emendation of "tabula" to "tabulae." I can't think of a way to resolve this question, but am assuming that Nicholas is the author of both the "tabula" in the sense of "picture," i.e., the 24-line staff, and the "tabula" in the sense of an "array" or "list" of numbers.[31]

It's too much to hope that even if we don't know who Nicholas was or when he flourished, we have his very cross-eyed likeness—the eyes, possibly modified by a mischievous reader, were charitably rendered normally by the engraver of Gerbert's frontispiece—in the tonsured person surrounded by the capital U of the text of the quasi-*explicit.* Several commentators have been of the reasonable opinion that, given the grossness of the copying errors found in the Barberini manuscript generally, we appear to be some steps removed from the authors represented therein—something supported by the errors in the numerical table—so I'm inclined to see the portrait as that of a generic wise man, not of Nicholas himself.

[30] Johann Georg Theodor Graesse, *Orbis latinus,* 1971 one-volume edition (Braunschweig: Klinkhardt & Biermann, 1971), lists Laodunum, Lodunum, Laudunum, Laudunensis urbs, and Lugdunum clavatum as Latin forms of modern French Laon. That "Luduno" may be an alternative for "Lauduno" is suggested by Angevin archival sources of the end of the thirteenth century; Paul Durrieu, *Les archives angevines de Naples: Étude sur les registres du roi Charles 1er (1265–85),* vol. 2, Bibliothèque des Écoles françaises d'Athènes et de Rome, fasc. 51, II (Paris: Thorin, 1887) lists the following: "LUDUNO, (Alexiardus de) v. Lodun . . . LODON ou de LODUN (Elisiart ou Helisier de) ou, dans les textes latins, Eliseus ou Alexiardus de Lauduno ou de Luduno, chevalier de l'Hotel, vice-justicier de la terre d'Otrante en 1277."

[31] To quote the *Oxford Universal Dictionary*: "An arrangement of numbers, words, or items of any kind, in a definite and compact form, so as to exhibit some set of facts, or relations in a distinct and comprehensive way, for convenience of study, reference, or calculation." "Table," *Oxford Universal Dictionary,* 3rd ed. (Oxford: Clarendon, 1955), 2118.

Now to the six lines of text between the *tabula* of musical notes and that of numbers. These are in fact six stanzas of a poem with the label "Cribrorum demonstratio" connected to each of the stanzas.[32] A "cribrum" is a "sieve," in the Middle Ages as in Classical Latin, so I assume that these stanzas are instructions for filtering out some of the notational signs in order to produce something that makes sense, not necessarily, but possibly a musical composition in the conventional sense. It's also conceivable that the 24-line staff is designated a "cribrum," although that seems to me less likely.[33] I offer my transcription of the text with some trepidation, inasmuch as a few important words are doubtful—and even so the detailed meaning is far from clear.

[CRIBRORUM DEMONSTRATIO]*

1. Ut pateat evidenter
Monochordi (quot) et quibus
Pleri—licet nescienter—
Diversis a communibus
Cordis canant decentibus,
Ut calculi fert ratio.

2. Omnes pandi differenter
Veteres has marginibus
Albis pure condecenter
Pure nigris has tractibus
Sed mediis coloribus,
Novas ut sit distinctio.

3. Inventasque consequenter
Puta non cum veteribus
Nec etiam tam recenter
Ac si cum novioribus
Pandi fustris tangentibus
Sese colore vario.

4. Ex notarum contingenter
Equivocarum <..>ibus
Cautis dare compellenter

**This phrase is attached to each stanza in the manner of a refrain*

[32] I actually read here "cribriorum," assuming that the curlicue at the end of the word is a sign for "-orum." "Cribrorum" seems to be the only reasonable emendation.

[33] The only musical writing known to be with this word in the title is the *Cribrum musicum ad triticum Siferticum* of Marco Scacchi (Venice, 1642). The word is otherwise known in ancient mathematics, in which the "cribrum Eratosthenes" is an algorithm for finding prime numbers. See Boethius, *De institutione arithmetica libri duo*, I.17, ed. Gottfried Friedlein (Frankfurt am Main: Minerva, 1966), 33, no doubt after Nicomachus.

Tetras formas temporibus,
Fictitiis absentibus
Ad quancunque, sed proprio.

5. Utque fiat vehementer
Confusio faventibus
Semiminimis patenter
Nequaquam possibilibus
Ac prorsus inutilibus,
Cuius tanquam probatio.

6. Transferendo diligenter
Primam notam ex omnibus
Ad quam placet eligenter
Ratas dando sequentibus
Quam diversis ex gradibus,
Una surgat prolatio.

One might hope that an adequate translation would enable a reasonable decipherment of the notation; but I'm not entirely sure this hope can be realized. The first stanza seems clear enough if one supplies a few words, although perhaps we shouldn't take the verb "canant" too literally: "In order to demonstrate the monochord, some people may sing pitches different from the usual ones, although ignorantly." Indubitably, the many sharped and flatted pitches indicated along the right-hand edge of the staff are surely different from the usual ones.

In the second stanza, the author claims to have distributed both the old and the new pitches so that a distinction is made between them. At first, I believed that the white borders or margins ("albis marginibus") and black lines ("nigris tractibus") simply referred to the fact that the pitch names of the degrees of the standard gamut, seen on the left hand side of the diagram, are alternately on lines and spaces, with those on lines written in red, those on spaces in black. This is in distinct contrast to the odd sharps and flats on the right hand side, which are not arranged in any such obvious order.

Interpretation of the third stanza is hampered by a word found in no lexica consulted by me, viz., "fustris." "Frustris" would make some kind of sense, meaning "little bits or pieces." Also possible would be "fustis," in the sense of note stems, derived from the root meaning of tree trunk or column. Worse yet, the syntax of the entire stanza is anything but clear. In plain language one might read "Pandi inventas [chordas]" ("I have laid out [or distributed] the discovered pitches"), apparently contrasting them with both old and newer pitches. "Fustis tangentibus" could then mean "with deceiving stems" and, what is more, "sese colore vario," "in differing color."

This interpretation is suggested by the language of the fifth stanza, which unequivocally proclaims the author's intention to confuse, citing particularly the semiminims. But the fourth stanza as well tells us that misleading or meaningless pitches of another sort have been included. The meaning there may be something to the effect that without "fictitious" pitches, four forms of definite *tempora* can be seen.

Of all the stanzas, the sixth appears to be least equivocal. I construe it as follows: "By transferring carefully the first symbol of all to whatever [note] it may please you to choose, and by giving definite [values/pitches] to those following, one prolation will emerge from these most diverse levels [of mensuration]."

Needless to say, I've made various attempts at deciphering this puzzle. The first thing one is inclined to try, inspired by the expression "fictitiis absentibus" of the fourth stanza, is to omit all of the chromatic steps, with the exception of *b fa* and *b mi*. Nothing even remotely convincing emerges from this filtration, nor from the next most obvious procedure, i.e., omitting all of the useless and impossible semiminims which we are told, so it seems, have been included to confuse the "faventibus." At the other end of the temporal spectrum, although the grouping of the rests would appear to indicate, for example, *maximodus perfectus* and *maximodus imperfectus*, one doesn't find note groupings that correspond to those mensurations. Anyway, would these really correspond to the "tetras formas temporibus" of stanza four?

One might well be tempted to take a "stupider" approach to the puzzle, simply by examining the distribution of time values to each of the indicated pitches. The disconcerting result is that the temporal density of the upper octave is rather lower than that of the lowest; and that many important diatonic pitches have virtually no time values allocated to them. This is perhaps just a more detailed and roundabout way of restating Hammond's conclusion—based, it's true, on Gerbert's and Koller's quasi-facsimiles—"it is difficult to conceive exactly how the piece could be read, since the great variety of neumes and notes, in black and red notation, of which it consists are notated on a continuous staff marked off to show a system *gamma* to ee."[34]

In all of these attempts at a solution, one assumes that there is one, that the notation is not just a fourteenth-century leg-pull. But one wonders whether a prankster would have had the patience to plan, compute, and annotate the following table of numbers. Perhaps what is most interesting—

[34] Corpus Scriptorum de Musica 27:11.

barring a resolution of the riddle—is that the author attempted an integration of his arithmetical fantasy with something resembling a piece of music.[35]

The *tabula numerorum* has its own historical interest quite apart from the riddle of the *tabula figurarum,* particularly given the intense recent interest in questions of *musica ficta,* of added hexachords, and of tuning generally. The basic structure of the *tabula* is easily described: a list of pitches from ee down to *gamma,* with the interpolation of sharped forms (*acuata*) and flatted ones (*aggravata)* of A (sharped in the lowest octave only), C (flatted in the upper two octaves only), D, and G. F is only sharped, not flatted and E is only flatted. Otherwise put, the gamut offers us, in addition to the traditional diatonic pitches, 5 flats (viz., E, A, D, G, and, remarkably, C) and 5 sharps (F, C, G, D, and A—the last-named only in the lowest octave and keeping company with B *fa,* normally found only in the higher octaves.)

The *tabula* is, to be sure, rather more complicated than this abbreviated description might indicate. It can be thought of as consisting of six columns, as follows. In column one our dogged author or scribe repeats the radix value, i.e., a lowest common denominator for *gamma* for each pitch. The second column uses the technical vocabulary of Boethian proportional arithmetic, telling us in effect how to perform the required calculations for deriving the numerator of the given pitch; it also designates the interval in terms of the usual Greco-Latin nomenclature, diapason, and so forth. There are some details of considerable interest buried in what might seem totally conventional; we will return to these.

The third column gives in black ink—actually rather greenish, but which I assume was once black—the appropriate integer for the pitch relative to the radix, and in red, the difference between successive pitches. These steps are also designated *limma* or *comma* depending (obviously) on how far apart they are.

The fourth column gives the standard Latin A–G pitch name with, in the appropriate places, the additional comments "per ♮ acuata quantitate apothomes" or "per ♭ aggravata quantitate apothomes," comments which may testify to a relatively advanced stage in the conversion of the signs for *b mi* and *b fa* to sharps and flats.

[35] While the famous circle and heart of Baude Cordier do not seem to be particularly comparable, the somewhat less known *harpe de mélodie* by Senleches found in the Chantilly codex and the Newberry Library theory manuscript seems at least a distant cousin, in that each harp string represents a distinct diatonic pitch, a point given due recognition in the poem telling us how to develop the second canonic part from the written texted part: "premiere note en .d. prent son ressort; harpe toudis sans espasse blechier." To be sure, this is rather different from the *cribrum* in which omitting all lines or all spaces will still not produce a reasonable melody.

The fifth column gives the appropriate Greek pitch names according to the *systema teleion*, with apparent neologisms for double e ("epypantiys") and for *gamma* ("ypopanthos"). The alternative of "prosmelodos" is also offered for "proslambanomenos." None of these non-traditional terms has, to my knowledge, any Classical Greek authority, nor am I familiar with them from other medieval contexts . . . with one exception to be mentioned below.

One might well ask how all of the normal diatonic pitches between A and dd—two octaves and a fourth—manage to have the traditional names of Classical Greek theory, inasmuch as the Greater Perfect System has only enough names for two octaves. The answer is rather startling, namely that the *synemmenon* tetrachord, rather than being an alternative, is grafted into the system along with the usual four tetrachords of the Greater Perfect System.

The sixth and final column associates numbers with the Greek pitch names, numbers taken from Boethius, Book IV, but altered due to the drastic change wrought by our author to the Greater Perfect System. Thus *proslambanomenos*, 9216 to Boethius, is here doubled to 18432. This doubling is required in order to accommodate the odd numbers which appear in the topmost tetrachord (. . . but which in Boethius were found only in the *synemmenon* tetrachord). Additionally, the numbers and names are those of the enharmonic genus, with its nongeometric, non-proportional division of the semitone into two *dieses*, equal only in terms of the numerical differences, but not in sound.[36]

Were it not for the fact that our author appears to be quite well acquainted with Boethian teaching regarding the integers representing steps of the Greater Perfect System, one might be inclined to suggest that the apparently obtuse—if not stupid—revision of the Greek double octave to conform to the medieval two octaves and a sixth rested on a misunderstanding of the diagrams linking pitch names with notational signs in Boethius, Book IV. There, in fact, we see following in order: *Mese, Trite synemmenon, Paranete synemmenon* (in all three genera), *Nete synemmenon, Paramese, Trite diezeugmenon*, and so forth.[37] On the other hand, it may also be regarded as a rather interesting attempt to adapt the Greater Perfect System to the standard medieval *gamma*-to-ee gamut. I incline to the latter.

[36] The difference, admittedly, is hardly detectable by the human ear.

[37] Friedlein, *De institutione*, 313, and table between 342 and 343; Calvin Martin Bower, "Boethius's *The Principles of Music:* An Introduction, Translation, and Commentary" (Ph.D. diss., George Peabody College for Teachers, Baltimore, 1966), 127 and 155.

In any event, the entire array is something of an intellectual *tour de force* presupposing thorough acquaintance with Greek theoretical nomenclature and proportional number theory as well. It also involves numerical calculations that go considerably beyond anything encountered in Latin (or Greek!) music theory prior to the fourteenth century. Since the system is Pythagorean in its principles, i.e., entirely based on the 2:3 perfect fifth, there's no difficult conceptual problem; the actual computation, however, required uncommon ambition.[38]

There are any number of ways in which the specific numerical results may have been arrived at. Suffice it to say that the radix or fundamental value (i.e., 644,497,544) which must be assigned to *gamma* in order that all the higher pitches be represented by integers is correct, as are also the other values, barring a few copying errors. One observes that all the numbers are even save the one designating double C flat (viz., 129,140,163 or more simply three to the seventeenth power) in the highest octave. Similarly large or larger numbers are used in musical treatises of considerably later date, as in the calculations of the lengthy treatise *Sicut omnis ars* found in Ghent Universiteitsbibliotheek 70/71, known to have been copied shortly after 1500. Here the author arrives at a fundamental value (or radix) for the lowest G of 42,467,328.[39] Far more spectacularly, Zarlino, dealing with powers of 81 required to demonstrate that the whole tone is larger than 9 commas, lays out for our astonishment in his *Dimonstrationi harmoniche* a number of 21 digits (109,418,989,131,512,359,209, if you must know).[40]

Why on earth one would want to operate with such large numbers without rounding them off may not be immediately clear to our twentieth-century minds. From the point of view of a fourteenth-century intellectual, however, those numbers are unavoidable. As the very essence of Pythagorean arithmetic is its avoidance of irrational quantities—which accounts for its stubborn insistence that the whole step can't be divided into equal half-steps—it also must insist that every proportion, consequently every

[38] When attacking this problem a few weeks prior to the delivery of the paper at the conference, it took me half a day to figure out how to make my shareware spreadsheet calculate the appropriate table. Once I did that, it took about 2 seconds to make the calculations, another 20 to 30 seconds to print out the result.

[39] A partially or fully chromatic gamut does not appear to be involved. For a photograph of the relevant page and an informed discussion see Joseph Smits van Waesberghe, *Musikerziehung: Lehre und Theorie der Musik im Mittelalter,* Musikgeschichte in Bildern 3 (Leipzig: VEB Deutscher Verlag für Musik, 1969), 162f. The theorist suggests division by 72 if one doesn't want to work with such large numbers and is willing to tolerate fractions.

[40] Gioseffo Zarlino, *Dimostrationi harmoniche* (Venice: Francesco dei Franceschi Senese, 1571; facsimile repr., Ridgewood, N.J.: Gregg, 1966), 123. I've not checked his multiplication.

Table 4

Sample Instructions of the Tabula numerorum

[ee]	644972544	Tonus cum dyapente et bisdyapason proportio sextupla supertripartiens quartas. Dux radicum 27, comes 4; eorum differentia quinquies 4 et 3	185551488 [41]
			5111808
[dd♯]	644972544	Apothome cum dyapente et bisdyapason proportio sextupla super417partiens 1024as. Dux radicum 6561, comes 1024; eorum differentia quinquies 1024 et 41.	190663296 [42]
			1373376
[ee♭]	644972544	Limma cum dyapente et bisdyapason proportio sextupla. Dux radicum 6, comes 1; eorum differentia quinquies 1.[43]	102036672
			5458752
[dd]	644972544	Diapente cum bisdyapason, proportio sextupla. Dux radicum 6, comes 1; eorum differentia quinquies 1.	107495424
			5750784
[cc♯]	644972544	Tritonus cum bisdyapason, proportio quintupla super89partiens 128as. Dux radicum 729, comes 128; eorum differentia quater 128 et 89.	113246208
			1545048
[dd♭]	644972544	Semitritonus cum bisdyapason, proportio quintupla super451partiens 729as. Dux radicum 4096, comes 729; eorum differentia quater 3 et 1.[44]	114791256
[cc♭]	644972544	Tonus minimus cum communi et bisdyapason proportio quadrupla super6524partiens 6561as. Dux radicum 32768, comes 6561; eorum differentia ter 6561 et 6524.	129140162

[41] Incorrect; should be 95551488.

[42] Incorrect; should be 100663296.

[43] Obviously incorrect; the text for the following pitch was copied in error.

[44] Incorrect; should be "quater 729 et 451."

musical pitch, be represented as a ratio of integers. The Pythagorean legitimacy of any of the sharps or flats of a gamut like the one here under examination can be established simply by displaying the numbers—assuming that the skeptic is susceptible to such an advanced argument, "ut calculi fert ratio."

Nothing so far helps us make a link with any specific author of the later Middle Ages. Careful reading of the instructions of the second column, however, is productive in this regard. I include here a selection of the 48 instructions, seen in table 4. Inasmuch as all of them follow the same pattern, it would be otiose to include them. But that pattern deserves explication. Thus, in the recipe for deriving ee, viz., "Tonus cum dyapente et bisdyapason proportio sextupla supertripartiens quartas. Dux radicum 27, comes 4, eorum differentia quinquies 4 et 3," we're given first of all the standard musical nomenclature for the interval between *gamma* and the pitch, i.e., two octaves plus a sixth. Then follows the formal arithmetical name for the proportion of the interval, i.e., a sextuple proportion (6 times 4) plus another 3 (*supertripartiens quartas*). Finally, this proportion is stated in its lowest possible terms, considering only the two pitches of the interval, in this case 27:4 (table 4).

The one rubric or instruction of those included above that helps in linking Nicholas to a known author is that for double C flat, with the ratio of 129140162 : 644972544. Its deciphering gave a bit of trouble at first, due to the tinyness of the script and an abbreviation that was not immediately obvious. Finally, however, *Sitzfleisch* was victorious: "Tonus minimus cum communi et bisdyapason proportio quadrupla super6524partiens 6561," and so forth. The octave of double C flat uses the same nomenclature, as also G flat: "Tonus minimus cum communi supra diapente et diapason," and so forth. To be explicit: *gamma* to g is a double octave, g–aa an ordinary whole step (*tonus communis*), and aa–cc flat larger than either a minor or a major semitone, but smaller than the ordinary whole step aa–bb.[45] Besides the unusual "tonus minimus" another rare technical term is found in the

[45] It might have been possible to describe the interval as a double octave (*gamma* to g) plus a whole step (g to aa) plus a minor semitone (aa to bb flat) plus another minor semitone (bb flat to cc flat). In any event, an interesting problem of nomenclature arises, as a whole step above aa ought to be some kind of b. However, the name of b flat is naturally assigned to the minor semitone above a, while b natural is the normal whole tone. Thus we have the odd interval of aa to cc flat, consisting of 2 minor semitones, or, alternatively, a comma less than a normal whole step. Once having created cc flat, one is led to consider the oddest interval of all, that between aa sharp and cc flat, otherwise a doubly-diminished third, a comma less than a minor semitone. This interval does not exist in Nicholas's gamut, since A sharp is found only in the lowest octave, which does not have the C flat.

instructions for dd flat and its octaves, namely, "semitritonus cum bisdyapason."

This is the language of Jacques of Liège/Mons/Audenaarde in the forty-third chapter of the second book of the *Speculum musicae*, entitled *Toni divisio in partes subjectivas.* Here are defined three kinds of *tonus*, the *tonus minor*, consisting of two minor semitones, the *tonus medius perfectus vel integer*, consisting as usual of a minor plus a major semitone, and the *tonus maior vel abundans* of two major semitones. Jacques freely admits that "although these tones are unused and useless for practical music, one should not spurn their theoretical consideration."[46] They're useless because, in the theorist's opinion, no one can sing two minor or major tones in a row; furthermore, the "normal" tone can be notated, the others not.

Quite a few chapters further on, this opinion is repeated and it's made clear that the *tonus minor* and the *tonus minimus* are one and the same: "Tacti duo toni, minor scilicet vel minimus, maior vel maximus, etsi in natura possibiles sint . . . in usu tamen non sunt quia sensus et humana vox vel ea proferre non valet, vel non faciliter; ideo notis nostris notari nequeunt et in monochordo non habent locum."[47]

This same urge towards theoretical comprehensiveness is manifested in regard to the analogous distinction between the tritone, which if between F and B or B flat and E, consists of three whole tones; and the semitritone of two whole steps and two minor semitones, as between E and B flat, or B natural and F.[48]

We shouldn't finish without mentioning a paragraph included at the very end of the *tabula*, in the hand of the original scribe as distinguished from the other hands seen in two annotations in the bottom margin of the same folio. It consists of a concise statement—or restatement, since the vocabulary and the doctrine corresponds with that already used in column 2

[46] "Qui [toni], etsi inusitati sunt et musicae inutiles sint practicae, ipsorum tamen non est spernenda theoria." Jacobus Leodiensis, *Speculum musicae*, ed. Roger Bragard, Corpus Scriptorum de Musica 3 ([Rome]: American Institute of Musicology, 1955–73), 2:104ff.

[47] *Speculum musicae*, Book II, chapter 72 (Corpus Scriptorum de Musica 3, 2:175).

[48] The urge to comprehensiveness doesn't stop there. Jacobus is even willing to contemplate such tonal monstrosities as the *tetratonus*, *pentatonus*, and *hexatonus*, even though they can't be found on the monochord unless *musica ficta* is used. For example, the *hexatonus* is illustrated by a diagram showing an ascending scale F flat, G flat, A flat, B flat, C, D and E, an interval larger than the octave by a comma. It's hard to imagine why he draws the line at the *hexatonus* ("The other following consonances, constructed of seven, eight, etc. whole steps should not be spoken of further, because the knowledge of them is not so useful as of the preceding ones"). Another important fourteenth-century figure to be considered in this context is Johannes Boen in his so-called *Musica;* see *Johannes Boens Musica und seine Konsonanzlehre*, ed. Wolf Frobenius, Freiburger Schriften zur Musikwissenschaft 2 (Stuttgart: Musikwissenschaftliche Verlags-Gesellschaft, 1971).

of the *tabula*—of the relationship between *limma*, *comma*, and *apotome* and might eventually be helpful in determining antecedents and descendants of Nicholas's work. As nearly as I can make out from my photograph of the manuscript this text reads:

> Lima [. . . .] lima et coma est proportio tonalis. Lima simpliciter est proportio semitonalis minus. Lima et coma proportio apothomes. Lima et [diesis?] dicitur tonus minus. Apothomes dicitur semitonus maius.

As already mentioned above, some of the technical terms found in the *tabula* appear to receive little or no sanction from either Classical or medieval Greek or Latin sources known to me. But there exists one text copied considerably later which contains this nomenclature and is clearly derived from or otherwise related to the Sankt Paul fascicle. This is found on fol. 116 recto and verso of the manuscript now in Catania, copied in 1473, probably in the kingdom of Naples, i.e., Southern Italy or Sicily. Its principal contents are Boethius on music, the *Commentum super cantum* of Roger Caperon, the *Lucidarium* of Marchetto of Padua and the *Expositiones tractatus practice cantus mensurabilis magistri Johannis de Muris* of Prosdocimo de' Beldemandis.[49]

Direct kinship is shown by the gamut itself, *gamma* to ee with the selfsame non-diatonic steps of Sankt Paul; the three odd Greek-derived terms (albeit rather different orthographically), viz., "eperipapancos," "ypapanchos," and "prosmelelos"; the *systema teleion* nomenclature, together with the numbers between 3456 and 18432 and the insertion of the *synnemenon* tetrachord between the *meson* and the *diezeugmenon* tetrachords. A minor difference is found in the specification of the distances between the steps of the gamut, here by "comma" and "diesis," rather than by "comma" and "limma." The major differences are the omission of the huge numbers, as well as the detailed instructions for deriving them from a radix value.[50]

[49] To give the manuscript its full name: Catania, Biblioteche Riunite Civica e Antonio Ursino Recupero, Ursino Recupero D.39. For further details consult Jan Herlinger's edition, *The Lucidarium of Marchetto of Padua*, ed. Jan Herlinger (Chicago: University of Chicago Press, 1985), and in more detail, his edition of Prosdocimo de' Beldemandis, *A Short Summary of Ratios Insofar as They Pertain to Music and A Little Treatise on the Method of Dividing the Monochord*, ed. Jan Herlinger (Lincoln: University of Nebraska Press, 1987). My thanks to Professor Herlinger for sending me a copy of the pages discussed here.

[50] These pages are edited and interpreted by Herlinger in Appendix D of his edition of Prosdocimo's *Brief Treatise on Ratios*. The suggestions for emendation of the Greek neologisms (?) should be rethought in the light of Nicholas's *tabula*. Christian Meyer has very recently invoked the Catania table as related to a complex of earlier monochord divisions which interposed new chromatic tones between the traditional diatonic ones. See Meyer, "Le *De synemmenis* et sa tradition," 83–95. While Meyer's arguments are not always easy to follow, the

Needless to say, the southern origin of the Catania manuscript lends further support to an origin in the region of Naples for Barberini 307.

I regret not having made in this essay much attempt to discuss the reconstituted manuscript in terms of the graphic imagination manifested therein. A few belated words will have to suffice. The rather wonderful trees of Johannes Vetulus—a regrettably monochrome reproduction is readily accessible[51]—are not only visually appealing, they make a strong impact on the imagination and memory, and do not undermine the theoretical conceit they attempt to illustrate. Well, not quite, inasmuch as they also embody the four solmization syllables, *ut re mi fa*, which, Johannes would have it, could replace the traditional hexachord. The connection between these is never explained, nor is it at all clear to me what it might be.[52]

The wheel seems to me to be less effective in capturing our imagination. We might be willing to accept a connection between the perfection, the comprehensive simplicity of the circle as a geometric figure, and a theoretical statement which also attempted an analogous kind of comprehensiveness. But that doesn't explain the four-fold cycle, even though it is reinforced by the four vignetted heads at each corner of the page. (One might also mention that the need to employ very small and abbreviated writing as one approaches the hub of the wheel renders the text nearly illegible.)

Which brings us to the tower . . . which, in my opinion, surcharges the diagram of the relationship of time values at various levels of rhythmic organization with philosophical dichotomies that are by no means characteristic of the usually quite matter-of-fact explications of mensural notation and rhythmic organization found after Franco. And this even though it was apparently not finished, to judge from the sketchy arches or gate at the bottom of the structure. Perhaps we have here a presage of Robert Fludd's *templum musices* some two centuries later, a graphic marvel which although vastly richer than the Sankt Paul tower, nonetheless makes contact with it

manuscripts and texts he cites will have to be considered in a more complete treatment of the work of Nicholas of Luduno.

[51] Smits van Waesberghe, *Musikerziehung*, 175.

[52] Hammond does not attempt an explanation of the inclusion of the syllables in his introduction to Corpus Scriptorum de Musica 27. Smits van Waesberghe, *Musikerziehung*, 172–75, offers facsimiles of five of Johannes's trees, along with an interpretation which I find not very convincing. It boils down to the notion that Johannes's system depends completely on the numbers 3 and 4, as manifested, respectively, in the system of rhythmic notation and in the tetrachord represented by *ut*, *re*, *mi*, and *fa*. Smits freely admits, "die Erklärung dazu ist ziemlich kompliziert."

via the emphasis on mensural notation.[53] (Fludd's temple uses the triangle diagram attributed to John Torkesey ca. 1400.)[54]

Finally, a similar tendency to overabundance, to excess and exaggeration, to the synthesis of concepts, to the devising of attractive yet somewhat bewildering visual metaphors seems present not only in the arithmetic exaggeration of the numerical *tabula* of Nicholas, but also in the notational *tabula*. One wonders, in the end, whether we are in the presence of a school of thought, rather than a mere propensity (and a pocketbook) for decorative ornament.[55]

These *tabulae* of Nicholas of Luduno are remarkable attempts to rationalize a fully chromatic gamut, once through arithmetic and again through the bizarre panoply of notation that obviously intrigued Gerbert, to judge by his choosing it for the frontispiece of the third volume. (Perhaps I should qualify the term "fully chromatic" inasmuch as that term cannot be applied *stricto sensu* to any Pythagorean cyclical tuning.) A dating in the last half of the fourteenth century seems appropriate although hardly obligatory. That Nicholas's work had no known repercussions could be attributed to difficulty in integrating it with conventional monochord divisions or with hexachord theory, as well as to the off-putting nine-digit numbers.

On the other hand, the work of Johannes Vetulus, as well as the wheel and the tower, also found no echoes,[56] so perhaps texts and diagrams were hidden away in a library to which interested scholars or copyists had little or no access. Perhaps also geography had as much to do with such neglect as

[53] For a reproduction of Fludd's *templum* see *Die Musik in Geschichte und Gegenwart* 4, pl. 22.

[54] André Gilles and Gilbert Reaney, eds., *Ms. Oxford, Bodley 842 (Willelmus): Breviarium regulare musicae Ms. British Museum [sic] Royal 12. C. VI: Tractatus de figuris sive de notis, Johannes Torkesey, Declaratio trianguli et scoti*, Corpus Scriptorum de Musica 12 ([Rome]: American Institute of Musicology, 1966).

[55] Smits van Waesberghe, *Musikerziehung*, 172, suggests that the copyist was more of an artist and illuminator than a music theorist. It is, however, difficult for me to imagine a mere copyist developing the *tabula notarum* from the *tabula numerorum* on his own. Of course, Smits was dealing only with Barberini 307 and not the Sankt Paul fascicle in writing what he did.

[56] Since we are at the end of this essay, it seems not inappropriate to mention the brief treatise added (so it would seem) in a different book hand nearly at the end of Barberini 307, on fols. 37^{v}–38^{r}. This *Ars et modus pulsandi organa secundum modum novissimum inventum per magistros musicos modernos* (and edited by Casimiri in *Note d'archivio*) is actually a set of transposition rules beginning categorically, "Nota quod omnes voces totius organi tam toni quam semitoni possunt esse fa et mi." There follow detailed, if not redundant, instructions for basing a descending S T T tetrachord on every step of the twelve-step-to-an-octave gamut diagrammed at the start of the treatise. Although the first octave (C to C) has no semitones other than the "normal" ones of E–F, A–B flat, B–C, the second and third octaves insert semitones—indicated only by a crux—between each whole step. If, as seems quite necessary, we assume

the factors already mentioned, that is to say, copying and subsequent preservation in Southern Italy, for all that much of the contents, possibly including the work of Nicholas of Luduno, was of French origin. I find it difficult to resist the temptation to invoke the Angevin regime and its musicians, or a school of music theory centered at the University of Naples, as the locus for the interests represented by these two parts of one manuscript, much as one must admit that the destruction of the Angevin archives and the dearth of surviving documents from that University will make it difficult to move from possibility to probability.

that all the tetrachords are alike, then this scheme would seem to require equal temperament, or as near to it as one could get by keeping the traditional minor semitones E–F, A–B flat, B–C. In fact not only are each of the normal diatonic fifths said to be "bona quinta" but also all of the others ("et sic de aliis"). This insouciance regarding the size and nomenclature of semitones is rather at odds with the scenario for the rather orderly addition of sharps and flats to the keyboard described by Karol Berger, *Musica ficta*, 48ff.

DAVID HILEY

The Repertory of Sequences at Winchester

The following observations have been occasioned by work on a critical edition of the sequences in the two well-known Winchester manuscripts Oxford, Bodleian Library, Bodley 775 (hereafter *Ob*) and Cambridge, Corpus Christi College 473 (hereafter *Ccc*). Compared with the enormous strides made in recent years in the study of Winchester's tropes and organum, study of the sequences has remained somewhat on the sidelines. It is true that Frere, in his book *The Winchester Troper*,[1] listed and cross-indexed the melodies and texts of the sequences (including those in some other early sources). He also gave facsimiles of most of the melodies and transcriptions of some, but devoted his editorial effort to the tropes. Since most of the texts had been edited by Misset and Weale, Frere judged another text edition to be unnecessary. Bannister then took up the task for *Analecta Hymnica*.[2]

[1] Walter Howard Frere, *The Winchester Troper, from Mss. of the 10th and 11th Centuries, with Other Documents illustrating the History of Tropes in England and France*, Henry Bradshaw Society 8 (London: Henry Bradshaw Society, 1894).

[2] Possibly Frere may have lacked the enthusiasm for sequences which he brought to the study of other parts of the liturgy. J. H. Arnold said that Frere thought sequences dull; cf. *Walter Howard Frere, Bishop of Truro: A Memoir*, ed. C. S. Phillips (London: Faber & Faber, 1947), 168. Yet from the catalogues in *The Winchester Troper* it is clear that Frere spent a lot of time collecting and identifying sequences in early sources (see in particular *The Winchester*

In this paper I propose to discuss three aspects of the Winchester sequence repertory. First of all I shall identify the pieces taken over from other repertories and those which appear to be the result of local initiative. Secondly I shall inspect the basic melodic plan of some of the sequences, that is, the number and length of their verses, in order to identify which versions of some well-known sequence melodies were known to the Winchester musicians. Finally I shall present some observations on the liturgical assignment of the sequences.

Imported and Local Compositions

Ob and *Ccc* do not have quite identical collections. (Both also contain a number of later additions, but here I intend to discuss only the basic tenth- and eleventh-century repertories.) Table 1 presents a complete list of the melodies with their Winchester names and texts. I have given each melody and each text a number for ease of reference. I have also stated the order in which these pieces occur in the two manuscripts, so that the original order can be reconstructed from table 1 if desired. (This information is already available in Frere, presented somewhat differently.)[3] The order in which I have listed the texts is determined by the order of the melodies, so that texts for the same melody are grouped together. Thus melody no. 3, called *Iustus ut palma maior* at Winchester, was used with three different texts, nos. 3–5: *Oramus te*, *Laus armonie*, and *Organicis canamus*. (The list does not give the original melody titles in a critical edition, so that differences between the two manuscripts are ignored unless substantial.)

Between them the two sources are witness to 59 different melodies, including two melodies, so far untraced, for which organal voices were added in *Ccc*.

Troper, 227–46). Is it symptomatic that the sequentiary of London 12194 is omitted from the facsimile *Graduale Sarisburiense?* This was no emulation of Solesmes practice, for the first volume of *Paléographie musicale* where a sequentiary was omitted from the facsimile (vol. 4, containing Einsiedeln 121) appeared only in the same year, 1894. In both cases the exclusion reflected the needs of the post-Tridentine Roman liturgy. Frere would not have wished to emphasize the local as opposed to the Roman qualities of Sarum chant.

[3] *The Winchester Troper*, 70–83.

Table 1

Melodies sung at Winchester and their Texts

	Melody	Ccc	Ob		*Text*	Ccc	Ob
1	Musa	1	1	1	Celica resonant	1	1
2	Beatus vir	2	2	2	Gloriosa dies	2	2
3	Iustus ut palma ma.	3	3	3	Oramus te	3	
				4	Laus armonie	4	3
				5	Organicis canamus		4
4	Pura deum	49	4	6	Pura deum	5	5
5	Multifarie	4	5	7	Nato canunt	6	6
6	Chorus	5	6	8	Epiphaniam domino	7	7
7	Adorabo (mi.)	6	7	9	Claris vocibus	8	8
8	Fulgens preclara	7	8	10	Fulgens preclara	9	9
9	Eduxit dominus	8	10	11	Prome casta concio	10	10
10	Pascha nostrum	9	9	12	Pange turma	11	11
11	Cithara	10	11	13	Rex omnipotens	12	12
12	Benedicta sit	11	12	14	Benedicta sit beata	13	13
13	Mater	12	13	15	Exulta celum	14	15
					Exulta celum		62
				16	Alle caeleste	15	14
14	Sanctus Petrus	13	14	17	Sanctus Petrus	16	17
				18	Agmina leta	17	16
15	In omnem terram	14	15	19	Laude iocunda	18	18
16	Hieronima	15	31	20	Arce superna	19	36
17	Hodie Maria virgo	16	16	21	Aureo flore	20	19
18	Post partum virgo	17	17	22	Hac clara die turma	21	20
19	Maris stella	18	18	23	Salve porta	22	21
20	Angelica	19	19	24	Candida contio	23	22
21	Pretiosa	20	20	25	Gaudet clemens	24	23
				26	Alme caelorum	25	24
				27	Laudes . . .		63
22	Lira pulchra	21	27	28	Lira pulchra		31
				29	Ecce pulchra canorum	26	32
23	Iustus ut palma mi.	22	24	30	Ave pontifex Haedde	28	
				31	Laudem dicite		30
24	Letabitur iustus	23	23	32	Laurea clara		27
				33	Fulget dies	27	
25	Mirabilis deus	24	25	34	Mirabilis deus	29	28
26	Iusti epulentur	25	26	35	Arguta plectro	30	29
27	Adducentur	26	32	36	Alme Hiesu	31	
				37	Deo promat		37
				38	Laude Christum modulemus		56
28	Ostende mi.	27	33	39	Precamur nostras	32	38
29	Ostende ma.	28	34	40	Salus aeterna	33	39
30	Letatus sum	29	35	41	Regnantem sempiterna	34	40
31	Excita domine	30	36	42	Qui regis sceptra	35	41
32	Dominus regnavit	31	37	43	Nostra tuba nunc tua	36	42
33	Hec est sancta	32		44	Christicolarum sacrosancta	37	46
34	Quoniam deus mi.	33	22	45	Caelum mare tellus	38	26

	Melody	Ccc	Ob		*Text*	Ccc	Ob
35	Quoniam deus ma.	34	21	46	Promere chorda	39	25
36	Domine refugium	35	51	47	Laude canora	40	43
37	Laudent te pie	36	42	48	Laudent condita	41	49
38	Tuba vel fistula	37	38	49	Alma chorus domini	42	44
39	Ploratum	38	41	50	Gloria resonante	43	48
40	Ecce quam bonum, Prota	39	28	51	Laude resonet	44	
				52	Cantent te Christe		33
41	Stans a longe	40	39	53	Stans a longe	45	45
42	Tractus iocularis	41	44	54	Consona caterva	46	51
43	Tympanum	42	29	55	Aule celestis/rutile	47	34
44	Vaga varia	43	46	56	Laus inclita	48	
				57	Aule celse lux summa		53
45	Dulce lignum	44	40	58	Laus surgat	49	
				59	Gaudeat fidelis plebs		47
46	Via lux veritas	45	30	60	Laude celebret		35
47	Omnes sancti	46	43	61	Omnes sancti		50
48	Bucca excelsa		45	62	Ad te pulchra		52
				63	Laude pulchra	50	
49	Berta vetula	47	48	64	Arce summa		55
50	Adorabo ma.	48	47	65	Angelice turme		54
51	Scalam ad celos	50	49	66	Scalam ad celos		57
52	Planctus cigni	51	50	67	Plangant filii		58
53	? (added)	52					
54	?			68	Aulae plebs ethereae	51	
55	Exultate deo			69	Exultate deo agmina fidelia		59
56	Adorabo (another)			70	Salve mater Christi		60
57	?			71	. . . Aurea celi pandat . . . (end of a mostly erased piece)		61
(58)	Planctus sterilis	(added in *Ccc*, only *vox organalis* entered)					
(59)	Simon obediens	(added in *Ccc*, only *vox organalis* entered)					

	Melodies for which Ccc *has no text*		Text *in* Ob
46	Via lux veritas	60	Laude celebret
47	Omnes sancti	61	Omnes sancti
49	Berta vetula	64	Arce summa
50	Adorabo ma.	65	Angelice turme
51	Scalam ad celos	66	Scalam ad celos
52	Planctus cigni	67	Plangant filii
53	? (added)		

The 59 melodies known at Winchester may be divided into several groups:

19 known all over Europe, in both West and East Francia (table 2);
25 well known in West, but not in East Francia (table 3);
2 importations from East Francia (table 4);
4 found only in a few English and North French sources (table 5);
3 found only at Winchester (table 6);
– sequences which remain problematical, because of having their notation erased, or for some other reason (table 7).

Wherever Winchester used a well-known text for these melodies, I have shown this by placing a left-facing arrow in the appropriate column of tables 2 and 3. Table 2 lists 25 texts sung at Winchester, of which 13 were commonly sung elsewhere, hence 13 left-facing arrows. Of the 34 texts listed on table 3, 14 were commonly sung elsewhere.

It is clear that the Winchester repertory was firmly rooted in West Frankish traditions. The two East Frankish sequences are quite exceptional, with melodies unknown in West Francia, taken over at Winchester complete with Notker's texts.

As already mentioned, only three of the melodies (apart from those in table 7) are peculiar to the Winchester manuscripts (table 6). This means that for the present they remain, alas, untranscribable, as does the melody *Bucca* in table 5. Some other melodies survive in transcribable notation only by the slenderest of threads, for example nos. 35 and 43 (table 5), for which we have transcribable sources only from Nevers and Reims, respectively.

While rather few new melodies can be attributed to Winchester musicians, there is no doubt that new texts were composed in abundance, about half the total number, in fact: a striking if not quite Notkerian proportion. In some cases the two Winchester manuscripts actually have different texts from each other, for example for the melody *Adducentur*, no. 27 in table 1: *Ccc* has the text *Alme Hiesu*, *Ob* has *Deo promat*, both for virgins, both at the same point in the respective series. Later *Ob* has yet another text, *Laude Christum modulemus*, also for virgins. The traditional associations of the melody seem to have determined the subject matter of the text. None of these texts is known elsewhere. One has the impression that new texts continued to be written during the time these collections were being compiled.

Table 2

Universally Known Melodies

Melody		*Texts*		*Texts elsewhere (selection)*	
Winchester		*Winchester*		*West Francia*	*East Francia*
1	Musa	1	Celica resonant	<	Cangaudent angelorum chori
2	Beatus vir	2	Gloriosa dies	<	Sacerdotem Christi
3	Iustus ut palma maior	3	Oramus te		Sancti baptiste
		4	Laus armonie		
		5	Organicis canamus	<	
6	Chorus	8	Epiphaniam domino	<	Hanc concordi
7	Adorabo (minor)	9	Claris vocibus	<	Eia recolamus
10	Pascha nostrum	12	Pange turma	Hec est vera redemptio Beata tu virgo	Gaude Maria virgo
11	Cithara	13	Rex omnipotens	<	Sancti spiritus
12	Benedicta sit	14	Benedicta sit	<	Benedicta semper
16	Hieronima	20	Arce superna	Nunc exultet	Laudes salvatori
20	Angelica	24	Candida contio	<	Johannes Jesu Christo
23	Iustus ut palma minor	30	Ave pontifex	Precursor Christi	Dilecte deo Gallo
		31	Laudem dicite		
27	Adducentur	36	Alme Hiesu	Iubilemus omnes	Stirpe Maria regia
		37	Deo promat	En virginum agmina	
		38	Laude Christum		
29	Ostende maior	40	Salus aeterna	<	Clare sanctorum
30	Letatus sum	41	Regnantem	<	Psallat ecclesia
31	Excita domine	42	Qui regis sceptra	<	Angelorum ordo
32	Dominus regnavit	43	Nostra tuba nunc	<	Nostra tuba regatur
33	Hec est sancta	44	Christicolarum	Haec est sancta	Haec est sancta
41	Stans a longe	53	Stans a longe	<	Sancti belli celebremus
55	Exultate deo	59	Exultate deo	In cithara Davidis	Laeta mente canamus

Table 3

West Frankish Melodies

Melody Winchester	*Texts Winchester*	*Texts elsewhere*
5 Multifarie	7 Nato canunt	<
8 Fulgens preclara	10 Fulgens preclara	<
9 Eduxit dominus	11 Prome casta concio	<
13 Mater	15 Exulta celum	
	16 Alle caeleste	<
14 Sanctus Petrus	17 Sanctus Petrus	<
	18 Agmina leta	
15 In omnen terram	19 Laude iocunda	<
17 Hodie Maria virgo	21 Aureo flore	<
18 Post partum virgo	22 Hac clara die	<
19 Maris stella	23 Salve porta	<
21 Pretiosa	25 Gaudet clemens	O alma trinitas deus es
	26 Alme caelorum	
	27 Laudes . . .	
22 Lira pulchra	28 Lira pulchra	
	29 Ecce pulchra	<
24 Letabitur iustus	32 Laurea clara	Concelebremus
	33 Fulget dies	
25 Mirabilis deus	34 Mirabilis deus	<
26 Iusti epulentur	35 Arguta plectro	Alludat letus, Precelsa seclis
28 Ostende minor	39 Precamur nostras	<
34 Quoniam deus minor	45 Caelum mare tellus	Rex magne deus
36 Domine refugium	47 Laude canora	Succinat cantibus
38 Tuba vel fistula	49 Alma chorus domini	<
40 Ecce quam bonum, Prota	51 Laude resonet	Laudum carmina
	52 Cantent te Christe	
44 Vaga varia	56 Laus inclita	Iubilans concrepa, Pro nobis ora
	57 Aule celse	
45 Dulce lignum	58 Laus surgat	Salve crux sancta
	59 Gaudeat fidelis	
46 Via lux veritas	60 Laude celebret	Celsa polorum
49 Berta vetula	64 Arce summa	Alme sanctorum
50 Adorabo maior	65 Angelice turme	Observanda, Letetur et concrepet
52 Planctus cigni	67 Plangant filii	<

Table 4

East Frankish Melodies Known at Winchester

Melody		*Text*	
47	Omnes sancti	61	Omnes sancti
51	Scalam ad celos	66	Scalam ad celos

Table 5

Rare Melodies Found in North France and England

Melody Winchester		*Text Winchester*		*Text elsewhere*
4	Pura deum	6	Pura deum	< (N. France)
35	Quoniam deus maior	46	Promere chorda	Deus quoniam magnus (Nevers)
43	Tympanum	55	Aule celestis/rutile	Psallat mens nostra (Reims)
48	Bucca excelsa	62	Ad te pulchra	– (melody "Musca" in Cambrai 75)
		63	Laude pulchra	

Table 6

Melodies known only from Winchester

Melody		*Text*	
37	Laudent te pie	48	Laudent condita
39	Ploratum	50	Gloria resonante
42	Tractus iocularis	54	Consona caterva

Table 7

Other Melodies

Melody		*Text*	
53	? (added)	–	
54	?	68	Aule plebs ethereae
56	Adorabo? (another)	70	Salve mater Christi o inclita (incomplete)
		71	. . . Aurea celi pandat et astra . . . (end of a mostly erased piece)
(58)	Planctus sterilis	–	(only *vox organalis* entered)
(59)	Simon obediens	–	(only *vox organalis* entered)

Only twice, as far as I know, does a rare Winchester text turn up in a later English manuscript. Text no. 18, *Agmina leta*, is to be found with its music in the Crowland gradual (London, British Library, Egerton 3759), and the text is also known from the *Book of Cerne* (Cambridge, University Library, Ll.ii.10) and the Sherborne missal (manuscript of the Duke of Northumberland, now on loan to the British Library). Most surprisingly, text no. 26, *Alme caelorum*, appears in a late-fourteenth-century Sarum unnoted missal, British Library, Lansdowne 432. In both cases the melody is known from other sources. That is one indication of how little of the Winchester repertory passed into the post-Conquest repertory of other English churches. (The cleavage introduced into English traditions by the Norman Conquest causes some difficulty when one wishes to find sources with staff notation which can be used in transcribing the Winchester neumes. I have described elsewhere my identification of suitable later sources.)[4]

Variants in Melodic Plan

One of the most important contributions to sequence studies of recent years has been Richard Crocker's exploration of the differences of melodic plan in Aquitainian and St. Gall sequences with the same melody.[5] In a number of cases the version of the melody known at St. Gall was apparently modified, rationalized even, in Aquitaine. How do the Winchester versions of such sequences match up to their foreign counterparts?

In a number of cases there is no substantial variance in the melodic plan assumed by several texts for the same melody. This is the case, for example, with Winchester text no. 35, *Arguta plectro*, which has West Frankish counterparts in *Alludat letus* and *Precelsa seclis*. Nor does the text of *Arguta plectro* offer any obvious clue that it was modeled on one of the other texts.

The Winchester texts no. 58, *Laus surgat*, and no. 59, *Gaudeat fidelis plebs*, have the same syllable count as the more widely known West Frankish text *Salve crux sancta*. These three texts are given as examples 1a–c.

[4] David Hiley, "Editing the Winchester Sequence Repertory of ca. 1000," in *Cantus Planus*, ed. L. Dobszay et al. (Budapest: Hungarian Academy of Sciences, Institute for Musicology, 1990), 99–113.

[5] Richard Crocker, *The Early Medieval Sequence* (Berkeley: University of California Press, 1977).

Example 1a
Salve crux sancta
(London British Library Royal 8.C.xiii fol. 20^r)

A	Salue crux sancta arbor digna		
1a	Cuius robor pretiosum	mundi ferret talentum	
1b	Vt hostis per lignum uictor	ligno reuinceretur	
2a	Quodque exortu	mortis primis erat terrigenis	paradiso propulsis
2b	Causa etiam uite	foret cunctis Christi morte	uere uiuificatis
3a	Horrificum	tu es semper signum	inimicis crux sacra seuis
3b	Quam mors pauet	inferusque timet	que Christo suos reconsignans
Z	Cui laus sit in euum		

Example 1b
Gaudeat fidelis plebs universa (Ob *fol.171^r)*

A	Gaudeat fidelis plebs uniuersa		
1a	Clara cantans cum gloria	fulgida crucis dona	
1b	Hostis que strauit imperia	liberauit et arua	
2a	Salus iocunda nobis	ex qua floret	felicitas fulget atque serena
2b	Ex qua munera sancta	. . . stillant	pax procedit uita micat et alma
3a	Siderea	per quam regna patent	gaudia manant et superna
3b	O crux sancta	te laude canentes	uirtute tua rege pia
Z	Omnia per tempora		

Example 1c
Laus surgat ubique Christo iocunda (Ccc *fol.132^v)*

A	Laus surgat ubique Christo iocunda		
1a	Cuius aegro praelibauit	mundo mors uite hausta	
1b	Cuius pepulit pomiferae	cause crux atque dampna	
2a	Scala ac porta celi	Laus et decus	que refulget orbis salus et ampla
2b	Per quam uenia fluxit	Pax processit	et libertas uita fulsit et alta
3a	Hec est alma	protectio secli	Gloria fidelium et summa
3b	Que uirtus	generosa splendens	muniat salvet firmet et regat
Z	Nos cuncta per tempora		

Laus surgat, in *Ccc*, seems to contain echoes of *Salve crux sancta:* compare verse 2 of *Salve crux sancta*, "paradiso propulsis, causa . . ." with verse 1b of *Laus surgat*, "pepulit pomiferae causae." But the author of *Laus surgat* also knew *Gaudeat fidelis:* compare verse 2b in these two texts, "pax procedit vita micat et alma" (*Gaudeat fidelis, Ob*) and "pax processit et libertas, vita fulsit et alta" (*Laus surgat, Ccc*). *Gaudeat fidelis* in *Ob* is less artful, more conventional, and I should guess that *Laus surgat* in *Ccc* was designed to replace it, bringing in stronger images. Thus in verse 1b of *Laus surgat* Christ's cross drives out the harm caused by the apple-bearing woman, in 2a the cross is a ladder up to and also the gate of heaven, and in 2b through this gate peace and liberty go forth and a noble life shines.

Musically more interesting than these cases are those where there are differences in the melodic scheme known in different areas of Europe. My first examples are from sequences listed in table 2, whose melodies were known all over Europe, St. Gall included (which means they were discussed by Crocker). Example 2 gives the Winchester sequence *Christicolarum sacrosancta* (text no. 44), which has among its counterparts the West Frankish *Haec est sancta*, the East Frankish *Haec est sancta*, and *Quid tu virgo* (discussed by Crocker, 116ff.).[6]

The West and East Frankish versions of the melody are on the whole similar, except that for verses 4 and 5 the West Frankish version runs on into an f-g-g cadence. Winchester ignores this cadence. Crocker considered that Notker could have "improved" his model (the West Frankish *Haec est sancta*) in this respect, that is, by eliminating the favorite West Frankish cadence. Are we then to assume that Winchester also eliminated the cadence of its own accord, or that it adopted the St. Gall version of the melody? It is perhaps more logical to assume that the melody was known in these different versions before being texted. Certainly we could imagine that purely musical preferences played a part in deciding whether or not to use the ubiquitous f-g-g cadence.

Example 3 illustrates the sequence sung with the Winchester texts no. 30, *Ave pontifex Haedde*, and no. 31, *Laudem dicite*, and with the West Frankish text *Precursor Christi* and the East Frankish *Dilecte Deo Gallo* and *Rex regum*, among others (Crocker, 262ff.).

[6] I have attempted no critical editions of the sequences reproduced here, but have simply transcribed from a single representative source. In the case of Winchester sequences I have been guided partly by the pitch readings of the second source cited. In the case of examples 4b and 5d the notation of *Ob* was revised, so that consultation of an additional source is almost unnecessary. I have omitted opening Alleluia melismas, where present, and also in example 5b the melismas which appear between texted verses in Paris 1119.

There are two main melodic traditions. The Winchester *Laudem dicite*, example 3b (and *Ave pontifex*), corresponds almost exactly with the one Notker knew, while the Aquitainian *Precursor Christi*, example 3a, stands apart. The main differences are the following:

- in verse 2 *Laudem dicite* and the rest have a short, rather easily memorable phrase, *Precursor Christi* a longer one;
- verse 4 of *Precursor Christi* is practically double the length of the other version;
- verse 6 of *Precursor Christi* is absent from *Laudem dicite* and the East Frankish tradition;
- in *Precursor Christi* verse 8 is treated as one long double-versicle, as opposed to the two shorter double-versicles 7 and 8 in *Laudem dicite*.

In verse 1 Winchester rounds out the melody to make an exact pair, instead of the 13 + 16 notes or syllables everywhere else. On the other hand it agrees with the scheme Notker knew even, for example, in the thrice repeated a at the start of 4b. I would argue from the agreement of East Francia and Winchester alone that this was the mainstream version of the melody, and this is confirmed by the early source Chartres, Bibliothèque municipale 47 (with 13 + 16 syllables for verse 1).

As Crocker pointed out (p. 269), "the early [West Frankish] sources furnish two versions." By this he meant on the one hand example 3a here and on the other the melody in Paris, Bibliothèque Nationale lat. 1118, fol. 139^{r}, given here as example 3c. The similarities and dissimilarities between example 3c and the versions just discussed need not be pointed out in detail here. Crocker thought that a now lost version of *Precursor Christi* might have existed for the melody in example 3c, and he put forward various possible models and adjustments which might have led to Notker's version and the West Frankish example 3a, without committing himself to any one solution. It seems equally likely to me that the version of the melody known in St. Gall, Brittany, and Winchester (example 3b), established over a wide area, is as old as any other, being texted differently in different centers as required, and that the two Aquitainian versions are of merely local significance. They could be seen as further evidence of that Aquitainian propensity to adapt and recast which we know well from the transmission of tropes in Aquitaine.[7] Or they could reflect a period of expansion in the repertory

[7] See for example Alejandro Enrique Planchart, "On the Nature of Transmission and Change in Trope Repertories," *Journal of the American Musicological Society* 41 (1988): 215–49.

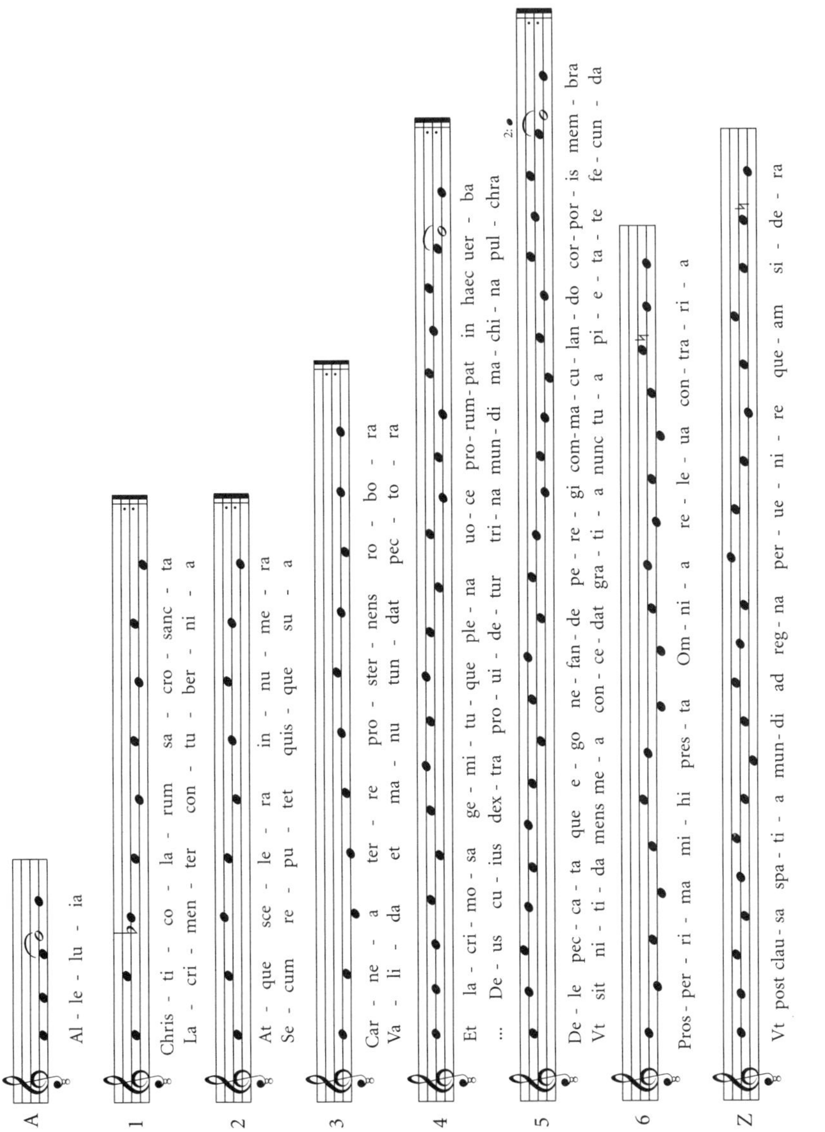

Example 2: *Christicolarum sacrosancta* (*Ob* fol. 170v; Reims, Bibliothèque municipale 285 fol. 104r *Hec est sancta* <East Frankish>).

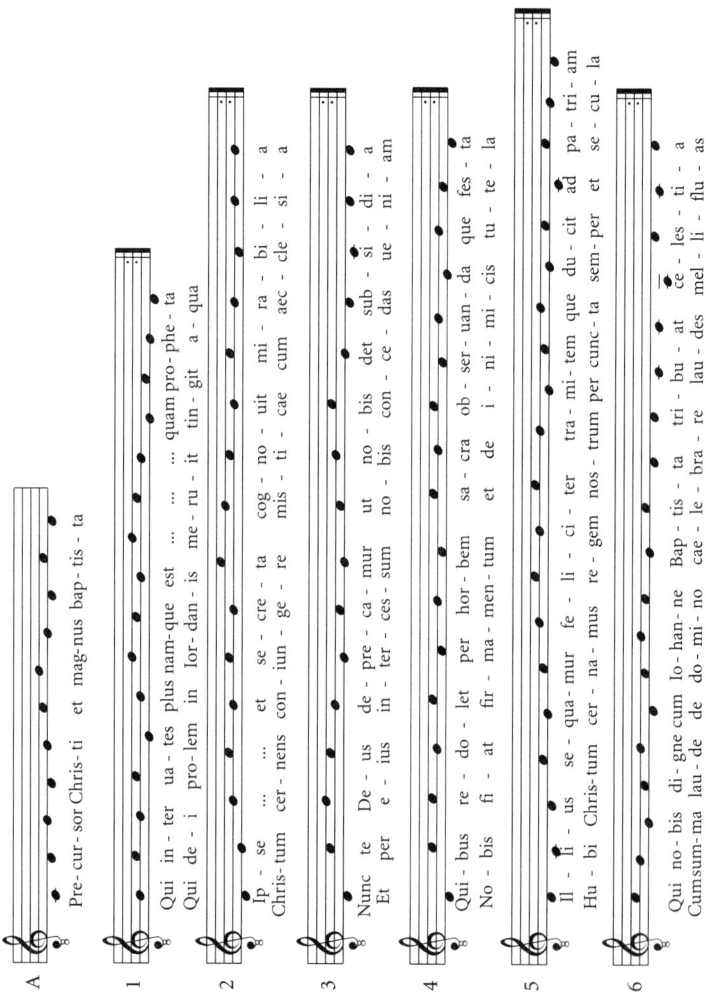
A
Pre - cur - sor Chris - ti et mag - nus bap - tis - ta
1
Qui in - ter ua - tes plus nam - que est ... ... quam pro - phe - ta
Qui de - i pro - lem in Ior - dan - is me - ru - it tin - git a - qua
2
Ip - se ... ... et se - cre - ta cog - no - uit mi - ra - bi - li - a
Chris - tum cer - nens con - iun - ge - re mis - ti - cae cum aec - cle - si - a
3
Nunc te De - us de - pre - ca - mur ut no - bis det sub - si - di - a
Et per e - ius in - ter - ces - sum no - bis con - ce - das ue - ni - am
4
Qui - bus re - do - let per hor - bem sa - cra ob - ser - uan - da que fes - ta
No - bis fi - at fir - ma - men - tum et de i - ni - mi - cis tu - te - la
5
Il - li - us se - qua - mur fe - li - ci - ter tra - mi - tem que du - cit ad pa - tri - am
Hu - bi Chris - tum cer - na - mus re - gem nos - trum per cunc - ta sem - per et se - cu - la
6
Qui no - bis di - gne cum Io - han - ne Bap - tis - ta tri - bu - at ce - les - ti - a
Cumsum - ma lau - de de do - mi - no cae - le - bra - re lau - des mel - li - flu - as

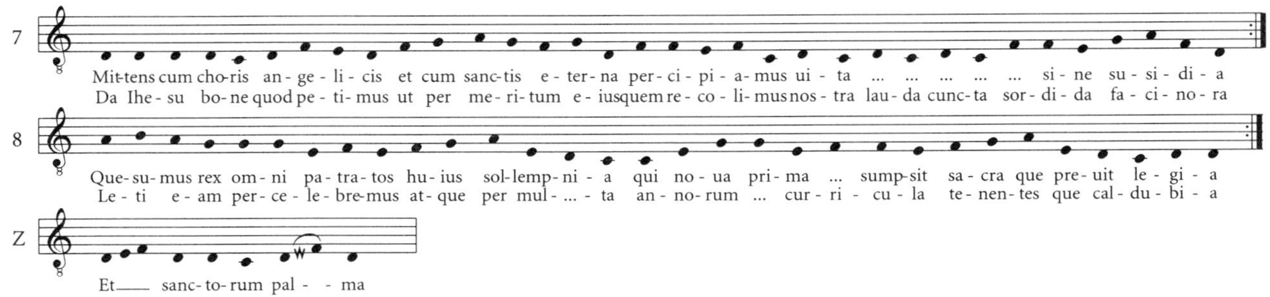

Example 3a: *Precursor Christi* (Paris, Bibliothèque Nationale lat.1118 fol. 206^{r}).

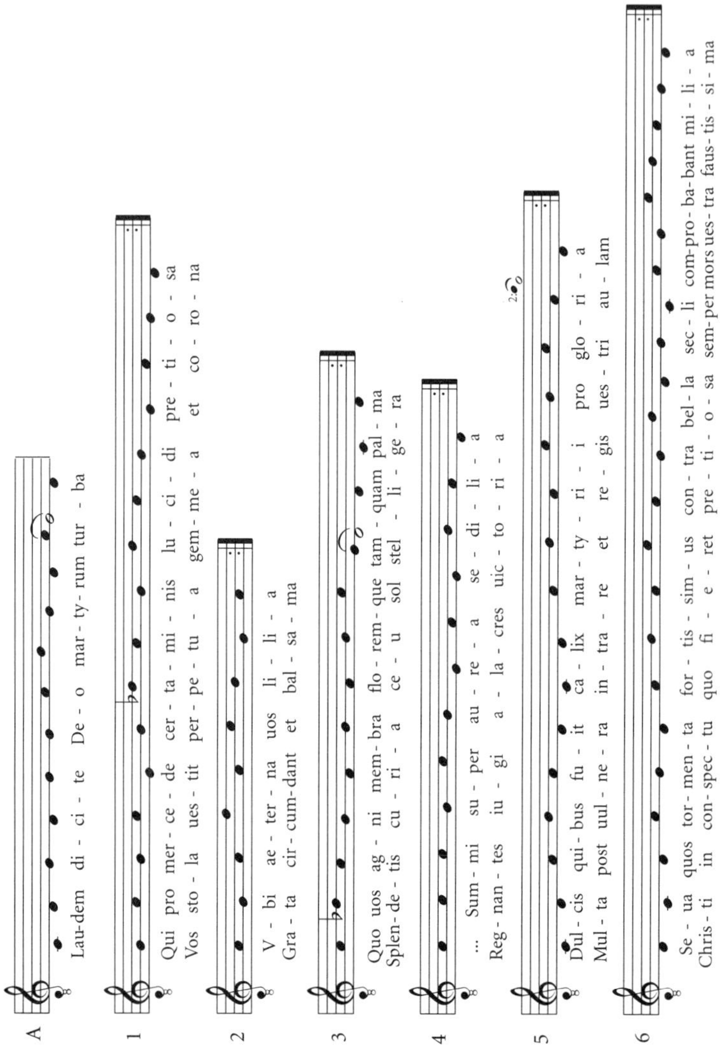
A
Lau-dem di - ci - te De - o mar - ty - rum tur - ba
1
Qui pro mer - ce - de cer - ta - mi - nis lu - ci - di pre - ti - o - sa
Vos sto - la ues - tit per - pe - tu - a gem - me - a et co - ro - na
2
V - bi ae - ter - na uos li - li - a
Gra - ta cir - cum-dant et bal - sa - ma
3
Quo uos ag - ni mem - bra flo - rem - que tam - quam pal - ma
Splen-de - tis cu - ri - a ce - u sol stel - li - ge - ra
4
... Sum - mi su - per au - re - a se - di - li - a
Reg - nan - tes iu - gi a - la - cres uic - to - ri - a
5
Dul - cis qui - bus fu - it ca - lix mar - ty - ri - i pro glo - ri - a
Mul - ta post uul - ne - ra in - tra - re et re - gis ues - tri au - lam
6
Se - ua quos tor - men - ta for - tis - sim - us con - tra bel - la sec - li com-pro - ba-bant mi - li - a
Chris - ti in con - spec - tu quo fi - e - ret pre - ti - o - sa sem-per mors ues - tra faus - tis - si - ma

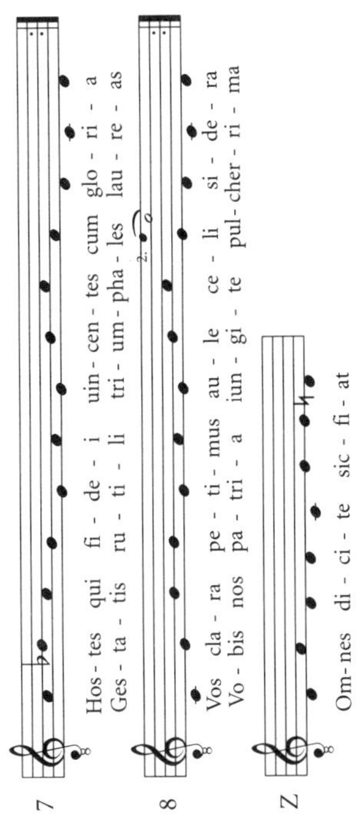

Example 3b: *Laudem dicite* (*Ob* fol. 162r; Brussels, Bibliothèque Royale II.3824 fol. 169r *Rex Regum*).

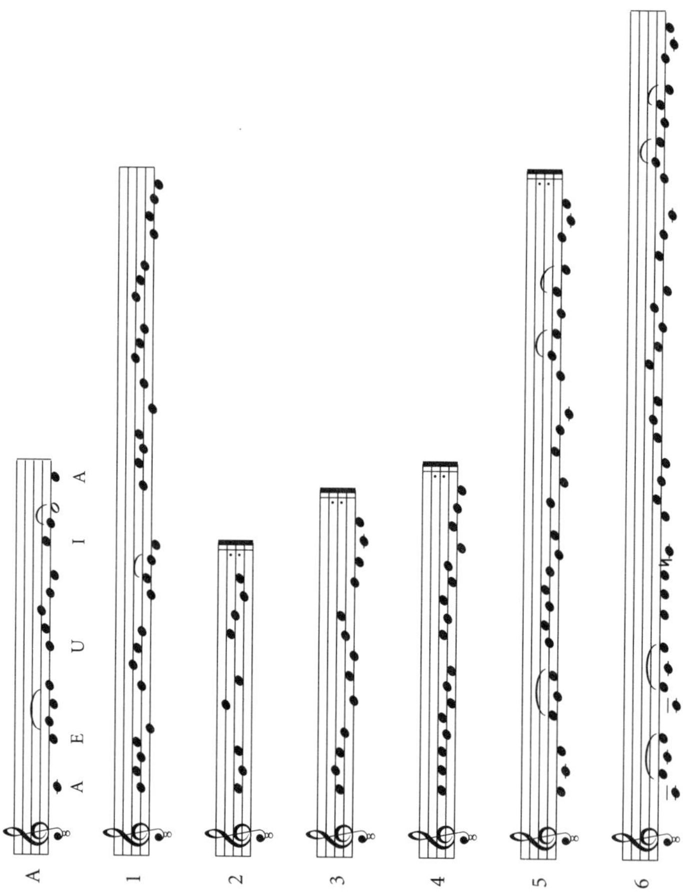
A
A E U I A
1
2
3
4
5
6

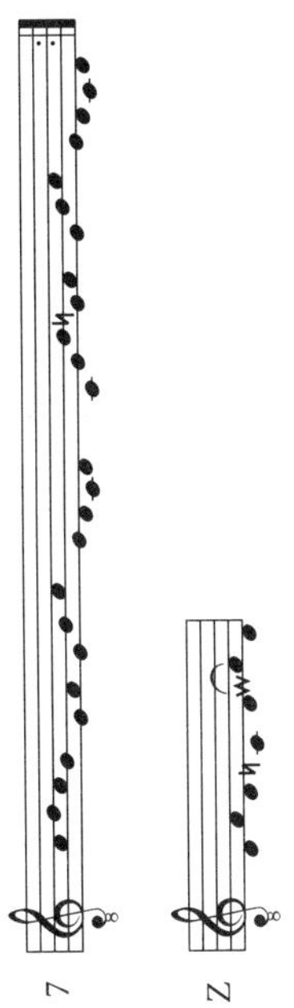

Example 3c: (Paris, Bibliothèque Nationale lat.1118 fol. 139^{r}).

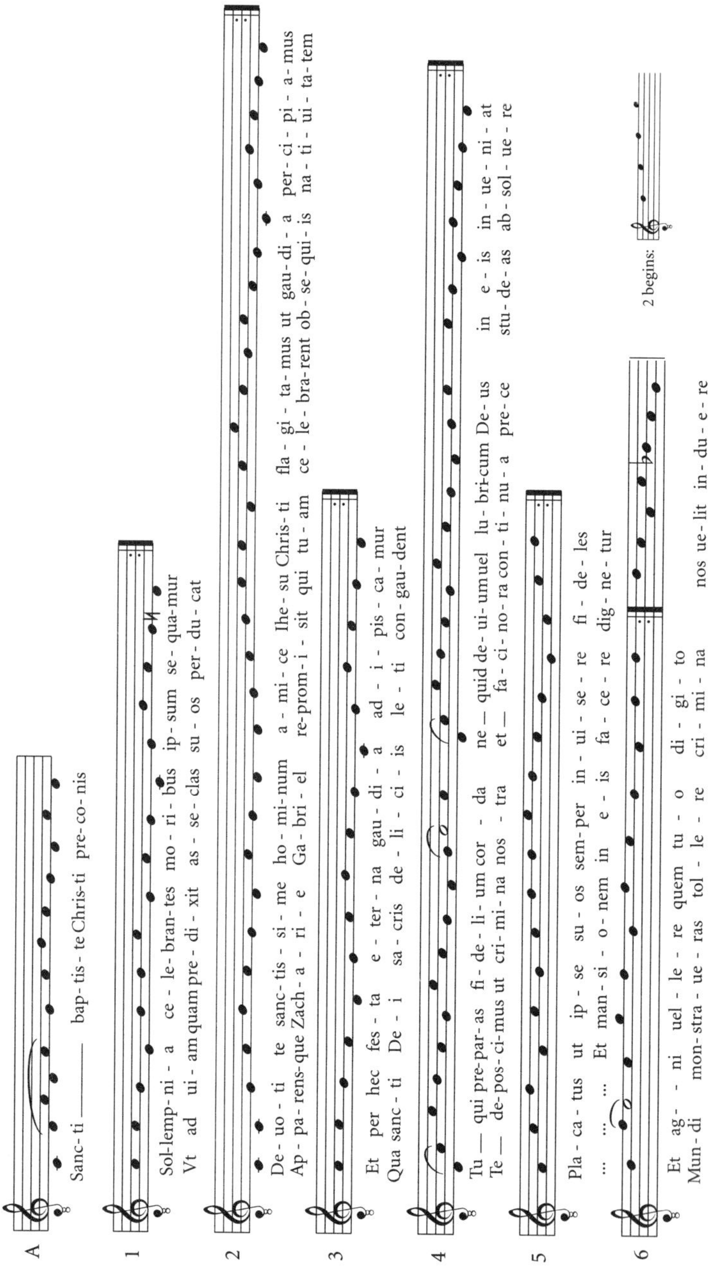
A
Sanc-ti ______ bap-tis-te Chris-ti pre-co-nis
1
Sol-lemp-ni-a ce-le-bran-tes mo-ri-bus ip-sum se-qua-mur
Vt ad ui-am quam pre-di-xit as-se-clas su-os per-du-cat
2
De-uo-ti te sanc-tis-si-me ho-mi-num a-mi-ce Ihe-su Chris-ti fla-gi-ta-mus ut gau-di-a per-ci-pi-a-mus
Ap-pa-rens-que Zach-a-ri-e Ga-bri-el re-prom-i-sit qui tu-am ce-le-bra-rent ob-se-qui-is na-ti-ui-ta-tem
3
Et per hec fes-ta e-ter-na gau-di-a ad-i-pis-ca-mur
Qua sanc-ti De-i sa-cris de-li-ci-is le-ti con-gau-dent
4
Tu __ qui pre-par-as fi-de-li-um cor-da ne __ quid de-ui-um uel lu-bri-cum De-us in e-is in-ue-ni-at
Te __ de-pos-ci-mus ut cri-mi-na nos-tra et __ fa-ci-no-ra con-ti-nu-a pre-ce stu-de-as ab-sol-ue-re
5
Pla-ca-tus ut ip-se su-os sem-per in-ui-se-re fi-de-les
... ... Et man-si-o-nem in e-is fa-ce-re dig-ne-tur
6
Et ag-ni uel-le-re quem tu-o di-gi-to
Mun-di mon-stra-ue-ras tol-le-re cri-mi-na nos ue-lit in-du-e-re
2 begins:

Example 4a: *Sancti baptiste Christi preconis* (Aachen, Bischöfliche Diözesanbibliothek 13 (XII) fol. 160[v]).

Example 4b: *Laus armonie* (*Ob* fol. 137v; London, British Library Cotton Caligula A.xiv fol. 46v *Oramus te*).

of melodies before they assumed codified and texted form, a period where the differences between West and East Frankish versions seem to have arisen. To put it bluntly, I see no reason to assume that a now lost West Frankish version of *Precursor Christi* served as Notker's model.

Example 4 concerns the Winchester texts no. 3, *Oramus te*, and no. 4, *Laus armonie* (example 4b), and their continental counterparts, the West Frankish *Organicis canamus* (sung at Winchester) and the East Frankish *Sancti baptiste* (example 4a), *Laus tibi Christe cui sapit*, etc. (Crocker, 279ff.).[8]

The scheme of *Organicis canamus*, which was in any case known at Winchester, is almost identical to that of *Oramus te* and *Laus armonie*. This West Frankish scheme differs from the East Frankish ones and other West Frankish ones in having the characteristic sub-tone cadence (c-d-d) at the end of the first two double-versicles and in omitting the third double-versicle. In early Aquitainian sources of *Organicis canamus*, and in Chartres 47, the last verse before the "Z-phrase" is a double, but in Winchester and many other places it is a single.

The multiple repeats of the figure which begins verses 4 and 5 in example 4b seem not to have been wanted at Winchester. In the fascicle of sequence melodies the melody is copied in both *Ob* and *Ccc* with verse 4 as a single. In the text *Oramus te* verse 4 is a single. For the text *Laus armonie* verse 4a is copied in the margin in both manuscripts. In *Organicis canamus* (*Ob* only) a double is nevertheless retained, probably because of the strong parallelism in the text.

Evidently the Winchester compositions entered the tradition at a stage when it was felt inappropriate to alter radically a traditional melodic plan. Whatever led to the differences between West and East Frankish schemes was no longer operative here.

On the other hand, compositions such as Winchester text no. 20, *Arce superna*, with West Frankish counterparts including *Nunc exultet* and *Cantemus organa pulchra*, and the East Frankish *Laudes salvatori* (Crocker, 94ff.), exemplify strikingly the differences which can exist between melodic schemata. In this case Crocker included the Winchester text in his discussion, and further comment is unnecessary here. Winchester's version corresponds to that of the early source Autun, Bibliothèque municipale 28S, with a scheme of repetitions different again from that in *Nunc exultet* or Notker's piece. *Cantemus organa* is different again.

[8] In some sources *Oramus te* has the opening *O rex summe*, the first double being *A quo bonitas* in both cases.

Do these various schemes result from alteration of a texted model sequence, to suit the exigencies of the new texts, or do they stem from different conceptions of the melody, a melody known in different forms before being texted? In other cases the exact fitting of a new text to an old melodic scheme appears to have been regarded as a normal procedure, even to the retention of the same note/syllable-groupings, and there is no compelling reason to suppose that a new text must necessarily have caused recasting of the melody. In this case Autun 28S is a ninth-century witness to the melody as it was known at Winchester. One is tempted to ask why the melody need have come to Winchester (or St. Gall for that matter) with a now-lost text.

The last two examples are taken from among the sequences in table 3, that is, those whose melodies were not known in East Francia. Example 5 gives four versions of a common West Frankish melody: two versions of *Rex magne deus* (example 5a-b), one of *Magnus deus* (example 5c), and the Winchester *Caelum mare tellus* (example 5d).

The only text for this melody in the early Aquitainian sources is *Rex magne deus*, which has a rather complicated manuscript tradition. What appears to be the oldest version of *Rex magne deus* is to be found in Paris, Bibliothèque Nationale lat. 1118 (but altered by a later scribe), Paris 1138 (given in example 5a), and in all non-Aquitainian sources known to me.[9] Other Aquitainian sources have what appears to be a revised version, given here from Paris 1119 (example 5b).

In the version of Paris 1138 (example 5a) verse 2 appears to have too many notes for the syllables available (or too few syllables for the notes available), a "deficiency" partly rectified in Paris 1119. The same is true of the end of verse 8, where again Paris 1119 has a syllabic rendering.

In all sources of *Rex magne deus* there is considerable evidence of textual and melodic revision, in what was evidently a problematic composition. Part of the trouble seems to lie in the existence of another text with a much more unified manuscript tradition: *Magnus deus in universa terra*. This appears only in later Aquitainian sources, but is already in the Autun troper Paris, Bibliothèque de l'Arsenal 1169. In *Magnus deus* there is a more orthodox, syllabic disposition of the text in verses 2 and 8. It may be that the author of the revised Aquitainian version of *Rex magne deus* (example 5b) had *Magnus deus*, or its form of the melody, in mind. It is true that for verse 4

[9] Angers, Bibliothèque municipale 96 omits 6b, probably mistakenly. The other northern sources are Limoges, Bibliothèque municipale 2, Paris, Bibliothèque Nationale lat. 10508 and London, British Library, Cotton Caligula A.xiv. The piece also made its way into the Norman-Sicilian repertory and Benevento, Archivio Capitolare 34.

in example 5b the revisor has opted for a greater amount of repetition of a key recurring phrase (to be heard in verses 6 and 7 as well). But this may be because he wants a simpler version of verse 5, one more like *Magnus deus;* and then his verse 6 is the same as that in *Magnus deus.*

The text for this melody in Winchester is *Caelum mare tellus,* for St. Birinus. Clearly the version of the melody in *Magnus deus* is intended for this text. What is more, *Caelum mare tellus* has distinct echoes of the text *Magnus deus.* The start of *Magnus deus* refers to the "whole earth" ("universa terra") and then to "celo" and "terra" in verse 2a. At the start of *Caelum mare tellus* we have "heaven, sea, and earth and everything that is," and again "caelos" in 2a. In *Magnus deus,* a Stephen sequence, Stephen teaches "verissima dogmata," Birinus "doctrina catholica." The texts go their own ways where *Magnus deus* relates the story of Stephen's martyrdom, though it is faintly possible that the reference to the "impious people of the Jews" in verse 7 of *Magnus deus* has stimulated mention of the baptism of the heathen king Cynegils and the people of Wessex in the corresponding verse of *Caelum mare tellus.*

If the foregoing is correct, then *Magnus deus* can be dated back into the middle of the tenth century, as early as *Rex magne deus.* More importantly, it shows that one version of a melody could influence another: hence the conflicting Aquitainian versions. In this as in other cases, the Aquitainian musicians were willing to rewrite items in their repertory.

Example 6 gives the West Frankish sequence *Ad te cuncta / Succina cantibus* (example 6a) and the Winchester text for the same melody, no. 47 *Laude canora* (example 6b).

The melody is an old one, recorded in Autun 28S (but with verse 6 as a single), and it also appears in Angers, Bibliothèque municipale 144. None of the texts has more than a fragile hold on the written tradition. There is a puzzle about the beginning. *Succina cantibus* appears partially notated in Paris 1118, fully notated in Paris 1338, and unnotated in Paris 9449 (from Nevers). This text begins not at the start of the sequence melody but only after the first double verse. If this were the "original" text for the sequence, why should it start thus? In Angers 97 the text starts in the "normal" place, *Ad te cuncta* (transcribed in example 6a), then continues at verse 2 with *Succina cantibus.* If *Ad te cuncta* were the original, why should the first verses have been omitted in Aquitaine?[10]

[10] The melody title at Winchester, *Domine refugium,* encourages comparison with melody 383 in Karlheinz Schlager, *Thematischer Katalog der ältesten Alleluia-Melodien aus Handschriften des 10. und 11. Jahrhunderts, ausgenommen das ambrosianische, alt-römische and alt-spanische Repertoire* (Munich: Ricke, 1965) and Schlager's edition of *Alleluia Domine*

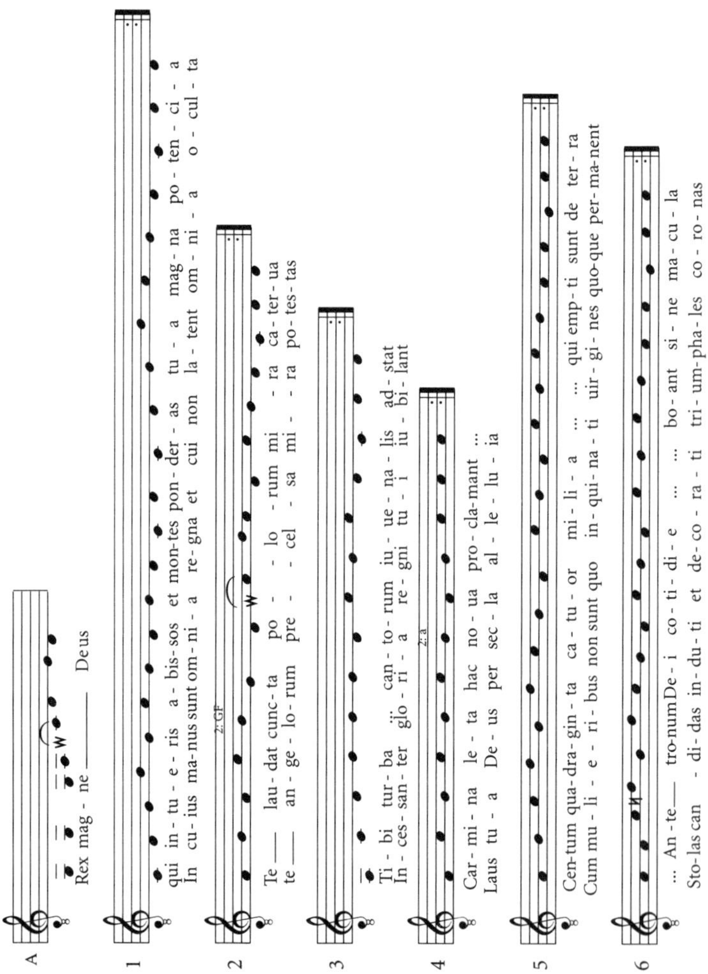
A
Rex mag - ne ___ Deus
1
qui in - tu - e - ris a - bis-sos et mon-tes pon - der - as tu - a mag - na po - ten - ci - a
In cu - ius ma-nus sunt om - ni - a re - gna et cui non la - tent om - ni - a o - cul - ta
2
2: GF
Te ___ lau - dat cunc - ta po - - lo - rum mi - - ra ca - ter - ua
te ___ an - ge - lo - rum pre - - cel - sa mi - - ra po - tes - tas
3
Ti - bi tur - ba ij can - to - rum iu - ue - na - lis ad - stat
In - ces - san - ter glo - ri - a re - gni tu - i iu - bi - lant
4
2: a
Car - mi - na le - ta hac no - ua pro - cla-mant ...
Laus tu - a De - us per sec - la al - le - lu - ia
5
Cen-tum qua-dra-gin - ta ca - tu - or mi - li - a ... qui emp - ti sunt de ter - ra
Cum mu - li - e - ri - bus non sunt quo in - qui - na - ti uir - gi - nes quo-que per - ma-nent
6
... An - te ___ tro-num De - i co - ti - di - e ... bo - ant si - ne ma - cu - la
Sto - las can - di - das in - du - ti et de - co - ra - ti tri - um - pha - les co - ro - nas

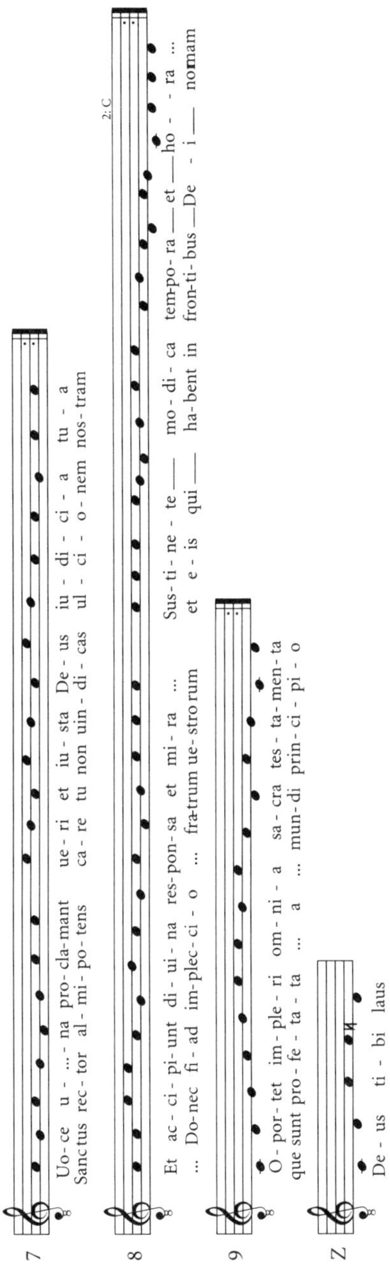

Example 5a: *Rex magne Deus* (Paris, Bibliothèque Nationale lat.1138 fol. 62[v]).

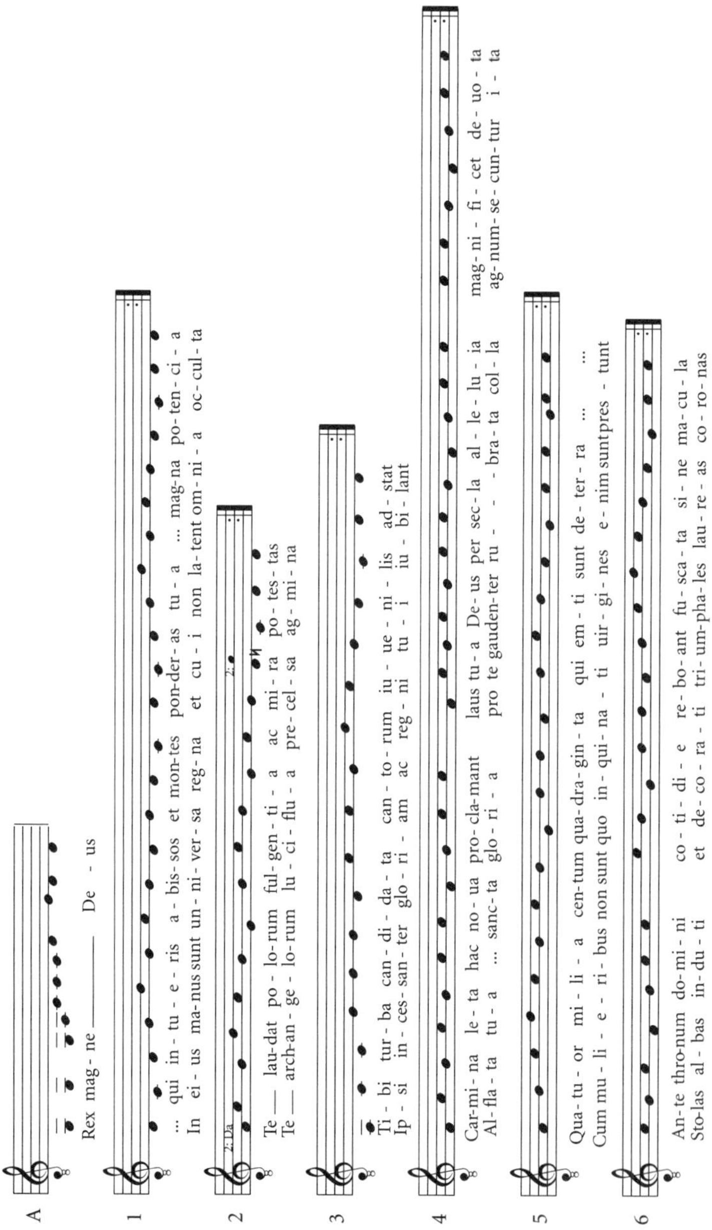
A
Rex mag - ne ——— De - us
1
... qui in - tu - e - ris a - bis - sos et mon-tes pon-der - as tu - a ... mag - na po - ten - ci - a
In ei - us ma - nus sunt un - ni - ver - sa reg - na et cu - i non la - tent om - ni - a oc - cul - ta
2
Te — lau - dat po - lo - rum ful - gen - ti - a ac mi - ra po - tes - tas
Te — arch-an - ge - lo - rum lu - ci - flu - a pre - cel - sa ag - mi - na
3
Ti - bi tur - ba can - di - da - ta can - to - rum iu - ue - ni - lis ad - stat
Ip - si in - ces - san - ter glo - ri - am ac reg - ni tu - i iu - bi - lant
4
Car - mi - na le - ta hac no - ua pro - cla - mant laus tu - a De - us per sec - la al - le - lu - ia mag - ni - fi - cet de - uo - ta
Al - fla - ta tu - a ... sanc - ta glo - ri - a pro te gau - den - ter ru - - - bra - ta col - la ag - num - se - cun - tur i - ta
5
Qua - tu - or mi - li - a cen - tum qua - dra - gin - ta qui em - ti sunt de - ter - ra ... ...
Cum mu - li - e - ri - bus non sunt quo in - qui - na - ti uir - gi - nes e - nim sunt pres - tunt
6
An - te thro - num do - mi - ni co - ti - di - e re - bo - ant fu - sca - ta si - ne ma - cu - la
Sto - las al - bas in - du - ti et de - co - ra - ti tri - um - pha - les lau - re - as co - ro - nas

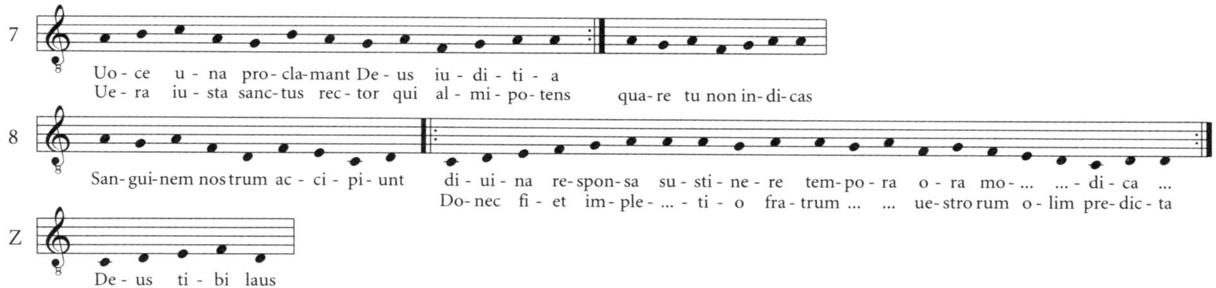

Example 5b: *Rex magne Deus* (Paris, Bibliothèque Nationale lat.1119 fol. 156r).

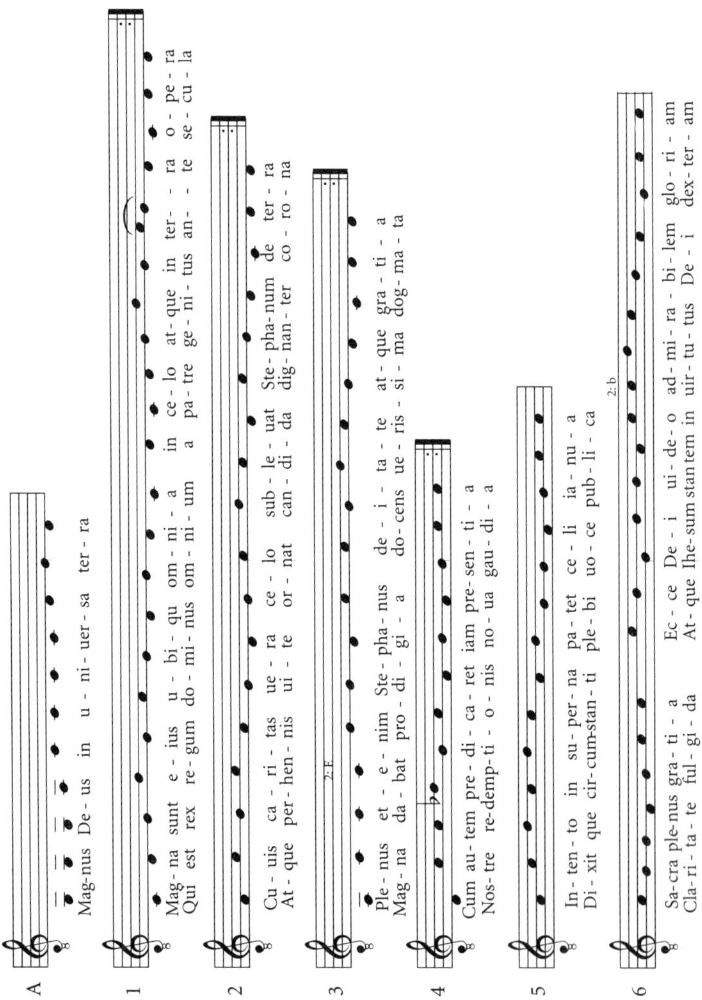
A
Mag-nus De-us in u-ni-uer-sa ter-ra
1
Mag-na sunt e-ius u-bi-qu om-ni-a in ce-lo at-que in ter- - ra o-pe-ra
Qui est rex re-gum do-mi-nus om-ni-um a pa-tre ge-ni-tus an- - te se-cu-la
2
Cu-uis ca-ri-tas ue-ra ce-lo sub-le-uat Ste-pha-num de ter-ra
At-que per-hen-nis ui-te or-nat can-di-da dig-nan-ter co-ro-na
3
2: E
Ple-nus et-e-nim Ste-pha-nus de-i-ta-te at-que gra-ti-a
Mag-na da-bat pro-di-gi-a do-cens ue-ris-si-ma dog-ma-ta
4
Cum au-tem pre-di-ca-ret iam pre-sen-ti-a
Nos-tre re-demp-ti-o-nis no-ua gau-di-a
5
In-ten-to in su-per-na pa-tet ce-li ia-nu-a
Di-xit que cir-cum-stan-ti ple-bi uo-ce pub-li-ca
6
2: b
Sa-cra ple-nus gra-ti-a Ec-ce De-i ui-de-o ad-mi-ra-bi-lem glo-ri-am
Cla-ri-ta-te ful-gi-da At-que Ihe-sum stan-tem in uir-tu-tus De-i dex-ter-am

Example 5c: *Magnus Deus in universa terra* (Angers, Bibliothèque municipale 97 fol. 103r).

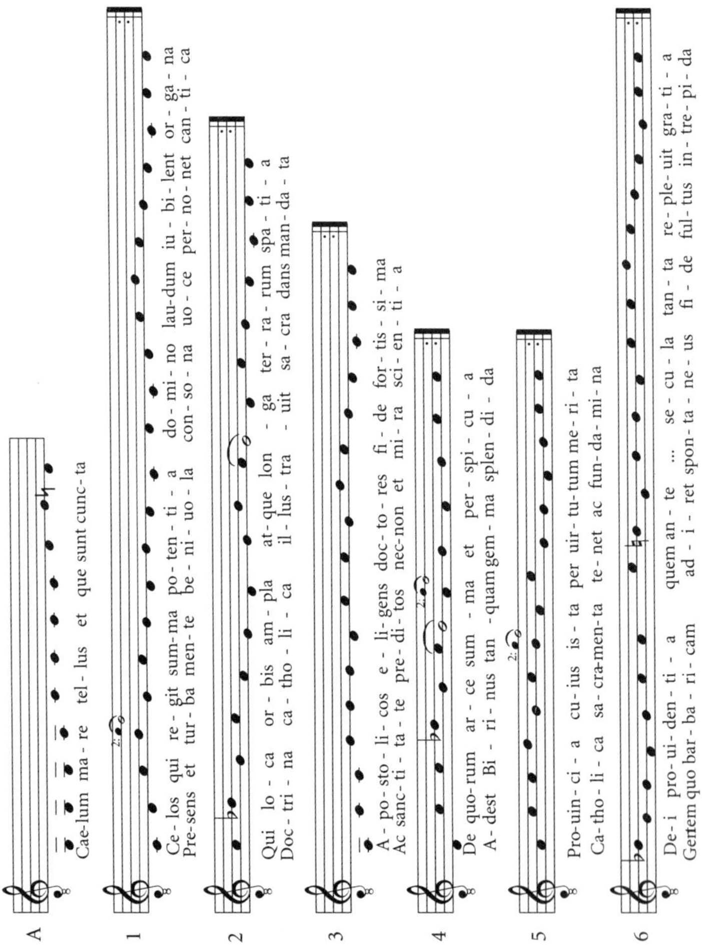
A
Cae-lum ma-re tel-lus et que sunt cunc-ta
1
Ce-los qui re-git sum-ma po-ten-ti-a do-mi-no lau-dum iu-bi-lent or-ga-na
Pre-sens et tur-ba men-te be-ni-uo-la con-so-na uo-ce per-no-net can-ti-ca
2
Qui lo-ca or-bis am-pla at-que lon-ga ter-ra-rum spa-ti-a
Doc-tri-na ca-tho-li-ca il-lus-tra-uit sa-cra dans man-da-ta
3
A-po-sto-li-cos e-li-gens doc-to-res fi-de for-tis-si-ma
Ac sanc-ti-ta-te pre-di-tos nec-non et mi-ra sci-en-ti-a
4
De quo-rum ar-ce sum-ma et per-spi-cu-a
A-dest Bi-ri-nus tan-quam gem-ma splen-di-da
5
Pro-uin-ci-a cu-ius is-ta per uir-tu-tum me-ri-ta
Ca-tho-li-ca sa-cra-men-ta te-net ac fun-da-mi-na
6
De-i pro-ui-den-ti-a quem an-te ... se-cu-la tan-ta re-ple-uit gra-ti-a
Gentem quo bar-ba-ri-cam ad-i-ret spon-ta-ne-us fi-de ful-tus in-tre-pi-da

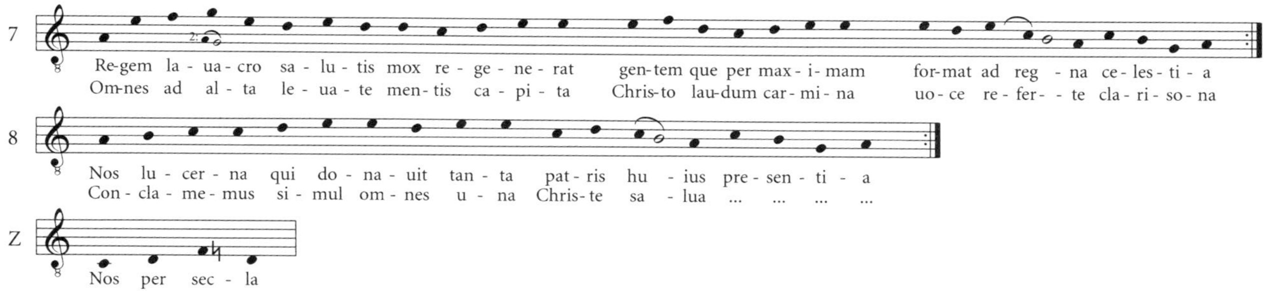

Example 5d: *Caelum mare tellus* (*Ob* fol.159[r]; Angers, Bibliothèque municipale 97 fol. 103[r] *Magnus Deus*).

Example 6a: *Ad te cuncta tendunt lumina* (Angers, Bibliothèque municipale 97 fol. 116r).

Example 6b

Laude canora (Ob *fol. 169*[r])

A	Laude canora uox pulchra	sileat nulla	
1a	Gaudenda dare preconia	per arua per sidera	
1b	Fecunda mittenti nuntia	mox partum sequentia	
2a	Virginis ad aures concipiendas munera gaudiflua		
2b	Spes unde lux uita prodit uenia libertas et gloria		
3a	Hinc stupet mater	miratur uirgo	currunt per orbem miracula
3b	Pax celiflua	uestit secula	noua capit dona natura
4a	Tanta sed fremit	ad insignia	plebs sola Iudaica
4b	Sibi nocua	nobis commoda	parat ac suspendia
5a	Hinc maxima iterum	laus micat soliflua	mortis iura cadunt improba
5b	Sacra cruce munera	deferente uiuida	bis bina orbis per climata
6a	Exultat hinc dignissima	triumphans fide iocunda	sponsa aecclesia lucida
6b	Fraus luget hinc spoliata	antiqua serpentis dira	Christi clementie subdita
7	Promissa ad supera ducat nos caelica post busta		
Z	Vbi alleluia redditur per secla		

Two other texts are known from Aquitainian manuscripts, and both use the whole melody but have the music for verses 4 and 5 the other way round. These texts are *Haec est festivitas magna* (Paris 1084, 1118, and 1138) and *Eia simul agmina* (Paris 1121). The text *Eia summe sator* appears to be unique to the Noyon liturgy; it texts the melody from the beginning but repeats one verse and has two others in reverse order: compared with *Ad te cuncta* the order is 1 2 3 6 3 4. The Winchester sequence has the melodic ordering of *Ad te cuncta.*

For completeness's sake, one or two other variants in the transmission of this melody may be mentioned. In Autun 28S verse 4 is shorter, omitting the equivalent of notes 8–11 here. The other main differences concern the ending. As can be seen in example 6, *Ad te cuncta* has verse 6 with the form a-a'-b (twice), verse Z with the form a'-c. This is also the arrangement in Angers 144 and at Winchester. Autun 28S has verse 6 as a single, while verse Z starts with a double phrase, thus a-a'-b, a-a'-c altogether. This version of 6 and Z is also that in the Noyon sequence *Eia summe sator* and in the

refugium in *Alleluia-Melodien* 1: *bis 1100*, Monumenta Monodica Medii Aevi 7 (Kassel: Bärenreiter, 1968), 135. But no melodic relationship with the opening of the sequence melody is discernible.

Aquitainian sequences *Haec est festivitas* and *Eia simul agmina.* (The copy of the melody alone in the sequentiarium of Paris 1118 actually gives 6 as a double, then 6 again as a single before proceeding to Z.)

The *Winchester* text *Laude canora* may have been composed with *Ad te cuncta* in mind, for both use the words *arva* and *sidera* in the first double verse. Those opening lines make conventional reference to the whole of creation praising the Lord. *Succina cantibus* is directed to confessor saints: Albinus in the Angers manuscript, Martial in Paris 1118, Aunarius in Paris 1338 and 9449.[11] I do not detect any further obvious links between the texts, *Laude canora* having a distinct flavor of its own, marked by words such as "gaudiflua," "celiflua," and "soliflua." The Winchester text is one of a relatively large number with no obvious liturgical destination, which the editors of *Analecta Liturgica* and *Analecta Hymnica* assigned simply to Sundays in general.

Liturgical Assignment

Laude canora is but one of many sequences in the Winchester collections whose liturgical assignment is unclear. These sequences are composed of conventional laudatory expressions of a general nature, which give no clue as to the particular feast day on which they might be sung. Such pieces are not uncommon in the early repertory as a whole, but the number of them at Winchester is relatively large. The editors of *Analecta Hymnica,* whose lead I have usually followed, classed no less than ten texts in *Ccc* and thirteen in *Ob* as being simply for Sundays. The manuscripts have no rubrics to help us, and there seems little alternative. Sequences for unspecified saints are also relatively numerous. There are four in *Ccc,* while *Ob* has four rubricated for martyrs or virgins and five unrubricated pieces which seem to fall into the same general category of the *Commune sanctorum.* Table 8 lists each text in manuscript order with liturgical assignments. I have given a tentative assignment in brackets where there is no help from a rubric in the sources, or from a specific reference in the text itself, or from the position of the sequence in the series.

Neither series follows the order of the church year consistently. I have placed dotted lines where some of the main divisions seem to fall. *Ccc* proceeds logically up to All Saints' Day. *Ecce pulchra* is usually an All Saints sequence, but in *Ccc* it is unexpectedly rubricked for St. Michael, out of

[11] Aunarius or Aunacarius was bishop of Auxerre (561–605?) with feast day on 25 September. He was brother of Austrenus, bishop of Orléans and uncle of Lupus, bishop of Sens.

Table 8

Liturgical assignment of sequence texts at Winchester

Ccc		Ob	
Celica resonant	Christmas (25/12)	Celica resonant	Christmas (25/12)
Gloriosa dies	Stephen (26/12)	Cloriosa dies	Stephen (26/12)
Oramus te	John Evang. (27/12)	Laus armonia	John Evang. (27/12)
Laus armonie	John Evang. (27/12)	Organicis canamus	John Evang. (27/12)
Pura deum	Innocents (28/12)	Pura deum	Innocents (28/12)
Nato canunt	Circumcision (1/1)	Nato canunt	Circumcision (1/1)
Epiphaniam domino	Epiphany (6/1)	Epiphaniam domino	Epiphany (6/1)
Claris vocibus	Purification (2/2)	Claris vocibus	Purification (2/2)
Fulgens preclara	Easter	Fulgens preclara	Easter
Prome casta concio	Easter	Prome casta concio	Easter
Pange turma	Easter	Pange turma	Easter
Rex omnipotens	Ascension	Rex omnipotens	Ascension
Benedicta sit beata	Pentecost	Benedicta sit beata	Pentecost
Exulta celum	John Bapt. (24/6)	Alle caeleste	Annunciation (25/3)
Alle caeleste	Annunciation (25/3)	Exulta celum	John Bapt. (24/6)
Sanctus Petrus	Peter and Paul (29/6)	Agmina letra	Peter and Paul (29/6)
Agmina leta	Peter and Paul (29/6)	Sanctus Patrus	Peter and Paul (29/6)
Laude iocunda	Peter and Paul (29/6)	Laude iocunda	Peter and Paul (29/6)
Arce superna	Benedict (Tr. 11/7)		
Aureo flore	Assumption (15/8)	Aureo flore	Assumption (15/8)
Hac clara die turma	Assumption (15/8)	Hac clara die turma	Assumption (15/8)
Salve porta	Nativity (8/9)	Salve porta	Nativity (8/9)
Candida contio	Germanus (1/10)	Candida contio	Germanus (1/10)
Gaudet clemens	All Saints (1/11)	Gaudet clemens	All Saints (1/11)
Alme caelorum	All Saints (1/11)	Alme caelorum	All Saints (1/11)
		Promere chorda	Martin (11/11)
Ecce pulchra	Michael (29/9)	Caelum mare tellus	Birinus (3/12, Tr. 4/9)
Fulget dies	Iustus (10/11)	Laurea clara	Lawrence (10/8)
		Mirabilis deus	Martyrs
Ave pontifex Haedde	Confessors (Haedda 7/7)	Arguta plectro	Martyrs
Mirabilis deus	Martyrs	Laudem dicite	(Martyrs)
Arguta plectro	Martyrs	Lira pulchra	(All Saints?)
Alme Hiesu	Virgins	Ecce pulchra	(All Saints? Michael?)
		Cantent te Christe	(Confessors)
		Aule rutile micantem	Augustine (26/5)
		Laude celebret	Ethelwold (1/8, Tr. 10/9)
		Arce superna	Benedict (21/3, Tr. 11/7)
		Deo promat	Virgins
Precamur nostras	Advent	Precamur nostras	Advent
Salus aeterna	Advent	Salus aeterna	Advent
Regnantem sempiterna	Advent	Regnantem sempiterna	Advent

Qui regis sceptra	Advent
Nostra tuba nunc tua	(Christmas)
Christicolarum	(Sunday)
Caelum mare tellus	Birinus (3/12, Tr. 4/9)
Promere chorda	Martin (11/11)
Laude canora	(Sunday)
Laudent condita	(Sunday)
Alma chorus domini	(Sunday)
Gloria resonante	(Sunday)
Laude resonet	Birinus and Swithun (2/7)
Stans a longe	(Sunday)
Consona caterva	(Sunday)
Aule celestis micantem	Augustine (26/5)
Laus inclita	(Sunday)
Laus surgat	Holy Cross (3/5, 14/9)
Laude pulchra	(Sunday)
Aulae plebs ethereae	(Sunday)

Qui regis sceptra	Advent
Nostra tuba nunc tua	Christmas
Laude canora	(Sunday)
Alma chorus domini	(Sunday)
Stans a longe	(Sunday)
Christicolarum	(Sunday)
Gaudeat fidelis plebs	Holy Cross (3/5, 14/9)
Gloria resonante	(Sunday)
Laudent condita	(Sunday)
Omnes sancti	(All Saints)
Consona caterva	(Sunday)
Ad te pulchra	(Sunday)
Aule celse lux summa	(Sunday)
Angelice turme	(Sunday)
Arce summa	(Sunday)
Laude Christum	Virgins
Scalam ad celos	Virgins
Plangant filii	(Sunday)
Exultate deo	(Sunday)
Salve mater Christi	BMV
Exulta celum (again)	John Bapt.
Laudes . . .	All Saints

calendric order. Restoring it to All Saints only prolongs the calendric order of the series as far as St. Iustus, whereupon there follow four sequences for the *Commune.* (*Ave pontifex* is rubricked for confessors but contains Haedda's name; almost any other saint's name could be substituted, for the text is couched in quite anonymous terms.) The four well-known Advent sequences are then followed by a miscellany of Sunday sequences and items from the Sanctorale.

Ob is calendric up to Birinus, whereupon Lawrence starts a miscellaneous group of Sunday and saints' items. As in *Ccc*, nothing after the Advent group seems to be liturgically ordered.

Perhaps upon further reflection a few more instances of logical succession in these series may become clear. The order in which the melodies are recorded must also be taken into account, for this does not always correspond to the order of the texts using those melodies. The differences between the two sources must also be explained. Yet it seems unlikely that the impression of liturgical disorder will be effaced to any large degree. Apparently we have to do with a large number of local, newly composed texts, deliberately couched in general terms to make them suitable for a variety of feast days. This runs somewhat counter to the oft-remarked tendency of medieval chant texts, to make the liturgies of important feast days more specific, topical.

Let us recollect that a sequence melody is made proper to a particular feast by its text. Some melodies are strongly associated with a particular feast, so that several texts composed for it will all treat the same theme, at least texts composed in the same area of Europe. Yet just as noticeable are the cases where a melody, through its text, becomes assigned to quite different occasions. Crocker has rightly drawn attention to the almost constant dissonance in this respect between West Frankish and East Frankish assignments. And we can see an instance of it here, where the texts for the melody known as *Hieronyma* or *Frigdola* are *Nunc exultet* and *Laudes salvatori* for Easter in West and East Francia respectively, but *Arce superna* for St. Benedict at Winchester (melody no. 16 in table 2).

So melodies in themselves need not be associated with particular feasts. This is borne out by one of the earliest collections of sequence melodies, in Chartres 47. The 29 melodies appear at the end of the manuscript, after a series of Alleluias. They have no texts in this source; and try as one may to find texts which would suggest a possible liturgical order for these melodies, nothing adds up.

Chartres 47 is not the only early collection of melodies alone: Angers 144 and Cambrai 75 are two others. Of course, the absence of texts in such sources is not conclusive—the texts may simply have been copied on other leaves, now lost—but we do know that at Cluny sequences were sung without texts except on the highest feasts of the year.[12]

I believe, therefore, that we should reckon with the possibility that the singers in some churches, perhaps peripheral ones, but perhaps not, knew and performed sequence melodies without text, making individual decisions about their liturgical assignment. The impulse toward liturgical fixity would have come primarily from the texts.

In fixing the text, one was at the same time fixing the shape of the melody, hence the tendency of later texts for that melody to observe the same syllable sound and even syllable grouping. Could we therefore understand the opposite phenomenon, the fact that some melodies take on different shapes in different areas of Europe, as evidence that these melodies were at one time transmitted independently of a text, with correspondingly greater freedom to respond to local musical taste?

The Winchester sequence collections suggest to me a repertory composed partly of well-established melodies and texts with a fixed place in the church year, and partly of melodies without standard texts, melodies traditionally available in a sort of pool for deployment in the church year as deemed appropriate. It seems possible to me that this pool might once have included many of the other melodies as well, before their assignment became fixed. The different versions of the better-known melodies which we find in different parts of Europe might be explained as the result of adaptation for new texts; yet to me the possibility seems equally plausible that those different forms arose during a period of oral, textless transmission.

To hypothesize about the early history of the sequence on the basis of late tenth-century sources is obviously somewhat tendentious (though this is precisely what we are obliged to do with important Aquitainian sources such as Paris 1084 and 1118). But the Winchester repertory is large, and from an area of Europe otherwise poorly represented by early sequence sources. (Many elements of the Winchester liturgy reproduce Northern French use, more specifically that of Corbie and related monasteries.[13]

[12] See my papers "The Sequentiary of Chartres, Bibl. Municipale, ms. 47," in *La Sequenza medievale: Atti del Convegno internazionale sulla sequenza, Milano, 7–8 aprile 1984*, ed. A. Ziino and S. Malgarini (Lucca: Libreria musicale italiana, 1992); and "The Sequences Sung at Cluny and Elsewhere," in *De Musica et Cantu: Studien zur Geschichte der Kirchenmusik und der Oper: Helmut Hucke zum 60. Geburtstag*, Musikwissenschaftliche Publikationen, Hochschule für Musik und Darstellende Kunst 2, ed. Peter Cahn and Ann-Katrin Heimer (Hildesheim: Olms, 1993); also "Cluny, Sequences and Tropes," in *La tradizione dei tropi liturgici*, ed. C. Leonardi and E. Menesto (Spoleto: Centro italiano di studi sull'alto medioevo, 1990), 125–38.

[13] Out of what is by now a fairly extensive literature I cite here only three recent studies which impinge upon Winchester's continental affiliations, with references to previous research. David Hiley, "Thurstan of Caen and plainchant at Glastonbury: Musicological Reflections on

There seems little reason to suppose that its sequence repertory would not follow this pattern.) Since only about two dozen sequentiaries altogether can be dated to the first millenium or the first two decades of the eleventh century, there is every reason for adding the evidence of the Winchester repertory to our consideration of the early medieval sequence. The Winchester poet-musicians appear to follow their melodic models closely, where these can be identified. To establish triangular comparisons between St. Gall, Winchester, and Aquitaine can illuminate all three repertories; and what we can learn about Winchester may help us understand what was happening at churches for which the evidence is not as plentiful.

the Norman Conquest," *Proceedings of the British Academy* 72 (1986): 57–90; Susan Rankin, "Neumatic Notations in Anglo-Saxon England," in *Musicologie médiévale: Notations et séquences*, ed. Michel Huglo (Paris: Champion, 1987), 129–44; K. D. Hartzell, "An Eleventh-Century English Missal Fragment in the British Library," *Anglo-Saxon England* 18 (1989): 45–97.

MICHEL HUGLO

The Origin of the Monodic Chants in the Codex Calixtinus

The Codex Calixtinus, preserved at Santiago de Compostela, is the only witness to the full monophonic and polyphonic musical repertory composed in celebration of St. James that contains musical notation. The other manuscripts of this office which are known to us are either partial copies or texts without any musical notation. Although these compositions have been published several times as a whole or in part, they still present many unsolved questions. It is consequently in the context of multi-disciplinary research that musicological analyses, based on codicology and iconography, have had the greatest chance of moving forward.

The compositions with musical notation in the Codex Calixtinus may be divided into three different categories. First, the Gregorian compositions, that is the antiphons, responsories, and hymns, together with psalms and lections, formed the framework of the canonical office and have a clear liturgical function. Second, the post-Gregorian compositions were grafted on to the preceding material, as if to gloss it, either by introducing individual chants or to conclude the hours of the office. These are the tropes for the ordinary of the mass, the tropes introducing the Introit, those for the *Benedicamus Domino*, at the end of vespers, and lastly the processional *versus* and the *conductus*. The function of these supplementary pieces is not always clearly defined: they were not essential for the celebration of an office. They were sung in some churches, while in others, notably at Cluny and at St. Denis, they were almost completely unknown. The third category is that of polyphonic compositions, namely liturgical compositions sung by two voices, the *cantus* or *vox principalis* and the second voice, the improvised *organum:* this improvisation according to well-defined rules was later fixed by being written down.

Whichever category each of the different compositions belongs to, the musical notation which accompanies it remains identical throughout the Codex Calixtinus. The melodies of the chant are notated on a set of four lines, ruled separately in red ink without the use of a rastrum. The notes and note groups or neumes are square-shaped neither when separate nor when combined, as was the practice in Northern France and in Italy from the mid-twelfth century. Instead the notation was drawn with a pen, so that the horizontal stroke of the neume could be fine and undulating, as seen in example 1:

Example 1

Musical notation in the Codex Calixtinus

Such neume forms were chiefly used in the region of "Lorraine notation" or "Metz notation," in one of the four branches of the Cistercian Order depending on the Abbey of Morimond; but they were also used, with some variations, along the "route des foires," that is, in the regions which linked Lorraine with the valley of the Loire, notably at St. Laurent-de-Longré, Troyes, St. Florentin, and further at Auxerre, Vézelay, and Nevers. Finally, one manuscript of Montier-en-Der contains an unedited *Conductus ad lectionem* for the feast of St. James (given as an appendix to the present article).

It is at Nevers that the notation is closest to that of the Calixtinus, as Peter Wagner remarked. In examining this similarity we must begin with the *custos*, which at the end of each line indicates the pitch of the following note at the start of the next line. Use of a such a sign was widespread in Italy and southern France, but it is almost unknown in northern France. It is only found in manuscripts from Nevers and, a little further south, in those of

Lyons. Paris did not use the *custos* until the end of the thirteenth century, and probably adopted it in imitation of Dominican practice since 1255.

One piece in the Calixtinus uses the system of notation of the Midi, namely a non-liturgical pilgrimage song on the last page; but this is the only instance of such notation. The use of non-Aquitainian notation in the remainder of the Calixtinus is most remarkable, for the sole notation adopted in Spain after the suppression of Mozarabic chant was precisely this Aquitainian notation from the south of France.

Gregorian Compositions

This category includes the group of antiphons and responsories of the canonical office, and masses in honor of St. James.

The compositions for the office are chiefly composed in rhythmical prose and in the order of the eight tones of Gregorian chant, following a procedure which was first used by Hucbald and Stephen of Liège at the beginning of the tenth century: the first antiphon and responsory use the first tone, the second antiphon and responsory use the second tone, and so on. This continues until the eighth composition for the eight tones, and then the sequence begins again with the first tone or any tone.

The office of St. James is characterized more by its use of the monastic scheme of twelve antiphons and twelve responsories, and not the canonical scheme of nine antiphons and nine responsories. This distinctive liturgical practice can be explained in two ways: either the office was composed by monks working for their Galician colleagues, a hypothesis which assumes that there was a monastery at the apostle's shrine, or the office was copied from a monastic model, and it was left to the recipients to reduce it so as to fit into the canonical scheme. This happened on other occasions during the Middle Ages when proper offices were created.

It is important to recognize that there were secular offices for St. James, with nine responsories, in existence at this time, notably at Angers, and that the canons of St. James could easily have procured such an office if necessary. The compiler of Book I of the Codex Calixtinus therefore knew what he was doing when he copied a monastic office!

The texts of the antiphons and responsories for this office are taken from the Bible or from the *Passio major* of St. James. Those which we regard as "ecclesiastical compositions" because the authors are unknown, are attributed to Pope Calixtus. But it is worth noting that the authority of the name of Calixtus conceals borrowings from other offices: thus responsory VIII, *Misit Herodes*, takes its text and melody from a response for the Beheading of St. John the Baptist. Further, the antiphon for the Magnificat of the Vespers, *Ad sepulchrum beati Jacobi*, is a simple transformation of the office of St. Germanus of Auxerre, a cathedral close to Vézelay.

The melody for the responsories is sometimes the standard flexible melody which could be applied to any new text, and sometimes a new melodic composition in the style of the responsories for Mary Magdalen, which were unique to Vézelay. This should not surprise us, for her feast, the 22nd of July, was two days before the first vespers for St. James, the 24th of July.

According to medieval rule, one polyphonic responsory was sung at the end of vespers and at the end of each nocturn. This is what happens in the Calixtinus for the responsory for the vespers *Dum esset;* the three other responsories for two voices are concentrated on the third nocturn and are sung after lessons IX, XI and XII, which are taken from a homily on the Gospel ascribed to Bede. In passing, let us recall that Bede's homily was still read at Vézelay in the fifteenth century.

The Mass Proper

The *Epistola beati Calixti*, at the beginning of the Calixtinus, points to a great variety of practices in the choice of the repertory adopted for the feast of St. James. This variety, which is confirmed by an analysis of the graduals and missals, enabled the compiler of the *Liber sancti Jacobi* to present a new mass proper, where the texts were adapted to fit preexisting melodies from the Gregorian gradual.

In 1173 a monk of Ripoll, Arnaud du Mont, came to Compostela to transcribe the *Missa sancti Jacobi;* but he transposed its French notation into the Aquitainian notation which was widespread throughout Spain at that time. He also left out the name of the "composer," Calixtus, for the first two Alleluias. If we compare the melodies in the Calixtinus with those in the Ripoll copy, as Peter Wagner has shown, we discover a large number of melodic variants; but since we do not know what the melodic version of the models for the music of the Ripoll *Missa sancti Jacobi* were, it is particularly difficult to judge what was going on.

Post-Carolingian Compositions

The tropes, sequences, and *conductus* found in the Calixtinus deserve a full-length study in their own right. Let us look at a few pieces so as to try to approach the sources from which they derive.

The Introit for the mass is preceded by an introductory trope, *Ecce adest nunc Jacobus;* this trope, at least at the beginning, is a plagiarism of the Christmas trope *Ecce adest de quo prophetae,* which was widespread in Germany and Aquitaine, and in use at Nevers.

The tropes of the Kyrie, Gloria, and Sanctus are adapted from very common melodies: the Hosanna of the Sanctus trope is a text found in Catalonia and at Moissac, while the Agnus dei trope *Qui pius ac mitis* is only known from a single source, the gradual of St. Cyran-en-Braine, close to Vézelay.

The compiler of this liturgical assemblage chose wisely from the important production of Paris, Aquitaine, and Burgundy for his selection of sequences and *conductus.* But why did he select three *conductus ad lectionem,* rather than a different one, such as the *conductus Columnarum trium* transcribed in the manuscript of Paris, which draws directly on the New Testament? We cannot explain this. Perhaps the answer is that, faced with the reluctance of monasteries of the Order of Cluny, north of the Loire, to write in the style of the post-Gregorian compositions, the compiler was forced to look at the repertoires of the Limousin and of Aquitaine—at Ste. Foy-de-Conques and especially at Moissac—so as to select pieces most fitting to honor the apostle.

The Polyphonic Compositions

The songs for two voices in the Codex Calixtinus, though they are transcribed after the "Pilgrims' Guide" in Book V, are directly related to the liturgical pieces in Book I, as we have already established in the account of the responsories. At the Pittsburgh Symposium Hendrik Van der Werf showed that the melodic make-up of the third Alleluia *Vocavit Jesus* implied a simultaneous composition for the *vox principalis* and the second voice.

We should also note that the counterpoint for the *conductus Congaudeant catholici* was added by a second hand at the same pitch as the *vox principalis.* This piece is attributed to the cantor of Notre Dame, Albert of Étampes, because this kind of composition for three voices seems to have been first introduced at Notre-Dame in Paris, around 1170. The name Magister Albertus Parisiensis is also written by the second hand; but this is not as clearly an addition as are the others, which are positioned between the lines or invade the space reserved for musical notation. This cantor, who directed the choir of the Cathedral of Paris for thirty-five years, had taken part in the coronation of Louis VII and of Queen Adele at Paris in 1161.

Most of the other names, apart from that of Calixtus II who had been Guy de Bourgogne before he was made Pope, are Burgundian in origin, and can be dated between 1123 and 1174. Table 1 shows a chronological list of composers.

In its present form the Codex Calixtinus cannot predate 1150 or post-date 1180. It copies a collection of five different books all treating of St. James, his miracles, his legend, his cult, and his pilgrimage, and this is why it has been called the *Liber sancti Jacobi.* The oldest copy of this collection, the Codex Calixtinus, enables scholars to track down the sources and to date the different parts, insofar as the anonymous compiler has not overly obscured the traces of their origins.

Book I, a full liturgical collection to honor the apostle, might well have been commissioned by the monks who served the basilica before the transfer of the episcopal seat from Iria to Compostela. The possibility that the office and the mass were composed at Vézelay should not surprise us if we study the importance of that abbey situated in the county of Nevers, at the beginning of the twelfth century. Not far from the abbey church stood the pilgrims' church, for those pilgrims who wanted to come and worship at the shrine of Mary Magdalen before leaving south for Spain. At the foot of the hill at Vézelay the church of St. James d'Asquins served as an assembly point for pilgrims departing for Compostela.

The Codex Calixtinus shows no traces that it was used, as Diaz y Diaz's close examination has shown, but we should not infer from that conclusion that the *Liber sancti Jacobi* was never used for worship: the frequent rubrics which give details of how the chants were to be performed imply just the opposite.

It is very likely that by 1173 the mass of the Calixtinus alone was celebrated in the presence of pilgrims as the *Epistola beati Calixti papae* prescribes. According to Alejandro Planchart, the same mass as that for the feast of St. James in the Calixtinus on the 25th of July is transcribed in the fifteenth century missal from St. Jacques-la-Boucherie in Paris, the Parisian church where the pilgrims assembled to walk to Compostela. This mass of

Table 1

The "Compositors" of the Polyphonic Songs in the Calixtinus

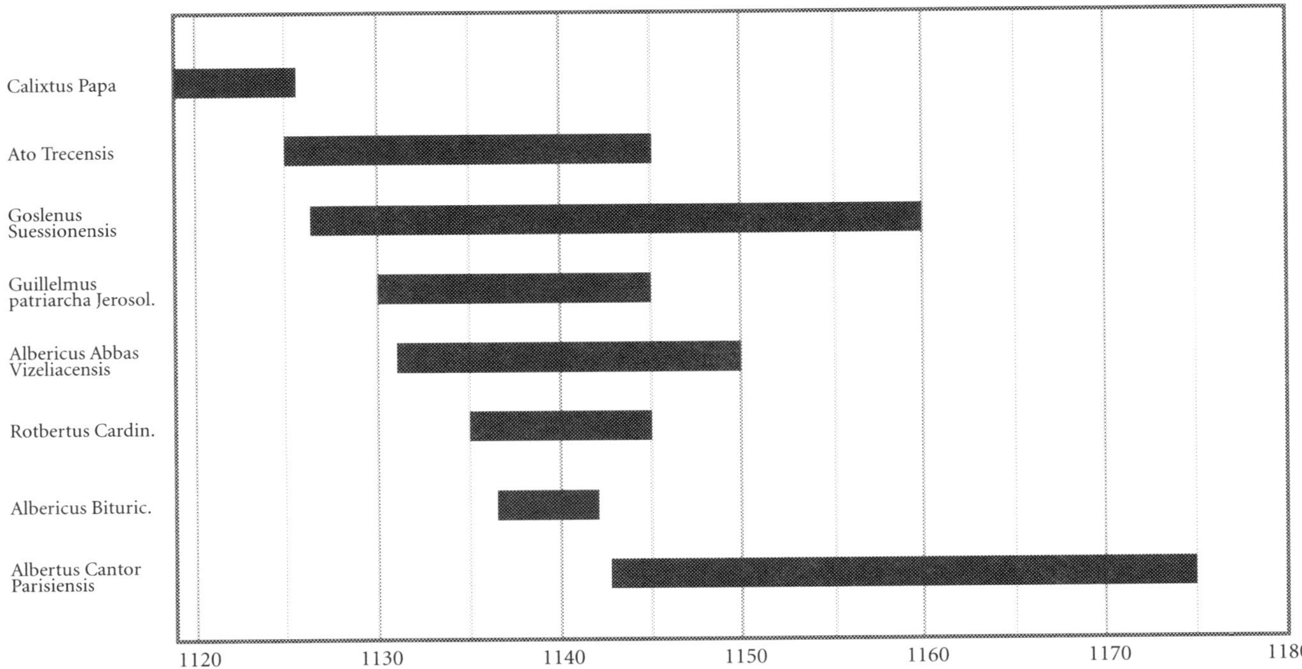

St. James includes one Tractus instead of the Alleluia, in case pilgrimages were made during Lent.

But in the same century, the monastic office of the Calixtinus was already disappearing. In 1494 the Austrian pilgrim Hieronymus Münzer quoted in his journal liturgical compositions which at that time were still current in the Breviaries of Compostela, in manuscript or printed versions. He was shown the Jacobus which contained "all that is needed for lections and chants for feast days."

In fact by that date, polyphony from Notre-Dame had already penetrated as far as Toledo and the *ars nova* was no longer practiced in Aragon, while tropes, *versus*, and *conductus* disappeared before they could enter the fourteenth century.

Nevertheless, the relations between Compostela and Vézelay remained very strong for the next three or four centuries: they even celebrated the dedication of their churches on the same date, the 21st of April. That may not at first seem very important, but I would like to give you another example.

In our own times, the abbey of Solesmes founded Quarr Abbey in England, Oosterhout in Holland, and Clervaux in Luxembourg, and these three foundations all use for the date of their dedications that of Solesmes.

Thus, the use of the same date by Compostela and Vézelay for the dedication of their churches may strongly suggest that the first monks at Compostela considered their community to have been founded by Vézelay.

Appendix A
[*Conductus ad lectionem*]
after Paris, B.N. lat. 2096, fol. 92v.

1. Columnarum trium   Jacobe media
   Quibus Christus Jesus   insigni gratia.

2. In montis vertice   dat testimonia
   Legis et gratiae   verba fidelia.

3. Quod luce claruit   in regni gloria
   Fulgebunt sicut sol   sanctorum millia.

4. In urbe pateris   qua Christus passus est
   Sed vide longius   triumphus datus est.

5. Te sol dum oritur   vidit occumbere
   Et idem occidens   audit astruere.

6. Dum cernit undique   gentes confluere
   A summo cardine   nubes convehere.

7. Quod in occidue   valeant pluere
   Cum nemo Jacobi   nesciat gratiam.

8. Et contra demones   eius potentiam
   Adferte domino   adferte gloriam.

9. Qui dicit canticum   ducat laetitiam
   Qui festum celebrat   pellat inertiam.

10. Jam LECTOR incipe   sancti notitiam
    Pandere populis   per dei gratiam.

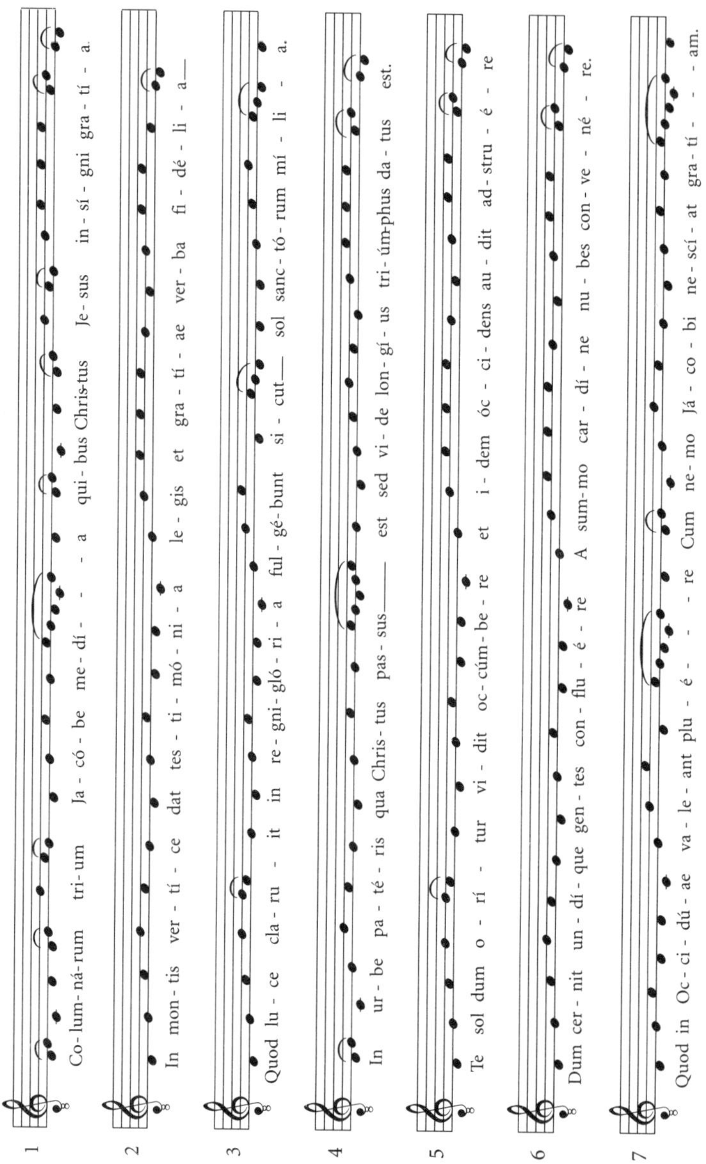
1 Co - lum - ná - rum tri - um Ja - có - be me - dí - - - a qui - bus Chris-tus Je - sus in - sí - gni gra - tí - a.
2 In mon - tis ver - tí - ce dat tes - ti - mó - ni - a le - gis et gra - tí - ae ver - ba fi - dé - li - a
3 Quod lu - ce cla - ru - it in re - gni - gló - ri - a ful - gé - bunt si - cut sol sanc - tó - rum mí - li - a.
4 In ur - be pa - té - ris qua Chris - tus pas - sus est sed vi - de lon - gí - us tri - úm-phus da - tus est.
5 Te sol dum o - rí - tur vi - dit oc - cúm - be - re et i - dem óc - ci - dens au - dit ad - stru - é - re
6 Dum cer - nit un - dí - que gen - tes con - flu - é - re A sum - mo car - dí - ne nu - bes con - ve - né - re.
7 Quod in Oc - ci - dú - ae va - le - ant plu - é - re Cum ne - mo Já - co - bi ne - scí - at gra - tí - am.

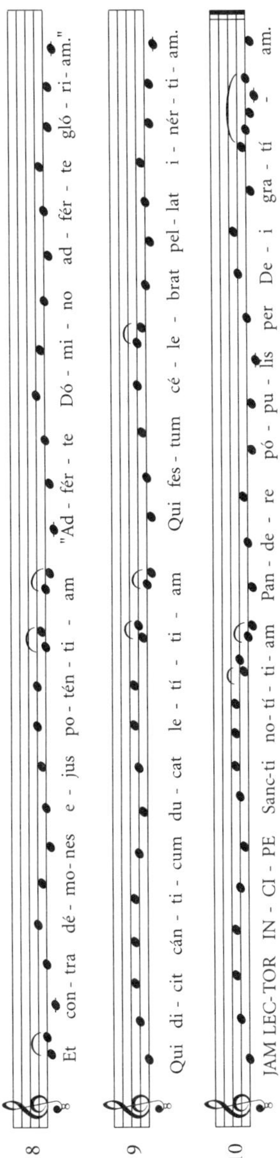

Appendix B: Melody for *Conductus ad lectionem*, after Paris, B.N. lat. 2096, fol. 92v.

PETER JEFFERY

Rome and Jerusalem: From Oral Tradition to Written Repertory in Two Ancient Liturgical Centers[*]

In the early medieval period, Jerusalem and Rome had much in common. Both were important administrative centers in the early Church, the sees of powerful bishops who could trace their authority back to the apostles. Both were visited constantly by pilgrims from all over the Christian world, eager to see and worship in (what were said to be) the actual places where many New Testament figures had lived and died. Both were surrounded by monasteries, many of them populated with those who had come as pilgrims but decided to stay. Both cities had impressive liturgical traditions, in which the bishop and clergy, the monks, the pilgrims, and the ordinary residents all took part, celebrating in all the different churches and holy places of the city successively, over the course of the liturgical year, to commemorate the awesome events that had taken place there.[1]

*Much of the research leading to this paper was supported by a Mellon Faculty Fellowship at Harvard University during the academic year 1982–83. I am grateful to Prof. David Hughes for his interest and support during that period.

[1] See John Francis Baldovin, *The Urban Character of Christian Worship: The Origins, Development, and Meaning of Stational Liturgy*, Orientalia Christiana Analecta 228 (Rome: Pont. Institutum Studiorum Orientalium, 1987).

Only when we seek to recover the musical history of these two cities do they begin to look dissimilar, indeed almost like opposites. From the city of Rome we have two fully-preserved liturgical chant traditions, the "Gregorian" and the "Old Roman," textually very similar but melodically more distantly related. Yet we know scarcely anything about the processes by which these two traditions were formed, and thus we cannot say how they are related or why they are not identical. From Jerusalem, on the other hand, we have no notated sources at all for most of the chant repertory.[2] Yet we have many textual sources dating from the early fifth century to the late tenth, amply documenting the historical processes by which this repertory was formed. We can thus say a great deal about how and when the texts of the Jerusalem chant repertory first passed from oral into written form, how they came to be assigned to specific services and feasts, and how the written chant collections grew and evolved over the course of more than half a millenium, stretching from the fourth to the eleventh centuries—the very period from which we have so little information about the development of chant in Rome.

The purpose of the present paper, then, is to see what could perhaps be learned from a hypothetical comparison of the two cities. Could we somehow put them together—the city with much recorded history but little music, and the city with much extant music but little recorded history—to form a more nearly complete, though hypothetical, picture of the emergence of medieval chant? Could the known history of the formation of the Jerusalem chant tradition help us reconstruct the unknown history of the formation of the Roman chant traditions? The answer is a qualified "yes." The early history of Jerusalem chant provides us with a unique model of the processes by which early Christian chant repertories developed, and the chronological stages through which this development unfolded. If we cautiously attempt to use the history of Jerusalem chant as a kind of template, and line up the very meager bits of Roman evidence around it, we will find that much of it falls into place quite naturally and meaningfully, although the fit is by no means perfect. To put it another way, what we know about the genesis of the Jerusalem chant tradition can help us determine where to look for comparable Roman evidence, and how to evaluate more objectively the rare bits of Roman evidence that we find. The result is a more firmly grounded and defensible picture of the genesis of Roman chant than has

[2] A partial exception is the Georgian *heirmologion*, preserved in tenth-century manuscripts. See my article: "The Earliest Christian Chant Repertory Recovered: The Georgian Witnesses to Jerusalem Chant," *Journal of the American Musicological Society* 47 (1994): 1–38.

ever been possible before, leading to a clearer recognition of where the remaining gaps are and what will be needed to fill them.

The history of the Jerusalem chant tradition can be divided into at least four developmental stages. To compare Jerusalem with Rome, we must proceed by looking for a Roman counterpart to each stage. Four tables summarizing important events and sources for each stage are located at the end of the article (pages 243–47).

Annual Cycles of Responsorial Psalms (Graduals) are Formed. Fifth Century (table 1, page 243)

Sermons[3] and pilgrim accounts[4] from late fourth-century Jerusalem already attest to the practice of singing responsorial psalms in conjunction with the readings from the Bible. At some time between 417 and 439 A.D., a complete cycle of readings, *prokeimena* (equivalent to Western graduals) and alleluias for all the feasts of the Jerusalem liturgical year, was written down in a type of liturgical book known as a *lectionary.* Though the original Greek text no longer survives, its contents are preserved in Armenian translation, in the oldest manuscript lectionaries of the Armenian Orthodox Church, which adopted the rite of Jerusalem as the basis of its own.[5]

Can we find evidence of a comparable development in Rome? Partially. The Eastern practice of singing responsorial psalmody appears to have been brought to Milan from the East about the year 386, and to have spread

[3] A most important source of information about the fourth-century liturgy of Jerusalem is the corpus of sermons by Cyril, who was bishop from about 349 to his death in 387. See, for example, Sebastià Janeras, "A propos de la catéchèse XIVe de Cyrille de Jérusalem," *Ecclesia Orans* 3 (1986): 307–18. See also my article "The Sunday Office of Seventh-Century Jerusalem in the Georgian Chantbook (Iadgari): A Preliminary Report," *Studia Liturgica* 21 (1991): 52–75. The use of sermons by Cyril and others for evidence about early Christian psalmody will be fully explained in my forthcoming book, *Prophecy Mixed With Melody: From Early Christian Psalmody to Gregorian Chant.*

[4] The most important pilgrim account is that of Egeria, a Latin-speaking woman who described the entire Jerusalem liturgical year as she witnessed it in 383. The most recent edition is *Égérie: Journal de voyage (Itinéraire),* ed. Pierre Maraval, Sources chrétiennes 296 (Paris: Éditions du Cerf, 1982). The best English translation with commentary is John Wilkinson, *Egeria's Travels to the Holy Land,* rev. ed. (Jerusalem: Ariel, 1981).

[5] The Armenian Lectionary is edited in Athanase Renoux, ed., *Le codex arménien Jérusalem 121,* 2 vols., Patrologia Orientalis 35/1 and 36/2 (Turnhout: Brepols, 1969, 1971). On the date and the manuscripts see especially 35/1:169–81 and 36/2:170–72. Many of the sources of the Jerusalem rite are listed and described in Charles Renoux, "Hierosolymitana: Aperçu bibliographique des publications depuis 1960," *Archiv für Liturgiewissenschaft* 23 (1981): 1–29, 149–75.

through much of the West within a generation. It seems to have been introduced into the Roman Mass by Pope Celestine I (422–32), who had been at Milan as a younger man.[6] It certainly was at Rome by the mid-fifth century, for it is mentioned in sermons of Pope Leo the Great (reigned 440–61),[7] and apparently also in the psalm commentary of Arnobius the Younger, a significant but underutilized source of evidence bearing on the fifth-century Roman liturgy.[8] On the other hand, Rome seems never to have had a full annual cycle of alleluias before the seventh century; like the other Western rites we know of, it seems originally to have made use of a very limited alleluia repertory, which may originally have been restricted largely to the Easter season.[9] The expansion of the Roman alleluia repertory to the rest of the year seems to have continued through the seventh and eighth centuries. The relatively late origin of many of these pieces is doubtless the reason that, in many early manuscripts of the Gregorian *graduale*, many alleluias are

[6] Peter Jeffery, "The Introduction of Psalmody into the Roman Mass by Pope Celestine I (422–432): Reinterpreting a Passage in the *Liber Pontificalis*," *Archiv für Liturgiewissenschaft* 26 (1984): 147–65.

[7] Leo describes the congregational singing of Ps. 109:4 (apparently as a responsorial refrain to Ps. 109) in two sermons he delivered on 29 September, the anniversary of his episcopal consecration: "Vnde et dauiticum psalmum, dilectissimi, non ad nostram elationem sed ad Christi Domini gloriam consona uoce cantauimus," and "totius Ecclesiae et omnium sacerdotum ore cantatur: 'Iurauit Dominus et non paenitebit eum: Tu es sacerdos in aeternum secundum ordinem Melchisedech.'" See *Sancti Leonis Magni Romani Pontificis Tractatus septem et nonaginta*, ed. Antoine Chavasse, Corpus Christianorum, Series Latina 138 (Turnhout: Brepols, 1973), 10, 23. A gradual with this refrain is used in the Gregorian and Old Roman chant repertories for feasts of popes. Less certain is Leo's reference to Ps. 21 in a sermon delivered on Passion Sunday in 454, though this psalm is the source of the tract *Deus Deus meus* assigned to this day in the Gregorian and Old Roman repertories (see ibid., 138A:408). In this article all psalms are cited according to the Latin Vulgate numbering. For more information on the use of sermon evidence, see my forthcoming book cited in n. 3 above.

[8] The new edition of Arnobius's *Commentarii in Psalmos*, ed. Klaus-Detlef Daur has just appeared in Corpus Christianorum, Series Latina 25 (Turnhout: Brepols, 1990). See Germain Morin, "Étude d'ensemble sur Arnobe le jeune," *Revue bénédictine* 28 (1911): 154–90, esp. 175–76. Angelo di Berardino, ed., *Patrology* 4: *The Golden Age of Latin Patristic Literature from the Council of Nicea to the Council of Chalcedon*, trans. Placid Solari (Westminster, Md.: Christian Classics, 1988), 567–69. Rosalba A. Rallo Freni, "Arnobio il Giovane fonte di Cassiodoro?" in *Flavio Magno Aurelio Cassiodoro (Cosenza-Squillace 19–24 settembre 1983): Atti della settimana di studi*, ed. Sandro Leanza (Soveria Mannelli [Cosenza]: Rubbettino, 1986), 421–33.

[9] See Terence Bailey, *The Ambrosian Alleluias* (Egham, Surrey: Plainsong & Mediaeval Music Society, 1983), 1–20; Thomas Forrest Kelly, *The Beneventan Chant* (Cambridge: Cambridge University Press, 1989), 76–77, 119–24; Peter Wagner, *Gregorianische Formenlehre: Eine choralische Stilkunde*, Einführung in die gregorianischen Melodien 3 (Leipzig, 1921; repr. Hildesheim: Olms, 1962), 397–417; Karl-Heinz Schlager, *Thematischer Katalog der ältesten Alleluia Melodien aus Handschriften des 10. und 11. Jahrhunderts, ausgenommen das ambrosianische, alt-römische und alt-spanische Repertoire*, Erlanger Arbeiten zur Musikwissenschaft 2 (Munich: Ricke, 1965), 1–9; Jean Claire and André Madrignac, "Les formules centons des *Alleluia* anciens," *Études grégoriennes* 20 (1981): 3–4 plus twelve unnumbered pp. of charts, and *Études grégoriennes* 21 (1986): 27–[45].

grouped together in an appendix at the end, instead of being assigned to specific feasts and distributed throughout the year, like the (apparently earlier) chants belonging to other genres.[10]

But if Rome had at least responsorial psalmody by about the year 450, when did it develop a complete annual cycle, fixed in writing like the one in the Jerusalem lectionary of 417–39? Probably this process operated somewhat differently than at Jerusalem, for Rome seems never to have used a book comparable to the Jerusalem lectionary. Lectionaries containing readings and responsorial psalms were used in the sixth-century Gallican church,[11] and part of one survives among the mysterious Latin liturgical fragments preserved on Mt. Sinai.[12] The Gallican fragments include respon-

[10] Egon Wellesz, "Gregory the Great's Letter on the *Alleluia*," *Annales musicologiques* 2 (1954): 7–26; Michel Huglo, "Les listes alléluiatiques dans les témoins du graduel grégorien," in *Speculum Musicae Artis: Festgabe für Heinrich Husmann zum 60. Geburtstag am 16. Dezember 1968, dargebracht von seinen Freunden und Schülern*, ed. Heinz Becker and Reinhard Gerlach (Munich: Fink, 1970), 219–27; Michel Huglo, *Les livres de chant liturgique*, Typologie des sources du moyen âge occidental 52 (Turnhout: Brepols, 1988), 104–05. On the origins of the alleluia more generally, see Aimé-George Martimort, "L'origine et signification de l'Alleluia de la messe romaine," in *Kyriakon: Festschrift Johannes Quasten*, ed. Patrick Granfield and Josef A. Jungmann (Münster: Aschendorff, 1970), 811–34, repr. in *Mens Concordet Voci: Pour Mgr. A. G. Martimort à l'occasion de ses quarante années d'enseignement et des vingt ans de la Constitution "Sacrosanctum Concilium"* (Paris: Desclée, 1983), 95–121; André Rose, "L'usage et la signification de l'Alleluia en Orient et en Occident," in *Gestes et paroles dans les diverses familles liturgiques: Conférence Saint-Serge, XXIVe semaine d'études liturgiques, Paris 28 juin–1 juillet 1977*, Bibliotheca «Ephemerides Liturgicae,» Subsidia 14 (Rome: Centro Liturgico Vincenziano, 1978), 205–33; James W. McKinnon, "The Patristic Jubilus and the Alleluia of the Mass," in *International Musicological Society Study Group Cantus Planus: Papers Read at the Third Meeting, Tihany, Hungary, 19–24 September 1988*, ed. Laszlo Dobszay et al. (Budapest: Hungarian Academy of Sciences, Institute for Musicology, 1990), 61–70.

[11] Alban Dold, ed., *Das älteste Liturgiebuch der lateinischen Kirche: Ein altgallikanisches Lektionar des 5./6. Jhs. aus dem Wolfenbüttler Palimpsest-Codex Weissenburgensis 76*, Texte und Arbeiten 26–28 (Beuron: Druck und Verlag der Kunstschule der Erzabtei Beuron, Hohenzollern, 1936), XCIV–XCVIII. It contains the refrains of responsorial psalms that were sung both between the epistle and the gospel (pp. 29, 38, 47, 51, 53, 54, 57, 58, 64), corresponding to the Gregorian graduals, but also the refrains of responsorial psalms sung after the gospel (pp. 10, 52, 57, 58), which may have corresponded to offertories, or perhaps to the Jerusalem handwashing chant and the Gallican/Ambrosian *antiphona post evangelium*. For evidence indicating the former existence of other similar books, see Cyrille Vogel, *Medieval Liturgy: An Introduction to the Sources*, NPM Studies in Church Music and Liturgy, trans. and rev. William G. Storey and Niels Krogh Rasmussen (Washington, D.C.: Pastoral Press, 1986), 303, 320–21, 393. Two reviews of the Vogel book were published by Peter Jeffery in *Worship* 62 (1988): 183–85 and by Victor Saxer in *Rivista di archeologia cristiana* 63 (1987): 387–407.

[12] Elias Avery Lowe, "Two New Latin Liturgical Fragments on Mount Sinai," *Revue bénédictine* 74 (1964): 252–83, esp. 280–83; Bonifatius Fischer, "Zur Liturgie der lateinischen Handschriften vom Sinai," ibid., 284–97; Elias Avery Lowe, "Two Other Unknown Latin Liturgical Fragments on Mount Sinai," *Scriptorium* 19 (1965): 3–29, esp. 10–13, 28–29. The Lowe articles are reprinted in Lowe, *Palaeographical Papers: 1907–1965*, ed. Ludwig Bieler (Oxford: Clarendon, 1972), 520–74. For two different views on the likely provenance of the fragments,

sorial refrains corresponding to the Roman graduals and perhaps also to the offertories, while the Mt. Sinai lectionary evidently contained graduals (before the epistles) and alleluias (before the gospels). But no such book survives from Rome itself. At Rome the epistles, the gospels, and the chants were each collected in separate books, reflecting the fact that each was the responsibility of a different liturgical minister. The earliest Roman manuscripts of the epistolary (used by the subdeacon) and evangeliary (used by the deacon) survive from the early eighth century, but represent seventh-century states of development.[13] The graduals, alleluias, and tracts were also collected into their own book, the *cantatorium* (used by the cantor). Though the existence of the *cantatorium* is attested in the early eighth century,[14] actual manuscripts of it survive only from the ninth century. This includes the famous *cantatorium* of Monza and its fragmentary "Schwesterhandschrift," once dated to the eighth century, but which Bernhard Bischoff has now redated to the second third of the ninth.[15]

At Rome, then, the first stage in the development of the chant repertory happened somewhat differently than at Jerusalem, and it also appears to have taken longer. Responsorial psalmody may have entered the Roman Mass only in the 420s under Pope Celestine I, by which time the repertory of the Jerusalem lectionary probably already existed. Because the epistles, gospels, and psalms of the Roman Mass were collected into independent books, rather than a single lectionary as at Jerusalem, the history of each

see Bernhard Bischoff, *Latin Palaeography: Antiquity and the Middle Ages*, trans. Dáibhí O'Cróinín and David Ganz (Cambridge: Cambridge University Press, 1990), 97–98, and Guy Dominique Sixdenier, "A propos de l'origine du psautier latin du Sinaï: Une piste?" *Scriptorium* 41 (1987): 129.

[13] See Vogel, *Medieval Liturgy*, 339–54; Antoine Chavasse, "L'Epistolier romain du Codex de Wurzbourg: Son organisation," *Revue bénédictine* 91 (1981): 280–331; idem, "L'évangéliaire de 645: Un recueil, sa composition (façons et matériaux)," ibid., 92 (1982): 33–75.

[14] This is in *Ordo Romanus* I, an early eighth-century description of the papal Mass (see Vogel, *Medieval Liturgy*, 155–60). The oldest form of the text states that after the epistle, "another person goes up [into the ambo] with the *cantatorium* and says the responsory" or gradual ("Deinde ascendit alius cum cantatorio, dicit responsum"); see Michel Andrieu, *Les Ordines Romani du haut moyen âge* 2, Spicilegium Sacrum Lovaniense 23 (Louvain: Spicilegium Sacrum Lovaniense, 1948), 86. No earlier use of the word "cantatorium" is recorded in *Mittellateinisches Wörterbuch bis zum ausgehenden 13. Jahrhundert* 2, fasc. 2, ed. Otto Prinz et al. (Munich: Beck, 1979), 187, 195.

[15] Peter Jeffery, "The Oldest Sources of the *Graduale:* A Checklist of MSS Copied Before About 900 AD," *Journal of Musicology* 2 (1983): 316–21. See also Huglo, *Les livres*, 94–100. Huglo's list of *cantatorium* manuscripts on p. 100 dates the Monza *cantatorium* to the early ninth century; Bischoff's dating to the mid-ninth century is given in Klaus Gamber, *Codices Liturgici Latini Antiquiores*, 2nd ed., Spicilegii Friburgensis Subsidia 1 (Freiburg, Switzerland: Universitätsverlag, 1968), 2:501. For the closely-related fragments, see Peter Siffrin, "Eine Schwesterhandschrift des Graduale von Monza," *Ephemerides Liturgicae* 64 (1950): 53–81.

collection has to be traced independently, because evidence relating to the origins and history of one book is of limited help for reconstructing the origins or history of the other books. In any case we cannot trace the Roman epistolary and evangeliary earlier than the seventh century, and we cannot trace the *cantatorium* earlier than the eighth.

The Core Chant Repertories are Completed and Written Down. Sixth to Eighth Centuries (table 2, page 244)

Over time the Jerusalem lectionary began to incorporate the texts, or at least the incipits, of other genres of chant, in addition to the graduals and alleluias that had always been part of it. These other genres included the introits of the Mass and of Vespers, and the handwashing chants, offertories, and communions of the Mass. This stage of development is preserved in the earliest lectionary manuscripts of the Georgian Orthodox church, which were translated from lost Greek texts representing the Jerusalem liturgy of the eighth century.[16] Already in the seventh century, however, perhaps even the sixth, someone had collected all these chant texts from the lectionary, supplemented them with the texts of the Office chants that had not been recorded in the lectionary, and produced a true chantbook, probably the first one ever created in any branch of Christendom. The original Greek of this book, too, is lost to us, for we have only the Georgian translation; as a result we do not know what its original Greek name was (in Georgian it is called *Iadgari*).[17] It contains not only the proper Mass and Office texts arranged in liturgical order, but identifies the modes to which many of their lost melodies belonged, the earliest substantial witness to the existence of the Oktoechos.[18]

To compare the second stage of the Jerusalem chant tradition to the Roman evidence is to ask two questions: (1) At what date can we first speak of

[16] Edited in Michel Tarchnischvili, *Le grand lectionnaire de l'église de Jérusalem (Ve–VIIIe siècles)*, 2 vols. in 4, Corpus Scriptorum Christianorum Orientalium 188–89, 204–05 (Louvain: Secrétariat du Corpus SCO, 1959–60).

[17] There are two editions: A. Šanije, A. Marṭirosov, A. J̌išiašvili, ed., *Çil-eṭraṭis Iadgari* [The Papyrus-Parchment Iadgari], Jveli kartuli enis jeglebi 15 (Tbilisi: Mecniereba, 1977); El. Meṭreveli, C. Çankieva, L. Xevsuriani, ed., *Ujvelesi Iadgari* [The Oldest Iadgari], Jveli kartuli mçerlobis jeglebi 2 (Tbilisi: Mecniereba, 1980).

[18] See Peter Jeffery, "The Sunday Office of Seventh-Century Jerusalem," 52–75, also "The Earliest Christian Chant Repertory Recovered."

an integral Roman repertory comparable to the *Iadgari*, and (2) by what process(es) was this repertory formed? These two questions must be dealt with separately.

The Date of the Roman/Gregorian Repertory

There are indications that at least the basic repertory of proper Mass chants already existed in the seventh century, and may thus be roughly contemporary with the *Iadgari* of Jerusalem. In the oldest manuscripts of the *graduale*,[19] the repertory of Mass chants is structured around the calendar of Roman stational churches, which had achieved its classic form by the early seventh century.[20] More recent feasts, introduced during the later seventh and early eighth century, are only inconsistently represented in these early *graduale* sources.[21] When they do occur these feasts rarely have chant texts

[19] The texts of selected early manuscripts are edited in parallel columns in René-Jean Hesbert, *Antiphonale Missarum Sextuplex* (Brussels, 1935; repr. Rome: Herder, 1968) and Paul F. Cutter, *Musical Sources of the Old Roman Mass*, Musicological Studies and Documents 36 (Neuhausen-Stuttgart: Hänssler, 1979). An attempt at a more complete list of the early sources is Jeffery, "The Oldest Sources." The still primitive state of research into this subject is evident from the fact that, already, this list is in need of revision, expansion, and improvement. See Michel Huglo's remarks in "Bulletin codicologique," *Scriptorium* 39 (1985): 52*. Further information and some new fragments are listed in Klaus Gamber et al., *Codices Liturgici Latini Antiquiores/Supplementum: Ergänzungs- und Registerband*, Spicilegii Friburgensis Subsidia 1A (Freiburg, Switzerland: Universitätsverlag, 1988), 128–44. I will publish a more detailed, complete, and accurate list after I have personally examined all the manuscripts and fragments that ought to be in it.

[20] Theodor Klauser, "Ein vollständiges Evangelienverzeichnis der römischen Kirche aus dem 7. Jahrhundert, erhalten im Cod. Vat. Pal. Lat. 46," *Römische Quartalschrift* 35 (1927): 113–34, repr. with further comments in Klauser, *Gesammelte Arbeiten zur Liturgiegeschichte, Kirchengeschichte und christlichen Archäologie*, ed. Ernst Dassmann, Jahrbuch für Antike und Christentum Ergänzungsband 3 (Münster: Aschendorff, 1974), 5–21; Winfried Böhne, "Eine neuer Zeuge stadtrömischer Liturgie aus der Mitte des 7. Jahrhunderts: Das Evangeliar Malibu, CA, Paul-Getty-Museum, vormals Sammlung Ludwig, Katalog Nr. IV 1," *Archiv für Liturgiewissenschaft* 27 (1985): 35–69. See also the following articles by Antoine Chavasse: "L'organisation stationnale du Carême romain avant le VIIIe siècle: Une organisation 'pastorale,'" *Revue des sciences religieuses* 56 (1982): 17–32; "Les oraisons pour les dimanches ordinaires: Vers une organisation préétablie: Premières tentatives, premières collections," *Revue bénédictine* 93 (1983): 31–70, 177–244; "Les grands cadres de la célébration à Rome 'in Urbe' et 'extra muros' jusqu'au VIIIe siècle," *Revue bénédictine* 96 (1986): 7–26; "Le sanctoral et le temporal grégoriens, vers 680: Distribution et origine des pièces utilisées," *Ecclesia Orans* 3 (1986): 263–88; "Le sacramentaire grégorien: Les additions et remaniements introduits dans le témoin P," in *Traditio et Progressio: Studi liturgici in onore del Prof. Adrien Nocent, OSB*, ed. Giustino Farnedi, Analecta Liturgica 12, Studia Anselmiana 95 (Rome: Pontificio Ateneo S. Anselmo, 1988), 125–48; "Les célébrations eucharistiques à Rome, V[e]–VIIIe siècle: Une double ossature, 'in Urbe,'" *Ecclesia Orans* 7 (1990): 69–75; "Après Grégoire le Grand: L'organisation des évangéliaires au VIIe et VIIIe siècle," in *Rituels: Mélanges offerts à Pierre Marie Gy, O.P.*, ed. Paul De Clerck and Eric Palazzo (Paris: Éditions du Cerf, 1990), 125–30.

[21] Theodor Klauser, in a review of Hesbert's *Antiphonale Missarum Sextuplex* in *Jahrbuch für Liturgiewissenschaft* 15 (1935): 467–69, observed that the feasts in Hesbert's manuscripts

of their own, but rather tend simply to re-use texts and melodies that were already in the repertory assigned to older feasts.[22] This suggests that, at the time their chants were assigned, there was already a core repertory that to some degree was regarded as "closed." As new feasts of non Roman origin were introduced it was becoming easier simply to "recycle" established chant texts than to create new ones. The last feast to be supplied with a completely new set of chants was the feast of the rededication of the Roman Pantheon as the church of Sancta Maria ad Martyres about the year 609[23]—

seemed to represent the state of the calendar as it was in the time of Pope Honorius I (625–38), with the addition of some (but not all) of the feasts introduced later, down to the reign of Gregory III (731–41). See also his "Die liturgischen Austauschbeziehungen zwischen der römischen und der fränkisch-deutschen Kirche vom achten bis zum elften Jahrhundert," *Historisches Jahrbuch* 53 (1933): 169–89, esp. 175; repr. in *Gesammelte Arbeiten*, 139–54, esp. 143–44. Unfortunately he never pursued this subject in the same rigorous way he did for the Roman evangeliary, in his book *Das römische Capitulare Evangeliorum: Texte und Untersuchungen zu seiner ältesten Geschichte* 1: *Typen*, 2nd ed., Liturgiewissenschaftliche Quellen und Forschungen 28 (Münster: Aschendorff, 1972), see esp. 184–85. For the most up-to-date account of Klauser's subject see Vogel, *Medieval Liturgy*, 342–54; also Antoine Chavasse, "L'épistolier romain du codex de Wurzbourg," and "L'évangéliaire roman de 645." Such a study of the *graduale* calendar is badly needed, and should be undertaken once the complete publication of all the early manuscripts has been completed (see n. 121 below).

[22] See Antoine Chavasse, "Évangéliaire, épistolier, antiphonaire et sacramentaire: Les livres romains de la messe au VIIe et au VIIIe siècle," *Ecclesia Orans* 6 (1989): 177–255. The caveat mentioned in n. 42 below applies to this article also.

[23] Louis Duchesne, ed., *Le Liber Pontificalis: Texte, introduction et commentaire*, ed. Cyrille Vogel, Bibliothèque des Écoles françaises d'Athènes et de Rome (Paris: Boccard, 1981), 1:317; *The Book of Pontiffs (Liber Pontificalis): The Ancient Biographies of the First Ninety Roman Bishops to AD 715*, trans. Raymond Davis, Translated Texts for Historians, Latin Series 5 (Liverpool: Liverpool University Press, 1989), 62. It is stated therein that Pope Boniface (608–15) held the dedication after successfully obtaining the permission of the Emperor Phokas (602–10), hence the date was ca. 609. See Pierre Jounel, "Le culte collectif des saints à Rome du VIIe au IXe siècle," *Ecclesia Orans* 6 (1989): 285–300; Aimé Georges Martimort et al., *The Church at Prayer, An Introduction to the Liturgy* 4: *The Liturgy and Time*, new ed., trans. Matthew J. O'Connell (Collegeville, Minn.: Liturgical Press, 1986), 100–01. In the following article James McKinnon argues that these chants are more likely to be of eighth-century origin, because the feast of the Dedication does not appear in sources that represent the seventh-century Roman liturgy: "The Emergence of Gregorian Chant in the Carolingian Era," in *Antiquity and the Middle Ages from Ancient Greece to the 15th Century*, ed. James McKinnon, Music and Society (Englewood Cliffs, N.J.: Prentice Hall, 1990), 88–119, see 108–09. But this is partly a matter of how one interprets the manuscripts: see Klauser, "Ein vollständiges Evangelienverzeichnis," 122 (repr. 12), Böhne, "Eine neuer Zeuge," 48 and 60, and Klauser, "Rom und der Kult der Gottesmutter Maria," *Jahrbuch für Antike und Christentum* 15 (1972): 120–35, esp. 122–23. There are also other explanations, such as the possibility that the dedication may originally have been commemorated only in the church of S. Maria itself before becoming part of the general Roman calendar, or that it may have been part of the papal stational liturgy but not the presbyteral liturgy that the Gelasian sacramentary represents. Even if it were true, however, that the Dedication chants date from the eighth century, it is still hard to avoid the conclusion that this was one of the very last times a complete new proper was created for a feast in the *graduale*, and thus that this particular group of chants marks a turning point in the

and even some of these chants show signs of dependence on earlier ones.[24] For feasts of later origin even the appearance of originality was largely abandoned. All the chants except the tract for the feast of St. Gregory, introduced at some time after his death in 604,[25] were borrowed from the feasts of other popes. The feast of St. Apollinaris, seemingly introduced by Pope Honorius I (625–38),[26] borrowed all its chants except the communion; indeed the introit and offertory (in the Old Roman tradition also the gradual) are the same ones used for St. Gregory. Hypapante, also called the Purification of St. Mary or the feast of St. Simeon, seems to have been introduced at Rome between about 650 and 680.[27] Only the communion seems to be original; the gradual is partly based on an older one and the other chants were borrowed outright from earlier feasts.[28] The feast of St. George,

formation of the repertory. The fact that the chants for other seventh-century feasts make even greater use of earlier material confirms that the period of originality was coming to an end. The question is only how accurately we can pinpoint the period when this was taking place.

[24] In particular, the gradual *Locus iste* borrows the second half of its verse, i.e., the words "exaudi preces servorum tuorum" and their music, from the gradual *Protector noster* of Monday in the first week of Lent. We know that *Protector* is the original because its text is adapted from Ps. 83:10, 9, to which these words belong. It is interesting that the alleluia *Adorabo* for this occasion seems to represent a transitional stage between the earliest type of alleluia (where the verse ends with the same music as the alleluia refrain) and the later, freer type. See Karl-Heinz Schlager, *Alleluia-Melodien* 1: *Bis 1100*, Monumenta Monodica Medii Aevi 7 (Kassel: Bärenreiter, 1968), 672.

[25] The earliest extant source that includes a feast of Gregory is an eighth-century English manuscript of the pseudo-Hieronymian martyrology. See H. A. Wilson, ed., *The Calendar of St. Willibrord from MS. Paris Lat. 10837: A Facsimile*, Henry Bradshaw Society 55 (London: Henry Bradshaw Society, 1918), pl. 3, pp. 5, 23–24, 26; Henri Quentin, ed., *Martyrologium Hieronymianum*, Acta Sanctorum, Novembris Tomi II Pars posterior (Brussels: [Société des Bollandistes], 1931), 138. The fact that that feast occurs in no Roman sacramentary before the *Hadrianum* suggests that it may not have been celebrated at Rome before the early eighth century; see Vogel, *Medieval Liturgy*, 128. See also my forthcoming article, "The Gregory Legend is from England."

[26] Duchesne, *Le Liber*, 1:323; Davis, *The Book*, 64. The text actually says that he built the basilica of St. Apollinaris and authorized weekly processions from there to St. Peter's, but this pope's particular interest in this Ravennate saint may also indicate that he was the one who introduced the feast at Rome. It certainly was not part of the older Roman calendar, and the manuscripts of the Roman evangeliary seem to support the inference that it came to Rome in the early seventh century; see Klauser, *Das römische Capitulare Evangeliorum*.

[27] The evidence suggesting this, from the Roman sacramentaries, evangeliaries, and homiliaries, is adduced on pp. 189–94 of Antoine Chavasse, "L'organisation générale des sacramentaires dit grégoriens," *Revue des sciences religieuses* 56 (1982): 179–200, 253–73; 57 (1983): 50–56.

[28] The introit *Suscepimus*, from the eighth Sunday after Pentecost, and the alleluia *Adorabo*, from the feast of the Dedication, were evidently borrowed because their texts refer to the Temple, where the events celebrated in this feast took place. The offertory *Diffusa* was used on many feasts of virgins. The text of the gradual *Suscepimus* may have been inspired by the introit; the music of the verse is adapted from the gradual *Discerne* of Tuesday in the fifth week of Lent—note that the words "in monte sancto" / "in montem sanctum" occur at the same point in the music.

apparently introduced under Pope Leo II (682–83),[29] and the feast of the Triumph of the Holy Cross, associated with Pope Sergius I (687–701), have no original chants in those manuscripts that contain them.[30] The other feasts of the Virgin Mary introduced during the seventh century (Annunciation, Assumption, Nativity)[31] have two chants that seem to be partly based on earlier models, but for the most part simply re-use texts and melodies from older feasts of Mary and other virgins.[32] The Thursdays in Lent, introduced by Pope Gregory II (715–31), derive almost all their chants from the Sundays after Pentecost.[33] Even if the chant assignments were not made

[29] Duchesne, *Le Liber,* 1:360; Davis, *The Book,* 79. The text credits Pope Leo II only with building the church of St. George in Velabro, but this may be a clue that the feast of this Greek saint was introduced at that time, a possibility which seems to be supported by Klauser's work on the Roman evangeliary. However, this information about Pope Leo occurs in only one manuscript of the *Liber pontificalis,* Vatican, Biblioteca Apostolica Vaticana, MS. Lat. 3764 of the eleventh century; see Duchesne, *Le Liber,* 1:CXCV. The communion is unique in the Gregorian sources but shared with other feasts in the Old Roman.

[30] Duchesne, *Le Liber,* 1:374. Davis, *The Book,* 85. See also Martimort et al., *The Church,* 99–100. The *Liber pontificalis* actually states that Pope Sergius discovered a relic of the cross which has been venerated on this feast ever since, but it is quite plausible that this feast, which originated in Jerusalem, would have been brought to Rome by a pope of Syrian background. The offertory was borrowed from the second (dawn) Mass of Christmas, and the other chants from Holy Week.

[31] On the origins of these feasts see Martimort et al., *The Church,* 88–90, 95–96, 134–36. According to the *Liber pontificalis,* Pope Sergius I ordered processions on these days and on the feast of the Purification (Duchesne, *Le Liber,* 1:376; Davis, *The Book,* 87). The Old Roman graduals have processional antiphons before Mass on Purification, Assumption, and Nativity, but the Gregorian manuscripts have them only for Purification, a trait that suggests the Gregorian tradition is more archaic at this point. See also *Ordo Romanus* 20 in Michel Andrieu, *Les Ordines Romani* 3, Spicilegium Sacrum Lovaniense 24 (Louvain: Spicilegium Sacrum Lovaniense, 1951), 235–36.

[32] The gradual *Propter veritatem* includes several common fifth-mode melodic formulas, but the music for the last half of the verse seems to be drawn from the end of the verse of *Viderunt omnes* of Christmas. There is however no shared text as in the graduals *Locus iste* and *Suscepimus.* The communion *Dilexisti* may owe something to the melody of *Ab occultis* for Monday after the fourth Sunday in Lent. Chants that were borrowed from older feasts include the introit *Rorate,* the gradual *Tollite,* the communion *Ecce virgo,* and perhaps the offertory *Ave Maria* from Ember Wednesday in Advent (a traditionally Marian day), the introit *Vultum,* gradual *Diffusa,* offertory *Diffusa,* and communion *In salutari* from the feasts of St. Agnes and St. Euphemia, and the offertory *Offeruntur* from the feast of St. Lucy.

[33] Duchesne, *Le Liber,* 1:402. For confirmation from the Roman sacramentaries and ordinaries see Vogel, *Medieval Liturgy,* 69, 116, 128, 159, 209–10. The Thursday after Ash Wednesday drew its introit, offertory, and communion from the tenth Sunday after Pentecost, its gradual from the third. Thursday in the first week, which had St. Lawrence in Panisperma as its stational church, drew its introit *Confessio* from the feast of St. Lawrence, the gradual from the tenth Sunday after Pentecost, and the offertory and communion from the fourteenth. Thursday in the second week drew its introit and offertory from the twelfth Sunday, its gradual from the fourth, and its communion from the fifteenth. Thursday in the third week drew its introit, offertory, and communion from the nineteenth week (the introit *Salus populi* recalling the tradition that SS. Cosmas and Damian, the patrons of the stational church, were

at the time the feasts were first introduced, but years or even decades afterward, the general pattern is still clear: during the seventh century it was becoming less and less common to expand the repertory by the addition of new chants, and more and more common to simply re-use material that was already in the tradition. After the early eighth century, new additions to the Gregorian repertory seem to be of Frankish rather than Roman origin, and even these were often derived from older material rather than completely original. The chants for Trinity Sunday, for instance, are mostly contrafacts of older Gregorian chants.[34]

The repertory of proper chants for the Roman Office, on the other hand, seems to have taken longer to solidify. The *antiphonale*, containing the proper chants of the Divine Office, is more poorly attested in early sources than the *graduale*, so that it is much more difficult to imagine what it may have been like in the seventh century.[35] But the smaller number of sources

physicians) and its gradual from the twentieth. Thursday in the fourth week drew its introit from Ember Friday in September, its gradual from the thirteenth Sunday, and its offertory and communion from the sixteenth. Thursday in the fifth week drew its introit, offertory, and communion from the twentieth Sunday; its gradual, *Tollite hostias*, is the only chant for any of these Thursdays that has no other liturgical assignment.

[34] The introit *Benedicta sit* takes its melody from *Invocabit me* of the first Sunday in Lent. The gradual *Benedictus es* and the offertory *Benedictus sit* are from the two *Constitues eos* of the feast of SS. Peter and Paul. The communion *Benedicimus Deum* is adapted from *Feci judicium* from the feast of St. Prisca. The alleluia *Benedictus es*, though not a contrafact, may have been inspired by one or more of the several melodies of the *Cantus trium puerorum*, with which it shares both its text and its mode. See Schlager, *Alleluia-Melodien*, 48–51, 589, 648–49. On melodic traditions of the *Cantus trium puerorum* see Ruth Steiner, "Antiphons for the Benedicite at Lauds," *Journal of the Plainsong and Medieval Music Society* 7 (1984): 1–17. On the origins of the feast see Martimort et al., *The Church*, 102–03, also P. Browe, "Zur Geschichte des Dreifaltigkeitsfestes," *Archiv für Liturgiewissenschaft* 1 (1950): 65–81.

[35] There appear to be two complete antiphoners of the Roman/Gregorian tradition from the ninth century: Paris, Bibliothèque Nationale, MS. fonds lat. 17436 (on which see the next n.) and Albi, Bibliothèque municipale, MS. 44, described in Michel Huglo, "La tradition musicale aquitaine: Répertoire et notation," in *Liturgie et musique (IXe – XIVe s.)*, Cahiers de Fanjeaux 17 (Toulouse: Privat, 1982): 253–68, and in a forthcoming publication by John Emerson. Fragments of other early manuscripts will be found listed in Gamber, *Codices*, 238, 254, 495–500 (antiphoners) and 606–12 (breviaries), and in the *Supplementum*, 56–57, 126–27, 164–65. These and other fragments are further described in Iso Müller, "Karolingische Pergament-Fragmente," *Bündnerisches Monatsblatt* (1936): 331–35; Alban Dold, "Ein merkwürdiges Liturgiefragment aus HB Inc 3513 der Württemburgischen Landesbibliothek zu Stuttgart," *Sacris Erudiri* 4 (1952): 280–92; idem, "Was ein 8zeiliger Fragmentstreifen eines einstigen Doppelblattes uns alles berichten kann," *Sacris Erudiri* 7 (1955): 237–56; idem, "Zwei sonderbare, ja teilweise regelswidrige, aber deutlich monastische Brevierfragmente," *Sacris Erudiri* 7 (1955): 257–66; idem, "Ein Brevierfragment aus der Quadragesima mit Genesislesungen in der 2. Nokturn des 1. Sonntags und an den Wochentagen bis zum Quatembermittwoch und die Probleme, zu denen es anregt," *Sacris Erudiri* 10 (1958): 142–50; idem, "Wiederum 'Brevierfragmente' mit Abraham-Lesungen in der ersten Fastenwoche (und Isaac-Jakob-Lesungen in der zweiten) mit eigenartigem Sonntagsformular," *Sacris Erudiri* 11 (1960):

may in itself be evidence that the Office repertory stabilized more recently than that of the Mass, and thus that the few early sources we do have witness to a more primitive stage in the development of the complete and fully-organized book. Inconsistencies in the earliest extant complete *antiphonale* (later ninth century) suggest that this manuscript may have been compiled from separate *libelli*,[36] small collections covering one or a few feasts that were originally independent of each other.[37]

The Formative Processes

Some evidence suggests that, at Rome, antiphonal and responsorial chants were originally brought together in separate collections. Two well-known documents of the eighth and ninth centuries seem to state quite clearly that the Roman Office repertory was originally divided into two different collections: one for the responsories (the responsorial), the other for the

212–19; idem, "Teile einer alten Nacht– und Tagesliturgie für den ersten Quadragesima–Sonntag," *Archiv für Liturgiewissenschaft* 6 (1959): 85-89; Karl Drew Hartzell, "An English Antiphoner of the Ninth Century?" *Revue bénédictine* 90 (1980): 234–48; Klaus Gamber, "Ein Brevier-Fragment aus der 1. Hälfte des 9. Jahrhunderts," *Revue bénédictine* 95 (1985): 232–39; Franz Unterkircher, "Fragmente eines karolingischen Chorantiphonars mit Neumen," *Codices Manuscripti* 11 (1985): 97–109.

[36] This is the Compiègne MS (Paris B.N. lat. 17436), edited in the first column of René-Jean Hesbert, *Corpus Antiphonalium Officii* 1: *Manuscripti "Cursus Romanus,"* Rerum Ecclesiasticarum Documenta, Series Maior: Fontes 7 (Rome: Herder, 1963). Apparent inconsistencies include: (1) a stray responsory, seemingly for the feast of St. Peter's Chair (Jan. 18), for which there are no other chants in the manuscript (p. 86), (2) the feast of St. Benedict (July 11) follows the monastic arrangement of antiphons and responsories even though the rest of the manuscript follows the Roman arrangement (pp. 266–68), (3) there are two different offices for the feast of St. Andrew (November 30; pp. 330–32 and 340–44), (4) some important feasts are absent, even though many local feasts from various centers were included (see pp. XVIII–XIX). The order of the contents also suggests that the scribe was putting this book together from disparate sources, for he did not fully succeed in integrating the temporal and sanctoral cycles. Following the Christmas cycle, there are offices only for the feasts of the Purification (Feb. 2) and St. Valentine (Feb. 14) before Septuagesima. After Pentecost the *sanctorale* recommences with the feast of St. Germanus (May 28) and continues through, with some unexpected omissions, to the feast of St. Thomas (Dec. 21). The fact that the scribe left a great many blank lines and open spaces throughout the antiphoner section of the manuscript suggests he may have expected to enter further material at a later date. Thus I disagree with the article of Jacques Froger, "Le lieu de destination et de provenance du 'Compendiensis,'" in *Ut Mens Concordet Voci: Festschrift Eugène Cardine zum 75. Geburtstag*, ed. Johannes Berchmans Göschl (St. Ottilien: EOS, 1980), 338–54. The peculiar calendar does not represent the usage of any one place, but is due to the fact that many of the separate *libelli* available to the compiler contained offices for local patron saints from various places.

[37] On liturgical *libelli* see Huglo, *Les livres*, 64–75; Vogel, *Medieval Liturgy*, 37–39, 54–56; Éric Palazzo, "Un 'Libellus Missae' du Scriptorium de Saint-Amand pour saint Denis: Son intérêt pour la typologie des manuscrits liturgiques," *Revue bénédictine* 99 (1989): 286–92.

antiphons (the *antiphonale* strictly speaking).[38] We have no extant examples of such manuscripts, for all the medieval sources of Gregorian and Old Roman Office chants include both the antiphons and the responsories. However, these sources often exhibit greater variability in the responsory repertory than they do in the antiphon repertory, a phenomenon that would not be surprising if the two were originally collected in separate books with different histories.[39] Research into the origins of the *antiphonale* has unfortunately been sidetracked by Dom Hesbert's attempt to reconstruct the original archetype,[40] consuming years of effort and massive amounts of computer time in a project that was fundamentally misconceived.[41]

[38] The earlier is a letter of Pope Paul I to Pippin, written between 758 and 763, which states in the postscript: "Direximus itaque excellentissime praecellentiae vestrae et libros, quantos reperire potuimus: id est antiphonale et responsale, insimul artem gramaticam Aristolis, Dionisii Ariopagitis geometricam, orthografiam, grammaticam, omnes Greco eloquio scriptas, nec non et horologium nocturnum." *Monumenta Germaniae Historica, Epistolarum* 3: *Epistolae Merowingici et Karolini Aevi* 1, ed. Ernst Dümmler (Berlin: Weidmann, 1892), 529. From the early ninth century there is the remark of Amalarius of Metz in the prologue to his revision of the *antiphonale:* "Notandum est volumen quod nos vocamus antiphonarium, tria habere nomina apud Romanos: quod dicimus graduale, illi vocant cantatorium; qui adhuc iuxta morem antiquum apud illos in aliquibus ecclesiis in uno volumine continetur. Sequentem partem dividunt in duobus nominibus: pars quae continet responsorios, vocatur responsoriale, et pars quae continet antiphonas, vocatur antiphonarius. Ego secutus sum nostrum usum et posui mixtim responsoria et antiphonas secundum ordinem temporum, in quibus solemnitates nostrae celebrantur." See J. M. Hanssens, *Amalarii Episcopi Opera Liturgica Omnia* 1, Studi e testi 138 (Vatican City: Biblioteca Apostolica Vaticana, 1948), 363.

[39] Huglo, *Les livres*, 87–88, 90.

[40] In my view Hesbert's work was based on at least four erroneous assumptions: (1) All manuscripts of the *antiphonale* derive from a common archetype. (2) The manuscripts he happened to use in his database adequately represented the totality of the tradition, so that those he did not use could be safely ignored for purposes of recovering the archetype. (3) The period of Advent was representative enough that one could extrapolate from it to the rest of the *antiphonale.* (4) The original common archetype could be recovered by quantitative statistical methods with the help of a computer. Hesbert's own explanation of his method is in *Corpus Antiphonalium Officii* 5: *Fontes earumque prima ordinatio*, Rerum Ecclesiasticarum Documenta, Series Maior 11 (Rome: Herder, 1975), 19–22. There he frequently railed against "suffrage universel," by which he meant the assumption that any reading found in the majority of sources should be regarded as original. But his own method is only a slight variation of this idea. Instead of considering each manuscript as a unit, he merely considered each Sunday of Advent individually, determined the majority readings, strung these majorities together in liturgical order, and dubbed the resulting hypothetical collection the archetype.

[41] For other discussions of Hesbert's work, see Jacques Froger, "La méthode de Dom Hesbert dans le volume V du *Corpus Antiphonalium Officii*," *Études grégoriennes* 18 (1979): 97–143; Jacques Froger, "La méthode de Dom Hesbert dans le volume VI du *Corpus Antiphonalium Officii*," *Études grégoriennes* 19 (1980): 185–96; Hartmut Möller, "Auf dem Weg zur Rekonstruktion des Antiphonale S. Gregorii? Kritisches zu den Klassifizierungen des *Corpus Antiphonalium Officii*," *Die Musikforschung* 37 (1984): 207–15; Michel Huglo, "L'édition critique de l'Antiphonaire grégorien," *Scriptorium* 39 (1985): 130–38; Pierre-Marie Gy, "Le 'Corpus Antiphonalium Officii' et les antiphonaires carolingiens," in *Grégoire le Grand: Chantilly,*

In the Mass repertory, also, there is evidence that the graduals were transmitted "separately (not to say independently)" from the introits, offertories, and communions.[42] This is indeed what we might expect if, as at Jerusalem, the responsorial psalms of the Mass were the first repertory to form or be written down, while the repertories of the other genres were fluid for a longer period of time. One is tempted of course to identify this hypothetical writing down with the origins of the *cantatorium*, which included the responsorial graduals and alleluias and the tracts, but excluded the responsorial offertories and the antiphonal introits and communions (which may therefore have first been collected separately). How and when, then, did Rome make the transition from the repertory underlying the *cantatorium*, with its roots in the fifth century, to the complete Mass proper repertory of the seventh century that underlies the *graduale?* If at Jerusalem the newer chants were added to the lectionary, perhaps at Rome the *cantatorium* served in much the same way, so that over time the introits, offertories, and communions, or at least their incipits, came to be inserted in the margins of the *cantatorium*, until it was eventually expanded into the full *graduale*. If such a process took place, we may detect an echo of it in the *cantatorium* of St. Gall,[43] in which the introit, offertory, and communion chants are cited only by textual incipit, while the traditional contents of the *cantatorium* are given in full. In other words, this manuscript looks as if it were descended from a transitional type of book, in which the introits, offertories, and communions were just beginning to coalesce around the core repertory of the *cantatorium*, still written down only by incipit as in the

Centre culturel Les Fontaines, 15–19 septembre 1982, ed. Jacques Fontaine, Robert Gillet, and Stan Pellistrandi, Colloques internationaux du Centre national de la recherche scientifique (Paris: Éditions du Centre national de la recherche scientifique, 1986), 645–48; Jean Claire, "La musique de l'office de l'Avent," ibid., 649–59; Michel Huglo, "L'Antiphonaire: Archétype ou répertoire originel?" ibid., 661–69; Knud Ottosen, *L'antiphonaire latin au moyen-âge: Réorganisation des séries de répons de l'Avent classés par R.-J. Hesbert*, Rerum Ecclesiasticarum Documenta, extra seriem (Rome: Herder, 1986); and Hartmut Möller, "Research on the Antiphoner—Problems and Perspectives," *Journal of the Plainsong and Medieval Music Society* 10 (1987): 1–14.

[42] The most detailed attempt to deal with this evidence is Antoine Chavasse, "Cantatorium et Antiphonale Missarum: Quelques procédés de confection, dimanches après la Pentecôte, graduels du sanctoral," *Ecclesia Orans* 1 (1984): 15–55, our quote from p. 55. However, Chavasse's work is somewhat flawed by the facts that he restricts himself to only a few manuscripts, mainly the ones that have been published in Hesbert's *Antiphonale*, and that he regards the Monza *cantatorium* as dating from the mid-eighth century, whereas it has now been redated to the middle of the ninth. Thus his imagined chronological progression from the Monza *cantatorium*, to the Mont-Blandin *graduale*, to the *gradualia* of Compiègne, Corbie, and Senlis is in fact much too simplistic.

[43] St. Gall, Stiftsbibliothek, MS. 359, published in *Paléographie musicale*, ser. 2, vol. 2 (Tournai: Desclée, 1924, 1968, 1988).

Georgian lectionary of Jerusalem. However the St. Gall manuscript is not itself a "transitional book" of this sort, because it is later in date than many manuscripts and fragments of the complete *graduale*—it does not date from a time when the other chants were just beginning to be added to the *cantatorium;* the most that can be argued is that it is a copy or a more distant descendant of such a manuscript.[44]

However, the evidence we have does not conclusively prove the hypothesis that the *cantatorium* crystallized first and then was expanded by the addition of new chants of other genres. It is also possible, for instance, that the introits, offertories, and communions may once have existed in written collections of some other kind. They may have been included in early antiphonaries for the Office, for instance,[45] or each chant genre may have been collected separately, as we find in a fragment of about the year 1000 now in Munich.[46] Whatever happened, the entire process of collecting and writing down must have happened before the late eighth century, from when the earliest manuscripts of the *graduale* survive.

How and when were the early Roman repertories of responsorial and antiphonal Office chants combined to produce the *antiphonale* of the Office? If the Roman church originally kept responsorial and antiphonal Office chants in separate collections, were the two first merged in Rome itself, or somewhere outside it,[47] as part of the process of exporting Roman chant

[44] Tree rings indicate that the wooden portion of the cover was made from an oak tree cut down between the years 923 and 931, according to Johannes Duft and Rudolf Schnyder, *Die Elfenbein-Einbände der Stiftsbibliothek St. Gallen* (Beuron: Beuroner Kunstverlag, 1984), 117–18. On the methodology see G. L. Baillie, *Tree-Ring Dating and Archaeology* (Chicago: University of Chicago Press, 1982). For more on the dating of the St. Gall manuscripts, see the paper by Susan Rankin in this volume.

[45] See the opinion in Huglo, *Les livres,* 80, 98–99.

[46] Alban Dold, "Neuentdeckte Bruchstücke neumierter liturgischer Handschriften des Mittelalters aus Codex latinus Monacensis 18036," *Gregorius-Blatt* 53 (1929): 33–39, 54–64, 70–73, plus two plates between 66–67. The fragment contains a section of alleluias for the common of saints (i.e., the end of an alleluia collection) and a section of offertory verses for the liturgical year from Advent through Annunciation (i.e., the beginning of a collection of offertory verses). For two similarly organized manuscripts (Munich, Bayerische Staatsbibliothek Clm 14083 and 14322) see Moines de Solesmes, eds., *Le Graduel romain* 2: *Les sources* (Solesmes: Abbaye St. Pierre, 1957), 80, 82.

[47] The sending of a responsorial and antiphonal to Pippin (see n. 38 above) suggests that this was still the customary arrangement in Rome. However, two Anglo-Saxon sources of the same century could be interpreted to suggest that there was only one Roman book. The Council of Clofesho in September 747 decreed, "Ut uno eodemque modo Dominicae dispensationis in carne sacrosanctae festivitates, in omnibus ad eas rite competentibus rebus, id est . . . in cantilenae modo celebrantur, juxta exemplar videlicet quod scriptum de Romana habemus Ecclesia. Itemque ut per gyrum totius anni natalitia sanctorum uno eodemque die, juxta martyrologium ejusdem Romanae Ecclesiae, cum sua sibi convenienti psalmodio seu cantilena venerentur." Arthur West Haddan and William Stubbs, eds., *Councils and Ecclesiastical Docu-*

traditions to other parts of Europe? If the merger took place outside of Rome, it may have reflected an attempt to compromise, between the Roman tendency to keep different material in separate books, and a non-Roman tendency to combine everything into a single book. For the Ambrosian, Mozarabic, and other Latin rites, like the rite of Jerusalem, consistently placed all the chants for the Mass and Office into a single collection, usually designated by some form of the word "antiphonale" or "antiphonarius."[48] The earliest actual copy of such a book, representing the Ambrosian tradition, is preserved in a fragmentary double palimpsest at St. Gall, and shows that complete antiphoners already existed by the beginning of the eighth century.[49] But only one eighth-century source of the Gregorian chant tradition includes all the Mass and Office chants in a single collection.[50] Gregorian collections that contained both antiphons and responsories for the Office seem to have been common by the early ninth century, when Amalar, Agobard, and Helisachar prepared their own revisions of the *antiphonale*.[51] But the inexact use of the word "antiphonale" throughout the Middle Ages, when it was applied indiscriminately to both the book of Office chants and the book of Mass chants or *graduale*, may reflect a historical

ments Relating to Great Britain and Ireland 3 (Oxford, 1871; repr. Oxford: Clarendon, 1964), 367. A *De Institutione Catholica Dialogus* attributed to Archbishop Egbert of York (d. 766) argues for keeping the Ember days "ut noster didascalus beatus Gregorius, in suo Antiphonario et Missali Libro, per pedagogum nostrum beatum Augustinum transmisit ordinatum et rescriptum . . . . Hoc autem jejunium idem beatus Gregorius per praefatum legatum, in Antiphonario suo et Missali, in plena epdomada post Pentecosten Anglorum aecclesiae celebrandum destinavit. Quod non solum nostra testantur Antiphonaria, sed et ipsa quae cum Missalibus suis conspeximus apud apostolorum Petri et Pauli limina" (Haddan and Stubbs 3:411). For more see Thomas Talley, "The Origin of the Ember Days: An Inconclusive Postscript," in *Rituels: Mélanges offerts à Pierre Marie Gy*, 465–72.

[48] Fragments of an antiphoner of this sort survive also among the Mount Sinai fragments edited by Lowe, cited above, n. 12.

[49] The basic bibliography is given in Gamber, *Codices* 276–77, no. 550. See also Michel Huglo et al., *Fonti e paleografia del canto ambrosiano*, Archivio Ambrosiano 7 (Milan: Scuola tipografica San Benedetto, 1956), 5–6.

[50] Jacques Froger, "Le fragment de Lucques (fin du VIIIe siècle)," *Études grégoriennes* 18 (1979): 145–55.

[51] Michel Huglo, "Les remaniements de l'Antiphonaire grégorien au IXe siècle: Hélisachar, Agobard, Amalaire," in *Culto cristiano, politica imperiale carolingia, 9–12 ottobre 1977*, Convegno del Centro di studi sulla spiritualità medievale 18 (Todi: Presso l'Accademia tudertina, 1977), 87–120. On the revision of Amalarius see R. J. Hesbert, "L'Antiphonaire d'Amalaire," *Ephemerides Liturgicae* 94 (1980): 176–94. The preface to Agobard's antiphoner is edited by L. Van Acker in *Agobardi Lugdunensis Opera Omnia*, Corpus Christianorum, Continuatio Mediaeualis 52 (Turnhout: Brepols, 1981), 335–51. On Helisachar see Huglo, "Trois livres manuscrits présentés par Helisachar," *Revue bénédictine* 99 (1989): 272–85.

memory in non-Roman areas that at one time, before the general adoption of the Gregorian repertory, there had been only one chant book.[52]

In sum, the Roman chant repertory developed somewhat differently from that of Jerusalem. There is some evidence, though not enough to ensure certainty, that responsorial and antiphonal chants were collected separately, both for the Mass and for the Office. If so, the only book of this kind to survive was the *cantatorium*. Independent collections of introits, offertories, and communions for the Mass, or of Office antiphons, or of Office responsories—if they ever existed—do not survive. All other extant manuscripts of Gregorian or Old Roman chant contain the complete repertory of either the Mass or the Office. Both Gregorian and Old Roman chant, however, retained the principle of keeping Mass and Office repertories in separate books, despite the practice of the other Western rites and Jerusalem whereby proper Mass and Office chants were all collected in a single *antiphonale*. A basic repertory of chants for the Roman Mass seems to have been in existence by the seventh century, about the same date as the Jerusalem chantbook that survives in the Georgian *Iadgari*. The repertory for the Roman Office, on the other hand, may not have solidified until somewhat later. The earliest Gregorian antiphoner, from the ninth century, shows signs of having been compiled from independent *libelli*, each containing one or a few feasts or a portion of the liturgical year.

The Core Repertories Are Expanded by Expert Singers/Hymnodists. Seventh to Ninth Centuries (table 3, page 245)

After its early strata were formed in the seventh century, the Jerusalem chant repertory was greatly expanded by new hymns, composed in Greek by monastic authors. Of those whose compositions survive in the Byzantine chantbooks, one of the earliest is Sophronios, monk and then bishop of Jerusalem from 634–39.[53] But the most famous of these hymnographers were John of Damascus (John Damascene, died ca. 749, also known as John

[52] On the terminology see Huglo, *Les livres*, 79–108. However Dom Hesbert did not introduce the term "Antiphonale Missarum" (99), which goes back at least to Paul Cagin, *Un mot sur l'«Antiphonale Missarum»* (Solesmes: Imprimerie Saint-Pierre, 1890).

[53] On his hymnographic activity see W. Christ and M. Paranikas, eds., *Anthologia Graeca Carminum Christianorum* (Leipzig: Teubner, 1871), LIII, 96–97; Karl Krumbacher, *Geschichte der byzantinische Literatur von Justinian bis zum Ende des oströmischen Reiches (527–1453)*, Handbuch der klassischen Altertums-Wissenschaft 9/1, 2nd ed., 2 vols. (Munich: Beck, 1897;

the Monk), Cosmas Melodos (also called Cosmas of Maiuma and of Jerusalem), and Andrew of Crete (ca. 660–740, also known as Andrew of Jerusalem), all monks of the monastery of St. Sabas or Mar Saba near Jerusalem, men who wrote in Greek although they were of Semitic origin, born in Damascus.[54] These hymnodists are among the first who we can be reasonably sure composed according to the modal system.[55] The rediscovery of the Georgian *Iadgari*, however, gives us access to a vast amount of hymnody composed before they were active, and makes it clear that the modal system was already fully developed and being applied to the chant repertory before their time.[56] A century after John and Cosmas, Mar Saba was still producing hymnodists, even though the center of hymn composition had by this time shifted to the monastery of St. Studios in Constantinople. The most famous of these later Mar Saba hymnodists are the brothers Theodore (d. 840s) and Theophanes (d. 845), each surnamed "Graptos" or "the inscribed one" because they were branded with heretical verses by an emperor who favored the Iconoclastic heresy.[57]

Very few of these Greek poetic and musical compositions ever reached the West,[58] and indeed they are easier to compare with Western rhymed offices, strophic hymns, or sequences than with the main Western chant

repr. New York: Burt Franklin, 1970), 672–73. For a thumbnail sketch of his career and other writings see Frederick W. Norris, "Sophronius," in *Encyclopedia of Early Christianity*, ed. Everett Ferguson et al. (New York: Garland, 1990), 861.

[54] On the Sabaitic school see Jean-Baptiste Pitra, *Analecta Sacra Spicilegio Solesmensi Parata* 1 (Paris: Jouby et Roger, 1876, repr. Farnborough: Gregg, 1966), XXXVII–XL; Christ and Paranikas, *Anthologia*, XLII, XLIV, XLIX–L, 97, 147, 117, 205, 161; Krumbacher, *Geschichte*, 673–76; Egon Wellesz, *A History of Byzantine Music and Hymnography*, 2nd ed. (Oxford: Clarendon, 1971), 204–28; Siméon Vailhé, "Les écrivains de Mar-Saba," *Echos d'Orient* 2 (1898–99): 1–11, 33–47, and "Le monastère de S.-Sabas," ibid. 2 (1898–99): 332–42 and 3 (1899–1900): 12–28, 168–77; Ioannes Phokulides, *He Hiera Laura Saba* ['Ιωάννης Φωκυλίδης, *'Η 'ιερά λαύρα Σάβα*] (Alexandria: Patriarchikon Typographeion ['Εκ τοῦ Πατριαρχικοῦ Τυπογραφείου], 1927); Everett Ferguson, "Andrew of Crete," Michael P. McHugh, "Cosmas Melodos," George C. Berthold, "John of Damascus," in Ferguson, *Encyclopedia*, 38, 237, 498–99 (respectively).

[55] Aelred Cody, "The Early History of the Octoechos in Syria," in *East of Byzantium: Syria and Armenia in the Formative Period: Dumbarton Oaks Symposium 1980*, ed. Nina Garsoïan et al., Dumbarton Oaks Papers 36 (Washington, D.C.: Dumbarton Oaks Center for Byzantine Studies, 1982), 89–113.

[56] See my article, "The Earliest Christian Chant Repertory Recovered."

[57] See Christ and Paranikas, *Anthologia*, XLIV, 236; Wellesz, *A History*, 198–204; Margaret Mullett, "Writing in Early Mediaeval Byzantium," in *The Uses of Literacy in Early Medieval Europe*, ed. Rosamond McKitterick (Cambridge: Cambridge University Press, 1990), 156–85, esp. 156. The Studite hymnographers of the same period are discussed in Wellesz, *A History*, 229–39.

[58] For a few that did, see Oliver Strunk, "The Latin Antiphons for the Octave of the Epiphany" (1964), reprinted in his *Essays on Music in the Byzantine World* (New York: Norton, 1977), 208–19.

repertory. Nor could Rome boast a comparable school of hymnographers, during the same period or indeed at any other time—in fact it is often asserted that the Roman church accepted the strophic office hymn only in the twelfth century.[59]

Notwithstanding medieval and modern attempts to credit certain hymns to Gregory the Great, what hymnographic activity there was in the West during the seventh and eighth centuries was going on far from Rome, and in any case few creations of this period found a place in the liturgy.[60] To the extent that we can infer from Italian and especially Anglo-Saxon evidence, the Roman church may originally have gotten by with a very limited repertory of about fifteen office hymns, built around the oeuvre of Ambrose (called by modern hymnologists the "Old Hymnal"). Only in ninth-century Frankish lands was this repertory expanded to form the basis of the standard repertory of over a hundred hymns (the "New Hymnal") that one finds in medieval breviaries. Even this standard medieval collection includes texts from more ancient authors like Prudentius, and some of its anonymous hymns may have been inherited from the old Gallican rite.[61] Thus it is fair to say that there was never a strictly Roman school of hymnography. Neverthless, the very absence of a close parallel between Rome and Jerusalem forces us to ask the reason, and to examine carefully the different situations in the two cities.

[59] Authors who make this claim are relying on Suitbert Bäumer, *Histoire du Bréviaire*, ed. Reginald Biron (Paris, 1905; repr. Rome: Herder, 1967), 2:34–37. The basis of Bäumer's argument is that such hymns are not mentioned in the twelfth-century works published by Mabillon as *Ordo Romanus* 11 and *Ordo Romanus* 12 (see Vogel, *Medieval Liturgy*, 194–95), and that hymns first appear in a Roman source (and then only a few of them) in the Old Roman antiphoner, MS. Vatican City, Biblioteca Apostolica Vaticana, Archivio di San Pietro B 79. Bäumer was relying on the edition published in Giuseppe Maria Tommasi, *Opera Omnia*, ed. Antonio Francesco Vezzosi, vol. 4: *Responsorialia et Antiphonaria Romanae Ecclesiae* (Rome, 1749; repr. Farnborough: Gregg, 1969), 1–170, esp. n. A on p. 168. A recent discussion of the manuscript and of Tommasi's edition is Edward Nowacki, "The Performance of Office Antiphons in Twelfth-Century Rome," in *International Musicological Society Study Group Cantus Planus*, 79–91.

[60] See Josef Szövérffy, *Die Annalen der lateinischen Hymnendichtung: Ein Handbuch* 1: *Die lateinischen Hymnen bis zum Ende des 11. Jahrhunderts* (Berlin: Schmidt, 1964), 140–44, 167–261.

[61] This history is briefly outlined in Helmut Gneuss, "Latin Hymns in Medieval England: Future Research," in *Chaucer and Middle English Studies in honour of Rossell Hope Robbins*, ed. Beryl Rowland (Kent, Ohio: Kent State University Press, 1974), 407–24. This article moves beyond the conclusions of Gneuss's book *Hymnar und Hymnen im englischen Mittelalter: Studien zur Überlieferung, Glossierung und Übersetzung lateinischer Hymnen in England*, Buchreihe der Anglia 12 (Tübingen: Niemeyer, 1968), reviewed by Rossell Hope Robbins in *Speculum* 47 (1972): 759–61.

Seventh-century Rome certainly had expert singers, trained from boyhood. But because this subject has often been used as ammunition in the debate over Old Roman chant,[62] a dispassionate review of the evidence is in order. The training process was part of a complex educational system that trained ecclesiastical functionaries of all sorts.[63] As many as four popes of the seventh century may have experienced this training.[64] Of Pope Sergius (687–701), a Syrian born in Palermo who came to Rome as a boy, we are told that "because he was studious and capable in the office of *cantilena,* he was given to the prior of the cantors for training."[65] During the same century this kind of training was also made available in England, as we can read in certain well-known passages of the Venerable Bede, who completed his *Historia gentis Anglorum ecclesiastica* in the year 731. During the reign of Pope Agatho (678–81), a certain John, archcantor of St. Peter's and abbot of St. Martin's, was brought to England by Benedict Biscop, founding abbot of Wearmouth, to teach the monks "the yearly course of singing as it was done in St. Peter's in Rome."[66] Anglo-Saxon England boasted a number of singers

[62] See particularly S. J. P. Van Dijk, "Gregory the Great, Founder of the Urban *Schola Cantorum,*" *Ephemerides Liturgicae* 77 (1963): 345–56; Van Dijk, "Papal Schola *versus* Charlemagne," in *Organicae Voces: Festschrift Joseph Smits van Waesberghe* (Amsterdam: Institut voor Middeleeuwse Muziekwetenschap, 1963), 21–30. Other literature on this subject is discussed in Andrew Tomasello, "Ritual, Tradition, and Polyphony at the Court of Rome," *Journal of Musicology* 4 (1985–86): 447–71; Anthony Milner, "Liturgy, Church Music, and Politics in the Carolingian Empire," *Studies in Music from the University of Western Ontario* 5 (1980): 23–34.

[63] The various officials and their roles are outlined in Thomas F. X. Noble, *The Republic of St. Peter: The Birth of the Papal State, 680–825* (Philadelphia: University of Pennsylvania Press, 1984), 212–30; Noble, "Literacy and the Papal Government in Late Antiquity and the Early Middle Ages," in *The Uses,* ed. McKitterick, 82–108, though the liturgical information in this article is not always accurate. See also Riché, *Education,* 150–51, 174, 314–15, 350–51, 372, 378–83, 386–87; Henry Leclercq, "Chantres," *Dictionnaire de l'archéologie chrétienne et de liturgie* 3/1 (Paris, 1948), 344–65; Leclercq, "Schola," ibid., 15/1 (Paris, 1950), 1008–13; Paul Bayart, "Chantres," *Dictionnaire de droit canonique* 3 (Paris: Letouzey et Ané, 1942), 511–16.

[64] The evidence is least explicit for the first three. The epitaph of Honorius I (625–38) describes him as "divino in carmine pollens." See Amédée Gastoué, *Les origines du chant romain: L'Antiphonaire grégorien,* Bibliothèque musicologique 1 (Paris: Picard, 1907; repr. New York, 1975), 93–94. The full epitaph is conveniently given in Duchesne, *Le Liber,* 1:326–27. The *Liber pontificalis* describes Leo II (682–83) as "Vir eloquentissimus, . . . cantelena ac psalmodia praecipuus, et in earum sensibus subtilissima exercitatione limatus" and says that Benedict II (684–85) "se . . . in divinis scripturis et cantilena a puerili etate . . . exhibuit." Duchesne, *Le Liber,* 1: 359, 363; Davis, *The Book,* 77–78, 79.

[65] ". . . quia studiosus erat et capax in officio cantelenae, priori cantorum pro doctrina est traditus." Duchesne, *Le Liber,* 1:371; Davis, *The Book,* 82.

[66] ". . . cursum canendi annuum, sicut ad sanctum Petrum Romae agebatur." *Bede's Ecclesiastical History of the English People,* ed. Bertram Colgrave and R. A. B. Mynors (Oxford: Clarendon, 1969), 388–89. Cf. John Michael Wallace-Hadrill, *Bede's Ecclesiastical History of the English People: A Historical Commentary* (Oxford: Clarendon, 1988).

who learned and taught the chant "in the manner of the Romans or Kentish people."[67] At least one of them seems actually to have studied at Rome,[68] while others were said to have learned the tradition from "the disciples of the blessed Pope Gregory in Kent,"[69] whence it spread to other parts of England.[70] Kent, of course, was the location of Canterbury, where Augustine and the other missionaries sent by Pope Gregory had set up their headquarters. The tendency to see it as a kind of outpost of Rome, and hence as a place linked to Gregory, seemed quite natural in England, which regarded Gregory as its national apostle. It was in England that Gregory's cult first flourished,[71] for he "was unpopular in Rome at the time of his death."[72]

[67] For example a certain Jacobus Diaconus, who was at York in the second half of the seventh century, was a "magister ecclesiasticae cantionis iuxta morem Romanorum sive Cantuariorum" who instructed many. Colgrave and Mynors, *Bede*, 206–07, cf. 192–93.

[68] "Nam et ipse episcopus Acca cantator erat peritissimus, quomodo etiam in litteris sanctis doctissimus . . . cum quo etiam Romam ueniens multa illic, quae in patria nequiuerat, ecclesiae sanctae institutis utilia didicit." Colgrave and Mynors, *Bede*, 530–33. Acca, a contemporary of Bede, eventually became bishop of Hexham, where he brought in Maban, trained at Canterbury, to teach chant and reform the local practice (see the next n.).

[69] Putta, who was bishop of Rochester until its destruction by Aethelred in 676, was "maxime autem modulandi in ecclesia more Romanorum, quem a discipulis beati papae Gregorii didicerat, peritum." After the destruction he "went round wherever he was invited, teaching the songs of the church" ("ubicumque rogabatur, ad docenda ecclesiae carmina diuertens"). Colgrave and Mynors, *Bede*, 336–37, 368–69. Bishop Acca of Hexham is said to have brought in a certain Maban, who had studied with "Gregory's disciples" at Canterbury, and who restored the deteriorating local chant tradition to its "pristine state": "Cantatorem quoque egregium, uocabulo Maban, qui a successoribus discipulorum beati papae Gregorii in Cantia fuerat cantandi sonos edoctus, ad se suosque instituendos accersiit, ac per annos XII tenuit, quatinus et quae illi non nouerant carmina ecclesiastica doceret, et ea quae quondam cognita longo usu uel negligentia inueterare coeperant, huius doctrina priscum renouarentur in statum." Colgrave and Mynors, *Bede*, 530–31.

[70] One person involved in this spread was a certain Aeddi or Eddius Stephanus, the first *cantandi magister* in Northumbria, who taught a kind of singing that up to then had been known only in the Canterbury area. "Sed et sonos cantandi in ecclesia, quos eatenus in Cantia tantum nouerant, ab hoc tempore per omnes Anglorum ecclesias discere coeperunt . . . ." Colgrave and Mynors, *Bede*, 334–35.

[71] The most recent history of Gregory's cult is Pierre Jounel, "Le culte de saint Grégoire le Grand," in *Grégoire le Grand*, 671–80; an expanded version with the same title is in *Ecclesia Orans* 2 (1985): 195–209. However this article is weak on the Anglo-Saxon sources and seems not to recognize that Gregory's cult first grew up in England and was only later brought back to Rome; see Jeffrey Richards, *Consul of God: The Life and Times of Gregory the Great* (London: Routledge, 1980), 259–66. Among the Anglo-Saxon sources Jounel did not mention is *The Earliest Life of Gregory the Great by an Anonymous Monk of Whitby*, ed. Bertram Colgrave (Lawrence, Kan., 1968; repr. Cambridge: Cambridge University Press, 1985), which does not yet attribute to Gregory a role in the history of the chant repertory.

[72] John Norman Davidson Kelly, *The Oxford Dictionary of Popes* (Oxford: Oxford University Press, 1986), 68. One major reason for the unpopularity was Gregory's preference for placing monks in high ecclesiastical positions, leading to conflicts with the secular clerics and the noble families from which many of them came. Reading between the lines of the *Liber ponti-*

Since "the growth of his continental reputation was another of the Anglo-Saxon contributions to European thought in their penetration of the West during the late seventh and eighth centuries,"[73] it is no wonder that "the legend of the origin of Gregorian chant was certainly born in English ecclesiastical circles."[74]

Only in the early eighth century do we begin to encounter the term "schola cantorum,"[75] which may be a sign that the Roman way of training singers had now become more formalized, perhaps along the lines of the *schola defensorum*, which Gregory the Great had set up in imitation of the even older *schola notariorum*.[76] Thus the official who had been called the "prior of the cantors" in the seventh century was being called "the prior of the school of the cantors" in the eighth.[77] Whereas the future Pope Sergius I had been "given to the prior of the cantors" in the seventh century, the twelve-year-old orphan who would become Pope Sergius II (844–47) was given by Pope Leo III (795–816) "to the school of the cantors, for the learning of common letters and that he might be instructed in the mellifluous melodies of *cantilena*."[78] By the late ninth century it was apparently standard procedure that poor boys who could sing well be transferred from

ficalis, one can infer that this issue continued to dominate Roman and papal politics through at least the first half of the seventh century, with Popes Sabinian (604–06), Deusdedit (615–18), Severinus (640), and John IV (640–42) remembered for having "dearly loved the clergy," while Boniface IV (608–15), the former treasurer of Gregory I, and Honorius I (625–38) supported the monks. See Kelly, *The Oxford Dictionary of Popes*, 66–72; Duchesne, *Le Liber*, 315–30; Davis, *The Book*, 62–66. Further support for this interpretation is adduced in Peter Llewellyn, *Rome in the Dark Ages* (New York: n.p., 1971), 110–11, n. 10.

[73] Owen Chadwick, "Gregory of Tours and Gregory the Great," *Journal of Theological Studies* 50 (1949): 38–49, quotation from 38.

[74] Pierre Riché, *Education and Culture in the Barbarian West, Sixth through Eighth Centuries*, trans. John J. Contreni (Columbia, S.C.: University of South Carolina Press, 1976), 315. See my forthcoming article, "The Gregory Legend is From England."

[75] The term occurs in *Ordo Romanus* 1; see Andrieu, *Ordines*, 2:80, 81, 83, 84.

[76] The document by which Gregory did this is published in *S. Gregorii Magni Registrum Epistularum* 2: *Libri VIII–XIV, Appendix*, ed. Dag Norberg, Corpus Christianorum Series Latina 140A (Turnhout: Brepols, 1982), 534–35. For interpretation see Noble, *Republic*, 218–24; Llewellyn, *Rome*, 114–15.

[77] In a letter to Pippin written between 761–67, Pope Paul I apologized for recalling Symeon, *scholae cantorum prior*, back to Rome from Rouen, where he had been teaching certain monks of Bishop Remedius, Pippin's brother. He said he would not have done this had not Symeon's predecessor, Georgius, died, for which reason Symeon was needed to take his place. Meanwhile the Rouen monks had followed Symeon back to Rome because they had not had enough time to learn the *psalmodii modulatio* perfectly. Paul assured Pippin that the Rouen monks would remain with Symeon until they learned *ecclesiasticae doctrinae cantilena*. This well-known letter is published in *Monumenta Germaniae Historica, Epistolarum* 3:553–54.

[78] "Tunc praesul eum scolae cantorum ad erudiendum communes tradidit litteras et ut mellifluis instruetur cantilenae melodiis" (Duchesne, *Le Liber*, 2:86).

other schools into the *schola cantorum;* after being educated there they moved on to become papal *cubicularii* or chamberlains, joining the noble boys who could achieve this position without such training.[79] The earliest legal document that mentions the *schola cantorum* by name dates from about 919,[80] during the reign of John X (914–28). Thus the most conservative reading of the evidence leads us to see a gradual development. In seventh-century Rome there was some kind of program for training singers, and by the eighth century it had been fully organized and was being called the *schola cantorum.* Under that name it was still functioning in the ninth and tenth centuries, though a thorough and objective history of this shadowy organization and its northern European offshoots remains to be written.[81]

What and how were the boys in the *schola* actually taught? Unfortunately we have little information. Though we can name the textbooks used to teach some of the other subjects at the time, we cannot even confirm that the musical treatises of Augustine,[82] Martianus Capella,[83] Boethius,[84]

[79] "Primum in qualicumque scola reperti fuerint pueri bene psallentes, tolluntur unde et nutriuntur in scola cantorum et postea fiunt cubicularii." *Ordo Romanus* 36, in Michel Andrieu, *Les Ordines Romani du haut moyen âge* 4, Spicilegium Sacrum Lovaniense 28 (Louvain: Spicilegium Sacrum Lovaniense, 1956), 195; see also comments on 123–26. See also Andrieu, "Les ordres mineurs dans l'ancien rit romain," *Revue des sciences religieuses* 5 (1925): 232–74. Gregory's attempt "to end the practice of employing young laymen in the papal chamber as *cubicularii,*" part of his general favoritism toward monks, may perhaps be seen as evidence against the possibility that he founded the *schola cantorum.* See Llewellyn, *Rome,* 110.

[80] See Paul Fridolin Kehr, ed., *Regesta Pontificum Romanorum,* Italia Pontificia 1: Roma (Berlin: Weidmann, 1906; repr. 1961), 17–18.

[81] But see Enrico Josi, "Lectores—schola cantorum—clerici," *Ephemerides Liturgicae* 44 (1930): 282–90; Guilherme Schubert, "Scholae puerorum: sua história e organizaçao," *Revista eclesiástica brasileira* 9 (1949): 893–912.

[82] It will be easier to determine whether Augustine's *De musica* was known in Rome at that date when the recent dissertation of Patrick Le Boeuf is published. For now, see Le Boeuf, "La tradition manuscrite du 'De musica' de saint Augustin et son influence sur la pensée et l'esthétique médiévales," *École nationale de chartes: Positions de thèses* (1986), 107–15. See also the review of G. Folliot in *Revue des études Augustiniennes* 33 (1987): 353–54. See also Brian Brennan, "Augustine's *De Musica,*" *Vigiliae Christianae* 42 (1988): 267–81; Richard R. LaCroix, ed., *Augustine on Music: An Interdisciplinary Collection of Essays,* Studies in the History and Interpretation of Music 6 (Lewiston, N.Y.: Mellen, 1988).

[83] On the transmission and reception of this text see Cora Lutz, "Martianus Capella," in *Catalogus Translationum et Commentariorum: Medieval and Renaissance Latin Translations and Commentaries* 2, ed. Paul Oskar Kristeller (Washington, D.C.: Catholic University of America Press, 1971), 367–81; Lutz and John J. Contreni, "Martianus Capella: Addenda et Corrigenda," ibid. 3 (1976), 449–52; Haijo J. Westra, "Martianus Capella," ibid. 6, ed. F. Edward Cranz (1986), 185–86. While the bulk of the evidence comes from Carolingian times and later and from northern Europe, the extant text does seem to be descended from a revision made in Rome by Securus Felix in 534 (see Lutz, "Martianus Capella," 368). Thus it is possible that the text was available to the Roman *schola* during the seventh and eighth centuries.

[84] "There was a time prior to the Carolingian Renaissance when all that remained of the music treatise of Boethius was a single copy in an unidentifiable library of the West," perhaps

Cassiodorus,[85] or Isidore[86] were ever studied in the Roman *schola.* For each of these authors there is a possibility that his musical writings were known in Rome during the seventh and eighth centuries, but the possibility cannot be confirmed, and most of these works saw only limited circulation before the Carolingian Renaissance. Nor can we be sure that the students or the teachers made use of written chantbooks of any kind. The *cantatorium,* for instance, seems at first to have been more of a ceremonial object than a book to be actually consulted,[87] and most of the earliest *graduale* manuscripts have come down to us as sections or parts of early missals—manuscripts that would not have been used by singers at all, but by priests who recited the chant texts quietly at private Masses where there was no singing.[88] Thus it may well be that the *schola cantorum* taught a largely or completely oral art, and this is suggested further by one alumnus of the Canterbury school, who wrote in December 671 that he had learned "the right way to fit syllables to the musical modulations of *cantilena.*"[89]

"one of those Italian libraries destroyed by the Lombards," according to Ubaldo Pizzani, "The Influence of the *De Institutione Musica* of Boethius up to Gerbert d'Aurillac: A Tentative Contribution," in *Boethius and the Liberal Arts: A Collection of Essays,* ed. Michael Masi, Utah Studies in Literature and Linguistics 18 (Bern: Lang, 1981), 97–156, see 119–20. What Pizzani meant was that all extant manuscripts appear to be descended from such a hypothetical archetype. It is of course possible that this "unidentifiable library" was in Rome, and the possibility that there were other manuscripts available to the Roman *schola*—manuscripts which left no extant descendants—is not excluded, though there is no positive evidence for their existence either.

[85] It appears that some of Cassiodorus's library found its way to Rome, and thus the musical information in his *Institutiones divinarum et humanarum lectionum* may have been available there. See Pierre Courcelle, *Late Latin Writers and Their Greek Sources,* trans. Harry E. Wedeck (Cambridge, Mass.: Harvard University Press, 1969), 361–409; James J. O'Donnell, *Cassiodorus* (Berkeley: University of California Press, 1979), 240–41, 244–45; James W. Halporn, "Pandectes, Pandecta, and the Cassiodorian Commentary on the Psalms," *Revue bénédictine* 90 (1980): 290–300; Halporn, "The Editing of Patristic Texts: The Case of Cassiodorus," *Revue des études Augustiniennes* 30 (1984): 107–26. Evidence that the *Institutiones* were known to Gregory the Great makes it plausible, but hardly certain, that this writing was known to the *schola cantorum.* See Louis Holtz, "Quelques aspects de la tradition et de la diffusion des *Institutions,*" in Leanza, ed., *Flavio,* 281–312, esp. 285–86.

[86] Two Italian manuscripts of Isidore survive from the eighth century, one of which has been expanded with material from Cassiodorus. See P. K. Marshall, "Isidore," in *Texts and Transmission: A Survey of the Latin Classics,* ed. L. D. Reynolds (Oxford: Clarendon, 1983), 194–96, esp. 196. See also Bernhard Bischoff, "Die europäische Verbreitung der Werke Isidors von Sevilla," repr. in *Mittelalterliche Studien* 1 (Stuttgart: Hiersemann, 1966), 171–94.

[87] See the remarks in my book, *Re-envisioning Past Musical Cultures: Ethnomusicological Issues in the Study of Medieval Chant* (Chicago: University of Chicago Press, 1992), 65–67.

[88] See my remarks in "The Oldest." On private Mass see now Vogel, *Medieval Liturgy,* 156–59.

[89] ". . . et ad musica cantilenae modulamina recto sillabarum tramite lustrare, cuius rei studiosis lectoribus tanto inextricabilior obscuritas praetenditur, quanto rarior doctorum numerositas reperitur." Rudolf Ehwald, ed., *Aldhelmi Opera,* Monumenta Germaniae Historica, Auctores Antiquissimi 15 (Berlin: Weidmann, 1919), 477. For a translation and

Clearly the Roman *schola* did not produce hymnographers of the sort that flourished at St. Sabas near Jerusalem. In this respect the two centers were very different. Yet whatever Roman chant was like during the seventh and eighth century, it was undoubtedly made that way by the graduates of the *schola cantorum*, just as the Jerusalem chant of the same period was largely the product of the hymnographers of St. Sabas.

The Central Roman and Jerusalem Traditions are Exported Elsewhere. (table 4, pages 246–47)

Even while it was still developing, the Jerusalem liturgy was being exported, in whole and in part, to other churches throughout Christendom. Already in the fourth century, information about the services in Jerusalem was being carried elsewhere by pilgrims like Egeria (see n. 4). At some point in the fifth century, it seems, the Jerusalem lectionary of the years 417–39 was adopted by the Armenian church and translated into Armenian. However the three extant manuscripts differ from each other in some important respects, reflecting differences in their Greek originals due to changes made at Jerusalem itself.[90] Thus it is not that one manuscript was imported into Armenia and there became the archetype of the new Armenian rite. The process of translation and importation into Armenia happened repeatedly. Even after the Armenian liturgy began to develop independently, with the fifth-century Jerusalem lectionary as its basis, for centuries it continued to be influenced by new developments in Jerusalem.[91]

commentary of the complete letter see Michael Lapidge and Michael Herren, eds., *Aldhelm: The Prose Works* (Cambridge: Brewer, 1979), 152–53, 199. Aldhelm's letter describes his studies of meter in a way that suggests he was reading Servius, a commentator on Vergil of the fourth century A.D.; had his study of music included the reading of Boethius or other writers, he might have described it in language echoing one of them, rather than as a practical matter of fitting syllables to melodies, a subject that received little attention in the music treatises available at the time.

[90] Renoux, *Le codex*, 35/1, 30–32, 186–88, and 36/2, 152–54, 160–61. See also n. 5 above.

[91] See the following articles by Charles Renoux: "Liturgie arménienne et liturgie hiérosolymitaine," in *Liturgie de l'Église particulière et liturgie de l'Église universelle: Conférences Saint-Serge, XXIIe semaine d'études liturgiques*, Bibliotheca «Ephemerides Liturgicae,» Subsidia 7 (Rome: Edizioni liturgiche, 1976), 275–88; "La fête de la Transfiguration et le rite arménien," in *Mens concordet voci: Pour Mgr A. G. Martimort*, 652–62; "Čašoc' et tonakan arméniens: Dépendance et complémentarité," *Ecclesia Orans* 4 (1987): 169–201.

What is true of the Armenian rite is even more evident in the Georgian. Though the four main manuscripts of the Georgian lectionary generally seem to represent an eighth-century state of development, they and the several surviving fragments demonstrate that the Georgian church did not adopt the Jerusalem rite once, but rather many times, for each manuscript represents a slightly different Greek archetype, assignable to a somewhat different point in time between the fifth and the eighth centuries.[92] The Georgian homiliary presents an even more complicated picture; it seems to be a late seventh-century collection, made in Georgia itself, of saints' lives translated individually at many different dates and often repeatedly revised.[93] Comparisons of the sources of the *Iadgari* would doubtless show that they too reflect originals of somewhat different dates.

By the beginning of the ninth century, the monastic rite of Palestine, closely related to the urban rite of Jerusalem, had begun to be celebrated in the monasteries of Constantinople. In the course of a monastic revival led by Theodore the Studite (d. 826), the *typikon* (corresponding to the Western ordinal) of St. Sabas near Jerusalem was adapted and expanded at the Constantinopolitan monastery of St. Studios, producing the Studite *Typikon*.[94] The Studite *Typikon* spread everywhere the Byzantine liturgy was then in use, from Russia to southern Italy, but was itself further synthesized back at St. Sabas. The book that resulted, still known as the *Typikon* of Jerusalem, is the basis of the Byzantine Rite in use today. Even in Jerusalem itself it supplanted the older local liturgy, which is why we must rely on Armenian and Georgian sources to know what it was like. The only source of the local Jerusalem rite extant in the original Greek, a *typikon* for Holy and Easter Week, was copied in 1122, by which time the Jerusalem liturgy was already an anachronism, fast succumbing to the Studite-Sabaitic monastic

[92] ". . . chacun d'eux renvoie à une période différente de la liturgie hagiopolite"; see Renoux, "Hierosolymitana (1)," 4, and the list of sources (including many that Tarchnischvili did not use), 3–7.

[93] Michel Van Esbroeck, *Les plus anciens homéliaires géorgiens: Étude descriptive et historique*, Publications de l'Institut Orientaliste de Louvain 10 (Louvain: Université catholique de Louvain, 1975), esp. 348–49.

[94] Manuscripts reflecting various stages in the development of the rite of Constantinople, and its encounter with monastic usages, are described and partly edited in A. Dmitrievskij, *Opisanie Liturgicheskikh Rukopisej* 1: *Typika* [А. Дмитрієвскій, Описаніе Литургическихъ Рукописей: *Τυπικά*] (Kiev, 1895; repr. Hildesheim: Olms, 1965). See also Juan Mateos, ed., *Le typicon de la grande église: Ms. Sainte-Croix n° 40, Xᵉ siècle*, Orientalia Christiana Analecta 165–66 (Rome: Pont. Institutum Orientalium Studiorum, 1962–63); Miguel Arranz, ed., *Le typicon du monastère du Saint-Sauveur à Messine: Codex Messinensis Gr 115, A. D. 1131*, Orientalia Christiana Analecta 185 (Rome: Pont. Institutum Orientalium Studiorum, 1969).

synthesis.[95] Yet much of this process is quite difficult for us to trace accurately, for neither the Studite *Typikon* nor the earlier or later *typika* of St. Sabas are extant in pure, early copies from the monasteries themselves. They are known to us only from the countless adaptations made at other monasteries all over the Byzantine world, incorporating both local peculiarities and later developments of various origins.[96] Here again, then, the spread of the Jerusalem rite was not something that happened once and for all, but something that happened over and over, with a bewildering variety of results.

All this sounds complicated and confusing, but it resembles nothing so much as the current state of knowledge about Western chant, where even the very earliest manuscripts exhibit a great variety of textual recensions and notational types, and where no extant manuscript can be linked especially closely to a key historical milieu, such as the court of Charlemagne, the Cathedrals of Metz or Rouen with their Roman-trained singers, a particular Roman church, or the reign of a particular pope. Loss of sources no doubt accounts for some of this. However it is time to recognize that we are not dealing with a single historical event, but with a long historical period, during which repeated waves of Roman influence washed over many parts of the West at different times, with varying strengths, and with varying effects. This is in fact what the literary sources actually tell us: "The Germans and the Gauls, among the other peoples of Europe, were given a remarkable number of opportunities to learn and repeatedly relearn the sweetness of this modulation," complained John the Deacon, "yet because of their fickle souls, as well as their natural savagery, they were utterly unable to preserve it incorrupt, because they mingled things of their own into the Gregorian chants."[97]

[95] A. Papadopoulos-Kerameus, *Analekta Hierosolumitikes Stachuologias* [Α. Παπαδόπουλος-Κεραμεύς, Ἀνάλεκτα Ἱεροσολυμιτικῆς Σταχυολογίας] 2 (St. Petersburg: Kirsvaoum, 1894; repr. Brussels: Culture et Civilisation, 1963), 1–254.

[96] Robert Taft, *The Liturgy of the Hours in East and West: The Origins of the Divine Office and its Meaning for Today* (Collegeville, Minn.: Liturgical Press, 1986), 276; Alexander Schmemann, *Introduction to Liturgical Theology*, trans. Asheleigh E. Moorhouse (Crestwood, N.Y.: St. Vladimir's Seminary, 1986), 205–12. For the extant manuscripts of the various recensions of the St. Sabas *Typikon*, see A. Dmitrievskij, *Opisanie Liturgicheskikh Rukopisej* 3: *Typika* II [А. Дмитрieвскiй, Описанiе Литургическихъ Рукописей 3: *Τυπικά* II] (St. Petersburg, 1917; repr. Hildesheim: Olms, 1965).

[97] "Huius modulationis dulcedinem inter alias Europae gentes Germani seu Galli discere crebroque rediscere insigniter potuerunt, incorruptam vero tam levitate animi, quia nonnulla de proprio Gregorianis cantibus miscuerunt, quam feritate quoque naturali servare minime potuerunt." *Sancti Gregorii Magni Vita*, in *Patrologia Latina* 75 (Paris: J.-P. Migne, 1862), 90–91.

Attempts to export Roman liturgical practices are documented continually from the beginning of the fifth century.[98] Even the two most concerted efforts to spread the Roman liturgy, the Anglo-Saxon mission and the Carolingian reform, involved numerous trips back and forth in search of Roman books and Roman singers.[99] The Roman liturgy promoted by Boniface[100] (680–754) was not the Roman liturgy promoted by Chrodegang[101] (d. 766). Neither was quite the same as the Roman liturgy witnessed by Pippin when Pope Stephen II visited him in 754.[102] To put it another way, the process of exporting the Roman chant repertory was much like the better-documented processes involved in exporting the other

[98] See the material summarized in Vogel, *Medieval Liturgy*, 147–50, 61–105, 110–33, esp. nn. 131, 194. The earliest document advocating the adoption of Roman customs elsewhere is a letter of Pope Innocent I written in the year 416; Robert Cabié, *La lettre du pape Innocent Ier à Décentius de Gubbio (19 mars 416): Texte critique, traduction et commentaire*, Bibliothèque de la Revue d'histoire ecclésiastique 58 (Louvain: Publications universitaires de Louvain, 1973). It is important to recognize that many of these efforts were not initiated from Rome or by the popes, but rather by outsiders who, for reasons of their own, wished to draw closer to Rome. Pippin and Charlemagne were, in their time, only the most recent and successful of these Romanizers.

[99] On the manuscript traffic between Rome and the north, see Armando Petrucci, "L'Onciale Romana: Origini, sviluppo e diffusione di una stilizzazione grafica altomedievale (sec. VI–IX)," *Studi medievali*, ser. 3, 12 (1971): 75–134, with 20 plates; Paola Supino Martini, "Carolina romana e minuscola romanesca: Appunti per una storia della scrittura latina in Roma tra IX e XII secolo," *Studi medievali*, ser. 3, 15 (1974): 769–93, with twelve plates; Supino Martini and Petrucci, "Materiali ed ipotesi per una storia della cultura scritta nella Roma del IX secolo," *Scrittura e civiltà* 2 (1978): 45–101; Donald A. Bullough, "Roman Books and Carolingian *Renovatio*," in Derek Baker, ed., *Renaissance and Renewal in Christian History*, Studies in Church History 14 (Oxford: Blackwell, 1977), 23–50; Bischoff, *Latin Palaeography*, 81, 101, 115.

[100] On Boniface in general see Theodor Schieffer, *Winfrid-Bonifatius und die christliche Grundlegung Europas*, 2nd ed. (Darmstadt: Wissenschaftliche Buchgesellschaft, 1980). On his liturgical sources see *Sankt Bonifatius: Gedenkengabe zum zwölfhundertsten Todestag*, ed. Cuno Raabe et al. (Fulda: Parzeller, 1954), 58–101; Gamber, *Codices*, 227, 233; *Supplementum*, 49.

[101] Eugen Ewig, "Saint Chrodegang et la réforme de l'église franque" and Cyrille Vogel, "Saint Chrodegang et les débuts de la romanisation du culte en pays franc," in *Saint Chrodegang: Communications présentées au Colloque tenu à Metz à l'occasion du douzième centenaire de sa mort* (Metz: Éditions le Lorrain, 1967), 25–53, 91–109; John Michael Wallace-Hadrill, *The Frankish Church*, Oxford History of the Christian Church (Oxford: Clarendon, 1983), 170–74. Ewig's article is reprinted in his *Spätantikes und fränkisches Gallien: Gesammelte Schriften (1952–1973)* 2, ed. Hartmut Atsma, Beihefte der Francia 3/2 (Munich: Artemis, 1979), 232–59. Carol Heitz, "De Chrodegang à Cluny II: Cadre de vie, organisation monastique, splendeur liturgique," in *Sous la règle de Saint Benoît: Structures monastiques et sociétés en France du Moyen Age à l'époque moderne, Abbaye Sainte-Marie de Paris 23–25 octobre 1980*, École pratique des hautes études IVe section, Sciences historiques et philosophiques V, Hautes études médiévales et modernes 47 (Geneva: Droz, 1982), 491–97.

[102] For the sources see Vogel, *Medieval Liturgy*, 148–50.

Roman liturgical books. A few surviving manuscripts of the Gregorian Sacramentary appear to have been copied directly from the exemplar Pope Hadrian sent to Charlemagne,[103] but this textual tradition never fully supplanted the many other traditions descended from other Roman sources: the Old Gelasian, the Frankish Gelasian, and the non-Hadrianic Gregorian sacramentaries.[104] Competing textual traditions can also be traced for the *Ordines Romani*[105] and the Roman lectionaries,[106] homiliaries, and legendaries[107]—and this variety is not due merely to lapses in Frankish transmission, but to variations and changes made even within the city of Rome itself. Probably the Gregorian repertory does not descend from a single manuscript or singer, but was molded from a number of written and oral sources, differing somewhat among themselves, and brought north at different times by varying routes.

It is important to understand this varied transmission correctly. Despite recent attempts by revisionist historians "to contradict liturgical standardization and uniformity as major dimensions of the reality of Carolingian religious life" and to assert that "there is little consensus on what was 'Roman' in the liturgical world of the eighth and ninth centuries,"[108] there is no need to substantially modify the traditional view. The will to Romanize and standardize was indeed a central goal of the Carolingian reform. What was lacking was our modern conception of absolute uniformity, which we owe to the printing press. Only a relative unity was possible then, and it was relatively achieved. The Carolingian ideal was clearly expressed, among other places, in the *Libri Carolini*, a document drawn up by Carolingian theologians which purports to speak for Charlemagne himself:

[103] Ibid., 81–85.

[104] Ibid., 64–106.

[105] Ibid., 135–90.

[106] Ibid., 61–106, 110–34; 135–272; 339–54, 395–97.

[107] Réginald Grégoire, *Homéliaires liturgiques médiévaux: Analyse de manuscrits*, Biblioteca degli 'Studi medievali' 12 (Spoleto: Centro italiano di studi sull' Alto Medioevo, 1980), 127–244; François Dolbeau, "Notes sur l'organisation interne des légendiers latins," in Centre de recherches sur l'Antiquité tardive et le haut Moyen Age, Université de Paris X, *Hagiographie, cultures et sociétés, IVe–XIIe siècles: Actes du Colloque organisé à Nanterre et à Paris (2–5 mai 1979)* (Paris: Études augustiniennes, 1981), 11–31; Antoine Chavasse, "Un homiliaire liturgique romain du VIe siècle: L'homiliaire 'augustinien' du Parisinus 3798," *Revue bénédictine* 90 (1980): 194–233.

[108] Richard E. Sullivan, "The Carolingian Age: Reflections on Its Place in the History of the Middle Ages," *Speculum* 64 (1989): 267–306, esp. 293. Just because the variety among Carolingian liturgical sources seems bewildering to anyone who is not fully prepared to deal with them, does not mean that standardization was not being attempted by those who created them. Compare the more accurate account of Pippin's relationship with Rome in Wallace-Hadrill, *The Frankish Church*, 162–80.

> While from the early days of the faith [the Frankish church] stood firm with [the Roman church] in the union of sacred religion, and differed only a little from it in the celebration of the offices (which in any case is not contrary to faith), it is [now] joined to it even in the order of psalmody, by the care and industry of our father the illustrious and excellent man King Pippin of venerable memory, and since the coming into the Gauls of the most reverent and most holy man Stephen, bishop of the city of Rome. [This was done] so that there might not be an unequal order of psalmody where there was an equal order of believing, and so that [the Frankish and Roman churches,] which were united by the sacred reading of one sacred law, would also be united even by the venerable tradition of one chant [*modulamen*]—nor would those who were joined by pious devotion to a single faith be separated by a varied celebration of offices. Hence indeed we too, now that the kingdom of Italy has been united to us by God, have wished to raise the roof of the holy Roman church, and have pressed for submission to the salutary exhortations of Pope Hadrian, so that the many churches of this region, which formerly were refusing to receive the tradition of the Apostolic See in psalmody, might now embrace it with all diligence, and adhere in the order of psalmody as they also adhered to the obligation of faith. Thus not only all the provinces of the Gauls and Germany or Italy, but even the Saxons and certain peoples of the northern region are known to have been converted by us, with God's approval, to the rudiments of the true faith, and so they are careful to follow the See of Blessed Peter in all things, just as they desire to reach that [Heaven] to which [Peter] holds the keys.[109]

[109] "Quae dum a primis fidei temporibus cum ea perstaret in sacrae religionis unione et ab ea paulo distaret—quod tamen contra fidem non est—in officiorum celebratione, venerandae memoriae genitoris nostri inlustrissimi atque excellentissimi viri Pippini regis cura et industria sive adventu in Gallias reverentissimi et sanctissimi viri Stephani Romanae urbis antestitis est ei etiam in psallendi ordine copulata, ut non esset dispar ordo psallendi, quibus erat conpar ordo credendi, et quae unitae erant unius sacrae legis sacra lectione, essent etiam unitae unius modulaminis veneranda traditione nec seiungeret officiorum varia celebratio, quas coniunxerat unicae fidei pia devotio. Quod quidem et nos conlato nobis a Deo Italiae regno fecimus sanctae Romanae ecclesiae fastigium sublimare cupientes et reverentissimi papae Adriani salutaribus exhortationibus parere nitentes, scilicet ut plures illius partis ecclesiae, quae quondam apostolicae sedis traditionem in psallendo suscipere recusabant, nunc eam cum omni diligentia amplectantur, et cui adhaeserant fidei munere, adhaereant quoque psallendi ordine. Quod non solum omnium Galliarum provinciae et Germania sive Italia, sed etiam Saxones et quaedam aquilonalis plagae gentes per nos Deo annuente ad verae fidei rudimenta conversae facere noscuntur, et ita beati Petri sedem in omnibus sequi curant, sicut illo pervenire, quo ille clavicularius exstat, desiderant." *Monumenta Germaniae Historica*, Legum Sectio III: Concilia, Tomi 2 Supplementum: *Libri Carolini*, ed. Hubert Bastgen (Hannover: Hahn, 1924), 21–22. On the authorship and historical position of the *Libri Carolini*, see Judith Herrin, *The Formation of Christendom* (Princeton: Princeton University Press, 1987), 427–28, 435–40, 462, 467, 470–72; Helmut Feld, *Der Ikonoklasmus des Westens*, Studies in the History of Christian Thought 41 (Leiden: Brill, 1990), 14–20.

Thus both Jerusalem and Rome exported their local liturgical traditions within their respective spheres of influence: Jerusalem to Armenia, Georgia, and ultimately Constantinople; Rome to Anglo-Saxon England, the Carolingian realm, Germany, and eventually all of Western Europe. In both Jerusalem and Rome there may have been a significant variety of practices from one church to another; certainly the living tradition continued to develop even while it was being exported to places farther away. Thus it is not that one uniform tradition was exported once and for all, but that continually varying strains of it were brought out again and again, in slightly differing forms, officially and unofficially, by a succession of private individuals and public figures of all kinds.

This is why, when we turn to the earliest Gregorian chant manuscripts, we find too many differences in calendar, repertory, text, and notation to allow for the easy reconstruction of a common archetype, as if they were all descended from a single book that was brought once from Rome to (say) Aachen or Metz. It is true that all the manuscripts together, with all their variations, appear nearly identical compared to the welter of local Gallican traditions they supplanted. That is why so many have entertained the hope that an archetype can be reconstructed. But the differences are many and significant enough that efforts to reconstruct the archetype have not succeeded and cannot do so. In place of the classical approach to filiation, then, it would be better to try to arrange the earliest Roman chant manuscripts into what New Testament scholars would call "text types" or "profiles," groups of related manuscripts representing branches within the total tradition.[110] For the manuscripts of the *graduale* at least, preliminary investigations yield the following preliminary results:

(1) The most obvious and provocative text type, perhaps, would consist of those eighth- through tenth-century fragments that are textually closer to the well-known Old Roman manuscripts of the eleventh and twelfth centuries than they are to Gregorian manuscripts.[111]

[110] See my book, *Re-envisioning Past Musical Cultures*, 40–45. Bibliography on the manuscripts mentioned in the following discussion can be found in Jeffery, "The Oldest Sources of the *Graduale*."

[111] Michel Huglo has already pointed out the Old Roman character of the flyleaves that were formerly part of Kassel, Landesbibliothek MS. Theol. Fol. 36, in his "Le chant «vieux-romain»: Liste des manuscrits et témoins indirects," *Sacris Erudiri* 6 (1954): 96–124, see 107. For another example see Helene Wagenaar-Nolthenius, "Ein Münchener Mixtum: Gregorianische Melodien zu altrömischen Texten," *Acta Musicologica* 45 (1973): 249–55. An eighth-century fragment with Old Roman affinities, possibly the earliest extant *graduale*, is described in my forthcoming study "The Oldest Manuscript of Roman Chant."

(2) Others, though Gregorian in their textual affinities, exhibit some interesting archaic traits.[112]

(3) The *gradualia* of Compiègne, Corbie, and Senlis have long been recognized as "not entirely independent of each other";[113] the *graduale* Laon, Bibliothèque municipale MS. 118 could also be placed with this group.[114] Several fragments of north Italian origin, though perhaps not closely related to this "northern French" group, at least have no major textual disagreements with it.[115] Perhaps these northern French and northern Italian sources, taken together, represent a kind of "standard" or "central" kind of text.

(4) Other Italian fragments, however, seem to stand outside this "standard" text, in part because they are from plenary missals, in which the chant repertory has been modified to conform to the calendar of the sacramentary.[116]

(5) Two manuscripts copied at St. Amand tend to agree with each other against the "standard" group—yet they also disagree with each other in some important respects.[117]

[112] For example, the Vatican MS. Ottoboni 313 has unusually few alleluias, as if pointing back to a time before the expansion of the alleluia repertory. The Mass *Omnes gentes*, a more recent addition to the Gregorian repertory, occurs in an unusual place, between the last two Sundays after Pentecost; most manuscripts that have it place it after the Sixth Sunday after Pentecost. The different placement in the Ottoboni manuscript may perhaps reflect a desire to preserve the older sequence of Sundays undisturbed. The presence of these two archaic or conservative traits (if indeed that is what they are) does not necessarily mean we should regard the entire text as representing an earlier period than other manuscripts. Typically, every text type would be more archaic than others in some respects, but more developed in other respects.

[113] Jacques Froger, "The Critical Edition of the Roman Gradual by the Monks of Solesmes," *Journal of the Plainsong and Medieval Music Society* 1 (1978): 81–97, see 92. These are the graduals in the last three columns of Hesbert's *Antiphonale.*

[114] For instance on the feast of the Annunciation, where the Compiègne and Senlis graduals have different propers, Laon 118 has both of them. Laon 118 is also linked to the Corbie gradual and to the Mont Reynaud gradual edited in *Paléographie musicale* 16 (1955) by the system used to indicate the modes of the introit psalms: see Michel Huglo, *Les tonaires: Inventaire, analyse, comparaison* (Paris: Société française de musicologie, 1971), 90–93.

[115] Darmstadt, Hessische Landes- und Hochschulbibliothek MS. 752; Dublin, National Library, MS. 2291; Heidelberg, Universitätsbibliothek MS. 362a/28 I. The Dublin fragment has now been edited in Klaus Gamber, "Fragmenta Liturgica," *Sacris Erudiri* 21 (1972–73): 254–56.

[116] Thus the fragment in Vatican MS. lat. 10644 has an unusual alleluia for the feast of St. Michael the Archangel. See Klaus Gamber, "Fragment eines mittelitalienischen Plenarmissale aus dem 8. Jahrhundert," *Ephemerides Liturgicae* 76 (1962): 335–41. The flyleaves in Pistoia, Biblioteca Capitolare MSS. C 81 and C 132 have graduals after the readings of Ember Saturday after Pentecost instead of the usual alleluias. On the complex of fragments in Munich, Bayerisches Hauptstaatsarchiv, Manuskriptensammlung 586 and 587, see my forthcoming "The Wessobrun Fragments of a Ninth-Century Italian Missal."

[117] Paris, B. N., MS. lat. 2291, and Reims, B. M. 213. Their agreements include the offertory *Elegerunt* on the Feast of St. Stephen, the propers for Annunciation and the Ember Days after

(6) That some people were aware of different manuscript traditions even in the eighth and ninth centuries is clear from the *graduale* of Mont-Blandin, which represents a "conflationary" type of text. For instance it includes two different series of graduals for the period after Pentecost, and the famous rubric at the *Omnes gentes* Mass, "Ista ebdomata non est in antefonarios romanos."[118] The underlying tradition that served as the original basis for the Mont-Blandin text prior to conflation may have been related to a fragment in Munich.[119]

(7) The *graduale* of Rheinau represents an "abridged" type of text: it gives the chants for Sundays while omitting most of the other days; it gives the choir sections in full while usually citing the solo only by incipit. The corresponding *cantatoria* of this type would give the solo sections in full while citing the choir parts only by incipit.[120]

Clearly the Roman chant repertory was exported not once but many times, as different streams of the Roman tradition were transmitted according to different principles and produced different types of texts.[121] No doubt interaction with older local chant traditions also played a role. It may well be that, like the Ambrosian and Mozarabic rites, the local Gallican traditions included some texts and even melodies that were similar to parts of the Gregorian repertory brought in to supplant them.[122] This would have made it easy for the Carolingians to portray these traditions as "differing

Pentecost and in the Seventh Month, and many of the introit psalms. Their disagreements, however, include many alleluias, many chants of the sanctoral cycle, and the order of canticles on Holy Saturday.

[118] See Huglo, "Le chant «vieux-romain,» " 111; Hesbert, *Antiphonale*, 180, third column.

[119] Munich, Bayerisches Hauptstaatsarchiv, Kloster Holzen Kl. Lit. No. 104, described in Alfred Schröder, "Bruchstück eines Mess-Antiphonars aus dem neunten Jahrhundert," *Archiv für die Geschichte des Hochstifts Augsburg* 6 (1929): 795–806. It agrees with the Mont-Blandin MS in having the gradual *Venite fili* in the *Omnes gentes* Mass, and the gradual *Gloria et honore* on the feast of St. Menna. On the provenance of this fragment see Bernhard Bischoff, *Die südostdeutschen Schreibschulen und Bibliotheken in der Karolingerzeit* 2 (Wiesbaden: Harrassowitz, 1980), 206, 242.

[120] See the title of the Rheinau manuscript in Hesbert, *Antiphonale*, p. 2, second column: "Incipiunt Dominicales anni circulo." On a *cantatorium* fragment of the same type, Laon B. M. 266, see Peter Jeffery, "An Early Cantatorium Fragment Related to MS Laon 239," *Scriptorium* 36 (1982): 245–52, pl. 29–30.

[121] Therefore Hesbert's *Antiphonale* needs to be replaced by a new edition in which all the earliest manuscripts and fragments are presented in full. I hope to publish such a work eventually under the title *Graduale, vel potius Antiphonale Missarum Sacrosanctae Romanae Ecclesiae, S. Gregorio Papae I. vulgo adscriptum, ex omnibus codicibus antiquissimis nunc curatius editum.*

[122] A good example is the gradual *Probasti* for the feast of St. Lawrence. Apparently there was also a Gallican gradual with this text: see Michel Huglo, "Altgallikanische Liturgie," *Geschichte der katholischen Kirchenmusik* 1, ed. Karl Gustav Fellerer (Kassel: Bärenreiter, 1972), 219–33, esp. 225; also Huglo, "Gallican rite, music of the," *New Grove* 7:133–25, esp. 115, 123. The text

only a little" from the Roman (as the *Libri Carolini* put it) or as merely corrupt versions of the Roman chant, making it seem only reasonable that they should turn (to use the metaphor attributed to Charlemagne himself) from the stream to the source.[123]

Thus there are many similarities in the ways the Jerusalem and the Roman chant traditions were exported to other centers, leading to a comparable variety among the surviving manuscripts. In both cases the process was already under way in the fifth century, and the influence grew stronger until it had produced a fully hybridized tradition by the twelfth and thirteenth centuries. And just as the local Jerusalem rite was ultimately supplanted by one of its own descendants—the hybrid we call the Byzantine rite—so the local liturgy of Rome, with its Old Roman chant, was eventually replaced by what we call the Roman rite, the Carolingian synthesis as adopted by the thirteenth-century papal court, and spread throughout the West by the Franciscans.[124] More thorough investigation of the ways the Jerusalem chant was exported to Armenia, Georgia, and finally Constantinople (which investigation is sorely needed in any event) could provide us with useful models of the export and assimilation processes, models that could save us many false starts and missteps as we attempt to develop a clearer picture of the spread of the Roman rite to the rest of Europe.

Conclusion

The origins and early history of Gregorian and Old Roman chant have been so heavily worked over, so clouded and confused by controversy, that it is helpful to look away for a moment at another center—a center where many

also forms part of the Beneventan offertory *Adhesit* V. *In craticula*, which has its own Gregorian, Old Roman, and Milanese counterparts: see Kelly, *Beneventan Chant*, 178–81. This is hardly an isolated case.

[123] According to the story told by John the Deacon (*Patrologia Latina*, 75:91): "Sed et Carolus noster patricius, rex autem Francorum, dissonantia Romani et Gallicani cantus Romae offensus, . . . interrogasse fertur quis inter rivum et fontem limpidiorem aquam conservare soleret? Respondentibus fontem prudenter adjecit: Ergo et nos qui de rivo corruptam lympham usque hactenus bibimus, ad perennis fontis necesse est fluenta principalia recurramus."

[124] S. J. P. Van Dijk and Joan Hazelden Walker, *The Origins of the Modern Roman Liturgy: The Liturgy of the Papal Court and the Franciscan Order in the Thirteenth Century* (London: Newman, 1960); Van Dijk, ed., *Sources of the Modern Roman Liturgy: The Ordinals of Haymo of Faversham and Related Documents (1243–1307)*, 2 vols., Studia et Documenta Franciscana 1–2 (Leiden: Brill, 1963); Van Dijk and Walker, eds., *The Ordinary of Innocent III*, Spicilegium Friburgense 22 (Freiburg: Universitätsverlag, 1975).

of the same processes took place, but where they are much better documented and hence more easily traced. Once we have seen clearly how the Jerusalem chant repertory began in the fifth century with the responsorial psalms accompanying the annual cycle of readings, how this cycle became the nucleus around which chants of other genres accumulated, how it grew into the complete written chantbook of the seventh century and the fully developed lectionary of the eighth, how it was expanded further through the creativity of the eighth-century hymnodists, and how, after exerting strong influence on neighboring churches throughout its history, it finally overwhelmed and partly merged with the rite of Constantinople in the ninth century and later—then we can look again at the Roman tradition and see it from a new perspective. Allowing for the many differences between the two cities, an understanding of what happened in the East can help us imagine more realistically what might have happened in the West, by showing us how to sift through the much more meager Western evidence, what to look for as we go, and how to interpret what we find. If we try to do this we will begin to see that, in Rome as in Jerusalem, there was already a fifth-century repertory of responsorial psalmody that was somehow expanded into the core repertory of the seventh century that had been written down by the eighth. While the Jerusalem tradition was shaped especially by local monastic poets, the Roman tradition was shaped by the creativity of the well-trained singers of the *schola cantorum*, until, after exerting strong influence on neighboring churches throughout its history, it finally overwhelmed and partly merged with the other Western chant traditions beginning in the later eighth century.

Thus the investigation of Jerusalem chant will do much for the study of Roman chant, teaching us that the quickest route West begins by turning East. Simultaneously investigating the musical traditions of these two centers, the Holy City and the Eternal City, will bring to our efforts a kind of binocular vision by which each can be seen in its full three dimensions. This in turn will help us feel more confident about where to look, and about what to make of what we see. In short, it will create the beginning of a framework that can help organize and orient further explorations into the formation of the two Roman chant repertories.

Table 1

Fifth Century: Annual Cycles of Responsorial Psalms (Graduals) Are Formed

JERUSALEM		ROME	
Events	*Sources*	*Events*	*Sources*
417–39: The early lectionary completed, including full cycle of graduals and alleluias for the liturgical year.	Text survives only in Armenian translation, ed. Renoux 1969–71. See n. 5.	422–32: Pope Celestine I introduces graduals into the Roman Mass.	*Liber Pontificalis*, ed. Duchesne 1:89, 230 (see also n. 6).
		440–61: Pope Leo I cites texts of graduals in his sermons.	Ed. Chavasse 1973 (see also n. 7).

Table 2

Sixth–Eighth Centuries: Core Chant Repertories are Completed and Written Down

JERUSALEM		ROME	
Events	*Sources*	*Events*	*Sources*
6–7th c.: The oldest chantbook completed (Office and Mass in one book).	Text survives only in Georgian translation, ed. Metreveli et al. 1980. See n. 17.	ca. 609: Dedication—the last feast given a complete set of new proper chants. Feasts introduced in the 7–8th c., which borrow most of their chants from older feasts: 625–38. St. Apollinaris 682–3. St. George 687–701. Triumph of the Cross, Purification, Annunciation, Assumption, Nativity. 7–8th c. St. Gregory the Great	Dates of feasts indicated or implied by *Liber pontificalis*, confirmed by research on the development of the Roman sacramentaries and lectionary, see Klauser 1972:184–85, Vogel 1986:342–54, and nn. 22–33.
8th c.: The developed form of the lectionary includes many chant texts and incipits.	Text survives only in Georgian translation, ed. Tarchnischvili 1959–60. See n. 16.	715–31: Pope Gregory II institutes Masses on Thursdays in Lent: chants borrowed from older feasts.	

Table 3

Seventh through Ninth Centuries: The Core Repertories Expanded by Expert Singers/Hymnodists

JERUSALEM		ROME	
Events	*Sources*	*Events*	*Sources*
Sophronios, bishop of Jerusalem (639–39), composes hymns.	See Christ and Paranikas 1871:LIII, 96–97, and n. 53.	638: Epitaph of Pope Honorius I (625–38) calls him "divino in carmine pollens."	*Liber Pontificalis,* ed. Duchesne 1:326–27. See n. 64.
The hymnographer/monks of Mar Saba: St. Andrew of Crete (ca. 660–740); St. John Damascene (ca. 675–ca. 749); St. Cosmas of Maiuma (d. ca. 743)	See Pitra 1876:XXXVI–XL. Christ and Paranikas 1881:XLII, 97, 147; XLIV, 117, 205; XLIX–L, 161; and n. 54.	Popes Leo II (682–83), Benedict II (684–85) and Sergius I (687–701) trained in singing from boyhood by a "prior cantorum."	*Liber Pontificalis,* ed. Duchesne 1:359, 363, 371. See nn. 64–65.
		ca. 700: *Ordo Romanus* 1 uses the term "schola cantorum" for the Papal choir.	Ed. Andrieu 2 (1948) 80, 81, 83, 84. See n. 75.
Theophanes and Theodore Graptos, hymnographers (d. 840s)	Christ and Paranikas 1881:XLIV, 236, and n. 57.	795–816: The 12-year-old future Pope Sergius II (844–47) sent to *schola cantorum* by Pope Leo III.	*Liber Pontificalis,* ed. Duchesne 2:86. See n. 78.
		late 9th c.: *Ordo Romanus* 36 directs that poor boys who can sing well be transferred to the *schola cantorum.*	Ed. Andrieu 4 (1956) 195, see also comments on 123–26. See n. 79.

Table 4

The Central Roman and Jerusalem Repertories are Exported Elsewhere

JERUSALEM		ROME	
Events	*Sources*	*Events*	*Sources*
383: Egeria visits from West.	Ed. Maraval 1982, Wilkinson 1981. See n. 4.		
		416: Pope Innocent promotes Roman practices abroad.	Ed. Cabié 1973. See n. 98.
After 439: Jerusalem lectionary adopted by Armenian church.	Renoux 1969:30–32, 186–88; 1971:152–54, 160–61. See n. 5.		
7–8th c.: Jerusalem chantbook, homiliary, lectionary adopted by Georgian Church.	Metreveli 1980, Tarchnischvili 1959–60, Van Esbroeck 1975, Jeffery 1991. See nn. 16–18, 92–93.	7–8th c.: Roman sacramentaries and *ordines* brought into Gaul.	See Vogel 1986, nn. 102–106.
		731: Bede describes exchanges of books and singers between Rome and England, chant school at Canterbury taught by "disciples of Pope Gregory."	*Historia Gentis Anglorum Ecclesiastica*, ed. Colgrave & Minors 1969. See nn. 66–70.
		719–54: Mission of St. Boniface.	See Schieffer 1980, n. 100.
		753: Chrodegang introduces Roman chant at Metz.	See *St. Chrodegang* 1967, n. 101.
		754: Pippin meets Pope Stephen II.	Vogel 1986:148–50, n. 102.

Table 4 (cont.)

The Central Roman and Jerusalem Repertories are Exported Elsewhere

JERUSALEM		ROME	
Events	*Sources*	*Events*	*Sources*
		757–67: Pope Paul I sends books and singers to Pippin.	Ed. Dümmler 1892:529, 553–54, nn. 38, 77.
		784–85: Pope Hadrian I sends Gregorian Sacramentary to Charlemagne.	See Vogel 1986:80–85, n. 103.
8–9th c.: Monastic revival led by Theodore the Studite (d. 826) imports Palestinian monastic rite into Constantinople, producing the Studite *Typikon.*	Dmitrievskij 1 (1895), see n. 94.	8–9th c.: Earliest MSS of Roman and Gregorian chant texts.	Jeffery 1983, see nn. 15, 19.
		10th c.: Earliest notated Gregorian sources.	
1122: Last MS of Jerusalem liturgy.	Ed. Papadopoulos-Kerameus 2 (1894) 1–254, see n. 95.	11–13th c.: Notated Old Roman MSS.	
12–13th c.: Earliest MSS of Sabaitic *Typikon,* a new synthesis of Palestinian and Constantinopolitan monastic traditions.	Dmitrievskij 3 (1917), see n. 96.	13th c.: Liturgy of the Roman Curia (Gregorian) becomes basis of modern Roman rite and chant.	See Van Dijk and Walker, n. 124.

THOMAS FORREST KELLY

Structure and Ornament in Chant: The Case of the Beneventan Exultet

Even before my days as a student of David Hughes I was fascinated with those manuscript fragments that we all used to treat so casually: the framed page of an antiphoner that hangs over the photocopy machine in a departmental office that I won't name; the drawerful of uncatalogued vellum leaves used to illustrate "the medieval manuscript" in another music department; and the two pages that I must confess to owning myself. The fascination, of course, lies in wondering why one particular page, or one manuscript, should survive; in the amazing durability of medieval book-production as compared to modern efforts; in the contrast between what such a page's original purpose was and what it is doing hanging over a photocopy machine.

So it seemed particularly meaningful, when a friend of mine was recently dismembering a tenth edition of the *Encyclopaedia Britannica* (for reasons best known to himself), that I should be presented with a fragment including the article entitled "Plain Song." I was then beginning a study of the Exultet, and this fragment shared my enthusiasm for the subject. The author, the eminent William Smyth Rockstro, speaks of the Exultet as being "of extreme antiquity, and beautiful beyond all description. The melody of the Exultet is, indeed, very frequently cited as the finest example of plain song in existence."[1]

But despite Rockstro's admiration for the Roman Exultet, and indeed despite its undoubted beauty, we cannot be certain any longer about its extreme antiquity, particularly as we know that the Exultet was sung variously in different regions, and we have no evidence that the Roman Exultet is older than some others.[2]

In fact, it is a non-Roman melody that will occupy our attention here: the melody used in southern Italy, the Beneventan melody—which is not beautiful beyond description. It is a simple recitation on three pitches; and although it is not "frequently cited as the finest example of plain song in existence," it is a fine example of a highly-structured reciting tone with opening formulas, a flex, an intermediate cadence, and a final cadential phrase. An example of this melody can be examined in example 1.

Example 1
The Beneventan Exultet melody

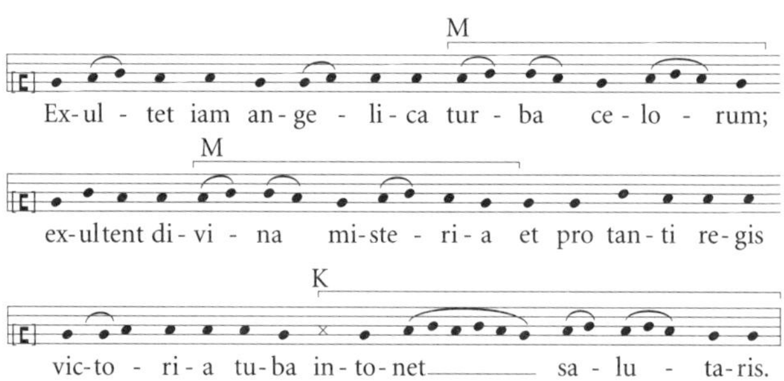

The Exultet—the extended praise of the Paschal candle sung by the deacon at the Easter Vigil—has a particular importance in the old Beneventan liturgy. Whereas the Exultet elsewhere is normally the first event of the Paschal Vigil, in the Beneventan liturgy it comes after the reading of the

[1] *Encyclopaedia Britannica*, 10th ed., s. v. "Plain Song," by William Smyth Rockstro.

[2] On the history of the Exultet and its ceremony in general see Jordi M. Pinell, "La benedicció del ciri pasqual i els seus textos," *Scripta et documenta* 10: *Liturgica* 2 (Montserrat: Abadia de Montserrat, 1958), 1–119; Georges Benoît-Castelli, "Le 'Praeconium paschale,'" *Ephemerides liturgicae* 67 (1953): 309–34; Bernard Capelle, "La procession du *Lumen Christi* au Samedi-Saint," *Revue bénédictine* 44 (1932): 105–19; Hermanus A. P. Schmidt, *Hebdomata sancta*, 2 vols. (Rome: Herder, 1956–57).

Table 1

Musical sources of the Exultet in southern Italy, in roughly chronological order

This table lists musical versions of the Exultet; thus some sources are included more than once, when they contain two texts (as do the fragments of Farfa and Trento), or when they were substantially revised from an earlier form to provide a later text (as were Vat. lat. 9820, Bari 2, and others).

(LS = Lower script; US = Upper script)

	Date	*Deposit*	*Text*	*Type*	*Provenance*
1.	10ex	Vat. lat. 9820	Ben	Exultet roll	Benevento
2.	10/11	Benevento, Bibl. cap. 33	Ben	Missal	provenance unknown
3.	11in	Vat. lat. 10673	Ben	Gradual	provenance unknown
4.	11in	Manchester, Rylands 2	Ben	Exultet roll	provenance unknown
5.	11in	Bari, Duomo, Exultet 1	Ben	Exultet roll	Bari
6.	11	Farfa-Trento A	Ben	Gradual	Veroli?
7.	11	Farfa-Trento B	Rom	Gradual	Veroli?
8.	11	Mirabella Eclano Exultet 1	Ben	Exultet roll	Benevento?
9.	11	Gaeta, Duomo, Exultet 1 (LS)	Ben	Exultet roll	Gaeta?
10.	11	Montecassino Exultet 1	Ben	Exultet roll	Amalfi (?)
11.	11med	Avezzano, Curia vescovile	Rom	Exultet roll	Montecassino
12.	11	Capua, Bibl. arcivescovile	Rom	Exultet roll	Capua? Montecassino
13.	11	Gaeta, Duomo, Exultet 2	Rom	Exultet roll	Gaeta?
14.	11	Pisa Duomo, Exultet 1	Rom	Exultet roll	Montecassino
15.	11 2/2	Vat. lat. 3784	Ben	Exultet roll	Montecassino
16.	11 2/2	Troia, Duomo, Exultet 1	Ben	Exultet roll	Troia
17.	11 2/2	Rome, Vall. C 32	Rom	Ritual	Montecassino?
18.	11 2/2	Mirabella Eclano Exultet 2	Rom	Exultet roll	Mirabella? Benevento?
19.	11ex	Bari, Duomo, Exultet 2 (LS)	Ben	Exultet roll	Bari
20.	11ex	Velletri, Museo capitolare	Rom	Exultet roll	Montecassino
21.	11ex	London, BL add. 30337	Rom	Exultet roll	Montecassino
22.	11ex	Oxford, Bodl. Can Bibl lat 61	Rom	Evangelistary	Zadar
23.	11ex	Vat. Barb. lat. 592	Rom	Exultet roll	Montecassino
24.	1082	Vat. Borg. lat. 339	Rom	Evangelistary	Dalmatian
25.	11/12	Gaeta, Duomo, Exultet 3	Rom	Exultet roll	Gaeta
26.	11/12	Paris, B.N., n.a. lat. 710	Rom	Exultet roll	Fondi
27.	11/12	Rome, Vall. F 29	Rom	Ritual	Farfa
28.	11/12	New York, Morgan M 379	Rom	Missal	Foligno
29.	12in	Troia, Duomo, Exultet 2	Ben	Exultet roll	Troia
30.	1106-20	Montecassino Exultet 2	Rom	Exultet roll	Sorrento
31.	12 in	Rome, Vall B 23	Rom	Missal	Norcia
32.	12 1/2	Berlin, Staatsb. Lat. Fol. 920	Rom	Missal	Kotor
33.	12	Subiaco XVIII	Rom	Missal	Subiaco
34.	12	London, BL Eg 3511	Rom	Missal	Benevento
35.	12	Troia, Duomo, Exultet 3 (LS)	Rom	Exultet roll	Troia

36.	12	Rome, Casanat. 724	Rom	Exultet roll	Benevento
37.	12	Vat. lat. 6082	Rom	Missal	Montecassino?
38.	12	Rome, Vall. B 43	Rom	Missal	Central Italy
39.	12ex	Naples VI G 34	Rom	Processional	Troia
40.	12ex	Bari, Duomo, Exultet 3	Rom	Exultet roll	Bari
41.	12/13	Salerno, Duomo, Exultet	Rom	Exultet roll	Salerno
42.	12/13	Vatican Ottob. lat. 576	Rom	Missal	Montecassino
43.	12/13	Vatican Barb. lat. 603	Rom	Missal	Caiazzo?
44.	13	Oxford, Bodl. Can. lit. 342	Rom	Missal	Dubrovnik
45.	13	Bari Exultet 2 (US melody 1)	Rom	Exultet roll	Bari
46.	13 2/2	Bari Exultet 2 (US melody 2)	Rom	Exultet roll	Bari
47.	13?	Naples VI G 38 (LS)	Rom	Missal	Franciscan
48.	14	Vat. lat. 3784A	Rom	Exultet roll	Naples
49.	15	Salerno 3	Ben	Missal	Salerno
50.	15	Salerno 4	Ben	Missal	Salerno
51.	15	Rome, Casanat. 1105	Rom	Missal	Montevergine

lessons and before the procession to the baptismal font.[3] Also peculiar to southern Italy is the phenomenon of the Exultet roll: some twenty-four surviving scrolls contain the text of the Exultet and its music, the oldest of them from the late tenth century.

An Exultet roll is made by sewing lengths of parchment together. Often pictures are painted on the roll, of three sorts: images from the text; or liturgical scenes of the ceremony at hand; or pictures of the ecclesiastical and secular rulers named in the Exultet. The illustrations are often painted upside-down with respect to the script so that viewers can see the pictures as they unroll from the top of the ambo (see plates 1–4).

These Exultet rolls have been given much scholarly attention, principally from art historians studying the beautiful illustrations they contain.[4] But scholars have often overlooked the many other appearances of the Exultet in southern Italy in missals, graduals, processionals, and the like (my own list of musical appearances of the Exultet in southern Italy appears as table 1); and nobody pays much attention to the music.

In what follows we shall give some close consideration to the melody of the Beneventan Exultet, and from it we can learn some simple but important facts about melodic transmission and about the process of embellishment. But even before that, I propose a brief survey of the surviving witnesses of the Exultet in southern Italy, for there is much to be seen of history and politics in this one occasional chant. In the space of less than two hundred years and in a limited area, the Exultet underwent many

[3] On the liturgical placement of the Exultet in the south Italian literature see René-Jean Hesbert, "L' 'Antiphonale missarum' de l'ancien rit bénéventain" (part 6, 'Le Samedi-Saint'), *Ephemerides liturgicae* 61 (1947): 153–210; idem, *Paléographie musicale* 14: *Le codex 10673 de la Bibliothèque Vaticane* (= *PM* 14, Tournai, 1931; repr. Bern, 1971), 240–60, 418–26.

[4] The art-historical bibliography on the south Italian Exultet rolls is vast, and will not be cited comprehensively here. The classic study is found in Émile Bertaux, *L'art dans l'Italie méridionale* (published as Tome 1; Paris, 1904); under the general direction of Adriano Prandi, Bertaux's work has been expanded and brought up to date as *L'art dans l'Italie méridionale: Aggiornamento dell'opera di Émile Bertaux,* 4 vols. (numbered IV–VI plus *Indici;* Rome: École française de Rome, 1978). Myrtilla Avery has published the surviving miniatures from Exultet rolls in *The Exultet Rolls of South Italy* (publ. as vol. II; Princeton: Princeton University Press, 1936); and more recently the Italian paleographer Guglielmo Cavallo has published a study and facsimiles of the rolls from Bari and Troia (*Rotoli di Exultet dell'Italia meridionale;* Bari: Adriatica, 1973) with substantial bibliography, 239–51. Additional facsimile volumes include Herbert Douteil, ed., *Exultet: Codex Vaticanus lat. 9820, Vollständige Facsimile-Ausgabe in Originalformat des Codex Vaticanus lat. 9820 der Biblioteca Apostolica Vaticana* (Graz: Akademische Druck- u. Verlagsanstalt, 1974), and Guglielmo Cavallo and Lucinia Speciale, eds., *Die Exultetrolle Codex Barberini latinus 592,* Codices e Vaticanis selecti 76 (Zurich: Belser, 1988), including essays by Cavallo and Speciale; for all the manuscripts cited here that are in Beneventan script, further bibliography can be found in Elias Avery Loew, *The Beneventan Script: A History of the South Italian Minuscule,* 2nd ed. Virginia Brown, 2 vols., Sussidi eruditi

Plate 1: Bari, Archivio del Duomo, Exultet roll 1 (detail). The deacon, on the ambo, sings the Exultet from a scroll while an attendant holds the Paschal candle. Note that the illustrations are reversed with respect to the text. Reproduced by permission.

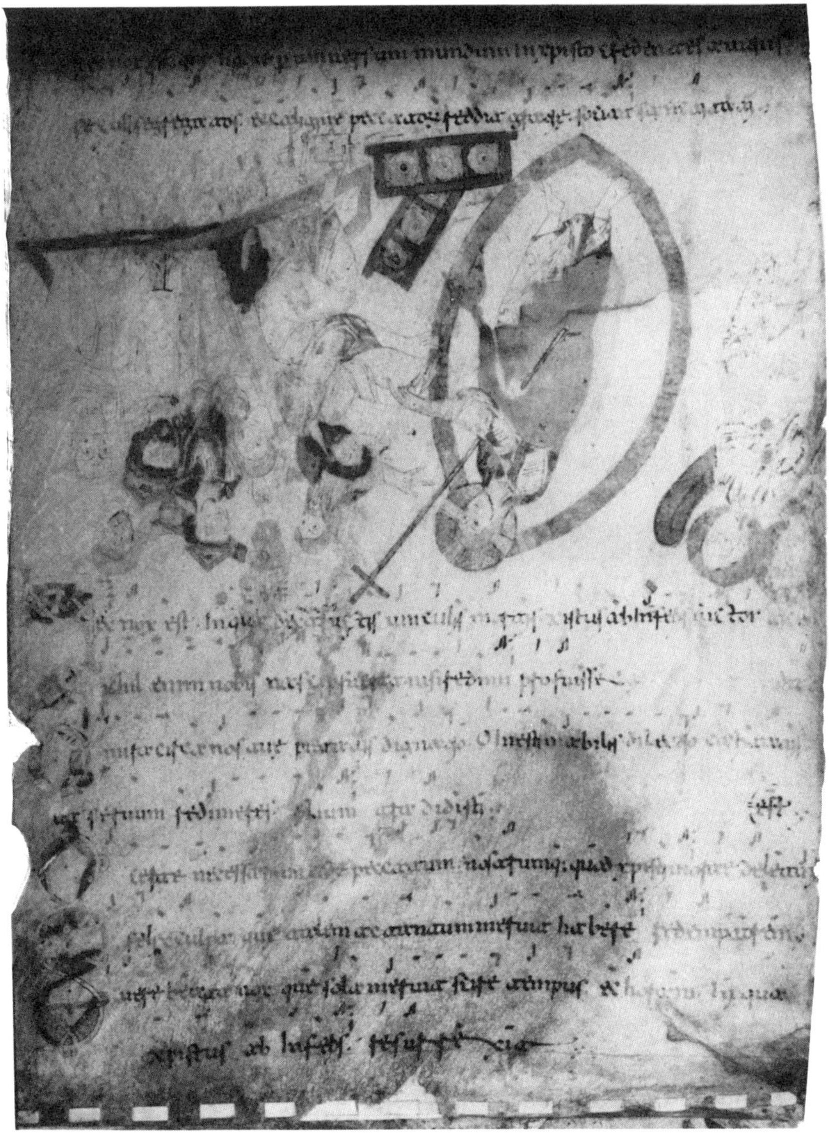

Plate 2: Montecassino, Archivio della Badia, Exultet roll 2 (detail). Two pieces joined together with a parchment strip. The illustration of Christ harrowing Hell is reversed so that it will appear right side up at the proper time. Reproduced by permission.

Plate 3: Troia, Archivio del Duomo, Exultet roll 3 (detail). Portraits of ecclesiastical and civil rulers for whom God's blessing is implored (Pope, Bishop, King); the roll concludes with the so-called Norman finale: "Qui semper vivis, regnas, imperas, necnon et gloriaris. . . ." Courtesy of the Istituto centrale per il catalogo e la documentazione, Rome.

Plate 4: Bari, Archivio del Duomo, Exultet roll 2 (detail). The original Beneventan script is visible for the first portion of the preface, but is erased beginning with *te invisibilem patrem;* the original notation has been erased throughout and replaced with square staff notation. Note the initial letters of the Beneventan text preserved on the left even though they no longer correspond to the substituted text. Reproduced by permission.

changes. Each new version, each alternative, owes its existence to a choice which reflects something of local history, and of cultural and even of political traditions.

Exultet rolls contain one of two texts, which we might call the Beneventan and the Roman versions (what Bannister called the *Vetus Itala* and the *Vulgate*).[5] The Beneventan text is a survival of the ancient liturgical rite of the area, associated with the Lombard duchy of Benevento at least as far back as the eighth century, and almost completely suppressed in the course of the eleventh century under the joint forces of Papal reform and Norman invasion. The Vulgate text reflects the rites of the church of Rome, whose authority only gradually asserted itself in southern Italy during the ninth and tenth centuries. Hence when we see, as we do in so many of the Exultet rolls, the old Beneventan text erased and the newer Roman text substituted, we see also the decline of Lombard power in the South and the increased importance of the Roman church.[6]

We notice also that Montecassino seems almost to be a factory for Exultet rolls with the newer Vulgate text. Montecassino, reaching the height of her power in the eleventh century, and no longer dependent on Lombard princes, is producing bishops, cardinals, and popes for the universal church: when a monk of Montecassino was made a bishop, the monastery often sent him out with a beautiful Exultet roll—using the Roman text—for use in his new diocese. Exultet rolls now at Velletri, Avezzano, the Vatican, the British Library, and probably others, are part of this phenomenon.[7] Montecassino, under Frankish and Papal influence, seems to have embraced all things Roman rather sooner than other places in the South, and these Exultets are an aspect of Montecassino's public stance.

The melody used for the Exultet in southern Italy is also clearly associated with the old Beneventan liturgy.[8] So it is no surprise that the oldest

33–34 (Rome: Edizione di storia e letteratura, 1980); see also Thomas Forrest Kelly, *The Beneventan Chant* (= *TBC;* Cambridge: Cambridge University Press, 1989), 46–48, 59–60, and Appendix 3 (298–319).

[5] Henry Marriott Bannister, "The *Vetus Itala* Text of the Exultet," *The Journal of Theological Studies* 11 (1910): 43–54, edits the Beneventan text, but incompletely and with errors. The Beneventan text is conveniently available in *PM* 14, 385–86, and in Cavallo, *Rotoli*, 26.

[6] On the Roman and Beneventan liturgies in the history of southern Italy see Kelly, *TBC*, 6–40; a classic article which deals with the changing role of the church at Benevento is Hans Belting, "Studien zum beneventanischen Hof im 8. Jahrhundert," *Dumbarton Oaks Papers* 16 (1962): 141–93, plus plates.

[7] The Exultets in question are Velletri, Museo capitolare, Exultet without shelf-mark (displayed under glass); Avezzano, Curia vescovile, Exultet without shelf-mark; Vatican City, Biblioteca Apostolica Vaticana MS. Vat. lat. 3784; London, British Library Additional MS. 30337.

[8] The demonstration that the melody considered here, and exemplified in example 1, is a melody from the old Beneventan liturgy, requires more space than is available here. Briefly, the

surviving Exultets have the local text and the melody associated with the regional liturgy; and these are among the very earliest musical documents in the area.

But because Exultet rolls are very beautiful and not easily replaced, they are not discarded, like so many other outmoded liturgical documents, when needs change. As a result, the Exultet rolls together, and many of them separately, reveal several layers of influence.

In cities which preserve more than one Exultet roll—Bari, Troia, Gaeta, and Mirabella Eclano—the successive documents reflect changing needs (these multiple rolls are summarized in table 2). The oldest roll in each city has the Beneventan text. This is, of course, a reason for the existence of multiple rolls in these cities, since the Beneventan text is soon replaced with the more widespread Vulgate. Sometimes, as at Bari and Troia, a second roll is designed probably to clarify the musical notation of the older Beneventan Exultet.

At some point in the late eleventh or early twelfth century, each center creates a new Exultet roll using the Roman text (these are Bari 3, Troia 3, Gaeta 2, Mirabella 2); but often—and here the musicologist can help the art historian in detecting Lombard conservatism—often the new text retains the old Beneventan melody.

At a still later stage, an older roll is sometimes re-used to fill the need for a "Roman" melody and a Vulgate text. Thus two old rolls were altered—Bari 2 in the thirteenth century, Gaeta 1 in the fourteenth—to preserve their illustrations while rejecting both their text and their melody. Similarly, Troia 3, whose text was already the Vulgate, had its Beneventan melody altered in the fourteenth century.

These two, separate, stages of transition—from the Beneventan to the Roman text, and from the Beneventan to the Roman melody—are to be seen also in many of the individual documents in other cities. The scribes of some of the Vulgate Exultets show a transitional stage when they include, in their new document, parts of the older Beneventan text: a south Italian roll now at Pisa, a Dalmatian gospel-book at Oxford, and an Exultet at Montecassino[9] all show a combination of texts. An intermediate stage in

use of the same melody for a variety of other functions specific to the Beneventan liturgy makes the connection clear. The melody of the Exultet is used also for a reading from the book of Jonah used either for Maundy Thursday or the Easter Vigil; for the introductory verses to the canticle of Azarias and the canticle of the Three Children from the book of Daniel, sung on Good Friday or Holy Saturday; and for the prayer of Jeremiah. See Kelly, *TBC*, 131–32. See also *PM* 14, 271–74, 318–21, and 417 n.1.

[9] These are Pisa, Duomo, Exultet roll without shelf-mark (now on display in the Museo dell'Opera del Duomo); Oxford, Bodleian Library MS. Canonici liturg. 342; and Montecassino, Archivio della Badia, Exultet 2.

Table 2

Cities with Multiple Exultets

Bari

11in	Bari 1	Beneventan text and melody
11ex	Bari 2	Beneventan text and melody; clearer notation
12ex	Bari 3	Roman text, Beneventan melody elaborated
13	Bari 2	revised, in Gothic hand (for those portions of text not matching Roman version) to Roman text, and elaborated melody on staff

Troia

11 2/2	Troia 1	Beneventan text and melody
12in	Troia 2	Beneventan text and melody, clearer notation
12	Troia 3	Roman text with Norman finale, Beneventan melody
14	Troia 3	Beneventan melody replaced with Roman

Gaeta

11	Gaeta 1	Beneventan text and melody
11	Gaeta 2	Roman text, Beneventan melody
11/12	Gaeta 3	Roman text, Beneventan melody
14	Gaeta 1	text and melody altered to Roman

Mirabella Eclano

11	Mirabella 1	Beneventan text and melody
11 2/2	Mirabella 2	Roman text, Beneventan melody

Other Later Alterations to Exultets

1. Vat. lat. 9820 (s. 10ex, Benevento) erased and reversed for Roman text, s. 12.
2. Farfa-Trento (s. 11 gradual) contains Beneventan and Roman texts together.
3. Vat. lat. 3784 (s. 11 2/2 Montecassino) amputated (s. 14) after prologue, replaced with Roman text and melody.

melodic change may be the twelfth- or thirteenth-century missal Vatican, Barberini lat. 603, whose Vulgate Exultet begins and ends with the Beneventan melody, but whose central portion has the now-usual preface-tone. A particularly interesting transitional stage is seen in four fragmentary folios, now divided between Farfa and Trento, from a single eleventh-century gradual which contained *two* versions of the Exultet—the one Beneventan with the usual melody, and the other Vulgate with a unique melody.[10]

One brutal way to change the text is simply to chop off the parts of an old roll that do not correspond to the Vulgate text, and to append new text and music; this is the fate of the Montecassino roll now Vatican, Barberini lat. 3784. A similarly drastic measure was taken with the Exultet of St. Peter's convent *extra muros* in Benevento (now Vat. lat. 9820), which in the twelfth century was erased and reordered to become a Roman text; by reversing the scroll the original pictures were now presented upside-down (that is, right-side-up to viewers), and in fact the initial letters of the older text survive upside-down in the present right margin.

A further layer of textual alteration is the so-called Norman finale of the Exultet, apparently imported into southern Italy and Sicily by the Normans in the later eleventh century.[11] This is an alternative ending to the Roman text, related, with its "qui semper vivis, regnas, imperas," to the Frankish *Laudes regiae;* it appears occasionally in Beneventan script, as in the processional Naples VI G 34; more often, however, it comes from the periphery of the Beneventan zone, where the confluence of traditions may be seen in many ways. An example is manuscript M. 379 in the Pierpont Morgan Library—a missal in ordinary minuscule that in many ways resembles those of Subiaco. The Exultet has the Roman text, but the melody is the old Beneventan one—at least at the beginning: but it switches to the Roman preface tone in the middle, at just the place where the two texts diverge. The Morgan missal may well reproduce an earlier source that physically substituted the Roman melody for the Beneventan, as in the amputated roll at the Vatican. And at the end comes the Norman finale. The rubric that follows demonstrates the foreign origin of what has preceded: "benedictione cerei

[10] These two fragments are Farfa, Biblioteca dell' Abbazia MS. AF.338 Musica XI (formerly AB.F.Musica XI) and Trento, Museo Provinciale d'Arte, s. n. (formerly Lawrence Feininger collection); the Farfa fragment is reproduced in *PM* 14, pls. XXVI–XXVII (in the first printing erroneously labeled "Cava"); the Exultet melodies from this manuscript are studied and transcribed in *PM* 14, 390–99.

[11] The name was coined by Ernst H. Kantorowicz in "A Norman Finale of the Exultet and the Rite of Sarum," *Harvard Theological Review* 34 (1941): 129–43; see also Eileen L. Roberts, "The Exultet Hymn in Twelfth Century Sicily as an Indicator of Manuscript Provenance," *Ecclesia orans* 5 (1988): 157–64.

finita, secundum teutonicum ordinem." It is not clear what is Teutonic about the foregoing: is it the Norman finale?

Is it possible, in fact, that the arrival of the Normans in the eleventh century, and their imposition of imported liturgical customs—including the Norman finale—provided the impetus for the change to the Roman melody? Evidently not: although the processional Naples VI G 34, one of only two sources in Beneventan script which have the Norman finale, uses the Roman melody, the third Exultet roll of Troia, which also has the Norman finale, was originally written with the Beneventan melody throughout; only in the fourteenth century was Troia 3's old notation replaced with the Roman melody. Three related missals from central Italy (Subiaco XVIII, Morgan M. 379, and Rome, Vallicelliana B 23) all have the Norman finale, and all use the Beneventan melody. These are sources peripheral to the Beneventan zone, written in ordinary minuscule; but they use the Beneventan melody for the first part of the Exultet, and the Roman preface-tone thereafter. The Norman conquest of south Italy, of which the Norman finale of the Exultet is a very small side effect, was not also the impetus for the change to the Roman melody. The cause for this change must be sought elsewhere; perhaps in the thirteenth-century standardization of Roman books by adopting Franciscan models.

All of these details contribute to underscore a single simple but important observation: for these scribes at least, changing the text does not necessarily mean changing the music. The Beneventan melody survives later and more frequently than its associated text. The arrival of the Vulgate text is not the moment of change to the Roman melody; we have already seen, in Bari, Troia, Gaeta, and Mirabella, that the earliest version of the Roman text retains the Beneventan melody. A new text, even if it arrives clothed in a new melody, can be selectively received, adapted to a well-known melodic formula, and the useless melody discarded. Melody and words can be, and are, transmitted separately. The older Beneventan melody survives for a long time—and because it is a formulaic reciting-tone it adapts easily to the needs of changing texts.[12]

[12] This facile reception of new texts is possible only when the melody is relatively formulaic—that is, adaptable to a variety of texts. A notable example of this is the adoption in most Gregorian chant traditions of the Gallican Psalter for formulaic verses such as those accompanying Introits, while retaining the Roman Psalter for all those pieces with more specific melodies; it is worth noting, however, that the southern Italian tradition either resists the Gallican Psalter, or never receives it in the chant tradition. See *PM* 14, 145–51.

This Beneventan melody deserves a little more of our attention. It is isolated in time and place, and in most of its appearances remarkably uniform; but in a few later sources, singers have developed, and scribes have recorded, ornamented versions of the Beneventan Exultet melody, and these can teach us much about how musicians of the time thought of embellishment, how they carried it out, and—what is often difficult to observe in other contexts—what precisely is the base material on which the embellishment is mounted.

The standard Beneventan Exultet tone is limited to the three pitches of a major third, reciting on the central pitch.[13] The music is arranged in periods, each of which ends with a characteristic final cadence (marked K in example 1 on p. 250); an intermediate cadence (marked M) divides the longer period into—usually—three phrases. Each phrase begins with an intonation, a special intonation being reserved for the opening of each period. In longer phrases, a descent of a tone precedes the *podatus* which marks occasional accents in the text, evidently for breathing pauses.

The final and medial cadences are based on a single accent, and vary only according to whether the final word is a paroxytone or a proparoxytone. For the final cadence (K) this is simply a matter of adding a single note at the end; but the medial cadence has two versions, in which the characteristic *torculus* of the paroxytone "caelorum" is subdivided for the proparoxytone "misteria." The rest of the cadential figure is applied to the syllables preceding the final accent without regard to their accentuation.

This melody is quite strictly applied to the text in almost 40 manuscripts. There are, of course, the occasional small variants which we find in almost all chant transmission, as in example 2, which shows the beginning of nine Exultets; all different, but all designed to emphasize the first accent of the text.

The first four are from the "standard" group presenting the original melody, but they are chosen to show a variety of openings. The leap of no. 1 is in fact the only leap in this otherwise entirely stepwise melody. The melody leaps a third, emphasizing the opening accent, before settling to the tenor on the central pitch. No. 2 compresses this leap to a single syllable, giving the further weight of length to the accented syllable. No. 3 keeps the weight but avoids the leap by filling in the third. No. 4, by beginning a step higher, eliminates the third altogether, but keeps the weight of the accent. No. 5 can be viewed as filling in the leap as presented in no. 2; and no. 6,

[13] The structure of the Beneventan Exultet was analyzed as long ago as 1894 by Dom Mocquereau in vol. 4 of the *Paléographie musicale* (Solesmes, 1894, 171–85), and considered also by Dom Hesbert in vol. 14, 388–90.

Example 2

Openings of selected Exultets

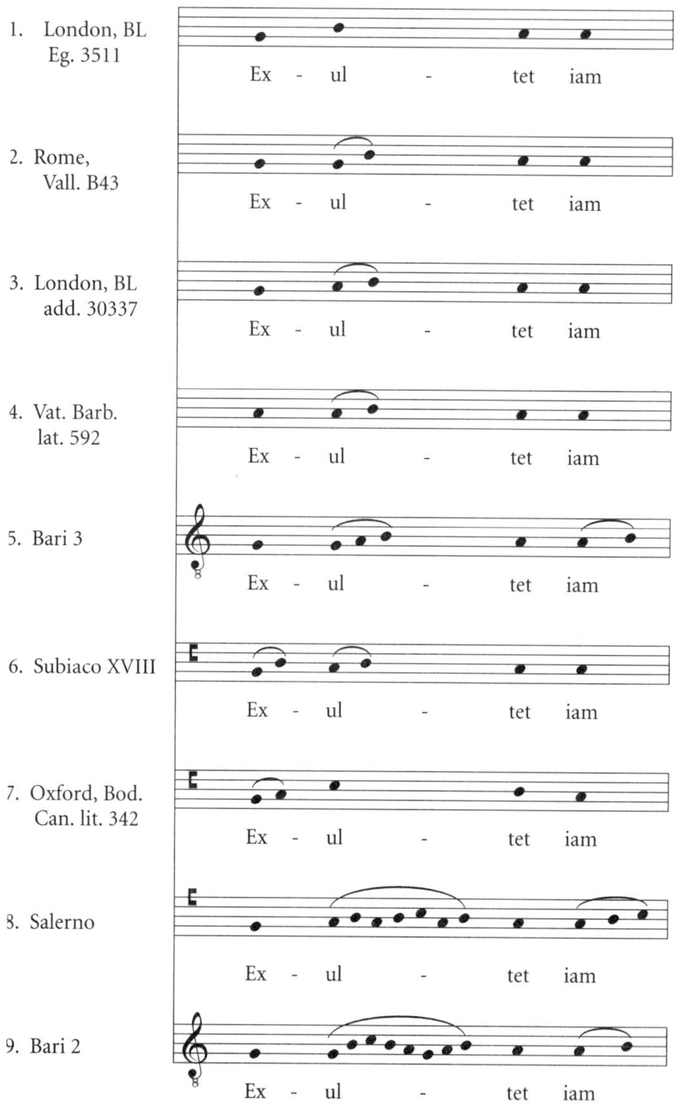

perhaps related to No. 3, creates a new leap on the first syllable, anticipating the high note of the second syllable. The last three openings are from later, consciously-embellished Exultets. No. 7 leaps beyond the range of the traditional Exultet on its first accented syllable; and nos. 8 and 9 use this high note as part of an extended flourish.

A comparative look at the principal cadences of elaborated Exultets will show many of these same principles at work. Example 3 shows typical cadences from eight Exultets. The two versions of the intermediate cadence appear in columns M1 through M9, and the final cadences in columns K1 through K8. I have selected a Montecassino Exultet of the late eleventh century, British Library Additional MS. 30337, as representative of the "standard" version of the melody, and its cadences are transcribed at the top.

In arranging these versions in order of ascending complexity it is important to avoid viewing them as a single development. Each version is, of course, a single way of singing the Exultet on a given occasion, and is not necessarily based on one or another slightly less decorated melody in another source. A better approach, in most cases, is to consider each version in comparison with the "standard" melody, whose widespread familiarity is certain.

The Dalmatian missal Berlin 920 is quite close to the standard melody. It does, however, alter the typical *torculus* in column M5 to provide an anticipation of the final; and in column K3 it sometimes, but not always, extends the range to the upper fourth. Subiaco XVIII, also a peripheral manuscript, uses in column M5 the same anticipation as seen in Berlin 920, and extends the range, not upward, but below the final at the end—in columns K6 and K7. The second Exultet of Troia extends the range in both directions: in the medial cadence at column M3 it precedes the standard *clivis* with another providing upper and lower auxiliaries and reaching the upper fourth; and in the final cadence the subfinal is reached by continuing the scale at K3, and the subfinal is repeated, at K7, in proparoxytone endings.

With the second and third Exultet rolls of Bari we are lucky to be able to study the progressive development of the Exultet melody in the same place: the three melodies of Bari are clearly related to one another. The first Exultet of Bari[14] is one of the oldest extant witnesses of the traditional melody and the Beneventan text. Later in the eleventh century, as we have

[14] Bari, Archivio del Duomo, Exultet roll 1 is reproduced in full in Cavallo, *Rotoli*, pls. 1–11, and discussed on 47–55; see also Avery, *The Exultet Rolls*, 11–13 and pls. 1–11; most recently, see Penelope C. Mayo, "Borders in Bari: The Decorative Program of Bari I and Montecassino under Desiderius," in *Monastica IV: Scritti Raccolti in memoria del XV centenario della nascita di S. Benedetto (480–1980)*, Miscellanea cassinese 48 (Montecassino: Pubblicazioni cassinesi, 1984), 31–67.

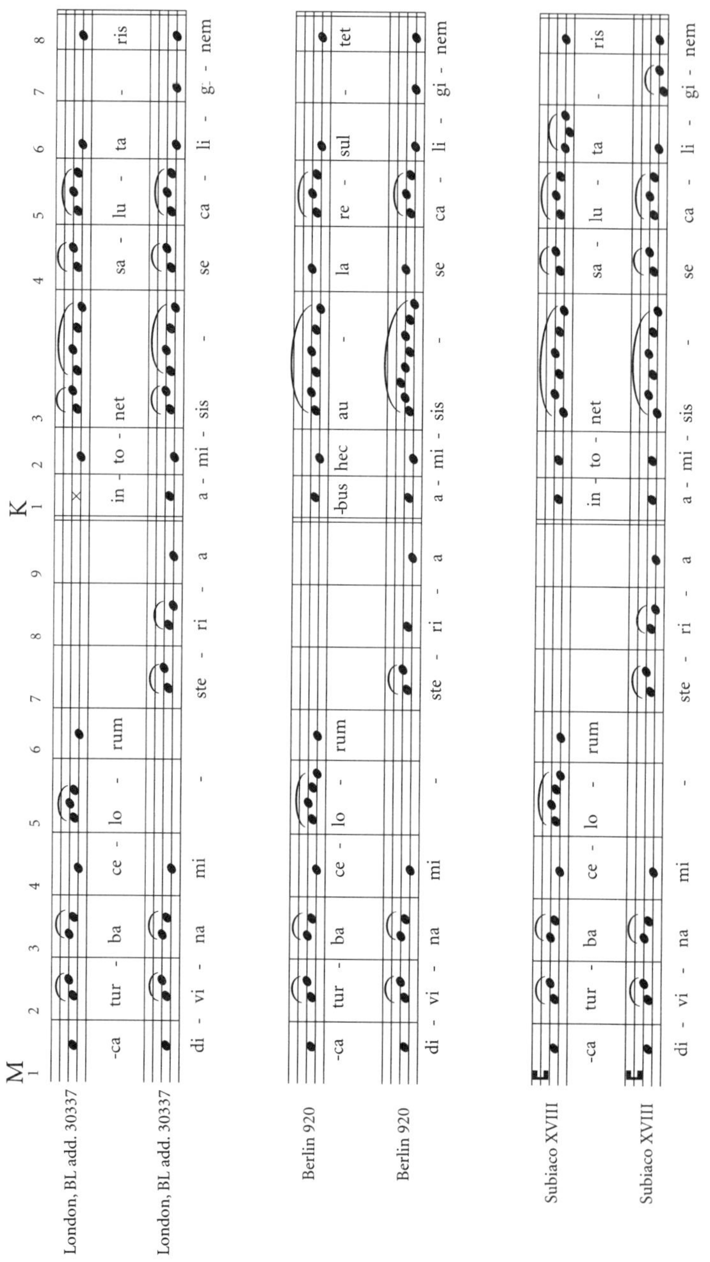

Example 3a: Cadential formulae of selected Exultets.

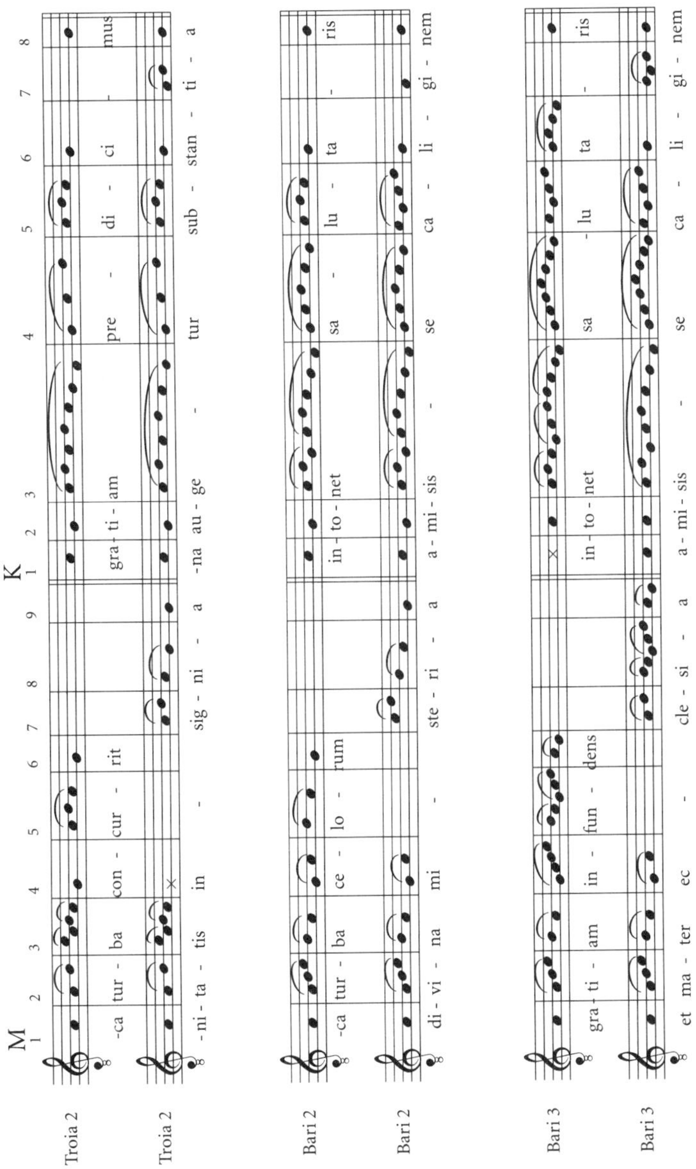

Example 3b: Cadential formulae of selected Exultets (continued).

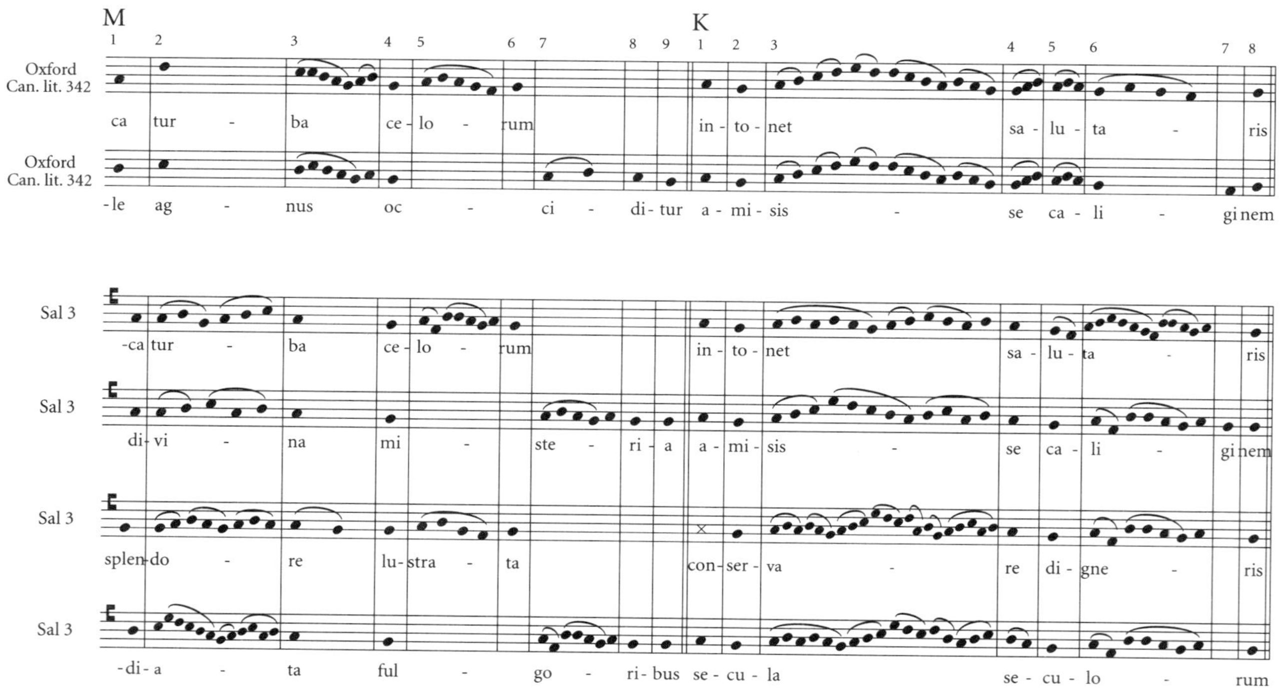

Example 3c: Cadential formulae of selected Exultets (continued).

seen, a second Beneventan Exultet was made at Bari with a clearer musical notation.[15] This second roll, however, was altered at a later date—somewhere around the turn of the thirteenth century; the Beneventan portions of its text were erased to provide for the Roman text in Gothic script, and its standard Beneventan melody was replaced throughout with a more elaborate version in an awkward square notation (see plate 4).

Bari also preserves a third Exultet roll, usually dated earlier than the revision of Bari 2, but whose melodic version clearly is a later development. This third roll has been little studied because it has no pictures; it is made, not too carefully, from an older scroll which once contained a Greek liturgical text (see plate 5).[16]

Example 4 compares these three Bari melodies. It is important to remember that, although Bari 2 and Bari 3 present embellished forms of the melody, they still follow the standard formal procedures for the Exultet: the formulas are regular, and consistently applied.

Bari 1 presents the "standard" melody—you may wish to compare it with the British Library roll in example 3. Noteworthy here, though, is the *quilisma* in column K4, which is not typical. Bari 2 shows a development of this basic melody. The intermediate cadence M reaches beyond the third at column M2, continuing the upward motion. On the word "celorum" (column M5), the typical *torculus* is divided, its first note given to the preceding syllable. This produces, by analogy, the *podatus* at the corresponding place in the proparoxytone cadence ("Misteria"), even though this version of the cadence lacks the original *torculus;* and the extra syllable allows a move to the upper fourth on the second syllable of "misteria"; this upper fourth is reached *only* on the three-syllable proparoxytone cadence. Bari 2 never reaches this upper fourth in the closing formula K. Instead, there is an elaboration of the figure at K3 with an opening *torculus* and a final scalewise continuation down to the subfinal. Bari 2's arch at K4, replacing the *quilisma* of Bari 1, has the effect of inverting the figure at K5. Note that the subfinal returns at the final cadence, but only where there is an extra syllable, as on "caliginem," column K7.

As for the melody of Bari 3, a glance will confirm that it is a development of what we have just seen in Bari 2, and not an independent branch from the original melody of Bari 1. One of the most striking developments is the "feminine ending" of the medial cadence (columns M6, M9),

[15] Cavallo, *Rotoli*, pls. 17–23 and pp. 99–102; Avery, *The Exultet Rolls*, pls. 17–23 and pp. 14–15.

[16] Avery, *The Exultet Rolls*, pl. 24 and pp. 15–16.

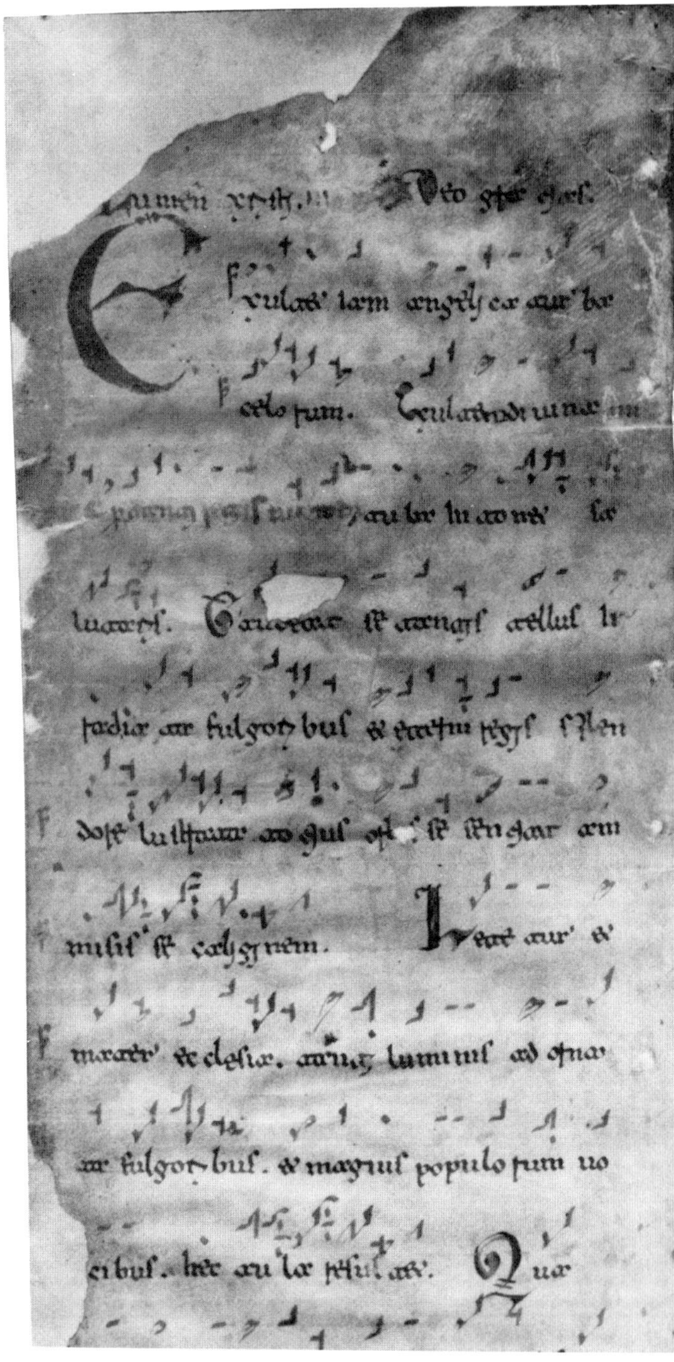

Plate 5: Bari, Archivio del Duomo, Exultet roll 3 (detail). Reproduced by permission.

Example 4

Cadences from Exultets of Bari

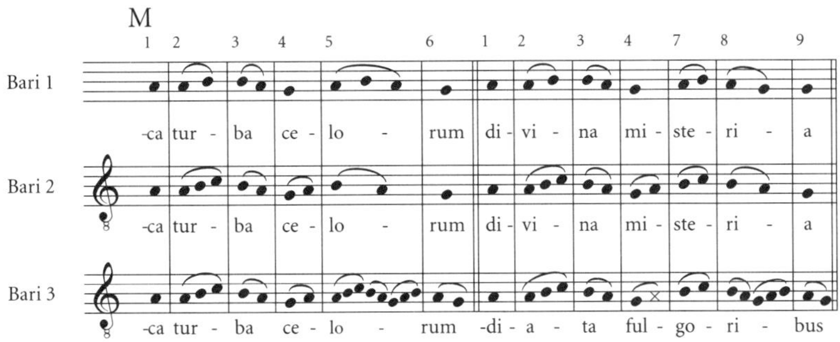

achieved by a reallocation of the last three pitches, giving two of them to the final syllable. The elaborated figure in column M5 surrounds the two-note figure of Bari 2 with two rising three-note *scandicus.* The result is, in fact, that the last two syllables are a reprise of the whole phrase: or more exactly, of the precise notes of "turba celorum" in Bari 2. The similar figure in column M8 (on "fulgo*ri*bus") is simpler because the phrase has already risen to the upper fourth on the previous syllable.

The final cadences of Bari 3 show some typical developments from Bari 2. On "intonet," column K3, Bari 3 fills in a gap in the version of Bari 2. The arched figure at K4 is taken one step higher in Bari 3, to the upper fourth; and the final cadence, in both its accentuations, elaborates the subfinal, which in Bari 2 was only used in the three-syllable cadence.

Two further versions of the Exultet remain to be considered. These are the thirteenth-century Dalmatian missal now in the Bodleian Library, Canonici liturg. 342, and the Exultet preserved in two fifteenth-century missals of Salerno. Both of these differ from the versions presented so far in that they show a loosening of the formulaic understanding of the melody and present rather extravagant and florid melodies. The Oxford version was studied in some detail by Dom Hesbert,[17] so we will concentrate here on the Salerno missals, which until recently were inaccessible.

These twin missals,[18] though they are written in Gothic script with occasional square notation, seem to be retrospective books, representing the liturgy of the twelfth century at Salerno, probably the liturgy as reorganized by archbishop Romualdo Guarna.[19] They contain many elements of the old Beneventan rite for Holy Week—including, as it happens, one antiphon

[17] *PM* 14, 399–416.

[18] Salerno, Archivio del Museo del Duomo, manuscripts without shelf-number. They will here be referred to as Salerno 3 and Salerno 4, according to the order in which they are described in Arturo Capone, *Il Duomo di Salerno* (Salerno, 1927–29), 2:261–63 ("Capo 3"), 265–66 ("Capo 4"); the Exultet from these missals was described, and partially transcribed, in Agostino Latil, "Un 'Exultet' inedito," *Rassegna gregoriana* 7 (1908): cols. 125–34; facsimiles of both manuscripts, including the complete Exultet from Salerno 4, appear in Thomas F. Kelly, ed., *Les témoins manuscrits du chant bénéventain,* Paléographie musicale 21 (Solesmes: Abbaye St. Pierre, 1992).

[19] An *ordo officii* (Capone no. 6) in the Salerno library carries the incipit "Incipit compendiosa pronuntiata officii ecclesiastici secundum salernitanae ecclesiae quam dominus Romualdus venerabilis Salernitanus archiepiscopus cum voluntate sui capituli ordinavit." According to Capone (2:271–72) this is Romualdo II Guarna (116?–1181); the *ordo officii* was copied by the same Guglielmo da Roma who copied Salerno 3 in 1431; this group of fifteenth-century manuscripts may represent a codification of the twelfth-century liturgy as then preserved and understood.

whose melody is known nowhere else.[20] The Exultet has the Beneventan text—extremely unusual for the fifteenth century, but not so rare for the twelfth; and the Exultet is placed, in Beneventan fashion, after the lessons. The Beneventan antiphons and tracts transcribed in these missals are not so different from those preserved in eleventh- and twelfth-century manuscripts—except for the Exultet, whose exuberance probably represents not so much the development of several centuries as it does a Salerno practice of great virtuosity on the part of the deacon (see illustration in plate 6).

Some typical cadences are transcribed at the end of example 3. Despite the melodic prolixity, and the fact that the cadences are not identically formulaic, we can see elements of the basic Beneventan melody. The decoration in column M5 and the elaborations in K3 occur at places where the Beneventan melody has its longest figures. Indeed in column K3 we can recognize the original Beneventan melody in the first six notes of three of the cadences.

But the Salerno melody seems more attentive to accented syllables than is the standard melody. The original Beneventan final cadence is entirely oriented to the single accent in column K6, though the syllable itself is an undecorated arrival on the final; but the Salerno singers give the accented syllable an extended figure. They do the same in column M2 for a syllable which is often, but not always, accented, and the results are not always happy.

The Salerno Exultet, then, follows the outline, and the general formulaic shape, of the Beneventan melody. But it does not limit itself to repeating the same formula when the same situation recurs. Indeed it seems a part of the singer's duty to vary these inflections as his virtuosity makes possible. Some clear examples of this process of immediate variation and development are transcribed in example 5, the Salerno versions of the threefold "Lumen christi," and the passage in the Beneventan text beginning "Flore utuntur," whose short repetitive phrases surely seem to cry out for virtuosity, at least to a singer in the Salerno style.

This is virtuoso solo singing. Indeed, even the standard Beneventan Exultet is no easy matter to sustain. The singer must be an expert, and it is easy to imagine a temptation to embroider the melody at hand. One wonders how many of the "standard" Exultets were sung precisely as written; perhaps in the hands of an adventurous and capable deacon the Beneventan melody served only as a framework for extempore embellishment. Perhaps

[20] This is the antiphon *Transivimus per ignem et aquam*, which was formerly known only from a rubric in the Farfa fragments ("postea pergat sacerdos vel episcopus ad altare canente antiphona haec: Transivimus per ignem et aqua"): see *PM* 14, pl. XXVII.

Plate 6: Salerno, Archivio del Museo del Duomo, manuscript without shelf-number (Capone 3), fol. 136v. Missal, 15th century; beginning of the Exultet. Reproduced by permission.

Example 5

From the Salerno Exultet.
Salerno, Archivio del Museo del Duomo,
manuscript without shelf-number (Capone 3)

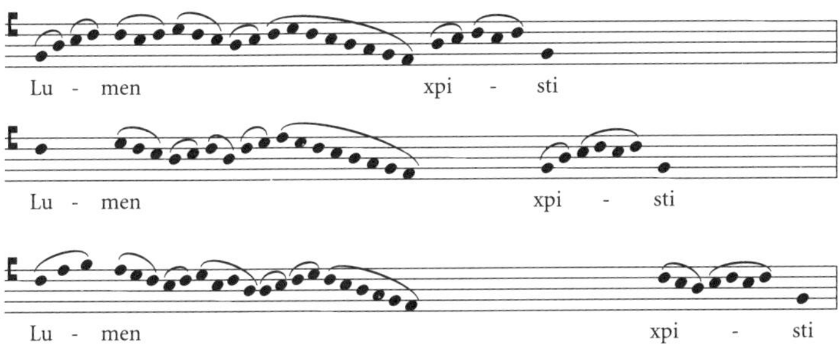

it is a change of writing habit, not of performance style, that gives us our few decorated melodies. They are perhaps records of a singer's performance, rather than the framework on which he builds.

In any case, the survival of these ornamented melodies allows us to consider at close range the nature of medieval musical elaboration. It is remarkable how often we speak of a decorated melody, of a melodic embellishment—and how seldom we actually can compare framework and ornamentation. This melody gives us such an opportunity, and it is a rare one. With further study we may come closer to a medieval, rather than a modern, appreciation of this and other music; and the music of the Exultet rolls of southern Italy may once again take its rightful place with the illustrations in our esteem for the beauties of these extraordinary documents.

KENNETH LEVY

Gregorian Chant and Oral Transmission

At the Rutgers conference on plainchant transmission, organized by Helmut Hucke in 1986, I projected a series of papers that would deal at large scale with issues of Gregorian chant and its transition from orality to written record.[1] The basic questions were obvious enough. Under what conditions were the conversions made, and how close to the oral deliveries were the neumed substances that resulted? Those questions have long awaited answers. David Hughes was a participant at the Rutgers conference, and I had the pleasure of conversing with him and discovering that we were in essential agreement on some important points. Now I am approaching the end of my series, with most of the papers already in print.[2] Two full-scale discussions have yet to appear. One concerns the editing of plainchant and

[1] "Transmission Problems in Medieval Chant," conference held at Rutgers University, New Brunswick, N.J., April 4–5, 1986.

[2] Preliminary papers include "A Gregorian Processional Antiphon," *Schweizer Jahrbuch für Musikwissenschaft*, Neue Folge 2 (1982): 91–102; "Toledo, Rome, and the Legacy of Gaul," *Early Music History* 4 (1984): 49–99; then "Charlemagne's Archetype of Gregorian Chant," *Journal of the American Musicological Society* 40 (1987): 1–30; "On the Origin of Neumes," *Early Music History* 7 (1987): 59–90; "On Gregorian Orality," *Journal of the American Musicological Society* 43 (1990): 185–227; involved by extension are three "Communications" to *Journal of the American Musicological Society* 41 (1988): 566–79 by Leo Treitler, David Hughes, and myself; the article by Hughes, "Evidence for the Traditional View of the Transmission of

the nature of the written input in the versions we have.[3] The other concerns the partnership between neumes and memory and its effect on the emergence of distinctive neumatic and melodic styles during the ninth through twelfth centuries.[4] My remarks here will anticipate fuller discussions of these and related matters, yet with many of the Rutgers participants again gathered together, it seems an appropriate time for an overview of my broader result. This falls into two historical stages, the first of them early and unwritten, the second later and written, but for the sake of clarity I will begin with the melodies as transmitted in writing and then move back to the oral developments that lay before. In a short space, I can endeavor to set out only a skeleton, without the flesh of document and analysis that appear elsewhere.

My point of departure is that an authoritative neumed repertory of Gregorian mass chants was circulated by the Carolingians: with some likelihood before the beginning of the ninth century, and with some certainty before about 840.[5] Such use of neumes for the Gregorian propers has been placed a half-century or even a whole century later, but there are arguments for the earlier dates, and though none of them is decisive, when taken together they have a certain force. Speaking generally, it makes sense for the Carolingian liturgists of the late eighth century to have cast the musical component of their ecclesiastical reform in a written state that supported the melodies' accurate spread to the corners of the Empire. It also makes sense for the many similar neumatic traditions of the tenth through twelfth centuries to have a common neumatic source, rather than for them to issue separately from late, local initiatives.[6]

What I project is an authoritative noted collection of Gregorian mass propers compiled toward the end of the eighth century, a "visual model" whose neumatic shapes were decisive for all later recensions. The difficulty with such a model has been that no single neumatic *ductus* seemed capable of generating the diversity of styles among the eventual neume-species.[7] In

Gregorian Chant," *Journal of the American Musicological Society* 40 (1987): 377–404; also involved are two "Communications" to *Journal of the American Musicological Society* 42 (1989): 432–37, by Hughes and Hendrik van der Werf.

[3] "Centonate Chant and Carolingian Editorial Process."

[4] "The Carolingian Visual Model."

[5] Levy, "Charlemagne's Archetype"; see n. 2.

[6] Levy, "On The Origin of Neumes" (see n. 2) outlines the argument; a fuller discussion will appear in "The Carolingian Visual Model."

[7] This is illustrated in *Le graduel romain: Édition critique par les moines de Solesmes*, 4: *Le texte neumatique*, 2: *Les relations généalogiques des manuscrits* (Solesmes: Abbaye de St. Pierre, 1962), 92, by Dom Froger's diagram showing a "zone brumeuse" between the "original" neumation and the eventual neume–species.

a departure from previous explanations, my proposed model was not only early in date, but its neumatic shapes were conjunct and nuance-poor.[8] By "conjunct" I mean the kind of notation found in the *Editio vaticana* or at St. Gall, where the pitches tend to be grouped together in ligatures rather than disposed as individual dots or strokes. By "nuance-poor" I mean that the visual model had few specifiers of length, pitch, and delivery, such as the letters, *episemata*, or neumatic disjunctions that eventually played a large role at St. Gall and elsewhere. The great majority of tenth- through twelfth-century neumations, representing origins in both the eastern and western zones of the Empire, are in fact conjunct and nuance-poor. And there is enough agreement among them to point to a common neumed source whose formulation can with some likelihood be placed before the Treaty of Verdun.[9]

For the neumatic provisions in the visual model and all its descendent neume-species, I have suggested an operating rationale that can be described as "gestural"; or to give this a more familiar technical name, it was "chironomic": that is to say, the neumes' behavior was like that of the melody-descriptive hand-gestures that were used around the Mediterranean basin for conducting and teaching since antiquity.[10]

This gestural rationale, however, would not reach back to the "origin" of Latin neumes. There have been many theories about origin: the "accent" theory, "punctuation" theory, "Byzantine" theory, "ekphonetic" theory, etc.; also the "chironomic" theory.[11] Some of the factors involved, and perhaps even all of them, were operating in proximity to the musical environment at the time when neuming began. Alexandrian accents and chironomy were there, both going well back in time; and—depending on suppositions about the starting-date for melodic neumes—there may have been Byzantine neumatic models, and Byzantine and Latin ekphonetic and punctuation signs as well; there was also the ancient concern for the "liquid" pronunciation of certain consonants and half-vowels, and that is reflected in the earliest neumings.[12] Yet in my theory none of these factors, either singly or in

[8] Levy, "On the Origin of Neumes."

[9] This point has been adumbrated by Michel Huglo, most recently in his *Les livres de chant liturgique*, Typologie des sources du moyen âge occidental 52 (Turnhout: Brepols, 1988), 84.

[10] Concerning the description of the rationale as "gestural" see my "On the Origin of Neumes," 76; concerning the phenomenon of chironomy see Michel Huglo, "La chironomie médiévale," *Revue de musicologie* 49 (1963): 153–71, and Hucke, "Die Cheironomie und die Entstehung der Neumenschrift," *Die Musikforschung* 32 (1979): 1–16.

[11] Levy, "On the Origin of Neumes," 62–65.

[12] Heinrich Freistedt, *Die Liqueszierenden Noten des Gregorianischen Chorals*, Veröffentlichungen der Gregorianischen Akademie zu Freiburg (Schweiz) 14 (Freiburg, Switzerland: St. Paulsdruckerei, 1929), remains the authoritative discussion, with an assemblage of the main texts.

combination, accounts for the notion of melodic neumes. I have proposed instead that an "original" stage of neuming, earlier and distinct from the Carolingian gestural model, came into being with the adoption of a "graphic" rationale.[13] That is, the musical notation began by using a principle whose aim and method was a picturing of pitch positions. Each pitch was rendered as a dot, or as an implied point on a line or curve connecting two or more dots. The roster of graphic signs was completed with other simple picturings of length, phrasing, and nuanced deliveries, representing prototype-forms of the *oriscus*, *quilisma*, *strophici*, liquescences, etc. These original "graphics" survive only in the archaic Paleofrank neumes. For the first users of neumes, the graphic rationale was a practical means of recording dictations from oral deliveries and of editing the raw written melodic record. It tended, however, to produce many dots, and these formed images that were shapeless to a novice's eye. That led to the replacement of the graphic rationale by the gestural rationale, and with it a greater reliance on conjunct forms. The gestural neumes' more plastic counterparts of melodic flow were better suited to memorizing and conducting.

Staffless neumes, whether generated under the earlier graphic or the replacement gestural rationale, supplied only an incomplete record of actual melodic substances. They showed accurate profiles of pitch-motion and nuances of length and delivery, but specific pitch-levels were beyond them. In view of the precision with length and ornament, it can scarcely be that just the choice of pitches was left to the vagaries of local reimprovisers.[14] It must rather be that in the early stage of neuming the full melodic substances were thought secure enough in professional memories for the pitch-levels to be slighted by the notation. The real seat of melodic transmission then lay in memory, and for so long as staffless neumes continued as the basic medium of written transmission, memory continued as the guarantor of full melodic substance. This reliance on written means, however, led to weakened memories, and musicians began using the neumes to record sometimes aberrant impressions of melodic detail. The local variants among tenth- through thirteenth-century descendents of the Carolingian visual model would in large measure be the result of such processes. Yet the variants tend only to affect details, and it is remarkable how uniform the transmissions are, from Calabria through Anglo-Saxon Kent, and from Brittany through the Carpathians.[15]

[13] Levy, "On the Origin of Neumes," 70–79.

[14] Theories of improvisational input or "reimprovisation," continuing after the introduction of neumes, have been proposed by Treitler, Hucke, and Van der Werf; they are considered in my "On Gregorian Orality," 188–90.

[15] The paper "The Carolingian Visual Model" will examine the question in some detail.

A major question remains. By what process were the neumes changed from their conjunct, nuance-poor shapes in the visual model around 800 to the variety of disjunct and nuance-rich shapes that flourish around 900? This took place, as I see it, under the umbrella of the gestural rationale. Many scribes were content to reproduce in essential facsimile the model's picturings of melodic events. That sort of copy could be executed even by scribes who were unmindful or ignorant of the musical substances being represented. Yet there were other scribes whose musical faculties were more actively engaged in the copying-writing process. They undertook to stylize and improve the received neumatic representations. The melodies remained unchanged, with the full musical substance ostensibly secure in memory. It was only the scribes' picture of the well-remembered melos that was subject to alteration. They turned to disjunct neumes to increase pitch-specificity, and to letters, *episemata*, neumatic disjunctions, and comprehensive heighting for other improvements in accuracy; and yet, for so long as the notation remained based in staffless neumes, each act of neuming would remain the gestural fixing of some well-remembered melodic detail.

Now let me turn back from the first written stages to the oral stages that went before. There is no real access to the melos of plainchant before neumes. At best one hopes to intuit backward from the preserved written forms. In that way a range of oral options can be imagined. On the one hand would be deliveries that were free and exuberant, with little of the premeditated to them. On the other hand would be melodies that while still orally produced were largely fixed and memorized. In-between them would be deliveries that were "free" yet considerably dependent on rule and custom. A further range of options can be imagined in the conversion from oral to written. On the one hand would be the verbatim transcription of an oral delivery, whatever it was. On the other hand would be melodies that reached much or all of their eventual shape in the written medium. In-between would be melodies whose oral shape underwent considerable change during written stages before the final one that is all we have. These two ranges were intertwined on the way to the ultimate written version, and the combined range of possibilities is large. To trace a path here, I have suggested dividing the repertory tentatively into three classes that are described as *psalmic*, *idiomelic*, and *centonate*.[16]

[16] The division is considered in "On Gregorian Orality," 217–18; a fuller discussion will appear in the paper "Centonate Chant and Carolingian Editorial Process."

Psalmic chants have elements of psalm-structure—intonations, reciting tones, and cadences—in their melodic fabrics. As variants of a simple, well-known pattern such chants may, perhaps more than any others, represent oral deliveries that were in large measure "freely improvised" and then so-to-speak quick-frozen in the medium of neumes. The psalmic class is comparatively small.

Idiomelic chants have no single shape like the psalmic matrix. Instead, each idiomelic chant is turned out as a distinctive melody, with a shape of its own. The music calls on familiar turns of modal phrase, but these are given distinctive twists. The emphasis is on melodic niceties, and that says the differences mattered. In effect, it says the idiomelic chants were identifiable, memorized entities. There are indications that this memorability went back of the written formulations to a prior oral stage. These rest chiefly in cases of "close multiples," where a chant managed to elude the homogenizing scalpel of Carolingian liturgists and survive in two or more versions that are unrelated in their notation but close in music. This suggests, as surely as anything can, that behind the preserved written melos there was a common oral substance with the shape of a fixed, memorized melos. Idiomelic chants represent the bulk of the repertory.

The third class contains the chants often described as "centonate."[17] Their fabrics incorporate amounts of pithy material that reappears in other musical contexts in other corners of the repertory. The density of centonate texture is greatest among Graduals and Tracts, but the technique runs through the whole repertory, and to the extent that it involves chants which might otherwise be classifed as psalmic or idiomelic, what can be inferred about the nature of the centonate process should apply there as well. The use of recombinable elements represents a different stance than in music whose genesis is written and whose thrust is continuous. Here the constraint is not the usual linear exposition, and the possibility has long been considered that the origins of centonate chants lay outside the written medium, in the realm of improvised performance.[18] Any conjectures about

[17] Paolo Ferretti began this musical use of the term *cento; Estetica gregoriana, ossia Trattato delle forme musicali del canto gregoriano* 1 (Rome: Pontificio istitutio di musica sacra, 1934; in French, *Esthétique grégorienne* [Paris: Société de saint Jean l'Évangeliste, 1938]); Peter Wagner, *Einführung in die Gregorianischen Melodien* 3: *Gregorianische Formenlehre* (Leipzig: Breitkopf, 1921), 353–96 was the first to offer comprehensive analyses of the phenomenon.

[18] P. Wagner, *Gregorianische Formenlehre*, 391, on the verses of the Graduals of the fifth mode: "Die Sänger wurden nicht müde, immer neue Fassungen für die Initialen der Soloverse zu suchen und erfreuten sich an dem Wohlwollen, das die Kirche ihrer Kunst so reichlich spendete." Wagner considered the possibility of Hebrew antecedents: of ". . . Zusammenhanges der Gradualmelismatik mit dem jüdischen Kantorengesang," and that "die Technik der wandernden Melismen mit Interpunktionssinn ist [for the Tracts] ein Erbteil aus der

oral antecedents, however, are based on the received Carolingian musical text, and that not only is written, but it has in its fabric marks of considerable editorial intervention. There were alterations to chants that began in an irregular modal environment, tailoring them to the symmetries of the eight-mode system.[19] There were adjustments to chants that once were "chromatic," fitting them to the more angular skeleton of a diatonic tonal system.[20] There were homogenizations of centonate melismas, giving them the same melodic contour and neumatic dress wherever they appeared in the repertory.[21] There were adjustments when chants employed as musical models were accommodated to fresh texts (as was common with the second-mode Graduals), and these show great sensitivity to conditions of text-accent and syllable-count.[22] There were attachments of particular words to particular musical elements throughout the repertory.[23] All these are indications of written-editorial activity. Above all, with the isolated centonate correspondences, the likelihood that the Carolingian recension's neumed forms amount to shapshots of oral, improvisational deliveries seems remote. Much that appears in the written versions may go back to prior unwritten practice. As Peter Wagner intimated, there are echoes of oral hot-wirings, generated by volatile, artful memories. Yet in the neumed

synagogalen Psalmodie" (ibid., 396). Musical speculation took further impetus from the literary theory of Balkan epic developed by Milman Parry and Albert B. Lord (cf. Lord's *The Singer of Tales* [Cambridge: Harvard University Press, 1965]), as in Leo Treitler, "Homer and Gregory," *The Musical Quarterly* 60 (1974): 333–72 and "Centonate Chant: *Übles Flickwerk* or *E pluribus unus?*" *Journal of the American Musicological Society* 28 (1975): 1–23.

[19] An ample background is supplied by Michel Huglo, *Les tonaires: Inventaire, analyse, comparaison* (Paris: Société française de musicologie, 1979); cf. Harold S. Powers, "Mode," in *The New Grove:* ". . . the idea of an eightfold system of modes in a four-by-two matrix was adapted by Carolingian theorists to an existing body of traditional song with which it had not originally been associated."

[20] Hughes, "Evidence for the Traditional View," has reopened this issue; cf. 394–98.

[21] Gregori M. Sunyol, *Introducció a la paleografia musical Gregoriana* (Montserrat: Abadia de Montserrat, 1925), pl. F, illustrates melodic homogeneity (repr. in the expanded French edition, *Introduction à la paléographie musical grégorienne* [Paris: Société de saint Jean l'Évangeliste, Desclée, 1935]); that of neumation is clear from many of the comparative tables illustrating semiological studies; e.g., that of Walter Wiesli, *Das Quilisma im Codex 359 der Stiftsbibliothek St. Gallens* (Immensee: Verlag Missionshaus Bethlehem, 1966); Johannes B. Göschl, *Semiologische Untersuchungen zum Phänomen der Gregorianischen Liqueszenz*, Forschungen zur Älteren Musikgeschichte: Veröffentlichungen des Institutes für Musikwissenschaft der Unversität Wien 3/1–2 (Vienna, 1980); also in many issues of the *Beiträge zur Gregorianik* (Regensburg: Bosse), of which Heft 8 appeared in 1989.

[22] Dom Eugène Cardine's classic *Semiologia gregoriana* (Rome: Pontificio Istituto di Musica Sacra, 1968), nos. 333–37, offers a clear example of the practice (same numbering in the French edition of 1970).

[23] D. Johner, *Wort und Ton im Choral* (Leipzig: Breitkopf & Härtel, 1940; 2nd ed., 1952), 101–04.

chants that we have, the decisive shape-giver was deliberate and text-critical. The Gregorian chants in this respect show much the same editorial preoccupations as the biblical, prayer-book, and homiletic texts that were their partners in the Carolingian ecclesiastical reforms.[24] Linkages of nature and process have been proposed between Gregorian chant and oral epic.[25] Yet if analogies are to be credited between materials that are so different as melody-based plainchant and word-based epic, then the closer counterparts for the Gregorian repertory would rather be found in authored epics such as the *Aeneid* or *Ossian* than in the eponymous oral creations of Homeric and latter-day Balkan bards. The written epics have their postures of orality, but like the fine-tooled fifth-mode graduals of the Gregorian tradition they are the outcome of deliberate written process.

[24] Charlemagne's concern for emending and careful copying is voiced in the seventy-second paragraph of his *Admonitio generalis* addressed to the Frankish clergy in 789. Priests are admonished, "ut scolae legentium puerorum fiant. Psalmos, notas, cantus, compotum, grammaticam per singula monasteria vel episcopia et libros catholicos bene emendate: quia saepe, dum bene aliqui Deum rogare cupiunt, sed per inemendatos libros male rogant. Et pueros vestros non sinite eos vel legendo vel scribendo corrumpere; et si opus est evangelium, psalterium et missale scribere, perfectae aetatis homines scribant cum omni diligentia" (Alfred Boretius, ed., *Capitularia Regum Francorum* 1, Monumenta Germaniae Historica, Legum Sectio 2 [Hannover: Hahn, 1883], 60). This is further documented in Charlemagne's *Epistola* (between ca. 786–800) recommending the newly compiled Homiliary of Paul the Deacon: "Igitur quia curae nobis est, ut nostrarum ecclesiarum ad meliora semper proficiat status, oblitteratam pene maiorum nostrorum desidia reparare vigilanti studio litterarum satagimus officinam, et ad pernoscenda studia liberalium artium nostro etiam quos possumus invitamus exemplo. Inter que iam pridem universos veteris ac novi instrumenti libros, librariorum imperitia depravatos, Deo nos in omnibus adiuvante, examussim correximus. Accensi praeterea venerandae memoriae Pippini genitoris nostri exemplis, qui totas Galliarum ecclesias romanae traditionis suo studio cantibus decoravit, nos nihilominus solerti easdem curamus intuitu praecipuarum insignire serie lectionum. Denique quia ad nocturnale officium compilatas quorundam casso labore, licet recto intuitu, minus tamen idonee repperimus lectiones, quippe quae et sine auctorum suorum vocabulis essent positae et infinitis vitiorum anfractibus scaterent, non sumus passi nostris in diebus in divinis lectionibus inter sacra officia inconsonantes perstrepere soloecismos, atque earundum lectionum in melius reformare tramiten mentem intendimus. Idque opus Paulo diacono, familiari clientulo nostro, elimandum iunximus, scilicet ut, studiose catholicorum patrum dicta percurrens, veluti e latissimis eorum pratis certos flosculos legeret, et in unum quaeque essent utilia quasi sertum aptaret" (Boretius, *Capitularia*, 80–81). A general discussion appears in Cyrille Vogel, "La réforme liturgique sous Charlemagne," in *Karl der Grosse: Lebenswerk und Nachleben*, ed. Helmut Beumann et al. (Düsseldorf: Schwann, 1965–68), 2:217–32. The literature is surveyed by Klaus Gamber, *Codices liturgici latini antiquiores*, 2nd ed. (Freiburg, Switzerland: Universitätsverlag, 1968), 347–49, 438–39, 583–85; and by Cyrille Vogel, *Medieval Liturgy: An Introduction to the Sources*, rev. and trans. William G. Storey and Niels Krogh Rasmussen (Washington, D.C.: Pastoral Press, 1986), 70–85, 363–65.

[25] Chiefly by Treitler in the papers cited in n. 18 above; most recently in his "Communication" to *Journal of the American Musicological Society* 41 (1988): 566–75; also by Hucke, "Der Übergang von mündlicher zu schriftlicher Musiküberlieferung im Mittelalter," in *Report of the*

Summing up now, let me rearrange these proposals in a straighter historical line. While still oral, most of the Gregorian repertory became firm as to melody and fixed in memory. Cases of "close multiples" suggest there was little margin left for free improvisation. The practice of neuming began at an uncertain place and time. Likeliest would be the third quarter of the Frankish eighth century, the time when, according to Charlemagne, much of the Romanizing of Carolingian church music was done. Yet an earlier time, and an ultimate origin in Italy or Rome, cannot be excluded. Neumatic practice would not originate from "accents," "chironomy," text-punctuation, or any of the other familiar options. It would come from adopting a graphic rationale, whose simple pictorial renderings of melodic events as a series of points were suited to recording dictations from oral delivery. By around 800, the neumes underwent a change from the graphic rationale (which is reflected only in the Paleofrank notations) to one that was gestural or chironomic. This was incorporated in a neumed "visual model" whose copies were circulated as the authoritative reference-documents of the Carolingian musical reform. By their means, a nuclear repertory of Carolingian–"Gregorian" mass propers (and perhaps office propers as well) spread quickly among Frankish dependencies. This visual model was the likely product of some liturgical-musical atelier in the zone between the Meuse and the Rhine-Moselle, with Aachen to the north and Metz to the south.[26] The melodic substances that its neumes described were fully fixed in memory. Its notations were specific with regard to every musical factor except for pitch. They left no license for continuing improvisation; and for so long as neumes continued in unheighted forms, verbatim memory served as the repository of the full melodic information, including pitch. The visual model's neumatic forms were themselves gestural, conjunct, and nuance-poor. Its closest paleographic descendents may perhaps be found in the diocese of Trier in the Carolingian heartland: in the neumatic species of

Twelfth Congress of the International Musicological Society, Berkeley, 1977, ed. Daniel Heartz and Bonnie Wade (Kassel: Bärenreiter, 1981), 180–90. The current position of literary specialists was reviewed in a plenary address for the Medieval Academy of America in 1989, by Dennis H. Green, published as "Orality and Reading: The State of Research in Medieval Studies," *Speculum* 65 (1990): 267–80.

[26] Dom Cardine's definition of the region as lying "between the Seine and the Rhine," in "Vue d'ensemble sur le chant grégorien," *Études grégoriennes* 16 (1977): 174, would be further focussed here, but the possibility remains of neumatic beginnings farther to the West (say at Tours) or at Rome.

Echternach[27] or Prüm,[28] rather than in the conjunct, nuance-rich species of more distant St. Gall, or the disjunct, nuance-rich species of Lorraine, Brittany, or the Aquitaine. All neume-species of the ninth through twelfth century (other than the Paleofrank), however, would be outgrowths of this visual model: they all would implement its gestural rationale. For many scribes, it was enough to produce near-facsimiles of the model's neumatic forms. Yet the model formulation also served as a point of departure for local and personal neumatic stylizations. Musician-scribes regestured the model's gestural neumatic shapes, producing their own preferred images of the well-remembered melodies. As for the musical substances that were represented by the neumes, most of the written versions amount, with but minor retouchings, to melodic formulations that were already essentially firmed during oral transmission. With the more intricately "centonate" chants, however one can reckon on larger amounts of calculation and assembly during written stages prior to the final one.

In closing, let me observe that dealing with prehistory, as I have done here, is a difficult, dangerous game. It is no easy task to shape proofs of what was "oral" and "early" out of a thin surviving record that is "written" and "late." Flaws will appear in my construction, and because all of us tend to be loyal to our own mistakes, it may be that I am discounting some considerations that deserve fairer treatment. All the same, I believe this offers a better account than there has been of the Gregorian transition from oral to written.

[27] This is represented around the year 1000 in Darmstadt, Hessische Landesbibliothek, MS. 1946; facs. ed. in *Echternacher Sakramentar und Antiphonar*, Codices selecti 74 (Graz: Akademische Druck- und Verlagsanstalt, 1982). See also Paul Ulveling, *Essai historique et musicologique . . . suivi d'un commentaire introductif au Sacramentaire et Antiphonaire d'Echternach* (Luxemburg: Ministère des arts et des sciences, 1982).

[28] As in Paris, B. N. lat. 9448, compiled ca. 1000; many facsimile plates are given by Margaretha Rossholm Lagerlöf, "A Book of Songs Placed upon the Altar of the Saviour Giving Praise to the Virgin Mary and Homage to the Emperor," in *Research on Tropes: Proceedings of a Symposium Organized by the Royal Academy of Literature, History and Antiquities and the Corpus Troporum, Stockholm, June 1–3, 1981*, ed. Gunilla Iversen, Konferenser 8 (Stockholm: Almqvist & Wiksell, 1983), 126–78.

EDWARD NOWACKI

Antiphonal Psalmody in Christian Antiquity and Early Middle Ages[*]

The definition of the antiphon and its companion concept, antiphonal psalmody, is a familiar conundrum in the history of medieval music.[1] If the current definition begs the question of the relation of these two concepts to each other, it is even less adequate as a description of their history. It is difficult enough to understand how psalmody performed in alternation by two halves of a divided choir should require the addition of an antiphon to be considered antiphonal. But an understanding of how such a contrived method of performance should have emerged out of the performing conditions of the early Church seems almost unattainable, given the allusive nature of the testimony. Contemporary witnesses to early Christian liturgies have plenty to say about the content and spiritual meaning of the rituals,

[*]I am especially indebted to Joseph Dyer for information generously shared and for many helpful suggestions. I also wish to thank Peter Jeffery for calling my attention to the Antiphonary of Bangor and the Mozarabic orational of Verona.

[1] The following abbreviations will be used. *CCSL* = *Corpus Christianorum: Series Latina* (Turnhout: Brepols, 1954–); *CSEL* = *Corpus Scriptorum Ecclesiasticorum Latinorum* (Vienna, 1866–); *MECL* = James McKinnon, ed., *Music in Early Christian Literature* (Cambridge: Cambridge University Press, 1987); *PG* = *Patrologiae Cursus Completus . . . Series Graeca*, ed. J. P. Migne, 166 vols. (Paris, 1857–1904); *PL* = *Patrologiae Cursus Completus . . . Series Latina*, ed. J. P. Migne, 221 vols. (Paris, 1844–1904); RB = Rule of Benedict; RM = Rule of the Master.

but about particulars of performing style, especially those that concern music historians, they are almost uniformly silent.

In spite of these obstacles, scholars have been able to coax from the testimony more than it intended to say. Baumstark, Gelineau, and Hucke, for example, have been able to show that antiphonal singing at the time of its adoption in the fourth century did not refer primarily to the balanced alternation of odd and even verses that later became the norm in monasteries.[2] Leeb reinforces this view by showing that St. Ambrose (ca. 339–97) does not once mention balanced antiphony in any of his writings, even though he is the one alleged by Isidore of Seville (ca. 559–636) to have introduced it to the West.[3] However, the alternative proposed by these authorities—that antiphonal singing entails some kind of alternation between verses and refrains—only raises further questions. Why would a method of performance already well known in the fourth century as "singing in response" (ὑπηχεῖν, ὑποψάλλειν) attract the entirely new term "antiphon"?[4] While Baumstark and Gelineau tried to explain the term as designating an enhanced form of responsorial psalmody in which the refrain is sung in two halves by a divided assembly, Hucke has argued, more convincingly in my opinion, that the difference lay in the nature of the texts (nonbiblical), the composition of the ensemble (a congregation led by a group rather than by a single cantor), and the sites where antiphonal songs were first sung (out of doors).

[2] Anton Baumstark, *Nocturna Laus*, Liturgiewissenschaftliche Quellen und Forschungen 32 (Münster: Aschendorff, 1957), 124; Joseph Gelineau, *Chant et musique dans le culte chrétien* (Paris: Fleurus, 1962), 128; Helmut Hucke, "Die Entwicklung des christlichen Kultgesangs zum Gregorianischen Gesang," *Römische Quartalschrift für christliche Altertumskunde und Kirchengeschichte* 48 (1953): 152–62. For a critical summary of these views see Helmut Leeb, *Die Psalmodie bei Ambrosius*, Wiener Beiträge zur Theologie 18 (Vienna: Herder, 1967), 18–20.

[3] The designation of St. Ambrose as the Father of Church Music may be justified in connection with his contribution to Western hymnography, but his reputation as the one who introduced balanced antiphony to the West appears to be no older than Isidore. The contemporary reports of St. Augustine and Paulinus mention Ambrose only as a participant in the musical innovations of 386, not as their originator. And regardless of Ambrose's involvement, the new musical forms had nothing to do with the kind of balanced antiphony taken for granted by Isidore. Leeb, *Die Psalmodie*, 103–10, esp. 107.

[4] Philo's frequently cited reference to "antiphonal harmonies" in the music of the Alexandrian Jewish sect known as the Therapeutae around the first decade A.D. probably should not be considered a precedent for the use of the term by Christians in the fourth century. Besides the lack of a continuous tradition for this term in Christian circles during the intervening period, we should bear in mind that the songs to which Philo refers are dance songs.

> They all rise up together and form two choirs in the middle of the banquet, one of men and one of women. A leader and intoner who is the most respected and musical is chosen for each. Then they sing composed hymns to God in many meters and melodies, now sounding together, now gesturing and dancing to

General studies of liturgical and monastic history have tended to treat the distinction between antiphonal and responsorial psalmody as one of little consequence, or have simply transmitted received opinion without acknowledging its inherent contradictions. *The Liturgy of the Hours in East and West* by Robert Taft presents the antiphon in the Jerusalem Office of ca. 400 as "a trope or refrain, a piece of ecclesiastical poetry," to be inserted between the verses of a psalm chanted by a soloist;[5] and later, in his description of the Rule of Benedict, Taft presents antiphonal psalmody as an enhanced form of responsorial, with verses and refrains distributed to two choirs and two soloists in a pattern that is a little too complex to be entirely credible.[6] The collaborative *RB 1980: The Rule of St. Benedict in Latin and English with Notes* follows the respected authority of de Vogüé in presenting antiphons in Benedictine monasticism as mere refrains.[7]

Since the context for the later development of the antiphon was monastic psalmody, it seems only reasonable that we should set as a condition for our research a full understanding of how monks knew and said psalms. Joseph Dyer's thorough revision of the received view, in which he concludes that all monastic psalmody from its beginnings in the Egyptian desert until the Carolingian epoch was performed by individual monks taking turns in the order of precedence, provides an important basis for this discussion.[8] With that in mind, I would like to propose a new look at the antiphon and

> antiphonal harmonies (τῇ μὲν συνηχοῦντες, τῇ δὲ καὶ ἀντιφώνοις ἁρμονίαις ἐπιχειρονομοῦντες καὶ ἐπορχούμενοι).

The connection of "antiphonal harmonies" to songs sung by facing rows of dancers suggests that it was a term of choreography. It is not at all clear that Philo understood it to refer to alternating hymnody in general, or that there is any connection between its choric and later ecclesiastical uses beyond mere coincidence. Philo of Alexandria, *De vita contemplativa*, ed. Leopold Cohn and Siegfried Reiter, in *Opera quae supersunt* (Berlin: Reimer, 1915), 6:69.

[5] Robert F. Taft, *The Liturgy of the Hours in East and West: The Origins of the Divine Office and Its Meaning for Today* (Collegeville, Minn.: Liturgical Press, 1986), 54.

[6] "The congregation, divided into two choirs, responds to the verses alternately, sometimes with the same refrain, sometimes each choir with its own refrain, to the verses chanted by the soloist or, at times, by two soloists alternating the verses, one at the head of each choir.

"Note that the refrain or antiphon was repeated after each verse and not just at the beginning and end of the psalm, and that two soloists, not two choirs of monks, alternated the verses, contrary to what one sees in more recent Latin usage. The evidence is not always clear, but I would take modern Western antiphonal usage, with the soloist's role and the repetition of the antiphon after each verse suppressed, to represent but the debris of the pristine structure of this liturgical unit as intended by Benedict in the *Rule*" (Taft, *The Liturgy*, 139).

[7] *RB 1980: The Rule of St. Benedict in Latin and English with Notes*, ed. Timothy Fry et al. (Collegeville, Minn.: Liturgical Press, 1981), 401–03.

[8] Joseph Dyer, "Monastic Psalmody of the Middle Ages," *Revue bénédictine* 99 (1989): 41–74; idem, "The Singing of Psalms in the Early-Medieval Office," *Speculum* 64 (1989): 535–78.

antiphonal psalmody, and to urge a new application of musical common sense to our reading of the contemporary testimony.

1

The circumstance, all too often ignored, without whose acknowledgment no sense can be made of this subject, is memorization. Monks knew the psalms by heart and recited the psalmic portions of their Offices from memory. The followers of Pachomius and Horsiesius in Upper Egypt in the fourth century were required to recite scriptural passages, including the psalms, from memory. The semianchoritic monks of Lower Egypt are described in the *Lausiac History* of Palladius (ca. 364–425) as reciting psalms and other scriptures while on journeys and while standing throughout the night in religious trances, presumably without benefit of light to read by. And the Palestinian nuns whom Jerome advised were forbidden not to know the psalms, which they recited in sequence at a formal cycle of daily and nightly assemblies.[9]

The Rule of the Master (late sixth century)[10] has numerous and detailed references to the obligation of monks to memorize the psalter and refers to those who have fulfilled it as *psalterati:*

> During these three hours the boys, in their deanery, are to learn letters on their tablets from someone who is literate. Moreover, we also exhort illiterate adults up to the age of fifty to learn letters. Again, we wish it kept in mind that during these same periods the psalms are to be studied [*meditari*][11] by those who do not know them, directed by the deans in their respective deanery. So during these three hours they are to read and listen to one another, and take turns teaching letters and the psalms to those who do not know them. (50.12–15)

> But the brothers may have permission at any time, provided the abbot is not present, to rehearse [*meditari*] the psalms and to repeat the scriptures and to speak about God, if it is done humbly and quietly. (50.26)

> When they have mastered and memorized [the psalms] perfectly [*memoria perfecte tenuerint*], let their deans take them to the abbot to recite by heart the psalm or canticle or lesson of any kind. (50.65)

[9] Dyer, "Monastic Psalmody," 44–46; *MECL*, nos. 112, 119–20, 327.

[10] On the date, see n. 50.

[11] Meditation means repeating a text aloud. See Fry, *The Rule of St. Benedict*, 446. The same word root (*meditatio, meditare*), denoting a similar routine of repetition and memorization, may be found in RB 8.3 and 48.23.

> But if he is sent on a longer journey, let him take with him from the monastery a small book containing some readings, so that he can do at least a little reading whenever he takes a rest along the way. But only if he knows the psalter. [*Ita tamen si fuerit psalteratus.*] If he does not, let him take along tablets on which psalms have been transcribed by the superior, so that when he stops to have his meal or take up lodging he may, insofar as he has opportunity, do at least a little memorizing [*meditetur*], in order to give the rule its due each day. (57.4–9)
>
> To be seated at the abbot's table are the seniors, visiting outsiders, and, taking turns as the abbot wishes, those who know the psalter [*fratres psalterati*]. (84.1–2)[12]

Memorization is implicit in the drilling prescribed in the Rule of Paul and Stephen (central Italy, late sixth century):

> Let the younger ones and especially those who are still practicing to learn the psalms [by heart] recite them in choirs consecutively and without distraction, so that when they are away from that place [i.e., where they practice] apart from which they have been hitherto ignorant as children, these juniors, who now have finished the psalter, may succeed one another in reciting, each in his turn. (chap. 6)[13]
>
> Let those who are learning letters or the psalms take care to be heard by those to whom they have been assigned, for they are to be chided by them for negligence or approved for their learning and zeal. (chap. 15)[14]

The Rule of Ferreolus (mid-sixth century) provides one of the most lapidary statements of the principle:

> Let no one who wants to claim the name of monk be permitted to be ignorant of letters. Nay let him even memorize the entire psalter, and let him not defend himself with any excuse at all why he should not be occupied with this holy endeavor. (chap. 11)[15]

[12] *The Rule of the Master*, trans. Luke Eberle (Kalamazoo, Mich.: Cistercian Publications, 1977). *La Règle du maitre*, original text ed. with intro., French trans., and notes by Adalbert de Vogüé, 3 vols., Sources chrétiennes 105–07 (Paris: Éditions du Cerf, 1964–65).

[13] "Iuniores, et maxime qui adhuc psalmos discere meditantur, per choros ex ordine et sine neglegentia dictent, ita ut ab eo loco a quo adhuc minores ignorant, hi iuniores qui iam psalterium finierunt, per ordinem sibi in dictando succedant." *Regula Pauli et Stephani: Edició crítica i Comentari*, ed. J. Evangelista M. Vilanova (Montserrat: Abadia de Montserrat, 1959), 110.

[14] "Hi qui litteras uel psalmos discunt, illis obseruent ad excipiendum, quibus fuerint deputati; qui pro eis aut de neglegentia arguendi sunt, aut in eorum eruditione et studio adprobandi" (Vilanova, *Regula Pauli*, 114).

[15] "Omnis qui nomen vult monachi vindicare, litteras ingorare non liceat. Quin etiam psalmos totos memoriter teneat: neque se quacunque excusatione defendat, quominus sancto hoc studio capiatur" (*PL* 66:963).

The consequence of memorization was to create a situation exactly opposite to the one that prevailed among the laity. The congregation of monks could sing as much of the psalmody as it chose to do. It did not need an invariant refrain to insure a minimal level of participation. Antiphons may have served a theological purpose, or a ceremonial or musical one, but they were not needed as the only practical alternative to passive listening.

Recognizing this, we may want to reconsider possibilities that have long been dismissed, as it turns out, for reasons no better than pure assumption. What is to prevent us, for example, from considering antiphonal psalmody as alternation between a group singing verses and another singing antiphons? Or between a congregation singing verses and an individual singing antiphons? Or, finally, between a group singing verses and antiphons and part of that group singing only verses? Several early monastic rules, including those of Cassian, Aurelian and Caesarius of Arles, Benedict, and the Master, provide no less of a basis for adopting these assumptions than they do for retaining the more familiar ones.

2

One obstacle to reconsideration of this question has been the presumptive interpretation of technical terms. One such term, common in the sixth century to designate the soloist's function, is the verb *imponere* and its noun equivalent *impositio.* In my opinion the most noncommittal interpretation, "to impose," is also the one closest to the original sense. By interpreting the word as "to chant" (i.e., to sing an entire chant by oneself), we categorically exclude possibilities of group performance before we have had an opportunity to weigh them on their merits; and by interpreting *imponere* as "to intone," the most common translation, we impute to the sixth century a kind of formality that is probably anachronistic. Fry comes closest with "to lead," but "to impose" does the job better. With this interpretation we can include within our understanding of the rules of Benedict and the Master a soloist's function that does not rule out informal participation by the brethren, some entering on pitch after the first few syllables, others waiting longer to enter and muttering the words softly to themselves. But it would be the imposer's function to see that the psalm prescribed by the rule got sung, and he would be the one to control the pauses where the antiphon might be inserted. In the case of the antiphons themselves, interpreting *imponere* as "to impose" is even more apt, since before the days of formal antiphonaries, the antiphon may have been an excerpt imposed on the congregation for its devout consideration at the soloist's discretion.[16]

3

A second consequence of memorization is the preference it creates for continuous recitation. Constant interruption of the psalmody by a refrain, unless very short, might break the train of thought and make recitation from memory awkward. (It certainly would for modern performers.) One can imagine the dull brother excused from imposing the psalms, because he has to start over at verse 1 every time he pauses to sing an antiphon. The Rule of Paul and Stephen, anticipating such difficulties, makes provision for rehearsals in which young monks may practice the psalms straight through, *ex ordine*, without the interruptions for refrains and prayer that occur in the Office (see nn. 13 and 14). How much, one wonders, did this practical attitude toward memorization affect the Office itself and the number of interruptions that even experienced monks were willing to impose upon themselves?

Amalar's reference in chapter 3 of the *Liber de ordine antiphonarii* to the six antiphons of ferial matins as chants "which the choirs repeat in turn after each verse" ("quas vicissim chori per singulos versus repetunt") is the only testimony known to me from this entire period describing such fre-

[16] Dyer supports his interpretation of *impositio* as solo chanting with citations from the RM in which the brethren are forbidden under certain conditions to impose psalms, antiphons, readings, or verses: "Tamdiu antifanam et uersum aut lectionem non inponat" (13.66); "Tamen psalmum et responsorium aut lectionem aut uersum tamdiu non inponat" (73.17). Here no distinction is made between psalms and antiphons, and readings, which unquestionably demand solo performance. But the Master uses "imposition" in a variety of senses, one of which indicates a unit of psalmody, prostration, and silent prayer. The twenty-four impositions that the Master requires to be completed each day and night must be made up of these units. One may not count readings, which are evidently something different. See Adalbert de Vogüé, "Le sens d''antifana' et la longueur de l'office dans la 'regula magistri,'" *Revue bénédictine* 71 (1961): 119–24; and Odilo Heiming, "Zum monastischen Offizium von Kassianus bis Kolumbanus," *Archiv für Liturgiewissenschaft* 7 (1961): 92–98. A similar injunction may be found in the RB: "Ita sane ut psalmum aut lectionem vel aliud quid non praesumat in oratorio imponere nisi iterum abbas iubeat" (44.6). But the same rule in another place states that those excommunicated from the common table may not impose psalms or antiphons, *nor recite readings:* "Psalmum aut antiphonam non imponat, neque lectionem recitet" (24.4). This suggests that the author did indeed understand there to be a distinction between the different solo functions, and that imposing psalms and antiphons was not the same kind of solo activity that reading lessons was.

quent repetition. It may be a special case, for he does not allude to this kind of repetition at all in his much more detailed description of antiphonal psalmody in Book 4, chapter 7, of the *Liber officialis*, where one would expect to find it (see section 12 below). Amalar may have thought the frequent repetition useful for prolonging the relatively short night Office on ferias, and the ferial antiphons known from Carolingian times may indeed be short enough not to disturb the continuity of the psalm despite frequent insertion.[17]

If antiphons are examples of the constant rumination of scriptural passages that the culture of memorization fostered, it is possible that their frequent repetition during psalmody was intended to formalize such rumination and raise it to a state of extreme concentration. On the face of it, I find that hypothesis an attractive one, but it begs the question of how often the antiphon needed to be repeated in order to achieve that objective. Lacking clear testimony for any scheme of repetition other than Amalar's in the ninth century, and in the light of the psychological considerations mentioned above, I consider the common assumption that antiphons were inserted after every verse in primitive antiphonal psalmody to be without foundation.

4

To be sure, frequent repetition of refrains was well known during the epoch of the Greek and Latin Fathers, but it occurred in cathedral psalmody, where the lay congregation responded to a reader reading the verses from a book. And even there, we cannot be certain that the refrains were inserted after every verse, although Ambrose's comparison of a congregation singing refrains to the rhythmic roaring of waves does suggest it.[18] Such psalmody is

[17] *Amalarii Episcopi Opera Liturgica Omnia*, ed. Jean Michel Hanssens (Vatican City: Biblioteca Apostolica Vaticana, 1948–50), 3:24 and 2:433 respectively.

A rare example of written-out psalmody with refrain may be found in the Antiphonary of Bangor (680–91), where the Canticle of Moses, "Audite coeli quae loquor," is divided into paragraphs usually comprising two verses with a repetition of the refrain between each paragraph. However, it is a difficult example from which to generalize, for it seems to be a kind of invitatory and may be subject to special performing rules. See Warren, *The Antiphonary*, 2:1–3 and 2:35 (full citation, n. 67).

We are better informed about specific repetition schemes from the tenth century on. See Edward Nowacki, "The Performance of Office Antiphons in Twelfth-Century Rome," in *International Musicological Society Study Group "Cantus Planus": Papers Read at the Third Meeting, Tihany, Hungary . . . 1988*, ed. Laszlo Dobszay et al. (Budapest: Hungarian Academy of Sciences, 1990), 79–91; and Peter Wagner, *Einführung in die gregorianischen Melodien: Ein Handbuch der Choralwissenschaft* (Leipzig, 1911–21; repr. Hildesheim: Olms, 1962), 1:145–46.

known generally as responsorial. In the East it was referred to with verbs meaning "to sing in response" (ὑπηχεῖν, ὑποψάλλειν), while the responses themselves were called "answer" (ὑπακοή, ὑπήχησις), "saying" (ῥῆσις), and "ending" (ἀκροτελεύτιον).[19] In Latin, responsorial psalmody was referred to with the expressions *psalmum respondere* (literally "to respond the psalm"), *responsorium psalmi,* and *psalmus responsorius.*[20] The term "antiphon" does not come up in most discussions of cathedral psalmody, and that suggests that the responsorial style of performance found there was familiar and not in need of a special name.[21]

Whether responsorial psalmody at that time was a familiar practice, however, is not entirely certain, for references to it before St. John Chrysostom (ca. 347–407) and St. Ambrose (ca. 339–97) are rare. Moreover, St. Augustine, a protégé of Ambrose's, and Paulinus, a younger contemporary, both state that the form of psalmody introduced in Ambrose's church in 386 and imitated thereafter "throughout the world" was a novelty borrowed from the East.[22] Since the only form of psalmody ever mentioned by Ambrose is responsorial, we are compelled to agree with Leeb that responsorial psalmody was as much a novelty to Augustine and Paulinus as the new antiphonal chant currently spreading to the West through monastic channels. Leeb goes on to argue that Paulinus simply lumped all such innovations together, calling them "antiphons," but intending by it nothing more than an acknowledgment of their supposed eastern origins.[23]

[18] *Hexameron* 3.5.23; *MECL* no. 289.

[19] Examples may be found in Chrystostom, *In psalmum 41,* 1; *In psalmum 117,* 1; *In psalmum 144,* 1; *Homilia habita in magnum hebdomadam* 2; *In Matthaeum,* Hom. 11, 7; *In Corinthios,* Hom. 36, 5–6 (trans. *MECL* nos. 163, 170, 172, 175, 178, 184 respectively); also Eusebius, *Ecclesiastical History* 2.17.22 (trans. *MECL* no. 208); and Sozomen, *Ecclesiastical History* 5.19 and 8.7 (trans. *MECL* nos. 221, 223).

[20] The transitive use of *respondere* and the substantive *responsorium* replacing *responsum* and *responsio* are late Latin formations not known before Ambrose. However, one may doubt, contrary to Leeb, *Die Psalmodie,* 53 and 63, that these usages differ enough from the classical ones to qualify as technical terms comparable to the loanword *antiphona,* with its distinctly Greek complexion. For a full discussion see Leeb, *Die Psalmodie,* 53–69.

[21] One could offer as a contrary example the Jerusalem Office described by Egeria around the year 400, a cathedral Office according to Taft, *The Liturgy,* 54, yet with an abundance of antiphons. In my opinion, however, this was not a pure cathedral Office, but a mixed one, in which the monastic elements are especially evident in the assemblies of monks and nuns keeping vigil before the arrival of the bishop and singing not just responsorial psalms, but hymns and antiphons too; that is, chants requiring monastic experience.

[22] Augustine, *Confessions* 9.7.15, trans. *MECL* no. 351; Paulinus, *Vita sancti Ambrosii* 13, trans. *MECL* no. 393. For an exegesis of their testimony, see Leeb, *Die Psalmodie,* 91–103.

[23] Leeb, *Die Psalmodie,* 103.

But Paulinus's apparent mixing of meanings is an anomaly, and the fact remains that references to responsorial psalmody do occur—albeit with extreme scarcity—in pre-ambrosian testimony, including that of Athanasius of Alexandria (d. 373), Pachomius (d. 346), Eusebius (d. ca. 340), Tertullian (late second or early third century), and the Apostolic Tradition of Hippolytus (also late second or early third century).[24] These references equate the refrain of responsorial psalmody with the word "alleluia" or the phrase "Quoniam in aeternum misericordia eius," whose repetition after every verse is an explicit part of the biblical text (Ps. 135). It is probable that occasional responding to a psalmist, using the word "alleluia" or the biblical response to Psalm 135, was a commonplace in various early Christian churches, and that what contemporaries perceived as new in the responsorial psalmody of Ambrose was not the principle of alternation between a psalmist singing verses and a congregation singing an invariant refrain, but the formality and complexity of the responses now being taught. For the ambrosian refrains are proper to each psalm, and their texts are composed of whole verses.[25] Responsorial psalmody, then, was both new and old—new enough to justify Augustine's and Paulinus's belief that it had been imported from the East, but old enough to present a standard against which another performing style, antiphonal, could be recognized as different and in need of a special name. The fact that that name, *antiphona*, was applied in the West to monastic practices, but not—except by Paulinus—to cathedral ones is significant.

An important thing to remember about cathedral psalmody sung in the responsorial manner is that the cantor read the psalm from a text and therefore was in no danger of losing his place on account of the interruptions caused by the refrain. This observation forms the basis of an important technical distinction between responsorial and antiphonal psalmody. Proof of it may be found in several passages from Ambrose and Augustine that make express use of the root *legere*, "to read," in the context of responsorial psalmody:

[24] The references may be found translated in *MECL* as follows: Pachomius, no. 111; Athanasius, no. 102; Eusebius, no. 208; Hippolytus, no. 89; Tertullian, no. 78. Compare these with the abundance of references to responsorial psalmody in Ambrose and Chrysostom (*MECL*, 78–90 and 125–34, respectively).

[25] Leeb, *Die Psalmodie*, 62, lists seven actual citations of responses that he has been able to find in all of the writings of Ambrose. They are Pss. 39.2, 37.22, 50.12, 44.3a, 42.4, 22.5a, and Canticles 5.1, of which five comprise two hemistichs and two comprise only one. For a sampling of responsory refrains in Chrysostom and Augustine, see *MECL* nos. 163, 170, 172, 175, 190, 354, 357, 372, and 374. Note that all of these examples are complete psalm verses comprising two hemistichs.

> With what great effort is silence maintained in church during the readings [*cum lectiones leguntur*]! If just one person recites, the entire congregation makes noise; but when a psalm is read [*legitur*], it is itself the guarantor of silence because when all speak [in the response], no one makes noise. (Ambrose, *Explanatio psalmi* 1, 9)[26]

> At the morning Office, as you will recall, brethren, there was read [*lectum*] what we sang in response [*respondemus*] with great sorrow of spirit: "O God, the heathen have come into thy inheritance." (Ambrose, Epistle 20, 20)[27]

> First, regarding what we have sung in response to the reader [*legenti respondentes*], although it is from the middle of the psalm, let me take from it nevertheless the opening of my sermon: "My enemies have spoken evil against me: 'When shall he die, and his name perish?'" (Augustine, *In psalmum* 40, 1)[28]

5

The term "antiphon" in most Latin writers of the fifth and sixth century refers to a song or kind of singing that is different from responsorial psalmody, though in most cases, nothing more can be learned from the reference beyond the mere fact of the difference. But that is not insignificant, especially in view of the common modern assumption that the two forms are the same. Below are several citations from the *Itinerarium* of Egeria (ca. 400), the *Institutes* of Cassian (between 417 and 425), and the rule of Aurelian of Arles (before 551), in which "antiphons" are mentioned as something distinct from the normal psalmody. In these sources psalms are chanted responsorially by a soloist and congregation, or directly by a soloist alone, while antiphons are performed in some other way not specified:

> From that hour until it is light, hymns are sung and psalms responded to, and likewise antiphons; and with every hymn there is a prayer. For two or three priests, and likewise deacons, who say these prayers with every hymn and antiphon, take turns to be there each day with the *monazontes*. (*Itinerarium Egeriae* 24.1)[29]

[26] *PL* 14:924–25; *CSEL* 64:7–8; trans. *MECL* no. 276.

[27] *PL* 16:1000; trans. *MECL* no. 291.

[28] "Primo quod legenti respondentes cantauimus, quamquam de medio psalmo sit, hinc tamen sermonis ducamus exordium: 'Inimici mei . . .'" (*PL* 36:453; *CCSL* 38:447). See also *MECL* no. 357.

[29] "Et ex ea hora usque in luce dicuntur ymni et psalmi responduntur, similiter et antiphonae: et cata singulos ymnos fit oratio. Nam presbyteri bini uel terni, similiter et diacones,

Though Egeria states in the *Itinerarium* that the psalms and antiphons are always appropriate to the time of day, forming—she seems to say—a body of select psalmody of the kind that Taft considers to be the special mark of the cathedral Office,[30] they are presented in the excerpts cited here and elsewhere as an indeterminate number lasting as long as necessary to fill up the time until the arrival of the bishop.

> Again at the sixth hour all come down to the Anastasis in the same way, and sing psalms and antiphons until the bishop is called. (24.3)[31]

That suggests the monastic practice of *lectio continua*, or some version of it, not the limited number of fixed psalms well known to the laity for their topical allusions to the time of day. This fact needs to be borne in mind, for our interpretation of Egeria's testimony on the antiphon depends on what we can infer about the general context. To the extent that we infer a monastic context, we can assume knowledge of the psalms and a level of congregational involvement that would have been quite impossible in a purely cathedral Office.

Though Egeria, in the passage quoted below, describes only the first of the three psalms expressly as responsorial, it is probable on the basis of context and precedent that all three form a liturgical unit of similar elements.[32] From that we may conclude that when she used the term "psalm," she took responsorial performance for granted. I cannot say with any certainty what she means by "antiphons," except that they are evidently different from "psalms."

> On the seventh day, however, that is the Lord's Day, all the people gather before cockcrow, as at Easter. . . . Hymns are sung and also antiphons, and there are prayers with each hymn and antiphon. . . . As soon as the first cock crows, straightway the bishop comes down and enters the cave in the Anastasis. All the gates are opened, and the entire throng enters the Anastasis, where already countless lamps are burning, and when the people are within, one of the priests sings a psalm and all respond, after which there is a prayer. Then one of the deacons sings a psalm, similarly followed by a prayer, and a third psalm is sung by one cleric, followed by a third prayer and the commemoration of all. (24.8–9)[33]

singulis diebus uices habent simul cum monazontes, qui cata singulos ymnos uel antiphonas orationes dicunt" (*CCSL* 175:67; trans. *MECL* no. 242).

[30] *Itinerarium*, 25.5 (trans. *MECL* no. 252); Taft, *The Liturgy*, 54.

[31] "Item hora sexta denuo descendent omnes similiter ad Anastasim et dicuntur psalmi et antiphonae, donec commonetur episcopus" (*CCSL* 175:68; trans. *MECL* no. 244).

[32] Taft, *The Liturgy*, 53.

[33] "Septima autem die, id est dominica die, ante pullorum cantum colliget se omnis multitudo, . . . ac si per pascha. . . . Et dicuntur ymni nec non et antiphonae, et fiunt orationes

In the following description of a Friday-night vigil there can be no doubt that antiphons are not ornaments to psalms, but distinct liturgical items:

> All night responsorial psalms are sung in turn, antiphons in turn, and various readings in turn, all of which continue until morning. (27.8)[34]

The following passages from Cassian's *Institutes* continue to treat antiphons as Egeria did, that is, as chants distinct from psalms with responses:

> And what we have seen in this province, that after one sings to the end of the psalm all stand and sing aloud "Glory be to the Father and to the Son and to the Holy Spirit," we have never heard throughout the entire East. Instead, when the psalm is finished, there follows a prayer by the one who sings, all the others remaining silent, and only the antiphon is ordinarily terminated with this glorification of the Trinity. (*Institutes* 2.8)[35]

This is one of the earliest statements that antiphons were sung with any kind of verse at all, and it is a doxology. Whether other verses, from the psalms or from ecclesiastical poetry, were also sung with chants called "antiphons" cannot be determined.

Cassian also describes the monastic practices of Palestine and Mesopotamia, where the novelty of antiphons was welcomed as a relief from ordinary psalmody. During "antiphons" the monks sang together ("concinuerint") in a standing position, while for "psalms" they sat and responded to a soloist singing the verses ("psalmos uno modulante respondent"). The element of relief or "pleasure" can hardly be accounted for by a change of text type—from scripture to ecclesiastical poetry—much less by the change in posture. A heightened level of participation or musical interest or both seems more likely. Note too that the antiphons are not appendages to the psalms, one antiphon for each psalm, but three elements of a

cata singulos ymnos uel antiphonas. . . . Mox autem primus pullus cantauerit, statim descendet episcopus et intrat intro speluncam ad Anastasim. Aperiuntur hostia omnia et intrat omnis multitudo ad Anastasim, ubi iam luminaria infinita lucent, et quemadmodum ingressus fuerit populus, dicet psalmum quicumque de presbyteris et respondent omnes; post hoc fit oratio. Item dicit psalmum quicumque de diaconibus, similiter fit oratio, dicitur et tertius psalmus a quocumque clerico, fit et tertio oratio et commemoratio omnium" (*CCSL* 175:69).

34 "Tota autem nocte uicibus dicuntur psalmi responsorii, uicibus antiphonae, uicibus lectiones diuersae, quae omnia usque in mane protrahuntur" (*CCSL* 175:74).

35 "Illud etiam quod in hac prouincia uidimus, ut uno cantante in clausula psalmi omnes adstantes concinant cum clamore 'gloria patri et filio et spiritui sancto,' nusquam per omnem Orientem audiuimus, sed cum omnium silentio ab eo, qui cantat, finito psalmo orationem succedere, hac uero glorificatione trinitatis tantummodo solere antiphona terminari" (*CSEL* 17:24; trans. *MECL* no. 340).

liturgical unit that is completed before the next unit, comprising responsorial psalms, begins:

> Hence they divide [the vigils] into threefold offices, so that the effort thus broken up with variety might relieve the exhaustion of the body with a sort of pleasure. For when they have sung three antiphons while standing, after this while sitting on the floor or on low benches they respond to three psalms sung by one of their number, each of them performed by a single brother succeeding another in turn, and to these they add three readings while still sitting in silence. (*Institutes* 3.8)[36]

Another reference to antiphons in the *Institutes* leaves little doubt that one of their distinguishing features was their melodiousness, elevated in some way above ordinary psalm-singing:

> For some have decided that twenty or thirty psalms ought to be recited each night, and that these ought to be prolonged by the melodies of antiphons and the addition of certain rhythms. (*Institutes* 2.2)[37]

Like Cassian, Aurelian of Arles makes clear that "antiphons" are not refrains appended to psalms but separate liturgical items sung as a group after the part of the service comprising "psalms" is over:

> On the first day of Easter at terce say *Kyrie eleison* three times, [then] twelve psalms, that is, each of four brethren say two psalms and a third alleluiatic psalm apiece. When the psalms are finished, [say] a *Kyrie eleison*, six antiphons, and three lessons. (*Regula ad monachos*, app.)[38]

It cannot be stressed enough that since "antiphons" and "psalms" are separate chants rather than parts of a compound form, they must exhibit some kind of tangible difference. Otherwise the application to them of different names, especially in a list of items to be performed in a single Office, would be nonsensical. What could that difference be? The one alleged by Isidore of Seville, that "in responsories a soloist says the verses, while in antiphony the choirs alternate verse by verse,"[39] is probably inapplicable to

[36] "Ideoque eas tripertitis distingunt officiis, ut labor hac diuersitate diuisus delectatione quadam defectionem corporis releuet. Nam cum stantes antiphona tria concinuerint, humi post haec uel sedelibus humillimis insidentes tres psalmos uno modulante respondent, qui tamen singuli a singulis fratribus uicissim succedentibus sibi praebentur, atque his sub eadem quiete residendi ternas adiciunt lectiones" (*CSEL* 17:42–43; trans. *MECL* no. 349).

[37] "Quidam enim uicenos seu tricenos psalmos et hos ipsos antiphonarum protelatos melodiis et adiunctione quarundam modulationum debere dici singulis noctibus censuerunt" (*CSEL* 17:18; trans. *MECL* no. 336).

[38] *PL* 68:393. See also Heiming, "Zum Monastischen," 117.

[39] "Inter responsorios autem et antiphonas hoc differt, quod in responsoriis unus versum dicit, in antiphonis autem versibus alternant chori" (*Etymologiarum* 6.19.8; *PL* 82:252). English trans. after Leeb, *Die Psalmodie*, 104.

earlier times. The assumption that antiphons and responsories differ in their textual origins, the former being ecclesiastical, the latter biblical, is probably inapplicable as well. All the evidence suggests that when antiphons became domesticated in western monasticism, they shed their eastern élan and became simple excerpts from the Bible—fruits of the rumination of scripture that monks and nuns were urged to practice without ceasing.[40] This view is reinforced by Jeffery's contention that *antiphonatim* in the sixth century meant "in excerpts."[41]

Absent these two possibilities, a likely alternative is that the difference was one of performing style. If responsories were based on alternation between a soloist singing verses and a congregation singing an invariant refrain, antiphons were probably something opposite to that. A pattern in which verses sung by the whole congregation, or part of it, alternate with antiphons sung by those who could, seems a distinct possibility.

6

I have presented the adoption of antiphon singing in eastern monasticism and its migration to the West around the year 400, without having first considered the circumstances of its origins. For that we must turn to Antioch and Asia Minor in the decades immediately preceding.

St. Basil in a letter written in 375 refers to two practices in the same office: responsorial psalmody between a soloist and undivided congregation, and psalmody without refrain in which verses are sung in alternation by the two halves of a divided choir. Defending these practices, he claims that they are common in Asia Minor, Egypt, and the Near East as far as Mesopotamia. Significantly, he avoids the term antiphon entirely, describing balanced alternation as ἀντιψάλλουσιν ἀλλήλοις, "singing opposite one another."[42]

St. John Chrysostom mentions neither alternating psalmody nor the term antiphon. His writings do, however, contain references to responsorial psalmody. The refrain texts that he cites are scriptural, comprising entire psalm verses identical in length and function to those adopted in Milan

[40] "Quodcumque operis feceritis, quando lectio non legitur, de divinis scripturis semper aliquid ruminate." Caesarius of Arles, *Regula Sanctarum Virginum* 22; see *Sancti Caesarii Episcopi Arelatensis Opera Omnia* 2: *Opera Varia*, ed. Germain Morin (Maredsous: n.p., 1942), 106. See also *PL* 67:1110.

[41] Peter Jeffery, "The Introduction of Psalmody into the Roman Mass by Pope Celestine I (422–432)," *Archiv für Liturgiewissenschaft* 26 (1984): 163–65.

[42] Basil, Letter 207, 3; *PG* 32:764; trans. *MECL* no. 139.

around the same time and understood by Latin writers to be of eastern provenance.[43]

The Greek ecclesiastical historian Socrates is a central witness to the origins of antiphonal hymnody in the East. Writing in Constantinople in the first half of the fifth century, he bears witness to the events with just enough ambiguity to defy definitive interpretation. Referring to the sectarian strife in Antioch while St. John Chrysostom was a priest of that city (386–98), he states that the Arians sang "antiphonal hymns" (ᾠδὰς ἀντιφώνους) and cites a short refrain of new composition and polemical intent as a component of such hymns: "Where are they who tell of the three as one power?" Nowhere does he suggest that antiphonal means balanced alternation. Yet the obvious alternative—that "antiphonal" means "polemical"—is not at all certain, for antiphonal hymns are also sung, he says, by angels adoring the Trinity, and it is hard to believe that he would have presented angels in the divine presence singing hymns whose main intent was to persuade or mock theological opponents. The mention of a leader of the orthodox singers who was struck by a projectile in a mêlée with the Arians bears witness to a cantorial function at least among the orthodox, but since it is the Arians who are mentioned expressly as singing antiphonal hymns, we cannot even be certain of this implied connection between the soloist's role and antiphonal singing.[44]

From Socrates's testimony we can extract that Antiochene antiphonal hymns were composed in an atmosphere of intense zealotry and therefore probably had attractive, perhaps even popular melodies, that they were sung in processions through the streets, that they had nonscriptural texts, and that their performance involved a group of singers perhaps under the leadership of a cantor.[45]

Sozomen, a contemporary of Socrates and probably dependent on him, confirms the connection of antiphonal singing to the Arian sect. He mentions the division of the ensemble into groups (εἰς συστήματα μεριζόμενοι)—without saying how many or what their composition was—and the devising of apologetic refrains. But in describing the practice generally as being "in the manner of antiphons" (κατὰ τὸν τών ἀντιφώνων τρόπον), he does not specify which aspect is antiphonal, the division into groups, the use of

[43] For a sample of relevant excerpts in translation, see *MECL* 78–90.

[44] Socrates, *Ecclesiastical History* 6.8, in *PG* 67:688–92; trans. *MECL* no. 218. On the meaning of ἀντιφωνία as "contradiction," note that Eusebius uses the term in that sense about a hundred years earlier in his *De vita Constantini* 6.37 (Hucke, "Die Entwicklung," 159).

[45] The demotic character of Antiochene antiphons has been stressed by Hucke, who imagines them as the fourth-century equivalent of Salvation Army hymns. Hucke, "Die Entwicklung," 160.

refrains, both aspects, or some other aspect simply taken for granted. We have no way of knowing with certainty that "in the manner of antiphons" did not refer to a special melodic style, to the sites at which such songs were sung, or to the apologetic content of their words. The refrains are designated ἀκροτελεύτια, "endings," suggesting the responsorial form of performance already well known since apostolic times, in which all the lines or strophes terminate with an invariant refrain.[46]

In an unrelated anecdote Sozomen describes an incident of public psalmody that sheds some light on practices then current. A crowd bearing the relics of the martyr Babylas to a new burial site responds with an invariant refrain (Ps. 96.7) to verses sung by those who knew the psalms. Even if not expressly antiphonal, the singing has the same ring of sectarianism, and the refrain, though psalmic, has the same tendentious purpose, as songs sung "in the manner of antiphons":

> Those who knew them well took the lead in the psalms for the benefit of the others, and the crowd joined in in unison, adding this saying: "Disgraced are they who worship sculpted things, who pride themselves in idols."[47]

Theodoret of Cyrus (449/50) passes on the tradition that credits Flavian and Diodorus with introducing in Antioch the practice of singing the biblical psalms in some kind of alternation, but he does not use the term antiphon, and his allusion to clergy and laity suggests an uneven division that does not correspond to the common concept of balanced antiphony.[48] Akominatos (thirteenth century), citing a lost text of Theodore of Mopsuestia (fourth century, second half) as his source, repeats the same legend, but now calls the new kind of psalmody "antiphons," claiming further that they were translated from the Syrian. If this hearsay testimony is accepted at face value, it implies that antiphons entailed nonbiblical texts, since biblical ones would not have had to be translated from the Syrian, but could have been taken directly from the Septuagint.[49]

In the late fourth century the East knew various kinds of participatory hymnody involving a soloist and congregation, the two halves of an equally divided congregation, and a small group alternating with a larger one. The refrains themselves are referred to in a variety of ways: ὑπακοή, ὑπήχησις ("answer"), ῥῆσις ("saying"), and ἀκροτελεύτιον ("ending"), but not as antiphons. Psalms performed in balanced alternation are not called

[46] Sozomen, *Ecclesiastical History* 8.7; *PG* 67:1536; trans. *MECL* no. 223.

[47] (Sozomen, 5.19; *PG* 67:1276). See also *MECL* no. 221.

[48] Theodoret, *Ecclesiastical History* 2.24.8–9; *PG* 82:1060; trans. *MECL* no. 224. For interpretation see Hucke, "Die Entwicklung," 154–55.

[49] Hucke, "Die Entwicklung," 155–56.

antiphonal either, at least not in orthodox monasticism. The term "antiphon," at least at first, seems to be associated with heretical and apologetic singing. While it does not exclude refrains, it seems to imply something larger, encompassing both invariant and variable elements—the whole form, in other words, along with its popular, nonscriptural texts and various schemes for group participation.

In the light of our current knowledge, it seems prudent not to define "antiphon" too narrowly. It may have involved various types of participatory singing, and various types of alternation, and was probably associated at first with the sites at which such singing was heard and the spirit of contentiousness that underlay it. It is probable, but not certain, that it differed from responsorial singing as described by Chrysostom. Yet even that was relatively new, for the responses recorded in the first three centuries of Christian liturgical practice are mostly limited to the biblical "Alleluia" and "Quoniam in aeternum misericordia eius."

7

The two Italian rules of the sixth century, St. Benedict's (ca. 530) and the Master's (late in the century),[50] represent an important turning point in the history of monastic psalmody. Dyer has argued that psalmody in these two rules was performed by individual monks in turn while their brothers responded with a refrain or antiphon—in other words, following a tradition established by the monks of the Egyptian desert.[51] There is much to recommend this opinion, especially the frequent insistence on observance of rank: in the RM (Rule of the Master) psalms are to be "imposed" first by the abbot, then the deans, and then the brothers "one at a time" ("singuli fratres").[52] But that argument does not satisfy all doubt. If we take *imponere* to mean not to chant by oneself, but literally to impose a chant on the community and lead in its singing (see section 2 above), the indubitably solo nature of imposing becomes irrelevant, for it does not rule out that others might join in in a subordinate capacity. Furthermore, why would two dif-

[50] Marilyn Dunn presents a strong case for discarding the old date of ca. 500–25, and placing the composition of the RM in the latter part of the sixth century, in any case after the RB. This dating may actually be unnecessarily cautious. Dunn's arguments showing the RM to be dependent on the Rule of St. Columban seem to rule out a date earlier than the 590s since Columban, who eventually founded a monastery at Bobbio in northern Italy, only arrived on the continent in 590 or 591. Marilyn Dunn, "Mastering Benedict: Monastic Rules and Their Authors in the Early Medieval West," *English Historical Review* 105 (1990): 567–94.

[51] Dyer, "Monastic Psalmody," 59–61.

ferent terms, *antiphona* and *responsorium*, be applied to two categories of psalmody whose performing styles did not differ—that is, if both entailed solo verses periodically interrupted by a congregational refrain?

Singulars and plurals in the RM and RB (Rule of St. Benedict), as Dyer has observed, do not help: rules governing collective psalmody could be addressed to the individual, as in "It behooves the psalm singer [*psallentem*] to stand erect with bowed head . . .," and rules governing solo psalmody could be addressed to all collectively, as in "Let us sing [*psallamus*] therefore with voice and mind in accord."[53]

But there are other passages in the RM which, because of the concrete circumstances to which they refer, can hardly be interpreted in more than one way. When brothers say the Office on journeys, they withdraw from the road and kneel for a moment; then returning to the road, they suppress all ordinary conversation, and after a blessing has been asked, they "break into the psalm as soon as it is imposed" ("inpositum prorumpant in psalmum").[54] The plural *prorumpant* in particular is hard to explain as a characterization of solo chanting while the rest of the group devoutly listens.

Returning from a journey and finding the community in the oratory, they are to ask the brothers to pray for them. But if they find them in the midst of chanting (*psallentes*), the returning brothers, "after saying a prayer, should immediately sing along with them" ("orantes mox psallant cum ipsis").[55] The contrast between *orantes* and *psallant* and the emphatic *cum ipsis* would all seem unnecessary if participation in the Office entailed nothing more than paying prayerful attention to the chanting of a soloist.

A brother with aching limbs but no fever may enter the oratory with the others at the customary hour and "chant while lying on a mat as if in prayer" ("iacens in matta uelut in oratione psallat").[56] It seems unthinkable that a brother in that position would be permitted to chant a solo psalm for the edification of the whole community. It is with good reason that the text of the Rule says *psallat* and not *imponat*, for while he may sing along, he does not lead the singing.

Other remarks in the Rule seem to make more sense when some kind of communal recitation is assumed. Those occupied with urgent work elsewhere in the monastery are instructed to fulfill the *opus Dei* "softly to themselves" ("lente sibi") right there where they are occupied, "following the

[52] RM 22.13–14, 46.1–2, and 92.36; see also RB 47.2–3 and 63.4.
[53] RM 47.6 and 19. See also RB 19.7.
[54] RM 56.2.
[55] RM 67.1–2.
[56] RM 69.10.

voice of the oratory."[57] If merely listening in devout attention was all that was required to fulfill the obligation of the Office, what would be the point of *lente sibi*, since listening is quiet by definition?

Though the rules of Benedict and the Master do not expressly describe how to perform antiphonal psalmody, the performing style may be inferred from assumptions that they make about its opposite, *psalmi directanei* or *in directum*. Depending on whether "direct" means "without alternation" or "without interruption," we may reasonably conclude that ordinary psalmody—antiphonal psalmody—is alternated by two choirs, or interrupted periodically with a refrain. (The latter entails alternation too, but not necessarily between equal performing forces.) In some cases the wording of the rules is ambiguous. Does "sine antiphona in directum" (RB 12.1) mean without antiphon *and* directly, or are the two expressions merely pleonastic? The latter seems to be the case, for the Master stipulates that the individual brother compelled by urgent work to say the Office in private should say the psalms directly in order to save time.[58] That allowance would be absurd if saying them not directly meant saying them in alternation—something an individual could not do in any case. The obvious alternative is that direct psalmody means uninterrupted psalmody. That meaning seems quite inescapable in RB 17.6, where the two expressions are placed as opposites: "Si maior congregatio fuerit, cum antiphonas, si vero minor, in directum psallantur." Accordingly, the normal performing style, and the referent of "antiphonal," is not balanced alternation of verses, but periodic interruption of the verses with an antiphon.

That Benedict permits only small congregations to chant the little hours directly has a bearing on the performance question. What would be gained from this permission? No time is saved by chanting together instead of alternating from side to side, and two can do that as easily as twenty. But in a small community where every brother is responsible for some urgent task (feeding the livestock, baking bread, and so forth), and none can afford the long interruption of a fully antiphonated service, the brevity of direct psalmody makes sense. Furthermore, in such a community there might be a dearth of monks able to impose antiphons or join in their singing, whereas all monks could manage the unadorned psalms.

The rules of Benedict and the Master bear witness to a conspicuous departure from tradition in the distribution of responsorial and antiphonal

[57] RM 55.17.

[58] "Aut si urguet fratrem quaeuis opera facienda, . . . psalmos sibi, tamen cum gloriis suis, conternent . . . psalmos uero directaneos dicens, propter, ut supra diximus, urguentem laboris operam" (RM 55.5–7).

psalmody—a tradition represented by the rules of Aurelian and Caesarius of Arles. Those rules, though roughly contemporary with Benedict's, depend on the lost Rule of the Monastery of Lérins (off the southeast coast of France, opposite Cannes) established by Cassian's disciple Honoratus (d. ca. 430). They are thus indirect descendants of the tradition that Cassian brought from Egypt and Palestine in the early fifth century.[59] In Aurelian's rule for monks the proportion of "psalms" to "antiphons" in festal Offices (not counting *directanei*) is as follows:

terce	sext	none	lucernarium	duodecimam	nocturns	matins
12:6	12:1	12:1	0:3	18:3	18:3	0:12

The aggregate is 72:29. The Arlesian rules preserve a tradition in which the norm is solo psalmody—with or without "alleluia" as a congregational response—while "antiphons" entail some kind of musical or participatory enhancement added to most hours in small proportion after the "psalms" are finished. Only matins and lucernarium (our lauds and vespers) consist primarily of psalms called "antiphons."[60]

In the rules of Benedict and the Master these proportions are reversed. The bulk of the psalmody at each hour is in the form of antiphonal psalms—in the RB they are called "psalmi cum antiphonas" [sic], in the RM simply "antifanae." Responsories are sung afterward and in much smaller proportion. In fact, the enumeration of psalms in chapter 18 of the RB, intended to insure that all 150 psalms are said each week, is stated entirely in terms of antiphonal psalms. Responsories are not taken into account. In both the RM and the RB responsorial psalms are routinely abbreviated—at the little hours in the RM (46.9) and at nocturns of the short nights of summer in the RB (10.2). That abbreviation in the RB is a sure sign that the responsorial psalms are not part of the sacred duty, or *pensum*, to say the entire psalter once each week.

[59] Taft, "The Liturgy," 101.

[60] Aurelian of Arles, *Regula ad monachos*, *PL* 68:387–96. All four Arlesian rules, one apiece for monks and nuns by Aurelian and Caesarius, present basically identical forms of the Office. For Aurelian's *Regula ad virgines* see *PL* 68:399–406. For Caesarius's *Regulae virginum ac monachorum* see Morin, *Regula*, 97–155; see also *PL* 67:1099–1104, and 1107–21. "Antiphons" in these rules almost certainly mean antiphonated psalms, probably whole ones. "Dicite antiphona de psalmis in ordine" implies at least that "antiphons" were psalmic extracts, if not whole, antiphonated psalms, and that they were sung in their biblical order. All four rules say in various ways that the psalms and canticles of matins are said *in* or *cum antiphonis*, and Heiming has pointed out that the allowance for *antiphonae parvulae* at certain hours implies not a shorter refrain, but fewer verses, suggesting that the normal "antiphon" included a psalm with all its verses (Heiming, "Zur Monastischen," 118).

In fact, responsorial psalmody, once the form employed by default when special forms were not prescribed, has become the special form in the RB. Responsories are referred to in chapters 9 and 11 as belonging to the lections that precede them ("lectiones cum responsoriis suis"). This suggests that responsory texts were chosen for their topical relevance to the preceding reading and that they—like the gradual responsories of the Roman Mass on which they are evidently modeled—were not necessarily even psalmic. If not, that would have presented no problem to the cantor who had to sing them, for the RB implies that they were not sung from memory, but read from a book along with the readings: "legantur in codice . . . quattuor lectiones cum responsoriis suis" (11.2).

The rules of Benedict and the Master represent a fundamental shift in the medium through which monks satisfy their sacred obligation to recite the psalms. In the light of this change of medium, is it too much to propose that the performing style changed as well? More—that the difference of performing style is what motivated the change? Antiphons have advantages. They give scope to the culture of quotation, allowing every monk in turn to select a favorite passage as the theme of the psalmody. And they allow the rest to avoid fatigue and boredom by singing along with the leader, making use of a competence that they have invested much personal energy to acquire.

The Rule of Paul and Stephen is alone among the rules of late antiquity in providing vivid and unequivocal testimony to choral recitation of the Office.[61]

> When chanting by choirs, let the priors who stand in them begin the verses; or if they are afflicted with some infirmity, let those do it whom the abbot orders. And when they have begun, let everyone immediately on the first or second syllable—if that is possible—join in evenly, in unison, and with one voice, so that there is no dissonance among the singers, which is especially apt to happen from a disorganized beginning or any contentious diversity. (5.1–4)[62]

[61] Although Vilanova places the composition of the rule in the latter part of the sixth century on the basis of its contents, the actual manuscript tradition goes back no further than the ninth century, making it impossible to rule out that the references to choral recitation are later additions (Dyer, "Monastic Psalmody," 67).

[62] "Initium uersuum, per psallentium choros, priores qui in eis stant incipiant; aut si eis aduersatur infirmitas, hi incipiant quibus iusserit pater. Quibus incipientibus, mox omnes, si potest fieri, in prima aut secunda syllaba pariter unanimiter et uno ore subiungant; ut non sit dissonantia cantantium, quae maxime ab inordinato initio et quodammodo contentiosa uarietate solet accidere" (Vilanova, *Regula Pauli*, 110).

8

The number of Latin antiphons that survive from the period before 680 is extremely small. I know of only three. They are all from around the year 600 or shortly before. The first is from Gregory the Great's fourth dialogue; the other two are from the writings of Gregory of Tours, the historian of the Franks under the Merovingians. The texts are long and obviously not suitable for congregational participation. And their apparent spontaneity suggests that they were solo chants intended in some way to complement psalms sung by a group.

> [The monk John, summoning his brothers to his deathbed, asked them to sing psalms,] but he himself imposed on them the antiphon, saying: "Aperite mihi portas iustitiae et ingressus in eas confitebor Domino. Haec porta domini; iusti intrabunt per eam." (Ps. 117.19–20)[63]

> As the boys made haste and approached the place next to the royal headquarters, they entered the holy basilica, and while they did so, the one who was the leader [*primicirius*] spontaneously [*ex inproviso*] imposed this antiphon: "Praecinxisti me, Domine, virtutem ad bellum, subplantasti insurgentes in me subtus me et inimicorum meorum dedisti mihi dorsum et odientes me disperdedisti." (Ps. 17.40–41)[64]

> [During a famine the people implored St. Quintinian to impose an antiphon, believing that the prayer, coming from him, would be especially effective.] And he fell prostrate on his cloak right there in the street and prayed with tears for a very long time. Then rising, he imposed the antiphon for which they were pleading, for it was a virtuous thing. And his words were these from the speech given by Solomon: "Si clauso caelo pluviae non fuerint propter peccata populi, et conversi deprecati fuerint faciem tuam, exaudi, Domine, et dimitte peccata populi tui et da pluviam terrae, quam dedisti populo tuo ad possedendum." (2 Paral. 6.26–27)[65]

The rule of Paul and Stephen forbids brothers to sing responsories or antiphons of their own invention, adding that it is the custom for some to do this:

> Let no one presume to do what some do, that is, for their own pleasure to sing in chapel, or ruminate, or say any responsories or antiphons of composed character not taken from the canonical scriptures. (14.1)[66]

[63] Dialogues 4.36, in *Grégoire le Grand: Dialogues*, ed. Adalbert de Vogüé, Sources chrétiennes 265 (Paris: Éditions du Cerf, 1980), 118.

[64] *Gregorii Turonensis Opera*, Monumenta Germaniae Historica 1 (Hannover: Hahn, 1885), 100.

[65] Ibid., 676.

[66] "Nullus praesumat responsoria uel antiphonas quae solent aliqui composito sono pro suo

This adds further weight to the assumption that antiphons in the late sixth century could be improvised, and therefore, that they were for soloists, not the ensemble.

9

The first surviving collections of Latin antiphons come from around the year 700. They are the Mozarabic orational preserved in Verona, Biblioteca capitolare, MS. 89, and the Antiphonary of Bangor, preserved in Milan, Biblioteca Ambrosiana, MS. C.5 inf.[67] The Antiphonary of Bangor contains seventy-four antiphons, of which forty-five are psalmic or derived from biblical canticles, two are from other biblical sources, and twenty-seven are of ecclesiastical origin, including some in verse. The psalmic antiphons usually comprise whole biblical verses, though a few are limited to a single hemistich. The poetic antiphons have from two to five lines, the following three-line example being typical:

> Fornacis flammas pueri contempserunt,
> Christo jugiter immolaverunt,
> Viam iniquam dereliquerunt.[68]

The antiphons in the Bangor Antiphonary are neither numerous nor especially long and present no insurmountable obstacle to memorization. Yet they do go beyond the repertory of psalm verses that monks were expected to know by heart as a condition of their vocation. The book is not a pure antiphonary, but a miscellany for the abbot or prior, containing the hymns, collects, and antiphons that he would need to know in order to conduct the service.[69] The appearance, in such a book, of antiphons written out in full suggests that they were indeed read, and that the readers were probably the abbot or individual brothers with his permission. Performance by

libito, non ex canonica scriptura assumpta, canere in congregatione ista uel meditari uel dicere" (Vilanova, *Regula Pauli*, 113).

[67] For the Mozarabic orational, Claveras has given the date of late seventh or early eighth century, but in all events before 711; *Oracional Visigotico*, ed. D. José Vives, with paleographic study by D. Jeronimo Claveras, Monumenta Hispaniae Sacra: Serie Liturgica 1 (Barcelona: Consejo Superior de Investigaciones Cientificas, Instituto Padre Enrique Flórez de Historica Eclesiàstica, 1946), xxxiv. Gamber agrees in general but gives a *terminus ante quem* of 732; Klaus Gamber, *Codices Liturgici Latini Antiquiores* (Freiburg, Switzerland: Universitätsverlag, 1968), 206. For the Antiphonary of Bangor, Warren gives the date of 680–91; *The Antiphonary of Bangor*, ed. Frederick Edward Warren (London: Harrison and Sons, 1893), 1:viii. Gamber, *Codices*, 146, accepts this date without reservation.

[68] Fol. 32^r; Warren, *The Antiphonary*, 2:29.

[69] Fernand Cabrol, "Bangor, Antiphonaire de," *Dictionnaire d'archéologie chrétienne et de liturgie* (Paris: Letouzey et Ané, 1907–53), 2:183–91.

individuals is also suggested by the book's small size, which Warren gives as about 7 by 9 inches.

The Mozarabic orational in Verona is more difficult to evaluate. Its antiphons are not whole; it gives only incipits. The texts to which the incipits refer, however, can be found in Mozarabic antiphonaries. A further difficulty is that the incipits, as well as rubrics, are written in the margins of the manuscript and by a hand other than the two that filled the normal writing area. But since all three hands employ the same Visigothic minuscule script,[70] it is reasonable to accept as a working hypothesis that the antiphon incipits form part of the manuscript's original conception. That view is reinforced by the many verbal concordances between the antiphons and the orations with which they are paired.

The Mozarabic antiphons include psalmic, biblical nonpsalmic, and ecclesiastical texts. They are long by antiphonal standards, easily comprising whole biblical verses, and sometimes several, as shown in the following antiphon for Matins of Christmas based on Luke 2.10–11:

> Ecce annuntio vobis gaudium magnum, quod erit omni populo; quia hodie natus est nobis salvator qui est Christus Dominus; regnabit in domo Iacob in eternum, et regni eius non erit finis.[71]

But they are not only remarkable for their length; they are also remarkably abundant, numbering over four hundred. Most of the arguments that apply to the Bangor Antiphonary apply with even greater force here, for not only does the Mozarabic repertory include nonpsalmic and ecclesiastical material, but it is more extensive than the Irish, presenting real practical obstacles to choral recitation from memory. If solo performance of antiphons seems apt in the Bangor Antiphonary, it must seem all the more so here.

10

The familiar ferial antiphons of the Benedictine and Roman *cursus* are very short, usually half-verses. That is much shorter than the antiphons cited by Gregory the Great and Gregory of Tours around the year 600, shorter than those in the Mozarabic and Irish collections from around the year 700, shorter than most of the antiphons in the earliest Gregorian sources of the ninth and tenth centuries. The Hartker Codex (ca. 1000), with its ninety-five ferial antiphons, is the first Gregorian source to transmit a complete list. Regino's tonary (early tenth century) transmits about a third of that

[70] Vives, *Oracional*, xxxii and xxxv–xxxvii.

[71] Incipit, Vives, *Oracional*, 93; full text, León, Biblioteca catedral, MS. 8, fol. 69^r, in *Antiphonarium Mozarabicum de la Catedral de León* (León: n.p., 1928), 36.

number, while the Carolingian Tonary of Metz (ca. 870) and the *Musica disciplina* of Aurelian of Réôme (840s) give a tenth or less. The antiphonary of Compiègne (ca. 860–80) lacks the ferial list entirely. Although it is generally assumed that the ferial antiphons constitute the repertory's most primitive layer,[72] the evidence does not compel that conclusion. It does show that many of the longer proper antiphons are of ninth-century origin or later—mainly because their feasts were only introduced at that time—but it does not rule out that the short ferial antiphons may be equally recent. In other words, brevity in antiphons—a quality making them apt for collective performance—may be a relatively late adaptation.

11

The repertory of antiphons was growing in the ninth and tenth centuries. The Carolingian tonary of Metz transmits about 1440, the Hartker Codex over two thousand. While the division of the repertory into chronological layers of ferial, psalmic but proper, and biblical nonpsalmic antiphons is based on surmise, there can be little doubt that many proper antiphons and nearly all nonbiblical ones are no older than the Carolingian era. These topical antiphons presented to the monk an array of texts that extended far beyond his fund of memorized psalm verses. Apart from the difficulty of learning the melodies, the type and sheer number of texts make it unlikely that they were sung by the whole choir. It seems more probable that they were performed by a soloist reading them from a book.

12

The state of antiphonal psalmody at the beginning of the Middle Ages is summed up in Book 4, chapter 7, of Amalar's *Liber officialis:*

Antiphona dicitur vox reciproca. Antiphona inchoatur ab uno unius cori, et ad eius symphoniam psalmus cantatur per duos coros; ipsa enim, id est antiphona, coniunguntur simul duo cori.

"Antiphon" means alternating sound. The antiphon is begun by one member of one choir, and to its harmony the psalm is sung by two choirs; for it is precisely by it—that is, by the antiphon—that the two choirs are joined together into one.

[72] Edward Nowacki, "The Gregorian Office Antiphons and the Comparative Method," *Journal of Musicology* 4 (1985–86): 243–75, esp. 249–59; Jean Claire, "Les répertoires liturgiques latins avant l'octoéchos," *Études grégoriennes* 15 (1975): 5–192.

Quanto enim melior est anima corpore, tanto melior est cantus animae quam corporis. Igitur intendendum est quae sit antiphona animae. Videtur nobis virtus delectionis esse quae coniungit opera duorum fratrum simul.	For as the soul is better than the body, so the chant of the soul is better than that of the body. Therefore we need to turn our attention to what the antiphon of the soul may be. It seems to me that it is the virtue of love, which joins together the works of two brothers into one.
Psalmi ad opera referuntur, antiphona ad illam dilectionem, qua unusquisque fratri suo porrigit suum opus. Verbi gratia, unus legit et discit doctrinam in scola, alter seminat in campo; tempore fructus doctor seminanti porrigit doctrinam, sator doctori panem.	Psalms refer to the works and the antiphon to the love by which each offers his work to his brother. For example, one reads and studies doctrine in school, another sows in the field; at harvest time the teacher offers to the sower doctrine, and the sower to the teacher bread.
Duobus coris alternatur antiphona, quoniam non potest minus esse caritas quam inter duos. Hanc vicissitudinem caritatis significant cantores, qui alternatim ex utraque parte antiphonas levant. Hos duos coros designaverunt pennae animalium invicem porrectae, quae vidit Iezechiel in figura adventus Christi et novi testamenti. Coniunctio duarum pennarum antiphona est, quae vicem tenet caritatis.	The antiphon is alternated by two choirs, for charity cannot exist between less than two. This exchange of charity is signified by the singers who alternately from either side raise the antiphons. These two choirs are symbolized by the wings of living creatures reaching out to each other, which Ezechiel saw in prefigurement of the coming Christ and the New Testament. The conjoining of the two wings is the antiphon, which stands for charity.[73]

The psalm verses are sung by the whole assembly divided into two choirs ("per duos choros"). Reinforcing this interpretation is the allegory of good works ("Psalmi ad opera referuntur"), with its implication of reciprocity ("unusquisque fratri suo porrigit suum opus").

Amalar says that the antiphon is "begun" by "one"; he does not say how many finish it. In such an elaborate analogy, if one of the choirs or both of them joined the soloist in finishing the antiphon, we would expect Amalar to mention it. That he fails to do so suggests that he was indifferent to this detail or that joining the cantor in finishing the antiphon was *ad libitum* and not predictable.

[73] Ed. Hanssens, *Amalarii*, 2:433; trans. by the author.

Amalar does say that the antiphon "is alternated by the two choirs," but this is almost immediately balanced by the statement that "singers," not choirs, alternately from either side "raise" the antiphons. The reason that Amalar mentions this fact apparently is to turn aside an anticipated objection to his analogy. He knows that the choirs take turns originating the antiphons. Lest someone say that this weakens his image of the antiphon as a kind of unifying virtue, he responds that the antiphon must be alternated because you cannot have charity between less than two. The meaning, as in the RM (22.13), is that the first antiphon is sung by someone from the first choir, the second antiphon by someone from the second, and so forth.

Amalar's actual text states that the choirs become one not by singing the antiphon, but by singing the alternate psalm verses to the antiphon's harmony. The allegory reinforces this interpretation: harmony is like charity, an incorporeal aspect of actions which on their corporeal surfaces are separate, reciprocal acts.

In general, Amalar must mean something like the following. A soloist begins the antiphon, establishing the mode of the psalmody to follow. Others may join in, but their doing so has no bearing on the allegory of reciprocal charity. The antiphon will establish the harmony to which the verses are sung regardless of how it is performed. That is a practical matter dependent on rehearsal and the ability of the participants to see and read from the antiphonary. When the antiphon is finished, the two choirs sing the psalm verses in choral alternation according to the mode established by the antiphon, being united in common harmony, just as the reaper and teacher are united by the virtue of charity.

"Antiphons" began in the region of Antioch in the mid-fourth century. What distinguished them at first from other kinds of singing was probably not a particular performing style, but the subject and intent of their texts, the sites where they were sung, and their popular musical character. By the early fifth century they were adopted into western monasticism, where they were treated as whole antiphonated psalms, not just as refrains, and formed distinct parts of the Office separate from the parts comprising ordinary psalms. Except by Paulinus, they were considered different from responsorial psalms, which were read by a soloist from a book while the congregation responded with an invariant refrain. It is reasonable to infer that the difference entailed a reversal of those roles—something that was possible because of the obligation of all monks to memorize the psalter. The refrain in such "antiphons" was probably a quotation from scripture imposed on the congregation by the monk whose turn it was to lead the psalmody.

The RB introduces a change of medium in which the obligation to recite a weekly quota of psalms is satisfied not by the traditional solo psalms, but by antiphonal ones. Many descriptions of daily life in the RB and RM are compatible with that assumption, although, to be sure, neither rule addresses the question expressly. Amalar of Metz does, and leaves little doubt that the antiphonal psalmody known to him entailed verses chanted in alternation by a divided choir and antiphons intoned, and probably completed, by a soloist.

The repertory of Latin antiphons around the year 700 was already large and by the millennium had grown considerably larger. Such a repertory is not one that the average monastic congregation is likely to have known well enough to sing chorally, nor would such congregations have possessed more than a single antiphonary from which to conduct the service. It makes more sense to assume solo performance of antiphons, joined by the whole congregation on more solemn occasions. The whole point of antiphons was to make the psalmody more ceremonious and to connect it to particular themes—not to enable ordinary monks to participate. There was no need of that, for all monks knew the psalms by heart. The different functions of psalms and antiphons in monastic life were well served by choral performance of the former and solo performance of the latter. The testimony of the period seldom contradicts, often corroborates, and almost always is compatible with that conclusion.

NINO PIRROTTA

A Sommacampagna Codex of the Italian Ars Nova?

Gidino da Sommacampagna is not a new name to any scholar who has dealt with the history of the Trecento madrigal, its owner being the author of a late fourteenth-century treatise on Italian poetic forms, too easily dismissed by many as an uncritical imitation of the older treatise by Antonio da Tempo.[1] What is new is the association of this name with a musical manuscript. The manuscript itself is not new: it is simply that I have found expedient for the purpose of a title to use a single name in place of two different bibliographical references, those pertaining to the Vatican fragment Rossi 215 and to the two related folios preserved in the library of the Opera Pia Greggiati of Ostiglia. My listeners and readers will judge whether or not the name might come to be permanently associated with the manuscript.

To explain my reasons for selecting the topic of my present contribution and for adding Sommacampagna's name to its title I must state that I am presently involved in the task of preparing a new facsimile edition of the

[1] Da Tempo's *Summa artis rithimici vulgaris dictaminis* has recently been reedited by Richard Andrews (Bologna: Commissione per i testi di lingua, 1977), while Gidino's text is still only available in the old edition by Giovanni Battista Carlo Giuliari, *Gidino da Sommacampagna: Trattato inedito dei ritmi volgari: da un codice del sec. XIV della Biblioteca Capitolare di Verona* (Bologna: Romagnoli, 1870; repr. Bologna: Commissione per i testi di lingua, 1968).

two fragments.[2] This has led to a close re-examination of their codicological connotations, beginning with their beautiful handwriting—a very regular, most energetic hand whose style we Italians call "cancelleresca" for its prevailing connection with the practice of chancery scribes. Other specimens of this style, many of them coming from the Venetian region, include the only extant source of Sommacampagna's *Tractato de li Rithimi Volgari*, codex CCCCXLIV of the Biblioteca Capitolare of Verona. It pleases me to think that a connection may have existed between the two musical fragments and the Veronese milieu in which Sommacampagna conceived his treatise, or even with his own musical experiences—a connection in favor of which also speak the dialectal connotations observed by many scholars in the literary texts of the two fragments.[3]

Sommacampagna's tract is dedicated to Antonio della Scala, the last Veronese lord of that family who ruled alone from 1381 to 1387, and must have been completed between these two dates. This fact has led the author of a recent dissertation on our two fragments to place them at about the same time.[4] I do not go that far and still maintain the date of about 1370, which I had previously suggested,[5] my main reason being that all the *ballate* in my so-called Sommacampagna codex are monophonic, while we have only polyphonic *ballate* in the older section of the Reina codex, thought to have been written shortly before 1400. Even my date, however, does not agree with the general assumption that the repertory of the two fragments represents a very early phase of Italian polyphony.[6] I have, myself, shared this view in the past and contributed to it by interpreting the madrigal "Dal bel castel se parte de Peschiera" as referring to Alberto and Mastino della

[2] *Il Codice Rossi 215,* ed. Nino Pirrotta (Lucca: Libreria Musicale Italiana, 1992).

[3] Most particularly by Ugo Sesini, "Il canzoniere musicale trecentesco del Cod. Vaticano Rossiano 215," *Studi medievali* 16, n.s. (1943–50): 212–36.

[4] Gian Carlo Brioschi, "Struttura e cronologia del codice Vaticano Rossi 215 e del frammento Greggiati di Ostiglia" (Ph.D. diss., Università "La Sapienza," Rome, 1989), 28–29.

[5] See my article "'Arte' e 'non arte' nel frammento Greggiati," in *L'Ars Nova italiana del Trecento* 5, ed. Agostino Ziino (Palermo: Enchiridion, 1985), 211. F. Alberto Gallo, "Antonio da Ferrara, Lancillotto Anguissola e il madrigale trecentesco," *Studi e problemi di critica testuale* 12 (1976): 41, places it shortly after 1350.

[6] Already the first short musicological notice on the Rossi fragment, Heinrich Besseler, "Studien zur Musik des Mittelalters, II: Die Motette von Franko von Köln bis Philipp von Vitry," *Archiv für Musikwissenschaft* 7 (1927): 233, describes its contents as "29 anscheinend sehr frühe Madrigale und Cacce." Following this statement and similar ones contained in the articles on the same subject of Fernando Liuzzi and Johannes Wolf, Kurt von Fischer, *Studien zur italienischen Musik des Trecento und frühen Quattrocento* (Bern: Haupt, 1956), 95, also states briefly: "Das Repertorium von *Rs* gehört vermutlich in die Zeit von 1330–1340."

Scala and to events of the "thirties."[7] I am now inclined to reconsider, to think that not all the pieces in the two fragments need to be that old, and to give a different explanation of the so-called archaic features of the source.

Such features are essentially three: 1) the musical notation, strictly adhering to the principles of Italian notation and said to be near to the principles expounded by Marchettus de Padua, or even, according to Apel, to represent "a link between the Petronian system and the fully developed Italian notation";[8] 2) the handling of polyphony, often interspersed with crudities, such as parallel unisons, fifths and octaves, frictions between the voices, and strange motions of the tenors;[9] 3) the presence in the manuscript of one isolated *rondello* and of a number of madrigals whose metrical schemes, diverging from the most usual patterns, are more consistent with the variety of forms described by da Tempo in 1332.

Let us take the three points one by one. The Italian system of notation seems to me fully developed in the two fragments. Consistently applied is the habit of using letters to indicate the number of *semibreves minimae* contained in each *brevis*, a habit typically Italian but diverging from Marchettus's suggestions.[10] *Puncti divisionis* frame the content of each *brevis* value, within which the *semibreves maiores, minores,* and *minimae* are distinguished *via artis* by the addition of upward or downward tails if their arrangement is not already evident *via naturae.*[11] *Puncti perfectionis* and *augmentationis* are never used, except that a few perfect *longae* are so marked in the ritornello of the madrigal "La disiosa brama."[12] Distinctive in

[7] Nino Pirrotta, "Marchettus de Padua and the Italian Ars Nova," *Musica disciplina* 9 (1955): 68. Giuseppe Corsi, *Poesie musicali del Trecento* (Bologna: Commissione per i testi di lingua, 1970), 331–32, has objected that Padua, where Alberto usually lived at that time, is not on the river Po, mentioned in the madrigal; but I refer to a time when Alberto was trying to gain possession of some salines near the mouth of the Po. The ensuing war against Venice led to the loss of Padua (1337) and to Alberto's emprisonment for some time in Venice.

[8] Willi Apel, *The Notation of Polyphonic Music 900–1600*, 5th ed. (Cambridge, Mass.: Mediaeval Academy of America, 1953), 382. The chapter is entitled "The Early Stage of Italian Notation."

[9] Some of this I have mentioned in "'Arte' e 'non arte' nel frammento Greggiati" (see n. 5). More will be shown presently.

[10] See Marchettus de Padua, *Pomerium*, ed. Giuseppe Vecchi (Florence: American Institute of Musicology, 1961), 164, on the habit of some composers of using the letters *.i.* and *.p.* (or else *.b.* and *.t.*, or even "alia signa secundum beneplacitum eorum") to indicate *tempus imperfectum* or *perfectum*. Later on (179–80), he also speaks of using *.g.* and *.y.* for his *modus cantandi gallicus* and *italicus* (see below, n. 13).

[11] This is the subject of lengthy discussions in *Pomerium*, 107–55.

[12] One of two places in the manuscript where a letter *.t.* suggests a *ternaria* division. Here the use of *puncti* is equivocal, however, for at a certain point one of them is placed after a *longa* made imperfect *a parte ante* by a *brevis*, making it work as a *punctus divisionis* between two units of a perfect *modus*. The letter *.t.* cannot be taken here to indicate the *modus* because the

the source is the use of the letters *.sg.* and *.sy.*, meaning *senaria gallica* and *senaria italica*, for the measures usually called *senaria imperfecta* and *senaria perfecta;* but although the two adjectives recall a passage in the *Pomerium*, Marchettus's distinction between a French and an Italian way of singing, for which he suggests the use of the letters *.g.* and *.y.*, has a completely different meaning.[13] Irrelevant is the occasional presence of an *.m.*, which I interpret as meaning *maior*, added to the letters of *duodenaria* and *octonaria* in some *superius* part in which semiminims are present; the corresponding tenors have only the usual letters. Finally, a *ternaria* division is marked by a *.t.* in two pieces whose fast motion however implies, respectively, a binary and a ternary *modus*.[14]

Up to this point I do not see what deserves to be deemed archaic in this notation, if we consider it in the general frame of faithfulness to the Italian system that is evident in the northern Reina and Lucca codices or in the works of such late composers as Bartolino and Johannes Ciconia in his Paduan period.[15] The same applies to the use of some *plicae* and of ligatures between notes of the same pitch. Both are mentioned by Marchettus;[16] but *plicae* are still present in at least one of Jacopo's madrigals, "Si come al canto della bella Iguana," in the Florentine manuscript London 29987; and ligatures between notes of the same pitch (together with letters and *puncti divisionis*) are present in the Lucca manuscript in works by Bartolino, Ciconia, and Anthonellus Marot as well as in the Squarcialupi Codex in works by the Florentines Giovanni, Lorenzo, and Landini and by the Northerners Jacopo and Bartolino.[17]

other passage in which it also occurs, the *ritornello* of "Du' ochi ladri," seems to imply a binary *modus*.

[13] According to Marchettus, *Pomerium*, 172–80, both letters refer to what we call *senaria imperfecta:* singing *more gallico* the unmarked *semibreves* must be read as placing larger values ahead of smaller ones, singing *more italico* just the opposite.

[14] See above, n. 12.

[15] In both sources this applies to works by Northerners, or anyway composed in northern Italy, much less or not at all to pieces of possible Florentine or Tuscan provenance. Quite different in fact is the tendency of Florentine scribes to use letters sparingly and to eliminate the *duodenaria* and *octonaria* measures (replaced by the so-called *Longanotation* in *quaternaria*) as well as the *punctus divisionis*. The latter is made unnecessary by the reduction of the *semibreves* to only two forms, one of them simply called *minima*.

[16] See for the former the chapter *De plicis* in *Pomerium*, 191–95. Marchettus violently objects to the latter in the chapters entitled *De errore circa ligaturas et primo in universali* and *Reprobatio cuiusdam erroris in speciali*, ibid., 195–200. Nevertheless an obscure final sentence on p. 200 sounds to me like a reluctant admission.

[17] In the case of Ciconia and Anthonellus a sharp distinction is to be made, both from the notational and from the compositional point of view, between the works they conceived in the spirit of the *ars subtilior* (at the court of Giangaleazzo Visconti, according to John Louis Nádas and Agostino Ziino, *The Lucca Codex* [Lucca: Libreria Musicale Italiana, 1990], 39–42) and such other pieces as Ciconia's "Poi che partir mi convien," "La fiamma del to' amore," and "Li

Coming to the second point, irregular contrapuntal procedures, I should like to stress that not all the pieces in the manuscript present striking irregularities. One *caccia* by Piero, two madrigals by Giovanni, plus another one which might also be by him are also found in such late and discriminating sources as Panciatichi 26 or Squarcialupi; and as composers' names are never given in the two fragments, the possibility exists that other pieces also belong to known masters.[18] For the rest, to get an idea of what I call unusual procedures—not mistakes, for we have no idea of the existence of established rules—let us see some examples, beginning with the madrigal "Su la rivera dove 'l sol agiaza" (example 1).[19] From its very beginning it is striking to find the usual opening with sustained notes replaced by the energetic participation of the tenor in the fast motion of the upper part, later repeated in a number of other passages. Also announced in the first line of music is the propensity for parallel fifths, while the last measure of the penultimate line gives a striking example of parallel octaves. Then we have, at m. 4, the strange friction of a d in the *superius* against an e in the tenor, which cannot be a scribal error for it is repeated two more times at mm. 11 and 13. All the same I find the piece attractive in its coherent compactness, the briskness of its pace, and the directness of its melodic contours.

The lack of long sustained notes at the beginning is even more evident in example 2, the beginning of the madrigal "Bella granata fra le fioro sete"; I use this excerpt to call attention to the initial gesture of an upbeat unison, followed at mm. 6 and 7 by another upbeat motion in octaves, not to speak of the presence here and there of other parallel perfect intervals and unexpected frictions. Upbeat gestures are also found in example 3, the madrigal "E con cavalché," to which I shall return later for other considerations.[20]

cani sono fuora," or Anthonellus's "Con dogliosi martiri" and "Or tolta pur mi sei," all included in the Lucca codex. In the latter a conscious adherence to the Italian tradition of forms and notation is evident and, in the case of Ciconia, quite consistent with the spirit of the Paduan milieu in which he spent his final years, while we know nothing of Anthonellus's whereabouts; should we hypothesize a Paduan sojourn for him as well? For the Squarcialupi Codex see John Louis Nádas, "The Transmission of Trecento Secular Polyphony" (Ph.D. diss., New York University, 1985), 454–58.

[18] See, for instance, the madrigals "De soto il verde," "Seguendo un me sparvero," and "Involta d'un bel velo," as well as the *caccia* (which I have already suggested to be possibly by Piero) "Or qua, compagni."

[19] The text of this madrigal speaks of salines located near an unnamed "riviera," possibly the river Po, thus adding strength to the interpretation of "Dal bel castel" given above, n. 7.

[20] See the beginning of the segments A and B (the latter's coming back as B[1] provides another example of the kind of non-structural repetition to be discussed below). The piece is particularly rich in parallel octaves.

Example 1: "Su la rivera dove 'l sol agiaza" (madrigal). From *The Music of Fourteenth-Century Italy*, vol. 2, ed. Nino Pirrotta, Corpus Mensurabilis Musicae 8:2 ([Rome]: American Institute of Musicology, 1960), 29.

Example 2: "Bella granata fra le fioro sete" (madrigal). From *The Music of Fourteenth-Century Italy,* vol. 2, ed. Nino Pirrotta, Corpus Mensurabilis Musicae 8:2 ([Rome]: American Institute of Musicology, 1960), 19. © by American Institute of Musicology/Hänssler-Verlag. Reproduced by permission.

Strange procedures can be seen in many of the pieces in the two fragments, with a tendency to increase the more we advance in their pages, more particularly then in the Ostiglia fragment. The question is whether such features need to be seen as indicating an early date of composition; and once more my negative answer finds support in the nearest North Italian source, the first section of the Reina codex. In an article of 1983 entitled "Rhapsodic Elements in North Italian Polyphony of the 14th Century," I drew attention to a number of pieces in that source also showing irregular features similar in nature to those observed in my Sommacampagna manuscript;[21] we cannot speak of "archaic" features in these pieces, for most are polyphonic *ballate* and I do not know of any *ballata* text that might have received a polyphonic intonation before, more or less, 1370. My explanation for such appearances, which we can also apply to the pieces in the Reina codex which I have indicated as would-be *siciliane,*[22] is that side by side with the "regular" masters, better known through the critical selections of the Florentine manuscripts, lesser composers of various provenance and aptitude and of less systematic habits existed, whose works are fairly

[21] *Musica disciplina* 37 (1983): 83–99.

[22] See Nino Pirrotta, "Musica polifonica per un testo attribuito a Federico II," in *L'Ars Nova italiana del Trecento* 2, ed. F. Alberto Gallo (Firenze: Bandettini, 1968), 97–112; idem, "New Glimpses of an Unwritten Tradition," in *Words and Music: The Scholar's View* [. . .] *in Honor of A. Tillman Merritt,* ed. Laurence Berman (Cambridge, Mass.: Department of Music, Harvard University, 1972), 271–91.

represented in the northern sources, less selective than those coming from Florence.

The third point under discussion concerns the texts of the works included in our fragments, whose metrical schemes often diverge from the types prevailing in other sources. "Gaiete, dolce parolete mie" is the only known example at this time of a polyphonic *rondello*, the equivalent of the French *rondeau*, never found elsewhere and yet known to both da Tempo and Sommacampagna and to the author of the so-called *Capitulum de vocibus applicatis verbis*, a short garbled tract on the relationship between words and music thought to have been written during the first quarter of the century.[23] The question is whether the presence of a *rondello* is to be related to chronology or geography. The latter seems to me more likely since the three tracts speaking of *rondelli* all come from the Venetian region and one of them is later than our source. The same applies to the unusual madrigal forms present in my Sommacampagna codex: madrigals without a *ritornello* and others in which a *ritornello* is inserted after each one of the strophes; madrigals showing a prevalence of seven-syllable lines and others in which the first line of each strophe is repeated to conclude it; not to speak of the extreme case of "E con cavalché," whose metrical scheme is unrecognizable but for the certain lack of a *ritornello*. Such schemes are not always consistent with the descriptions and examples provided by da Tempo and Sommacampagna, but certainly agree with the indication both theorists give that a variety of schemes was acceptable, an indication that pertains up to the end of the century, when Sommacampagna wrote his *Tractato*. Once more I see here a geographical discrimination; this variety is typical of the northern regions (and is evident to some extent also in the works by Jacopo and Giovanni), while our image of the established forms derives from the models offered by such Florentine poets as Soldanieri and Sacchetti and by the pieces in the Florentine sources.

After so much insistence on the geographical connotations of our fragments it should have become evident that there is more in my relating them to Sommacampagna than pure expediency for the purpose of a title. Actually, I find it impossible to dismiss his treatise as an uncritical imitation of the older one by da Tempo, an imitation unrelated to what was still practiced after fifty years. The Veronese court at whose service Sommacampagna spent

[23] Anonymous and without a title in the MS. Venice, Biblioteca Nazionale San Marco, Lat. cl. 12, 97, where it is added as a sequence to a copy of da Tempo's *Summa artis rithimici vulgaris dictaminis* (hence the copyist's use of the term *mandrialis*). It was given a title by Santorre Debenedetti, "Un trattatello del secolo XIV sopra la poesia musicale," *Studi medievali* 2 (1906–07): 59–82.

all his life is the very one about which we have most numerous and persistent indications of polyphonic performances. Already Cangrande, who ruled from 1311 to 1329, is known to have had some *intonatori* among the different kinds of musicians attracted to this splendid court.[24] Alberto, to whom da Tempo dedicated his *Summa*, was described by historians as a music lover.[25] His brother and co-ruler Mastino was the "tyrant" who, according to Filippo Villani, amused himself pitting Jacopo and Giovanni against each other in a competition in which, unknown to Villani, Piero also took part.[26] Cansignorio, who ruled from 1359 to 1375, was the dedicatee of a three-voice madrigal of good quality, "La dolce Scala del signor lombardo"; and Antonio, his successor, that of Sommacampagna's treatise in which polyphonic performance is described as an ordinary practice. How then could it be possible that Sommacampagna dealt with madrigal forms just by hearsay?

He does not say, however, who the performers or composers were who contributed to the practice he knew; and this is a pity, for I think he would have given a sensibly different picture from the one prevailing in Florence. There we know the principal practitioners of secular polyphony to have been clergymen attached to some religious institution who either taught or influenced each other, and their art to have been the sport of an upper middle class of intellectuals—I think of Sacchetti and of the narratives in the *Paradiso degli Alberti.*[27] Landini himself, however, had experienced the different conditions prevailing elsewhere when, in his youth, he had described himself as "peregre canens" ("singing while traveling abroad") in a motet for a Venetian doge, or when also in Venice his playing on the organ had won him a laurel from the king of Cyprus. There in northern Italy, we hear of madrigal singing at the lordly courts of Milan, Verona, or Padua, but we know very little about who the performers and composers were and how they acquired whatever skills they possessed. Some, once more like Jacopo,

[24] See the poem "Bisbidis di Manoello Giudeo a magnificenza di messer Cane della Scala" in Vincenzo De Bartholomaeis, *Rime giullaresche e popolari d'Italia* (Bologna: Zanichelli, 1926), 68–70, quoted in my article "Back to Ars Nova Themes," in *Music and Context: Essays for John M. Ward*, ed. Anne Dhu Shapiro (Cambridge, Mass.: Department of Music, Harvard University, 1985), 173, n. 33.

[25] See Torello Sarayna, *Le historie e fatti de Veronesi nelli tempi d'il popolo et signori Scaligeri* (Verona: Antonio Portese, 1542), fol. 40^{v}, repeated and amplified by Girolamo Della Corte, *Istorie della città di Verona* (Venezia, 1744), 2:168.

[26] The story is well known. For a comparison between two old renditions of Villani's text reporting it see Ettore Li Gotti, "Il più antico polifonista italiano del secolo XIV," *Italica* 24 (1947): 196–200.

[27] See Giovanni da Prato [Giovanni Gherardi], *Il Paradiso degli Alberti: ritrovi e ragionamenti del 1389*, ed. Alessandro Wesselofsky (Bologna: Gaetano Romagnoli, 1867).

Giovanni, and Piero, all three apparently laymen, must have received some solid training; many others, whose names were not remembered, must have learned by themselves by trial and error, perhaps much error; and yet they did not hesitate to compete to gain favor, if for a single day, with some courtly or academic audience.[28] Jacopo himself, whose competitive attitude transpires from a few of his madrigal texts,[29] significantly lamented the competition in the twice-set text of his madrigal "Oselleto salvagio": a beautiful song, he says, needs mastery, but:

> Pochi l'ànno e tutti se fa maistri
> fa ballate, matrical e muteti;
> tuti en Fioran, Filipoti e Marcheti.
>
> Sì è piena la terra de magistroli
> che loco più non trovano i discipuli.

("Few have it and all pretend to be masters; they set *ballate*, madrigals and motets; they all think to be like Floriani, Filippotti and Marchetti. So teeming is the place with little masters that no more space is left to willing pupils.") This is a poetic exaggeration; yet it is to such peripatetic little masters, wandering like jesters from one place to another, that we must refer in order to assess the repertory of the Sommacampagna codex. After all, even in Florence there existed a different level of artists from the serious masters, a level represented by such odd persons as Rosso da Collegrana, the painter Bonaiuto Corsini, or the shoemaker Jacopo, whose works were mostly rejected by the discriminating tastes of the best Florentine scribes.

I see most northern composers not as permanent employees in a court, but as occasional visitors attracted by the mirage of a good gift; and in this sense I have spoken of "rhapsodic elements in North Italian polyphony."[30] An indication that some of these people had limited powers of invention can be seen in the fact that a few of them tended to use their music more than once. Repetition has an artistic meaning in such pieces as "Dal bel castel se parte de Peschiera" or "Quando i oselli canta," where it is used to underline the return of the first line of text; it lacks justification in the case of the quasi-madrigal "E con cavalché" (example 3), illustrated in a short

[28] F. Alberto Gallo, in the above-mentioned article "Antonio da Ferrara," mentions the singing of madrigals as an object of Antonio's regret while obliged to leave Bologna. The same university city was remembered for its music by Nicolò de' Rossi, by Petrarch, and by Giovanni da Ravenna; the latter cites the singing of "canciones balatas sonicia madrigalia ac vulgaria reliqua note deliramenta."

[29] See, for instance, the texts of "I' mi son un che per le frasche andando," "Tanto che sit' aquistati nel giusto," and "Vestissi la cornacchia d'altru' penne."

[30] See above, n. 21.

Example 3: "E con cavalché" (quasi-madrigal).

article by W. Thomas Marrocco.[31] I have also shown similar instances in my article "'Arte' e 'non arte' nel frammento Greggiati,"[32] and prefer now to give an example coming from the Rossi section of the source. This is the madrigal "Pianze la bella Iguana" (example 4), in which a section starting in the middle of line 1 of the text and embracing the whole of line 2 and the first measure of line 3 is then repeated starting in the middle of line 3 and covering the whole of line 4 plus the first measure of the *ritornello*. The latter, whose music comes back with a different text after each one of the strophes, also includes a short element twice heard before. Repetition here has no structural or musical meaning.

Having discarded notation, metrical forms, and contrapuntal techniques as acceptable criteria for assigning an early date to the repertory, we are left with very little in our hands in our attempt to give dates to the pieces in the Sommacampagna manuscript. We are lucky with two of them, the anonymous "Du' ochi ladri" and Giovanni's "La bella stella," for these are mentioned in poems of the northern poet Antonio da Ferrara, through which quotation Alberto Gallo has been able to determine that they were sung, respectively, ca. 1344 and ca. 1354.[33] A little older might be the already mentioned "Dal bel castel," which I relate to events of ca. 1337. For the rest I find very unconvincing some late dates suggested by Giuseppe Corsi, also on the basis of the texts.[34] Since my date of 1337 is only seven years earlier than the date c. 1344 given by Gallo also to Jacopo's madrigal "In su' bei fiori,"[35] I would say that we are still far away from the beginning and early development of the madrigal.

All we know of the new genre is that the early texts in which it is mentioned all come from the Venetian region. So do the anonymous *Capitulum* and da Tempo's *Summa;* so does the quotation by Francesco da Barberino, a Tuscan who was writing ca. 1313, an exile in Venice.[36] Even Barberino, however, does not list the madrigal among the kinds of poetry "which are just coming out" ("qui de novo emergunt"); he mentions it as a "rudium

[31] W. Thomas Marrocco, "The Newly-Discovered Ostiglia Pages of the Vatican Rossi Codex 215: The Earliest Italian Ostinato," *Acta musicologica* 39 (1967): 84–91.

[32] See above, n. 5.

[33] Gallo, "Antonio da Ferrara."

[34] Corsi, 27, interprets "Gaiete dolze parolete mie" (a *rondello*) as referring to a Ghidola Malaspina; on p. 331 he also relates the madrigal "Dal bel castel" to the wedding of Verde della Scala with Niccolò II d'Este in 1362.

[35] Once more, see Gallo, "Antonio da Ferrara," 41; the madrigal is mentioned by Antonio as being sung in Bologna, presumably at that date.

[36] In the "glosse" (comments) to his *I Documenti d'Amore*, ed. Francesco Egidi (Rome: La Società, 1905–27), 2:263. A notary in Florence, Barberino was exiled from 1304 to 1314 for political reasons and spent most of this time in Venice and in Padua.

Example 4: "Pianze la bella Iguana" (madrigal). From *The Music of Fourteenth-Century Italy,* vol. 2, ed. Nino Pirrotta, Corpus Mensurabilis Musicae 8:2 ([Rome]: American Institute of Musicology, 1960), 30.

inordinatum concinium" ("an unorderly singing together of vulgar matters") and as an example of a "voluntarium," an arbitrary poem. The two essential characteristics of the northern madrigal thus announced with terse clarity—its formal freedom and its preference for rural or pastoral themes—bring me back to an old hypothesis of mine of an analogy existing between the origins of the madrigal and of the French motet.[37]

To clarify further my thinking, let us examine a French text from the motet "Quant revient—L'autre jour—Flos filius eius":

> Quant revient et fuelle et flor
> contre la saison d'esté
> dès adonc me souvient d'amors
> qi torjours m'a cortoise et douce esté.
> Mout aim son secours
> q'a ma volenté
> m'aliège de ma dolour.
> Mout en vient bien et honor
> d'estre à son gré.

We have here nine lines of 7, 7, 8, 10, 5, 5, 7, 7, and 5 syllables, the last ones providing a generalization which might resemble the *ritornello* of many a madrigal. We can call it, in Barberino's words, a "rudium inordinatum concinium" because there is no order in its assemblage of lines and rhymes. And its words, like those of so many motets, speak "of country girls, of flowers, of bushes, of garlands and fertility" as prescribed by the above-mentioned *Capitulum de vocibus applicatis verbis.*[38] The obvious explanation for the lack of any rule in the poem comes from the fact that the music is that of a preexisting *clausula* and the length of each line was determined by the length of the musical phrase to which the words were added.[39]

I omit quoting the text of the *motetus* for which similar considerations could be made. But I ask myself whether it could have been possible for a similar process to have given origin to the first madrigals. We have hints that some Notre-Dame music was known in Italy, including motets.

[37] Nino Pirrotta, "Una arcaica descrizione trecentesca del madrigale," in *Festschrift Heinrich Besseler*, ed. Institut für Musikwissenschaft der Karl-Marx-Universität (Leipzig: VEB Deutscher Verlag für Musik, 1961), 158–59.

[38] "Una arcaica descrizione," 158: "Cuius verba volunt esse de villanellis, de floribus, arbustis, sertis, ubere et similibus, dummodo sit bona sentencia, loquela et sermo."

[39] Friedrich Gennrich, *Bibliographie der ältesten französischen und lateinischen Motetten* (Darmstadt: n.p., 1957), 65, indicates that it is set to the same music as the motet "Stirps Iesse progreditur—Virga prodit celitus—Flos filius eius," which in turn derives from a three-voice *clausula* in the MS. Florence, Biblioteca Laurenziana, Pluteus 29.1, fol. 11.

Whether a knowledge of their origin as a genre also existed is difficult to say. This might have suggested adding words to preexisting music—with a basic difference, however, for the motet texts were usually added to *clausula* music at the rate of one syllable per note, while the tendency is evident for the upper parts of the early madrigal to have been melismatic. As the oldest examples of Italian organ music also show a tendency to melodic effusion in the upper parts of a two-voice polyphony, my suggestion was and is that some kind of organ music, somewhat similar to the *clausula* but more melismatic in the upper part, might have been the matrix of the madrigal. The term matrix is also included in my hypothesis for it has the advantage of providing a plausible etymology of madrigal.[40] Indeed, dismissing da Tempo's arbitrary derivation from *mandria*, a derivation probably suggested by the prevailing rural connotations of the poetry, all the ascertained forms of the term are compatible with a derivation from *matrix* or *mater*, or from the latter's Italian or dialectal equivalents *madre*, *matre*, or *mare*. To the former correspond the Tuscan forms *madriale* and *matriale*, to the latter the Venetian *maregale* and *marigale* used by both da Tempo and Sommacampagna in spite of their having suggested the derivation from *mandria*.

An organ *clausula* functioning as the matrix of the new madrigal fits well with the earliest description of the musical aspects of the genre, the one given by the *Capitulum*, according to which, I translate, "madrigals are words applied to many voices, one of which must consist of all *longae*, and this is called tenor, while the other or the others must consist of all minims, and one of them in particular must go up to the twelfth or fifteenth note and proceed melodiously."[41] According to this passage such madrigals would be nearer to the original pattern that have a fast moving *superius* and a tenor in slow equal notes. No one madrigal in our fragments strictly adheres to the formula, while many have tenors in fast motion. This is one more reason for me to dismiss the notion that my Sommacampagna manuscript has an archaic content. And the name I have adopted for the two fragments seems to agree with their mirroring a situation whose variety of aspects was still consistent with Sommacampagna's musical experiences.

[40] That is, the Latin *matricalis* from *matrix;* hence the various Italian and dialectal forms listed below. The etymology from *matrix* had already been advanced but with a different interpretation—as meaning a poem in *lingua materna*, that is, in the vulgar tongue.

[41] The Latin original, given in my article "Una arcaica descrizione," 157, reads: "Mandrigalia sunt verba applicata pluribus cantibus, quorum unus debet esse de puris longis, et hic appellatur tenor, alter vel alii volunt esse de puris minimis, et unus specialiter vult ascendere ad duodecimam vel quintadecimam vocem et ire melodiando."

ALEJANDRO ENRIQUE PLANCHART

Notes On The Tropes in Manuscripts of the Rite of Aquileia

In an earlier study dealing with tropes in Italian sources, I sought to trace the nature and general characteristics of the trope repertories of the peninsula.[1] There I left out of consideration a group of sources stemming from the region of the Veneto and from southern Austria which, in terms of the notation of the earlier manuscripts as well as in terms of their trope repertory, appeared to be related to a south German tradition closely allied to that of St. Gall.[2] In their general liturgical characteristics virtually all these manuscripts follow the rite of the Patriarchate of Aquileia, and they range in date from the early twelfth to the late fourteenth century. I list them below in alphabetical order:

Ber 40608	Berlin, Stiftung Preußischer Kulturbesitz, MS. Mus. 40608. Gradual with tropes and Sequences. Venice, San Marco, 14th c.
Civ 56	Cividale del Friuli, Museo Archeologico, MS. LVI. Gradual with tropes and sequences. Cividale del Friuli, Santa Maria Assunta, 14th c.

[1] Alejandro Enrique Planchart, "Italian Tropes," *Mosaic* 18/4 (1985): 11–31.
[2] Ibid., 15.

Civ 58	Cividale del Friuli, Museo Archeologico, MS. LVIII. Gradual with tropes and sequences. Cividale del Friuli, Santa Maria Assunta, 14th c.
Civ 79	Cividale del Friuli, Museo Archeologico, MS. LXIX. Gradual with tropes and sequences. Cividale del Friuli, Santa Maria Assunta, 14th c.
Gor I	Gorizia, Seminario teologico Centrale, MS. I. Gradual with tropes and sequences. Aquileia, 14th c.
Ox 340	Oxford, Bodleian Library, MS. Canonici lit. 340. Gradual (winter part) with tropes and sequences. Moggio, San Gallo, early 12th c.
Ox 341	Oxford, Bodleian Library, MS. Canonici lit. 341. Gradual, Kyriale, Troper, Sequentiary. Innichen, San Candido, middle 12th c.
Ud 2	Udine, Biblioteca Archivescovile, MS. 2. Gradual, Troper, Proser. Aquileia, early 12th c.
Ud 79	Udine, Biblioteca Archivescovile, MS. 78. Gradual, Troper, Proser. Aquileia, early 12th c.
Ud 234	Udine, Biblioteca Archivescovile, MS. 234. Gradual (summer part) with tropes and sequences. Moggio, San Gallo, early 12th c.

Some of these sources, particularly the Graduals from Santa Maria Assunta, are well-known sources of "primitive polyphony," and some *ars antiqua* motets.[3] In addition two of them contain in their flyleaves fragments of an early fifteenth-century polyphonic manuscript that reflect the repertory of the papal chapel under Gregory XII. But thus far no study of them as sources for the trope and sequence repertories of northern Italy has appeared and they have been little noted. My purpose here is to present the repertory of proper tropes in these manuscripts and note briefly some of its main characteristics.

Given the relatively late date of most of these manuscripts, the number of proper tropes that they transmit comes as something of a surprise. The

[3] See Pierluigi Petrobelli and Cesare Corsi, eds., *Le polifonie primitive in Friuli e in Europa: Atti del congresso internazionale Cividale del Friuli, 22–24 agosto 1980,* Miscellanea Musicologica 4 (Rome: Torre d'Orfeo, 1989).

total repertory consists of fifty-seven "tropings" distributed as follows: fifty-three tropes to the introit, one *Visitatio sepulchri,* one trope to the gradual, and two tropes to the communion. These are listed in the appendix in the order of the liturgical year. The appendix gives the incipit and cue for each trope verse, the sources for the piece in the manuscripts listed above, a summary concordance, and the pages where the verses appear in those volumes of the *Corpus Troporum* that have been published to date.[4] Six of the introit tropes include among their internal verses lines that usually serve as introductory verses elsewhere and have a concordance that is quite independent of that of lines with which they appear in the Aquileian manuscripts. The verses in question are:

Forma speciocissimus	Epiphany
Terrigenis summis	Ascension
Ex numero frequentium	Ascension
Spiritus sanctus descendit	Pentecost
Quem prophetae caecinerunt	Saint John Baptist
Hodie exsultent iusti natus	Saint John Baptist

The first three of these do indeed appear in one or another of the Aquileian manuscripts also as introductions, but the last three do not. Nevertheless, for the purposes of the concordance they must be counted independently thus bringing the total repertory to sixty pieces.

The presence of communion tropes is unusual since these fell into disuse relatively early and from the start met with little favor in Italy. Both communion tropes are of German origin, but one of them, *Magnus et felix,* appears also in two of the Nonantola tropers. The second one, however, *Adducite vitulum,* has a very narrow concordance, even in Germany, and thus the Aquileian sources are the only non-German manuscripts that transmit it. Unfortunately the one Aquileian source that gives all four verses, Ox 340, is, like the German manuscripts, copied in staffless neumes, but the Cividale Graduals provide us with a transcribable version of the first verse of the melody.

In contrast to the case of the communion tropes, the absence of tropes to the offertory is not surprising since Italy was from the beginning not receptive to them.[5] The trope to the gradual is one of those small anomalies

[4] *CT* 1 = Ritva Jonsson, ed., *Corpus Troporum* 1: *Tropes du propre de la messe* 1: Cycle de Noël, Studia Latina Stockholmiensia 21 (Stockholm: Almqvist & Wiskell, 1975); *CT* 3 = Gunilla Björvall, Gunilla Iversen, and Ritva Jacobsson, eds., *Corpus Troporum* 3: *Tropes du propre de la messe* 2: Cycle de Pâques, Studia Latina Stockholmiensia 25 (Stockholm: Almqvist & Wiskell, 1982).

[5] See Planchart, "Italian Tropes," 17–21.

that can be found mostly in the Aquitanian manuscripts but are extremely rare elsewhere.[6] Its presence in the Aquileian manuscripts suggests that at one time the trope repertory of the region must have been quite rich, since such exceptional pieces are found elsewhere in regions that had an extensive trope repertory. The trope to the gradual is also unusual in that its lone concordance is a German manuscript. Once again, the Aquileian sources provide us with the only transcribable version of the melody.

The concordance pattern of the Aquileian repertory orients it strongly towards Germany. Of sixty pieces, forty-five turn up in German manuscripts. Twenty of these appear outside the region of Aquileia only in Germany and eleven more are found elsewhere only in German and Italian sources.[7] In contrast, thirty-five of the pieces are found in Italian sources, and only four of these are uniquely Italian concordances.[8] Concordances with sources from other regions are as follows: fourteen each in Aquitanian and English manuscripts, sixteen in north French manuscripts, and two each in Spanish and Norman-Sicilian manuscripts. None of the concordances among those in Aquitanian, English, north French, Spanish, or Norman-Sicilian manuscripts is exclusive. Finally, there are three *unica* in the Aquileian repertory, all of them in the gradual from San Marco.[9]

In virtually every case where we have sources from outside Aquileia, the Aquileian versions of the melodies follow closely one or another of the melodic traditions for each trope. This stands in a relatively sharp contrast to the behavior of many of the other Italian repertories, where received texts were often provided with entirely new melodies. In any event, there seems to be no pattern of preference in the Aquileian pieces with multiple melodic traditions outside Aquileia except for the fact that a good number of the

[6] The most common of these exceptional tropes are the Aquitanian tropes to the prose or the *sequentia* studied by Paul Evans in "The Tropi ad sequentiam," in *Studies in Music History: Essays for Oliver Strunk,* ed. Harold Powers (Princeton: Princeton University Press, 1968), 73–82, but tropes to the gradual and to the fraction antiphon also survive in Aquitanian manuscripts, see Alejandro Enrique Planchart, *The Repertory of Tropes at Winchester* (Princeton: Princeton University Press, 1977), 1:71–72. It should be noted that the relatively numerous tropes to the gradual reported in Clemens Blume, *Tropi Graduales: Tropen des Missale im Mittelalter* 2: *Tropen zum proprium Missae,* Analecta Hymnica Medii Aevi 49 (Leipzig: Reisland, 1906; repr. New York: Johnson Reprint, 1961), 211–65, are for the most part *prosulae* to the melismata of the graduals, together with a few offertory tropes that were misinterpreted by Blume, and some polyphonic *conductus* of the twelfth century.

[7] The Italian concordances in this group are distributed as follows: one in Benevento, two in Benevento and northern Italy, seven in northern Italy, and one in the Roman Gradual of Santa Cecilia in Trastevere as a verse *ad repetendum.*

[8] Two in Benevento and northern Italy, and two in northern Italy alone.

[9] These are *Beatus Petrus apostolus, Hodie exsultent caelicolae,* and *Haec est dies caelestis.*

German pieces in the Aquileian repertory show here the same kind of textual and melodic stability that characterizes the German repertory once the St. Gall tradition settles down.[10] Further, the French and English concordances clearly appear to have been filtered through German or north Italian intermediaries. Nonetheless, despite the German orientation of the repertory in terms of its concordances, the actual structure of the individual tropings reflects strong Italian traits in the ways the verses are combined and in the melodic and poetic structure of those pieces that do not appear to have been imported from elsewhere. A few examples may serve to illustrate this point.

In most Italian sources, but particularly in those from southern Italy, we encounter two relatively common approaches to the construction of a trope. The first, exemplified by such pieces as the Beneventan version of *Adest alma virgo parens*, for the feast of the Purification, combines an international introduction with internal lines apparently of local origin:[11]

Tropos

[1]	Adest alma virgo parens adest verbum incarnatum proclamemus omnes laudes in excelso patri	*Suscepimus*
[2]	Lumen aeternum Christum dominum	*In medio*
[3]	Gaude virgo beatissima quae de verbo nobis hominem offers infra templi moenia.	*Secundum*
[4]	Offers die ista in templo senis Symeonis brachio.	*Ita*
[5]	Hinc erigendo capita pro signo tibi laudes et odas voce publica rex sabaoth.	*In fines*

In this trope the first two verses belong to the international tradition associated with this introduction (albeit with uniquely Beneventan variants in lines two and four), but verses three and four appear only in Ben 34 and Ben 35. Verse five presents another trait confined largely to trope collections of the Italian peninsula, that of pulling of a verse entirely out of its liturgical and literary context. Indeed, the verse has no verb and nothing in the

[10] The early St. Gall repertory found in SG 381 and SG 484 shows a great number of small variants, anomalous pieces, and so on. But the German repertory becomes extremely stable already with sources such as SG 376 and the St. Emmeram cantatories, that is, by the early eleventh century. This is not the case in Aquitaine.

[11] Ben 34, fol.47r, facsimile in *Le codex VI. 34 de la Bibliothèque Capitulaire de Bénévent*, Paléographie musicale 15 (Tournai: Desclée, 1937; repr. Bern: Lang, 1972).

surrounding introit text provides the verb: *Ita et laus tua* [trope] *in fines terrae; iustitia plena est dextera tua.* But the original locus of the trope line, the Gloria *Prudentia prudentium,* which was known in England, northern France, Aquitaine, and northern Italy,[12] does provide the verb to the trope's sentence with its acclamation *glorificamus te.*

If the Aquileian sources give us no example comparable to that of verses three and four of the Beneventan trope, they do provide us with cases of the kind of liturgical transposition found in verse five. The first of these is *In Bethlehem Iudae salvator* (appendix, no. 1), for the midnight mass at Christmas. In the Gregorian sources it appears in Vro 107, fol. 84ʳ, and To 18, fol. 29ʳ, not as a trope but rather as the *antiphona ante evangelium* for Epiphany. It survives also with the same liturgical function in the books of the Ambrosian rite.[13] James Borders published a perceptive study of the different versions of this work before that of Ber 40608 was known.[14] The Venetian trope adds yet further complications to the liturgical, textual, and melodic transmission of the piece. The four sources transmit four closely related texts and three melodies, as shown in examples 1a–d. Note that, as written in the manuscript, the music of the trope (example 1b) lies a fifth above that of the *antiphona ante evangelium;* thus in order to facilitate a comparison I have transposed the music of examples 1c and 1d up so that they will have the same final as the trope.

As Borders indicates, the text of the different versions is paraphrased from a number of passages in the Gospels: Matthew 2:1, 2:3, Mark 1:4–5, and John 1:27.[15] In other words, the text of the antiphon brings together biblical passages and newly composed text to form what Kenneth Levy has aptly called a chant "libretto,"[16] a characteristic that he associates with plainsong repertories that fall outside of the classical Gregorian tradition.

The earliest surviving source for the piece is Vro 107 (ca. 1000), which has no music, but already the text there has problems. The opening sentence in all other sources is a simple statement: "The savior is born in

[12] See the concordance in Alejandro Enrique Planchart, *The Repertory of Tropes at Winchester,* 2:297–300.

[13] See Lo 34209, p. 110. Facsimile in *Antiphonarium Ambrosianum du Musée Britannique,* Paléographie musicale 5 (Solesmes: Abbaye de Saint-Pierre, 1896; repr. Bern: Lang, 1972). See also *Antiphonale Missarum iuxta Ritum Sanctae Ecclesiae Mediolanensis,* ed. Grègori Maria Sunyol (Rome: Desclée, 1935), 68.

[14] James Borders, "The Northern Italian Antiphons ante evangelium and the Gallican Connection," *Journal of Musicological Research* 8 (1988): 16–19. While Borders's transcriptions of To 18 and Lo 34209 are accurate, the texts presented in his table 3 have a number of errors.

[15] Borders, "Northern Italian Antiphons," 18–19.

[16] Kenneth Levy, "Toledo, Rome, and the Legacy of Gaul," *Early Music History* 4 (1986): 66. Levy's argument is presented in detail on 61–66.

Example 1a

Ber 40608, fols. 9v-10r
In nocte Tropha

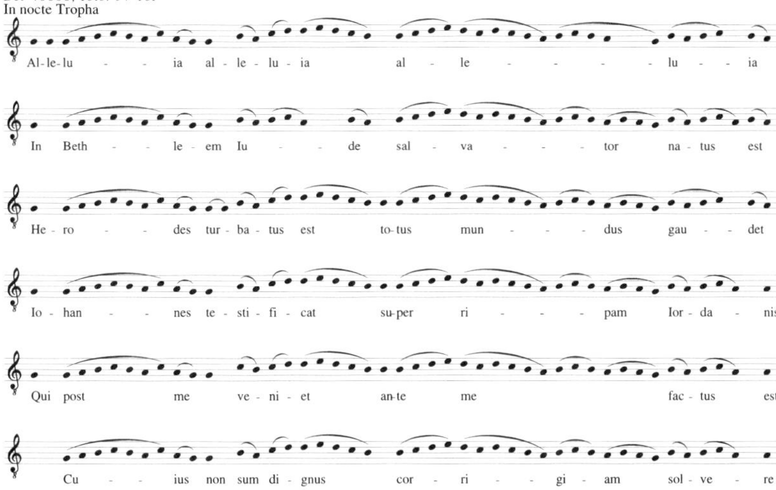

Example 1b

Vro 107, fol. 84v
EVG

In Bethleem Iude salvator natus est totus mundus gaudet
Herodes turbatus est de Hiesu qui natus est
Iohannes testificat super flumen Iordanis
qui post me veniet ante me factus est
cuius non sum dignus corrigiam calciamenti solvere
Alleluia alleluia

Example 1c

To 18, fol. 29r
(transposed up a fifth)
A Ante evanglm

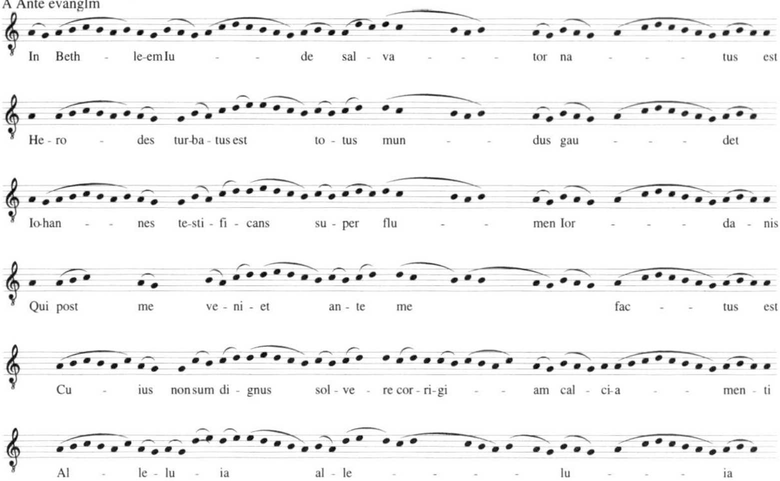

Example 1d

Lo 34209, p. 110
(transposed up a fifth)
A An evg

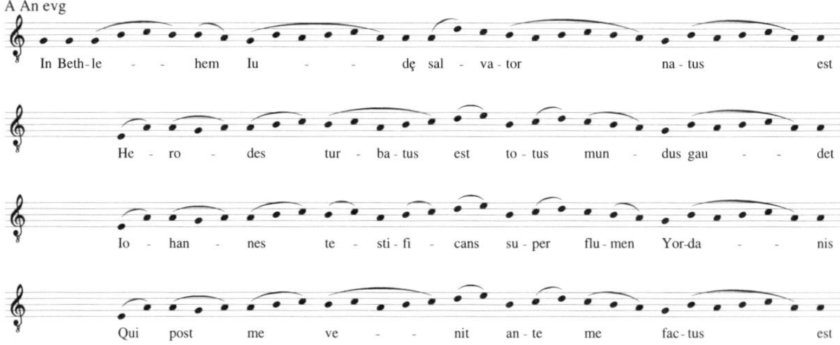

Bethlehem of Judea," immediately followed by a sentence that sets up in the starkest possible manner the contrast between Herod's reaction and that of "the whole world" to this event: "Herod is troubled; the whole world rejoices." This is, in fact, an almost direct contradiction of the passage in Matthew, which shows a considerable portion of "the world" sharing Herod's reaction: "When Herod the King heard these things he was troubled, and all of Jerusalem with him." The contrast, as set in the antiphon text, is a master stroke in terms of Christian exegesis; but nonetheless some scribe in the tradition leading to Vro 107, by a possible misunderstanding of the highly elliptical phrasing in the antiphon that would posit Herod's discomfort rather than Jesus's birth as the immediate cause of the world's rejoicing, inverted the two halves of the second sentence and added a further clause that clarifies the source of Herod's annoyance but also destroys the verbal balance of the entire text and renders it unsingable to any of the surviving melodies.

The first two sentences of the text deal with the visit of the magi, the last three set the stage for the baptism of Christ. Thus it is not hard to see that the main liturgical connection of the work is with Epiphany and that its placement as a trope to the introit of the first Christmas mass in Ber 40608 is an adaptation. This feeling is strengthened by the transferral of the final alleluia of the antiphon to serve as the opening of the trope, and the lengthening of that line by the inclusion of a third alleluia.[17] Thus when this trope was sung the Christmas liturgy would begin with a singing of a triple alleluia by the cantors, a particularly felicitous opening for the feast.

Musically the trope and the two versions of the antiphon are related. They share the same ambitus (the low opening of lines 2–4 of the Milanese antiphon being the only exception), the same general melodic *ductus*, and some of the gestures and their neumation. The trope and the Milanese antiphon have the same extended cadence for each line, though the variations in the trope cadence seem to be textually generated, and the same line ends generate small differences in the cadences of the version from Bobbio. Similarly, the Bobbio antiphon and the trope show the same small change in the first extended neume of each line, from a second A–B at the end of the neume in the first three lines, to the third A–C in the final three lines.[18] Also,

[17] Once the alleluia is transposed to the beginning of the piece, the third repeat makes eminent sense in terms of the balance of the text. The five lines, each a complete sentence, contain 12, 13, 14, 12, and 12 syllables respectively. A concluding double alleluia with eight syllables reads smoothly enough and belongs in a long tradition of shorter final lines that permeates Latin and Romance prose and verse. But such a short opening line for so regular a text would be something of an anomaly; the third alleluia provides a twelve-syllable first line.

[18] It may well be that the much shorter neume at "qui post me" in the Bobbio antiphon is a scribal error.

despite the transposition of the final alleluia of the antiphon to the beginning of the trope, it would appear that the repeated-note opening of one version contaminated the other. Borders makes a convincing case for the Milanese antiphon being farther away from a putative archetype than either of the two north Italian versions of the antiphon,[19] but the trope is clearly an even later adaptation.

Nonetheless, in this trope we have yet another example of the way in which the trope repertories of Italy, and indeed throughout the European continent, appear to have served as a repository of non-Gregorian repertories and poetic and melodic styles that might have disappeared entirely otherwise. In previous studies I have noted a number of instances of this, including another case of an *antiphona ante evangelium* transformed into an introductory trope.[20] Melodically all versions of *In Bethlehem* share the hymn-like structure of much of the Italian repertory that shows no apparent connection with the Gregorian or Roman traditions of chant.

A further example of the kinds of melodic and textual reworking of a chant in order to produce a trope can be seen in the case of the Aquileian introit trope for the Purification found in the gradual from San Marco. The piece in question is *Responsum accepit,* and its immediate model appears in several of the other Aquileian sources. In the graduals from Santa Maria Assunta, the piece is the processional antiphon sung at the door of the church during the Candlemass procession right before entering. In the San Marco gradual its place in the procession has been taken by several stanzas of the hymn *Laetetur omne saeculum,*[21] and the text of *Responsum accepit* now serves as a trope to the introit *Suscepimus.* The text of the introit has been broken into four or possibly five segments,[22] that connect with the trope with varying degrees of grammatical infelicity. This in itself can also be taken as an Italian trait, since Italian cantors often viewed tropes as

[19] Borders, "Northern Italian Antiphons," 16. See also Levy's observation in "Toledo, Rome," 83, that among the offertories the Milanese texts are less complete than those of the parallel Mozarabic and the putative Gallican versions.

[20] Alejandro Enrique Planchart, "On the Nature of Transmission and Change in Trope Repertories," *Journal of the American Musicological Society* 41 (1988): 238–42, and "Fragments, Palimpsests, and Marginalia," *Journal of Musicology* 6 (1988): 315–17.

[21] Bruno Stäblein, ed., *Hymnen* 1: *Die mittelalterlichen Hymnenmelodien des Abendlandes,* Monumenta Monodica Medii Aevi 1 (Kassel: Bärenreiter, 1956), 440. The hymn is ascribed to Peter Damian (d. 1070); see Joseph Szöverffy, *Die Annalen der lateinischen Hymnendichtung* (Berlin: Erich Schmidt, 1956), 1:393–94.

[22] In the trope the verses *Non visurum se mortem* and *Et cum inducerent,* each of which ends with the same extended cadence, are provided with ornamental capitals in the manuscript, but there is no chant cue after *Non visurum se mortem.*

Example 2

Ber 40608, fols. 45v-46r.
Tropha

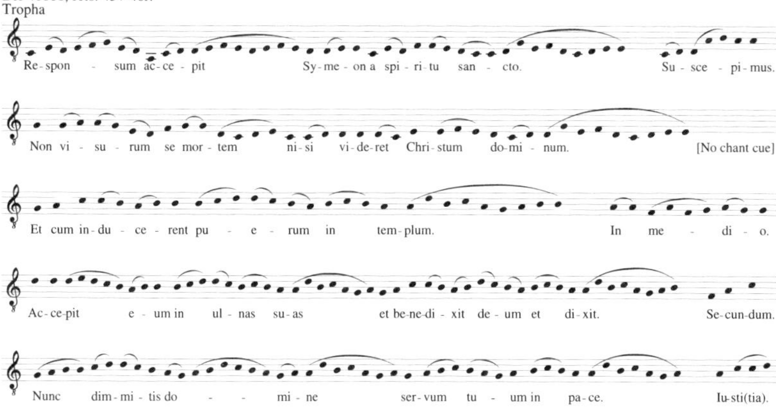

pieces that merely coexisted with the introit and told their own self-contained story.[23] The melody of the antiphon has been reworked extensively in the trope, but a number of its characteristics remain, including the melismas at the end of each verse (although the trope's melismas seem to be summaries of those found in the antiphon and have been made far more regular), the beginning motives of a number of verses (albeit transposing those for *cum inducerent* and *accepit eum* up a fifth), and the exceptional dip to the low A at *accepit Symeon.* The music of the trope appears in example 2.

In the case of *Responsum accepit* we can talk of an actual reworking of the antiphon as a trope because unlike the previous example, where the possible models for the trope come from distant centers and the transmission to the region of Aquileia is not clear, for *Responsum accepit* we have the antiphon preserved in the Aquileian sources and with a relatively stable textual and musical tradition. The model, then, was ready at hand, was well known, and had a clear liturgical position. It is significant that in reworking the piece, both text and melody were preserved closely, but the model was entirely removed from its place in the liturgy and was replaced by *Laetetur omne saeculum.*

The nature of the revisions of the trope repertory in the Aquileian manuscripts is also revealed by the lone trope for the feast of the Circumcision in Civ 56 and Civ 58. The mass for this day in the Aquileian sources, whether called the feast of the Circumcision as in the Cividale graduals or

[23] Planchart, "On the Nature of Transmission," 238.

Example 3

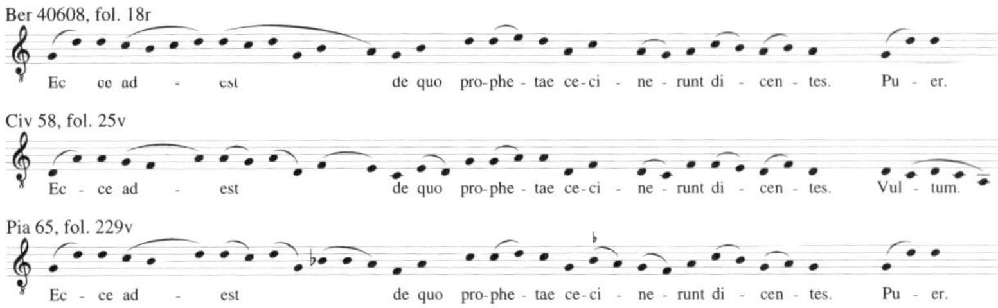

the Octave of Christmas as in the San Marco gradual, is not the expected repetition of the third Christmas mass, but rather the Marian mass *Vultum tuum,* which has an ancient but complex and ambiguous pedigree for this calendric position.[24] Now, the introit *Vultum tuum* was not particularly rich in tropes, there are less than a dozen introductions to it for all the Marian feasts throughout Europe between 950 and 1300, and the tropes that were written for it are largely narrowly Marian in their language. Thus in Cividale the most widespread of all the introductions to *Puer natus* was adapted to serve as the trope to *Vultum tuum.* Musically the adaptation is relatively simple; it involves a simple transposition of the melody of the trope down a fourth, as shown in example 3.

But *Ecce adest* has one of the most complex and ambiguous modal histories of any trope. Originally it seems to have been firmly centered on A, even though it is a trope to a seventh-mode introit. Different manuscript traditions transpose either part or the whole of the melody to G, sometimes preserving the minor third above the final by the use of a B flat and sometimes ignoring this aspect of the melody and assimilating it to the seventh mode of the introit itself.[25]

The one version of *Ecce adest* as a trope to *Puer natus* in the Aquileian sources, that of the San Marco gradual, is one of the most drastic of such accommodations, where even the F, A, C rise at *de quo prophetae,* which survives in virtually all the other adaptations of the melody to a G final, is moved up to G, B, D, so that the internal tonal balance of the melody is disturbed. This version, however, is not the version that seems to be behind the

[24] See René-Jean Hesbert, ed., *Antiphonale Missarum Sextuplex* (Brussels: Vromant, 1935; repr. Rome: Herder, 1967), lxxx–lxxxii and no. 16bis.

[25] See Ellen Reier, "The Introit Trope Repertory at Nevers: MSS Paris, B. N. lat. 9449 and B. N. n. a. lat. 1235" (Ph.D. diss., University of California at Berkeley, 1981), 1:99–102.

trope in the Cividale graduals. Instead the Cividale version seems to be closely derived from a common northern Italian version where the melody on A was simply transposed down a tone and its intervallic integrity was preserved by the use of a B flat. Among the manuscripts that transmit this version is Pia 65, and its melody is given in example 3 as a means of comparison. The differences between a strict transposition of the melody in Pia 65 down a fourth and the melody of Civ 58, for example, the A at the end of *prophetae* and the series of F's at *caecinerunt dicentes,* are probably intentional and modally generated. They make the trope into something that could pass for a second-mode melody by emphasizing the reciting tone in the second half of the melody. Textually the trope makes a surprisingly smooth connection with the introit, although "the prophet" of the trope is no longer Isaiah, who wrote *Puer natus,* but King David, the author of *Vultum tuum,* and the one who is to appear is not Christ but his mother.

The melodic differences between the versions of a trope as common as *Ecce adest* within a relatively circumscribed region that shared a common liturgy indicate not only how complex the interrelationships among trope repertories were, but also how fluid the repertory remained in some regions to the end of its existence.

The three unique proper tropes in this repertory, *Beatus Petrus apostolus, Hodie exsultent caelicolae,* and *Haec est dies caelestis,* all found in Ber 40608, present no consistent stylistic picture. *Beatus Petrus apostolus* has the extended melodic repetitions typical of so much of the Italian repertory, *Haec est dies caelestis* shows the kind of continuous melodic writing that one finds in large-scale ultramontane tropes, and *Hodie exsultent caelicolae* is undistinguishable from the hundreds of modest introit introductions found in every trope collection. Its verbal conceit, *Hodie exsultent caelicolae et nos christicolae: Gaudeamus omnes* is obviously modeled on the very popular trope for All Saints, *Hodie mundo festivo.*[26]

To end it may be useful to present here a brief conspectus of the ordinary tropes in the Aquileian manuscripts. The sources transmit fourteen Kyries with Latin verses or with actual tropes.[27] Eight of these have concordances only in German sources, while the other six belong to the

[26] See Planchart, *Repertory,* 2:97–98.

[27] *Canamus cuncti laudes, Cunctipotens genitor deus, Firmator sancte firmamenti, Immense caeli conditor, Ineffabilis et interminabilis, Kyrie fons bonitatis, Kyrie o theos critis, Kyrie sabaoth iudex, Lux et origo lucis, Omnipotens genitor lumenque, Orbis factor, Pater cuncta, Pater infantium,* and *Rex virginum amator.* See Clemens Blume, ed., *Tropi Graduales: Tropen des Missale im Mittelalter* 1: *Tropen zum Ordinarium Missae,* Analecta Hymnica Medii Aevi 47 (Leipzig: Riesland, 1905; repr. New York: Johnson Reprint, 1961).

pan-European repertory. The two Gloria tropes, *Pax sempiterna* (in Ber 40608) and *Spiritus et alme* (a late addition to OxC 340) present a stark contrast. Though both have essentially a pan-European tradition, *Pax sempiterna* belongs to the oldest layer of tropes and may date from the ninth century,[28] while *Spiritus et alme* is virtually the last of the Gloria tropes to come into existence and the only one to survive into the sixteenth century. There are nine Sanctus tropes:[29] three have concordances only in German sources, three more have pan-European concordances but appear to have reached Aquileia through their German versions, and of the final three one is a French trope and the other two have concordances only in Italy. The Aquileian repertory of Agnus tropes consists of seven pieces:[30] one is a purely Italian piece, three other are German (and more specifically St. Gall) pieces, and the remaining three are widely distributed international tropes. Finally, OxC 341 transmits five tropes to the *Benedicamus domino*[31] and seven tropes to the *Ite missa est.*[32] The concordances for these two groups are restricted to German and Italian sources, and the entire repertory seems to be of German origin.

In their surprising mixture of old and new, in the survival of ninth-century pieces such as *Pax sempiterna,* of reworked *antiphona ante evangelium,* or of odd pieces such as a true trope to the gradual, together with very recent works such as the Gloria *Spiritus et alme,* the Aquileian sources suggest that there was once a rich and large repertory of tropes sung in the churches of the region, and that it was a repertory where the formal and stable tradition of Germany, and particularly of St. Gall, was mixed with works imported from France and elsewhere in Italy as well as with a local repertory that, as in much of the peninsula, reflected local traditions that went back

[28] See Planchart, *Repertory,* 2:292–97, and Keith A. Falconer, "Early Versions of the Gloria Trope *Pax sempiterna Christus,*" *Journal of the Plainsong and Medieval Music Society* 7 (1984): 18–27.

[29] *Admirabilis splendor, Deus fortis, Divinum mysterium, Genitor omnium, Genitor summi fili, Factor omnium, Qui regnas sine fine, Sancte ingenite genitor,* and *Summus et invisibilis.* For a detailed concordance see Gunilla Iversen, ed., *Corpus Troporum* 8: *Tropes du Sanctus,* Studia Latina Stockholmiensia 34 (Stockholm: Almqvist & Wiskell, 1990).

[30] *Ad dexteram patris resides, Caelitus informans, Christe redemptor orbisque, Cui Abel iustus, Iustus Abel, Qui resides in caelis, and Qui sedes . . . solus.* See Gunilla Iversen, ed., *Corpus Troporum* 4: *Tropes de l'Agnus Dei,* Studia Latina Stockholmiensia 26 (Stockholm: Almqvist & Wiskell, 1980).

[31] *Deus adoratur rex, Iohannes postquam senuit, Iugiter regnanti, Laudanti caelestibus,* and *Mundo salus gratia.*

[32] *Caelesti domino signati, Cum pace semper domino, Deo dignus simul, Deo servite sancto spiritus, Sine dolo et lite,* and *Sit rex caelestis.* See Blume, Analecta Hymnica 47.

before the advent of Gregorian chant to the region. Indeed, the strong localism of the Aquileian tradition would for a time survive even the reforms of the Council of Trent, and its rite affected the liturgical music of Venice at the height of the republic's glory as a cultural center.[33] Such localism has left its own imprint in the surviving fragments of the Aquileian trope repertory.

[33] See James H. Moore, "The *Vespro delli Cinque Laudate* and the Role of the *Salmi Spezzati* at Saint Mark's," *Journal of the American Musicological Society* 34 (1981): 258–61.

Appendix

Inventory of Proper Tropes in Aquileian Sources

Christmas (Midnight Mass)

1. In Bethlehem Iudae salvator *Dominus dixit*

Aquileian sources: Ber 40608, 9v.

Concordances

As a trope: none
As *antiphona ante evangelium*: Lo 34209, 110; To 18, 29r; Vro 107, 84v.

Christmas (Mass of the Day)

1. Ecce adest de quo prophetae *Puer natus*
2. Quem virgo Maria genuit *et filius*
3. Nomen eius Emmanuel vocabitur *cuius imperium*

Aquileian sources: Ber 40608, 18r.
CT 1: 82, 144, 175.

Concordances

Aquitanian: Apt 17, PaN 779, PaN 887, PaN 903, PaN 909, PaN 1084, PaN 1118, PaN 1119, PaN 1121, PaN 1240, PaN 1871.
Beneventan: Ben 34.
English: CC 473, Lo 14, OxB 775.
German: Ba 5, Be 11, Ka 15, Lo 19768, Lo 19768, MuB 14083, PaN 10510, PaN 9448, Stu 160, Stu 160, 56r.
North French: Apt 18, Cai 75, Me 452, Me 452, PaA 1169, PaN 1235, PaN 13252, PaN 9449, Pro 12.
North Italian: BoU 2824, Ivr 60, Mod 7, Mza 75, Mza 76, OxD 222, PdC 16, PdC 20, PdC 47, PdC 57, PdS 697, Pia 65, Pst 121, RoA 123, RoC 1741, RoN 1343, To 18, To 20, Vat 10645, Vce 146, Vce 161, Vce 162, Vce 186, Vce 56, Vol 39, Vro 107.

1. Hodie cantandus est nobis puer *Puer natus*

Aquileian sources: Civ 56, 16r; Civ 58, 17v; Civ 79, 10v; Gor I, 3r; Ud 2, 149r; Ud 78, 123v.
CT 1: 107.

Concordances

English: CC 473, L0 14, OxB 775.

German: Ba 5, Ba 6, Ba 9, GrU 756, GrU 807, Ka 15, Ka 25, Klo 73, Klo 588, Kre 309, Li 125, Lo 19768, MuB 27130, MuB 14083, MuB 14322, MuB 14845, MuU 156, OxS 27, PaN 9448, PaN 10510, SG 376, SG 378, SG 380, SG 381, SG 484, Stu 160, Utr 417, Vie 1845.
North French: Cai 60, Cai 75, Cai 78, Me 452, PaN 1235, PaN 9449, PaN 13252.
North Italian: NYM 797, OxD 222, PdC 16, PdC 57, PdS 697, Vro 107.

Saint Stephen

1. Christum cernentis patitur dum verba — [No cue]

Aquileian sources: Ud 78, 123v.

Concordances
German: Ber 11, OxS 27, SG 381, SG 484
CT 1: 66.

1. Domine Iesu Christe summe — *Etenim sederunt*
2. Qui se existimabant legis esse — *et adversum*
3. Me seductorem legisque mosaycae — *et iniqui*
4. Cum lapidibus interficientes — *adiuva me*
5. I quo omnem spem meam fiduciamque — *quia servus*
0. —— — *Ps. Beati*
6. Quam iste adeo servabit ut morti — *Gloria patri*

Aquileian sources: Ber 40608, 22r (1-5); Civ 56, 17r; Civ 58, 19r; Civ 79, 112r; Gor I, 3v (1-6)[1] no music; OxC 340, 18r (1-4/6-5); OxC 341, 59r; Ud 2, 149v (1); Ud 78, 132v.[2]
CT 1: 74, 82, 121, 137, 168, 182.

Concordances
German: Ba 6. Ba 9, GrU 756, GrU 807, Ka 15, Ka 25, Klo 73, Klo 588, Li 125, MuB 14083, MuB 14322, MuB 27130, MuU 156, OxS 27, SG 381, SG 484, Vie 1845, Zu 97.

1. Pro qua venerandus Stephanus — *Etenim sederunt*

Aquileian sources: OxC 340, 19r;[3] OxC 341, 59r; Ud 78, 123v.[4]
CT 1: 163.

[1] Cue to verse 6: *Ps. Beati.*
[2] Cue to verse 7: *Gloria patri*, probably a scribal error.
[3] Cue: *Gloria patri.*
[4] Cue: *Gloria patri.*

Concordances

German: Ba 6, Ba 9, Ber 11, GrU 756, GrU 807, Ka 15, Ka 25, Klo 73, Klo 588, Li 125, MuB 14083, MuB 14322, MuB 14845, MuB 27130, MuU 156, SG 376, SG 378, SG 380, SG 381, SG 382, SG 484, Vie 1845, Zu 97.

1. Magnus et felix fuerat nimium — *Video caelos* (Communion)

Aquileian sources: Civ 56, 20^r; Civ 58, 21^r; Civ 79, 13^r.
CT 1: 135.

Concordances

German: Ka 15, Ka 25, MuB 14083, OxS 27.
North Italian: RoC 1741, RoN 1343.

Saint John Evangelist

1. Dilectus iste domini Iohannes	*In medio*
2. Eructat puro pectore fluenta	*et implevit*
3. Os tuum inquiens aperi	*spiritus*
4. Quia omnia quae dixit	*et intellectus*
5. Intellectum quod dabo tibi	*stolam gloriae*
6. Milibus argenti melior laus	*induit eum*

Aquileian sources: Ber 40608, 25^v; Gor I, 4^v (1); OxC 341, 59^r (1);[5] Ud 2, 149^v (1); Ud 78, 124^r (1).
CT 1: 81, 88 123, 153.

Concordances

German: Ber 11, Ka 25, MuB 14083, OxS 27, SG 376, SG 378, SG 380, SG 381, SG 484, Vie 1609, Zu 97.
North French: Apt 18.
North Italian: BoU 2824, Pst 121.

1. Quoniam dominus Iesus Christus	*In medio*
2. Ut sacramentum fidei et verbum	*et implevit*
3. Qui eum in tantum dilexit	*spiritus*
0. ——	*Ps. Bonum est*
4. Quo inspirante evangelizabit	*Gloria patri*
5. Quam trinitatis gloriam	*sicut erat*

[5] Entered as the *repetendum* of *Quoniam dominus Iesus.*

6. Inde nos moniti peccata nostra *In medio*

Aquileian sources: Civ 56, 21r (1-4/6);[6] Civ 58, 21v (1-4/6);[7] Civ 79, 14r (1-4/6);[8] OxC 340, 19v; OxC 341, 59r (1-4/6-5);[9] Ud 78, 123 (1-4).[10]
CT 1: 118, 169, 178, 186, 210.

Concordances
German: Ba 5, Ba 6, Ba 9, Ber 11, GrU 756, GrU 807, Ka 15, Ka 25, Klo 73, Klo 588, Li 125, MuB 14083, MuB 14322, MuB 14845, MuB 27130, MuU 156, OxS 27, RoA 948, SG 376, SG 378, SG 380, SG 381, SG 382, Utr 417, Vie 1845, Zu 97.
North Italian: Vce 186.

Holy Innocents

1. Hodie parvulorum cunnulae *Ex ore infantium*

Aquileian sources: Oxc 341, 59v; Ud 78, 124r.
CT 1: 111.

Concordances
German: Be 5, Ber 11, GrU 807, Ka 15, Klo 73, Klo 588, MuB 14083, MuB 14845, OxS 27, RoA 948, SG 376, SG 378, SG 380, SG 381, SG 382, SG 484, Zu 97.
North Italian: Vce 186, Vro 107.

1. Hodie pro domino perempta sunt *Ex ore infantium*

Aquileian sources: Gor I, 5r; OxC 341, 59v; Ud 2, 149v.
CT 1: 111.

Concordances
Beneventan: Chi 2.
German: Ba 5, Ber 11, GrU 756, Ka 25, Lo 19768, MuB 27130, MuU 156, OxS 27, SG 381, SG 484, Vie 1845, Zu 97.

Circumcision

1. Ecce adest de quo prophetae *Vultum tuum*

Aquileian sources: Civ 56, 25r; Civ 58, 25v.
No concordances in this context, but see the entry for Christmas.

[6] Cue to verse 4: *Ps. Bonum est.*
[7] Cue to verse 4: *Ps. Bonum est,* cue to verse 7: *Gloria patri.*
[8] Cue to verse 4: *Stolam gloriae.*
[9] Cue to verse 6: *Gloria patri;* verse 5, incipit, no cue.
[10] Cue to verse 4: *Stolam gloriae.*

Epiphany

1. Ecclesiae sponsus illuminator[No cue] (later addition)
2. Iesus quem reges gentium[No cue] (later addition)
4. Cui soli debetur honor gloria[No cue] (later addition)
3. Vidimus stellam eius in oriente[No cue] (later addition)
5. Deus pater deo aeterno regi[No cue] (later addition)
6. Forma speciocissime manuque[No cue] (later addition)

Aquileian sources: OxC 341, 40v.
CT 1: 85.

Concordances[11]
Aquitanian: Apt 17, PaN 887, PaN 909, PaN 1084, PaN 1118, PaN 1119, PaN 1121, Wo 77.
English: CC 473, Lo 14, OxB 775.
German: Ba 5, Ber 11, Ka 15, Lo 19768, MuB 14083, OxS 27, PaN 9448, PaN 10510, SG 376, SG 378, SG 380, SG 381, SG 484, Stu 160, Utr 417, Zu 97.
North French: Apt 18, Cai 75, Me 452, PaA 1169, PaN 1235, PaN 9449, PaN 13252, Pro 12.
North Italian: PdC 16, PdC 20, PdC 57, PdS 697, Pia 65, Pst 121, RoA 123, To 20, Vce 186, Vro 107, Vol 39.

1. Forma speciocissimus manuque *Ecce advenit*

Aquileian sources: Civ 56, 27r; Civ 58, 27v; Civ 79, 17v; Gor I, 5v; OxC 349, 23r; Ud 78, 124r.
CT 1: 96.

Concordances
German: Ba 6, Ber 11, Ka 25, MuB 14083, MuU 156, OxS 27, SG 376, SG 378, SG 380, SG 381, SG 382, SG 484, Vie 1609, Vie 1845, Zu 97.
North Italian: BoU 2824, PdC 16, PdC 20, PdC 57, PdS 697, RoC 1741, RoN 1343, Vro 107.

1. Haec est praeclara dies tribus *Ecce advenit*
2. In Iordane a Iohannes baptizatus *dominator*
3. Naturas lympheas hodie mutavit *et potestas*
0. —— *Ps. Deus iudicium*
0. —— *Gloria patri*
4. Forma speciocissimus manuque *Ecce advenit*

Aquileian sources: OxC 341, 59v.
CT 1: 103, 119, 141.

[11] Verses 1-5 only, verse 6 has an independent concordance given in the following entry.

Concordances[12]

Aquitanian: Apt 17, PaN 779, PaN 887, PaN903, PaN 909, PaN 1084, PaN 1118, PaN 1119, PaN 1121, PaN 1871.
English: Lo 14.
North French: Apt 18.
North Italian: Ivr 60, NYM 797, OxD 222, RoC 1741, RoN 1343, To 18, Vce 56, Vce 146, Vce 161, Vce 162, Vce 186, Vic 106, Vol 39, Vro 107.

1. Hodie clarissimam secuti stellam — *Ecce advenit*
2. Olim quem vates antiqui — *dominator*
3. Qui montes in plana valles — *et regnum*
4. Et regat populum suum — *et potestas*
5. Ad domandum anguem saevum — *et imperium*

CT 1: 53, 108, 148, 210.
Aquileian sources: Ber 40608, 32v; Gor I, 5v (1); Ud 2, 150r (1).

Concordances

Beneventan: Ben 35.
German: Ber 11, Ka 25, MuB 14083, MuB 14322, MuB 14845, MuB 27130, MuU 156, OxS 27, RoA 948, SG 381, SG 484, Zu 97.
North Italian: Vro 107.

Purification

1. Hodie quemadmodum patriarchis — *Suscepimus deus*

Aquileian sources: Ud 78, 124r.

Concordances

English: Lo 14.
German: Ba 6, Ber 11, Ka 15, Ka 25, MuB 14083, MuB 14322, MuB 14845, OxS 27, SG 376, SG 378, SG 380, SG 381, SG 382, SG 484, Vie 1845, Zu 97.

1. Responsum accepit Symeon — *Suscepimus deus*
2. Non visurum se mortem nisi — *in medio*
3. Accepit eum in ulnas suas — *secundum*
4. Nunc dimittis domine servum — *iustitia*

Aquileian sources (A) As a trope: Ber 40608, 45v; (B) As an antiphon: Civ 56, 39r; Civ 58,[13] 41v; Civ 79, 98v; OxC 340, 28v.

Concordances

None as a trope.[14]

[12] Verses 1-3 only, verse 4 has an independent concordance given in the previous entry.
[13] Civ 58 has an incorrect rubric labeling the piece a responsory.
[14] The antiphon was widespread throughout Europe and there are several hundred sources

Easter Eve

1. Quis revolvet nobis lapidem ——
2. Quem quaeritis o tremulae mulieres *Surrexit enim*

Aquileian sources: Gor I, 65^{r};[15] Ud 2, 150^{r}; Ud 234, 1^{r}.[16]
CT 3: 217.

Concordances
German: Ba 5, GrU 756, MuB 14083, MuB 14845, Zu 132.
Norman-Sicilian: Ma 288, Ma 289.
North French: Cai 78.

Easter

1. Hodie resurrexit dominus Iesus [*Resurrexi*]

Aquileian sources: Gor I, 210^{v}; Ud 78, 124^{r}.
CT 3: 113.

Concordances
German: Ba 6, Ka 25, MuB 14083, MuB 14845, MuU 156.
Roman: Bod 74.

1. Postquam factus homo tua iussa *Resurrexi*
2. In regno superbo tibi coaequalis *posuisti*
3. Laudibus angelorum que te laudant *mirabilis*
4. Cui canunt angeli *alleluia*

Aquileian sources: Ber 40608, 107^{v}; Civ 56, 128^{r} (1); Civ 58, 131^{r} (1); Civ 79, 67^{r} (1); OxC 340, 77^{r} (1); OxC 341, 59^{v} (1); Ud 234, 4^{r}.
CT 3: 127, 132, 162.

Concordances
English: CC 473, Lo 14, OxB 775.
German: Ba 6, Ka 25, Kre 309, Lo 19768, MuB 14083, MuB 14322, MuB 14845, MuB 27130, OxS 27, PaN 9448, PaN 10510, RoA 948, SG 378, SG 381, SG 382, SG 484, Stu 160, Utr 417, Vie 1845, Zu 97.
North French: Ba 30, Me 452, PaA 1169.
North Italian: Vro 107.

for it. The Aquileian melody is identical to that found in the modern chant books such as the *Graduale Triplex* (Solesmes: Abbaye de Saint-Pierre, 1979), 541-42.

[15] No cue.

[16] The manuscript adds the cue to the *Te deum* after *Surrexit enim.*

1. Quem quaeritis in sepulchrum *Resurrexi*
2. Gaudeamus omnes resurrexit *posuisti*
3. Vicit leo de tribu iuda radix *mirabilis*

Aquileian sources: Ber 40608, 107ᵛ.
CT 3: 104, 211, 217.

Concordances

A. *Versus* or trope

Aquitanian: Apt 17, PaN 779, PaN 887, PaN 909, PaN 1084, PaN 1118, PaN 1119, PaN 1120, PaN 1121, PaN 1240, PaN 1871.
Beneventan: Ben 34, Ben 35, Ben 38, Ben 39, Ben 40.
German: SG 381, SG 484, Zu 97.
North French: Ba 30, Apt 18, PaA 1169.
North Italian: BoU 2824, Ivr 60, Mod 7, Mza 11, Mza 76, Mza 77, OxD 222, Pia 65, Pst 121, Pst 121, RoA 123, RoC 1741, RoN 1343, To 18, To 20, Vat 4770, Vce 56, Vce 146, Vce 161, Vce 162, Vro 90, Vro 107, Vol 39.
Spanish: Hu 4, Vic 105, Vic 106.

B. *Visitatio sepulchri*

Aquitanian: PaN 1139.
English: CC 473, OxB 775.
German: Ba 5, Ba 6, Ba 10, Be 11, Be 15, Da 3183, Ein 366, Eng 1003, GrU 211, GrU 756, GrU 763, GrU 770, GrU 778, GrU 1549, Ka 25, Klo 1013, Kre 21, Mlk 109, MuB 14083, MuB 14845, MuB 23037, OxS 27, OxC 297, PaN 9448, PaN 9488, PaN 10510, SG 339, SG 374, SG 376, SG 387, SG 388, SG 391, Stu 36, Ud 2, Ud 234, Utr 406, Utr 407, Vie 1888, Wo 1008, Wo 1109, Zu 65, Zu 132.
Norman Sicilian: Ma 20.4, Ma 288, Ma 288, Ma 289.
North French: An 96, Cai 75, Cai 78, La 263, 15 Me 452, PaG 117, PaN 1064, PaN 1235, PaN 9449, Re 265.
Spanish: Lo 30848, Lo 30850.

1. Qui crucifixus eram manus *Resurrexi*
2. Trusi tartareas spoliato *posuisti*
3. Quaeque sub occulto tecum *mirabilis*

Aquileian sources: Ud 78, 124ʳ.
CT 3: 169, 177, 206.

Concordances
German: Ba 6, Ka 25, Kre 309, MuB 14083, OxS 27.

1. Haec est dies quam excelsus *Haec dies* (Gradual)[17]

Aquileian sources: Civ 56, 128ᵛ; Civ 58, 131ᵛ; Civ 79, 67ʳ.

Concordances
German: Ka 25.

[17] Clemens Blume, *Tropi Graduales: Tropen des Missale im Mittelalter* 2: *Tropen zum*

1.	Adducite vitulum saguinatum	*Pascha* (communion)
2.	Comedite et bibite amici mei	*itaque epulemur*
3.	Quotiens calicem hunc bibitis	*alleluia*
4.	Ut sit omnibus nobis caritas	*alleluia*

Aquileian sources: Civ 56, 129ᵛ (1); Civ 58 133ʳ (1); Civ 79, 68ʳ (1); OxC 340, 78ʳ (over an erasure).
CT 3: 55, 71, 186.

Concordances
German: Ber 11, Vie 1609, Ka 25.

Ascension

1.	Ex numero frequentium qui obviarunt	*Viri galilei*

Aquileian sources: Gor I, 212ᵛ; OxC 341, 59ᵛ; Ud 78, 124ᵛ.
CT 3: 99.

Concordances
Beneventan: Ben 35, Ben 39, Ben 40.
German: Ber 11, Kre 309, Ka 15, Ka 25, MuB 14083, MuB 14322, MuU 156, OxS 27, SG 376, SG 378, SG 380, SG 381, SG 382, SG 484, Vie 1609.
North Italian: Vro 107.

1.	Hodie redemptor mundi caelos	*Viri galilei*
2.	Terrigenis summi affatur	*quid admiramini*[18]
3.	Hic deus et dominus	*quemadmodum*
4.	Ut reddat cunctis gestorum	*ita veniet*
5.	Ex numero frequentium	*alleluia*[19]

Aquileian sources: Ber 40608, 137ᵛ; Civ 79, 76ᵛ (1); Gor I 212ʳ (1).
CT 3: 99, 109, 113, 204, 209.

Concordances (verse 1 only)
Aquitanian: Apt 17, PaN 887, PaN 909, PaN 1084, PaN 1118, PaN 1119, PaN 1120, PaN 1121, PaN 1240, PaN 1834, PaN 1871.
English: CC 473, Lo 14, OxB 775.
North French: Lei 33, PaN 9449, PaN 13252, Pro 12.

Proprium Missae, Analecta Hymnica Medii Aevi 49 (Leipzig: Reisland, 1906; repr. New York: Johnson Reprint, 1961), 222, prints this text as a gradual prosula, but in the manuscripts it is a trope with its own independent melody.

[18] Normally an opening verse.

[19] Normally an opening verse.

North Italian: BoU 2824, Ivr 60, Mod 7, Mza 76, Mza 77, OxD 222, PdC 16, PdC 20, PdC 46, PdC 57, PdS 697, Pst 121, RoA 123, RoC 1741, RoN 1343, To 18, To 20, Vce 56, Vce 146, Vce 161, Vce 162, Vce 186, Vro 107.

1. Terrigenis summis affatur *Viri galilei*
2. Hic deus et dominus caelorum *quemadmodum*
3. Ut reddat cunctis gestorum *ita veniet*

Aquileian sources: Ud 78, 124r; Ud 234, 17r.
CT 3: 109, 113, 204, 209.

Concordances

Aquitanian: Apt 17, PaN 779, PaN 887, PaN 903, PaN 909, PaN 1084, PaN 1118, PaN 1119, PaN 1120, PaN 1121, PaN 1240, PaN 1834, PaN 1871.
Beneventan: Ben 39.
English: CC 473, OxB 775.
German: Ba 5, Kre 309, Lo 19768, MuB 14083, PaN 9448, PaN 10510, RoA 948, Stu 160.
North French: Apt 18, Cai 75, Me 452, PaA 1169, PaN 9449, PaN 13252.
North Italian: BoC 7, Ivr 60, Mod 7, PdC 47, Pst 121, RoA 123, RoC 1741, RoN 1343, To 18, To 20, Vat 4770, Vol 39, Vro 107.

Pentecost

1. Consubstantialis patri et sempiterno *Spiritus domini*

Aquileian sources: Gor I, 213r; OxC 341, 59v; Ud 78, 124v.
CT 3: 73.

Concordances

German: Ber 11, Ka 25, Kre 309, MuB 14083, MuB 14322, MuB 14845, MuB 27130, MuU 156, OxS 27, SG 376, SG 368, SG 380, SG 381, SG 382, SG 484, Vie 1609, Vie 1845.

1. Discipulis flammas infudit caelitus *Spiritus domini*

Aquileian sources: Ud 234, 19r (incipit only).
CT 3: 83.

Concordances

Aquitanian: Apt 17, PaN 779, PaN 887, PaN 903, PaN 909, PaN 1084, PaN 1118, PaN 1119, PaN 1120, PaN 1121, PaN 1240, PaN 1834, PaN 1871.
Beneventan: Ben 34, Ben 35, Ben 38, Ben 39, Ben 40.
English: CC 473, Lo 14.
German: Ba 5, Ka 15, Lo 19768, MuB 14083, PaN 9448.
North French: Apt 18, Cai 75, Me 452, PaA 1169, PaN 13252.

North Italian: Vol. 39, Vro 107.
Spanish: Vic 105, Vic 106.

1. Doctorum perfectissimus procedens — *Spiritus domini*

Aquileian sources: OxC 340, 92^{v}.
CT 3: missing.

Concordances

German: GrU 756.

1. Hodie spiritus sancti gratia — *Spiritus domini*
2. Missus a sede patris — *replevit orbem*
3. Igneis linguis — *et hoc quod*
4. Penetralia intuendo — *omnia*

Aquileian sources: Ud 234, 19^{r}.
CT 3: 115. 121. 138, 158.

Concordances

Verse 1-4

German: Ba 5 (1-3), Lo 19768, MuB 27130, OxS 27 (1), RoA 948 (1), SG 381 (1), SG 484 (1), Stu 160 (1).

Verses 2-4

Aquitanian: Apt 17, PaN 779, PaN 887, PaN 909, PaN 1084, PaN 1118, PaN 1119, PaN 1120, PaN 1121, PaN 1240, PaN 1871.
North Italian: Vce 186.

1. Hodie spiritus sanctus procedens — *Spiritus domini*
2. Apostolorum pectora invisibiliter — *et hoc*[20]
3. Spiritus sanctus descendit super — *omnia*[21]

Aquileian sources: Ber 40608, 124^{v}; Gor I, 213^{r}.
CT 3: 116, 198.

Concordances

Verses 1-2

Beneventan: Ben 38.
North Italian: BoU 2824, Ivr 60, Mod 7, Mza 76, Mza 77, NYM 797, OxD 222, PdC 16, PdC 20, PdC 57, PdS 697, Pst 121, RoA 123, RoC 1741, Ron 1343, To 18, Vce 146, Vce 161, Vce 162, Vce 186, Vro 107.

Verse 3

German: Ba 5, Lo 19768, MuB 14083.

[20] This line is normally part of the opening verse, *Hodie spiritus sanctus.*
[21] Normally an opening verse.

1. Hodie spiritus sanctus processit. *Spiritus domini*

Aquileian sources: Civ 56, 151r; Civ 58, 158v; Civ 79, 78v; Ud 234, 19r.
CT 3: 116.

Concordances

German: Ber 11, Kre 309, RoA 948, SG 376, SG 378, SG 380, SG 381, SG 382, SG 484.
North Italian: BoU 2824, RoC 1741, RoN 1343, Vro 107.

Saint John Baptist

1. Angelo praenuntiante magnus *De ventre*

Aquileian sources: Gor I, 213v; OxC 341, 59v; Ud 78, 124v; Ud 234, 24r.

Concordances

German: Ba 5, Ber 11, Ka 25, Kre 309, MuB 14083, MuB 14322, MuU 156, OxS 27, SG 376, SG 378, SG 380, SG 381, SG 382, SG 484, Vie 1845, Zu 97.
North Italian: Vol 39, Vro 107.

1. Audite insulae et attendite *De ventre*
2. Quem prophetae caecinerunt[22] *et posuit*
3. Honestavit verbum suum ore meo *sub tegumento*
4. Constitues me super gentes *quasi sagittam*

0. —— *Ps. Bonum est*

5. Hodie exsultent iusti natus est[23] *Gloria patri*

Aquileian sources: Ber 40608, 151v; Gor I, 214r (1/3-4).[24]

Concordances

Verse 1

Aquitanian: Apt 17, PaN 1118.
Italian: BoU 2824, Ivr 60, Mza 76, OxD 222, PdC 16, PdC 20, PdC 57, Pia 65, RoC 1741, RoN 1343, To 18, To 20, Vat 4770, Vce 146, Vce 161, Vce 162, Vol 39, Vro 107.
North French: Apt 18, PaA 1169.

Verses 2-4

Beneventan: Ben 34; Ben 35; Ben 38; Ben 39; Ben 40.
Aquitanian: Apt 17, PaN 779, PaN 887, PaN 909, PaN 1084, PaN 1118, PaN 1119, PaN 1120, PaN 1121, PaN 1240, PaN 1834, PaN 1871.
English: CC 473, Lo 14, OxB 775.

[22] Normally an opening verse.
[23] Normally an opening verse.
[24] Cue to verse 3: *et posuit.*

German: Lo 19768.
North French: Apt 18, Cai 75, Me 452, PaN 13252.
North Italian: Ivr 60, Mza 76, PdC 16, PdC 20, PdC 57, PdS 697, Pia 65, To 18, To 20, Vat 4770, Vce 146, Vce 161, Vce 162, Vce 186, Vro 107.

Verse 5

Italian: BoU 2824, Ivr 60, Mod 7, Mza 76, OxD 222, PdC 47, Pst 121, RoA 123, RoC 1741, RoN 1343, Vce 186.

Saint Peter

1. Beatissimus Petrus catenis — *Nunc scio*
2. Lux iustitiae in tenebris — *et eripuit*
3. Liberavit me salvator meus — *et de omni*

Aquileian sources: Gor I, 214v.

Concordances

Verse 1

Italian: BoU 2824, Ivr 60, Mza 76, OxD 222, PdC 16,PdC 20, PdC 57, PdC 59, PdS 697, Pia 65, Pst 121, RoC 1741, RoN 1343, To 18, To 20, Vce 146, Vce 161, Vce 162, Vce 186, Vol 39, Vro 107.

Verses 2-3

Aquitanian: PaN 1240.
Beneventan: Ben 39, Ben 40.
English: CC 473, Lo 14.
North French: Apt 18, Ba 30, PaA 1169, PaN 13252, PaN 9449.
North Italian: BoU 2824, Mod 7, PdC 16, PdC 20, PdC 47, PdC 57, PdS 697, RoA 123, RoC 1741, RoN 1343, To 18, To 20, Vat 4770, Vro 107.

1. Beatus Petrus apostolus — *Nunc scio*
2. De manu laqueantis praedonis — *et eripuit*
3. Tua pietate ab omni spectaculo — *et de omni*

Aquileian sources: Ber 40608, 155r.

Concordances

None.

1. Divina beatus Petrus ereptus — *Nunc scio*

Aquileian sources: Ud 234, 26r.

Concordances

Aquitanian: Apt 17, PaN 779, PaN 887, PaN 909, PaN 903, PaN 1084, PaN 1118, PaN 1119, PaN 1120, PaN 1121, PaN 1240, PaN 1834, PaN 1871.

Beneventan: Ben 39, Ben 40.
English: Lo 14.
German: Ba 5, Ka 25, Kre 309, Lo 19768, MuB 14083, MuB 14322, MuU 156, OxS 27, PaN 10510, RoA 948, Vie 1845.
North French: Apt 18, Ba 30, Me 452, PaA 1169, PaN 9449, PaN 13252.
North Italian: BoU 2824, Mod 7, OxD 222, PdC 47, Pia 65, RoA 123, RoC 1741, RoN 1343.

1. Eductus quidem sanctus de carcere — *Nunc scio*

Aquileian sources: OxC 341, 59^{v}; Ud 78, 124^{v}.

Concordances
German: Ba 5, Ka 25, Kre 309, Vie 1845.

Saint Lawrence

1. Hodie caelesti igne succensus — *Confessio*

Aquileian sources: Ud 78, 124^{v}.

Concordances
German: Ber 11, Ka 25, Kre 309, MuB 14083, MuB 14322, MuU 156, OxS 27, SG 376, SG 378, SG 380, SG 381, SG 484, Vie 1845, Zu 97.

1. Vox domino laudem ferat — *Confessio*
2. Ex quibus ornatus flammam — *sanctitas*
3. His caelum geminis scandit — *in sanctificatione*

Aquileian sources: Ber 40608, 164^{v}.

Concordances
Aquitanian: Apt 17, PaN 1084, PaN 1118.
English: CC 473, Lo 14, OxB 775.
German: MuB 14083.
North French: Cai 75, Me 452, PaN 1235, PaN 9449, PaN 13252, Reg 222.
North Italian: PdC 16, PdC 20, PdC 57.

Assumption

1. Gaude virgo gaude sancta — *Vultum tuum*
2. Gaude regina mundi et domina — *adducentur*
3. Intercede ad tuum filium — *adducentur*

Aquileian sources: Ber 40608.

Concordances

Beneventan: Ben 34, Ben 35, Ben 38, Ben 39, Ben 40, Urb 602.[25]
North Italian: Mod 7.

1. Hodie assumpta est Maria — *Gaudeamus omnes*
2. Qui tamquam sponsus — *diem festum*
3. Cives poli invocantes turma — *de cuius*
4. Laetentur in hac die — *et collaudant*

Aquileian sources: Gor I, 215^v^.

Concordances

German: PaN 9448, PaN 10510.
North Italian: PdC 16, PdC 20, PdC 57, PdS 697.

1. Hodie sanctissima virgo virginum — *Vultum tuum*

Aquileian sources: Civ 56, 175^r^; Civ 58, 262^r^;[26] OxC 341, 59^v^; Ud 78, 124^v^; Ud 234, 32^r^.

Concordances

German: Ba 5, Ba 6, Ber 11, Ka 25, Kre 309, MuB 14083, MuB 14322, MuB 14845, MuU 156, OxS 27, SG 376, SG 378, SG 380, SG 381, SG 382, SG 484, Stu 160, Vie 1845, Zu 97.
North Italian: Mod 7, RoA 123, Vol 39.

Nativity of the Virgin

1. Nativitatem venerandam sanctae — *Gaudeamus omnes*

Aquileian sources: Civ 56, 178^v^; Civ 58, 186^v^;[27] OxC 341, 59^v^; Ud 78, 124^v^; Ud 234, 32^r^.

Concordances

German: Ber 11, Ka 25, Kre 309, MuB 14083, MuB 14322, MuU 156, OxS 27, SG 376, SG 378, SG 380, SG 381, SG 382, SG 484, Vie 1845, Zu 97.

Saint Michael

1. Hodie fratres angelici pangamus — *Benedicite*

Aquileian sources: OxC 341, 59^v^; Ud 234, 34^v^.

[25] Palimpsest, only partially visible.
[26] Copied out of sequence at the start of the proser and cued by a cross reference at the appropriate place in the gradual.
[27] Only a cross reference in the gradual, but not the trope survives in the manuscript.

Concordances
German: Ber 11, Ka 25, Kre 309, MuB 14083, MuB 14322, MuU 156, SG 381, SG 484.

All Saints

1. Hodie exsultent caelicolae	*Gaudeamus omnes*

Aquileian sources: Ber 40608, 190^{r}.

Concordances
None

1. Hodie gaudet in excelsis	*Gaudeamus omnes*

Aquileian sources: OxC 341, 59^{v}.

Concordances
German: OxS 27.

1. Sollemnitatem venerandam omnium	*Gaudeamus omnes*
2. Ipsum cordibus solum canamus	*diem festum*
3. Non escis epulis vel luxu	*sub honore*
4. Cui in axe stelligero reddunt	*de quorum*
5. Caeli cives celebrat laeta	*et collaudant*

Aquileian sources: Ber 40608, 190^{r}; Civ 56, 183^{v} (1); Civ 58, 192^{r} (1); Ud 78, 124^{v} (1); Ud 234, 36^{r} (1).

Concordances
German: Ber 11, Ka 25, Kre 309, MuB 14083, MuB 14322, MuU 156, Oxs 27.

Saint Candidus

1. Hodie festum recolamus in qui est	*Laetabitur iustus*[28]

Aquileian sources: OxC 341, 60^{r}.

Concordances
German: MuU 156, OxS 27.

Saint Martin

1. Haec est dies caelestis micat	*Statuit ei*

[28] Cue for *Statuit ei* added in the margin.

2. Qua mente amplectendo sedula — *et principem*
3. Caelicolarum[29] in monarchia — *ut sit illi*

Aquileian sources: Ber 40608, 192r.

Concordances
None

1. Hodie laetemur fratres devoti — *Statuit ei*

Aquileian sources: Ud 78, 124v.

Concordances
German: MuU 156, OxS 27.

Saint Andrew

1. Hodie amicus dei et apostolus — *Mihi autem*
2. Domestici dei exaltati sunt — *amici tui*
3. Et glorificati in solio sancti — *Ps. Domine*

Aquileian sources: Ber 40608, 196v.

Concordances
North Italian: Mod 7, SeZ 2, Vol 39.

Dedication of the Church

1. Agmina perenniter iubilant — *Terribilis est*
2. In quo sceptra poli factor — *hic domus*
3. Intrant per quam iustorum — *et porta*
4. Per quam credentes veniam — *et vocabitur*

Aquileian sources: Ber 40608, 134v.

Concordances
Aquitanian: PaN 909, PaN 1084, PaN 1118, PaN 1119, PaN 1120, PaN 1121, PaN 1871.
North Italian: Mod 7, PdC 47.

1. Ante dei vultum penetrant — *Terribilis est*[30]

Aquileian sources: Ud 234, 64v.

[29] MS: *Mellicolarum.*
[30] Without music.

Concordances

German: Ka 25, Kre 309, MuB 14083, MuU 156, OxS 27.

1. Hodie revolvat annua ista plebs — *Terribilis est*
2. Rex quia magnificus templum — *hic domus*
3. Annua nempe dies sacratae — *et vocavit*
4. Quam manus omnipotentem petra — *et porta*

Aquileian sources: Civ 56 (1), 156^{v}; Civ 58 (1), 174^{r}; OxC 341 (1), 60^{r}; Ud 78 125^{r} (1); Ud 234, 15^{v} (1);[31] Ud 234, 64^{v}.

Concordances

German: Ka 25, Kre 309, MuB 14083, MuU 156, OxS 27, Vie 185.

[31] Without music.

List of Manuscripts in Alphabetical Order by Sigla

An 96	Angers, Bibliothèque Municipale, MS. 96 (88).
Apt 17	Apt, Basilique de Sainte Anne, MS. 17 (5).
Apt 18	Apt, Basilique de Sainte Anne, MS. 18 (4).
Ba 5	Bamberg, Staatsbibliothek, MS. Lit. 5 (Ed. V. 9).
Ba 6	Bamberg, Staatsbibliothek, MS. Lit. 6 (ED. III. 7).
Ba 9	Bamberg, Staatsbibliothek, MS. Lit. 9 (Ed. V. 3).
Ba 10	Bamberg, Staatsbibliothek, MS. Lit. 10 (Ed. V. 10).
Ba 30	Bamberg, Staatsbibliothek, MS. Msc. Bibl. 30.
Ben 34	Benevento, Biblioteca Capitolare, MS. 34 (olim 25).
Ben 35	Benevento, Biblioteca Capitolare, MS. 35 (olim 26).
Ben 38	Benevento, Biblioteca Capitolare, MS. 38 (olim 27).
Ben 39	Benevento, Biblioteca Capitolare, MS. 39 (olim 28).
Ben 40	Benevento, Biblioteca Capitolare, MS. 40 (olim 29).
Ber 11	Krakow, Biblioteka Jagiellonska, MS. theol. lat. 4° 11.
Ber 40608	Berlin, Preußischer Kulturbesitz, MS. Mus. 40608.
BoC 7	Bologna, Civico Museo Bibliografico Musicale, MS. Q 7.
Bod 74	Cologny-Geneva, Bibliotheca Bodmeriana, MS. 74.
BoU 2824	Bologna, Biblioteca Universitaria, MS. 2824.
Cai 75	Cambrai, Bibliothèque Municipale, MS. 75 (76).
Cai 78	Cambrai, Bibliothèque Municipale, MS. 78 (79).
CC 473	Cambridge, Corpus Christi College, MS. 473.
Chi 2	Chieti, Biblioteca Capitolare, MS. 2. Flyleaves.
Civ 56	Cividale del Friuli, Museo Archeologico, MS. LVI.
Civ 58	Cividale del Friuli, Museo Archeologico, MS. LVIII.
Civ 79	Cividale del Friuli, Museo Archeologico, MS. LXXIX.
Da 3183	Darmstadt, Landes- und Hochschulbibliothek, MS. 3183.
Ein 366	Einsiedeln, Stiftsbibliothek, MS. 366.
Eng 1003	Engelberg, Stiftsbibliothek, MS. 1003.
Gor I	Gorizia, Seminario Teologico Centrale, MS. I.
GrU 211	Graz, Universitätsbibliothek, MS. 211 (40/90 4°).
GrU 763	Graz, Universitätsbibliothek, MS. 763 (40/81 4°).
GrU 770	Graz, Universitätsbibliothek, MS. 770 (40/49 4°).
GrU 778	Graz, Universitätsbibliothek, MS. 778 (40/97 f°).
GrU 1549	Graz, Universitätsbibliothek, MS. 1549 (40/6 8°).
Ivr 60	Ivrea, Biblioteca Capitolare, MS. 91 (Bollati LX).
Ka 15	Kassel, Murhardsche Bibliothek, MS. theol 4° 15.
Ka 25	Kassel, Murhardsche Bibliothek, MS. theol 4° 25.
Klo 73	Klosterneuburg, Stiftsbibliothek, MS. CCI 73
Klo 588	Klosterneuburg, Stiftsbibliothek, MS. CCI 588.

Klo 1013	Klosterneuburg, Stiftsbibliothek, MS. CCl 1013.
Kre 21	Kremsmünster, Stiftsbibliothek, MS. CC 21.
Kre 309	Kremsmünster, Stiftsbibliothek, MS. CC 309.
Kre 390	Kremsmünster, Stiftsbibliothek, MS. CC 390.
La 263	Laon, Bibliothèque Municipale, MS. 263.
Lei 33	Leiden, Universiteitsbibliotek, MS. Voss lat. 4° 33.
Lo 14	London, British Library, Cotton MS. Caligula A. xiv.
Lo 19768	London, British Library, Additional MS. 19768.
Lo 30848	London, British Library, Additional MS. 30848.
Lo 30850	London, British Library, Additional MS. 30850.
Lo 34209	London, British Library, Additional MS. 34209.
Ma 20.4	Madrid, Biblioteca Nacional, MS. Vitrina 20-4 (C 132).
Ma 288	Madrid, Biblioteca Nacional, MS. 288 (C 151).
Ma 289	Madrid, Biblioteca Nacional, MS. 289 (C 153).
Me 452	Metz, Bibliothèque Municipale, MS. 452.
Mlk 109	Melk, Stiftsbibliothek, MS. 109.
Mod 7	Modena, Biblioteca Capitolare, MS. O. I. 7.
MuB 14083	Munich, Bayerische Staatsbibliothek, MS. clm 14083.
MuB 14322	Munich, Bayerische Staatsbibliothek, MS. clm 14322.
MuB 14845	Munich, Bayerische Staatsbibliothek, MS. clm 14845.
MuB 23037	Munich, Bayerische Staatsbibliothek, MS. clm 23037.
MuB 27130	Munich, Bayerische Staatsbibliothek, MS. clm 27130.
MuU 156	Munich, Universitätsbibliothek, MS. 156.
Mza 75	Monza, Biblioteca Capitolare, MS. c. 12/75.
Mza 76	Monza, Biblioteca Capitolare, MS. c.13/76.
Mza 77	Monza, Biblioteca Capitolare, MS. c. 14/77.
NYM 797	New York, Pierpont Morgan Library, MS. 797.
OxB 775	Oxford, Bodleian Library, MS. Bodley 775.
OxC 297	Oxford, Bodleian Library, MS. Canonici liturgical 297.
OxC 340	Oxford, Bodleian Library, MS. Canonici liturgical 340.
OxC 341	Oxford, Bodleian Library, MS. Canonici liturgical 341.
OxD 222	Oxford, Bodleian Library, MS. Douce 222.
OxS 27	Oxford, Bodleian Library, MS. Selden supra 27.
PaA 1169	Paris, Bibliothèque de l'Arsenal, MS. 1169.
PaG 117	Paris, Bibliothèque de St. Geneviève, MS. 117.
PaN 779	Paris, Bibliothèque Nationale, fonds latin, MS. 779.
PaN 887	Paris, Bibliothèque Nationale, fonds latin, MS. 887.
PaN 903	Paris, Bibliothèque Nationale, fonds latin, MS. 903.
PaN 909	Paris, Bibliothèque Nationale, fonds latin, MS. 909.
PaN 1064	Paris, Bibliothèque Nationale, n. a. lat., MS. 1064.
PaN 1084	Paris, Bibliothèque Nationale, fonds latin, MS. 1084.
PaN 1118	Paris, Bibliothèque Nationale, fonds latin, MS. 1118.
PaN 1119	Paris, Bibliothèque Nationale, fonds latin, MS. 1119.
PaN 1120	Paris, Bibliothèque Nationale, fonds latin, MS. 1120.

PaN 1121	Paris, Bibliothèque Nationale, fonds latin, MS. 1121.
PaN 1139	Paris, Bibliothèque Nationale, fonds latin, MS. 1139.
PaN 1235	Paris, Bibliothèque Nationale, n. a. lat., MS. 1235.
PaN 1240	Paris, Bibliothèque Nationale, fonds latin, MS. 1240.
PaN 1834	Paris, Bibliothèque Nationale, fonds latin, MS. 1834.
PaN 1871	Paris, Bibliothèque Nationale, n. a. lat., MS. 1871.
PaN 9448	Paris, Bibliothèque Nationale, fonds latin, MS. 9448.
PaN 9449	Paris, Bibliothèque Nationale, fonds latin, MS. 9449.
PaN 10510	Paris, Bibliothèque Nationale, fonds latin, MS. 10510.
PaN 13252	Paris, Bibliothèque Nationale, fonds latin, MS. 13252.
PdC 16	Padua, Biblioteca Capitolare, MS. B 16.
PdC 20	Padua, Biblioteca Capitolare, MS. A 20.
PdC 47	Padua, Biblioteca Capitolare, MS. A 47.
PdC 57	Padua, Biblioteca Capitolare, MS. E 57.
PdC 59	Padua, Biblioteca Capitolare, MS. C 59. Flyleaf.
PdS 697	Padua, Biblioteca del Seminario, MS. 697.
Pia 65	Piacenza, Biblioteca Capitolare, MS. 65.
Pro 12	Provins, Bibliothèque Municipale, MS. 12.
Pst 121	Pistoia, Biblioteca Capitolare, MS. C 121.
Re 265	Reims, Bibliothèque Municipale, MS. 265 (261).
Reg 222	Vatican, Biblioteca Apostolica Vaticana, MS. Reg. lat. 222.
RoA 123	Rome, Biblioteca Angelica, MS. 123 (B. III. 18).
RoA 948	Rome, Biblioteca Angelica, MS. 948 (R. IV. 38).
RoC 1741	Rome, Biblioteca Casanatense, MS. 1741 (C. VI. 2).
RoN 1343	Rome, Biblioteca Nazionale, MS. 1343 (Sessorianus 62).
SeZ 2	Seville, Biblioteca de Rodrigo de Zayas, MS. 2.
SG 339	St. Gall, Stiftsbibliothek, MS. 339.
SG 374	St. Gall, Stiftsbibliothek, MS. 374.
SG 376	St. Gall, Stiftsbibliothek, MS. 376.
SG 378	St. Gall, Stiftsbibliothek, MS. 378.
SG 380	St. Gall, Stiftsbibliothek, MS. 380.
SG 381	St. Gall, Stiftsbibliothek, MS. 381.
SG 382	St. Gall, Stiftsbibliothek, MS. 382.
SG 387	St. Gall, Stiftsbibliothek, MS. 387.
SG 388	St. Gall, Stiftsbibliothek, MS. 388.
SG 390-1	St. Gall, Stiftsbibliothek, MS.S 390-391.
SG 484	St. Gall, Stiftsbibliothek, MS. 484.
Stu 36	Stuttgart, Württembergisches Landesbibliothek, MS. 4° 36.
Stu 160	Stuttgart, Württembergisches Landesbibliothek, MS. Brev. 160.
To 18	Turin, Biblioteca Nazionale Universitaria, MS. 897 (F.IV.18).
To 20	Turin, Biblioteca Nazionale Universitaria, MS. 1088 (G.V.20).
Ud 2	Udine, Biblioteca Archivescovile, MS. 2.
Ud 78	Udine, Biblioteca Archivescovile, MS. 78.
Ud 234	Udine, Biblioteca Archivescovile, MS. 234.

Urb 602	Vatican, Biblioteca Apostolica Vaticana, MS. Urb. lat. 602.
Utr 406	Utrecht, Bibliotheek van de Rijksuniversiteit, MS. 406.
Utr 407	Utrecht, Bibliotheek van de Rijksuniversiteit, MS. 407.
Utr 417	Utrecht, Bibliotheek van de Rijksuniversiteit, MS. 417.
Vat 4770	Vatican, Biblioteca Apostolica Vaticana, MS. Vat. lat. 4770.
Vat 10645	Vatican, Biblioteca Apostolica Vaticana, MS. Vat. lat. 10645.
Vce 56	Vercelli, Biblioteca Capitolare, MS. 56.
Vce 146	Vercelli, Biblioteca Capitolare, MS. 146.
Vce 161	Vercelli, Biblioteca Capitolare, MS. 161.
Vce 162	Vercelli, Biblioteca Capitolare, MS. 162.
Vce 186	Vercelli, Biblioteca Capitolare, MS. 186.
Vic 105	Vich, Museo Episcopal, MS. 105 (CXI).
Vic 106	Vich, Museo Episcopal, MS. 106 (Rip. 31).
Vie 1609	Vienna, Österreichische Nationalbibliothek, MS. 1609.
Vie 1845	Vienna, Österreichische Nationalbibliothek, MS. 1845.
Vie 1888	Vienna, Österreichische Nationalbibliothek, MS. 1888.
Vol 39	Volterra, Biblioteca Guarnacci, MS. L. 3. 39.
Vro 107	Verona, Biblioteca Capitolare, MS. CVII (100).
Vro 90	Verona, Biblioteca Capitolare, MS. XC (85).
Wo 1008	Wolfenbüttel, Herzog-August-Bibliothek, MS. Helmst. 1008.
Wo 1109	Wolfenbüttel, Herzog-August-Bibliothek, MS. Helmst. 1109.
Wo 77	Wolfenbüttel, Herzog-August-Bibliothek, MS. Helmst. 77.
Zü 65	Zürich, Zentralbibliothek, MS. Rh. 65.
Zü 97	Zürich, Zentralbibliothek, MS. Rh. 97.
Zü 132	Zürich, Zentralbibliothek, MS. Rh. 132.

SUSAN RANKIN

Ways of Telling Stories

The best stories begin with something familiar, and mine is no exception:

> The more perfect art of chant, which now almost the whole of France loves, was introduced by Pope Stephen, when he had come to Pippin, the father of Emperor Charlemagne, in France in order to take back from the Lombards that which belonged to St. Peter. [The chant was introduced] on request by the same Pippin, through his clerics, and since then its use has everywhere and always grown strong.[1]

[1] "Cantilenae vero perfectiorem scientiam, quam iam pene tota Francia diligit, Stephanus papa, cum ad Pippinum, patrem Caroli magni imperatoris, in Franciam pro iustitia Sancti Petri a Langobardis expetenda venisset per suos clericos petente eodem Pippino invexit, indeque usus eius longe lateque convaluit." Walafridi Strabonis, *Liber de exordiis et incrementis quarundam in observationibus ecclesiaticis rerum*, ed. Aloisius Knoepfler (Munich: Stahl, 1890), ch. 26, 84. For the translation of this passage and another below, I am indebted to Ritva Jacobsson. The Pope in question is Stephen II, who had come to France in 753 to ask Pippin III for aid and for protection of the church's interests in Italy; on their meeting see Rosamond McKitterick, *The Frankish Kingdoms under the Carolingians, 751–987* (London: Longman, 1983). Fundamental studies of the liturgical exchange between Rome and the northern countries include Theodor Klauser, "Die liturgischen Austauschbeziehungen zwischen der römischen und der fränkisch-deutschen Kirche vom achten bis zum elften Jahrhundert," *Historisches Jahrbuch* 53 (1933): 169–89, and Rosamond McKitterick, *The Frankish Church and the Carolingian Reforms, 789–895* (London: Royal Historical Society, 1977); see also the brief survey of the relation of the political to the musical situation in the eighth century by Kenneth

—this as told by Walafrid Strabo, monk of Reichenau and Fulda, and intimate of the Carolingian court. His version of the famous story, written before 850, is certainly the least dressed up, and probably the closest to historical truth.[2] But it is not accuracy which initially concerns me, rather the "story" of this story. Its next telling is in the words of a Roman, and contains many insults against the Franks:

> Alpine bodies do not properly make the sweetness of the melody they have adopted resound, since with their voices they make high-sounding noises like thunder. Because the barbarian fierceness, belonging to a drinker's throat, emits rough hard voices when it attempts to produce a soft tone with inflections and repetitions, and does so with a kind of natural roar of the voice, sounding confused, as if you were to throw carts down steps. And so, through bewildering and terrible bawling, it [the adopted melody, i.e., Roman chant] rather disturbs the listeners' minds, which it ought to please . . .[3]

In this version—incorporated into his *Vita Gregorii Magni* written between 872 and 875—John the Deacon gives the major credit for the establishment of the Roman chant north of the Alps not to Pippin III but to his son Charlemagne.[4] His account has a new twist: following the model of Bede, John explains *how* the business of introducing Roman chant was accomplished. First, two Frankish cantors were trained in Rome and returned

Levy, "Toledo, Rome and the Legacy of Gaul," *Early Music History* 4 (1984): 49–99, esp. 49–50. Finally, the history of the "Roman chant story" is studied in some depth in Stephen J. P. Van Dijk, "Papal Schola versus Charlemagne," in *Organicae voces: Festschrift Joseph Smits van Waesberghe, angeboten anlässlich seines 60. Geburtstages, 18. April 1961*, ed. Pieter Fischer (Amsterdam: Instituut voor Middeleeuwse Muziekwetenschap, 1963), 21–30.

[2] Pupil of Hrabanus Maurus at Fulda, appointed teacher in 829 of the future Charles the Bald, and in 838 Abbot of Reichenau, Walafrid was closely in touch with the Carolingian court during much of his life; his direct personal knowledge of past and present elements of Carolingian theological politics is beyond question.

[3] "Alpina siquidem corpora, vocum suarum tonitruis altisone perstrepentia, susceptae modulationis dulcedinem proprie non resultant, quia bibuli gutturis barbara feritas, dum inflexionibus et repercussionibus mitem nititur edere cantilenam, naturali quodam fragore, quasi plaustra per gradus confuse sonantia rigidas voces jactat, sicque audientium animos, quos mulcere debuerat, exasperando magis ac obstrependo conturbat." Johannes Diaconus, *Vita Sancti Gregorii Magni*, ed. Jacques–Paul Migne, Patrologia Latina 75 (Paris: n.p., 1862), col. 91.

[4] The preface explains how, on the eve of the feast of St. Gregory in 873, the Pope, knowing the Saxon and Longobard *Vitae* of Gregory, had expressed surprise at the lack of one composed in Rome, and straightway commissioned John to produce one. To this end, John had access to the papal archives. The intended four books (corresponding to the four of Gregory's *Liber pastoralis*) were completed soon after Easter 875. On John the Deacon's literary work see Max Manitius, *Geschichte der lateinischen Literatur des Mittelalters* 1: *Von Justinian bis zur Mitte des zehnten Jahrhunderts*, Handbuch der Klassischen Altertumswissenschaft, Abt. 9, t. 2, 1 (Munich: Beck, 1911), 689–95.

north to teach. But their influence did not last beyond their own lifetimes and Charlemagne had to start all over again. Then Pope Hadrian sent two *Roman* cantors, who were more effective, and everyone lived happily ever after.

The next version of the chant story was written very shortly after John's, probably in the 880s, and by someone who reacted strongly against John's scorn. The story forms part of Notker Balbulus's *Gesta Karoli*, a life of Charlemagne composed at the behest of Charles the Fat (Emperor, 881–87).[5] With concrete physical evidence, it is possible to prove that Notker knew John's *Life of Gregory*, because it is his own hand which begins every gathering of the St. Gallen house copy. Plate 1 shows p. 54 of St. Gallen, Stiftsbibliothek 578, with John's version of the story of the introduction of Roman chant into Gaul; Notker's hand can be seen in the left-hand column, lines 1–14.[6] A crucial difference between Notker's and John's accounts is the reversal of the roles of Frankish and Roman cantors. Notker blamed the Romans for bad teaching, but his story had to end correctly; so he introduced the two Frankish cantors *after* the Romans.[7]

John had placed the two Roman cantors at Metz; Notker sent one to Metz, and one to accompany Charlemagne. In a fourth version of the story, part of which appears in the margins of the St. Gallen copy of John the Deacon's *Vita*, the story takes on a more specific local content. In the upper margin of p. 54 of Cod. 578 (plate 1), beside a neume composed of a *torculus* and two *puncta*, the hand of the monastic historian Ekkehard IV names the two successful cantors as Petrus and Romanus![8] Here and in his *Casus sancti Galli*, completed in the middle years of the eleventh century,

[5] It was apparently during a visit to the Abbey of St. Gallen between 6 and 8 December 883 that the Emperor made the request of Notker. Charles the Fat's predecessor as Emperor, Charles the Bald, had visited Rome late in 875, to be crowned Emperor. John the Deacon's prominence in the Roman situation is such that his *Vita* is likely to have been brought to Charles's attention. Thus, it is likely that (if not already by other means) a copy of the *Vita* was carried north of the Alps by the early part of 876.

[6] On Notker's hand see Susan Rankin, "Ego itaque Notker scripsi," *Revue bénédictine* 101 (1991): 268–98.

[7] A translation of this portion of Notker's account can be found in Van Dijk, "Papal Schola versus Charlemagne," 27. It was probably Notker himself who enlarged the number of Roman cantors mentioned in the story from two to twelve. Far from trying to snipe at the Romans, however, he must have had in mind that the twelve apostles went out from Jerusalem to preach the gospel, but since Rome was the center of the Christian church, and the seat of St. Peter, he transferred the idea. The biblical passage which tells how the ministry of the apostles began reads "And they were all filled with the Holy Ghost, and began to speak with other tongues, as the Spirit gave them utterance" (Acts 2.4). The idea that the Roman cantors should teach different ways of singing thus had a sound biblical model!

[8] The neume appears in the main text beside the phrase "duos in Galliam cantores emisit."

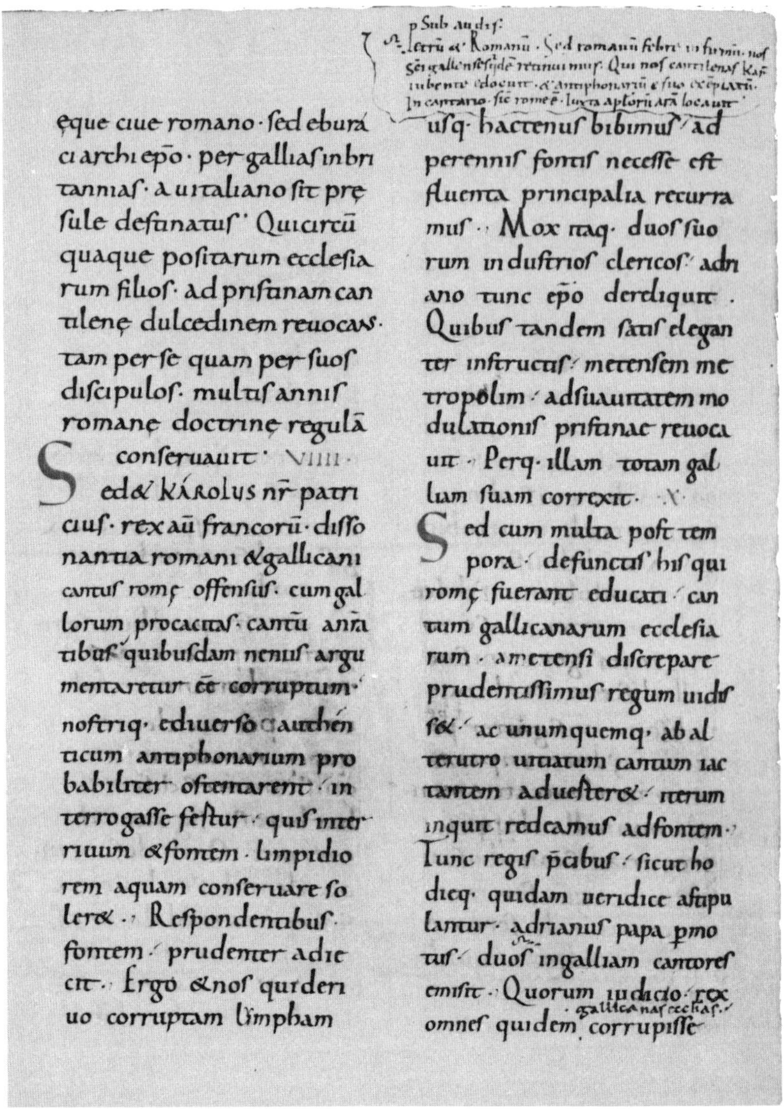

Plate 1: Stiftsbibliothek St. Gallen, Codex sang. 578, p. 54. Reproduced by permission.

Ekkehard explains that Romanus fell ill of a fever while travelling north, and remained at St. Gallen rather than continue his journey. Keeping one of two antiphoners brought from Rome, he taught the monks the Roman chant. The other book was taken by Romanus to Metz.[9]

In identifying the "successful travelling cantors" as two Romans, Ekkehard has returned to the substance of John the Deacon's story, rather than Notker's. Yet, in respect of the destiny of the cantors, Ekkehard's story has taken a new direction, rendering it especially significant in the history of St. Gallen. While the outline remains substantially the same from one version of the story to another, each new variation casts light on the situation in which it was told—and, following the circle around, the context of each may help to explain the variations. By the mid-eleventh century, there had grown up at St. Gallen a perception that the abbey had received and maintained an especially good transmission of Roman chant, allowing it to rival Metz; and Ekkehard's story can be read as intended to reveal how this came about.

In both implicit and explicit senses this perception has persisted in the modern world. The famous Cantatorium, published by Père Lambillotte in 1851 as the *Antiphonaire de Saint Grégoire*,[10] is now thoroughly the worse for wear, so much has it suffered the attentions of reverend pilgrims. But, as Jacques Handschin asked fifty years ago, how *did* the Roman-Frankish chant come to St. Gallen?[11] Was it direct from Rome, or via Metz, or how? What lies behind the nuance-rich St. Gallen neumes? To what extent are the patterns of manuscript sources, and the musically notated repertories they contain, typical? Against a background of extreme interest in and contact

[9] St. Gallen 578, p. 54, upper margin: "Sub audis. . Petrum et Romanum. Sed Romanum febre infirmum. nos Sancti Gallenses quidem retinuimus. Qui nos cantilenas Karolo iubente edocuit. et antiphonarium e suo exemplatum. In cantario. sicut Rome est. Iuxta apostolorum aram locavit." These words read as notes made in relation to (and possibly the preparation of) the longer account in Ekkehard's *Casus:* Ekkehardi IV, *Casus Sancti Galli*, ed. Hans F. Haefele, in *Ausgewählte Quellen zur deutschen Geschichte des Mittelalters* 10 (Darmstadt: Wissenschaftliche Buchgesellschaft, 1980), ch. 47, 106–08.

[10] P. Louis Lambillotte, *Antiphonaire de Saint Grégoire, facsimilé du manuscrit de Saint-Gall (VIIIe siècle)* (Paris: Poussielgue-Rusand, 1851); a superior facsimile was subsequently published as *Cantatorium No 359 de la Bibliothèque de Saint-Gall (IXe siècle)*, Paléographie musicale, 2nd ser. 2 (Tournai: Société de Saint-Jean L'Évangéliste, Desclée, 1924).

[11] Jacques Handschin, "St. Gallen in der mittelalterlichen Musikgeschichte," *Schweizerische Musikzeitung* 85 (1945): 244–48; see also his "Geschichte der Musik in der Schweiz bis zur Wende des Mittelalters," in *Schweizer Musikbuch* 1, ed. Willi Schuh (Zurich: Atlantis, 1939), 11–53. The most substantial modern *critique* of St. Gallen's importance is by Rombaut van Doren, *Étude sur l'influence musicale de l'abbaye de Saint-Gall, VIII. au XI. siècle* (Louvain: Librairie universitaire, 1925).

with St. Gallen manuscripts, one might imagine that the story of the Abbey's place as a musical center had been well and thoroughly told; and yet, nowhere in modern literature can one disentangle the specific situation of St. Gallen from the general picture of early medieval music, so often has the secondary literature tended to take St. Gallen as its point of departure. One need only cite the semiological neume studies. It is not that I want to move the spotlight somewhere else, but that I want to understand what is special about the musical traditions of St. Gallen, and to be able to distinguish these from other institutional patterns in the Carolingian and Ottonian periods.

"Then we, too, who until now drank from the troubled waters of the stream, must go back to the clarity of the source . . .": thus Charlemagne. As the starting point of a new evaluation of the Abbey of St. Gallen as a musical center, we need to go back to the sources. It is entirely characteristic of the late twentieth-century situation in St. Gallen that one should go looking for something, and immediately find hard rock—as in the case of Notker's copying of John the Deacon's text. While its stock of classical texts was much diminished by the raids of delighted humanists visiting the Council of Constance in the early fifteenth century, the Abbey's copies of patristic texts and liturgical books are uniquely well-preserved. Through study of the Abbey as a center in itself, and the minutiae of its musical sources—set within the larger context of contemporary St. Gallen books—we have a chance to build up a new framework of knowledge about how the monks of St. Gallen perceived and treated the Roman chant, and what significance they attributed to written sources.

In the remaining part of this study I will tell something of my own changing picture of the musical history of the Abbey of St. Gallen, based on the manuscripts in the Stiftsbibliothek. There are simply more early St. Gallen sources with musical notation than many people realize, a total of at least six dating from the late ninth and first half of the tenth century.

St. Gallen, Stiftsbibliothek Codex 342

The most substantial early source copied at St. Gallen containing musical notation—besides the famous Cantatorium—is a Gradual, Cod. 342. As such, it provides melodies for the Introit, Offertory, and Communion chants, as well as the Graduals and Alleluias found in the Cantatorium, and is thus of considerable interest.

The Gradual belongs within a composite manuscript, whose other main parts are a Kalendar and Sacramentary. The Kalendar (pp. 2–20) dates from the first part of the eleventh century (before 1034),[12] and is immediately followed by gatherings containing prayers, chants, and other liturgical material added by various late tenth- and eleventh-century hands (pp. 21–108). The Gradual (pp. 109–272) and Sacramentary (pp. 277–843) were dated by both Scherrer and the art-historian Adolf Merton to the tenth century;[13] Merton specifically associated the Gradual and Sacramentary with each other, and dated the latter as early as 920.[14] Misreading of Merton's comments led the *indexer* of his study to place the Gradual in the eleventh century;[15] and several subsequent publications, notably Bruckner's *Schreibschulen der Diözese Konstanz* (1938) and *Le Graduel Romain* (1957), have affirmed the later date.[16]

[12] P. Emmanuel Munding, *Die Kalendarien von St. Gallen* (Beuron, Hohenzollern: Beuroner Kunstverlag, 1948); Munding dates this Kalendar between 1031 and 1034 on the grounds that it includes an entry by the first hand for Aribo of Mainz (d. 6.IV.1031), but has the Remaclus feast—observed in St. Gallen after 1034—added by a later hand. In fact, the Aribo entry is *not* part of the first layer of copying of the Kalendar. Using these kind of criteria (rather than palaeographical guesses), it is hard to bring the date limits for copying this Kalendar any closer than 993 (the Kalendar includes an original entry for Udalrici, canonized 993) and 1034.

[13] Gustav Scherrer, *Verzeichniss der Handschriften der Stiftsbibliothek von St. Gallen* (Halle, 1875), 120; Adolf Merton, *Die Buchmalerei in St. Gallen vom neunten bis zum elften Jahrhundert* (Leipzig: Hiersemann, 1923), 53.

[14] Merton's commentary is mainly concerned with the decoration of initials in the Sacramentary, but those parts of his text which refer to the Gradual are without ambiguity as to his assessment of the date: "Eine ganz verspätete Arbeit karolingischen Charakters ist der Codex 342 der St. Galler Stiftsbibliothek. . . . Nach einem jüngeren Teil (Seite 1 bis 108), der unter anderem einen Kalendar des beginnenden 11. Jahrhunderts enthält . . . beginnt der ursprünglich erste Hauptteil, ein Graduale (Seite 109 bis 272) . . . . Da die Schrift relativ späten Charakter hat, gehört der Codex sicher schon tief ins 10. Jahrhundert. Die enge Verwandtschaft mit den Werken von der Jahrhundertwende ist wohl um das Jahr 920 noch denkbar" (*Die Buchmalerei in St. Gallen*, 53–54).

[15] Merton, *Die Buchmalerei in St. Gallen*, 105: "Codex 342, Graduale, saec. XI, Mitte, und Sacramentar, saec. X in St. Gallen."

[16] Albert Bruckner, *Schreibschulen der Diözese Konstanz: St. Gallen*, Scriptoria Medii Aevi Helvetica: Denkmäler Schweizerischer Schreibkunst des Mittelalters 2–3 (Geneva, 1936 and 1938), 2:98; *Le Graduel Romain: Édition critique*, 2: *Les sources* (Solesmes: Abbaye Saint-Pierre, 1957), 131 (GAL 7). The comments made in the latter appear to draw on the work of Munding, but he, albeit without exact dates for the Gradual and Sacramentary, had remarked on the fact that letter forms used in the Sacramentary were conspicuously older than those of the Kalendar, continuing "Somit ist das Kalendar etwas jünger als das Graduale und Sakramentar" (*Die Kalendarien von St. Gallen*, 13). Two other studies are concerned with more than details of drawings in the Codex: Derek H. Turner, "Sacramentaries of Saint Gall in the Tenth and Eleventh Centuries," *Revue bénédictine* 51 (1971): 186–215 (where the Gradual is linked with the Kalendar and dated in the eleventh century), and *Die Abtei St. Gallen: Ausgewählte Aufsätze in überarbeiteter Fassung von Johannes Duft*, eds. Johannes Duft, Peter Ochsenbein, and Ernst Ziegler (Sigmaringen: Jan Thorbecke, 1990), 254 (where *the whole book* is dated to the late tenth and early eleventh century).

It was probably for other reasons, however, that the editors of *Paléographie musicale* chose to publish the later Gradual, Cod. 339 (dated variously, but mainly to the early eleventh century) as an example of an *Antiphonale missarum* notated in the splendidly detailed St. Gallen neumes, rather than this. Like the Cantatorium, the first layer of Cod. 342 has no liturgy for local saints (Gall, Otmar, Wiborada), nor indeed for many others included in the eleventh-century liturgical books of St. Gallen. Further, Cod. 342 contains extensive marginalia dating from the eleventh and late twelfth centuries, rendering it much less clear to read and work with than the later manuscripts. And third, the scholars of Solesmes doubted its St. Gallen provenance, stating in *Le Graduel Romain*, "La série des versets alléluiatiques diffère de celle des autres manuscrits de Saint-Gall."[17] I will return to these points in the detailed discussion below.

Date of copying of the Gradual

My assessment of the date of copying of the Gradual is based on two categories of palaeographic evidence—characteristics of the text hand and of the decorative initials—as well as on the association between the Gradual and the Sacramentary. The Gradual was copied by one main text hand, with responsibility for the music notation shared out among several different scribes. This main hand is not as gracious and well-formed as that of the Cantatorium (which, dated on palaeographical criteria alone, belongs to the first quarter of the tenth century). Nor was the first scribe of the 342 Gradual as well-educated as most liturgical scribes of St. Gallen; here there are spelling mistakes and words omitted, frequently occasioning corrections by musical scribes and later, eleventh-century emenders. The hand is typical of St. Gallen work of the Ottonian period, showing less differentiation between the letters and a more vertical aspect than those of the late ninth century (or, in a different sense, those of the eleventh century), mixing round and straight *d*'s, and finishing descending minims (on *n, m, i*) with a short, but pronounced horizontal stroke. It has none of the wedged and squashed qualities of the eleventh-century hands (especially those of the liturgical codices, as, for example, Hartker's).[18] Characteristics which place

[17] *Le Graduel Romain*, 131.

[18] Fine examples of such hands illustrate just what had changed in St. Gallen calligraphy over 100 years: see, for example, the reproduction of a page from Wolfenbüttel, Helmst. 1008 in Hartmut Hoffmann, *Buchkunst und Königtum im ottonischen und frühsalischen Reich* (Stuttgart: Hiersemann, 1986), vol 2, pl. 215; this was one of the several liturgical books copied for Bishop Sigebert of Minden between 1022 and 1036. Its script, which is more regular and well-formed than that of any of the liturgical books remaining in the Stiftsbibliothek, and may thus stand as a prime example for the period, has a much more square and "horizontal" appearance than the tenth-century scripts with which it could so easily be confused.

this script earlier rather than later include the use of three forms of *a:* the standard "St. Gallen" form , the open *a*,  (which appears in the Cantatorium also, but which harks back to St. Gallen scripts of the early ninth century), and a frequently misformed *a*,  (almost like an insular majuscule). The hand of the Sacramentary,[19] while easily confused with the heavier high grade St. Gallen script of the second half of the tenth century, still retains the variation of stroke directions and rounder quality of earlier St. Gallen work, showing its high grade not only through elegance, but through a general absence of ligatures, in particular the ubiquitous *rt* ligature.[20] All that stands between this hand and that of the Folchart Psalter (copied in the last quarter of the ninth century), for example, is the effort (not always successful) to stop the descending *r* and *s* strokes from going below the horizontal base line, and the squareness of the little finishing strokes on descending minims.[21]

As with the discussion of text hands, any attempt to date decorative work immediately encounters an extreme stability of practice. Some general trends are nevertheless discernible. The most significant decorated initials in the Gradual are those for the beginning (*Ad te levavi*, p. 109), for the third Christmas mass (*Puer natus est*, p. 120, see plate 2) and for Easter (*Resurrexi*, p. 192). None are more than simple, but large and decorative inked capitals. Besides the formal similarity between these initials and securely dated earlier work, they clearly do not share with the late tenth- and eleventh-century decorative work a tendency to fill up every available inner space with weaving interlace, as in the Kalendar of Cod. 342, which must, on the grounds of internal evidence, be dated in the first third of the eleventh century.[22] This same interest in knotting and weaving patterns, which often fill the entire available space, is apparent in the large decorated

[19] For reproductions of this see Merton, *Die Buchmalerei in St. Gallen*, pls. XLVII–XLVIII; Bruckner, *Schreibschulen der Diözese Konstanz* vol 2, pl. XLVI; and, most recently, Duft, *Die Abtei St. Gallen*, pls. 18 and 19.

[20] For examples of St. Gallen script "on either side" of that of the Sacramentary, pl. 209 and 195 in Hoffmann, *Buchkunst und Königtum* 2, suffice. Pl. 209 (Stuttgart, Landesbibliothek HB VII 57, fol. 1) shows a very late example of the most characteristic late carolingian "Grimald" hand: since this is the hand of Notker Balbulus, it can be dated before 909, but the evident shakiness of the writer's hand, as well as the link with younger types of script in the same manuscript, suggest that this was written close to 909. Pl. 195 (London, British Library Add. 21170, fol. 2), dating from the second half of the tenth century, shows the same types of strokes as those of the Sacramentary, but now making a more solid impression.

[21] St. Gallen, Stiftsbibliothek 23; for reproductions and commentary see Peter Ochsenbein and Beat von Scarpatetti, *Der Folchart-Psalter aus der Stiftsbibliothek St. Gallen* (Freiburg-im-Breisgau: Herder, 1987).

[22] See n. 12 above.

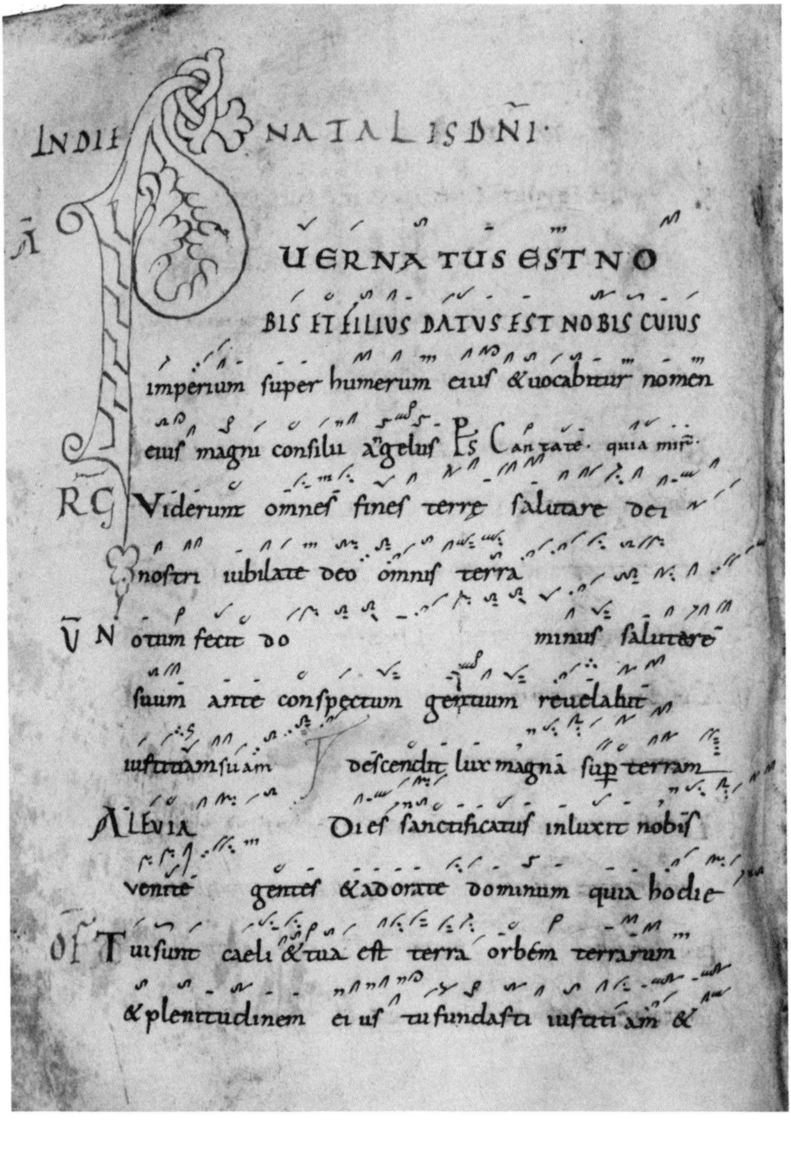

Plate 2: Stiftsbibliothek St. Gallen, Codex sang. 342, p. 120. Reproduced by permission.

initials in Hartker's Antiphoner and the Gradual, Cod. 339. The cleaner, more foliage-dominated lines of the initials in Cod. 342 correspond to those of the Cantatorium and many other late ninth- and early tenth-century sources. Lastly, the decorative initials in the Sacramentary, although painted in silver and gold, show the same degree of mediation between interlace and foliage, and in many cases use the same basic outlines as those in the Gradual.

Although palaeographical study can never provide exact information about dates, it is certainly beyond dispute that the two main parts of Cod. 342, the Gradual and Sacramentary, were copied in the tenth century. Moreover, they are more closely tied to examples of late ninth- and early tenth-century work, than to anything of ca. 1000.[23]

The liturgy of the Gradual

As noted above, the writers of *Le Graduel Romain* voiced doubts about the St. Gallen origin of Cod. 342, on the grounds that it did not contain, except as marginal additions, feasts for St. Gallen, and that the Alleluia series did not concord with that in other St. Gallen sources. The first objection can be dismissed, once the date of copying is rectified: had Cod. 342 been copied in the eleventh century, it would indeed have been odd that no St. Gallen saints were included in the first layer. But it is a much earlier manuscript, and includes *exactly* the same festal series as the Cantatorium. This more or less "pure Roman" series of feasts included none of the local, Irish, Saxon, and other saints whose feasts amplified the later liturgical books of St. Gallen. And, when the marginal material—most of it added by one hand in the late tenth or early eleventh century—is collated with the later Graduals, Cod. 339 and 376, it becomes clear that the marginal incipit lists (usually including Introit, Epistle, Gradual, Gospel, Offertory, and Communion) bring Cod. 342 directly into line with the later manuscripts by supplying all that was missing from the earlier liturgical books of St. Gallen.

The story of the Alleluia verse series leads to a similar conclusion, in that it illustrates a process of liturgical change, the development from a received Roman-Frankish liturgy to a St. Gallen "house version" during the tenth century. First, some indication of stability comes from the Alleluia verses for the week following Easter; the Cantatorium, Cod. 342, and the eleventh-

[23] While hands and writing styles of the ninth century may be linked with dated extant charters of the monastery (now preserved in the Stiftsarchiv), so few examples of tenth-century charters of St. Gallen survive that it is difficult to use them as more than a general guide to changing script practices, let alone achieve any degree of certainty concerning dates.

century Graduals (of which Cod. 339 and 376 may be taken as representative) all have the same list:

Pascha	Alleluia V. Pascha nostrum
Feria II	V. Surrexit dominus vere
Feria III	V. Obtulerunt discipuli
Feria IV	V. Surrexit altissimus
Feria V	V. Cantate domino
Feria VI	V. Eduxit dominus
Sabbato	V. Laudate pueri
Dom. I post Pascha	V. Pascha nostrum

In the series of post-Pentecost Alleluias, however, there are some differences not only between Cod. 342 and the other St. Gallen sources, but also between the Cantatorium and the eleventh-century Graduals.[24] The three series of Alleluia verses are as follows:

Codex 359	*Codex 342*	*Codices 339 and 376*
	1 Verba mea	1 Verba mea
1 Deus iudex	2 Deus iudex	3 Deus iudex
2 Diligam te	3 Diligam te	4 Diligam te
	4 Domine deus meus	2 Domine deus meus
3 In te domine speravi	5 In te domine speravi	5 In te domine speravi
4 Omnes gentes	6 Omnes gentes	6 Omnes gentes
etc. (from this point in agreement)		

All three series are of the type which follows the numerical order of psalms; although the series in Cod. 359 matches a standard well-known model, neither of the other two appear to.[25] Crucially, the 359 series is *not* retained in the later books. Since the set of Alleluias copied in Cod. 342 matches that in Cod. 339 and 376, with a small adjustment to the order of the first four pieces (*Domine deus meus* being moved forwards in the later series), it seems a relatively small step to see the 342 series as an expansion of that in 359, and the later series as a rearranged version of the second list. In fact, a series of Hebrew numerals in the margin of Cod. 342, p. 257—beside the

[24] On the post-Pentecost Alleluia lists see Michel Huglo, "Les listes alléluiatiques dans les témoins du Graduel Grégorien," in *Speculum Musicae Artis: Festgabe für Heinrich Husmann zum 60. Geburtstag*, eds. Heinz Becker and Reinhard Gerlach (Munich: Fink, 1970), 219–27; the difference between various St. Gallen lists is here mentioned in passing (225).

[25] Several possibilities are tabulated in Huglo, *Les livres de chant liturgique*, Typologie des sources du moyen âge occidental 52 (Turnhout: Brepols, 1988), 105.

first four Alleluias—reads 1 (*Verba mea*), 3 (*Deus iudex*), 4 (*Diligam te*), 2 (*Dominus deus meus*), suggesting exactly the rearrangement found in 339 and 376. Unfortunately, the annotating hand cannot easily be dated!

There are many interesting examples of alterations to an older liturgical practice evident in the emendations and marginalia of Cod. 342; it is a source which would richly repay detailed study. I will mention just two cases here. The Trinity Gradual *Benedictus es domine* has the verse *Benedicite deum caeli* in both the Cantatorium and the main text of 342 (as well as in west Frankish books). The later St. Gallen Graduals follow an east Frankish tradition in using the verse *Benedictus es in throno;* and, in the appropriate place in the margin of the tenth-century Gradual (342, p. 241), the main eleventh-century emending hand has added the verse *Benedictus es in throno*—with the rubric *Aliter* (plate 3).

On p. 133 this same marginal hand has appended a list of proper items for the feast *In cathedra sancti Petri* (18 January). By the time of the transfer of Roman liturgy north in the eighth century, this old Roman feast had disappeared from Roman use—hence its absence from Cod. 359 and from the main corpus of Cod. 342. But it had remained in the Gallican liturgy, and its inclusion by the marginal hand indicates a process of re-integration of Gallican material into a liturgy entirely based on a Roman model.

The musical notation of Cod. 342

With this new understanding of the complexities of Cod. 342, the seeming contradiction between palaeographical evidence of origin and the liturgical content disappears. A context for the production of the book has thus been provided. This is especially significant since the Gradual reveals a practice of music copying which has not, to my knowledge, been observed in any other music book of the early Middle Ages. The musical notation of the first layer was accomplished by five different scribes, each working through whole gatherings, as follows:

Gathering		*Notator*
pp. 109–26	I	A
pp. 127–46	II	B
pp. 147–66	III	C
pp. 167–82	IV	B
pp. 183–202	V	D
pp. 203–22, 223–42	VI + VII	B
pp. 243–62	VIII	E
pp. 263–72	IX	All by later scribes

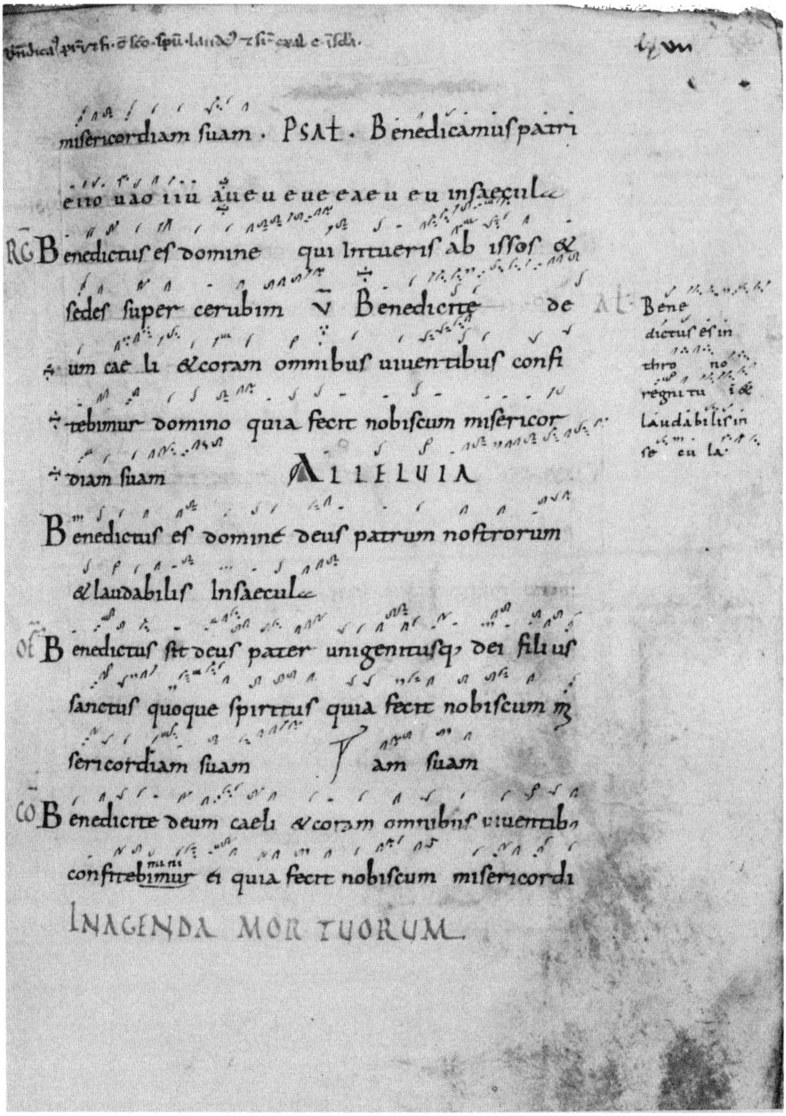

Plate 3: Stiftsbibliothek St. Gallen, Codex sang. 342, p. 241. Reproduced by permission.

The handover from one music scribe to another takes place exactly at the break from one gathering to another, often right in the middle of a chant.[26] Even more striking than the way in which gatherings were simply given out to different scribes, however, is the realization that, at the time when this Gradual was copied, the monastery at St. Gallen could boast a minimum of five music scribes, all competent to notate the complex chants of the mass.

The similarities and differences between the notating hands—which are really quite distinct—raise questions about the copying process. All five scribes are able to use the whole range of neumes found in the Cantatorium; while differentiation between the hands depends on observation of all the signs used, it is principally through their ways of writing the *oriscus*, *quilisma*, and *pes quassus*, as well as the axes of script that each can be distinguished. Each has idiosyncrasies: B, for example, consistently writes the *trigon* upside down '.' , rather than the more usual .'. . But the most marked differences in the work of these five scribes are to do with the use or not of episemas and *litterae significativae.* Where scribe C uses letters consistently and abundantly (even some of the rarest, such as *f*), scribes A, B, and D use none at all (and E a few). Only scribes C and D use episemas regularly; they appear with some frequency in E's work, but only very rarely in portions copied by A and B. What this variance might indicate about the exemplar(s) available to these scribes, and about scribal freedom and competence, belongs to future speculation and intensive study of the notation. At the very least, it is clear that the more musically trained the scribe, the more likely he was to notate a specific reading of each chant.

The later history of Codex 342

The Gradual, which appears to have been associated with the attached Sacramentary from the beginning, continued to be actively used over the next two hundred years; the process of "updating" continued into the twelfth and thirteenth centuries. But the most important phase of expansion of both Gradual and Sacramentary belongs to the end of the tenth and early eleventh century. An intensive project to bring the basic Roman-

[26] Such a division of copying tasks is, of course, entirely familiar in text copying. Similar procedures have been recognized in a fourteenth-century music book compiled at the monastery of Engelberg: see Wulf Arlt, "Repertoirefragen 'peripherer' Mehrstimmigkeit: Das Beispiel des Codex Engelberg 314," in *Trasmissione e recezione delle forme di cultura musicale: Atti del XIV Congresso della Società Internazionale di Musicologia, Bologna 1987*, 1: *Round Tables*, eds. Angelo Pompilio, D. Restani, Lorenzo Bianconi, and F. Alberto Gallo, 2: *Costituzione e conservazione dei repertorii polifonici nei secoli XIV e XV* (Torino: EDT, 1990), 97–123, and *Engelberg Stiftsbibliothek Codex 314*, facs., ed., and commentary by Wulf Arlt and Matthias Stauffacher (Winterthur: Amadeus, 1986), 25–27 and passim.

Frankish liturgical framework of the Gradual into line with a more developed local liturgical practice involved the addition of a host of saints' feasts, as well as the supplementing, clarification, and alteration of the main corpus. Eventually, with a final phase of expansion of the Sacramentary, the Kalendar was added. In this as in other things, Cod. 342 stands at a point of changeover in the process of book-copying, from a standardized Roman-Frankish liturgy to a more specific version, tailored to the needs and traditions of the local community. Nevertheless, the larger part of the mass chant repertory was notated earlier than the more well-known Cod. 339; Cod. 342 *is* the earliest extant St. Gallen Gradual. And, because of its easily-observable layers, it offers a special chance for the study of changes and developments in liturgical practice during the Ottonian period.

St. Gallen, Stiftsbibliothek Codex 18, pp. 21–40

A third substantial early source notated at St. Gallen appears not to have been noticed by musicologists until now: it is a collection of processional antiphons and hymns in one gathering—a typical *libellus*—now pp. 21–40 of a composite manuscript, catalogued as Codex 18 in the Stiftsbibliothek.[27] The Stiftsbibliothek catalogue of 1875 describes the contents of pp. 21–40 as "Antiphonen mit Neumen; und einige Hymnen von Theodulph und Ven. Fortunatus."[28] Of course, the hymns referred to are *Gloria laus* (sung on Palm Sunday) and *Crux fidelis* for the Adoration of the Cross (sung on Good Friday). There has never been any doubt expressed about the date of copying of these pages: both Scherrer and Bruckner placed them in the tenth century without demur, Bruckner describing the hand as "very fine and beautiful."[29] One hand copied the text and neumes throughout the whole (excepting nine lines added on pp. 39–40 by a twelfth-century hand). Although an entirely different hand from that of Cod. 342, this shares many characteristics with the main text hand of the Gradual, and with the notation of the Gradual's first music scribe (A). Thus, the processional *libellus* may also be placed in the early to middle years of the tenth century.

[27] I intend shortly to publish a report on this source, with detailed analysis of the repertory of processional pieces.

[28] Scherrer, *Verzeichniss*, 6.

[29] A. Bruckner, *Schreibschulen der Diözese Konstanz* 2:57: "von sehr feiner, schöner Hand, 10. Jh."

Both codicologically and in terms of content, the collection is complete in itself: within one gathering are copied antiphons and hymns for the major processions of the Temporale, Sanctorale, and Common, under the following rubrics:

[For the Major Litany (25.IV), rogations, Sanctorale, and Common]

Page	*Rubric*
21–24	[Antiphonae in laetania maiore]
24–25	Antiphonae ad pluviam postulandum
25	Ad serenitatem
25	Ad mortalitatem
25–26	De poenitentia
26	In natalitiis sanctorum
26–27	Ad reliquias ducendas
27–28	Antiphonae de quacumque tribulationem
28	De uno confessore

[Communion antiphons]

Page	*Rubric*
28–29	Ad communicandum in natale domini
29	Item ad communicandum [in pascha]

[Sanctorale]

Page	*Rubric*
29–30	Antiphona quando volueris
30	De sancta Maria
30–31	De sancto Petro
31	De sanctis apostolis
31	De sancto Gallo

[Easter procession]

Page	*Rubric*
31–32	In dominica sancta paschali ad processionem
32–33	De dominica resurrectione

[Palm Sunday procession]

Page	*Rubric*
33	Versos Thiotolfi presbiteri in palmis

[Maundy Thursday]

Page	*Rubric*
33–35	Antiphonae ad mandatum in cena domini

[Palm Sunday procession]

Page	*Rubric*
35–37	Antiphonae in palmis

[Good Friday, Adoration of the Cross]

Page	*Rubric*
37	Ad salutandum crucem
37–39	Versos Furtunati [sic] presbiteri
39–40	[Improperia, added in s. xii]

Although the phenomemon of a separate book of processional chants did not emerge until the end of the eleventh/early twelfth century,[30] the bringing together of this type of material in a discrete part of the Gradual (usually at the end) may already be observed in ninth-century books: the Compiègne Mass and Office Antiphoner (Paris, Bibliothèque Nationale lat. 17436) and another book of the same type from Albi (Albi, Bibliothèque municipale 44), both copied in the late ninth century, are the most obvious early examples.[31] But the actual content of such collections is variable, in terms of both feasts entered and the actual items included. In this sense, the St. Gallen *libellus* is the earliest example of a specific east-Frankish pattern and repertory, its selection of pieces and occasions conforming closely to those brought together at the end of two Graduals from the Benedictine monasteries of Einsiedeln (Einsiedeln, Stiftsbibliothek 121, copied in the second half of the tenth century) and St. Emmeram of Regensburg (Bamberg, Staatsbibliothek lit. 6: copied ca. 1000).[32] And the ten-folio *libellus* has the standard medium format of graduals copied at St. Gallen over a period of two hundred years; it could easily have been intended as a supplement to such a book.

Notwithstanding this possibility, one aspect of the St. Gallen *libellus* suggests a lack of fixed procedure in the copying process. For the jumbled order of the pieces is somewhat surprising; all of the material relating to Easter feasts, for example, is mixed up:

Easter Sunday procession
Palm Sunday procession (*Gloria laus*)
Holy Thursday *Mandatum* antiphons
Palm Sunday procession (antiphons)
Good Friday (*Ad salutandem crucem*)

[30] Pierre-Marie Gy, "Collectaire, Rituel, Processionnal," *Revue des sciences philosophiques et théologiques* 44 (1960): 441–69 (esp. 467), and Huglo, *Les livres de chant liturgique*, 10.

[31] The Compiègne Antiphoner is edited in *Antiphonale missarum sextuplex*, ed. René-Jean Hesbert (Rome: Herder, 1935) as C; for details of the Albi manuscript I am indebted to John Emerson, who will shortly publish an edition.

[32] *Le Codex 121 de la Bibliothèque d'Einsiedeln*, facs. ed., Paléographie musicale 4 (Solesmes: Abbaye Saint-Pierre, 1894; repr. Bern: Herbert Lang, 1974); facs. ed., *Die Handschrift BAMBERG Staatsbibliothek Lit.6*, Monumenta Palaeographica Gregoriana 2 (Münsterschwarzach: Studien des Gregorianischen Chorals, 1988).

The *libellus* may thus represent some sort of experimental copy, the attempt to bring together, in a clearly laid-out form, a full collection of processional pieces. Unlike the later Einsiedeln and Regensburg books, the practice of copying this material together was *not* followed in later St. Gallen books, which instead follow the older models, collecting the major litany and votive antiphons after an Alleluia fascicle, but placing the Palm Sunday, Good Friday, and Easter Sunday processional chants with the rest of the proper for those feasts.

One other detail of the content of this *libellus* intensifies one's sense that it might not represent internal practice at St. Gallen: this is its inclusion of the fraction antiphon *Emitte spiritum* (for Christmas), commonly found in west Frankish and Italian books, but, outside of Cod. 18, entirely absent from St. Gallen books. Where the Easter equivalent, *Venite populi*, is regularly copied after the Easter propers, *Emitte spiritum* never accompanies the Christmas propers. Against this foreign element, however, must be balanced the inclusion of an antiphon *De sancto Gallo*, "Suffragante domino beato Gallo."

What the processional *libellus* actually represents as liturgical practice thus remains a puzzle: and yet, this in itself is extremely interesting, since once again it reveals a situation of some fluidity concerning the liturgy of the monastery, and the way it was written in books. Here, it is important to distinguish between what the monks *actually* performed in their liturgy, and the content of their books. It is far from clear that these two matched before the eleventh century.

Codification of the Repertories of Tropes and Sequences

Moving over from the Roman-Frankish chant to the new repertories of trope and sequence, St. Gallen again occupies a prominent place in any catalogue of early sources. For the sequence, it can boast two of the earliest extant: Paris, Bibliothèque Nationale lat. 10587, a fragment of Notker's *Liber Ymnorum*, and St. Gallen, Kantonsbibliothek Vadianische Sammlung 317, fols. 13^{v}–15^{v}, where a group of six Notker sequences are copied, with some musical notation.[33] The Parisian source was only recently recognized

[33] A detailed study of both sources is made in Susan Rankin, "The Earliest Sources of Notker's Sequences: St. Gallen, Vadiana 317, and Paris, Bibliothèque Nationale lat. 10587," *Early Music History* 10 (1991): 201–33.

by a German paleographer as wrongly dated in the standard literature.[34] His arguments imply that this may be the earliest extant example of St. Gallen notation. The fragment consists of eight folios, containing the prefatory material and all or parts of four sequences (*Natus ante saecula, Hanc concordi, Laus tibi christe qui humilis, Festa christi*) from Notker's *Liber Ymnorum*. These pages belonged to a high quality book, written on fine, smooth parchment by an excellent hand.

Three facts about this source are of significance in the present discussion. First, although a small fragment, it appears to represent a discrete copy of the *Liber Ymnorum*, thus showing the format of the model from which later east-Frankish sequence sources took their cue. Second, it has the special two-column ruling—wide for text, and thinner for music—used in east-Frankish sequence collections, implying that this type of presentation *allowing for music notation* goes right back to the beginnings of the writing down of sequences at St. Gallen. Third, its melodic readings, down to the precise details of neumation, are identical with those of the eleventh-century St. Gallen sources, implying that the written transmission of sequences was closed, that is, it did not allow of variation introduced from practice (apart from the addition of episemas and *litterae significativae*). The dedication copy of Notker's *Liber Ymnorum* was prepared in 884; but Notker speaks in his preface of discussions with his teachers Iso and Marcellus (Moengal), both of whom died in 871. The use of musical notation at St. Gallen may hypothetically be traced back to this point.

The other early sequence source, now in the Vadiana collection, is perhaps less interesting in itself, except as an illustration of another type of transmission in St. Gallen. On some pages of a composite codex, a hand of the early tenth century copied six of Notker's sequences. Musical notation was added in the margins for part of one only—and then by a hand unused to copying neumes. This tiny collection includes sequences for Epiphany, Ascension, SS. Laurence, Gall, and Otmar, and for a martyr. Although musical notation can hardly be described as a major feature of this source, its fitful appearance, copied by an unpracticed hand, underlines the implications of the Paris fragment, that is, that at St. Gallen, music was recognized as an integral part of the written transmission of sequences from the beginning on.

Given what we now know of Notker's involvement with the copying of books, it is no surprise to discover such a stable form of written transmission—later adopted in its format, contents, and details by the whole east-Frankish realm. It was one of Notker's many interests/duties to plan and

[34] Hoffmann, *Buchkunst und Königtum* 1:390 and 2: pl. 202.

oversee the work of other scribes,[35] and he himself may have been responsible for conceiving the small-format, double-column layout of sequence collections.

Not so the tropes, however. It was to be another hundred years before these achieved an equal degree of stability of transmission. There are three separate trope collections of the tenth century associated with St. Gallen, two actually copied at (and presumably for) the monastery itself, and a third—the earliest—with very strong connections to the monastery, on grounds of repertory, context, and provenance. The trope collection in Vienna, Nationalbibliothek 1609 constitutes, in fact, the earliest east-Frankish example extant. It was probably copied at Freising in the very early years of the tenth century, but may stem directly from a St. Gallen exemplar.[36] It contains a concise repertory of 100 or so trope elements, and has all the appearance of a specially-compiled repertory, sufficient for the main *temporale* feasts of the liturgical year. It could be argued that its total lack of tropes for saints' feasts is the result of the gathering's loss of at least two folios; but, since saints' tropes were often integrated into the *temporale* cycle in St. Gallen books, it seems more likely that no tropes for saints' feasts were ever included.

All of the tropes copied here reappear in two mid-tenth-century St. Gallen tropers, Stiftsbibliothek 484 and 381. But the contrast between the earlier and later trope collections could not be more extreme. Where the Vienna collection is self-contained, stylistically limited, and copied in a non-liturgical context, Cod. 484 and 381 may have as many as thirty sets of tropes for a specific Introit, mixing many diverse types of trope; and both Cod. 484 and 381 are, as complete books, specific to their purpose of recording repertories of new liturgical compositions. Almost the tiniest liturgical book I have ever seen, Cod. 484 shows one fastidious monk at work, collecting as many tropes as he can, but evidently from a variety of exemplars.[37] He simply did not know at the beginning what the total size and subdivisions of his eventual collection would be, and ended up with the oddest, most irregular gatherings anyone could imagine. But he seems in Cod. 484 to have accomplished his object of bringing order to a large and

[35] On this see Rankin, "Ego itaque Notker scripsi," passim.

[36] An inventory of the trope repertory appears in Susan Rankin, "Notker und Tuotilo: Schöpferische Gestalter in einer neuen Zeit," *Schweizer Jahrbuch für Musikwissenschaft* 11 (1991): 17–42; on the origin of the manuscript see also Hermann Menhardt, "Die Überlieferung des althochdeutschen 138. Psalms," *Zeitschrift für deutsches Altertum und deutsche Literatur* 77 (1940): 76–84, and Natalia Daniel, *Handschriften des zehnten Jahrhunderts aus der Freisinger Dombibliothek,* Münchener Beiträge zur Mediävistik und Renaissance-Forschung 11 (Munich: Arbeo, 1973), 70–72.

[37] Such small books are common in the later Middle Ages; this was, for example, a popular format for the book of hours. But the size is certainly unusual for the Carolingian and Ottonian periods, even for a troper.

varied trope collection, for he then proceeded to copy the whole lot out again, in a larger higher quality format, with regular gatherings—this survives as Cod. 381. And here he brought together with the trope repertory a collection of *versus*, a whole year's repertory of Introit and Communion verses, a collection of sequences, and various other bits and pieces. In more than one sense, Cod. 484 and 381 make visible a process of gathering and sorting of liturgical compositions, the results of their compilation evident in the more streamlined eleventh-century trope collections of St. Gallen, which contain very little not already present in the tenth-century books.[38]

Certainly, other tenth-century tropers exhibit in their repertories (and, sometimes, in their codicological presentation also) "collecting" aspects: London, British Library 19768 from Mainz and Paris, Bibliothèque Nationale lat. 1240 from St. Martial-de-Limoges are two obvious examples. In this sense the selected, concise nature of the collection in Vienna 1609 sets it apart. Given its undeniable connection to Notker, *and* its lack of any trope attributed to Tuotilo, I am inclined to see the Vienna repertory as representing a special Notker "project." The implication of this hypothesis is that, in the early years of the tenth century, the whole repertory of St. Gallen tropes was *not* assembled in any one book. Only in the middle of the century was this exercise undertaken.

The process of exploration and integration of material into written sources is thus evident not only in the main chant sources, but in the tropers also. The two books Cod. 484 and 381 tell eloquently of the problems encountered by an enthusiastic trope hoarder, who tried to bring order to his material; and the adventures of that most famous liturgical *arriviste*, *Quem quaeritis*, in the St. Gallen sources illustrate the consequences of the monks' determination to fashion their liturgy in their own way. Of course, *Quem quaeritis* is not in the processional *libellus* in Cod. 18. It appears to have come to St. Gallen in a wave of trope transmission, and was copied as such in Cod. 484 and 381. By the time Hartker copied his Antiphoner (ca. 1000), *Quem quaeritis* had been put into the Easter morning procession, and there it stayed in the later books.

Setting the seven ninth- and tenth-century liturgical books of St. Gallen (Paris 10587, Vadiana 317, Stiftsbibliothek 359, 342, 18, 484, and 381) against those copied at the end of the tenth and the beginning of the eleventh centuries (beginning with Hartker's Antiphoner, through Stiftsbibliothek 339,

[38] On the physical structure and repertory of these two manuscripts see Susan Rankin, "From Tuotilo to the first manuscripts: the shaping of a trope repertory at St. Gall," in *Recherches nouvelles sur les tropes liturgiques*, eds. Wulf Arlt and Gunilla Björkvall (Stockholm: Almqvist & Wiksell, 1993), and *St. Gallen, Stiftsbibliothek Codices 484 and 381*, facs. ed. with commentary by Wulf Arlt and Susan Rankin (Winterthur: Amadeus, forthcoming).

376, and several other mass and office books), we can perceive the major liturgical task of the tenth century as the cultivation and secure recording in script of a "home" liturgy, with all its Roman and Frankish, old and new, foreign and native, dimensions. The end result of that process was the ability and inclination to produce liturgical books in large numbers, occasionally of an astonishingly high grade. The summit of St. Gallen production of liturgical books was reached in those prepared for Bishop Sigebert of Minden between 1022 and 1036.

Musical Notation in Non-Liturgical Sources

Mention of two other sources completes the story of musical notation at St. Gallen in the late Carolingian period. The more significant of these sources is a miscellany, Naples, Biblioteca nazionale IV.G.68, compiled in St. Gallen towards the end of the ninth century. Containing Boethius's *Consolatio*, Prudentius's *Psychomachia*, and part of Martianus Capella's *De nuptiis philologiae*, it also has the texts of fourteen hymns and *versus*, nine with musical notation.[39] These were added on empty pages by various scribes, from the late ninth century until well into the tenth.[40] The newest Carolingian verse (*Gratuletur omnis caro / nato christo domino*) is here mixed with hymns by classical authors (Prudentius's *O triplex honor*). There is an earlier transmission of some of the same pieces, without notation, in a St. Gallen manuscript of ca. 800 (Leiden, Bibliotheek der Rijksuniversiteit, Vos. lat. 69). An outstanding characteristic of the Naples notations is a concern with heighting techniques. Not only are significative letters used in abundance, but the open space above the written text is well exploited as representative of a spectrum of pitches.

[39] The main descriptions and discussions of this source dealing with the hymns and *versus* are Claudio Leonardi, "I codici di Marziano Capella," *Aevum* 34 (1960): 412–14; Dieter Schaller, "Frühmittelalterliche lateinische Dichtung in einer ehemals St. Galler Handschrift," *Zeitschrift für deutsches Altertum* 93 (1964/65): 272–91, and Ewald Jammers, "Rhythmen und Hymnen in einer St. Galler Handschrift des 9. Jahrhunderts," in *Festschrift Bruno Stäblein zum 70. Geburtstag*, ed. Martin Ruhnke (Kassel: Bärenreiter, 1967), 134–42; this last includes reproductions of all *versus* with music notation.

[40] In *Buchkunst und Königtum* (1:402), Hoffmann raises doubts about the origin and subsequent fate of the manuscript; undoubtedly, the whole source merits a careful palaeographical study. On the evidence currently available to me, I have to disagree with his proposal that it is not from St. Gallen. As far as can be judged from extant sources, several of the Latin *versus* stem from pure St. Gallen traditions (see Schaller, "Frühmittelalterliche lateinische Dichtung"); further, two late medieval entries of the note "Liber Sancti Galli" imply that the Codex had remained at the monastery throughout the medieval period.

Despite the sketchiness of these remarks, the Naples source deserved inclusion in this outline discussion because of the way in which it broadens the whole picture of musical literacy at St. Gallen in the late ninth and early tenth centuries. From an earlier period, there is only one example of musical notation in the Stiftsbibliothek: this appears in Cod. 397, the *vademecum* of Grimald, Archchaplain to Louis the German and Abbot of St. Gallen, 841–72.[41] The book contains shorter and longer entries made by as many as forty different hands, the last datable entry from 867, three years before Grimald's departure from court. Musical notation for the beginning of *Vere quia dignum* on p. 30 of this book is unlikely to have had anything to do with St. Gallen. But the book came to St. Gallen *with* Grimald, who died there in 872.

This is precisely the point to which my story of the earliest notated sources of St. Gallen had led back—on the supposition that Notker's early attempts at writing down sequences resembled those of ca. 900. From this point on, we witness an explosion of interest in musical notation, moreover, notation of a uniquely precise nature. Right across the spectrum of texts associated with music, sung in the liturgy and in school, notation appears. On the basis of sources which can be seen and touched, it can be deduced that the consistent and competent integration of musical notation into writing techniques at St. Gallen dates from the last quarter of the ninth century.

My story finishes with a moral, its subject the dedicatee of this book, David Hughes. I first encountered him in the Stiftsbibliothek at St. Gallen—surrounded by every available Gradual—painstakingly copying version after version of a melody, checking a word here and a neume there; and this reminded me of nothing so much as one of Ekkehard IV's anecdotes, which tells how Notker, Tuotilo, and Ratpert had obtained the permission of the abbot to spend the hour between the night offices in the library, collating texts. I believe that that kind of critical work, comparing and evaluating written texts, going back to read the sources, has never lost its value or interest.

[41] For a detailed study of the manuscript see Bernhard Bischoff, "Bücher am Hofe Ludwigs des Deutschen und die Privatbibliothek des Kanzlers Grimalt," in his *Mittelalterliche Studien* 3 (Stuttgart: Hiersemann, 1981), 187–212, esp. 201ff. The page with musical notation is reproduced and discussed by Handschin, "St. Gallen in der mittelalterlichen Musikgeschichte."

FRITZ RECKOW

Guido's Theory of Organum after Guido: Transmission—Adaptation—Transformation

"Est autem quaedam diaphonia grossa, ut Guidonis, et quaedam subtilis, ut Franconis et eorum qui ipsum secuti sunt in posteritatem." This assessment appears in an anonymously transmitted music treatise probably from the first half of the fourteenth century, recently ascribed to Jacques de Liège.[1] The statement is noteworthy primarily on two grounds.

First, the author not only mentions side by side two completely different conceptions of polyphony chronologically separated from one another by more than two centuries, but also compares them with one another, invoking the aesthetic categories "grossus" (rude, unformed) and "subtilis" (delicate, differentiated). This is an explicit aesthetic judgment quite unusual for the Middle Ages, one perhaps influenced by Guido's own distinction between a "modus durus" and a "modus mollis" in polyphony.[2]

[1] MS. Brussels, Bibliothèque Royale Albert Ier 10162/66, fol. 54; ed. Joseph Smits van Waesberghe, Eddie Vetter, and Erik Visser, *Jacobi Leodiensis . . . Compendium de musica*, Divitiae musicae artis, A.IX.a (Buren: Knuf, 1988), 117: III, 1, 8.

[2] Cf. *Guidonis Aretini Micrologus*, ed. Joseph Smits van Waesberghe, Corpus Scriptorum de Musica 4 (Rome: American Institute of Musicology, 1955), 201: XVIII, 15. Citations from this edition, here and elsewhere in this essay, are reproduced by permission of American Institute of Musicology/Hänssler-Verlag. The *Compendium* continues with information on concrete details of musical technique (including their aesthetic evaluation): "Est autem Franconis et

Second, however, the author's statement is remarkable because he speaks in the present tense: the traditional polyphony *à la* Guido is apparently still so familiar and current in the fourteenth century that it stands up to comparison with the far more elaborate polyphony of Franco's time and after. This view of things corresponds to that of Jacques de Liège who, in his *Speculum musicae*, argues for a polyphony based principally on consonances. Jacques calls to witness the traditional parallel organum of the early and high Middle Ages with the *vox organalis* doubled at the octave, just as it may be found in Guido—characterized as "modus durus"; and this type of polyphony is not, as one might expect, described as old-fashioned or forgotten, but rather—as one common type among others—as "multum simplex."[3]

Another example: the manuscript Bruges, Stadsbibliotheek 528, written in the first half of the fourteenth century, transmits the *Musica mensurabilis* of Johannes de Garlandia as a "core text," surrounded by extensive marginalia in the scholastic manner.[4] It is not so remarkable that this basic formulation of a new conception of polyphony—polyphony now as a rhythmically measurable "musica mensurabilis"—receives commentary; this had been the case even earlier, with Guido's *Micrologus*, for example.[5] But it is remarkable that here passages from Guido's organum theory and from the Milan organum treatise (the definitions of *diaphonia* and *organum*, for a start) are

sequentium, quando scilicet cavetur discordia notabilis vel soni inutilis identitas seu nugatio, puta continuando plures octavas, duas vel tres quintas, vel illas quas bonas, meliores, optimas supra retulimus, vel quas malas, peiores, pessimas descripsimus. In Guidonica [i.e., diaphonia] vero non hoc omnino cavetur" (117: III, 1, 9–10).

[3] *Speculum musicae*, ed. Roger Bragard, Corpus Scriptorum de Musica 3 (Rome: American Institute of Musicology, 1973), 7:12 (VII, 5, 6–7): "In tacto exemplo diapason continetur inter extremas voces, scilicet inter altissimas et gravissimas, diapente inter supremas et medias, diatessaron inter medias et inferiores. . . . Tactus modus discantandi multum simplex est, cum eundem cantum sub et supra similiter et in medio contineat, et vox sola contra vocem solam decantatur."

That criteria such as becoming old-fashioned or decaying were also recognized in the Middle Ages is shown for example by Aribo in his critical remarks about the supposed (earlier) tendency both to compose and to perform music "proportionaliter" as much as possible. This idea is now not only dead but actually buried: "Quae consideratio iam dudum obiit, immo sepulta est." Cf. *De musica*, ed. Joseph Smits van Waesberghe, Corpus Scriptorum de Musica 2 (Rome: American Institute of Musicology, 1951), 49.

[4] Descriptions of the manuscript in Hans Heinrich Eggebrecht and Frieder Zaminer, *Ad organum faciendum: Lehrschriften der Mehrstimmigkeit in nachguidonischer Zeit*, Neue Studien zur Musikwissenschaft 3 (Mainz: Schott, 1970), 33–37, and Erich Reimer, *Johannes de Garlandia: De mensurabili musica* 1: *Quellenuntersuchungen und Edition*, Beihefte zum Archiv für Musikwissenschaft 10 (Wiesbaden: Steiner, 1972), 19–24; facs. of fol. 54^{v} in Eggebrecht/Zaminer, pl. 17.

[5] Cf. *Expositiones in Micrologum Guidonis Aretini*, ed. Joseph Smits van Waesberghe, Musicologica medii aevi 1 (Amsterdam: North-Holland, 1957).

cited as supplementary material of clearly topical interest and placed beside the more modern concepts of Garlandia. Like Hieronymus de Moravia in his compilation from the late thirteenth century—in which Garlandia's *Musica mensurabilis* also appears—the redactor of this annotated version of Garlandia seems to have proceeded on the principle that "una positio declarat aliam" and "una [i.e., positio] super aliam in aliquibus addit scientiam"—that each treatise explains and can to some extent supplement or enrich the others.[6] What we have before us is a simultaneous presentation of important statements about polyphony from across a period of more than two hundred years, assembled and brought into visual relation with one another as much as three hundred years after the appearance of Guido's *Micrologus.*

For a historiography of music oriented one-sidedly according to criteria of "innovation," such "Gleichzeitigkeit des Ungleichzeitigen" ("contemporaneity of the uncontemporaneous") is a rather marginal phenomenon in history, typical of a traditionalistic—if not actually tradition-dependent—mentality, but not very illuminating for what is called the "course of history." Thus Frieder Zaminer, in his commentary on the marginalia in the Bruges manuscript, made no serious effort to find positive reasons—reasons which make sense, so to speak, in contemporary terms—for connections of this type. On the contrary, he asserts that "no concrete relation exists between the individual citations from the Milan treatise [and accordingly those from Guido's organum theory] and the main text [i.e., Garlandia's text]." Consequently he contents himself with the suggestion that the Bruges manuscript comes from "a rather peripheral region." The marginalia themselves are dismissed as relics of a time long past: "What had long since lost all authority in musical centers could still awaken some interest outside of those centers."[7]

We could, however, think less about steps and accomplishments in the course of "innovation," and more about the entire horizon of musical experience and the full range of musical interest in a given period. We could try to reconstruct what, in that period, was simultaneously known and familiar, appreciated and practiced, held worthy of acquisition and preservation—how, in short, the specific musical culture of a period was, so to speak, laid out in its entirety. Then such witnesses attain their own distinctive significance. For while it is all too easy to consider them old-fashioned, they were

[6] Hieronymus de Moravia O.P., *Tractatus de musica*, ed. Simon M. Cserba O.P., Freiburger Studien zur Musikwissenschaft, 2nd ser., 2 (Regensburg: Pustet, 1935), 189, 19–21.

[7] *Ad organum faciendum*, 182 ("Was in den musikalischen Zentren längst keine Geltung mehr besaß, konnte außerhalb dennoch die Aufmerksamkeit beanspruchen").

taken seriously by the period itself. These very witnesses have something to say about the fullness, the complexity, and also the disparity of simultaneously available possibilities. They attest to the multifarious knowledge and interests, orientations and preferences, and thereby characterize the intellectual climate of periods that experience and treasure such "Gleichzeitigkeit des Ungleichzeitigen" primarily as the differentiated riches of their own musical cultures.

When we consider the influence of Guido of Arezzo on the high and even on the late Middle Ages, we find particularly numerous points of departure from which to study more closely that intellectual climate—convictions, attitudes, and methods—and to analyze its character in the light of these diverse conceptions of polyphony.

For Guido's *Micrologus* is not only exceptionally widely disseminated, having been continuously recopied into the late Middle Ages (some eighty manuscript sources are preserved today, of which about half are from after 1200). Even more characteristic of the "active presence" of this text through the centuries is the profusion of citations and allusions in newly composed texts, and the numerous excerpts and commentaries transmitted separately; it is these above all that witness direct familiarity and direct engagement with this basic text of practically oriented music theory.

Most conclusive historically, however, are those texts of the high and late Middle Ages that begin with Guido's theories but modify them according to new ideas, altered ideals, and novel practices—whereby they *adapt* Guido's formulations to altered circumstances, even *transform* his theories outright. For on the one hand these texts manifest vividly the character, the direction, and the causes of changes (as deliberate modifications of the given text), and on the other hand they also highlight the specific theoretical achievements of Guido. To summarize what follows, one could say that this accomplishment consists in preserving the rigorous theoretical standards and demands of the older writings on polyphony (represented above all by the *Musica enchiriadis*) and at the same time giving pragmatic encouragement to experimentation and facilitating all sorts of change in direction.

Yet at the same time Guido's own conception of polyphony remains present and real. It is not only continuously recopied—often more or less mechanically—as an integral part of the *Micrologus:* more than that, as we shall see here, it was formulated entirely anew, probably as late as the thirteenth century, signifying that the thing itself was of binding interest—polyphony *à la* Guido. Hence, into the late Middle Ages Guido remains not only familiar as a "classic," but also active and relevant to musical consciousness and apparently even to musical practice through his own conception of polyphony and its specific realization.

The paper that follows, about "Guido after Guido," so to speak, attempts to trace the complexity of medieval music history, and to take the "Gleichzeitigkeit des Ungleichzeitigen" no less seriously than those who experienced it. I hope thus to do justice to the multiplicity of musical possibilities then available, theoretically and practically, and thereby to help reconstruct the multifaceted richness of musical cultures, not in the interest of pedantic completeness nor in the spirit of naïve historical "democratization," but rather in the hope of a better understanding of diverse, even contradictory phenomena; in the hope of a better evaluation than is possible with the one-sided criterion of "innovation," which is so often overstretched, if not helpless with respect to medieval music; and also in the hope of recovering step by step a music-historical context in which it can be more clearly established what may have been new at a given time and how this related to what was traditional. I shall be dealing with two main questions:

> In what respects does Guido remain current?
> How can this remarkable currency be explained?

I

Guido did not really alter the outward appearance of polyphony from what it had been in early medieval sources: as far as the resulting sound is concerned, the *Musica enchiriadis* and the *Micrologus* stand very close to one another. But Guido did alter significantly the methods of dealing with polyphony—of describing it, rationalizing it, and teaching it. On the one hand (as noted already) he introduced his readers to the rigorous theoretical standards and demands of the older writings on polyphony, and on the other encouraged a variety of practical experiments.

Traditional here is the fundamental role of the *symphoniae* in polyphonic performance, as well as the limitation of vertical range to a fourth. The adherence to two terms used and discussed in connection with polyphony since the early Middle Ages is also traditional:

> *diaphonia* as a general designation for "sounding separately," the "poly" in "polyphony," so to speak;
>
> *organum*, by contrast, as a specialized and precise designation that fixes the distance between the "separately sounding" voices as one of "concordant" sounds (in the theoretical sense of *symphoniae* or perfect consonances).

Guido's definition runs as follows (included in the comparative chart in table 1, column 1):

> Diaphonia "vocum disiunctio" sonat, quam nos "organum" vocamus, cum disiunctae ab invicem voces et concorditer dissonant et dissonanter concordant.[8]
>
> *The word "diaphonia" means "disjunction of pitches/lines," which we call "organum" if (and only if) these pitches/lines sound separately to make concords and at the same time make concords in sounding separately.*

This suggested translation of Guido's definition[9] agrees for the most part with Sarah Fuller's solution: "Diaphony sounds as a disjunction of pitches/lines which we call 'organum' *because* these pitches, which are distinct from each other, sound separately harmoniously and concord in sounding separate."[10] For in fact the early Middle Ages associated specifically with the word *organum* the idea of a strictly consonant structure, based on *symphoniae:* where, for example, other intervals smaller than the fourth occur, one can, according to several texts, speak of *organum* only in an inauthentic, misapplied (or even abusive) sense ("abusivum organum").[11] In this respect, Guido's logical linking of the two definitions—most likely phrased in the conditional with the conjunction "cum" (*cum explicativum*): "*if* these pitches/lines . . . make concords in sounding separately"—is strikingly precise and consistent: it takes up an essential differentiation between

[8] *Micrologus*, 196–97: XVIII, 2–3. As a linguistic term, the verb *sonare*—"diaphonia 'vocum disiunctio' sonat"—points up the "etymologically" relevant fact that the meaning can be derived from the sound and the components of the words themselves; *dis-sonantia* is a literal translation of "dia-phonia" into Latin.

[9] On this point and its historical background see Fritz Reckow, "Organum-Begriff und frühe Mehrstimmigkeit: Zugleich ein Beitrag zur Bedeutung des 'Instrumentalen' in der spätantiken und mittelalterlichen Musiktheorie," in *Forum Musicologicum* 1 (Bern: Francke, 1975), 138.

[10] Sarah Fuller, "Theoretical Foundations of Early Organum Theory," *Acta Musicologica* 53 (1981): 62. Other translations have overlooked precisely this crucial point of the logical connection: "Diaphonia heißt disiunctio der Töne, die wir Organum nennen. *Denn* die disjunkten Töne klingen übereinstimmend auseinander bzw. stimmen auseinanderklingend überein" (Frieder Zaminer, *Ad organum faciendum*, 51); "Diaphonia heißt die Trennung von Tönen, die wir organum nennen, *indem* die voneinander getrennten Töne zusammenstimmend verschieden erklingen und verschieden klingend zusammenstimmen" (Ernst Ludwig Waeltner, *Die Lehre vom Organum bis zur Mitte des 11. Jahrhunderts*, Münchner Veröffentlichungen zur Musikgeschichte 13 [Tutzing: Schneider, 1975], 91); "Diaphony sounds as a separateness of [simultaneous] sounds, which we also call organum, *in which* notes distinct from each other make dissonance harmoniously and harmonize in their dissonance" (Warren Babb, *Hucbald, Guido, and John on Music*, Music Theory Translation Series 3 [New Haven: Yale University Press, 1978], 77).

[11] Relevant passages are discussed in Reckow, "Organum-Begriff," 118ff.

diaphonia and *organum*, and makes plain that with respect to the available range of possible simultaneities, not every *diaphonia* is automatically *organum*.

Guido leaves undetermined, however, the breadth of the concept *concors/concordia*, as he himself uses it: meaning, that is, either a general "congruence" or a specific perfect "consonance" (*symphonia*). To be sure, he immediately goes on to a description of pure "symphonic" parallel singing in fourths, doubled at the octave—a manner of performance he characterizes, because of its strictness, as "modus durus." But when he then proceeds to speak of his own, intervallically flexible "modus mollis," which he prefers, he takes up without preliminaries all four of the simultaneities he has discussed—*tonus, ditonus, semiditonus, diatessaron*—as *concordiae.* Thus, in this context, *concordiae* are all intervals (including non-*symphoniae*) approved for use in polyphony along the conceptual lines just laid out. The traditional theoretical link between the concept of *organum* and the *symphoniae* is thereby quietly loosened: it expands, so to speak, (or is absorbed) into a more comprehensive—and, at the same time, less specific—concept of *organum*, which in turn leaves all the more room for individual ideas and decisions:

> Superior nempe diaphoniae modus durus est, noster vero mollis, ad quem semitonium et diapente non admittimus, tonum vero et ditonum et semiditonum cum diatessaron recipimus, sed semiditonus in his infimatum, diatessaron vero obtinet principatum. His itaque quattuor concordiis diaphonia cantum subsequitur.[12]

Guido's writing in the first person plural is symptomatic in this context: "more quo *nos* utimur," "modus *noster*," "semitonium et diapente non admitti*mus*," "tonum vero et ditonum et semiditonum cum diatessaron recipi*mus*." Guido does not present an abstract norm (as did the *Musica enchiriadis*), but rather reports, in the "we"-form, a concrete procedure, for which—so it appears—he personally assumes responsibility.

Thus Guido documents traditional theoretical ideals, concepts, and criteria, and orients himself according to these—without, however, remaining subservient to them. On the contrary, his teachings seem like an offer, or even a challenge, to engage both with traditional directives and, to an equal extent, with possibilities currently available—to consider alternatives never before discussed, and to draw individual, unforeseeable conclusions; and this possibility of further thought and further working-out obtains as well, to be sure, for the teaching of the *Micrologus* itself. In any case, Johannes

[12] *Micrologus*, 201–02: XVIII, 15–18.

Table 1

Comparative Chart: Definitions of Diaphonia and Organum

Guido, *Micrologus* (*ed. Smits van Waesberghe, CSM 4, 1955, p. 196f.*)	*Milan organum treatise* (*ed. Zaminer, 1970, p. 46*)
	[7] Organum est uox sequens precedentem sub celeritate diapente uel diatessaron.
	quarum uidelicet precedentis et subsequentis fit copula. aliqua decenti consonantia.
[2] Diaphonia 'vocum disiunctio' sonat	[8] Dyaphonia 'uocum disiunctio' sonat.
quam nos 'organum' vocamus, [3] cum disiunctae ab invicem voces et concorditer dissonant et dissonanter concordant.	quam nos 'organum' uocamus. cum disiuncte ab inuicem uoces concorditer dissonant et dissonanter concordant.
[4] Qua quidam ita utuntur, ut canenti semper quarta chorda	[9] Qua organizatores ita utuntur. quatinus diapente uel diatessaron
succedat ut .A. ad .D.	discurrant. ut .A. ad .D.
[5] ubi si organum per acutum .a. duplices, ut sit .A.D.a.,	Vbi si organum per acutum .a. duplices.
resonabit .A. ad .D. diatessaron, ad .a. diapason.	resonabit .A. ad .D. diatessaron. ad acutum .a. diapason.

Berlin treatise B *(ed. Eggebrecht, 1970, p. 159)*	[Guido, *Micrologus*] *London, British Library, MS. Harl. 281* *(CSM 4, p. 196f., App. crit.)*	*Florence, Biblioteca Medicea Laurenziana* *MS. Ashburnham 1051* *(fol. 94^{v}b)*
[5] Organum est uox sequens precedentem sub celeritate diapente uel diatessaron uel dittoni uel semidittoni. quarum id est precedentis uel subsequentis fit copula aliqua decenti consonantia.		
[6] Diaphonia 'uocum disiunctio' dicitur. quam nos 'organum' uocamus. Disiuncte enim uoces ab inuicem concorditer dissonant uel dissonanter concordant.	Diaphonia 'disiunctio vocum' sonat, consonanter dissonans et dissonanter consonans. nam in ea disiunctione ab invicem voces et concorditer dissonant et dissonanter concordant. Hanc vero... tripartitam dicere possumus. primam a natura remotam, secundam naturalem, tertiam planissimam... [infra]*	Est autem duplex symphonia, que nisi a duobus cantantibus fieri potest, quam uulgo 'organum' uocamus, quam etiam quidam 'dyaphoniam' nuncupant. Dia enim grece latine 'duo', phone 'cantus' uel 'uox' interpretatur. 'Organum' uero abusiue dicitur; nam organum proprie est uocabulum omnium instrumentorum musicorum.
[7] qua organizatores ita utuntur quatinus per diapente uel diatessaron uel dittonum uel semidittonum discurrant.	Hac autem diaphonia quidam ita utuntur, ut canenti semper quarta chorda succedat ut .A. ad .D.	Sequitur itaque diaphonia cantum per omnes consonancias absque semitonio et diapente.
	ubi si organum per acutum .a. duplices, ut sit .A.D.a., resonabit .A. ad .D. diatessaron, ad .A. diapason.	Quamuis enim per diapason organum fiat, non tamen a principali uoce ultra diatessaron uel diapente elongabitur diaphonia. Est autem, ubi per diatessaron et diapente organum redditur, quando scilicet uno canente gemina diaphonia infra supraque resonat. Si enim sit cantus in .F., organum in utraque .c. resonabit, ab inferiori uero per diatessaron, a superiori uero per diapente cantu in media uoce id est .F. existente. Utraque uero .c. ad se inuicem resonabit diapason.

*(1) Remota [sc. est diaphonia] quando aliquis nimis lascive organizans voces et voces subtilitate arteriarum quasi quadam superfluitate multiplicat.
(2) Naturalis que armonicali mediocritate ducitur; in ecclesia habetur autentica.
(3) Planissima si cantus organo respondeat equali simphonia.

Affligemensis can already largely dispense with Guido's minute regulations, and describe the new situation at the start of the "multifarious" twelfth century (as Paul Lehmann put it)[13] with a single laconic phrase: "Ea [i.e., diaphonia] diversi diverse utuntur"—different musicians deal with *diaphonia* [or perform polyphony] in their own different ways.[14]

In synthesizing the formative principles, categories, models, and perspectives of his time, carefully, but without dogmatic force, Guido can serve in effect as an ideal point of departure for new, more far-reaching experiments and plans. Thus it is only natural that even well into the late Middle Ages writers should continue to make connections with Guido's teaching, even with his own words. The character of his teaching, at once informative and open, also renders it exceptionally suitable for adaptation and/or transformation, within the context and according to the conceptions of a new period—or new circumstances. The concise, accurate, painstakingly thought-out formulations of the *Micrologus* seem almost to force later readers and authors into more cautious, considered modes of thought and expression in their own modifications or re-writings of the text. For the historian, this is a stroke of good luck, in that through close comparison of texts, he can perceive not only the fact of change but also its character, direction, and intensity during a given period. Here it is precisely the concrete and literal relation between model and modification, their distance or proximity, that yields valuable insights. With the help of a comparative chart (see table 1) I would now like to consider briefly a few characteristic features of such adaptation and transformation.

1) The author of the Milan organum treatise (column 2) obstinately emphasizes the connection between the term *organum* and perfect-consonance structure: polyphonic song may only be termed *organum*—so runs the famous-infamous "dialectic" epilogue, magisterially analyzed and interpreted by Max Haas[15]—if it makes exclusive use of *symphoniae* as intervals (polyphony in consonances which are other than perfect "non est

[13] "Die Vielgestalt des 12. Jahrhunderts" (1953), repr. in Paul Lehmann, *Erforschung des Mittelalters: Ausgewählte Abhandlungen und Aufsätze* 3 (Stuttgart: Hiersemann, 1960), 225–46.

[14] *De Musica cum Tonario*, ed. Joseph Smits van Waesberghe, Corpus Scriptorum de Musica 1 (Rome: American Institute of Musicology, 1950), 159: XXIII, 23.

[15] Max Haas, "Der Epilog des Mailänder Organum-Traktates: Zum Problem von Dialektik und Sachbezug in der Musiktheorie des ausgehenden elften Jahrhunderts," *Schweizer Beiträge zur Musikwissenschaft* 2 (1974): 7–19. In a new general survey Hans Heinrich Eggebrecht refers to Max Haas's interpretation but actually misses its point. Cf. Eggebrecht, "Die Mehrstimmigkeitslehre von ihren Anfängen bis zum 12. Jahrhundert," in *Die mittelalterliche Lehre von der Mehrstimmigkeit*, Geschichte der Musiktheorie, ed. Frieder Zaminer, 5

organum").[16] Logically enough, the author abandons the traditional limitation to the fourth—he repeatedly mentions the fifth as representative of all intervals larger than the fourth. His own organum, though, consists of a succession of changing perfect consonances including even the eleventh. It follows that the singers of organum are not infrequently required to make unusually large leaps. A frankly bizarre "pan-consonant" creation results;[17] it appears to derive from a rigorously narrowly understood concept of organum (resulting from what is called, in the history of philosophy, "realism" ["Begriffsrealismus"]). This conception of polyphony enables the author of the Milan treatise to hold to Guido's definition almost word for word: only the "concorditer" ("cum . . . voces concorditer dissonant . . ." etc.) must be understood in a sense considerably more stringent than Guido's own.

2) While the author of the Milan treatise one-sidedly accentuates the strict theoretical demands conveyed (and to a certain degree corroborated) by Guido, the author of the Berlin treatise B (column 3) prefers an empirical-descriptive method, sharing Guido's own inclination in this respect. Thus right at the beginning, in his introduction, he repeatedly mentions the two thirds alongside the *symphoniae* (*diapente* and *diatessaron*). The word "concord" must, then, be understood here in a broader sense, extending beyond the *symphoniae*. Consequently the former distinction between *diaphonia* and *organum* loses much of its weight: these become—in a rather "nominalistic" manner—two equally plausible if not equivalent designations for polyphony.

The author accordingly eliminates the logical link through the conjunction "cum." It is true that the statement "Disiunctae *enim* voces . . . concordant . . ." ("For indeed, the voices concord"), modified now into an independent sentence, remains the central factor also in his definition of polyphony; but it appears in equally close association with *diaphonia* and *organum* as well (if the author had not intended it thus, he could have kept Guido's formulation as it stood). To be sure, the author retains much of Guido's own formulation while weakening the implicit theoretical principles; this is quite the opposite of the Milan treatise, which deliberately radicalizes those principles. In sum, here we have two clearly contrasting

(Darmstadt: Wissenschaftliche Buchgesellschaft, 1984), 49–50. It is not the alternation between fifths and fourths (thus Eggebrecht) that the Epilogue is driving at, but the consistently symphonious composition of the "new organum"!

16 *Ad organum faciendum*, 49.

17 See the examples in *Ad organum faciendum*, 50.

conceptions of polyphonic execution, both of them rooted in the same opening lines of Guido's treatise.

3) The excerpt from the early fourteenth century in column 4 is especially noteworthy because it comes not from an independent organum treatise, but from an expanded version of Guido's teachings on polyphony presented within the context of the complete *Micrologus.* (This is, moreover, a version of the *Micrologus* with which Jacques de Liège was well acquainted, as his several citations from it indicate.) The copyist or redactor endeavors to update the *Micrologus* in the light of the polyphonic repertories that have arisen in the interim, without, however, encroaching excessively upon its core substance. Thus he no longer refers simply to polyphony as such, but rather contrasts three different characteristic types.

The first may be interpreted as a (melismatic) sustained-note type ("nimis lascive organizare," "quadam superfluitate multiplicare"), the second as a note-against-note procedure, which appears to include Guido's flexible *modus mollis.* There remains a third type, namely pure parallel singing in "equali simphonia," which is classed as "diaphonia planissima"—not, for example, as "diaphonia vetustissima": the characterization seems more or less to match Jacques's *diaphonia* "multum simplex." Thus the redactor legitimizes Guido's *modus durus* along with the *modus mollis* in the context of modern polyphony, in that he deals with them in terms of certain independent types among others. He is thereby doubtless forced to reduce the older teaching's comprehensiveness, but at the same time he assures it a respectable place in contemporary musical consciousness—and, probably, in actual musical practice as well.

His modifications of wording are also revealing. These go several steps further than those of the other authors just considered—especially since we are dealing in this case not with an independent adaptation or transformation, but rather with an ostensibly straightforward transmission of the *Micrologus* itself. The term *organum* has vanished entirely from the definition of polyphony—perhaps because in the interim it had become a special designation for sustained-note style; and the formulation "concorditer dissonare" and so forth, which Guido had linked explicitly to the term *organum,* is now twice associated directly with the term *diaphonia.* Not *organum,* but rather *diaphonia* is presented right at the outset, without question, as "consonanter dissonans et dissonanter consonans"; and at this juncture—pleonastically enough—there is then no problem in following the traditional formulation "et concorditer dissonant et dissonanter concordant" with a connective "nam" (since the term *organum* is omitted, there is of course neither need nor function for the conjunction "cum"): "The word 'diaphonia' means a 'disjunction' 'consonanter dissonans et dissonanter consonans'; *for* in this 'disjunction' the pitches/lines 'et concorditer dissonant et dissonanter concordant.' " The main point here is no longer a differentiation of terminology and its theoretical implications, but rather a definition of the actual thing in question, framed as incisively as possible. (It is not clear that the redactor makes any substantial distinction between the terms *consonanter* and *concorditer*, nor would such a distinction be likely.) Moreover, the author seems to stress the importance of concords even for the Guidonian *diaphonia grossa*—perhaps with almost apologetic intent—vis-à-vis the more modern (and more consonant) *diaphonia subtilis*, mentioned earlier.

4) The passage in column 5, finally, comes from a hitherto unpublished florilegium, probably from the thirteenth century. Here the anonymous author or redactor has synthesized Guido's teachings on polyphony into a single chapter, presenting them anew in his own words. In spite of his concentration on Guido, he makes clear that he by no means considers Guido's as the only possible way of creating polyphony. Thus at the start he plainly implies that for him the traditional distinction between *diaphonia* and *organum* has become largely irrelevant. Recalling Augustine, he stresses above all the superfluousness of the term *organum*. By contrast, he defines the term *diaphonia* more precisely, subjecting it to etymological analysis and to that extent taking it more seriously. Yet in the term *duplex symphonia* the author also introduces an overarching concept, one completely neutral or indifferent with respect to the terminological tradition. (By analogy, Walter Odington also speaks repeatedly of a *harmonia multiplex* in a very general sense.)[18] He simply alludes to traditional nomenclatures: *diaphonia* and *organum* are scarcely more to him—to put it nominalistically—than "flatus vocis," without concrete relevance for essential characteristics of what is being discussed.

The opening description, for example, is indicative: "Sequitur itaque diaphonia cantum per omnes consonancias absque semitonio et diapente." From a purely technical standpoint, in view of the real "substance" here, this does indeed describe Guido's *modus mollis* (". . . ad quem semitonium et diapente non admittimus, tonum vero et ditonum et semiditonum cum diatessaron recipimus"). Nonetheless, the author's failure to allude to the genuinely perfect-consonant character of early organum and the original

[18] *Summa de speculatione musicae*, ed. Frederick F. Hammond, Corpus Scriptorum de Musica 14 (Rome: American Institute of Musicology, 1970), see esp. 92 and 127.

hierarchy of consonances is significant: Guido, after all, had explicitly assigned the "principatus" to the fourth ("diatessaron vero obtinet principatum"). This loosening up of definitions seems almost to suggest an "anything-goes" attitude: characteristic structural devices are not under discussion; rather, only exceptions and exclusions are individually cited.

Yet at the same time Guido is still present: even this passage could never have been written without him. For a not inconsiderable part of what is stated consists of formulations that rework Guido's older teachings on polyphony, even if they refer less literally to them than do the other passages we have examined. At the same time they thus imply a kind of distance from Guido or even a certain independence from him. It is such a reference—the "intertextual" link, so to speak, with Guido—that shows how, and to what extent, different authors made the traditional principles more stringent or more relaxed, expanded upon them or, as in the case we have just seen, limited their currency. And we may further assume that such modifications not only characterize the types and the directions of musical change, but could also to some extent have influenced the changes as well. In any case, they lead us to acknowledge how multifarious the possibilities were for inventing new polyphony, highly varied in character, on the basis of Guido's *Micrologus.*

II

It is indicative of the complexity and diversity of musical culture in his age (probably the thirteenth century) that the last author discussed (column 5), while attaching little importance to the conceptual fundamentals of Guido's organum teaching, takes the thing itself—polyphony, that is, as taught by Guido—with great seriousness; and he does so despite showing at every turn that he is familiar with newer trends.

What is immediately striking—and it is this that requires interpretation—is that this last author should go to such trouble to reformulate Guido's teachings, given that he hardly alters their substance. He undoubtedly demonstrates thereby that active interest in this kind of polyphony still existed even in his own time. For a reformulation, far more than a simple copy or even a set of quotations, presupposes a thoroughgoing study, even an internalization, through practical experience, of the text so treated. Indeed, the new text shows clearly not only its author's mastery of the technical aspects of his subject matter, but also his ability to set it forth in careful argumentation, skillfully rendering it more immediate for his contemporaries. Naturally the present paper can offer only a few selective indications as to the content and character of the chapter in question here. A detailed investigation, together with an edition, must await later publication.[19]

On a completely superficial level, the author's intent is apparent even from the way he synthesizes Guido's chapters 18 and 19 into a single chapter, taking Guido's appended examples and setting them directly into the exposition of principles. The text thereby becomes not only more compact, but also more closely coordinated with practice.

The manner in which the anonymous author or redactor now presents polyphony *à la* Guido as one type among others is already suggestive of the altered music-historical situation. Strangely enough, parallel motion in *modus durus* (to which he also refers in his text) is described explicitly as a special type of voice-leading:

> Et nota quod sicut ascendit et descendit cantus, ita etiam organum [the *vox organalis*] eodem modo eleuatur et deponitur. (fol. 94^{v}b)

Guido's *modus mollis* is expressly presented as a deliberate selection of component simultaneities all within the narrow space of a fourth. Further simultaneities are thus deliberately excluded; in "this type of organum" they are considered to be "inconsonancie," because their occurrence is simply not envisaged:

> Aliud uero genus organi quod "simplex" uocatur. Hoc est, ubi inferius unus tantummodo est subsecutor. In quo .iiii. consonancie recipiuntur id est tonus, ditonus, semiditonus (quamuis raro) necnon et diatessaron. Alie uero .iii. id est diapason, diapente et semitonium ad hoc organum uelud inconsonancie iudicantur. (fol. 94^{v}b)

[19] The surviving version of the anonymous text is a copy (Florence, Biblioteca Medicea Laurenziana, MS. Ashburnham 1051, fols. 89–95^{v}). Unfortunately, the copyist had absolutely no understanding of the musical examples. He gives only uncoordinated strings of letter notation (which are for the most part incomplete) and he generally omits the *vox organalis* of Guido's examples completely.

The chapter on polyphony (fols. 94^{v}–95^{v}) is entitled *De duplici symphonia id est organo;* the incipit runs: "Quia uero de simplici simphonia satis superius disputatum est. . . ." In the specialist literature the title and incipit have on more than one occasion been given in garbled form (confusion of title and incipit); perhaps this is the reason that the text has so far hardly been studied. Cf. "Quia vero de simplici fini organophonia . . ." (Joseph Smits van Waesberghe, in Corpus Scriptorum de Musica 1:8), or "De duplici symphonia id est organo. Quia vero de simpliciori organophonia . . ." (Pieter Fischer, in *RISM* B III^{2} [Munich: Henle, 1968], 46).

In accordance with the new situation, the anonymous also weakens some of Guido's formulations which still sound quite normative. For instance, where Guido writes, in a rather schoolmasterly, authoritarian manner, that the organum singer may not go below the "Grenztöne" (the "boundary pitches" C, F, G) unless the cantus-singer "permits" him to do so:

> Quorum [i.e., troporum] a trito, in quem vel finis distinctionum advenerit, vel qui proximus ipsi finalitati suberit, subsecutor numquam tamen descendere debet, nisi illo inferiores voces cantor admiserit (p. 203: XVIII, 23–24)

the anonymous chooses instead a rather sloppy, casual phrase:

> Siquidem enim per uocem, que sit triti modi, organum fit, ab ipsa uoce triti inferius nullatenus est recedendum. Sed semper in ea manendum, nisi quando cantus sub ipsa [i.e., voce] forsitan [!] descenderit. (fol. 95a)

The same is true for the conclusions of both texts. Guido ends with an indication that the rules just given—more or less automatically—"diaphoniam dabunt," that they (the rules) produce the polyphonic result of themselves:

> Diaphoniae praecepta donata sunt, quae si exemplis probes, perfecte cognosces. (p. 208: XVIII, 50)

> Curiosus itaque existas et in usum exercitando vertas, si symphoniam habeas, satis tibi hae regulae diaphoniam dabunt. (p. 214: XIX, 26)

The anonymous, by contrast, recommends an independent and creative consideration of the examples provided (though not without a recognizable reliance on Guido's formulation): the learner will then "ad istorum similitudinem"—according to the patterns, possibilities, and suggestions offered by the examples, not the rules (Guido's word "praeceptum" is dropped entirely)—arrive by himself at insights as to what it is convenient or rewarding to preserve:

> De diaphonia ista sufficiunt. Si enim frequenti usu hec (que dicta sunt) exempla meditari uolueris, ad istorum similitudinem facile peruidebis, quod in ceteris conseruari conueniat. (fol. 95va)

Finally, the fact that the anonymous lays greater weight than does Guido himself on the *occursus* as the main principle of articulation also fits into this picture. According to him, the voices should be led into a unison at the ends of even the smallest musical units. Guido can content himself as easily with caesuras on the fourth in problematic cases. Where a stepwise convergence of the voices is not possible because of a lack of suitable intervals, according to Guido the organum singer should preferably stick to the lower fourth, rather than leaping up a fourth to a unison:

> A diatessaron vero vix fit occursus, cum gravis magis placet illo loco succentus. (p. 204: XVIII, 30)

For other passages, Guido favors pure parallel motion at the fourth over an *occursus:*

> diatessaron succentus plusquam occursus placet. (p. 210: XIX, 7)

The anonymous author seeks to avoid such "compromises" and "inconsistencies": not only at the ends of pieces, but also, as a rule, at the ends of internal phrases he favors a unison to articulate and "round off" the phrase. He also cites precedent as authority, in an empirical, pragmatic fashion, noting that "many" others have similarly preferred the unison:

> In fine uero cantus maxime est cauendum, ne organum fiat per diatessaron, quia semper fini aut tono aut ditono occurrendum est; uel si non est occursus, cantor et subsecutor in una uoce manere debebunt. Per diatessaron uero cum non ualet esse occursus, erit subsecutori cum cantu ante finem ascendendum, ut congrua inter utrumque sit concinnencia . . .
>
> Quod non solum in fine, sed etiam in distinccionibus plerumque est faciendum sicut in ea (quam diximus) antiphona *Ipsi soli.* Multi in ea parte [of a previous example], que est *seruo fidem,* simul cum cantore usque ad .F. [the unison] ascendunt hoc modo: [example incomplete]. (fol. 95b)

Guido ends this example in the fourth C–F (p. 210: XIX, 5).[20]

Altogether, then, this exceptional text illustrates in several ways how polyphony *à la* Guido remained current and vital long after Guido. To emphasize the point, even in the thirteenth century a redactor strives, in his enthusiasm, to be more Guidonian than Guido himself.

III

The selected examples from the authors presented here document quite different manifestations and reinterpretations of Guido's teaching of polyphony: literal transmission within the context of the entire *Micrologus;* adaptation and transformation according to new ideas, altered ideals, and

[20] The critical commentary for the *Micrologus* nevertheless cites two sources from the twelfth century in which the *vox organalis* in *Servo fidem* stays on the pitch F and thus forms a unison ending F–F with the *vox principalis* (215).

novel practices; and finally a completely new formulation of the original teaching.

One might draw the conclusion that such a persistent, multifaceted, and creative interest in Guido's teaching is symptomatic of a corresponding need in musical practice itself. Unlike poetry, texts conceived with pragmatic intent are seldom copied for their own sake alone; and it is questionable whether in the centuries after Guido such a need persisted only on the so-called "periphery"—that is to say, in cultural backwaters. Statements even from the late Middle Ages demonstrate that polyphony was differentiated less according to historical layers than according to varying complexity. In this sense polyphony *à la* Guido was regarded as a particularly simple type, but one which could meet a practical need even in innovative centers. It could form an alternative to the more subtle polyphony of later times, for example that of Franco of Cologne. We might hazard that according to the rank of the liturgical feast day or according to the musical character of the respective liturgical genre, polyphony of varying degrees of complexity was employed. For instance, Guido in the *Micrologus* presents primarily antiphons as examples for polyphony, and these are passed down through the centuries with virtually no alteration.

But Guido's method of presentation and argumentation may also have contributed to his continued topicality and influence. He carefully absorbed the theoretical tradition, without absolute reliance on that tradition. He fixed no absolute norms, but rather offered pragmatic principles for the performance of polyphony. Further, not only did he make clear that these principles emanated from his own personal preference, but he also—and this is crucial—gave solid reasons for these preferences. In so doing he established a model for dealing with polyphony that allowed freedom for alternatives and alterations in a way which implied the necessity of providing those alternatives and alterations with a rational foundation.

In this context a short anonymous text of the twelfth century entitled *Quomodo organice moduletur*, to which Michael Bernhard recently drew attention, is extremely informative.[21] The author concludes his rules, in a passage relying on the Guidonian model (see the citation above, p. 401, concerning *modus mollis*), by listing simultaneities which are rare or "inadmissible": the two sixths and sevenths (". . . quos regulariter rarius . . . vel

[21] Michael Bernhard, "Ein weiterer Text zur Klangschritt-Lehre," in *Quellen und Studien zur Musiktheorie des Mittelalters* 1, ed. Michael Bernhard (Munich: Verlag der Bayerischen Akademie der Wissenschaften, 1990), 68–70. Bernhard mentions only the version in Wolfenbüttel, Herzog August Bibliothek, 334 Gud. lat. 8° (fols. 111ᵛ–12). The same text is also preserved, unfortunately in a very corrupt state, in Vienna, Österreichische National-Bibliothek, Cpv 787, fol. 59ᵛ.

numquam . . . admittimus"). But at the same time he reports that in the polyphonic practice of his day such concords are not only employed frequently but actually produce a thoroughly pleasant effect. Thus, in the very same empirical spirit as Guido, he does not dismiss this established "usus" as being contrary to the rules; he allows it to stand by appealing to the judgment of the "outer senses" (seeing and hearing)—which obviously approve:

> Et notandum, quod modos, quos regulariter rarius, ut diapente cum semitonio et diapente cum tono, vel numquam, sicut diapente cum semiditono vel ditono, admittimus, organa sepe et dulcius frequentant. Haec secundum usum hominum et exteriores sensus (id est, pro[ut] videre et audire possumus) protuli.[22]

It was precisely because Guido made it possible for others to transcend his own teaching, and to elaborate the appropriate rational bases for their endeavors, that he remained contemporary and useful as a model and stimulus for succeeding generations.

(Translation: Adelyn Peck Leverett)[23]

[22] Ed. Bernhard, 68.

[23] I also wish to thank David Hiley and Craig J. Westendorf for their help with some details of the English version of this paper.

ERNEST H. SANDERS

Rithmus

Having in 1962 questioned the applicability of the rhythmic modes to the syllabic portions of polyphonic *conducti*, I undertook to demonstrate their inapplicability in a more recent article. Investigation of the relevant statements of thirteenth-century writers on music as well as of a number of *conducti* confirmed the summary, first offered in 1979, that prior to "approximately the second decade of the thirteenth century and probably for some time thereafter most syllables in polyphonic genres other than the motet had the durational value of one perfect long, some more, none less."[1] Three scholars have recently provided excerpts of and commentaries on medieval treatises concerning Latin poetry of the Middle Ages, neglected by almost all musicologists, even though their relevance to the degree(s) of interrelation between poetry and music should surely be examined.[2] It is

[1] Ernest H. Sanders, "Duple Rhythm and Alternate Third Mode in the 13th Century," *Journal of the American Musicological Society* 15 (1962): 283–84; "Conductus and Modal Rhythm," ibid., 38 (1985): 467. For an illuminating treatment of the relationship of music and text in the Middle Ages, see Fritz Reckow, "rectitudo—pulchritudo—enormitas: Spätmittelalterliche Erwägungen zum Verhältnis von *materia* und *cantus*," in *Musik und Text in der Mehrstimmigkeit des 14. und 15. Jahrhunderts*, ed. Ursula Günther and Ludwig Finscher, Göttinger musikwissenschaftliche Arbeiten 10 (Kassel: Bärenreiter, 1984), 1–36.

[2] Paul Klopsch, *Einführung in die mittellateinische Verslehre* (Darmstadt: Wissenschaftliche Buchgesellschaft, 1972), esp. 27–32; John Stevens, *Words and Music in the Middle Ages* (Cambridge: Cambridge University Press, 1986), 413–23; Margot E. Fassler, "Accent, Meter, and

hoped that the problems both the treatises and the poetry have presented to the modern reader, the scantiness of twentieth-century comment on the treatises, and the question of their pertinence to medieval musical practice and theory will justify another approach to these related issues.

I

Prior to the eleventh century, writers on poetry and on music generally agree that *rithmus*[3] is, in the words of Maximus Victorinus's *Ars Palaemonis de Metrica Institutione*, "an arrangement of words [i.e., poetry] duly proportioned not by means of the metrical system, but measured by numerical scanning with regard to the judgment of the ears" ("verborum modulata compositio non metrica ratione, sed numerosa scansione ad iudicium aurium examinata"). He further states that "very often, however, you will, by some chance, encounter metrical ordering in *rithmus* as well, but as a result of the guidance of sound and of that duly proportioned order, and not of scrupulous observance of the [metrical] system" ("plerumque tamen casu quodam etiam invenies rationem metricam in rhythmo, non artificii observatione servata, sed sono et ipsa modulatione ducente"). Except for the substitution of *numero* for *numerosa scansione* and of *invenies etiam rationem* for *etiam invenies rationem metricam*, the treatise by the seventh-century grammarian Audax offers the same definition.[4]

Rhythm in Medieval Treatises 'De Rithmis'," *The Journal of Musicology* 5 (1987): 164–90. Twice the latter rightly points to her predecessors' disregard of these authors (166, n. 8, and 173, n. 38). Indeed, William G. Waite merely listed a modern edition (see n. 21 below) in the bibliography of his *The Rhythm of Twelfth-Century Music* (New Haven: Yale University Press, 1954), 132; Janet Knapp made relatively cursory reference to the same collection in nn. 21 and 22 of her "Musical Declamation and Poetic Rhythm in an Early Layer of Notre Dame Conductus," *Journal of the American Musicological Society* 32 (1979): 388; and for reasons that remained to be articulated this author chose not to consider them for his 1985 article cited in n. 1 above. Only Sarah A. Fuller gave more consideration to the matter ("Aquitanian Polyphony of the Eleventh and Twelfth Centuries," Ph.D. diss., University of California, Berkeley, 1970, 179–92). Disregard of these treatises is not confined to musicology; they are unmentioned in both Michel Burger's *Recherches sur la structure et l'origine des vers romans*, Société de publications romanes et françaises 59 (Geneva: Minard, 1957) and Dag Norberg's *Introduction à l'étude de la versification latine médiévale*, Studia Latina Stockholmiensia 5 (Stockholm: University of Stockholm, distr. by Almquist & Wiksell, 1958).

[3] This is the spelling in most treatises dealing with medieval non-metrical poetry; Klopsch, *Einführung*, 27–28.

[4] Henricus Keil, *Grammatici Latini* (Leipzig, 1857–80; repr. Hildesheim: Olms, 1961), 6:206–07, and 7:331–32. Victorinus, too, is likely to have been active in the seventh century. While we have no direct evidence—see *Bedae Venerabilis Opera*, Pars VI_1, ed. Ch. W. Jones, Corpus Christianorum, Series Latina 123A (Turnhout: Brepols, 1975), XXV—Bernhard Bischoff seems to place both authors in the same time frame, before Bede (ca. 700) and before

The Venerable Bede's formulation begins with a clause stating that *rithmus* "seems to be entirely similar to meters" ("Videtur autem metris esse consimilis"); thereafter it is identical to that of Audax, except for the clarifying insertion of *syllabarum* after *numero* and for the substitution of *moderatione* (arrangement) for *observatione.* Bede, however, amplifies his account by citing two hymns as examples of *modulata compositio* brought about through the observation of *sonus* for the *iudicium aurium. Rithmus,* therefore, is both technique and a poetic genre now labeled as such.

> And in that way that excellent hymn was so beautifully made after the likeness [in imitation] of the iambic meter (*Quo modo instar iambici metri pulcherrime factus est hymnus ille preclarus*):
>
> Rex eterne domine,
> rerum creator omnium,
> qui eras ante secula
> semper cum patre filius;
>
> and a good many other Ambrosian hymns. Likewise, they sing the abecedarian hymn about the Day of Judgment after the model of the trochaic meter (*et alii Ambrosiani non pauci. Item ad formam metri trochaici canunt hymnum de die iudicii per alphabetum*):
>
> Apparebit repentina
> dies magna domini,
> fur obscura velut nocte
> inprovisus occupans.[5]

Archbishop Julian of Toledo (680s); see his *Mittelalterliche Studien* 1 (Stuttgart: Hiersemann, 1966), 296 and 291. Victorinus's relegation to the fourth century (Wilhelm Seidel, "Rhythmus/numerus," *Handwörterbuch der musikalischen Terminologie,* 10, col. 2, and 13, col. 2; Fassler, "Accent," 168, n. 17) results from his identification with Marius Victorinus. Both the latter and Attilius Fortunatianus (also fourth century) do, however briefly, describe *rithmus* as verse structured numerically and without feet, on the one hand, and on the basis of *sonus,* on the other (Keil, *Grammatici Latini* 6: 44, 96, and 282). For a discussion of the early grammarians' statements regarding *rithmus* see Wilhelm Meyer, *Gesammelte Abhandlungen zur mittellateinischen Rhythmik* (Berlin: Weidmann, 1905–36), 3: 127–45, esp. his list with commentaries on 140–45. On 135 he provides a somewhat differently articulated interpretation of the *Palaemon* passage in his translation and commentary.

[5] Chapter 24 (*De rithmo*) of his *De arte metrica;* see *Bedae Venerabilis Opera,* Pars VI_1, 138–39. His initial clause is not without precedent; both Maximus Victorinus and Audax mention syllables (and time units) as the elements of measurement of the feet in metrical poetry and precede their definition of *rithmus* with the contention that it is something that "metro . . . videtur esse consimile." The definition given in the *Ars grammatica, poetica, et rhetorica* of Julian of Toledo is somewhat less informative; see Francisco A. de Lorenzana y Butron, Cardinal, ed., *SS. PP. Toletanorum quotquot extant opera . . .* (Madrid: Ibarra, 1782–93), *Auctarium* [=Supplement] for vol. 2 (Rome, 1797), XLIXa. Even though his treatise was written between 680 and 687—just ten or twelve years before Bede's—it may not have served as Bede's model, Charles H. Beeson's strong suggestion to the contrary notwithstanding; cf. the

The discussions of *rithmus* by Aurelian of Réôme (mid-ninth century)[6] and by Rémy of Auxerre (ca. 900)[7] bring nothing new. Omitting all reference to meter, the former, also citing *Rex eterne domini*, reformulates his predecessors' statement that the apparent metrical ordering in certain *rithmi* is not the result "of scrupulous observance of the [metrical] system": the hymn, he says emphatically, "has no system of feet, but is founded solely on proper rhythmic regulation" ("nullam tamen habet pedum rationem sed tantum contentus est rithmica modulatione").

In sum, all these definitions of *rithmus* specify that (1) it is not meter and that it involves (2) numerical scanning of syllables (3) on the basis of their sound as judged by aural perception. Since measurement of the syllabic components as long or short is a matter of metric versification,[8] numerical scanning implies durational equality of syllables, pronounced in accordance with the way words are normally sounded and perceived (in prose). That such arrangements would often chance to produce the semblance—but not the reality—of trochaic or, less likely, iambic meters is hardly surprising in view of Latin pronunciation. Metrical schemes such as the trochaic or iambic dimeter may even have been templates, but irregularities[9] as well as the writers' offhand mention of this feature show that they seem not to have been seen as essential and obligatory.[10] To our knowledge it was St. Augustine who, late in the fourth century, initiated the long medieval tradition of non-metrical poetry, because he knew that many people no longer had "knowledge of long and short syllables, as taught by the grammarians," and because the pertinent poem, his *Psalmus contra partem Donati* (393), intended for congregational instruction and

latter's "The Ars Grammatica of Julian of Toledo," *Miscellanea Francisco Ehrle* 1, Studi e testi 37 (1924), 51, 56.

[6] *Aureliani Reomensis Musica disciplina*, ed. Lawrence Gushee, Corpus Scriptorum de Musica 21 (Stuttgart: Hänssler, 1975), 67; the passage is quoted and translated by Fassler, "Accent," 169.

[7] *Remigii Autissiodorensis Commentum in Martianum Capellam*, ed. Cora E. Lutz (Leiden: Brill, 1962–65), 2:335; the relevant passage is quoted in Stevens, *Words and Music*, 417, n. 6.

[8] See n. 5 above.

[9] As, for instance, the initial catalexis of *Rex eterne domine*, which more than one modern editor "corrected" by prefacing the first verse with "O"; see Clemens Blume, ed., *Analecta Hymnica* 51 (Leipzig: Reisland, 1908–09), 6. It is puzzling that Bede's reiteration of his predecessors' observation regarding the appearance or semblance of metrical order in *rithmi* should have led Norberg, 133, to the conclusion that Bede here comments on the "occasional success" of poets of *rithmi* in also "composing regular quantitative poetry."

[10] See below, p. 431. In view of later medieval definitions of *rithmus* (see p. 421–28 below) it is unlikely that the writers cited so far were referring to the kind of syllable-counting metrical poems whose verses contained constant numbers of syllables rather than feet and evidently displayed varying arrangements of longs and shorts. As regards this ancient and widespread type of poetry (Greek, Vedic Sanskrit, Slavic, Irish) see Calvert Watkins, "Indo-European Metrics and Archaic Irish Verse," *Celtica* 6 (1963): 194–249.

participation, imposed the obligation to eschew the use of "certain generally less customary words that metrical necessity might compel."[11]

Not until the second half of the eleventh century are we given further information about the nature of rhythmic Latin poetry. Alberic of Monte Cassino, who in his *Rationes dictandi* summarily states that, in contrast to metric poetry and prose, "a rhythmic composition is what is put together syllabically by means of a fixed numerical standard" ("rithmicum sane dictamen est quod certa numerorum lege sillabatim colligitur"),[12] proceeds in his *De rithmis*[13] to present a detailed treatise. Generally speaking, he begins,

> there are some *rithmi* in which only the quantity [not in the metrical sense] of syllables is considered, without any consideration of length and brevity. There are others in which for a specific, limited number of syllables length and brevity are taken into account as well. That is, to speak more plainly, they are both *rithmi* and *metra* [metrical verses or poems].

> *Rithmorum alii sunt in quibus consideratur mensura tantum sillabarum sine omni longitudinis et brevitatis consideratione. Alii sunt in quibus cum certo et determinato numero sillabarum etiam longitudo et brevitas est prospecta. Quod est apertius dicere: rithmi pariter sunt et metra.*[14]

Alberic then adduces two hymn stanzas[15] as examples of the first category: the first stanza of a hymn imitating the Sapphic strophe (*Christe, sanctorum decus atque vita*)[16] and the third stanza of *Ave maris stella*, identified as *rithmus exasillabus*, consisting of hexasyllabic verses (*membra*) made up of three disyllables each. Thereafter he unsystematically presents seven other categories on the basis of their numerical syllable content (8, 7, 15, 12, 10, 5, 11), beginning with *rithmus octosillabus* and citing as one of *exempla*

[11] For the original Latin passages see Klopsch, *Einführung*, 4 and 5. For short samples of Augustinus's poem see Norberg, *Introduction*, 88 and 137. The entire *psalmus* is printed (with French translation) in *Oeuvres de Saint Augustin*, Bibliothèque Augustinienne 28 (Paris: Desclée, 1963), 135–91.

[12] Ludwig Rockinger, "Briefsteller und Formelbücher des eilften bis vierzehnten Jahrhunderts," *Quellen und Erörterungen zur Bayerischen und deutschen Geschichte*, Alte Folge, 9 (Munich: Franz, 1863–64; repr. Munich: Scientia, 1969), 9.

[13] Hugh H. Davis, "The 'De rithmis' of Alberic of Monte Cassino: A Critical Edition," *Mediaeval Studies* 28 (1966): 198–227.

[14] Davis, "The 'De rithmis,' "208. This passage is cited and translated by Fassler, "Accent." Her translation of the second sentence ("There are others with a sure and determinate number of syllables in which long and short duration is considered as well") leaves it open to misinterpretation. She also offers one other excerpt and discusses the treatise at some length; cf. 170–72.

[15] Not three, as Fassler, "Accent," 171, has it; cf. Davis, "The 'De rithmis,' "218.

[16] He calls it "rithmus phaleuticus" (i.e., Phaleucian or Phalaecian), but as Davis points out, this poem "is properly called Sapphic" ("The 'De rithmis,' "216). The word "pentasyllable" in that annotation must be corrected to read "hexasyllable."

innumerabilia the first stanza of Peter Damian's (1006–72) hymn *Maria virgo regia.* He adds the following comment:

> Hence [or, from the example it is clear that][17] such *rithmi* customarily take care that the penultimate syllable of each verse be shortened in sound. Some octosyllabic *rithmi* are made, however, in which the opposite is carefully observed, i.e., that the penultimate syllable of each verse is lengthened in sound . . .
>
> *Inde* [or, *Unde*] *huiusmodi autem consueverunt cavere quatenus penultima sillaba uniuscuiusque membri accentu corripiatur. Fiunt tamen quidam octosillabi rithmi in quibus res cavetur contraria, ut videlicet penultima sillaba uniuscuiusque membri accentu producatur . . .*[18]

To express the lengthening of the penultimate syllable, Alberic consistently uses the verb *producere.* Instead of *corripere* he once writes *breviare* and once *levare.* In place of *accentu* he uses each of the following phrases once: *prolatione et accentu* (delivery and sound); *accentu et sola prolatione* (sound and singular delivery); *accentu et sono* (sound production); *pronuntiatione et sono* (delivery and sound production).[19] The terminology shows the

[17] Davis, "The 'De rithmis,' "218.

[18] His example (*Luget mundus, plorat terra*) can be dated 1054; Davis, "The 'De rithmis,' "219. It is tempting, therefore, to date the treatise as from the third quarter of the eleventh century. For a summary of information on Alberic of Monte Cassino see Owen J. Blum, "Alberic of Monte Cassino and the Hymns and Rhythms Attributed to Saint Peter Damian," *Traditio* 12 (1956): 87–148.

[19] Davis, "The 'De rithmis,' "212–14. The statement that *rithmi* "reflected [metrical schemata] through accent rather than duration . . . at cadences" (Fassler, "Accent," 171) seems puzzling. For his second category of *rithmi* Alberic never mentions meters, but constantly emphasizes the duration of the penultimate.

Early medieval sources, beginning with Placidus's Glossary (one of the oldest to have come down to us), consistently define *accentus* as follows: *ratio metrica; sonus productus, acutus sonus in verbis; vox acuta sive producta* (*sonus* and *vox* can be synonymous); *sonus vocis correptae vel productae;* see Georgius Goetz, ed., *Thesaurus glossarum emendatarum* 1, Corpus glossariorum Latinorum 6 (Leipzig, 1899; repr. Amsterdam: Hakkert, 1965), 12, and the references given there. One commentator (fifth century) elaborately describes what Klopsch, *Einführung,* 3, calls "expiratory accent" (stress accent); but, as the latter points out, the definition implies that it must have been very weak. In any case, no other writer touches on the notion of stress, and accent is always defined in terms of duration and/or pitch, not loudness. This is also the meaning *accentus* still has for Franco (see *Journal of the American Musicological Society* 33 [1980]: 604a); it does not mean accent, i.e. stress accent, as Dolores Pesce seems to believe ("The Significance of Text in Thirteenth-Century Latin Motets," *Acta Musicologica* 58 [1986]: 102). For the further persistence of the traditional meaning of *accentus,* see n. 79 below. The terms *emphasis* (= stress) and *ictus* do not appear, and even Ben Jonson still defined the sounding of vowels as "in quantitie (which is Time) long, or short. Or, in accent, which is tune [= sound] sharp [= acute, high], or flat [= grave, low] . . ."; Ben. Johnson [sic], *The English Grammar* ([London]: n.p., 1640), 36. (His categories "sharp" and "flat" are applied to monosyllables, while "long" and "short"—i.e., long and short vowels—are exemplified only by trisyllables.) To be sure, he elsewhere (p. 54) talks of "the force of an *Accent.*"

treatise to be an instruction manual both for the delivery and for the facture of *rithmi.*

Alberic's work seems to indicate that the principle of cadential articulation of rhythmic verses on the basis of their concluding either paroxytonically or proparoxytonically (also at the caesuras in the three longest verse types) arose sometime in the tenth or early eleventh century. In fact, however, he bases his definition of cadential endings not on the pronunciation of Latin *words*, but solely on the penultimate syllable of each *verse*. This helps to confirm that the syllables preceding the cadence were pronounced isochronically. The same essential feature is indicated by the fourth verse of the first stanza of the early hymn *O crucifer bone* by Prudentius (d. after 405) that he cites as an example of decasyllabic *rithmus* with short penultimate: "sed prius in genitore potens." Here it cannot be a matter of the antepenultimate being lengthened, but solely, as he says, of the penultimate being shortened. (This poem still reflects quantitative metrical principles, which Alberic replaces with his rule of the penultimate.)[20] Why the first two poems cited by him should not (yet) be bound by the new rule of the penultimate is unclear. In the first (*Christe, sanctorum decus atque vita*) it might be due to the relative complexity of the versification, while, contrariwise, the repetitive simplicity of the second poem may have inhibited versual articulation.

To answer the question of "what *rithmus* is, how many syllables the verse should contain, and how many verses constitute a stanza and where consonance [i.e., rhyme] should be observed" ("quid sit rithmus et quot ex syllabis distinctio [Alberic's *membrum*] constare debeat, et ex quot distinctionibus clausula sit, et ubi sit observanda consonantia"), the twelfth-century author of *De rithmico dictamine* offers the following definition:

> *Rithmus* is the rhyming parity of a fixed number of syllables. A verse must consist of at least four syllables and of at most sixteen.... A stanza must consist of at least two and at most five verses.... With respect to rhyme one must realize that, if the penultimate syllable of a verse is pronounced with a high pitch, rhyme must be observed from the vowel of the penultimate syllable to the end.... If, however, it is pronounced with a low sound, rhyme must be observed from the vowel of the antepenultimate syllable to the end...
>
> *Rithmus est consonans paritas sillabarum sub certo numero comprehensarum. Distinctio debet constare ex quatuor sillabis ad minus, et ex sexdecim ad plus.... Clausula debet constare ex duabus distinctionibus ad minus, ex quinque ad plus.... Sequitur de consonantia. Unde sciendum est quod si*

[20] Davis, "The 'De rithmis,' "212. The irregularity in the poem demonstrating pentasyllabic verse (Davis, 213) is easily removed by reading *omnium queque*, rather than *omniumque que.*

penultima sillaba distinctionis proferatur acuto accentu, consonantia debet servari a vocali penultime sillabe usque in finem. . . . Si vero proferatur gravi accentu, consonantia debet servari a vocali antepenultime sillabe usque ad finem . . .[21]

The great novelty here is the mandatory codification of rhyme, which as an elective feature goes back to late Roman Christian poetry and seems to have become obligatory by the end of the eleventh century.[22] In addition to specifying equality of syllables, a feature only implied by his predecessors, the author expressly introduces the concept of the antepenultimate, from which rhyme has to proceed if the penultimate is lowered in pronunciation.[23] In other words, the nature of the final word of any verse as either paroxytonic or proparoxytonic governs the rhyme. All of his examples of verses ending proparoxytonically do so with words of three or more syllables, and clearly a verse like that just cited from the hymn by Prudentius is no longer admitted, because its use in such a context is compatible only with metrical concepts. Thus, in apparent contrast to Alberic, this author does not recognize the possible poetic conception and treatment of syllables as entities independent of the words they constitute, which would likely have come to be a solecism in the course of the twelfth century. (For an example see p. 428.)

A twelfth-century redaction of the *De rithmico dictamine*, titled *Regulae de rithmis*, defines *rithmus* somewhat more elaborately, though with no change in meaning:

[21] Giovanni Mari, *I trattati medievali di ritmica latina* (Milan, 1899; repr. Bologna: Forni, 1971), 11–12 (also in *Memorie del Reale istituto Lombardo di scienze e lettere, Classe di lettere* [Milan: Hoepli, 1899], 373–496). If Walter Map wrote one of the cited poems (see Mari, 12, n. 5) the treatise could not have been written before the second half of the twelfth century, probably its last quarter. (Its definition of *rithmus* seems to have become traditionally authoritative. As late as ca. 1332 Antonio da Tempo defines *rithimus* [sic] as "consonans paritas syllabarum certo numero comprehensarum," adding that this definition also applies to vernacular poetry; see his *Summa artis rithmici*, ed. Giusto Grion in his *Delle rime volgari trattato di Antonio da Tempo* [Bologna: Romagnoli, 1869], 71.)

The meanings of *acutus* and *gravis accentus* seem to be the traditional ones. The one passage cited in the *Mittellateinisches Wörterbuch*, vol. 1, col. 145, for *scharfbetonend* as the meaning of *acutus* nonetheless also definitely turns out to use the word to mean "high." The use of *haut* or *bas* for high and loud or low and soft instruments evidently came into being in the fourteenth century; see Heinz Becker, "Oboe," in *Die Musik in Geschichte und Gegenwart*, vol. 9, col. 1788.

[22] See Klopsch, *Einführung*, 38–45; also Meyer, *Gesammelte Abhandlungen* 2:124.

[23] The remainder of the treatise, commented upon at length by Fassler, "Accent," 175–78, deals with the distribution of rhyme patterns within one stanza or over a pair of stanzas. While she does not cite the original Latin passages concerning the interrelation of rhyme and the pronunciation of the last word of a verse, her English paraphrase shows her to perceive *accentus* as stress "accent or beat." Such accentuation may indeed have been practiced, though no medieval writer specifically refers to it; see n. 19 above. As to her view of this sort of poetry as "suspended . . . upon a stationary grid of accent or beat" (177), see Section III of this paper.

> *Rithmus* is congruous, rhymed ordering of [elements of] speech [i.e., syllables, words, phrases], continuously rendered with equality of syllables. . . . Number is thus to be observed in it, that is, first in the verses and then in the syllables and rhymes.

> *Rithmus enim est congrua diccionum ordinatio, consona, continenter sillabarum equalitate prolata. . . . Numerus ergo in ipso notandus est, primo quidem in distinccionibus, postmodum vero in sillabis et consonanciis.*[24]

Apart from the more explicitly Gothic reference to the all-governing power of number, neither this general definition nor the subsequent particulars (i.e., interrelation of rhyme and pronunciation, distribution of rhyme patterns) differentiate this redaction from its model.[25]

This would seem to have been the understanding of *rithmus* when Johannes de Garlandia (Anglicus)[26] set about to write his exhaustive treatise—or, rather, part of a treatise—on *rithmus*, his *Ars rithmica.*[27] After a brief introductory paragraph reporting the taxonomy of music, as inherited from Boethius and Cassiodorus, he proceeds to define *rithmus:*

> *Rithmus* is the rhyme of words similar in their endings, which is arranged by means of a fixed number without metrical feet . . .;[28] "arranged," because words [phrases?] have to end in a well-ordered way in a *rithmus.* According to some, *rithmus* originated from the rhetorical ornament known as "ending similarly."[29] But a certain type of *rithmus* ends as if it were an iambic metrical verse, and another as if it were a spondaic metrical verse. In this context iamb should be understood to mean a word whose penult is shortened (for an

[24] Mari, *I trattati,* 28. He also mentions the matter of cadential rhythm, first raised by Alberic.

[25] See Fassler's summary, "Accent," 178–79. She remarks that the author "seems to say that all syllables in a rhythmic poem are equal . . ." and characterizes this as a "possible attempt at clarifying a difficult point, . . . on which most twelfth-century authors are silent." Her survey shows, however, that the only other twelfth-century treatise (the original *De rithmico dictamine*) also specifically mentions equality (or parity, as the author puts it) of syllables (Fassler, "Accent," 174–75; see also 421–28 above).

[26] In view of Jerome of Moravia's designation of the music theorist Johannes de Garlandia as "Gallicus," it may be well to differentiate the two more or less contemporary Parisian teachers, both named Johannes and both living in the Clos de Garlande, as "Anglicus" and "Gallicus," respectively; see Erich Reimer, *Johannes de Garlandia: De mensurabili musica* 1, Beihefte zum Archiv für Musikwissenschaft 10 (Wiesbaden: Steiner, 1972), 4, 13–14, and 16–17.

[27] For bibliographic details and an extensive discussion of this treatise see Fassler, "Accent," 180–88. As regards the date (early 1230s, possibly ca. 1220), see her nn. 42 and 64 on 174 and 180.

[28] Cf. the formulation by Aurelian of Réôme, p. 418 above.

[29] For the history of this rhetorical figure see Klopsch, *Einführung,* 46. The term (*similiter desinens*) need not be understood only as rhyme, however, as Mari, *I trattati,* 36, n. 4, did. It could have been intended to stand, at least partially, for identical articulation. Fassler, "Accent," 182, states that John, in using "terminology borrowed from metrics . . . does not connect the patterns with rhyme." But Garlandia mentions rhyme as the primary aspect of *rithmus.*

iamb consists of a short and a long). Spondee here means a word standing in the manner of a spondee. . . .[30]

We will then have to begin with the simplest matters, that is, with that *rithmus* which consists of two units [i.e., rhythmic units or beats], inasmuch as that meter that is the shortest (since *rithmus* imitates meter in some respect) consists of two units, as for instance the iambic dimeter, which consists of two meters [i.e., dipodies], and the meter in turn of two units, as *Iam lucis orto sidere.*

Rithmus est consonancia dictionum in fine similium sub certo numero sine metricis pedibus ordinata . . . . Ordinata dicitur quia ordinate debent cadere dictiones in rithmo. Rithmus sumpsit originem secundum quosdam a colore rhetorico qui dicitur similiter desinens. Quidam vero rithmus cadit quasi metrum iambicum, quidam quasi metrum spondaicum. Iambus in hoc loco intelligatur dictio cuius penultima corripitur; iambus enim constat ex brevi et longa. Spondeus hic dicitur dictio stans ad modum spondei. . . . A simpliciori ergo erit inchoandum; scilicet a rithmo qui constat ex duabus percussionibus, quia, cum rithmus imitetur metrum in aliquo, illud metrum quod est brevius, constat ex duabus percussionibus, sicut iambicum dimetrum, quod constat ex duobus metris, et metrum ex duabus percussionibus, ut illud Iam lucis orto sidere.[31]

John's citation of a simple hymn—a specimen from a genre linked to the tradition of metrical poetry—serves the purpose of explaining the meaning of *percussio,* i.e., a rhythmical unit, in analogy to a metrical unit,[32] though the latter is of course commonly called *pes.* And indeed, after touching on some further taxonomic issues,[33] he begins with the simplest *rithmus,* i.e., the *rithmus dispondaicus,* as he calls it, "which contains four units consisting of four words or parts thereof" ("continet quattuor percussiones, que sunt ex quattuor dictionibus vel partibus earundem dictionum"). His example as well as subsequent examples of other categories make it clear that, unlike the cited hymn, a *rithmus dispondaicus,* in fact, as one would expect, consists of two units, each made up, more often than not, of two words:

[30] This apparently tautological sentence shows Garlandia's professional awareness of the transfer of metrical terminology to a different context. It also seems to make clear that the earlier theorists' (especially Alberic's) use of the word *producere* means a lengthening not beyond normal isochronism, but only in comparison with the shortening of the penult of a proparoxytonic word at the end of a verse.

[31] Traugott Lawler, ed., *The* Parisiana Poetria *of John of Garland,* Yale Studies in English 182 (New Haven: Yale University Press, 1974), 160; Mari, *I trattati,* 36. Lawler consistently translates *rithmus* as "rhymed poem" or "rhymed poetry."

[32] In so doing, he therefore does not "jump ahead of himself" (Fassler, "Accent," 182).

[33] They will be dealt with presently.

O Maria,
Vite via,
per hoc mare
singulare. . . .[34]

Thereafter, *rithmi trispondaici* and *rithmi tetraspondaici*, consisting of three and four "spondaic" units, respectively, are exemplified:

Rosa sine nota,
gemma pulcra tota,
lutum peccatorum
ablue nostrorum.

Eva mundum deformavit,
Ave mundum reformavit,
munda mundum emundavit. . . .

An iambic *rithmus*, he continues, sometimes contains eight syllables, sometimes seven. His examples are:

Ve, ve mundo a scandalis,
ve nobis ut acephalis.

Ave, plena gratia,
ave, culpe venia.

Maria, perge previa,
nos transfer ad celestia,
prius emundans vicia,
fons vite, culpe venia.

As in the case of "spondaic" *rithmi*, he remarks that the stanzas of a poem must consist of two, three, or four verses.[35]

Johannes had earlier[36] pointed out briefly that "one kind of *rithmus* is simple, the other composite" ("rithmorum alius simplex, alius compositus"). Now, having demonstrated eight kinds of *rithmi simplices* (i.e., *rithmi* consisting of verses exclusively ending either "spondaically" or "iambically"), he simply notes that *rithmi compositi* "result from their commingling in alternation" ("ex permixtione eorum octo ad invicem resultant compositi"). "So that this be made manifest, let us join the above examples in such a way that a *rithmus dispondaicus* has a variant iambic

[34] Lawler, *The* Parisiana Poetria, 160–61; Mari, *I trattati*, 37. Tetrasyllabic verses are not part of Alberic's system; see p. 419 above.

[35] Lawler, *The* Parisiana Poetria, 162 and 164; Mari, *I trattati*, 37. Unlike the more meticulous author of *De rithmico dictamine*, John applies rhyme only to the last two syllables of verses, even if the last word is proparoxytonic ("iambic").

[36] See n. 33 above.

ending in its third [verse]" ("Quod ut manifestum fiat, coniungamus predicta exempla ita quod dispondaicus rithmus habeat iambicum differenciam[37] in tercio . . ."):

O Maria,
vite via
nobis perge previa . . .

Rosa sine nota,
gemma pulchra tota,
nostra dele vicia;
lutum peccatorum
ablue nostrorum,
vite via, venia.[38]

Or for that matter,

O virgo, perge previa,
nos transfer ad celestia,
que mundum emundasti. . . .[39]

Composite *rithmi* are to be performed as follows:

And note that a variant spondaic ending in an iambic *rithmus* begins low and ascends in its declamation, and with the addition of one syllable, so as to resemble the iambic [*rithmus*]. In a spondaic *rithmus* a variant iambic ending begins high and descends in declamation, with the reduction of one syllable, so as to resemble the spondaic [*rithmus*].

Et nota quod spondaica differencia in iambico rithmo incipit ab imo et tendit in altum in scansione, et addicione unius sillabe, ut sit similis iambico. In spondaico rithmo iambica differencia incipit ab alto et tendit in imum scandendo, subtracta una sillaba, ut sit similis spondayco.

These rules offer significant clarifications. In the first place, John stipulates that variant iambic endings elide the vowel of the penult and variant spondaic endings repeat it. Secondly, he leaves no doubt that the cadential articulation of verses involves both the duration (long or short) and the pitch (relatively high or low) of the penult. And thirdly, his rule regarding pitch makes it apparent that all non-cadential syllables are declaimed equally, not only in duration, but also in pitch, in a manner similar to the reciting tone of psalmody (see example 1).[40]

[37] The meaning of the term is analogous to that familiar from psalmody.
[38] The sources have *vita*, as do the two editors.
[39] Lawler, *The* Parisiana Poetria, 164, 170, and 172; Mari, *I trattati*, 38 and 43–44.
[40] Lawler, *The* Parisiana Poetria, 172; Mari, *I trattati*, 44. Lawler and Fassler, "Accent," 185,

Example 1

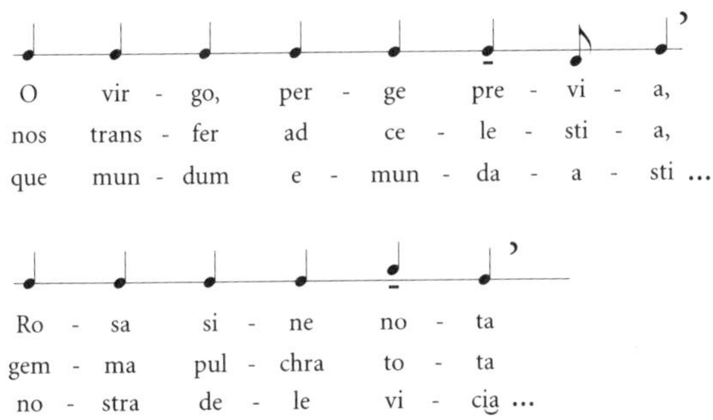

In sum, it seems that Garlandia's treatise does not contain anything essentially new when compared with *De rithmico dictamine.* To be sure, he codifies the *rithmi compositi*, a species left out of account by the earlier author; but the relative terseness of his treatise hardly needs to be taken as an indication of his ignorance of the mixed species. (A number of his poetic citations are, in fact, *rithmi compositi.*) Garlandia's use of the terms spondee and iamb in a non-quantitative context provides a new elucidation of the declamation of verse endings.[41] In addition, his coinage of *trispondeus* (or *trispondaicus*) and *tetraspondeus* (or *quadrispondaicus*)[42] gives names to the traditional isochronic syllabism of *rithmi* by extending the "spondaic" equality of paroxytonic verse endings backward to cover the entire verse.[43]

Of the three thirteenth-century treatises listed by Fassler[44] only that by Master Sion of Vercelli (before 1290) contains an interesting variant of John of Garland's codification. Instead of the latter's terms *spondaicus* and

translate *ab imo* and *ab alto* as "with an unstressed syllable . . . with a stressed syllable" and "with a weak syllable . . . with the strong," respectively.

The reduction of a syllable is a device that would seem to have arisen from the tradition of synizesis. (Elision was practiced ever since Roman antiquity; see Norberg, *Introduction*, 29–30). Adjacency of two vowels linking the last two syllables of a proparoxytonic word (e.g., *filius*) is, of course, quite common in Latin, and the preponderance of *rithmi iambici* given by Johannes de Garlandia end with such words.

The remainder of the treatise deals with ornamental rhetorical figures and with various rhyme patterns.

41 See the testimony of Nicolaus Tibinus (n. 79 below). The author of *De rithmico dictamine* does not discuss cadential durations.

42 A good many grammarians, beginning with Terentius Maurus (end of the second century) and ending with Isidore of Seville (ca. 600), report the *dispondeus*, but none knows any higher order of spondee; see "dispondeus" in *Thesaurus Linguae Latinae* 5, col. 1420, and the references given there.

43 Verses that both end paroxytonically and contain an odd number of syllables, such as Alberic's *rithmus epdasyllabus, pentasyllabus,* or *endecasyllabus* (see Davis, "The 'De rithmis,' "210 and 213–14), are impossible in Garlandia's square system.

44 Fassler, "Accent," 175. They are numbers III, VI, and II in Mari, *I trattati.*

iambicus he uses *spondaicus* and *dactylicus*, beginning his examples of both with verses of four and five syllables;[45] the "dactylic" verses are to be read as editorially indicated above the words (example 2).

Example 2

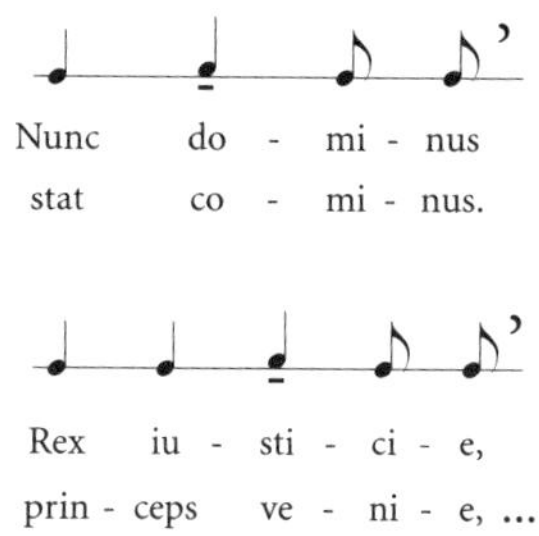

But the designation of such verse endings as dactylic is, in fact, a corruption, as ever since Alberic the deviation from syllabism could occur only on the penult, if the last word was proparoxytonic. Johannes de Garlandia expressly rejects the dactylic interpretation of such verse endings, in favor of his iambic designation.[46]

For verses containing seven to ten syllables Master Sion mandates first hemistichs ending spondaically—a significant increase in precisely measured organization, the more so as he does not recognize the terms trispondaic and tetraspondaic. Yet, the system does not always work cleanly, as for instance in the first verse of this example of spondaic endings after both the fourth and the eighth syllables of each verse:

Terret me dies terroris
ire dei et furoris,
dies luctus et tremoris . . .

II

More than a century ago Wilhelm Meyer "aus Speyer" (1845–1917), a great part of whose scholarly production was concerned with *rithmi*, characterized this genre as follows:

[45] Mari, *I trattati*, 17. Johannes de Garlandia recognized no *rithmi iambici* of fewer than seven syllables; see 425 above.

[46] Lawler, *The* Parisiana Poetria, 180; Mari, *I trattati*, 51.

In the examples above, the sign "_" under a notehead is intended, like an *episema*, to indicate an appropriate lengthening.

> But, in marked contrast to . . . quantitative poetry, the essence of rhythmic poetry is to be observed in the ordinary accentuation and pronunciation used in prose. This principle, that words are accented and pronounced as in ordinary speech, . . . was never given up, and we, too, must pronounce the individual words of rhythmic verses without regard and awareness of the verse pattern.[47]
>
> From the beginning to the end of Latin rhythmic poetry we face a striking phenomenon: if words are accented as ordinarily in prose, the endings of corresponding verses receive identical accentuation (either –́⏑– or –́⏑), but their preceding syllables very often display varying kinds of pronunciation [*verschiedenen Tonfall*].[48]

And, some twenty years later:

> I have always maintained this result of my research: the verses of rhythmic poetry are prose with a particular final cadence. As Latin accentuation knows only two types of word endings, dóminus and múltus, trochaic and spondaic terminations are imitated by the latter, while all terminations with short penult are imitated by the former. . . . Before these terminations one merely counted syllables.[49]

Apart from the conclusion (concerning prose articulation of verses with two types of cadential articulation) familiar from the medieval treatises, Meyer also discusses a great variety of verse schemes, which, as derivatives from classical quantitative patterns of versification, he considers to have been used by medieval poets as skeletal frameworks for their *rithmi*. "By far the greatest part of the *rithmi* of the earlier period [sixth century to twelfth century]," he says, "are composed in forms imitating forms of quantitative Latin poetry."[50] Alas, "to recognize the laws governing the construction of the inner part of the verse," he points out, "is as important as it is difficult."[51] The scholarly obligation of thus systematizing the profusion of *rithmi* from his "second period" (twelfth and thirteenth centuries) is no less challenging, the preservation of several manuals notwithstanding.

[47] Meyer, *Gesammelte Abhandlungen* 1:183. The original date of publication of this essay was 1882. For similar statements, applicable to "the entire corpus of rhythmic Latin poetry," see idem, 2:8–9.

[48] Meyer, *Gesammelte Abhandlungen* 2:52.

[49] Meyer, *Gesammelte Abhandlungen* 3:12. The original date of this essay was 1906. His use of metrical terms must of course be understood as adapted to rhythmical contexts, i.e., not quantitatively, but "qualitatively" (prose accentuation). Though he does not specifically stress equality of syllables, his references to syllable-counting and his frequent description of rhythmic verses as prose (except for their durationally emphasized cadences) can only be understood as equivalent to syllabism, prose and syllabic poetry being dictions without quantification of their syllabic ingredients.

[50] Meyer, *Gesammelte Abhandlungen* 1:197. See also 174 and 177.

[51] Meyer, *Gesammelte Abhandlungen* 1:179.

> These treatises, however, are late and, while dealing sparsely with a few verse types, offer us much useless material about the construction of the simpler stanzas. Consequently we have to glean everything ourselves from the poems.[52]

Meyer's copious analyses that follow this *schwer gefaßten Entschluß*, as well as the enormous collection of painstaking examinations of the repertoire from his "first period," persuaded him that the syllabism with prose accentuation found in *rithmi* is accommodated in the verse structures of classic poetry. Its regulatory quantitative patterns had given way to the regularity of syllabic counting, though it could not be said that accentual patterns had taken the place of quantitative patterns. He therefore formulated his concept of *Taktwechsel*[53] to account for the more or less frequent thwarting of the expectation of accentual regularity that had caused him to insist on prose accentuation in recitation (except for the cadences).[54]

Dag Norberg, in 1958, quoted the first sentence of Meyer's observation published in the third volume of his *Gesammelte Abhandlungen*,[55] in order to take issue with it. "But the idea that the syllables before the terminal cadences could have any rhythm whatever conflicts with several facts and must be revised. Indeed, as we are about to see, rhythmic verse had exactly the same accents as the corresponding quantitative [type of] verse."[56] While Meyer disdained the treatises published by Mari, Norberg disregards them. "Following the methods of modern scholarship," he states, "we'll do well, to the extent of what is possible, . . . to restrict ourselves to attempting to analyze and determine the facts," which are fundamentally that the historic basis of the poets of *rithmi* "was quantitative poetry, and from there they proceeded when they attempted to compose poetry in accordance with new principles."[57] This statement of policy is then followed by detailed analyses, arranged by types of perceived imitation. Although Norberg asserts that "it is only in rather rare cases that W. Meyer's rule proves valuable, i.e., that the accentuation before the terminal cadence is free,"[58] he is forced to acknowledge relatively frequent exceptions.[59]

[52] Meyer, *Gesammelte Abhandlungen* 1:245. According to a note added in 1905, six years after Mari's publication, "one learns nothing new from any of these treatises."

[53] Meyer, *Gesammelte Abhandlungen* 1:185; see also 261–74. As he points out (185–86), it can occur only in verses of more than six syllables.

[54] Quite in contrast, Fassler states that "accent and ictus coincided, and sharply marked accentual patterns prevailed"; "The Role of the Parisian Sequence in the Evolution of Notre-Dame Polyphony," *Speculum* 62 (1987): 346.

[55] See n. 49 above.

[56] Norberg, *Introduction*, 90–91.

[57] Norberg, *Introduction*, 92.

[58] Norberg, *Introduction*, 97.

[59] For instance, ". . . plus ou moins exacte" and "dans bien des cas" (Norberg, *Introduction*, 106); ". . . ne suivent pas ce système d'accentuation" (107); "imitation partielle de structure"

The issue is a matter of positing the existence of a system and then regarding its prosodic obligations, inherited and transformed from metrics, as either less or more viable. In other words, is prose pronunciation normal, or are the poets insensitive to the presumed demands of accentual regularity imposed by the metrically derived verse schemes? Is it proper, then, to set up the expectation of such patterns as an aesthetic criterion?

One must keep in mind that the medieval commentators give us no clue regarding the poets' presumable awareness of the structural traditions they are said to have imitated. All the treatises tell us that it is counting of syllables that is their concern. Nevertheless, we may wish to credit them with atavistic imitations of the traditional meters,[60] just as the sophistication of numerical motet construction cannot be denied, even though no detailed description of the various techniques seems to have been written by any medieval author. (Perhaps as conceptual fundaments these techniques were too self-evident to require comment.) That all the pronunciations that collide with the strictures of the verse systems should be thought of as accentual insensitivities[61] seems unlikely. It may be better to regard the notion of *iudicium aurium* as a continuing tradition supporting the concept of isochronous prose-like delivery of the syllables, except for the two defining types of cadential articulation. It is surely significant that the medieval

(113, 115, 117); "... souvent appliqué ..." (123). Curiously, in the case of Meyer's (1:224–25) and Norberg's (98) discussions of the same poem—the eleventh-century hymn *Mare, fons, ostium*—Norberg erroneously accuses Meyer of falsely mandating for it accentual equivalence to the quantitative meter both regard as being imitated. Meyer, however, had in his subtitle simply identified the classical meter in question; thereafter he meticulously listed all variants by categories, a few of which are cited by Norberg, who here proceeds to adopt Meyer's "to-be-revised" insight by stating that the poets "did not scan such verses, but read them with prose accents." It is bewildering to note this conclusion from an author (albeit in a specific case) who had previously criticized his predecessor for the same conclusion.

[60] Significantly, in the one extant case of specific metrical designation of a poem by a medieval writer, Alberic of Monte Cassino, the last not to report rhyme, makes a mistake; see n. 16 above.

Ewald Jammers maintains that the origin of rhythmic poetry lies in the tradition of psalmody, as quantitative principles began to lose force. The factors he adduces are compelling, as is the fact, not mentioned by him, that the earliest known *rithmus* was called a *psalmus* by its author (Klopsch, *Einführung*, 6 and 39; p 418 above). Moreover, his somewhat intuitive approach turns out to be supported by the testimony of Johannes de Garlandia (see p. 426 above). Though Jammers rejects Norberg's theory of *rithmi* as imitative derivations from quantitative meters, he credits the adaptation of psalmodic traditions to the frameworks of quantitative poetry for the rise of *rithmus;* see his *Ausgewählte Melodien des Minnesangs: Einführung, Erläuterungen und Übertragung* (Tübingen: Niemeyer, 1963), 36–39 (= "Der Vers der Trobadors und Trouveres und die deutschen Kontrafakten," in *Medium aevum vivum: Festschrift für Walther Bulst*, eds. Hans Robert Jauss and Dieter Schaller [Heidelberg: Winter, 1960], 148–50).

[61] That is the term Klopsch, *Einführung*, 61, uses in describing the poetry of Augustinus's *Psalmus contra partem Donati.* It is interesting that in this context no one comments on the systematic insensitivity of quantitative poetry to prose accentuation.

writers, who knew the classical meters thoroughly, seem to have regarded them as basically immaterial to their discussions of *rithmi*. Whether a line imitated the Phalaecian or the Lesser Asclepiadean verse[62] was irrelevant to them; the only thing that counted, literally, was that, in any case, such a line contained eleven syllables with paroxytonic verse ending. Quite possibly the treatises teach us all we need to know.

III

The chief modern investigators of *rithmus*, concerning themselves primarily, if not exclusively, with the poetry, are Meyer and Norberg. These two scholars are largely disregarded by those twentieth-century writers who have approached the subject by way of the treatises. Traugott Lawler, in his edition of John of Garland's *Parisiana poetria*, of which the *Ars rithmica* is the final chapter, translates a sentence from his definition of *rithmus* as follows: "Rhymed poems [sic] may be likened to quantitative meters: they are either quasi-iambic or quasi-spondaic."[63] In his editorial capacity as translator Lawler has here made cadential patterns applicable to the entire verse. His explanation: "Since it is not explicitly stated, one should note that it is the last word in a line that determines whether that line is iambic or spondaic. . . ."[64] In effect finding that John of Garland, professor of grammar and rhetoric (i.e., *ars dictaminis*) at the University of Paris,[65] did not know or value the difference between a spondee and a trochee, he adds:

[62] Meyer, *Gesammelte Abhandlungen* 1:224–25. In her recent book *Der musikalische Satz der Notre Dame-Conductus*, Münchner Veröffentlichungen zur Musikgeschichte 36 (Tutzing: Schneider, 1988), Roswitha Stelzle rightly puts it as a fundamental challenge for scholarship to determine "whether indeed it was the aim of any particular poet to produce a consistent verse rhythm" (185). She perceives the performer's dilemma of having to decide whether to follow a consistent verse pattern and sacrifice "the natural verbal accents" or to reorient oneself in accordance with the natural verbal accents, a dilemma whose unequivocal solution she regards as impossible (186). Even though she deals with poetic structure as "an essential matter, so as to clarify the mutual interaction of poetry and music" (11), in the end she offers no transcriptions, since, as she puts it in the regrettable spirit of editorial renunciation, "the question of the rhythmic identity of a melody must, in any case, remain open" (259).

[63] Lawler, *The* Parisiana Poetria, 161. His translation of the *Parisiana poetria*, praised as "excellent" by one reviewer, was criticized as "unsatisfactory" by another; see Winthrop Wetherbee in *Modern Philology* 74 (1977): 399, and Douglas Kelly in *Speculum* 52 (1977): 708–09. For another translation of this passage see p. 423 above.

[64] Lawler, *The* Parisiana Poetria, 265.

[65] For detailed information on Johannes de Garlandia (Anglicus) see Louis J. Paetow, ed., *Morale Scolarium of John of Garland*, Memoirs of the University of California 4/2, History 1/2 (Berkeley: University Press, 1927), 77–106. The subject of the new rhetoric is treated extensively by Paetow, *The Arts Course at Medieval Universities*, The University Studies, University of Illinois 3/7 (Urbana-Champaign: University Press, 1910), 70–91.

"(We would consider all of John's 'spondaic' types trochaic, and his 'iambics' as combining two trochees and a dactyl or a dactyl, a trochee, and a dactyl.)" That is the extent of his comment.

Professor Fassler similarly states that John of Garland, in "high-lighting the use of ictus or beat in rhythmic poetry," demonstrates that "quasi-spondaic lines are consistently patterned strong-weak throughout; word accent and beat are in perfect agreement."[66] In quasi-iambic *rithmi*, however, "the accents of individual words do not follow an iambic pattern of weak-strong throughout; only the cadences are consistently weak-strong:

> Ave, plena gratia,
> Ave, culpe venia."[67]

These verses, however, can only be classified as rhythmic imitations of the second hemistich of the trochaic septenarius (i.e., a catalectic trochaic verse);[68] it could not possibly in any way—except for the cadence—be related to the iambic pattern. Professor Fassler concludes "that what John calls spondaic lines (what we might [sic] call trochaic) are consistently patterned long-short and are described in terms of 'percussiones' or beats. What he calls iambic lines occasionally exhibit inconsistency in the patterns found throughout individual lines. . . . when he attempts to discuss lines of a weak-strong or quasi-iambic cast, he gets into trouble."[69] Subsequently she provides descriptions of his "attempts to extricate himself from the difficulties of working with quasi-iambic lines,"[70] of his seeming "to cover for this inadequacy," i.e., that "the lines he describes as 'iambs' in his examples do not always have consistent patterns of weak-strong throughout,"[71] of providing a "tortuous explanation" of *rithmi compositi*, and of his "clearly believing that the pattern of the cadence should be found consistently in the rest of the line," since he "wants word accents to fall in regular patterns so they can coincide with the beat or ictus."[72]

In her summation Fassler states "that the treatises 'De rithmis' offer no system of long and short syllables to composer/poets from the twelfth and early thirteenth centuries. Rhythmic poetry . . . appears to consist of

[66] The last clause is largely true, though there are exceptions. Fassler, like Lawler, is puzzled by Garlandia's terminology: "The reason he chose to call the pattern long-short 'spondaic' (what would usually be called 'trochaic') remains obscure" ("Accent," 182, n. 7; also "The Role of the Parisian Sequence," 361, n. 46).

[67] "Accent," 182–83.

[68] Norberg, *Introduction*, 117.

[69] Fassler, "Accent," 183.

[70] Ibid., 184.

[71] Ibid., 185.

[72] Ibid., 186.

syllables of equal duration."[73] Except for the omission of articulation of verse endings, this is entirely consistent with the evidence of the treatises, though it seems oddly inconsistent with her problematic evaluation of Johannes de Garlandia's definitions, as well as with her brief comment on the two treatises listed by her as nos. 4 and 6, i.e., nos. III and II in Mari's collection. Neither of these treatises, written under the influence of John of Garland's book, shows that "the theorists were trying to describe the force of the accent throughout the entire line. . . ."[74] In fact, Master Sion of Vercelli, the author of the second of these treatises, could not possibly have wanted to apply the dactylic pattern of his verse endings to the entire verse, since such a scheme cannot fit tetrasyllabic or pentasyllabic lines.[75]

As section I of this article has shown, all the treatises in their various ways transmit a thoroughly homogeneous account, beginning with Alberic of Monte Cassino and, with the addition of rhyme as a mandatory element, continued by the author of *De rithmico dictamine*. Modern scholarship has recognized for a long time (section II) that *rithmus* is syllabic rhymed poetry with systematic cadential articulation, either paroxytonic (´– –) or proparoxytonic (´– ⏑ –); the accentual emphases evidently were produced by duration and pitch.[76] But there is no indication that syllabism (prosaic equality of counted components) required regular accentual patterns or that it was affected, corroded, or replaced by quantification, whether systematic or not. As Janet Knapp has put it in a somewhat different context, "the equalizing of the syllables absorbs or accommodates the irregularity of the verses by neutralizing the stresses."[77] Even Nicolaus Tibinus, writing in the second half of the fourteenth century,[78] still explains *rithmus* in the Garlandian tradition, though in more individual language.[79] Therefore

[73] Ibid., 187.

[74] Ibid., 179, n. 60.

[75] See pp. 427–28 above. Janet Knapp's statement ("Musical Declamation," 388, n. 22) that three verses cited in the treatise of Master Sion of Vercelli (Fassler's no. 6) are there "identified, on the basis of the cadence as dactylic" must therefore be discounted. The same approach had been taken earlier by Sarah A. Fuller, who in her discussion of Master Sion's treatise ("Aquitanian Polyphony," 189–90) as well as of Garlandia's (192, n. 19) also simply and without comment identified spondees with trochees.

It should be pointed out in this connection that there is for Garlandia no such thing as a *triiambus* or a *quadriiambus*.

[76] Regarding accentuation, see n. 23 above and Nicholas Tibinus's statement quoted in n. 79 below.

[77] Knapp, "Musical Declamation," 392. There is, therefore, no need to comment on the "discrepancy between theory and actuality" and "confusion evident in the medieval theorist's treatment of stress within lines" (Fuller, "Aquitanian Polyphony," 192).

[78] Klopsch, *Einführung*, 35 and 40. The treatise is no. VIII in Mari.

[79] Briefly stated, his basic definition of *rithmus* involves a *mensura communis*, which concerns the number of syllables contained in each verse (p. 96), and a *mensura singularis*, which pertains to the rhyming syllables and therefore involves both *mensuram et accentum*. "By

he still singles out "inept accentuation" as a defect (*vicium*) only in conjunction with rhymes.[80]

Walther Bulst,[81] F. J. E. Raby,[82] and especially John Stevens in an admirable passage in his recent book[83] have given illuminating accounts of the nature of *rithmus.* The first two of these authors contend that before 1200 the rhythm that governs the cadence had come to control the whole verse. Bulst gives two twelfth-century verses to demonstrate the total coincidence of accentuation and (trochaic) verse ictus, while Raby contends that "progress towards verse of definitely rhythmical structure was slow" and that "it was not until the eleventh century that the principles of accentual verse were fully developed and fully mastered . . ." He describes "the Sequence in the later eleventh and early twelfth century" as having rhythm that "is regular and is based wholly on the word-accent, with occasional transpositions of stress. . . . The Sequence measure par excellence is the trochaic. . . ."[84] The easy coincidence of Latin accentuation with the long-short pattern of the trochee has been observed often. Even so, it seems that the incontestable appearance of quasi-trochaic regularity of the later sequence did not affect the isochronous tradition of *rithmus.* As it happens, one of the examples cited by the author of *De rithmico dictamine* is the seventh stanza (*Audi verbum novitatis*) of the prose *Missus Gabriel de celis,* while the first line of the well-known prose *Verbum bonum et suave* turns up in John of Garland's treatise

accent," he says, "I mean nothing more than the prolongation and abbreviation of syllables, i.e., their high and short [sic] rendition, so that a high or elevated sound is distinguished by the prolongation of a syllable, and its low, slight pronunciation by its abbreviation." His predecessors, he adds, express this by the use of the terms *iambicus* and *spondaicus,* the former meaning abbreviation, the latter prolongation (98).

[80] Mari, *I trattati,* 114. According to Mari, his examples are "'legere' "and "'rege' [sic]." The defective word must have been any of the roughly dozen verbs of the second conjugation ending *-gere,* such as *egere* or *vegere;* see Otto Gradenwitz, *Laterculi vocum latinarum* (Leipzig, 1904; repr. Hildesheim: Olms, 1966), 365.

[81] *Über die mittlere Latinität des Abendlandes* (Heidelberg: [Schneider], 1946), 18–20.

[82] F. J. E. Raby, *A History of Christian Latin Poetry from the Beginnings to the Close of the Middle Ages,* 2nd ed. (Oxford: Clarendon, 1953), 21–22.

[83] Stevens, *Words and Music,* 420. Jeremy Yudkin in his review (*Speculum* 64 [1989]: 765–69) describes Stevens's approach to the rendition of medieval non-quantitative poetry as his "isosyllabic rhythmic theory" and questions whether "formal speech [*dictamen*] [is] really isosyllabic." One should not, however, be led to infer from the review that Stevens, after stating his proposition "as the central hypothesis in the introduction" presents it "as a resounding conclusion at the end of the final chapter" (768) without adducing any evidentiary support. This essay cites additional medieval and modern testimony of what turns out to have been practice (rather than theory).

[84] Raby, *A History,* 347–48. Margot Fassler likewise has characterized the Parisian sequence as displaying "a relentless thrust of the trochaic accent" ("The Role," 360).

as an example of *quadrispondaic rithmus.*[85] Once again, then, it seems that, notwithstanding occasional "humanistic" traits in medieval musico-textual relationships, it was not until well into the fifteenth century that a decisive prosodic reorientation took place.[86]

IV

Professor Knapp has offered the conclusion that in the Notre-Dame *conductus* repertoire "trochaic" rhythmic poetry is not "invariably governed by the first rhythmic mode." Her example "can readily be seen to move in the longs of the fifth mode."[87] In fact, it turns out that the conclusion cited in the first paragraph of the present essay is, if not supported, certainly paralleled by the nature of *rithmus. Conducti* are *rithmi,* and as such the poems were declaimed syllabically (in the poetic sense of that word). Monophonic settings are known for two of the *conductus* poems cited by Master Sion of Vercelli, neither of which belongs to the Notre-Dame repertoire:[88] *Ex Ade vicio,* preserved in two related melismatic settings,[89] and the strictly non-melismatic *Patrem parit filia.*[90] Only the setting of the latter poem therefore allows the shortening of the penultimate of the proparoxytonic word at the end of each verse. The setting of *Ex Ade vicio,* on the other hand, like many Notre-Dame *conducti,* contravenes the rule of the correption of the penultimate. In fact, all musical settings tend to slow down the delivery of the poetry, even if they are not melismatic. The general inapplicability of the rhythmic modes—Gennrich's first-mode transcription of *Patrem parit filia* must, of course, be rejected—is thus not refuted by the poetic evidence. Nor is the corpus of rhythmic poetry of any consequence for the rise of the rhythmic modal system. *Conducti* and, for that matter, motets are not *vers mesurés.*

[85] Mari, *I trattati,* 13 and 37; Lawler, *The* Parisiana Poetria, 162. Since the first verse of the second stanza of *Missus Gabriel* also is *Verbum bonum et suave,* it may be that the same sequence was cited by both authors.

[86] Cf. Reckow, "rectitudo"; Sanders, "Conductus," 466 and n. 97.

[87] Knapp, "Musical Declamation," 400; as to the fifth mode, see Sanders, "Conductus," n. 101.

[88] Mari, *I trattati,* 18.

[89] Transcriptions by Jacques Handschin in *New Oxford History of Music* 2 (London: Oxford University Press, 1954), 173–74, and by Wulf Arlt in *Ein Festoffizium des Mittelalters aus Beauvais* (Cologne: Volk, 1970), Editionsband, 74.

[90] Transcriptions by Friedrich Gennrich in *Die Kontrafaktur im Liedschaffen des Mittelalters,* Summa Musicae Medii Aevi 12 (Langen-bei-Frankfurt: n.p., 1965), 259, and by Arlt, *Ein Festoffizium,* 156.

Under these circumstances it is not surprising that no Notre-Dame poems appear in the treatises. (Motet poetry could in any case not be expected to turn up in them.) According to a gloss to John of Garland's *Dictionarius* he wrote a *conductus* poem, datable ca. 1230,[91] which has not been preserved.[92] But the absence of all Notre-Dame poetry from his *Ars rithmica* not only lends support to Reimer's conclusion regarding the two Johannes,[93] but taken together with his bewildering brief excursion into musical theory[94] it also seems to indicate that in the context of the *studium generale* at the young University of Paris Johannes, the grammarian, was unlikely to have had much contact with Johannes, the musician, or much interest in the *musica practica* he represented. In accordance with tradition the study of music at the university was taken up with its quadrivial significance, i.e., Boethius. (In fact, we have no specific information just where in Paris Johannes "Gallicus" was active as a *magister*, though Notre Dame is a prime candidate.)[95] It was not until the late thirteenth century that syntheses of *musica speculativa* and *musica practica* began to be written by university professors, though before long, discussions of practical aspects of musical composition and performance predominated.[96]

Johannes de Garlandia, a man of considerable erudition, was in full command of the complexities of classical metrics. Alexander de Villa-Dei,

[91] Jacques Handschin, "Conductus-Spiciligien," *Archiv für Musikwissenschaft* 9 (1952): 115, n. 2.

[92] Gordon Anderson, "Notre Dame and Related Conductus—A Catalogue Raisonné," *Miscellanea Musicologica* 7 (1975): 34 (item R 1).

[93] See n. 26 above.

[94] See Lawler, *The* Parisiana Poetria, 267–68, for the frustration it caused him and others.

[95] The most comprehensive and up-to-date discussion of the medieval university is Alan B. Cobban's *The Medieval Universities* (London: Methuen, 1975); see also Gordon Leff, *Paris and Oxford Universities in the Thirteenth and Fourteenth Centuries* (New York: Wiley, 1968); still of considerable interest is Paetow, *The Arts Course.*

More recently, Christopher Page in an admirable book published after this essay was written (*The Owl and The Nightingale* [London: Oxford University Press, 1989]) has emphasized that the craft of music (notation, polyphony, rhythm, etc.) was not part of the curriculum in institutions of higher learning (137–54, especially 137–43) and that the title *magister* was not exclusively applicable to their faculty members, but designated anyone who, by virtue of his learning and expertise, was superior to most others in the exercise and teaching of his craft.

As regards the dating of the treatise by Anonymous IV as well as the translation of his term *abbreviatio* as "edition" (151), I refer to the conclusions I reached in 1984 ("*Sine littera* and *Cum littera* in Medieval Polyphony," in *Music and Civilization: Essays in Honor of Paul Henry Lang*, Edmund Strainchamps, Maria R. Maniates, Christopher Hatch, eds. [New York: 1984]): Anonymous IV, 1273 or shortly thereafter (223, n. 16); *abbreviatio* = abbreviation (216, n. 3).

[96] For an enlightening discussion of the coexistence or interrelation of these two branches of musical inquiry see Leo Schrade, "Das propädeutische Ethos in der Musikanschauung des Boethius," in idem, *De Scientia Musicae Studia atque Orationes*, ed. Ernst Lichtenhahn (Bern: Haupt, 1967), 35–44 (reprinted from *Zeitschrift für Geschichte der Erziehung und des Unterrichts* 20 [1930]: 179). See also Fritz Reckow's survey "Musica" in *Riemann Musik-Lexikon*, Sachteil (Mainz: Schott, 1967), 594–95, and Rebecca Baltzer, "Notre Dame Manuscripts and Their Owners: Lost and Found," *Journal of Musicology* 5 (1987): 392 and 394–95.

of whose work he had a very low opinion,[97] had in his *Doctrinale* of 1199 listed the following six meters as sufficient for an adequate knowledge of metrics: dactyl, spondee, trochee, anapest, iamb, and tribrach. Inevitably, since it seemed persuasive to regard the six rhythmic modes as analogues of the six poetic meters in question, the issue has been raised whether his arrangement had any influence on the rise of the modal system.[98] (The opposite seems a chronological impossibility.)[99] The circumstances referred to in the preceding paragraph do not help to support such a hypothesis. Neither does the order in which Alexander lists his six meters;[100] and neither does the notion of the fourth mode, which, in contrast to the third, "dactylic" mode, was not in use, according to the anonymous writer often called Dietricus in modern musicological literature. In the metrical system dactyls and anapests were of equal standing. Why then, if—without authorization from medieval authors—one transfers metrical nomenclature to the rhythmic modes, would anapests be included in that system?[101] The significance of the number 6 helped to frame both systems. But while it may be "hard to believe that educated men would not have recognized the parallel,"[102] nevertheless it seems that the modal system independently arose from musical, i.e., polyphonic, developments.[103]

Apparently it is due to both the independence of these disciplines and yet also to the tradition of equality of syllables in *rithmi* that Notre-Dame music had its way with them. Not only *conducti*, but, more strikingly, motets of the thirteenth and fourteenth centuries demonstrate the extent to which composers generally regarded the poets' words as raw material, whose syllabic constituents could be kneaded to fit the necessities of musical structure. To cite Ewald Jammers's penetrating observation, the system of rhythmic modes in conjunction with regularly structured poetry is simply "an especially distinct kind of syllable-counting."[104] Abundant

[97] Paetow, ed., *Morale Scolarium*, 98, 121, 122, and 124–25; also Paetow, *The Arts Course*, 41–43.

[98] See especially Rudolf Flotzinger, "Zur Frage der Modalrhythmik als Antike-Rezeption," *Archiv für Musikwissenschaft* 29 (1972): 203–08.

[99] Sanders, "Conductus," 449 and n. 54.

[100] See the discussion of this factor by Flotzinger, 206.

[101] See Sanders, "Conductus," 467, n. 101.

[102] Stevens, *Words and Music*, 429.

[103] "Undoubtedly," says Craig Wright, "such a system developed for purely musical reasons in a purely musical context . . ." ("Leoninus, Poet and Musician," *Journal of the American Musicological Society* 39 [1986]: 30). Flotzinger, Fassler's statement to the contrary ("The Role," 353 and n. 29) notwithstanding, comes to the opposite conclusion (Flotzinger, "Zur Frage," 208), with which Fassler necessarily agrees ("Accent," 188–90). In fact, she sums up that in *clausulae* "text is no longer present to . . . provide a relentless trochaic beat" ("The Role," 372). See also n. 84 above, as regards the credit she ascribes to the Parisian sequence for bringing about the rhythmic innovations of the Notre-Dame composers.

[104] Ewald Jammers, ed., *Aufzeichnungsweisen der einstimmigen außerliturgischen Musik des Mittelalters*, Palaeographie der Musik 1/4 (Cologne: Volk-Gerig, 1975), 37.

examples exist of what to a humanistic orientation would be horrendous declamatory solecisms.[105] Three specimens from ca. 1300—one French and two English—are cited here (example 3).[106]

Example 3

[105] For two examples from the Notre-Dame motet repertoire see Sanders, "The Medieval Motet," in *Gattungen der Musik in Einzeldarstellungen: Gedenkschrift Leo Schrade* (Bern: Francke, 1973), 511. For the treatment of text in *conducti* see idem, "Conductus," 460–66. Dolores Pesce's contention ("The Significance of Text," 91-117, specifically 101–17) that certain motets in the Bamberg codex "illustrate how . . . the creators of these motets, with few exceptions, work for agreement of musical and textual stress" (p. 106) seems less than tenably proven by the evidence she adduces. Of the third-mode motets, *Ba* no. 30, which, though "treating text declamation somewhat inconsistently" (p. 102), "brings to light the fact that consistent musical-textual treatment occurs only at line endings" (p. 103), nevertheless has a verse ending joining a word accent and a *brevis altera.* The conjunction of a stressed syllable and a *brevis altera* occurs eleven times in no. 77 (though not in the verses cited in figure 6), and while the appearance of four such cases in a total of sixteen *breves altere* (25%) in the triplum of no. 14 may constitute a relatively "low percentage of conflicts between textual and musical accents" (p. 104), it is hardly insignificant. No. 99, a first-mode motet, cited (though not discussed) as a composition with "texts whose regular stress patterns encounter minimum conflict in the musical setting" (p. 103), contains seven disyllables set to a breve followed by a long. Even in cases, such as nos. 2 and 96, that exhibit "fractio modi," consistency in musical patterning takes precedence over propriety of prosody, which in each instance could easily have been achieved by a slight shift in the *fractio.* In general, the relative frequency of good prosody, rather than proving composers' concerned awareness, should be seen as due to the above-mentioned easy coincidence of Latin accentuation with the pattern of the first mode. (The stiffness of third-mode articulation does not, in any case, evince solicitude for good declamation.)

[106] (a) Montpellier, Faculté de Médecine, MS. H 196, fol. 372^{v}. Transcriptions in Yvonne Rokseth, *Polyphonies du XIIIe siècle* (Paris: Oiseau-Lyre, 1936), 3:228; and in Hans Tischler, ed.,

For both *conductus* and motet the fundamental requirement was that the musical and poetic entities displayed structural concinnity so that the imperatives of *ordo* and *ratio* could be seen to have been fulfilled. Elements below the level of the properly constituted verse and of the properly constituted musical phrase were free and structurally insignificant, at least before the gradual development of ornamental isorhythmic procedures.

Even the Latin polyphonic songs (*cantilenae*) composed in fourteenth-century England, though clearly far more solicitous of the accents of the words,[107] occasionally still sacrifice them to the rhythmic regularity of the musical setting to which the syllables are tied. Nevertheless, the lilting musico-poetic lyricism of this usually non-melismatic genre may well have been an outstanding factor in the English music that so delighted Continental listeners in the early fifteenth century.[108] Its influence may justifiably be assumed to have at last given a strong impulse to composers' increasing attention to accentually correct declamation. Before that time, however, such tendencies are not significantly in evidence, and neither poetry nor treatises on poetry can be seen to have played a role.

The Montpellier Codex (Madison, Wis.: A-R, 1978), 3:195. Without explanation both editors chose to disregard the Franconian subdivision of the breve evidently mandated by the notation of most of the compositions preserved in the seventh and eighth fascicles of the manuscript. A reasonable rule of thumb would be to apply Franco's rule when the syllabic subdivision of the breve is both binary and ternary. But even in more conservative compositions the more modern (Franconian) notation might well be regarded as an indication of more modern performance practice. (b) Ernest H. Sanders, ed., *Polyphonic Music of the Fourteenth Century* 14 (Monaco: Oiseau-Lyre, 1979), 88. (c) Frank L. Harrison, ed., *Polyphonic Music of the Fourteenth Century* 15 (Monaco: Oiseau-Lyre, 1980), 30.

[107] As indicated also by the relatively frequent upbeat beginnings. Some English compositions of the late thirteenth century using breves as well as longs for their text settings (e.g., *Polyphonic Music* 14, nos. 32, 34, 36, and 43) already exhibit compelling sensitivity to accentual features.

[108] See Ernest H. Sanders, "Die Rolle der englischen Mehrstimmigkeit des Mittelalters in der Entwicklung von Cantus-firmus-Satz und Tonalitätsstruktur," *Archiv für Musikwissenschaft* 24 (1967): 39–41 and 52–53.

LEO TREITLER

Once More, Music and Language in Medieval Song

This is an occasion that calls for good colloquy, and I would like to address my contribution to a region where I think the possibility of that between David Hughes and myself is at hand. The entrance is his review of John Stevens's book, *Words and Music in the Middle Ages: Song, Narrative, Dance, and Drama, 1050–1350.*[1] But it is so characteristically courteous, soft-spoken, and understated that in order to gain access to the common ground I have in view, I have to angle a bit.

There is a very brief passage on page 407 of the review, of which I would like to remind you. Having just written "the last thing I intend is any suggestion that Stevens is not at home in matters of music," Hughes glances with momentarily raised eyebrow at a discussion in which Stevens compares two manuscript transmissions of a melody from Abelard's "Dolorum solatium," David's lament over Saul and Jonathan (see examples 1 and 2, transcriptions of the fourth strophe from Oxford, Bodleian 79 and Paris, n. a. lat. 3126).

[1] Cambridge: Cambridge University Press, 1986. Hughes's review appears in *Journal of the American Musicological Society* 42 (1989): 403–10.

Ve, ve tibi madida	Woe, woe to you, earth
Tellus cede regia	drenched with royal blood
Qua et te, mi Ionatha,	Where a hand of wickedness
Manus stravit impia.	felled you too, O my Jonathan.

Stevens is impressed by the emphasis on a g tonality expressed as a g triad in Oxford, while "variants in the Paris MS suggest a somewhat more modal, more 'medieval' view. While the melody remains basically as I have described it [that is, his description of the Oxford version], the g-tonality is counterbalanced by an f-triad which emerges clearly in the fourth phrase."

In Hughes's brief comment he first replaces the term "triad" with "chains of thirds," which we all know as the expression of choice for this phenomenon among adepts of medieval melody because it is more neutrally descriptive of this common property of the grammar of medieval melodic styles, less burdened with the distant sound of the approaching harmonic tonality. Hughes hints at "unnecessary problems" raised by the characterization of the Paris version as "more modal, more 'medieval.' " I don't know how far he would pursue those problems, but I think we ought to recognize in this expression the musty ideological aroma of the motif of the ultimately triumphant struggle of the major-minor tonalities of the northern European musical cultures against the ecclesiastical modes of Mediterranean and ultimately Greek background, a motif that was given full development in Hans Joachim Moser's 1914 article "Der Durgedanke als kulturgeschichtliches Problem."[2] I don't mean to suggest that Stevens would associate himself with that nationalist ideological background, any more than would the authors of current well-known textbooks of music history in which this motif is transmitted.[3] Still, awareness of that background allows us better to understand the persistence of this notion against "the truths of this foolish world," in Sir Philip Sidney's words,[4] and gives us some reason to think about whether it suits our social purposes to transmit it.

[2] Hans Joachim Moser, "Der Durgedanke als kulturgeschichtliches Problem," *Sammelbände der Internationalen Musikgesellschaft* 15 (1913–14): 270–95. I discuss this article in relation to the ideological background of modern studies in medieval melodic traditions, in "The Politics of Reception: Tailoring the Present as Fulfilment of a Desired Past," *Journal of the Royal Musical Association* 116 (1991): 289–98.

[3] E.g., "A northern influence on plainchant was that the melodic line became modified through the introduction of more skips, especially the interval of a third . . . . The tendency of Northern melody was toward organization by third." Donald Jay Grout and Claude Palisca, *A History of Western Music*, 4th ed. (New York: Norton, 1988), 64.

[4] E.g., against the results of the comparative study of actual melodies such as those conducted by Charlotte Roederer in "Can we Identify an Aquitanian Chant Style?" *Journal of the American Musicological Society* 27 (1974): 75–99. Roederer notes that a distinguishing

Example 1

Abelard, "Dolorum solatium," fourth strophe, in the version of Oxford, Bodleian 79

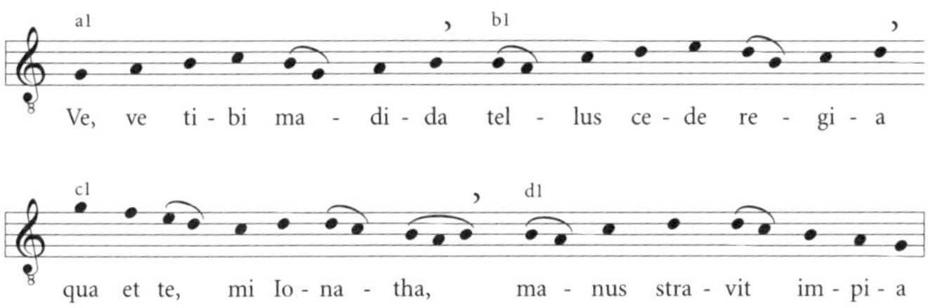

Example 2

Abelard, "Dolorum solatium," fourth strophe, in the version of Paris, B. N., n. a. lat. 3126

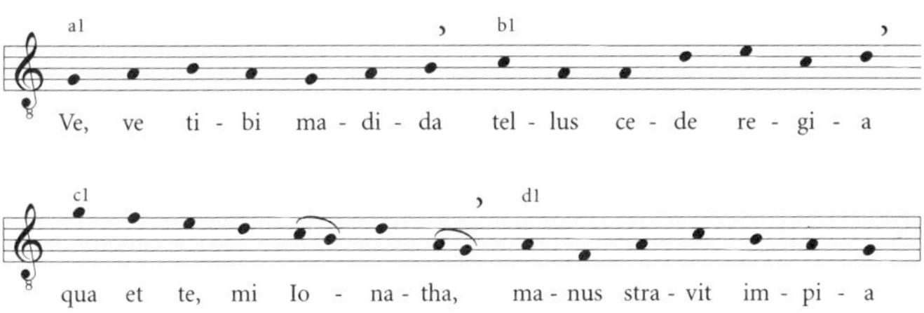

Hughes reminds us then that "many melodies, from classical chant onwards, are based on chains of thirds . . . ." He ends the passage with the observation that "Perhaps one whose basic discipline was music would have . . . been able to create a larger context for the alternation G-b-d with F-a-c" in the Paris version. He does not say what that context is, but I think he is justified in assuming a community of understanding about this in our discipline sufficient to allow him to refer to it. Without meaning to speak for Professor Hughes, I shall try to draw the general outline of that context with reference to the examples—something that I shall need in any case for the discussion of some other songs that are on my agenda. For this and all other recitations of fundamentals, I beg your indulgence.

The diatonic series may be traversed in medieval melody by way of two interlinked third-chains, polarized so that one, anchored in the final, is tonally primary and stable and the other, anchored in the tone below or above the final is secondary and unstable. This is a resource for ordering and contrasting juxtaposed passages of melody, which is to say for creating a dynamic of stability and instability and of tension and repose, also for motivating continuity and closure, and for creating melodic correspondence to dynamics of contrast, amplification, and reference in the phonetic, syntactic, and semantic aspects of language.

The other main resource for accomplishing the same purposes on the whole, especially for the lyric, is the disposition of the diatonic octave as pentachord and tetrachord, in either of the two positions relative to one another. To put it so sharply does of course pretend greater distinctness than melodies can always be depended upon to exhibit, but the two models are extremely useful for description, for example of the two versions of the melody from David's Lament.

The Oxford melody progresses through the g pentachord in the sequential phrases A and B a trichord at a time—g-a-b, b-c-d—then downward through the tetrachord in phrase C but continuing downward to b, and in phrase D reverses the movement through the trichord b-c-d before descending through the pentachord. The last two phrases are linked by this reversal, and the first two are linked through their complementarity with respect to the pentachord. In both cases the even-numbered phrase completes a melodic process and thereby underscores the completion of a sense unit of the poetry. The shaping and motivation of this melody by means of the pentachordal and tetrachordal segments of the octave is a perfectly normal "modal" procedure, no less so than the melodic process of the Paris version. And the correspondence of melodic with linguistic syntax is a

characteristic of this southern tradition is a much sharper organization of melody in third-chains than is the case in northern counterparts.

characteristic use of the resources of melody to clarify meaning in the performance of language. It is true what Stevens writes, that "the shape of the musical strophe coincides with the metrical; the musical phrase is the poetic line; each note or note-group has its corresponding syllable" (Hughes comments on the redundancy of that observation—how else would it be?). It is not true that "the relation between the words and the music is . . . purely formal." What is lacking behind that comment is attention to melodic process as it relates to language process in all its aspects.

The principal difference in the Paris melody is in its use of the third-chain principle within the larger framework of the octave-pentachord-tetrachord principle. Phrases A and B unfold through the pentachord, as in Oxford. But phrase B completes the process rather more subtly by way of a deviation into the secondary third-chain a-c-e before pausing on d. Phrase C traverses the whole octave lickety-split in two segments, tetrachord and pentachord. That having already been accomplished, phrase D destabilizes with the contrasting third-chain f-a-c before settling on the tonic. A different kind of linkage is made between phrases C and D, but a linkage nevertheless, which brings the syntax of the third and fourth lines of the poem to completion in its own way. It is the leap in the third phrase from d to a which is filled in the fourth phrase through the turn to c and the stepwise descent to g.

Late in his book Stevens writes ". . . it may be that the relationship between words and music in serious art-song (*chanson* and *cantio*) should be regarded as metaphysical rather than as physical—it goes beyond the 'musical potential of the poem' into the realm of the ideal. In plain language the musician did not set the words of the poem to music; he set its pattern. It was this pattern, a purely numerical structure of stanzas, lines, and syllables, which preceded both the melody and the poem. The pattern had to be realized in two media—the medium of words and the medium of notes—and it did not matter in the least which was realized first."

The point to which I have arrived so far, by following David Hughes's cue about the one musical example that he has picked out, persuades me that Stevens has not been sufficiently sensitive to the workings of medieval melody in such traditions to warrant this pre-emptive hypothesis. Consequently, against the merits of his interpretations on the theoretical side Stevens's book suffers on the empirical side, and the aesthetic he attempts to fashion for medieval song thus lacks a recognition of the ambiguity that is in the subject and of the contradictions between an expressive, rhetorical practice and a metaphysical theorizing that have yet to be reconciled. Just because I share completely Professor Hughes's belief in the "crucial importance of the relationship between words and music in the Middle Ages to our understanding of not only medieval music but later styles as well," I believe that Stevens's book should be approached with the greatest caution when it comes right down to the subject that it is supposed to be about.

We can build better understanding from different sides. I shall try to make a contribution by way of close interpretations of a few songs with attention to their aspect as sung poetry. I draw them from just the domain of lyric to which Stevens aimed his conclusion, two Latin *versus*, one Troubadour song, and one *Minnesang*.

Example 3 is my transcription of a song from the Aquitanian *versarius* Paris, Bibliothèque Nationale latin 1139, ca. 1100 (pp. 449–50). Example 4 is a separate edition of the poem, with my translation (p. 451).[5]

The poem exemplifies something that Wulf Arlt wrote recently about the poetry of such songs: ". . . an individual construction of form out of the unique character of the sounding verse; an astonishing multiplicity of form-construction."[6] I take only one exception to this formulation: I prefer not to use the word form, either for the song altogether or for the poem, because in our music-scholarly culture that word tends to evoke a sense that Carl Dahlhaus formulated in his *Esthetics of Music:* "Insofar as music is form, it attains its real existence in the very moment when it is past. Still held in memory it emerges into a condition that it never entered during its immediate present; and at a distance it constitutes itself as a surveyable plastic form."[7] But he writes that there is no expression of such an idea before the early sixteenth century, when we encounter for the first time the concept of the finished and absolute work, a concept which, he considers, suffused into the consciousness of "connoisseurs and amateurs" about 1800.[8] My preference is always to keep my eye (or ear) on the flow or process of the song or poem, in the sense of Fritz Reckow's distinction between process and structure.[9] (But I suspect that Arlt does not mean "form" in this strong sense, and that we do not really have a disagreement.)

From this viewpoint I think of the interplay of the sequence of syllables, beats (strong stresses), and vowel sounds (especially in the rhymed syllables), all of them changing their patterns from stanza to stanza in example 3, as activity at the phonetic level of language, rather than as the

[5] My thanks are due Drs. Gunilla Björkvall and Ritva Jacobsson of the Institute for Classical Languages at Stockholm University for their help with this difficult text.

[6] Wulf Arlt, "Das eine Lied und die vielen Lieder," in *Festschrift Rudolf Bockholdt zum 60. Geburtstag*, ed. Norbert Dubowy and Sören Meyer-Eller (Pfaffenhofen: Ludvig, 1990), 113–27.

[7] Carl Dahlhaus, *Esthetics of Music*, trans. William Austin (Cambridge: Cambridge University Press, 1982), 12.

[8] Dahlhaus, *Esthetics*, 11.

[9] Fritz Reckow, "Processus und Structura: Über Gattungstradition und Formverständnis im Mittelalter," *Musiktheorie* 1 (1986): 5–31.

parameters of a plastic form. The shifts in the patterning of these several sound qualities are coordinated with one another, and together they are coordinated with shifts in the meaning and expressive tone of the poetry, i.e., shifts at the semantic level. To the degree that the patterning at the phonetic level is matched in the melodic settings, these reflect the semantic shifts as well.

But it is on the syntactical plane of language that medieval musicians focussed most of all in reflecting and enhancing the meaning and expression of poetry through melody.

Syntax has to do with the ordering and patterning of words to form meaningful phrases and sentences, and the functional relationships among the words that enter into such units of meaning. Every meaningful phrase and sentence in a language depends for its coherence on the completion of normative syntactical patterns, but in the interest of poetic design the poet may control those patterns beyond what is required for coherence.

Consider for a moment the English translation of the Troubadour song, example 10 (p. 462–63). The second line could stand alone but the first line could not because of the conditional first word; it requires something like the second line to complete a coherent syntactical group, and in that sense it implies the second line. The first line lacks completeness, the second provides it. That links the two lines and the same relationship is repeated in the third and fourth lines. In that way all four lines enter into a larger semantic configuration. What is accomplished at the syntactical level—the correspondences of lines 1 with 3 and lines 2 with 4—is reinforced in the original language at the phonetic level through rhyme: *mai-lai* and *loing-loing.* The remaining three lines of the first stanza continue in a single longer syntactical unit, and again that is reinforced in the original by the rhyme scheme: *clis, -spis, -latz.* That rounds out the configuration of the stanza as a whole. Even if we think of all this as a matter of formal organization, it is not really separable from meaning. It would be hard to convey the sense of this stanza in some other form; the form of the two conditional clauses and their consequents, followed by the conclusion, is immanent in the idea of the stanza—not just the formal idea, but what it says. To the extent, therefore, that the melody brings out these formal arrangements, it contributes to the projection of meaning.

For all such aspects of coherence and design in poetry as I have just been observing, there are corresponding principles and resources of melody that make for the possibility of the closest matching between the two. I want to speak now about what those resources are: of what kinds of differentiations is the melodic idiom capable, what are the principles of coherence that operate within it, how can it suggest similarity and contrast, how does one melodic gesture imply another, and how are expectations satisfied? These are all questions about the options that are offered by the melodic idiom for responding to the poetry at the several levels of language utterance. I have already begun to address them with reference to the examples from Stevens, and I continue now by referring to the melodies of both the *versus* (compare examples 3 and 7, pp. 449 and 457). Their tunes appear to belong to the same family; they are productions of a single archetype, as I judge from their sharing of the following properties: (1) The functional range is the octave d-d'. (2) The octave is divided by the note a, the common boundary tone between the modules d-a and a-d', within which the phrases are mainly seated. There is a hierarchy of concluding tones, corresponding to a hierarchy of musical units which they conclude. Medieval writers described this sort of matched hierarchy of melodic tones and melodic units, and also its exact correspondence to the hierarchy of sense units of language, the hierarchy of what was called the comma and the period.[10] (3) Each song begins by declaiming repeatedly at the top of the range, then makes its way down to a. These opening phrases settle on a by way of a stereotyped circling ornamental figure that is typical for the style. (4) There is a tendency to move by step through the upper segment d'-a, and by thirds through the lower segment d-a.

Of course the first two properties make up one strand of what was described in the Middle Ages under the concept of "mode." It constitutes a principle of differentiation in the diatonic system that provides models for the composition of melodies: melodic modules for phrases, basis for dynamic contrast between phrases (statement and answer, open and closed, tense and relaxed), and a hierarchy of tones for differentiating degrees of closure. It is a basis for establishing a melodic syntax that engages linguistic syntax in a multiplicity of ways. The third characteristic—the declamatory beginning at the top of the range—outfits this melodic type for just the kind of poem that was sung to it in both our examples, one that begins with an announcement of something momentous that has happened, followed by a commentary about or reaction to that event. We may think of this as a formal relation within the melody, but it is motivated as a matching between melody and poetry at the semantic level of the latter.

The third-chain principle is exemplified again in the second phrase of the Troubadour song (example 9, p. 460). The melody rises through the primary chain from d to a, then turns back downward. On the way down it turns and pivots on e, and ends on c. Given the way that e is marked for attention, it hooks on to g in retrospect, and the c hooks on to both e and g.

[10] See Harold S. Powers, "Language Models and Musical Analysis," *Ethnomusicology* 24 (1980): 1–60.

So by the time the phrase has finished it has elaborated the third-chain g-e-c, and the progress of the phrase as a whole entails a shift from the primary to the secondary chain. When I return to this song in detail I shall want to interpret that shift in relation to the meaning of the words in this phrase.

The third-chain principle never received explicit theoretical description as such in the Middle Ages, but several modern writers have observed its importance for the formation of medieval melody.[11] Even though the principle of the octave/fifth/fourth species did receive such description, I prefer to think of both principles as constitutive properties of pan-European melodic traditions operating across a broad front, quite separately from the liturgical tradition that was the field of reference for modal theory as such. Questions and answers about "mode" in connection with such lyric traditions are in a sense beside the point.

I am ready now to focus on the four songs directly.

"Radix iesse castitatis lilium"

Example 3: "Radix iesse castitatis lilium," from Paris, B. N., lat. 1139

[11] Curt Sachs, "The Road to Major," *Musical Quarterly* 29 (1943): 381ff.; Joseph Smits van Waesberghe, *A Textbook of Melody: A Course in Functional Melodic Analysis*, trans. W. A. G. Doyle-Davidson (Nijrnegan, Netherlands: American Institute of Musicology, 1955); Leo Treitler, "The Aquitanian Repertories of Sacred Monody in the Eleventh and Twelfth Centuries" (Ph.D. diss., Princeton University, 1957), 36–44; Hendrik van der Werf, *The Extant Troubadour Melodies: Transcriptions and Essays for Performers and Scholars* (Rochester, New York: the author, 1984), 31–32.

C
no-va pro-fert ra - di-um vir-go de-i fi - li-um qui est sa-lus om - ni-um
D
qui non ha-bet i-ni-ti-um in hoc ve-nit e-xi-li-um da-re no-bis con-si-li-um
E
cu-ius in prae-co-ni-a in-to-net ar-mo-ni-a re-so-net sym-pho-ni-a
F
a pa-tri na-to a-tha-na-to a-tha-na-to de vir-gi-ne Ma-ri - a
G
er-go per haec gau - di - a gau-det cae-li-cu - ri - a gau-de-at ec - cle-si - a
H
vo - ci - fe-rans pro-di - gi - a per haec sa - cra so-lemp-ni - a
pa-trem na-tum de fi-li-a per haec sa-cra so - - lemp - ni - a

Example 4: Edition of the poem of "Radix iesse"

A 1	Radix iesse	The stem of Jesse, the chaste
2	castitatis lilium	lily, the new star, the gentle
3	Stella novum	rose, gives off a new ray of
4	nova profert radium	light, and [thereby she is]
5	Rosa mitis	crushing the weed under foot.
6	et conculcans lolium.	
B 1	Exulatis	The mother gave the reward of
2	Captivatis	life liberally to her children,
3	Morti datis	who were exiled, captured,
4	Mater natis	given up to death.
5	Dedit gratis	
6	Vitae bravium	
C 1	Nova profert radium	The star [who is] the Virgin
2	Virgo Dei filium	gives off a ray of light, the
3	Qui est salus omnium	son of God, who is the salvation of all.
D 1	Qui non habet initium	[He] who has no beginning has
2	In hoc venit exilium	come to this place of exile to
3	Dare nobis consilium	give us counsel.
E 1	Cuius in praeconia	Let harmony sing out, let
2	Intonet harmonia	symphony sound forth to
3	Resonet symphonia	proclaim him,
F 1	A patri nato	The immortal son, [born] of
2	Athanato	the immortal father through
3	Athanato	the Virgin Mary.
4	De virgine Maria	
G 1	Ergo per haec gaudia	Therefore, for this joyful
2	Gaudet caeli curia	occasion, the court of heaven
3	Gaudeat ecclesia	rejoices; let the Church rejoice,
H 1	Vociferans prodigia	Crying out the miracle of the
2	Per haec sacra solempnia	father born of the daughter
3	Patrem natum de filia	through this solemn ceremony.
4	Per haec sacra solempnia.	

This song, exuberant in language and melody, rich in vocabulary, and rhapsodic in form, celebrates the birth of Christ, which is announced metaphorically in stanza A. The Virgin Mary, identified through a string of traditional epithets that speak of her ancestry and her qualities (the stem of Jesse, the chaste lily, the gentle rose, the new star) has given off a new ray of light. The melodic beginning has the character of a proclamation, at the very top of the upper fourth of the authentic octave.

The first pair of lines brings the first two epithets, declaimed in the upper fourth. The next two melodic units (beginning *stella* and *rosa*) are identical. This emphasizes the syntactical parallelism—epithet/predicate clause, epithet/predicate clause—which helps the listener restore the continuity of syntax that has been interrupted by the artificial word order (following the sequence of semantic elements the order might have been lines 3, 5, 4, 6). Here melody helps to project meaning by responding directly to the abstract syntax of the language.

The proclamation of stanza A is followed in stanza B by a recollection of the hopelessness from which the great event has rescued mankind. The poem unrolls this as a series of rhymed four-syllable lines, closing it off in the last line with a rhyme that hooks onto the first stanza. The melody reflects this change of pace in the abrupt constriction of its range down to a third, but expands to the full range of a fifth with the shift to the predicate phrase ("mater natis . . ."), and reinforces the link to the rhyme of the first stanza by echoing the cadential figure of "radium" and "lilium" with "bravium."

Stanza C tells again of what has happened, now decoding the metaphors of A: the Virgin, Christ, and the miracle of salvation are identified directly. First (C1) there is a reiteration of A4, which predicates the whole event, in a melodic setting that refers back to the phrase to which it was initially sung. Lines C2 and C3 quickly spell out everything, with melodic variants of the same phrase—i.e., the melody keeps on referring back to that central line in the first stanza, of which the entire third stanza is an unpacking.

I call attention to a striking characteristic of this melodic phrase, which we have now heard four times. Its activity is in a restricted space: d-g, *not quite* the lower fifth of the octave. In its first occurrence, as A4, and its second, C1, it touches the a as a neighboring note. But it does not fill the space of the fifth, as does the melody all the way from A5 through B6. Then in C2 and C3 it is absolutely restricted to the space of a fourth. One hears it striking up against the g as a ceiling. There is a strong implication of a breakthrough to the a, which then comes in the next stanza (D), where the lines take on an additional syllable. This is a rhythmic expansion in the poetry, which is reflected as a satisfying expansion in the tonal space of the melody.

Choices in the melodic setting have been made in response to both semantic and phonetic aspects of the poetry.

The song picks up momentum through these expansions. The climax comes in stanzas E and F. Music itself (harmony and symphony) is evoked in proclamation of Christ. The melody is unusually mimetic, making a display of the "music" that is called for in the poem, something like a fanfare (I am reminded of the concretization of "music" in the "Possente Spirto" of Monteverdi's *L'Orfeo*). The movement is quickened through the progressive shortening of lines—from seven syllables through stanza E, to five syllables in F1, to four syllables in F2 and F3. (Phonetically F2, repeated in F3, is nearly a contraction of F1, through the removal of *patri.* That is exactly reflected in the musical setting of the two lines.) F4 provides the conclusion in sense and rhythm, slowing the pace through expansion back to seven syllables. The melody of F4 effects a conclusion, too, after the long anchorage on a through all of stanza E and F1–3, with its descent through g-f-e-d.

The question, after this fine moment, is how to bring about a suitable conclusion. In the last two stanzas both poetry and melody revert to an arrangement that had already been made in stanzas C and D: a run of seven-syllable lines, followed by one of eight-syllable lines, and in the melody a restriction to the lower fourth in stanza G, and then the implied expansion into the space of the fifth in the final stanza. The repetition of the second line of H provides the opportunity for a concluding melismatic flourish in the melody, a device that is a regular feature of the style.

A version of this song is preserved in two books copied in 1552 and about 1588 (example 5).[12] I would like to look first at variants in the poem, which I have listed as example 6. What strikes me about them is that, however they change the sense, they obey the same phonetic constraints as the Aquitanian version.

[12] Grenoble, Bibliothèque municipale MS. 4413 (1552) and Le Puy en Velay, Bibliothèque municipale A/V/7/009 (ca. 1588). The latter is identified under the title *Prosolarium ecclesiae aniciensis*, and is preserved in the *Grand seminar* of Le Puy en Velay. Our song is entered in both as "farsumen" (a kind of trope) for the second vesper service of the New Year office that was elaborately celebrated in the great Romanesque cathedral of Le Puy. The later manuscript also preserves other *versus*-type songs from the repertory of Paris 1139. An edition is soon to be published by Wulf Arlt, under the title *Lo Bozolari: Ein Klerikerfest des Mittelalters aus Le Puy: Lieder des 12. Jahrhunderts und Mehrstimmiges aus der Kathedrale des 16. Jahrhunderts* (Winterthur: Amadeus). I am grateful to Professor Arlt for providing me with bibliographic details and a transcription from Le Puy (virtually identical with the Grenoble version).

"Radix iesse"

Example 5: Alternative version of "Radix iesse"

Example 6: Variants in the poem "Radix iesse" from the Le Puy manuscript

A3	nova stella
A4	novum profert radium
B3	et dampnatis
B4	morti datis
C1	stella profert radium
D3	claret nobis consilium
E1	*omits* in
E2	intonet symphonia
E3	resonet harmonia
F1	Patris nato
F3	nobis dato
H2 *and* H3	*reversed*
H4	*lacking.*

Consider the second stanza. In dropping B4 the stanza loses a subject for the predicate in B5, which makes the stanza as a whole incoherent. But the line that replaces B4 ("et dampnatis") has the right number of syllables, the right stress pattern, and the right rhyme syllables. Similarly with the variant in D3 ("clare" in place of "dare") which makes no semantic sense, but has the right sound attributes. This is a clue to the importance of sound values in the transmission, even at the expense of sense values. The song was heard, and when it was sung again or remembered to be written down, words were substituted inadvertently which still followed the right sound patterns, even though they spoiled the sense of the passage. This could have happened even in the process of copying from one manuscript to another, as the scribe sounded out the words and wrote down their sound-alikes. In any case, the contribution of this comparison to our understanding of the nature of such traditions is the clue it provides to the role of hearing in the transmission, even when the material was preserved and passed about in writing.

But I do believe that there has been a deterioration in the tradition, and I would like to show something of that about the melodic tradition as well, even though our criteria for what makes melodic sense are weaker than they are for language. It will suffice to compare the melodies of just the first two stanzas in both versions, referring to melodic passages by stanza and line.

A1–2: LePuy sings in the upper fourth, like Aquitania, descending at the end to the co-final. The emphatic character of the repeated declamation on the d' is diluted in the two-note groups of LePuy. 3–4 (still LePuy) is a virtual repetition of 1–2. 5–6 makes a steady descent from the top to the bottom of the octave. The beginning of 6 is awkward, with its skip from b (flat?) to f. Even if sung with b-flat, the moment is tonally disorienting, i.e., obscuring what would be a clear shift from the upper fourth to the lower fifth. In any case, the melodic form of the whole stanza in LePuy can be designated MMN, as compared to the form MNN in Aquitania. Recall that the latter form corresponds to syntactical arrangements in the poetry, a correspondence that is lost in LePuy.

For B, the LePuy version again covers the entire octave span. While the phrase articulation in Aquitania reflects the list-like succession of short, rhymed lines in the poetry, LePuy runs in longer phrases (1, 2–3, 4–5, 6). Over all, the melody falls into two larger contrasting divisions, the first seated in the secondary third-chain e-g-b-d' (lines 1–3), the second in the principal chain d-f-a-c' (lines 4–6). In itself this is a normal and coherent process in the style, but it does not respond to anything in the poetry.

A final observation: the setting of lines 2 and 3 is virtually identical with that of stanza A, line 5 and the first two words of line 6. But there is no sense in that reiteration so far as the words are concerned (on the contrary in the first stanza it concerns the gentle rose, in the second the morbid conditions of life before the great event).

"Lilium floruit"

Example 7: *Versus,* "Lilium floruit"

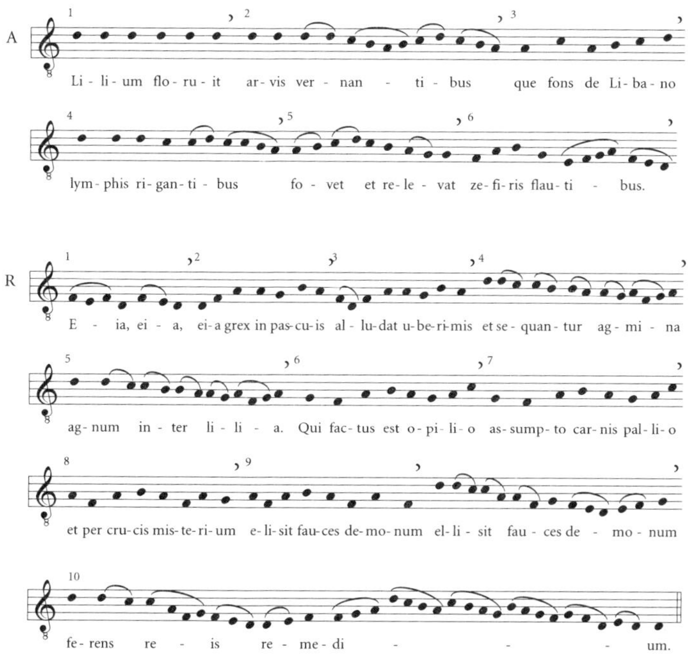

Example 8: The poem of "Lilium floruit," with translation

A 1	Lilium floruit	The lily has blossomed in
2	arvis vernantibus	the verdant fields. Thus the fountains of
3	Que fons de Libano	Lebanon, with their cleansing
4	lymphis rigantibus	waters, give warmth and comfort,
5	Fovet et relevat	as does the blowing zephyr.
6	zephyris flautibus	
R 1	Eia, eia	Eia, eia, eia! The flock
2	Eia grex in pascuis	plays in the most fertile
3	Alludat uberimis	pasture. And bid the
4	Et sequantur agmina	throng stream among the
5	Agnum inter lilia	lilies, following the

6	Qui factus est opilio	lamb who became a shepherd
7	Assumpto carnis pallio	by taking up the cloak of flesh,
8	Et per crucis misterium	and who crushed the demon
9	Elisit fauces demonum	through the mystery of
10	Ferens reis remedium	the cross, bringing healing to sinners.
B 1	Revisit thalamum	The bridegroom revisits
2	sponsi presentia	the bridal chamber, [He] who flew
3	Qui super cherubim	above the cherubs with wondrous
4	mira potentia	power, foreseeing all hidden things.
5	Volavit praevidens	
6	cuncta latentia	
R 1	Eia, eia . . .	
C 1	Electri species	At last the beauty of amber
2	tandem emicuit	shone forth, and the glassy sea flowed
3	Et mare vitreum	from Zion. The foul
4	de Sion exiit	serpent is now destroyed.
5	Anguis teterrimus	
6	nunc jam interiit	

The poem of this *versus* (example 8) is more regular, less rhapsodic in form than that of the first song. It alternates stanzas of one versification with a refrain of another.

The stanzas comprise paired two-beat verses of six syllables each; even-numbered verses are rhymed. The refrain begins always with the initial three-fold sounding of the vocables *eia*, and then goes in paired four-beat seven-syllable lines (three pairs), all rhymed in pairs. *Eia* provides good vowel sounds for a celebratory vocalise (like the vocables "ee-yi-ee-yi-o" in the folksong "Old MacDonald"), and it focusses on the singing itself, somewhat like the reference to "harmony" and "symphony" in the other *versus*. The effect of the alternation of verse forms is a shifting back and forth between two quite different rhythmic characters—the more flowing two-beat lines of the stanzas and the more percussive, rousing four-beat lines of the refrain. The difference is enhanced by the fact that the final syllables of the lines in the stanzas are unaccented, those of the lines in the refrain are accented, making an end-stop. (The eight-syllable lines begin with an unaccented syllable, an up-beat, so that the final syllable is always accented.)

The poet has set a pastoral scene and described it in rich, sensuous language. The elements are gathered from a poetic tradition that reaches back to antiquity—the tradition of poetry set in a "plaisance" (known in Latin antiquity and the Middle Ages as a *locus amoenus*, or "pleasant place"): a green meadow, a fountain, the west wind blowing, with shepherds, sheep, and an erotic element featuring a young couple.[13] Until the fifth and sixth lines of the refrain there is no explicit hint of the theological content that can be read only through metaphor until that moment. But then it emerges with great force and suddenness from the seventh line on. The effect of the theological plane settling over the naïve idyll is very powerful, and it informs the melodic setting. The poem celebrates in a richly sensual and sparkling way the exhilaration of Easter through a melodic setting of corresponding exuberance.

The melody is in the authentic disposition of the d tonality. It begins at the top in the same exclamatory style as the first song, hanging from that note most of the way through the setting of the stanza, making its way down to the bottom only at the conclusion of that setting; and at the end of the refrain it makes a spectacular tumbling, melismatic run from top to bottom.

Coming down now to detail, the setting of the first couplet (and the first sentence) declaims at the top of the range, then turns around in the upper fourth and stops at a. The setting of the second couplet begins there, rises to declaim again at the top, and falls again to the a. The melody of the third couplet begins like that of the second, then breaks out of the upper fourth, and pushes by step downward to the final.

In the refrain the rhymed couplets are melodically identified as repeating phrases, the first pair in the lower fifth, the second pair in the upper fourth. Both pairs converge on the co-final. Between them there is no resolution, the whole passage to this point is suspended on the a. The third and fourth pairs continue suspended on a, but with more constricted range—turning first up to c', then down to g and f. There is still no resolution here, only an increasing need for it. Release comes now with the repetition of the line "elisit fauces demonum." The melody breaks through its temporary boundaries to the top and bottom of the range and then at the last line repeats the melody of the penultimate line and ends with a long virtuoso descent from top to bottom. The melodic plan for the refrain as a whole is simple, and directly coordinated to the poetic idea: play in the melodic modules of the modal octave, but keep it in balance, without closure, until the strongest moment in the theological message—the message of salvation through the cross.

[13] See Ernst Robert Curtius, *European Literature and the Latin Middle Ages*, trans. Willard R. Trask (Princeton: Princeton University Press, 1952), 192ff.

"Lanquand li jorn"

Example 9: Troubadour song, "Lan qant li jorn" by Jaufré Rudel[14]

[14] The transcriptions and text editions for this example are from Hendrik van der Werf, *The Extant Troubadour Melodies*, 215*–19*. Reproduced by permission.

X
vains de ta - lant bruns et en - clin
R
vau de ta - lan en - brons e clis
W
vais de ta - lens bruns et en - clins
X
si que chant ne flors d'au - bes - pin
R
si que chans ni flors dels bels pis
W
si que chanz ne flors d'au - bes - pins
X
non mi vaut mai qu'i - vers je - laiz.
R
no.m val pus que l'y - vern in glat.
W
non val maiz que l'i - vers ge - laiz.

Example 10: The poem of "Lanquand li jorn," with translation[15]

I.
Lanquand li jorn son lonc en mai
M'es bęls douz chans d'auzęls de loing,
E qand me sui partitz de lai
Remembra·m d'un' amor de loing;
Vauc de talan enbroncs e clis,
Si que chans ni flors d'albespis
No·m platz plus que l'inverns gelatz.

1.
When the days are long in May,
I like the sweet song of birds from afar,
And when I have departed from there,
I remember a love from afar;
I go sad and bowed with desire
So that neither song nor hawthorn flower
Pleases me more than icy winter.

II.
Ja mais d'amor no·m gauzirai
Si no·m gau cest' amor de loing,
Qe gensor ni meillor non sai
Vas nuilla part ni pręs ni loing.
Tant es sos prętz verais e fis
Qe lai el renc dels Sarrazis
Fos eu per lięis chaitius clamatz.

2.
Never in love shall I rejoice
Unless I enjoy this love from afar,
For nobler or better I do not know
In any direction, near or far,
Her worth is so true and perfect
That there in the kingdom of the Saracens
I would, for her, be proclaimed captive.

III.
Iratz e gauzens m'en partrai
Qan veirai dest' amor de loing,
Mas non sai coras la·m veirai,
Car trǫp sonnǫstras tęrras loing:
Assatz i a portz e camis.
E per aissǫ no·n sui devis,
Mas tot sia cum a Dieu platz!

3.
Sad and rejoicing I shall depart
When I shall see this love from afar,
But I do not know when I shall see her
For our lands are too far.
Many are the ports and roads,
And so I cannot prophesy,
But may all be as it pleases God!

IV.
Be·m parrá jǫis qan li qerrai
Per amor Dieu l'amor de loing.
E s'a lięis plai, albergarai
Pręs de lięis, si be·m sui de loing.
Adoncs parrá·l parlamens fis
Qand drutz loindás er tant vezis
C'ab bęls digz jauzirái solatz.

4.
Joy will surely appear to me when I seek from her,
For the love of God, this love from afar.
And if it pleases her, I shall lodge
Near her, although I am from afar.
Then will appear fine discourse,
When, distant lover, I shall be so close
That with charming words I shall take delight in conversation.

[15] From Margaret Switten and Howell Chickering, eds. *The Medieval Lyric: A Project Supported by the National Endowment for the Humanities and Mount Holyoke College: Anthology 1*, (South Hadley, Mass.: Mount Holyoke College, 1988–89), 60–61. The edition and translation of the text for this example were made by Margaret Switten. Reproduced by permission.

V.
Ben tenc lo seignor per verai
Per q'ieu veirai l'amor de loing,
Mas per un ben qe m'en eschai
N'ai dos mals, car tant m'es de loing.
Ai! car me fos lai pelerís
Si que mos fustz e mos tapís
Fos pelz sieus bẹls huọills remiratz!

5.
I consider that Lord as the true one
Through whom I shall see this love from afar;
But for one good that befalls me from it,
I have two ills, because she is so far.
Ah! Would that I might be a pilgrim there
So that my staff and my cloak
Might be seen by her beautiful eyes.

VI.
Dieus qe fetz tot qant ve ni vai
E fermẹt cest' amor de loing
Me don poder, qe·l cọr eu n'ai,
Q'en breu veia l'amor de loing
Veraimen en locs aizís,
Si qe la cambra e·l jardís
Me resemblẹs totz temps palatz.

6.
God who made all that comes and goes
And established this love from afar,
Give me the power, for the desire I have,
Quickly to see this love from afar,
Truly, in agreeable places,
So that chamber and garden
Might always seem to me a palace!

VII.
Ver ditz qui m'apẹlla lechai
Ni desiran d'amor de loing,
Car nuills autre jọis tant no·m plai
Cum jauzimens d'amor de loing;
Mas sọ q'eu vuọill m'es tant ahis
Q'enaissi·m fadẹt mos pairis
Q'ieu amẹs a non fos amatz.

7.
He speaks the truth who calls me greedy
And desirous of love from afar,
For no other joy pleases me as much
As enjoyment of love from afar;
But what I want is so difficult,
For thus did my godfather decree my fate,
That I should love and not be loved.

VIII.
Mas sọ q'ieu vuọill m'es tant ahis . . .
Toz sìa mauditz lo pairis
Qe·m fadẹt q'ieu non fos amatz!

8.
But what I want is so difficult . . .
May the godfather be cursed
Who decreed my fate that I should not be loved.

The Troubadour song is transmitted in three sources.[16] Its composer is Jaufré Rudel, who has been called by Peter Dronke "the famous, indeed legendary, troubadour of love-longing."[17] The poem (example 10) is spun out around the phrase "amor de loing," "love from afar" or "distant love," and the differently shaded meanings through which that phrase passes. It has the sense of a distant and unattainable beloved, quite the sense that appealed to the romantics (Beethoven's *An die ferne Geliebte,* Berlioz's

[16] All are in Paris, Bibliothèque Nationale, fonds français: MS. 22543, known as R (ca. 1300); MS. 844, known as W (mid-thirteenth century, notated a fifth higher than the other versions), and MS. 20050, known as X (mid-thirteenth century).

[17] Peter Dronke, *The Medieval Lyric,* 2nd ed. (New York: Cambridge University Press, 1977), 119.

Symphonie fantastique). Much, but perhaps too much, has been said and written about the ideal of courtly love as unconsummated love for a lady not available—perhaps because she is married, or as far away as Tripoli—but admired, honored, served, protected, a love that is satisfying despite or perhaps because of the absence of emotional reciprocation and physical consummation (stanza VII: to "love and not be loved").

But this "love from afar" is painful. The poem is full of expressions of desire, and it becomes plain that "love" is not only what the poet feels, but an epithet for the lady who is the object of his quite carnal desires—the "love from afar" is the exotic woman. There is talk of captivity in the "kingdom of the Saracens" (II), of travel via "many ports and roads" (III), of pilgrimage (V). The double meaning is focussed in stanza VI. The context is the crusade. God, who "established this love from afar," is asked for the power "to see this love from afar, *truly* [Dronke reads 'naked'] in agreeable places," (perhaps a place like the *plaisance* of "Lilium floruit") and evidently to consummate the love in "chamber and garden," which would then be home to the poet and his lady. Once that has been made virtually explicit we can enjoy the irony of the lines "For no other joy pleases me as much as enjoyment of love from afar" (VII). But that irony, which also has an aspect of mystery or enigma, is implicit throughout the poem.

This poetic conceit plays into the sonority and form of the verses—the expression of meaning as form. In particular the enigmatic aspect is given musical expression. The word "loing" ends the second and fourth lines of every stanza. We can recognize that as a rhyme, but more than that, it is an obsessive idea and like a slow ostinato in the sound of the language. It alternates with the final *-ai* sounds of the first and third lines, and that makes the rhyme-pattern of the initial quatrain. The remaining three lines associate through their final sounds, *-is, -is, -atz.* The stanza unrolls in three segments: lines 1–2, 3–4, 5–7.

The song is strophic, and all stanzas were sung to the same melody. The beginning is with the low c that scoops up to the final of the d tonality that is suggested through the first two lines. Such an opening is a typical kind of intonation. It is also typical of melodies in d that from the final the melody skips to f, where it recites for a while. This defines the third d-f as a principal melodic module. Turning downward again, the melody takes the e that had been skipped on the way up and associates it with the low c (by way of d) as a contrasting module to the third d-f. The melody of the second line sharpens this contrast, extending to the third-chains d-f-a and g-e-c, and ending c. It amounts to a shift from the primary to the secondary third-chain, which is experienced as a de-stabilizing move. That is, after beginning with a tonally solid phrase in d the melody slips out of that stable place and into a contrasting place. At the very least that requires us, as we listen, to re-evaluate our initial impression about where the stability of the song lies; it is disorienting, and it is a kind of musical projection of the enigmatic character of the poem; the more so as this back-and-forth process is repeated throughout the song.

The polarization of the song into the two tonal sonorities is clearest, the contrast is sharpest, in the version of manuscript R, where the flourishes at the ends of phrases 1 and 2, 3 and 4, and 7 are identical but for the contrast with respect to the last note. But the dynamic process of the shift is the commanding idea in all the versions.

One way or another, phrases 5 and 6 make the climax of the melody, but here are the greatest differences among the versions. In R, phrase 5 imitates the melody of phrases 1 and 3 a fifth above, quite literally except for the last note. The third a-c, with recitation on c, echoes the third d-f, of phrases 1 and 3, with recitation on f. That reinforces the impression that the primary chain (d-f-a-c) is the anchorage of the song. But it also reinforces the disorienting effect of the turn down to c again in phrase 6, which comes only at the last moment; until then phrase 6 traces a descent within the framework c'-a-f. The shift is sudden.

The version of manuscript X follows a different course within the sense of the same general idea. The big difference is the ascent to d' at the beginning of phrase 6, expanding, that is, to the upper fourth of the octave on d. That is confirmed by the descent, which marks out the framework of that octave in a very sharp and explicit way and ends on d. The ending on c is thereby put off until the very end of the last phrase, and that makes it the most disorienting of all.

In this song the main poetic idea—the ironic presentation of the ideal of distant love—is carried out in all stanzas, so that the musical idea that interprets it is appropriate to each stanza.

Palästinalied

Example 11: Walther von der Vogelweide, *Palästinalied*[18]

Example 12: The poem of *Palästinalied*, with translation[19]

Nû alrêst lebe ich mir werde,
sît mîn sündic ouge siht
daz reine lant und ouch die erde
den man vil der êren giht.
Mirst geschehen des ich ie bat,
ich bin komen an die stat,
dâ got mennischlîchen trat.

Only now I live in dignity,
now that my sinful eyes have seen
that pure land and earth as well
which have been given such great honor.
To me has happened what I always hoped,
for I am come unto that place
where God once trod the earth as man.

[18] The transcription and text edition for this example are from Hendrik van der Werf, *The Extant Troubadour Melodies,* 215*–19*. Reproduced by permission.

[19] From Switten, ed., *The Medieval Lyric: Anthology I,* 62–63. Peter Frenzel was consultant in the preparation of this example. I take no position with respect to differences between textual versions in the editions of Switten and van der Werf. They do not affect the interpretations offered here. Reproduced by permission.

Schoeniu lant rîch unde hêre,
swaz ich der noch hân gesehen,
sô bist duz ir aller êre:
waz ist wunders hie geschehen!
Daz ein magt ein kint gebar
hêre über aller engel schar,
was daz niht ein wunder gar?

Lovely lands, rich and sublime
however many I have seen,
you are the glory of them all.
What wonders have happened here!
That a maiden bore a child
higher than all the hosts of angels,
was that not a wondrous thing?

Hie liez er sich reine toufen,
daz der mensche reine sî;
Dô liez er sich hêrre verkoufen,
daz wir eigen wurden fri,
anders waeren wir verlorn:
wol dir, sper, kriuz unde dorn!
wê dir, heiden, deist dir zorn!

Here in purity He let Himself be baptized,
that mankind might itself be pure.
Here too He, a lord, let Himself be sold,
that we, His vassals, might be free;
otherwise we would be lost.
So hail to you, spear, cross, and thorn!
and woe to you, Heathen, for your anger.

Hinnen fuor der sun zer helle
von dem grabe, da (e)r inne lac;
des was ie der vater geselle
und der geist, den niemen mac
sunder gscheiden: êst al ein,
sleht und ebener danne ein zein,
als er Abrahâme erschein.

From here to Hell the Son descended,
from the grave wherein He lay.
Ever was the Father His companion,
and the Spirit, whom no one may
break asunder: they are all one,
smooth and level as an arrow,
as He appeared to Abraham.

Do (e)r den tievel dô geschande.
daz nie keiser baz gestreit
dô fuor er her wider ze lande:
dô huob sich der juden leit,
daz er hêrre ir huote brach,
und man in sit lebendic sach,
den ir hant sluoc unde stach.

And after He had shamed the devil,
(no Kaiser had ever struggled better)
He journeyed back to this land.
And then began the pain of Jewry,
for He, the Lord, broke their guard,
and He has since been seen as a living man,
He whom their hands had struck and pierced.

In diz lant hât er gesprochen
einen angeslîchen tac,
dâ diu witwe wirt gerochen
und der weise klagen mac
und der arme den gewalt
der dâ wirt an ime gestalt:
wol im dort, der hie vergalt!

To this land He has spoken
a horrible day of wrath.
Then the widow will be avenged,
and the waif's complaint be heard,
and that of the poor man against brute force
which is imposed on him.
Lucky the man, whose sins are remitted.

Kristen, juden unde heiden
jehent daz diz ir erbe sî.
got sol uns ze rehte bescheiden
durch die sîne namen drî.
Al diu welt diu strîtet her:
wir sîn an der rehten ger,
reht ist daz er uns gewer.

Christians, Jews, and Heathen
declare this land their legacy.
But God must rightfully decide it,
by the three names He bears.
All the world is contending here:
But our desire is the right one,
and it is right that He should grant it us.

Walther von der Vogelweide's *Palästinalied* was composed 1224 or 1225, to generate support for the crusade of the Holy Roman Emperor, Frederick II.

The close parallel in the sound-configurations of the poetry with those of the Jaufré Rudel song (two pairs of four-beat lines with alternating rhyme sounds plus a three-line rhymed conclusion), and the close similarities in the melodic contour and phrase relationships suggested to Heinrich Husmann that this is a "contrafactum" of Jaufré Rudel's song.[20] The alternative would be to think that both men composed songs on their respective poems, using melodies of the same family. It is perhaps even more the differences between the two than their similarities that argue for the idea of a *contrafactum.*

Jaufré's poem turns on an ambivalence of feeling about what is far away. Walther's poem also concerns a faraway place, but without any ambivalence. It is the "pure land," "the glory of them all," and having once seen it the poet can live in dignity.

In Walther's melody we hear a process involving third chains like that in Jaufré's melody. The initial phrase marks out the third, d-f, but ends c. From that c the second phrase moves up through the secondary chain c-e-g, then peaks on a and re-descends via the principal chain to d. The movement of this pair of phrases, then, is *toward* the stable configuration of the d tonality. The two phrases are paired as antecedent and consequent, open and closed. It is in a sense a reversal of the dynamic of Jaufré's melody, and the effect is the opposite: rather than a feeling of disorientation, it is a feeling of integration, closure. The melodic process in the final three phrases is very clear: the third a-c' in 5, in 6 the reiteration of that third, then the descent through the chain c'-a-f-d, but then the continuation to c, as preparation for the concluding phrase that works exactly like the second and fourth phrases.

The phrase syntax in this song corresponds to the norms in the grammar of the style. It is possible to think that Walther simply gave his poem a conventional setting. But if we think of it as a *contrafactum*, then it entails a reversal of the melodic syntax of the melody, reflecting the contrast in the sense of the two poems. In any case the difference between them in itself constitutes a display of the expression of semantic quality through the syntax of melody.

I can conclude by citing the beginning of the recent paper of Wulf Arlt that I've already mentioned. "The suggestion that the history of song in the

[20] Heinrich Husmann, "Das Prinzip der Silbenzählung im Lied des zentralen Mittelalters," *Die Musikforschung* 6 (1953): 8–23.

strong sense, in all its artistic individuality, begins in the twelfth century, as a rule encounters scepticism or astonishment among music historians. . . . The perspective on older times continues to be determined by the view that the relation between music and language in the Middle Ages is limited to formal aspects." I wonder whether this rejectionist attitude, which has discouraged the sort of close observation of relationships beyond the formal that Arlt undertakes in his paper and that I have attempted here and elsewhere,[21] is not an extreme form of a nineteenth-century ideology of aesthetic autonomy under which music would be self-determining and self-referential, abstract and formalized, an enclave isolated from the images, feelings, desires, and relationships about which the poems speak. I say extreme form because it aims in the end to refine the song down to abstractions of melodic and speech elements that are altogether incapable of speaking. That seems more utopian even than was envisaged in the nineteenth century, and it has little relevance to the medieval world.

[21] Ritva Jonsson and Leo Treitler, "Medieval Music and Language: A Reconsideration of the Relationship," in *Studies in the History of Music* 1: *Music and Language* (New York: Broude, 1983), 1–23.

JEREMY YUDKIN AND TODD SCOTT

Ut Hic:
Announcing a Study of Musical Examples in Five Thirteenth-Century Music Treatises

An entire conference could be devoted to a discussion of all that remains to be done in the field of twelfth- and thirteenth-century polyphonic music and music theory. We still do not have a complete picture of the exact nature of the relationship between the music and the performers and the theorists, between the musicians and their audience, and the teachers and *their* audience. My research over the past several years has been founded on the belief that a close analysis of the surviving theoretical documents, concentrating carefully on the precise significance of every word, can provide us with some insights unobtainable by any other means. Only now are reliable editions of the principal treatises becoming available, and many smaller documents still await study.

In the course of preparing my new edition of the St. Emmeram treatise,[1] I undertook a study of all the musical examples cited or quoted in the course of the treatise. I have now widened the scope of my research to include all the musical examples given in the five principal treatises of the thirteenth century: Garlandia, Lambertus, the Anonymous of St. Emmeram, Franco, and Anonymous IV. Counting all the musical examples

[1] De musica mensurata: *The Anonymous of St. Emmeram: Complete Critical Edition, Translation, and Commentary* (Bloomington, Ind.: Indiana University Press, 1990).

that have a title or an incipit, or real music, and not counting those that simply show what a breve or *octonaria* look like, there is a total of one hundred and forty-one pieces.

My assistant in the current phase of the work is a graduate student in musicology at Boston University, Mr. Todd Scott. Our first and primary task was to track down the existence of these pieces—really fragments of pieces—in the actual musical sources of the time. In the end we examined a total of forty-six manuscripts, each of which contains one or more of these pieces. A list of these manuscripts is given as table 1.

Many pieces, of course, occur in several manuscripts, and we are tracing all such occurrences for each piece. In so doing we have been helped by some lists already made, such as those in the editions of Garlandia, Franco, and Anonymous IV.[2] All of these we have corrected and updated. Gilbert Reaney is at present engaged upon the production of a new edition of the Lambertus treatise,[3] and he has been kind enough to provide me with a complete typescript of his edition and a listing of those musical examples.

What most interested us, however, was the precise notation given in the treatise for each musical example. Since the main focus of the treatises (not the only focus, by any means, but the main focus) is musical notation, we thought it would be instructive to try to find those instances in which the notation of the example as given in the treatise is precisely reflected in an actual musical source. We are therefore examining every occurrence of every example and locating where possible a precise match between the example as given in the treatise and the fragment as it occurs in the music manuscripts.

Example 1 shows a musical example from the treatise of Johannes de Garlandia, illustrating the fourth mode. Below the notation of the fragment from a composition Garlandia identifies as "Docebit" is given a complete list of all the "Docebit" compositions we have been able to identify, arranged according to genre. After the siglum of each manuscript and its folio number we have given the ligature pattern of the music as it appears in the manuscript ("1" denotes a *simplex*, "2" a *binaria*, and so forth; a slash indicates a *tractus*). It will be noticed that of all these citations not one appears with the ligature pattern as given by Garlandia.

[2] Johannes de Garlandia, De mensurabili musica: *Kritische Edition mit Kommentar und Interpretation der Notationslehre*, ed. Erich Reimer, 2 vols., *Beihefte zum Archiv für Musikwissenschaft* 10–11 (Wiesbaden: Steiner, 1972); *Franco de Colonia, Ars cantus mensurabilis*, ed. Gilbert Reaney and Andre Gilles, Corpus Scriptorum de Musica 18 ([Rome]: American Institute of Musicology, 1974); *Der Musiktraktat des Anonymus 4*, ed. Fritz Reckow, 2 vols., Beihefte zum Archiv für Musikwissenschaft 4–5 (Wiesbaden: Steiner, 1967).

[3] Andre Gilles and Gilbert Reaney, ed., Corpus Scriptorum de Musica (forthcoming).

Table 1

A list of manuscripts containing compositions cited or quoted as musical examples in the five principal music treatises of the thirteenth century

A-V23	Vorau, Bibliothek des Augustiner Chorherrenstifts, 23
ArsA	Paris, Bibliothèque de l'Arsenal, 135
ArsB	Paris, Bibliothèque de l'Arsenal, 3517-3518
Ba	Bamberg, Staatliche Bibliothek, Lit. 115
Bes	Besaçon, Bibliothèque municipale, MS. I, 716
Bol	Bologna, Biblioteca G. B. Martini, Q 11
Boul	Boulogne-sur-mer, Bibliothèque municipale, 119
Ca	Cambrai, Bibliothèque municipale, A 410
Cb29	Cambridge, University Library, Ff. ii. 29
Châlons	Châlons-sur-Marne, Archives, 3.J.250
Cl	Paris, Bibliothèque Nationale, nouvelles acquisitions françaises 13521
Da	Darmstadt, Hessische Landes- und Hochschulbibliothek, 3471
Da2777	Darmstadt, Hessische Landesbibliothek, 2777
Da3317	Darmstadt, Hessische Landesbibliothek, 3317
F	Firenze, Biblioteca Laurenziana, Pluteus 29.I
F18	Firenze, Biblioteca Nazionale, Banco Rari 18
Fauv	Paris, Bibliothèque Nationale, français 146
Heid	Heidelberg, Universitätsbibliothek, 2588
Her	Louvain, Bibliothèque universitaire
Hu	Burgos, Monasterio de las Huelgas
LoA	London, British Museum, Egerton 2615
LoB	London, British Museum, Egerton 274
LoC	London, British Museum, additional 30091
LoD	London, British Museum, additional 27630
Ma	Madrid, Biblioteca Nacional, 20486
Mo	Montpellier, Faculté de Médecine, H 196
MüA	München, Bayerische Staatsbibliothek, Mus.ms.4775 (gallorom 42) and Berlin, Wolf fragments
MüB	München, Bayerische Staatsbibliothek, lat. 16444
N	Paris, Bibliothèque Nationale, français 12615
ONC	Oxford, New College, 362
P11266	Paris, Bibliothèque Nationale, latin 11266
P11411	Paris, Bibliothèque Nationale, latin 11411
P1337	Paris, Bibliothèque Nationale, latin 1337
R	Paris, Bibliothèque Nationale, français 844
R3025	Roma, Biblioteca Vaticana, Ottob lat. 3025 (Vatican Organum Treatise)

Reg	Roma, Biblioteca Vaticana, Reg. 1543
Sab	Roma, Santa Sabina XIV L3
StGA	Sankt Gallen, Siftsbibliothek, 383
StV	Paris, Bibliothèque Nationale, latin 15139
Tort	Tortosa, Biblioteca de la Catedral, C 97
Tu	Torino, Biblioteca Reale, Vari 42
V	Roma, Biblioteca Vaticana, Reg. 1490
W1	Wolfenbüttel, Herzog-August-Bibliothek, 628
W2	Wolfenbüttel, Herzog-August-Bibliothek, 1099
Westm33327	London, Westminster Abbey, 33327
Worc	London, British Museum, additional 25031; Oxford, Bodleian Library, Lat. liturg. d. 20; Worcester, Cathedral Library, additional 68

Example 1

Musical example "Docebit" from the treatise of Johannes de Garlandia; list of manuscripts and folios where different versions of "Docebit" may be found; ligature patterns of cited fragment.

2-pt. organum	F 163: 1/2,1/1/3/, etc.
	F 184^{v}: 1,2/2,3,2, etc., also Ma 136
	W1 45^{v}: = F 163
	StV 289: 1/1/1,2,2,2, etc.
	StV 289: 1/1/1/1, etc.
2-voice motet	Mo 260: 1/2,1/2,2,3/1, etc.
	F 399^{v}: 1/2/3/3/3/, etc.
	F 400: 1/2/3/3/3, etc.
	W2 132^{v}: = F 399^{v}
	W2 220^{v}: 3,2/3,2, etc.
	Ma 136: = F 400
	N 192: = W2 220^{v}
	MüA 5: 1,1,1,1,1,1,1/1,1,1,1, etc.
3-voice motet	F 389: 1/2,2/1,2,3, etc.
	W2 158^{v}: = F 389
4-voice motet	Westm33327 2: 1,1,1/1,1,1/1,1,1/, etc.

Example 2 shows a composite musical example from the treatise of Johannes de Garlandia, designed to demonstrate the third and fourth modes. Below the music is a list of all the "Regnat" pieces we were able to find, identified by manuscript and folio location. Since all these pieces were *clausulae*, the RISM number has also been given.[4] In this case, four selections were identified which were notated in the same patterns as those given in the treatise. These are identified by asterisks.

In order to establish some solid ground in a shifting sea of minute variants, we started by working with the musical examples as they have been established in modern editions. But it does appear to be necessary to check the manuscript tradition of the musical examples in the treatises themselves. This is particularly important in the cases of Garlandia and Franco, for whose treatises several manuscripts convey the musical examples in notation. Example 3 shows two musical examples from Garlandia's treatise as they appear in the published edition. In the first instance ("Regnat"), the editor has followed the version of the example as transmitted by the Vatican Library manuscript. In the second instance ("Angelus"), the musical example in the published edition conforms to neither of the extant manuscript versions. (Compare the fifth ligature group in each case.) The notation does, however, correspond to that preserved in the Bamberg manuscript, fol. 19^{v}. Whether this is what prompted the editor's decision in this case is unclear; Reimer is silent on this point.

Our aim is to find those instances in which the notation of the fragment in the treatise matches that in a musical source. We shall list those instances as main entries and all other occurrences of the passage as comparisons. We shall list all occurrences and all variants.

The treatise of Anonymous IV presents a special case, as the surviving manuscripts of the treatise preserve no notated musical examples. However, there are many pieces cited in the course of the work, and we shall trace all occurrences of these. Occasionally the treatise provides enough specific information in words about the notation of the example for us to have found a matching main entry.

For each example we shall also list the genre of the musical extract—motet triplum, hocket, polyphonic chant setting, and the like. In addition to all this, we shall also give, for each example, the verbal passage from the treatise that introduces the musical example itself. For instance:

[4] *Manuscripts of Polyphonic Music: 11th-Early 14th Century*, ed. Gilbert Reaney, Répertoire International des Sources Musicales B4/1 (Munich: Henle, 1966).

Example 2

Musical example "Regnat" from the treatise of Johannes de Garlandia; list of manuscripts where different versions of "Regnat" may be found; ligature patterns of cited fragment. Matching patterns identified by asterisks.

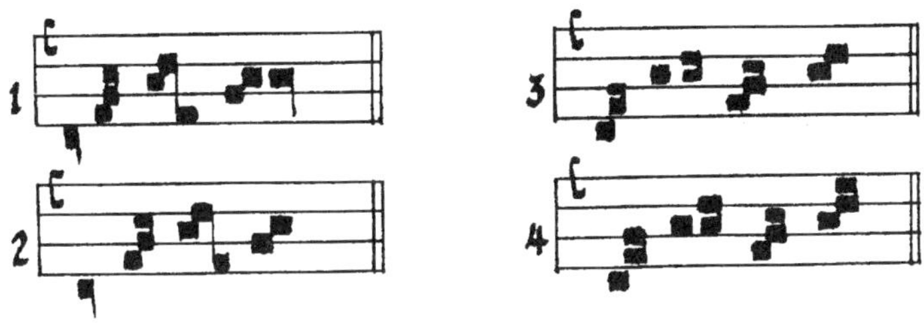

"*Regnat*" clausulae:

F 166 (330): 1,1,1,1 /1,1,1,1, etc.
F 166^{v} (331): 1,1,1,1,1/1,1,1,1,1, etc.
F 166^{v} (332): 1,1,1,1/1,1,1,1,1/1,1, etc.
F 166^{v} (333): 1,3/1/1,3/1/1/3, etc.
F 167 (336): 1,1/2,1/1/,1/2,1, etc.
F 167 (337): 1,2/1,4/1,3, etc.
*F 167^{v} (338): 1,3,3,2,1/ /1, etc.
*F 167^{v} (339): 1,3,3,2,1/ /1, etc.
*F 168 (341): 1,3,3,2,1,3,3, etc.
F 170^{v} (368): 1,1/2,1/1,1/2,1, etc.
F 176 (432): 1,1/2,1/1,1/2,1/, etc.
F 176^{v} (433): 1,1/2,1/1,1/2,1/, etc.
W1 51 (132): 1,1/2,1/1,1/2,1/1,1, etc.
W1 51 (133): 1,1/1,1,1/1,1/2,1/1,1, etc.
W1 51 (134): 1,1,1,1,1,1/1,1,1,1,1,1, etc.
W1 51 (135): 1,1,1,1,/1,1,1,1,1, etc. = F 166^{v} (331)
StV 291^{v} (61): 1,1,1,1,1,1,1,1,1,1, etc.
StV 292 (62): 3,1,1/1,1,1,1/, etc.

Example 3

Two examples comparing notation as given in the published edition and that given in two manuscripts preserving the treatise; beginning of "Angelus" tenor as notated in Bamberg, Staatliche Bibliothek, Lit. 115.

"Regnat" Edition:

Città del Vaticano, Biblioteca Apostolica Vaticana, vaticano latino 5325:

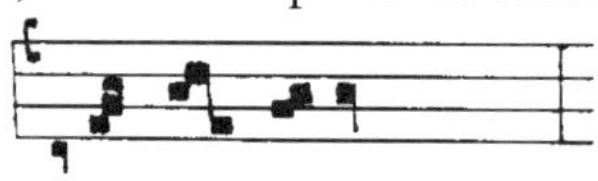

Brugge, Stadsbibliotheek, 528:

"Angelus" Edition:

Città del Vaticano, Biblioteca Apostolica Vaticana, vaticano latino 5325:

Brugge, Stadsbibliotheek, 528:

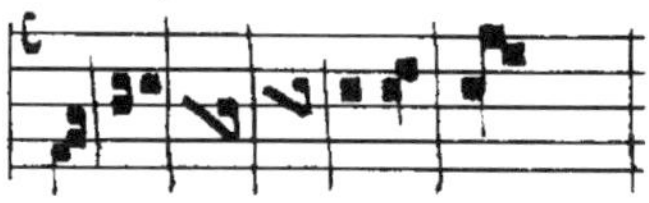

Bamberg, Staatliche Bibliothek, Lit. 115, fol. 19v:

> Unde primus modus imperfectus figuratur hoc modo: tres cum proprietate et postea cum duabus et duabus etc. cum proprietate et in fine tres sine proprietate, ut hic:
> (Garlandia V, 2; ed. Reimer: 57)
>
> *So the first imperfect mode is notated in this way: three with propriety and then two and two, etc., with propriety and at the end three without propriety, as here:*

These passages show the theorist's rationale for selecting the example and provide further control over the precise notational patterns of the music. Almost all such sentences end with the words "ut sumitur hic ("as is taken up here"), "ut patet hic" ("as appears here"), or simply "ut hic" ("as here").

Table 2 shows the beginning of a complete listing of the musical examples, arranged by treatise. The list will give the name of each example as it occurs in each treatise, the relevant verbal passage, a main entry where applicable, and a collation of comparable occurrences in other locations. In addition we shall list every folio cited in the study by manuscript, so that we can determine which manuscripts appear the most often. We shall also make a separate list restricted only to the manuscript folios appearing as main entries, with statistics as to how many main entries occur in each manuscript. We shall compile data on how the manuscript citations are divided among the individual theorists, with subsidiary information on the number of main entries per theorist. And we have begun to collect statistics on the relative frequency of each musical genre, both in the group as a whole and as represented by the individual treatises. Table 3 shows the frequency of genres appearing as musical examples in the treatises of Franco and Anonymous IV.

Finally, in the same way as we try to trace verbal or conceptual borrowings or imitations among the main theorists of the thirteenth century, it is instructive to trace those examples that are quoted or cited by more than one theorist. We shall trace all of these and give again in this context for each one the introductory verbal passage from the respective treatise, so that the individual rationales for the presentation of the musical example may be compared. Table 4 shows two musical examples, each of which appears in more than one treatise. The citation from each treatise is given, followed by the genre of the piece (if known) and the relevant introductory phrase or sentence. A condensed master list of the examples in alphabetical order will also show those items that overlap (see table 5). The orthography of each treatise has been maintained.

Table 6 shows the number of musical examples occurring in each treatise together with a total for all five treatises. Just these bare figures may

Table 2

Garlandia "Agmina" (Clausula/*motet tenor)*

V, 3: "Alia regula de eodem: duae ligatae et duae sine proprietate et cum pausatione longa et brevi, ut hic:" Not found exactly: pitch and ligature differences.

cf. clausulae: *StV 292*^{v}*; 2-voice motet: StV 258, LoA 91-2, LoB 45-46*^{v}*; 3-voice motet: Mo 149, Ba 4, F 397, Hu 90*^{v}*, ONC 82; 4-voice motet: Cl 377; Bes no. 18*

Alleluia Posui adiutorium (Duplum of three-part setting) IV, 11: "Alia regula de eodem, sed non probatur per istam artem, sed bene probatur per exemplum quod invenitur in *Alleluia. Posui adiutorium* in triplo, scilicet quatuor ligate cum proprietate et postea tres et tres cum proprietate etc., et hoc est exemplum, quod sumitur in supradicto *Alleluia.*" Not found with this ligature pattern.

cf. 3-part setting: Mo 16^{v}*, F 36 (fourth ligature is a* quaternaria*); cf. Anonymous of St. Emmeram:* Alleluya Posui; *Anonymous IV:* Alleluia Posui adiutorium, Posui adiutorium

"Angelus" 1 (Motet tenor) I, 37: "Exemplum secundae de perfecto modo:" 3-voice motet: Ba 19^{v} (different clef)

cf. 2-voice motet: W2 253, Ma 134, ArsB 117^{v}*, N 181*^{v}*; 3-voice motet: Mo 72, 175-6, Cl 390*^{v}*, Hu 87; Bes no. 4*

"Angelus" 2 (? Other motet tenor) I^{v}, 2: "Unde prima regula primi modi dicitur esse tres ligatae ad invicem in principio et in posterum cum duabus et duabus ligatis etc., et hoc totum cum proprietate et perfectione, ut hic:" Not found with this ligature pattern.

Table 3

Frequency of genres appearing as musical examples in the treatises of Franco and Anonymous IV

Franco

Hocket	1	-	1
Motet	3	1	4
Motet duplum	6	-	6
Motet tenor	1	-	1
Motet triplum	5	-	5
Three-part setting	1	-	1
Two-part setting	2	-	2
[?]	12	-	12
total	31	1	32

Anonymous IV

Chant	2	-	2
Clausula	-	3	3
Conductus	6	-	6
Four-part setting	2	-	2
Hocket	1	-	1
Motet	1	-	1
Motet tenor	1	-	1
Organum	1	1	2
Organum purum	5	-	5
total	19	4	23

Table 4

Two musical examples occurring in more than one treatise, together with the genre (if known) and the introductory passage from each treatise

"Poure socors"

Anonymous of St. Emmeram:

Cap. Ii 224, 37: (Motet triplum) "Si supra tenorem sit talis resecatio ordinata hoc erit sine littera, nisi aliquando eveniat in motellis, sicut patet . . ."

Franco:

IX, 21: (Motet triplum) "Si vero cum secundo, pausationes secundi habet, et in fine ante pausationem brevem sumit, ut hic: . . ."

"Regnat"

Garlandia:

I, 39: (? *Clausula*/motet tenor) "Exemplum tertiae de perfecto modo:" I, 40: (*Clausula*) "Exemplum tertiae de imperfecto modo" I, 41: (?) "Exemplum quartae de perfecto modo:" I, 42: (?) "Exemplum quartae de imperfecto modo:"

Anonymous IV:

33, 7: (? *Clausula*) "Sed ipse idem [quidam] posuit exemplum tertii et quarti modorum supradictorum per *Regnat* . . ." 59, 26: (? *Clausula*) "[Exemplum pausationis] Trium temporum patet aliter in *Regnat* tertio modo perfecto."

Table 5

Portion of master list of musical examples; showing several items occurring in more than one treatise

Posui adiutorium [A4] (3-part setting)
Poure socors [AE] (Motet triplum)
Povre secors ai encore recouvre [F] (Motet triplum)
Pro patribus [AE] (Hocket)
Quid plura credit natura [F] (Motet)
Regnat 1 [G] (? *Clausula*/motet tenor)
Regnat 2 [G] (*Clausula*)
Regnat 3 [G] (?)
Regnat 4 [G] (?)
Regnat [A4] (? *Clausula*)
Relegentur ab area [A4] (*Conductus*)
Respondi que ne lerroit [F] (Motet triplum)
S'en dirai chanconnette [L] (Motet triplum)
Salvatoris hodie [A4] (*Conductus*)
Sancti spiritus <assit> [L] (Chant)
Sanguine lavat [*stole gemine*] [F] (?)
Sederunt [A4] (4-part setting)
Superans omnia [F] (Motet duplum)
Tamquam [A4] (? *Clausula*)
Trop j'use ma vie [L] (Motet triplum)
Veni, sancti spiritus [L] (? Chant)
Viderunt omnes [A4] (3-part setting)
Viderunt omnes [A4] (4-part setting)

Table 6

Number of musical examples by theorist and total

Garlandia	31
Lambertus	16
Anonymous of St. Emmeram	32
Franco	32
Anonymous IV	30
total	141

Table 7

List of musical examples from the treatises not found in the musical sources; number by theorist; total

Aceto felle potari, Franco
Amen, Franco
Ave Maria, Anonymous of St. Emmeram (? Hocket)
Ave Maria gratia plena, Franco
Cruci corpus adap[*tari*], Franco
Dari, tradi, capi, flagellari, Franco
Dex ele ma tot motur emble, Anonymous of St. Emmeram
Domine, domine, domine, rex glorie, Lambertus, Anonymous of St. Emmeram
Dulcia, Franco (3-part setting)
Gaude, virgo mater Christi, Franco
Manere, Anonymous of St. Emmeram (Motet tenor, hocket)
Manus, pedes perforari, Franco
Mentibus vocibus, Franco
O virgo virginum, celi domina, Lambertus
Portare, Anonymous of St. Emmeram
Pro patribus, Anonymous of St. Emmeram (Hocket)
Quid plura credit natura, Franco
Recordare, virgo mater/Portare, Franco (Motet)
Sanguine lavat [*stole gemine*], Franco
Viderunt omnes, Anonymous IV (3-part setting)

Garlandia	0
Lambertus	2
Anonymous of St. Emmeram	6
Franco	12
Anonymous IV	1
total	21

themselves be significant. As can be seen, they show some consistency around the number thirty. The striking exception is Lambertus, who gives only sixteen. This may well give credence to the theory that the source for the mensural portion of the Lambertus treatise (B.N. lat. 11266) is defective. Indeed, it breaks off in the middle of the discussion of hocket (the theorist's second "species" of polyphony) and does not even reach the topic of organum, announced at the outset as a subject to be broached in the course of the treatise.

There are other things that I believe we might learn from this study. Separating out the musical examples for independent examination gives us further control over the issue of influence among treatises. Also, the fact that most of the pieces cited can in fact be found in extant music manuscripts suggests that most of the music that was considered important at the time seems to have survived. It is possible too that our main entry listings (those listings that indicate exact notational parallels between treatise and music manuscript), as broken down by treatises (and for treatises we have quite accurate dates), might help us to date more closely some of the thirteenth-century musical sources. On the other hand, there are pieces that simply cannot be found. These include French motets, Latin motets, hockets, and a three-part polyphonic chant setting. Table 7 gives the names of all the pieces whose name appears in the treatises (either with or without music) as a musical example, but that have not been located in a musical source. If nothing else, this list reminds us of something we occasionally forget: eight hundred years is a very long time.

This study is designed to provide insight into the extent and nature of the relationship between the theoretical documents and the musical repertoire they presume to discuss. It will give some indication of how much of the music considered important by the theorists has survived to our own time, and how familiar those writers were with contemporary musical compositions and the musical manuscripts themselves. (Some extracts come from the *middle* of compositions but are highly conspicuous in their physical manuscript locations.)

Finally, there are some cultural and aesthetic questions we shall be able to address. Among these it is important to consider the function of the musical examples in the setting of a written (usually prose) treatise. What are the contexts in which an author will turn to a musical example? When will he *not* do so? Does each author use the device for different pedagogical aims? When the same musical example appears in more than one treatise, is it used for the same purpose?[5]

[5] I am grateful to Profs. Leo Treitler and Fritz Reckow, who have made several useful suggestions for further research on this topic.

Manuscript Index

The index below does not take account of the manuscript lists found on pp. 108–14, 251–52, 348–69, and 473–74.

Aachen
Bischöfliche Diözesanbibliothek
13 (XII): 172–73

Albi
Bibliothèque municipale
44: 218n35, 388

Angers
Bibliothèque municipale
91: 39
96: 176n9
97: 177, 182–83, 184–86
144: 177, 187–88, 191

Autun
Bibliothèque municipale
28: 175–77, 187

Avezzano
Curia vescovile
Exultet without shelf-mark: 258n7

Bamberg
Staatsbibliothek
Lit. 6: 388–89
Lit. 115 (Bamberg Codex): 439n105, 478

Bari
Archivio del Duomo
Exultet roll 1: 254, 265, 269, 271
Exultet roll 2: 257, 259, 264–65, 267, 269, 271–72
Exultet roll 3: 264–65, 267, 269–72

Benevento
Biblioteca Capitolare
34: 39, 176n9, 337
35: 337

Berlin
Staatsbibliothek der Stiftung Preußischer Kulturbesitz
Lat. fol. 920: 265–66
Mus. 40608: 338–39, 341–46

Boulogne-sur-Mer (St. Omer)
Bibliothèque municipale
666: 35n40

Bruges
Stadsbibliotheek
528: 396–97, 478

Brussels
Bibliothèque Royale Albert Ier
10162/66: 395n1
II.3824: 168–69

Cambrai
Bibliothèque municipale
75: 191

Cambridge
Corpus Christi College
473: 153–57, 162–63, 175, 188–91
University Library
Ll.ii.10 (Book of Cerne): 161

Catania
Biblioteche Riunite Civica e Ursino Recupero
Ursino Recupero D.39: 149–50

Chartres
Bibliothèque municipale
47: 39, 164, 175, 191

Cividale del Friuli
Museo Archeologico

Cividale del Friuli
Museo Archeologico (cont.)
MS. LVI: 334–35, 343–45
MS. LVIII: 334–35, 343–45
MS. LXXIX: 334–35

Cologny-Geneva
Bibliotheca Bodmeriana
Codex 74 (St. Cecilia Gradual): 43–44, 49–50, 56–57, 103, 336n7

Compostela
Biblioteca de la Catedral
MS. without shelfmark (Codex Calixtinus): 195–202

Darmstadt
Hessische Landes- und Hochschulbibliothek
752: 239n115
1946: 286n27

Douai
Bibliothèque municipale
6: 35n40
246: 35n40

Dublin
National Library
2291: 239n115

Düsseldorf
Universitätsbibliothek
D.1: 35–40
D.2: 35n40
D.3: 35n40

Einsiedeln
Stiftsbibliothek
121: 388–89

Farfa
Biblioteca dell'Abbazia
AF. 338 Musica XI (AB.F Musica XI): 261, 273n20

Florence
Biblioteca Medicea-Laurenziana
Ashburnham 1051: 403, 409n19
Palatino 87 (Codex Squarcialupi): 320–21
Pluteus 29.1: 330n39
Biblioteca Nazionale Centrale
Panciatichi 26: 321

Gaeta
Archivio del Duomo
Exultet roll 1: 259

Ghent
Universiteitsbibliotheek
70/71: 145

Gorizia
Seminario teologico Centrale
MS. I: 334

Grenoble
Bibliothèque municipale
4431: 453n12

Heidelberg
Universitätsbibliothek
362a/28 I: 239n115

Kassel
Landesbibliothek
Theol. Fol. 36: 238n111

Laon
Bibliothèque municipale
118: 239
266: 240n120

Le Puy en Velay
Bibliothèque municipale
A/A/7/009: 453n12

Leiden
Bibliotheek der Rijksuniversiteit
B.P.L. 28: 35n40
Vos. lat. 69: 393

Limoges
Bibliothèque municipale
2: 176n9

London
British Library
Additional 19768: 392
Additional 21170: 379n20
Additional 29987: 320
Additional 29988: 45n3
Additional 30337: 258n7, 264–66, 269
Additional 34209: 338nn13–14, 340
Cotton Caligula A.xiv: 174, 176n9
Egerton 3511: 264
Egerton 3759: 161

London
British Library (cont.)
Harley 281: 403
Lansdowne 432: 161
Royal 8.C.xiii: 162

Lucca
Archivio di Stato
184 (Lucca Mancini Codex): 320
Biblioteca Capitolare
490: 223n50

Milan
Biblioteca Ambrosiana
C.5 inf. (Antiphonary of Bangor): 294n17, 310–11

Montecassino
Archivio della Badia
Exultet roll 2: 255, 259

Montpellier
Faculté de Médecine de l'Université
H 159: 51
H 196 (Montpellier Codex): 439n106

Monza
Tesoro della Basilica San Giovanni
cod. purpureo: 212, 221n42

Munich
Bayerische Staatsbibliothek
Clm 14083: 222n46
Clm 14322: 222n46
Clm 18036: 222n46
Bayerisches Hauptstaatsarchiv
Kloster Holzen Kl. Lit. No. 104: 240n119
Manuskriptensammlung 586 and 587: 239n116

Naples
Biblioteca Nazionale
MS. IV G 68: 393
MS. VI G 34: 261–62

New York
Pierpont Morgan Library
M. 379: 261–62

Ostiglia
Biblioteca Musicale Greggiati
MS. without shelf-mark: 317–18, 323

Oxford
Bodleian Library
Bodley 79: 441, 443
Bodley 775: 153–57, 162–63, 165, 168–69, 174–75, 184–85, 187–91
Canonici liturgical 340: 335, 346
Canonici liturgical 341: 346
Canonici liturgical 342: 259, 264, 268, 272

Padua
Biblioteca Capitolare
D 47: 100

Paris
Bibliothèque de l'Arsenal
1169: 176
Bibliothèque Nationale
fonds français 844: 463n16
fonds français 20050: 463n16
fonds français 22543: 463n16
fonds latin 903: 39
fonds latin 1084: 187, 192
fonds latin 1118: 33–4, 166–67, 170–71, 176–77, 187–88, 192
fonds latin 1119: 163n6, 176, 180–81
fonds latin 1121: 187
fonds latin 1138: 176, 178–79, 187
fonds latin 1139: 446, 449, 453n12
fonds latin 1240: 392
fonds latin 1338: 177, 188
fonds latin 2096: 203
fonds latin 2291: 30–35, 40, 239n117
fonds latin 2717: 35n40
fonds latin 7972: 35n40
fonds latin 9448: 286n28
fonds latin 9449: 177, 188
fonds latin 10508: 176n9
fonds latin 10587: 389–90, 392
fonds latin 10837: 216n25
fonds latin 12412: 72n21
fonds latin 15614: 35n40
fonds latin 17296: 78n1
fonds latin 17305: 35n40
fonds latin 17306: 35n40
fonds latin 17436 (Compiègne Antiphoner): 218n35, 219n36, 221n42, 239, 312, 388
nouv. acq. fr. 6771 (Codex Reina): 318, 320, 323
nouv. acq. lat. 1618: 35n40
nouv. acq. lat. 3126: 441, 443

Piacenza
Biblioteca Capitolare
65: 345

Pisa
Archivio del Duomo
Exultet roll without shelf-mark: 259

Pistoia
Biblioteca Capitolare
121: 51
C81: 239n116
C132: 239n116

Reims
Bibliothèque municipale
213: 30n32, 239n117
285: 165

Rome
Archivio di Stato
997: 49n10
Biblioteca Angelica
1383: 49–56
Biblioteca Casanatense
724: 45n4
Biblioteca Nazionale
Farfense 32: 48n8
Biblioteca Vallicelliana
B 23: 262
B 43: 264
C 52: 51
E 15: 49n10

Saint Gall
Kantonsbibliothek Vadianische Sammlung
317: 389–90, 392
Stiftsbibliothek
18: 386–89, 392
23: 379n21
339: 39, 378, 381–83, 386, 392
342: 376–86, 392
359: 221–22, 382–83, 392
376: 337n10, 381–82, 393
381: 337n10, 391–92
390–91 (Hartker's Antiphonale): 78n2, 311–12, 379, 381, 392
397: 394
484: 337n10, 391–92
578: 373–75

Salerno
Archivio del Museo del Duomo
MSS. without shelf-mark (Capone 3 and 4): 264, 268, 272–75

Sankt Paul (Austria)
Archiv des Benediktinerstiftes
135/1: 118–35, 138, 148–52

Stockholm
Kungliga Biblioteket
A 136: 30n32

Stuttgart
Landesbibliothek
HB VII 57: 379n20

Subiaco
Biblioteca del Protocenobio di Santa Scolastica
MS. XVIII: 262, 264–66

Trent
Museo Provinciale d'Arte
without shelf-mark (formerly Lawrence Feininger collection): 261

Troia
Archivio del Duomo
Exultet roll 2: 265, 267
Exultet roll 3: 256, 259, 262

Turin
Biblioteca Nazionale Universitaria
897 (F.IV.18): 338, 340

Udine
Biblioteca Archivescovile
2: 334
79: 334
234: 334

Valenciennes
Bibliothèque municipale
107: 35n40
148: 35n40, 41
294: 35n40
337: 35n40
399: 35n40

Vatican City
Biblioteca Apostolica Vaticana
Archivio di San Pietro B 79: 45n3, 226n59
Archivio di San Pietro C 92: 47–48
Archivio di San Pietro F 11: 45, 57
Archivio di San Pietro F 14: 49n10
Archivio di San Pietro F 22: 45n3
Archivio di San Pietro H 58: 56
Barberinianus latinus 307: 118, 120–29, 139, 150
Barberinianus latinus 587 (St. Cecilia Bible): 47–48
Barberinianus latinus 592: 264
Barberinianus latinus 603: 261
Barberinianus latinus 637: 46
Barberinianus latinus 3784: 261
Ottobonianus latinus 312: 99n27
Ottobonianus latinus 313: 239n112
Palatinus latinus 235 (Vatican Anonymous): 17–18, 42
Rossianus 215 (Codex Rossi): 317–19, 328
Vaticanus latinus 3764: 217n29
Vaticanus latinus 3784: 258n7
Vaticanus latinus 5319: 44, 50, 56–57, 95n24, 98
Vaticanus latinus 5325: 478
Vaticanus latinus 5465: 46–47, 57

Vatican City
Biblioteca Apostolica Vaticana (cont.)
Vaticanus latinus 9820: 261
Vaticanus latinus 10644: 239n116

Velletri
Museo Capitolare
Exultet without shelf-mark: 258n7

Venice
Biblioteca Nazionale San Marco
Lat. cl. 12, 97: 324n23

Verona
Biblioteca Capitolare
89: 310–11
MS. CCCCXLIV: 318
MS. CVII (100): 338–39, 341

Vienna
Nationalbibliothek
1609: 391–92
Cpv 787: 412n21

Wolfenbüttel
Herzog-August Bibliothek
334 Gud. lat. 8: 412n21
Helmstad. 1008: 378n18

Zürich
Zentralbibliothek
Rheinau 30: 99n26

Index

Aachen, 238, 285
Abelard, 441
Acca, bishop of Hexham, 228nn68–69
Ad organum faciendum (Milan organum treatise), 396–97, 404–05
Adele, queen of France, 200
Aethelred, 228n69
Agatho, pope, 227
Agobard, 223
Akominatos, 303
Alberic of Monte Cassino, 419–22, 424n30, 431n60, 434
Albert of Etampes, cantor of Notre Dame, 200
Alcaeus, 81n12
Alcuin of York, 19–20, 21n14
Aldhelm, 232n89
Alexander de Villa-Dei, 437–38
Amalar of Metz, 220n38, 223, 293–94, 312–15
Ambrose, St., 288, 294–97
Ambrosian rite, 223, 240
Amerus
  Practica artis musice, 103n39
Andrew of Crete, 225
Andrieu, Michel, 90, 99n27, 103
Anonymous IV, 437n95, 471–72, 476, 479
Anonymous of St. Emmeram, 471
Antioch, 301–03, 314
Antiphon, early history of, 297–304
Antonio da Ferrara, 326n28, 328
Antonio da Tempo, 317, 319, 324–25, 328, 331, 422n21
Apel, Willi, 319
Arian sect, 302
Aribo of Mainz, 377
Arlt, Wulf, 446, 468–69
Armenian rite, 209, 232
Arnaud du Mont, 198
Arnobius the Younger, 210
Athanasius of Alexandria, 296
Attilius Fortunatianus, 417n4
Audax, 416–17
Augustine of Canterbury, 228
Augustine, St., 230, 288n3, 295–97, 407, 418
Aunarius, bishop of Auxerre, 188n11
Aurelian of Arles, *see* Monastic rules
Aurelian of Réôme, 30, 40–42, 418, 423n28
  Musica disciplina, 35n40, 40–41, 312, 418n6
Austrenus, bishop of Orléans, 188n11
Bannister, Henry Marriott, 47, 153, 258
Bartolino, 320
Basil, St., 301
Baumstark, Anton, 288
Bede, 56, 198, 227, 372, 416n4, 417, 418n9
Benedict Biscop, abbot of Wearmouth, 227
Benedict II, pope, 227n64
Benedict, St., 105–06, 289n6; *see also* Monastic rules
Benedict VIII, pope, 105
Benevantan rite, 250, 258, 272
Benevento, 258
Berg, Knut, 47n7
Berger, Karol, 137n27
Bernhard, Michael, 412
Bischoff, Bernhard, 212
Boe, John, 88
Boen, Johannes
  Musica, 148n48
Boethius, Anicius Manlius Severinus, 25, 232n89, 423, 437
  De consolatio philosophiae, 393
  De institutione musica, 25, 144, 149, 230
Bohn, Peter, 29–30
Boniface IV, pope, 215n23, 229n72, 235
Borders, James, 338, 342
Bruckner, Albert, 377
Brunhölzl, Franz, 20n13
Bulst, Walther, 435
Burrows, David, 78
Byzantium, Byzantine rite, 88, 233, 241
Calixtus II, pope, 197–98
Camilla Battista da Varano, 71–73

Cantatorium, 212–13, 221–22, 224, 231, 240
Caperon, Roger
  Commentum super cantum, 149
Cardine, Eugène, 285n26
Casimiri, Raffaele, 121
Cassian, *see* Monastic rule
Cassiodorus, 60–61, 231, 423
  Institutiones divinarum et humanarum lectionum, 21, 231n85
Cecilia, St., 60, 64, 66–75
  depictions of, 73–75
  Passio Caeciliae, 60, 66–71
Celestine I, pope, 210, 212
Chant
  improvisation, 83–85, 196, 273, 280n14, 282–83, 285, 309–10
  melodic formulae, 83
  oral transmission, 277–86
Chant, repertories of
  Beneventan, 263–76, 337–38
  Gregorian, 80–82, 105, 197–98, 208, 217n31, 218, 220, 223–24, 238–40, 311, 338, 342
  Mozarabic, 197, 310–11
  Old Roman, 50–51, 56–57, 103, 105, 208, 216, 217n31, 220, 224, 238
Charlemagne, 18–19, 107, 234, 235n98, 236, 284n24, 371–73, 376
  Admonitio generalis, 284n24
Charles the Bald, 30n32, 372n2
Charles the Fat, 373
Chaucer, Geoffrey, 68–70, 72–73
Chavasse, Antoine, 99–100, 221n42
Chiti, Girolamo, 126–28
Chrodegang, St., 235
Ciconia, Johannes, 320
Claire, Jean, 82
Claudian, 80n11
Clausula, 330–31, 481
Clofesho, Council of, 222n47
Columban, St., *see* Monastic rules
Commemoratio brevis, 40
Conductus, 195–96, 199–200, 202, 415, 436, 438, 440, 481
Constantine I, emperor, 89, 92n15
Corbie, 192
Cordier, Baude, 143n35
Corsi, Giuseppe, 328
Cosmas Melodos, 225
Coussemaker, Edmond de, 121
Crocker, Richard, 161, 163–64, 175, 191
Cyril, bishop of Jerusalem, 209n3
Dahlhaus, Carl, 446
Damasus, pope, 106
Dante Alighieri, 59–66, 70, 72–73, 75
De Blaauw, Sible, 93
De Vogüé, Adalbert, 289
Delehaye, Hippolyte, 66–67
Della Scala
  Alberto, 318, 319n7, 325
  Antonio, 318, 325
  Cangrande, 325
  Mastino, 318, 325
  Verde, 328n34
Deshusses, Jean, 30n32, 100
Deusdedit, pope, 229n72
Dietricus, 438
Diogenes of Babylonia, 22n18, 24n22
Dionysios of Thrace, 22n18
Donatus, 21–28
Dronke, Peter, 463–64
Dunn, Marilyn, 304n50
Dyer, Joseph, 289, 293n16, 304–05
Egbert, archbishop of York, 223n47
Egeria, 209n4, 232, 295n21, 297–99
Ekkehard IV, 373, 375, 394
Ekkehard V of St. Gall, 100
Ellsworth, Oliver, 136
Este, Niccolò II d', 328n34
Eusebius, 296, 302n44
Exultet, 45n4, 249–76
Fassler, Margot, 427, 433
Fischel, Oskar, 74
Fludd, Robert, 150–51
Francesco da Barberino, 328–29
Franco of Cologne, 118, 150, 412, 420n19, 440n106, 471–72, 476, 479
Frederick II, emperor, 468
Frere, Walter Howard, 153
Fry, Timothy, 292
Fuller, Sarah, 129n13, 400
Gallican rite, 211, 226, 240n122
Gallo, F. Alberto, 121n5, 328
Ganshof, François Louis, 19
Gelineau, Joseph, 288
Gennrich, Friedrich, 436
Georgian rite, 213, 233
Gerbert, Martin, 118, 128, 142, 151
Giovanni da Firenze, 320–21, 324–26, 328
Giovanni da Prato (Giovanni Gherardi)
  Il Paradiso degli Alberti, 325
Giovanni da Ravenna, 326n28
Gregory I (the Great), pope, 49n9, 228–29, 230n79, 231n85, 309, 311
Gregory II, pope, 217
Gregory III, pope, 106, 215n21
Gregory IV, pope, 49
Gregory VII, pope, 49n9
Gregory XII, pope, 334
Gregory of Tours, 309, 311
Gribomont, Jean, 48
Grimald, abbot of St. Gall, 394
Guido of Arezzo, 45, 395–413
Haas, Max, 404
Hadrian, pope, 236–37, 373

Hammond, Frederick, 121, 126, 142
Handschin, Jacques, 30, 34–35, 40, 375
Hartker, 392
  Hartker's Antiphonale, 78n2, 311–12, 379, 381, 392
Heiming, Odilo, 307n60
Helisachar, 223
Hesbert, René-Jean, 103, 220
Hexachords, 132–33, 136–37, 143, 150
Hieronymus of Moravia, 397, 423n26
Hippolytus, Apostolic Tradition of, 296
Holman, Hans-Jürgen, 82–83
Holtz, Louis, 21, 22n18, 23n22, 25
Honoratus, 307
Honorius I, pope, 215n21, 216, 227n64, 229n72
Horace, 80n11
Horsiesius, 290
Hrabanus Maurus, 372n2
Hucbald de Saint Amand, 197
Hucke, Helmut, 288, 302n45
Hughes, David G., 117, 277, 394, 441–42, 444–46
Huglo, Michel, 212n15, 238n111
Husmann, Heinrich, 468
Iadgari, 213–14, 225, 233
Imbertus of France (Hubertus de Salinis?), 118, 129
Improvisation, *see* Chant
Innocent I, pope, 235n98
Isidore of Seville, 21, 23n21, 25–28, 231, 288, 300, 427n42
  Etymologiarum, 25–26, 300n39
Jacopo da Bologna, 320, 324–26, 328
Jacques de Liège, 136, 148, 395–96, 406
  Speculum musicae, 136, 148, 396
Jacques de Voragine, 68
Jammers, Ewald, 438
Jaufré Rudel, 463, 468
Jeffery, Peter, 51, 301
Jerome of Moravia, *see* Hieronymus of Moravia,
Jerome, St., 290
Jerusalem, 207–15, 224–26, 232–34, 241–47
  rite of, 208–09, 223, 232–34, 241
Johannes Affligemensis, 404
Johannes de Muris (Jehan des Murs), 118, 121n6, 129, 136
  Notitia artis musicae, 136
Johannes Gallicus, 437
Johannes of Garlandia, 396–97, 423–28, 432–37, 471–72, 476
Johannes Vetulus, 121, 127–29, 136, 150–51
John IV, pope, 229n72
John X, pope, 230
John XIX, pope, 45
John Chrysostom, St., 295, 301–02, 304
John of Damascus, 224–25
John the Deacon, 234, 241n123, 372–73, 375–76
Jounel, Pierre, 46, 49–50, 56, 104
Julian of Norwich, 70
Julian of Toledo, 417n4
Klauser, Theodor, 214n21
Knapp, Janet, 434, 436
Koller, Oswald, 120, 139, 142
Krautheimer, Richard, 88–89
Lambertus, Magister, 471–72, 485
Lambillotte, Père Louis, 375
Landini, Francesco, 320, 325
Landulf, bishop of Benevento, 45n4
Lawler, Traugott, 432
Leeb, Helmut, 288, 295
Lehmann, Paul, 404
Leo I (the Great), pope, 106, 210
Leo II, pope, 217, 227n64
Leo III, pope, 49, 229
Levitan, Joseph, 137n27
Levy, Kenneth, 107, 338
Liber pontificalis, 46, 49, 88n3, 217nn29–31, 227n64, 228n72
Liturgical reform
  Carolingian, 235–37, 278, 282, 284–85
  Council of Trent, 347
Lorenzo da Firenze, 320
Lothair, emperor, 100
Louis VII, king of France, 200
Lucius II, pope, 49
Lupus, bishop of Sens, 188n11
Lütolf, Max, 43n1
Map, Walter, 422n21
Marchetto of Padua, 129, 319–20
  Lucidarium in arte musicae planae, 149
  Pomerium in arte musicae mensuratae, 136n22, 319n9, 320
Mari, Giovanni, 430, 434
Marot, Anthonellus, 320
Marrocco, W. Thomas, 328
Martianus Capella, 21, 23n21, 25, 27–29, 34, 40n44, 230
  De nuptiis Philologiae et Mercurii, 27–28, 34, 230n83, 393
Martini, Giambattista (Padre Martini), 126–28, 137n28
Martini, Paola Supino, 48n8, 49, 56
Master Sion of Vercelli, 427–28, 434, 436
Matilda of Hackeborn, 65
Mauck, Marchita, 94
Maximus Victorinus, 416
McKinnon, James, 215n23
Meiss, Millard, 126
Melampous, 22n18

Merton, Adolf, 377, 386
Metz, 234, 238, 285
Meyer, Christian, 149n50
Meyer, Wilhelm, 428–30, 432
Michels, Ulrich, 120–21, 129, 136
Milan
  responsorial psalmody in, 209–10
Minnesang, 446, 466–68
Monastic rule
  of Aurelian of Arles, 292, 297, 300, 307
  of Benedict, 289, 292, 304–08, 315
  of Caesarius of Arles, 292, 307
  of Cassian, 292, 297, 299–300, 307
  of Columban, 304n50
  of Ferreolus, 291
  of Paul and Stephen, 291, 293, 308–09
  of the Master, 290–92, 293n16, 304–08, 315
  of the Monastery of Lérins, 307
Moser, Hans Joachim, 442
Motet, 436, 439n105, 440, 481, 485
Mozarabic rite, 223, 240
Münzer, Hieronymus, 202
Murethach of Auxerre, 20, 24–25
Musica enchiriadis, 24, 40, 398–99, 401
Musica humana, 60, 75
Musica instrumentalis, 60
Musica mundana, 60, 73
Nevers, 196, 199–200
Nicholas III, pope, 43–44, 46, 57
Nicholas of Luduno, 118, 126, 128, 137, 139, 147, 149, 150n50, 151–52
Nicolaus Tibinus, 427n41, 434
Norberg, Dag, 430, 432
Notation (chant)
  Aquitanian, 38–39, 197–98, 286
  Beneventan, 38–39, 45, 47–48
  Bretonic, 38–39, 286
  central-Italian, 44–45, 56–57
  French, 38–39, 198
  Lorraine, 196, 286
  origins of, 17–18, 29–42, 277–86
  Paleofrankish, 30–42, 280, 285–86
  Roman, 43–57
  St. Gall, 279, 286, 383, 385, 389–90, 393–94
Notation (polyphony)
  Italian, 319–20
Notker Balbulus, 157, 163–64, 175, 373, 375–76, 379n20, 390–92, 394
Odington, Walter, 407
Oktoechos, 213
Ordines Romani, 90–91, 101, 103, 212n14, 236
Organum, 396, 399–401, 404–08, 481, 485
Pachomius, 290, 296
Palladius, 290
Panvinio, Onofrio, 93
Paris
  churches
    Notre-Dame, 200, 202
    St. Jacques-la-Boucherie, 200
Paschal I, pope, 94–95, 102
Paul I, pope, 220n38, 229n77
Paul the Deacon, 20, 284n24
Paulinus of Antioch, 288n3, 295–96, 314
Paulinus of Aquileia, 19
Peter Damian, St., 66, 342n21, 420
Peter of Pisa, 19–20
Petrarch, 326n28
Philo of Alexandria, 288n4
Piero, Maestro, 321, 325
Pippin III, 19n5, 220n38, 222n47, 229n77, 235, 236n108, 237, 371–72
Pizzani, Ubaldo, 231n84
Placidus, 420n19
Planchart, Alejandro, 200
Prosdocimo de' Beldemandis
  Expositiones tractatus practice cantus mensurabilis magistri Johannis de Muris, 149
Prudentius, 226, 393, 421–22
Psalmody
  antiphonal, 287–315
    in Rule of Benedict and Rule of the Master, 304–08
    memorization, 290–94
  responsorial, 209–12, 295–98, 301
Putta, bishop of Rochester, 228n69
Quid est cantus (Vatican Anonymous), 17–18, 42
Quintilian, 23
Quomodo organice moduletur, 412–13
Raby, F. J. E., 435
Radulph de Rivo, 44n2
Raphael
  L'Estasi di Santa Cecilia, 73–75
Ratpert, 394
Reaney, Gilbert, 118, 126, 472
Reckow, Fritz, 446
Regino of Prüm, 311
Reichenau, monastery of, 21n14
Reimer, Erich, 437, 476
Remigius of Auxerre, 20, 418
Responsories, 77–78, 82–85, 197–98
Rithmus, 416–19, 428–30
Rockstro, William Smyth, 249–50
Rome, 87–89, 104–07, 207–09; *see also* Notation (chant)
  churches
    Lateran (Basilica Salvatoris), 89, 100, 102–04
    San Clemente, 92–93

Rome
  churches (cont.)
    Santa Prassede, 94–99
    St. Agnes, 90
    St. Lawrence extra muros, 90, 93, 104
    St. Mary Major, 90, 104
    St. Paul's, 90, 104
    St. Peter's, 56, 90, 100, 104, 106, 227
  monasteries, 105–06
    Abbey of San Saba, 49
    San Pancrazio, 106
    St. Crysogonus, 106
  "stational" liturgy, 89–91, 104, 214, 215n23
Romulado Guarna, archbishop of Salerno, 272
Rossi, Nicolò de', 326n28
Rouen, 234
Sabinian, pope, 229n72
Sacchetti, Franco, 324–25
Sacramentaries, 100, 236
  Gregorian, 100, 236
Sacramentary, 99, 102
  Gelasian, 95, 101, 215n23, 236
Saint Gall, monastery of, 21n14, 375–76, 385, 388–89
Salerno, 272–73
Salmon, Pierre, 101
Santiago de Compostela, 195, 198, 200, 202
Sappho, 81n12
Scherrer, Gustav, 377, 386
Schola cantorum, 92–3, 100, 229–32, 242
Scolica enchiriadis, 40, 78n6
Securus Felix, 230n83
Sedulius Scotus, 20, 25
Senleches, Jacob de, 143n35
Sequences, 435
  Aquitaine, 161, 164, 175–77, 187–88, 192–93
  Brittany, 164
  in the Codex Calixtinus, 199
  Saint Gall, 161, 163–64, 193, 389–91
  Winchester, 153–93
Sergius I, pope, 217, 227, 229
Sergius II, pope, 229
Severinus, pope, 229n72
Sigebert, bishop of Minden, 378n18, 393
Silverstein, Theodore, 120–21
Sixtus III, pope, 105
Smaragdous, 20
Smits van Waesberghe, Joseph, 150n52, 151n55
Socrates (historian, 5th c. A.D.), 302
Solage, 137
Soldanieri, Niccolò, 324
Solesmes, abbey of, 202
Sommacampagna, Gidino da, 317–18, 324–25, 331
Sophronios, bishop of Jerusalem, 224
Sozomen, 302–03
Stäblein, Bruno, 45
Stephen II, pope, 235, 237, 371
Stephen of Liège, 197
Stevens, John, 78, 435, 441–42, 445–46
Studite *Typikon,* 233–34
Taft, Robert, 106, 289, 298
Terentius Maurus, 427n42
Tertullian, 296
Theodonus de Caprio (Theodoricus de Campo), 121, 126, 129
Theodore and Theophanes "Graptos," 225
Theodore the Studite, 233
Theodoret of Cyrus, 303
Theodulf of Orléans, 19
Tonary
  of Metz, 312
  of Regino of Prüm, 311
Torkesey, John, 151
Tours, 20, 285n26
Tractatus de contrapuncto (Berkeley Manuscript, Anonymous), 136–37
Treitler, Leo, 29, 34, 42, 84–85
Trier, 285
Tropes, 335–37
  in the Codex Calixtinus, 195, 199, 202
  Saint Gall, 389, 391–92
Troubadour music, 446, 460–65
Tuotilo of St. Gall, 392, 394
Ugonio, Pompeo, 93
Urban I, pope, 68–69
Urban IV, pope, 44n2
Van der Werf, Hendrik, 199
Van Dijk, S. J. P., 103
Versification, Latin, 416–36
Versus, 195, 202, 446, 449–59
Vézelay, 196, 198–200, 202
Vilanova, J. Evangelista M., 308n61
Villani, Filippo, 325
Visconti, Giangaleazzo, 320n17
Vitalian, pope, 100–01
Vitry, Philippe de, 118, 129, 136n24
  Ars nova (Vitry?), 118, 129
Wagner, Peter, 17, 196, 198, 282n18, 283
Walafrid Strabo, 20, 372
Walther von der Vogelweide, 468
Warren, Frederick Edward, 311
Wenzel, Siegfried, 63
Wille, Gunther, 80
William of Dijon (Volpiano), 51, 56
Winchester, *see* Sequences
Zarlino, Gioseffo, 145